COMPUTER FORENSICS AND CYBER CRIME

COMPUTER FORENSICS AND CYBER CRIME

An Introduction

Second Edition

Marjie T. Britz, Ph.D.
Clemson University

Prentice Hall
Upper Saddle River, New Jersey
Columbus, Ohio

Library of Congress Cataloging-in-Publication Data

Britz, Marjie
   Computer forensics and cyber crime : an introduction/Marjie T. Britz.–2nd ed.
     p. cm.
   Includes bibliographical references and index.
   ISBN-13: 978-0-13-244749-2 (alk. paper)
   ISBN-10: 0-13-244749-5 (alk. paper)
   1. Computer security.   2. Computer crimes.   I. Title.
QA76.9.A25B77 2008
363.25–dc22

                             2008037077

Editor-in-Chief: Vernon Anthony
Acquisitions Editor: Tim Peyton
Editorial Assistant: Alicia Kelly
Director of Marketing: Dave Gesell
Marketing Manager: Adam Kloza
Marketing Assistant: Alicia Dysert
Production Manager: Wanda Rockwell
Creative Director: Jayne Conte
Cover Design: Bruce Kenselaar
Cover Illustration/Photo: Getty Images, Inc.
Director, Image Resource Center: Melinda Patelli

Manager, Rights and Permissions: Zina Arabia
Manager, Visual Research: Beth Brenzel
Manager, Cover Visual Research & Permissions: Karen Sanatar
Image Permission Coordinator: Vickie Menanteaux
Full-Service Project Management/ Composition: Integra Software Services, Ltd.
Printer/Binder: Bind-Rite, Robbinsville/ Command Web

Credits and acknowledgments borrowed from other sources and reproduced, with permission, in this textbook appear on appropriate page within text.

Pearson Education Ltd., London
Pearson Education Singapore, Pte. Ltd
Pearson Education, Canada, Inc.
Pearson Education–Japan
Pearson Education Australia PTY, Limited
Pearson Education North Asia, Ltd., Hong Kong

Pearson Educación de Mexico, S.A. de C.V.
Pearson Education Malaysia, Pte. Ltd
Pearson Education Upper Saddle River, New Jersey

Prentice Hall
is an imprint of

www.pearsonhighered.com

10 9 8 7 6 5 4 3 2 1
ISBN-13: 978-0-13-244749-2
ISBN-10:   0-13-244749-5

Dedication

This book is dedicated to my mother, Mary Ann Britz, the most amazing woman I know. Her strength of spirit, quiet fortitude, and generosity inspire me every day. Thanks, Mom. I love you.

CONTENTS

CHAPTER 11   SEARCHING AND SEIZING COMPUTER-RELATED EVIDENCE   296

CHAPTER 12 PROCESSING OF EVIDENCE AND REPORT PREPARATION 325

CHAPTER 13 CONCLUSIONS AND FUTURE ISSUES 349

I have never been accused of sugar coating my remarks, and I'm not about to start now. That is why when I say this book by Dr. Marjie Britz is an excellent text, I am sincere. This text is an excellent first step for anyone who wishes to learn about the investigation of computer crime, and the forensic processing of seized computer data. It is also an excellent reference for major cases involving computer prosecutions.

It is for persons who are just starting their exposure to and taking their first classes in computer crime and computer forensics. The text provides excellent information for students and those needing it for research and exposure to computer crime investigations. Fully explained for the newbie are technical terms that a person new to computer forensics needs to know. New terms are identified and defined with plenty of examples and explanations.

Dr. Britz provides an excellent background, history, and terminology of computer crime. She has gone step by step, and assumed the reader is a novice at computer investigation. The text starts out by explaining what Cyberspace is, how the Internet, criminal behavior, and computer crime have evolved, and how it all affects law enforcement.

She identifies the problems law enforcement has with maintaining state-of-the-art investigations and support for the investigations. The lack of law enforcement resources in both financial and management support is brought to light. In addition, she brings out problems identified with the lack of judicial consistency in both the laws and cases prosecuted.

When I first read this text, I was impressed by the amount of excellent legal research and references for cases and case law. Dr. Britz has done an excellent job of documenting the statutes and cases involving key issues in the investigation and prosecution of computer crimes. The primary federal computer statutes used for prosecuting computer crime are well identified.

Everyone involved in the investigation of any type of crime is well aware of the responsibility of the investigator to uphold and support the Constitution while performing the investigations. The safeguarding of a person's First and Fourth Amendment rights is covered throughout this text. There are entire chapters dealing with the First and Fourth Amendments as they relate to computer investigations, search warrants, and seizures of computers.

The legal chapters are followed with content concerning forensic and computer investigation terminology and procedures for conducting forensic analysis. Dr. Britz takes the reader though the basics of computer terminology relating to forensics and includes a significant number of technical terms which the investigator or analyst will have to know to conduct an analysis. Knowledge of these terms and how they related to computer analysis will help the analyst properly prepare a successful prosecution.

Chapters 10, 11, and 12 explain how to develop forensic capabilities and some standard operating procedures for processing computer evidence. A typical computer lab setup is discussed, so the novice will have a starting point with which to supply his/her lab.

The reader is given some basics on how to process computer evidence and how to build procedures that will allow the analyst to properly defend his/her activity against defense challenges. Problems involved with finding, preserving, and presenting digital evidence are discussed. One of the best parts is that the text provides an excellent overview of procedures and suggestions on how to create a forensic process and make your process defensible in court.

All in all, I found this book to be very informative and an excellent text for anyone wanting to expand his/her knowledge in the area of computer crime investigation and computer forensics.

It fills the gap between those texts that assume the reader already has a full understanding of both the legal and technical knowledge necessary to get involved with computer forensics and investigations and those who know very little about what computer forensics is.

By providing a good basis of the legal considerations along with a basic overview of forensic processing, the reader is shown the first steps necessary to expand his/her knowledge base and become a proficient computer examiner. After reading the book, the analyst/investigation will go on to the more technical issues involved with specific subjects that are encountered in day-to-day analysis.

Dan Mare,
IRS (ret.)
Owner, *Mares and Company LLC.*

The author thanks the reviewers of the second edition: Andrew Donofrio, Farleigh Dickinson University, and Jan Tudor, Butler County Community College. The author would like to thank all the men and women who work tirelessly to investigate and prosecute those involved in computer-related crime. The author would also like to thank all of those individuals who have graciously donated their time and energy to answer countless questions. Finally, the author would like to thank those individuals who have contributed articles or software for this text. They include, but are not limited to: Danny Mares, Maresware; Jon Hoskins; Clemson University Al Lewis, OIG; Jack Wiles, The Training Company; Steve Abrams, Abrams Computer Forensics; Joe Mykytn, JM Consulting; Amber Schroader, Paraben Software; Shauna Waters, Access Data; KeyGhost; and, James Lyle, Douglas White, and Richard Ayers, NIST.

Jon Hoskin—page 50–51 (Chapter 3)—A Short Introduction to Cryptography

Al Lewis—page 355–356 (Chapter 13)—Technology: The New Center of Gravity for Law Enforcement in the Information Age

Jack Wiles—page 63–64 (Chapter 3)—From the Experts: Social Engineering

Steve Abrams—page 123–125 (Chapter 5)—Computer Forensics and the Search for Virtual Adultery

James R. Lyle, Douglas R. White, and **Richard P. Ayers**—page 287–290 (Chapter 10)—Digital Forensics at the National Institute of Standards and Technology

Dr. Marjie T. Britz is an associate professor of criminal justice at Clemson University. She holds a bachelor of science degree in forensic science from Jacksonville State University, a master of science degree in police administration, and a doctorate of philosophy in criminal justice from Michigan State University. She has published extensively in the areas of computer crime, organized crime, and the police subculture. She has acted as a consultant to a variety of organizations and provided training to an assortment of law enforcement agencies. In addition, she has served on editorial and supervisory boards in both academic and practitioner venues. Her latest works include *Organized Crime: A Worldwide Perspective* (Prentice-Hall), *Criminal Evidence* (Allyn & Bacon), and *From Lucky Luciano to Tony Soprano: Italian Organized Crime in the United States* (Praeger Publishing).

Introduction

Chapter Outline

LEARNING OBJECTIVES

After reading this chapter, you will be able to do the following:

✓ Explore the changes in society associated with the advent of technological changes and the introduction of the Internet.

✓ Identify the challenges associated with the enforcement and prosecution of computer crime.

✓ Examine the extent of computer crime in society.

✓ Familiarize yourself with the categorization of computer-related crime.

KEY TERMS AND CONCEPTS

- computer crime
- computer-related crime
- cybercrime
- digital precious metals
- electronic purses
- Electronic Frontier Foundation (EFF)
- Information or Digital Revolution
- Internet
- Internet payment services
- Limited purpose or closed system cards
- mobile payments
- Multipurpose or open system cards
- phreaking
- physicality
- prepaid cards
- stored value cards

● INTRODUCTION

Historically, the world has experienced periods of great enlightenment and progress. The Industrial Revolution, for example, brought unprecedented knowledge and opportunities almost two centuries ago. This revolution, automating common tasks, provided previously unheard of privileges and advances. Advances in transportation increased the array of vacation destinations, enabled families to remain in contact with distant family members, and decreased infant mortality rates as prenatal care became more accessible in remote areas. In addition, sharp advances in communication improved police efficiency and radically changed the courting behavior of lovers. Individuals, families, and institutions were granted unprecedented access to luxury items like cooling systems, and household maintenance was made easier through power tools, yard equipment, and the like. The automation of printing and the introduction of mass media greatly enhanced information dissemination by increasing the availability of reliable and credible sources of knowledge. Unfortunately, it also increased levels of physical lethargy, obesity, complacency, desensitization, child poverty, and criminal behavior. Today, American society has experienced similar transformations as a direct result of the Information Revolution.

The introduction of the **Internet** has created unparalleled opportunities for commerce, research, education, entertainment, and public discourse. A global marketplace has emerged, in which fresh ideas and increased appreciation for multiculturalism have flourished. The introduction of computerized encyclopedias, international consortia, worldwide connectivity, and communications has greatly enhanced quality of life for many individuals. Indeed, the Internet can be utilized as a window to the world, allowing individuals to satiate their curiosity and develop global consciousness. It allows individuals to experience those things that they have only dreamed about. Interested parties can visit the Louvre, devouring priceless artifacts at their leisure or take an African safari without the heat or mosquitoes. They can find answers to the most complex legal or medical questions or search for their soul mates. They can download coupons for their favorite restaurants or search for recipes to their favorite dishes. In addition, individuals, corporations, public organizations, and institutions can more effectively advertise their products or services, using graphically highlighted information and providing links to supplemental information or support. In fact, computerized access to unprecedented information has cut across traditional boundaries of communication.

Like other institutions, law enforcement has also benefited. The Internet has successfully created a non-threatening platform for information exchange by community residents. In addition, the speed and efficiency has enabled agencies to communicate with other agencies on a global scale, solidifying relationships and increasing cooperation. Indeed, law enforcement has been able to further its mission by simply extending the range of audiences to whom it can communicate. Textual descriptions and graphic images of wanted suspects or missing persons can be viewed by anyone with an Internet connection, and concerned citizens can report suspicious activity in an efficient and effective manner. However, the Internet and the increasing reliance on digital technology and communications have also had negative repercussions—creating seemingly insurmountable obstacles for law enforcement. Indeed, the same technology that allows access to favorite recipes from Madagascar can be utilized to download blueprints for weapons of mass destruction. Those same individuals surfing the Web for vacation specials can stalk and harass targeted victims while enjoying the fruits of such searches. Indeed, the very advantages that make the Internet so attractive often pose the greatest risk.

Disadvantages to the Internet include an increasing dependence on cyber information. Many undergraduate students rely exclusively on "knowledge" gleaned from electronic sources. Unfortunately, the quality of information found in cyberspace is often questionable, and displacement of humanity has resulted from this dependence on artificial intelligence. More importantly, new technologies have a history of breeding new forms of socially undesirable behavior, while enhancing traditional ones. Just as the automation of the printing press and the introduction of mass media exponentially increased the distribution of and demand for criminal contraband, like pornography and illegal substances, the Internet has established a virtual cornucopia of child exploitation and obscenity and has created an underworld marketplace for drugs and weapons. In fact, the level and prevalence of criminal behavior and exchange of visual or informational contraband have never been this high. Such advances in technology are also being utilized to commit low-level predatory crime in a new environment known as cyberspace.

CYBERSPACE AND CRIMINAL BEHAVIOR

Cyberspace may be defined as the indefinite place where individuals transact and communicate. It is the place between places.[1] Although originally coined in 1984 by science fiction writer William Gibson, it is hardly a new concept. In fact, traditional electronic communications have always fallen within this existential space. Telephonic conversations, occurring across time and space, were pre-dated by wire exchanges. However, the new medium known as the Internet has monumentally increased the **physicality** of the virtual world, outpaced only by the exponential growth in the number of users. In fact, no other method of communication converges audio, video, and data entities so effectively. Unlike traditional methods, the Internet combines mail, telephone, and mass media. As stated previously, it exposes individuals to a myriad of new ideas and may serve as a social gathering place, a library, or a place to be alone. As such, the existential nature of the medium does not negate the reality of its consequences. Individual users have married, planned their lives, and stalked our children there. Unfortunately, this virtual world is often perceived as a painless alternative to worldly problems, where individuals shed their worries and become perfect in their profiles.

Privacy advocates have often overlooked the negative repercussions of this global medium, arguing zealously that the potentiality of emerging technology precludes governmental interests in monitoring citizens. The organization was co-founded by luminaries like The Grateful Dead's lyricist John Barlow and John Gilmore, co-founder/inventor of Cygnus Solutions, Cyberpunks, and DES Cracker. Both Barlow and Gilmore have been most vocal in their defense of some of the most notorious computer hackers in the United States and have championed the Bill of Rights. They argue that the original thrust of the frontier police, directed at ne'er-do-wells intent on compromising the privacy of American citizens, has been refocused on the very individuals that they originally protected. In fact, the two created the **Electronic Frontier Foundation** offering to "fund, conduct, and support legal efforts to demonstrate that the Secret Service has exercised prior restraint on publications, limited free speech, conducted improper seizure of equipment and data, used

In 1990, John Perry Barlow, of The Grateful Dead (pictured here) co-founded the Electronic Frontier Foundation. The group has been involved in numerous high-profile cases regarding privacy and the Internet. In one of its most recent cases, the group has filed a lawsuit against telecom giant AT&T for releasing calling and subscription information of consumers to the National Security Agency (NSA). (*Electronic Frontier Foundation*)

undue force, and generally conducted itself in a fashion which is arbitrary, oppressive and unconstitutional."[2] While early actions by the U.S. Secret Service may validate some of these early concerns, the efforts of this organization have often overlooked the negative potentiality of this global marketplace that has reunited a society that had increasingly removed itself through suburbanization.

Just as the Industrial Revolution created an environment conducive to street or predatory crime through the concentration of the urban population, the **Information** or **Digital Revolution** has created a new forum for criminal activity. Ironically, this new environment all but negates security measures taken by individuals wishing to protect themselves from traditional crime. In fact, the Internet is unlike other communication media, allowing predators to reach directly into a victim's home, circumventing the meanest of physical security systems. Such systems, a direct result of traditional street crime, are designed to protect individuals, families, and institutions from criminal victimization. They are characteristic of a growing suspicion of anyone unknown. This skepticism, not new or unique to the United States, has not established itself in cyberspace. In fact, the globalization of communications has led to a complacency diametrically opposed to traditional notions of privacy and security.

American society has long been characterized by its distrust of strangers. As media attention has focused on elevated levels of predatory crime perpetrated by non-acquaintances, this fear has been heightened. Cautionary admonitions to children have traditionally included warnings of strangers and locking of doors. However, the advent of technology has lowered traditional barriers and actually served as an informal invitation for unknown visitors. Many have recognized only too late the dangers of their inattentiveness—victims of theft, stolen privacy, and the like; while others, yet to suffer negative consequences, remain blissfully unaware of their own vulnerability. In fact, most individuals, young and old alike, are seduced by the soft hum of a device that appears to be the gateway to worlds previously restricted. Unfortunately, this fascination may be exploited by those we try most to avoid—criminals and predators.

CLARIFICATION OF TERMS

Just as debates rage over the appropriate codification of crime committed via electronic means, controversy surrounds the actual semantics associated with the phenomenon. For clarification purposes, then, it is necessary to define the historical usage of terms associated with technological or electronic crimes. **Computer crime** has been traditionally defined as any criminal act committed via

TECHNO-LINGO

Computer Crime, Computer-Related Crime, and Cybercrime

Computer crime—a general term that has been used to denote any criminal act which has been facilitated by computer use. Such generalization has included both Internet and non-Internet activity. Examples include theft of components, counterfeiting, digital piracy or copyright infringement, hacking, and child pornography.

Computer-related crime—a broad term used to encompass those criminal activities in which a computer was peripherally involved. Examples include traditional bookmaking and theft. **Cybercrime**—a specific term used to refer to any criminal activity which has been committed through or facilitated by the Internet.

computer. **Computer-related crime** has been defined as any criminal act in which a computer is involved, even peripherally. Finally, **cybercrime** has traditionally encompassed abuses and misuses of computer systems or computers connected to the Internet which result in direct and/or concomitant losses. While the first of these two terms will be used interchangeably throughout the text, cybercrime will only be used to describe that criminal activity which has been facilitated via the Internet. Additionally, students should be advised that a variety of definitions exist, and that such variations have resulted in confusion among legislators and investigators alike. Some authors, for example, argue that any crime that involves digital evidence may be characterized as a computer crime. This is misleading at best and self-serving at worst. Traditional kidnapping cases in which ransom demands are communicated via telephone will always represent a crime against a person and should not be characterized as a "telecrime." While it is desirable to establish an environment where computers are viewed as potential evidence containers in any case, to redefine traditional predatory crime as cybercrime or computer crime is absurd. Extortion is extortion and will remain such regardless of the method employed to communicate the threat. The result of such hyper-definition is to negate some emerging legislation. This is not to suggest that legislators should cease efforts to specifically criminalize computer-specific criminal activity. Indeed, further legislation should be pursued to enhance prosecutorial toolboxes, not to replace or supplant traditional mechanisms.

● TRADITIONAL PROBLEMS ASSOCIATED WITH COMPUTER CRIME

Individuals seeking a crime have always displayed a remarkable ability to adapt to changing technologies, environments, and lifestyles. This adaptability has often placed law enforcement at a disadvantage, struggling to keep up with criminal innovations. Indeed, the law-enforcement community has often failed to recognize the criminal potentiality of emerging technologies until it is almost too late. This trend has proven to be true in contemporary society. Fortunately, much computer-related crime involves non-specialist users (e.g., child pornographers, narcotics traffickers, and predators). In fact, the earliest computer crimes were characterized as non-technological. Theft of computer components and software piracy were particular favorites. Hacking and technologically complicated computer crimes came later.

Although the advent of technology has vastly changed the modus operandi of certain criminal elements throughout history, current advances have changed the very physical environment in which crime occurs. As such, the law enforcement community is experiencing unprecedented periods of uncertainty and ineffectiveness. Many of these problems are associated with the comprehension of the nature of the emerging technology, while others involve questions of legality and sovereignty. Unfortunately, legislative bodies and judicial authorities have been slow to respond to such inquiries, and law enforcement has been forced to develop investigative techniques without adequate legal foundations. At the same time, the lack of technological knowledge traditionally associated with the law enforcement community hampers even the most mundane investigation. So, while the investigators of computer-related crime must display levels of ingenuity comparable to sophisticated criminal entrepreneurs, traditional investigators are ill-equipped to do so.

Physicality and Jurisdictional Concerns

The physical environment that breeds computer crime is far different from traditional venues. In fact, the intangible nature of computer interaction and subsequent criminality poses significant questions for investigative agents. For example, what forensic tools are available for identifying entry points in data breaking and entering? Certainly, seasoned investigators recognize the utility of prymark analysis in home burglaries. But few recognize the how-to's and what-for's in abstract, intangible environments. In many cases, such differences in technique, and even approach, are

further complicated by the lack of precautionary boundaries and restraints—both physical and virtual. Indeed, the intangibility of such environments creates unlimited opportunities.

The lack of physical boundaries and the removal of traditional jurisdictional demarcations allow perpetrators to commit multinational crime with little fear (or potential) of judicial sanctions. For the first time, criminals can cross international boundaries without the use of passports or official documentation. Whereas traditional criminal activity required the physical presence of the perpetrators, cybercrime is facilitated by international connections that enable individuals to commit criminal activity in England while sitting in their offices in Alabama. In addition, electronic crime does not require an extensive array of equipment or tools. It does not require vehicular transportation, physical storage capability, or labor-intensive practices, all of which increase the potential for discovery and enforcement. In addition, this shift from a corporeal environment, where items can be seen, touched, smelled, etc., to a virtual world where

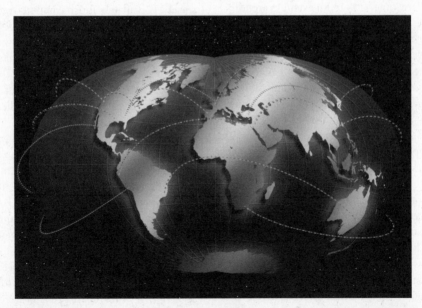

Schematic showing the lack of physical boundaries for cyberspace—to illustrate lack of jurisdiction. (*Hunt, Steven/Getty Images Inc.—Image Bank*)

boundaries, concrete barriers, and physical items are inconsequential has further insulated the criminal from law enforcement. In fact, the sheer intangibility of crime scenes has all but crippled many criminal investigations.

A further concern regarding the physical intangibility of computer crime involves the traditional lack of cooperation inherent in law enforcement investigations. Issues of funding, political platforms, and the like have traditionally reduced communication and cooperation among jurisdictions. These issues are further compounded when international components are considered. The lack of consensus among international entities regarding the criminalization of certain behaviors and the appropriate sanctions associated with same often negate cooperative agreements. While some countries rate computer crime as a high priority, for example, others have embraced computer criminals, protecting them from international prosecution. Antigua, Caracas, and the Dominican Republic, for example, have all

challenged American sovereignty over wagers placed by American residents through their online casinos and sports books. In addition, international councils that have been developed have been largely ineffective, and the momentum to develop such cooperation has waned in the wake of the Y2K nonevent.

Perceived Insignificance, Stereotypes, and Incompetence

Investigators and administrators have displayed great reluctance to pursue computer criminals. A lack of knowledge coupled with general apathy toward cyber-criminality has resulted in an atmosphere of indifference. Many stereotype computer criminals as non-threatening, socially challenged individuals (i.e., nerds or geeks) and fail to see the insidious nature of computer crime, and 36.3 percent of officers believe that the investigation of computer crime interferes with their ability to concentrate on "traditional" crime.[3] It

CASE IN POINT

The Internet's First Online Serial Killer

Photo of John Edward Robinson. (Matthew S. Hicks/Pool)

In a case that just goes to show you that you can find anything you want on the Internet, John Edward Robinson became the first known online serial killer. In the summer of 2000, investigators in rural Kansas and Missouri

discovered the decomposing remains of five women. Both discovery sites were owned by John Edward Robinson, Sr. Robinson, a married man and father of two, was considered to be an upstanding member of the community and devoted father. Using the screen name "Slavemaster," Robinson lured the young women to their death by soliciting sadomasochistic relationships while promising them financial incentives. The bodies were uncovered after several women filed complaints with law enforcement authorities, who stated that Robinson was far more brutal than he had advertised. Robinson was sentenced to death for the killing of three women in Kansas and pled guilty to five more killings in the state of Missouri, including that of paraplegic Debbie Faith, the teenaged daughter of one of Robinson's other victims. In addition, the "Slavemaster" admitted to killing Stasi, a young woman fleeing an abusive husband with a young child. Ironically, Robinson coordinated the adoption of his victim's child by his brother and sister-in-law.[4]

appears that the potentiality of weapons and narcotics trafficking, conspiracies of mass destruction, and the like are all but alien to those individuals not actively involved in computer investigations. In addition, those administrators and investigators who grudgingly admit the presence and danger of electronic crime tend to concentrate exclusively on child pornography, overlooking motivations and criminal behaviors apart from sexual gratification. Unfortunately, these perceptions are often directly opposed to the reality experienced by seasoned investigators.

In a study conducted by the Department of Justice, computer crime investigators recognized the threat posed by employees and insiders. Respondents indicated that businesses were perceived as the number-one target for computer crime. Individuals and financial institutions placed second and third, respectively. Their typology of employees or insiders consisted of longer-term workers with extended hours (male and female), between the ages of 20 and 45 years from a variety of social and economic backgrounds, with good computer skills, knowledge of company security procedures, and the ability to mask their intrusions. In fact, their commonality lies more in their motivations, which are usually characterized by revenge, greed, or resentment. Unfortunately, these individuals are most often trusted employees with authorized access. Thus, timely detection of their activities is often unlikely.[5]

A more recent study revealed that two-thirds of all agencies studied had dealt with or responded to a computer-related incident. Individual officer responses indicated that most viewed "harassment/stalking" via the Internet as the most prevalent of calls for assistance, with child pornography a close second. Other crimes reported to the police in the order of their perceived prevalence included forgery or counterfeiting, identity theft, e-commerce fraud, and the solicitation of minors.[6] This study indicates that hacking, a traditional concern for law enforcement personnel, did not constitute a significant perceived danger. At the same time,

earlier stereotypes of computer criminals were consistent. Typologies of these offenders (including child pornographers and hackers) included males between 16 and 57 (usually mid- or upper 30s to 40s) with a minimum of high school diplomas (although college degrees were also common). These individuals were likely to display moderate-to-high technical ability, few prior arrests, and possession of high-end computer equipment with large storage capacities. Unfortunately, the majority of Internet users fall squarely within this typology.[7] Recent studies suggest that identity theft is a growing concern among law enforcement investigators, although many perceive that investigation and prosecution of the crime is out of either their experience or purview.[8]

Even in situations where law enforcement authorities recognize the insidious nature of computer or cyber crime, many do not perceive themselves or others in their department to be competent to investigate such criminal activity. In fact, although 34.4 percent of agencies surveyed indicated that they had at least one individual who had received training in such investigations, only 18.8 percent felt that that person was competent to investigate computer-related crime, and only 12.3 percent indicated that that person was capable of forensic examinations. A more alarming statistic may be that almost 70 percent of those respondents who indicated that they had received training characterized it as "basic," "general," or "introductory."[9]

Prosecutorial Reluctance

Like their law enforcement counterparts, prosecutors across the country lack sufficient knowledge and experience to effectively prosecute computer crime. In addition, many do not perceive electronic crime as serious and often grant it the lowest priority. (As many prosecutors are strongly influenced by the concerns of their constituents, they are reluctant to deviate from the headline-catching cases of street crime or other violent crime.) This view is often created or exacerbated by the lack of judicial interest in these types of crime and the lack of training displayed by responding officers. Even those jurisdictions which have granted electronic crime high priority are often thwarted in their efforts by a lack of cooperation in extradition requests, the victim's reluctance to prosecute, the labor-intensive nature of case preparation, and/or the lack of resources for offender tracking.

Lack of Reporting

Although estimates vary, most experts agree that the vast majority of Fortune 500 companies have been electronically compromised to the tune of at least $10 billion/year, and 75 percent of all businesses have experienced some victimization, with 45 percent of that stemming from unauthorized access by insiders.[10] However, early studies indicated that only 17% of such victimizations were reported to law enforcement authorities.[11] At the same time, the number of reported incidents handled by Carnegie-Mellon University's Computer Emergency Response Team (CERT) has increased sixfold, from 21,756 in 2000 to 137,529 in 2003 (the year that the group stopped reporting).[12] It does appear that reporting is getting better; a survey of 521 security personnel from American companies, financial institutions, universities, and government agencies revealed that 32 percent of respondents reported electronic crime to law enforcement. This represented an increase of 15 percent from the previous study. However, computer intrusion is still vastly underreported.

One of the primary reasons that businesses fail to report computer intrusions is their need to assure consumers of data security. This represents an absolute necessity to most businesses, as individual consumers need to have faith in the company's infrastructure. And, more importantly, consumers need assurances that confidential information remains inviolate. Remember the chaos that erupted when ChoicePoint and the U.S. Office of Veterans Affair reported that the records of hundreds of thousands of Americans had been compromised. (Fortunately, emerging federal and state legislation requires the reporting of such occurrences, but complete disclosure has not yet been realized.) In addition, many corporations are uncomfortable with the release of information to any entity, including law enforcement, and want to maintain control of the investigation at all times. Unfortunately, law enforcement authorities cannot extend promises of confidentiality of findings as the sheer nature of the American judicial system makes it legally impossible to hide or fail to divulge results of an investigation (i.e., it is all available in the public record). Thus, many corporations choose to handle things internally, including disciplining perpetrators. Some naively assume that criminal prosecution, if preferred, can be accomplished by simply sharing the results of their investigations with law enforcement agencies. This assumption is based in large part on the perceptions of security professionals who decry the need for proper law enforcement procedures, arguing that corporate investigations should not "waste" time attempting to maintain the chain of custody. The "professionals" argue that only 2 percent of incidents that are investigated necessitate that type of detail.[13] Unfortunately, such internal investigations may all but negate the potential for criminal prosecution, as the incorporation and documentation of proper evidentiary procedures is essential in the judicial process.

A further reason that companies do not report is the perception that reporting will not result in capture or identification of a suspect. These companies fail to see a positive cost–benefit ratio. (Unfortunately, they may have a point, as 77 percent of surveyed departments reported that electronic crimes are assigned a low to medium priority at their agency, with the exception of child pornography.[14]) Many also find it difficult to determine the proper authorities or question the capabilities of law enforcement agencies, who are often stereotyped as technologically deficient or retarded. Interlapping and overlapping jurisdictions pose additional problems, as it is most rare that computer crimes occur within one state, let alone one jurisdiction. Even non-sophisticated computer criminals will access different services to disguise their location. Such circuitous activity often necessitates federal or international assistance. Finally, many intrusions are detected long after the violation occurred, making investigations more difficult.

Lack of Resources

Although computer intrusions have proven to be problematic within the corporate world, such institutions' unwillingness or inability to effectively communicate with judicial authorities has led to an increase in computer crime. Unfortunately, law enforcement and corporate entities desperately need to cooperate with one another. Unlike their civil service counterparts, the business communities have the resources (both financial and legal) necessary to effectively combat computer crimes. First, these companies, through their system administrators, have far more leeway in monitoring communications and system activities, and they have the ability to establish policies which enable wide-scale oversight. Subsequently, these entities have the ability to gather evidence with little or no resources expended (i.e., system monitoring software—used to track keyboard logging, scripting logging, password maintenance, etc.). Computer Anomaly Detection Systems (CADS), for example, are designed to use the power of the computer to detect suspicious activity. In addition, these companies have the

economic resources available to fund investigative efforts, while law enforcement agencies do not. Ideally, these two communities, sharing the same interests, should develop open lines of communication and cooperation. However, this has not yet occurred.

Due to the very nature of computer crime, an influx of economic support to local law enforcement agencies is sorely needed. Law enforcement has been seriously underfunded since its inception. This trend has been exacerbated with the advent of high-technology crime. Emerging technologies require perpetual training, as the potential for computer criminality has exponentially increased. Wireless technologies and emerging encryption and steganography programs, for example, are increasingly complicating law enforcement investigations. As law enforcement budgets remain strained, it is virtually impossible for administrators to allocate training funds to update their officers on today's technology without assurances that the training would not become obsolete by tomorrow. This never-ending cycle is further complicated by the sheer cost of the training available. With the exception of federally sponsored programs, much of the training available is offered by private companies who charge exorbitant fees for their services. It is not unusual, for example, for a one-week training course on computer forensics to exceed $1,500 per officer. It must be noted, however, that there are a variety of vendors who support law enforcement initiatives and who attempt to defray the costs associated with training or the acquisition

Collaborative Attempts

While both private and public entities have recognized the need for collaboration, attempts have been thwarted by traditional suspicions, stereotypes, and other baggage. However, there are some entities which have attempted to overcome these deficiencies. While some, like Carnegie-Mellon's CERT attempt to coordinate research between the two, others like the Training Company and the Southeast Cybercrime Summit attempt to pull the two together through networking and training. Both have displayed a measurable level of success, and investigators from both sectors have created and sustained lines of communication. However, organizational acceptance and cooperation has not been forthcoming.

of software. Some of them, for example, will extend free training offers with the purchase of their software, while others will offer law enforcement discounts or training scholarships. Unfortunately, some agencies are still incapable of affording adequate software or training even with these efforts and substantial discounts, as budgets are further strained by peripheral costs associated with training, like per diem expenses.

In addition to costs associated with training, administrators must consider three additional areas in support of computer crime investigations: personnel, hardware, and housing. By far, costs associated with staffing computer crime units far exceed the other two areas. While traditional expenses like salary and benefits are often overlooked, they become a very expensive component when establishing a new function. For every officer who is assigned new areas of responsibility, additional staff must be recruited, hired, and trained as a replacement in his/her original position. In addition, small agencies can scarcely afford to send officers to lengthy training courses or assign them exclusively to computer crime units, as their personnel resources are already stretched to the limit. As a result, many agencies have poorly trained computer investigators who are functioning in several capacities at once. Finally, the complexity of computer crime often necessitates the retention of individuals who exhibit a high level of technological competence and familiarity with computer infrastructures. Unfortunately, these skills are also highly prized within the private sector, placing poorly funded law enforcement agencies at a distinct disadvantage. While the private sector can offer elevated salaries and lucrative business packages, law enforcement, a civil service entity, is often precluded from offering differential packages to these individuals.

A further deterrent for many law enforcement agencies is the costs associated with the acquisition of appropriate equipment. As stated previously, technology is changing at a remarkable pace, and while computer components are decreasing in price, they quickly become obsolete, making large investments impractical for many departments. Twenty gigabyte hard drives, for example, were touted as a major revolution in 2000. Now, drives with four and five times that storage capacity are commonplace. Thus, it is essential for equipment to remain consistent with current technology, as imaging drives and storing criminal evidence require comparable space (and speed). Advances in microprocessors have also increased exponentially. Just as users were marveling over the speed of the Pentium IV, Intel introduced the Core™2 Duo family of processors. These devices are designed to

Law Enforcement—Friendly Vendors

As more and more corporations and private entities recognize the need for forensic and network software and training, discounts to law enforcement personnel for the same materials and products are forthcoming, as vendors can extend discounts as their bottom line and consumer base expand. Unfortunately, not all vendors have passed their good fortune on to law enforcement agencies. Some of those that do, however, are considered to be "friends" of law enforcement and have attempted to offset inadequate resources by offering discounted rates for software and scholarships for training. While the list below does not represent an exhaustive list of all such vendors, it does include a sample of companies known for their benevolence among computer crime investigators.

- Marsware
- The Training Company (Techno-Security Conference)
- Paraben Software
- Guidance Software
- Access Data
- dtSearch
- Intelligent Computer Solutions
- WetStone

enhance and promote energy-efficient perfomances due to their bifurcated architecture. However, CPUs are but one facet of the expense budget allocated for hardware. Printers, scanners, monitors, modems, storage devices, and the like are all necessary for investigations. And, as in other areas in computer technology, expenses associated with equipment updating can be enormous.

Updating software can also be quite expensive. Upgrades to many of the most popular programs can be as high as several hundred dollars per machine. Updates of operating systems can also be quite pricey. As with the update of hardware, it is absolutely imperative that investigative agencies remain abreast of developments in popular software, as criminal evidence may reside in these programs. In addition, investigative software is necessary to analyze and recover such evidence. At a minimum, agencies must invest in data duplication, data verification, data capture, data recovery, data preservation, and data analysis tools. Password cracking, text searching, and document viewing tools are also necessary. Unfortunately, many of the licenses to these programs, created exclusively for computer forensic purposes, require annual fees or significant costs for upgrades. New Technologies Incorporated (NTI), for example, grants licenses to individuals, not machines, and charges law enforcement annual fees for licensing and additional fees for upgrades. Thus, the majority of expenses associated with the creation of a computer crime unit are not only recurring, but increasing.

A further expense associated with establishing computer crime units concerns the creation of a computer laboratory. Unlike previous expenses, such expenditures should represent a non-recurring expense for an agency's budget. Software and hardware expenses aside, the most significant portion of lab start-up costs is a one-time investment in a physical site. As office space is always at a premium in police departments, this investment may be the hardest to come by. However, it is the most important due to the

unique and fragile characteristics of digital evidence and technological devices. These characteristics require the partitioning of traditional and technological evidence, with special consideration given to the fragility of digital evidence, including temperature, moisture, dust, and static controls. Unfortunately, such high maintenance support is almost impossible at the local level as most resources are only available at the federal level. (Although half of all agencies recently surveyed reported the presence of an electronic crime "unit," many of these units were staffed by a single officer, often acting part-time in this capacity, without the support of a forensic laboratory.)

Federal resources have been increasing by leaps and bounds; the creation of regional investigative offices at the FBI and child exploitation and pornography task forces are but a few examples. The Secret Service has invested a considerable amount of time, resources, and training in this area. Many of these programs have proven invaluable to local jurisdictions struggling with dwindling resources and outdated technology. Unfortunately, the federal resources are stretched extremely thin. The exponential increase in computer activity in violation of federal statutes coupled with the inundation from local agencies has resulted in extended turnaround time and a denial of cases which are not deemed significant (i.e., those that do not threaten public safety, involve exploitation of children, or the like). In addition, this same lack of resources has led to an inability to respond proactively to the dawning era of the technocriminal. Resources are so constrained that federal assistance traditionally is reserved for only the most serious of cases, avoiding local jurisdiction. (It must be noted, however, that the federal government has made a concerted effort to stem the flow of child pornography, aggressively investigating known offenders and surveying areas ripe for child pornographers.) In addition, many libertarians argue that this increasing reliance on federal resources violates constitutional safeguards that mandate jurisdictional

CASE IN POINT

Child Pornography—The Scourge of the Internet

Child pornography continues to be perceived by many individuals as the most serious of computer crimes. It has been argued that the introduction of the Internet has exponentially increased the proliferation and accessibility of such materials. High-profile cases are recounted on what seems to be a daily basis, and include little league coaches, public officials, police officers, members of the clergy, and university professors. Here are just a few examples:

- July, 2006—A former Orange County Deputy pled guilty to possession of child pornography, after authorities found hundreds of images of child pornography on his computer. The case against Patrick Francis Calcagno was initiated after U.S. Immigration and Customs Enforcement (ICE) shut down Regpay, a Belarus-based Internet billing firm that operated child porn Web sites and provided credit card billing services for 50 child pornography Web sites worldwide. Along with Calcagno, ICE has made over

1,200 cases from tracking down the purchasers of child porn subscriptions.

- September, 2006—Law enforcement authorities arrest University of Pennsylvania professor Lawrence Scott Ward, with receiving child pornography. It is alleged that some of the images actually depict Ward engaging in sexual activity with his male victim. The images were seized after Ward sent them to himself at his university office.

- November, 2006—Long Island priest Thomas G. Saloy, an administrator at the Queen of the Most Holy Rosary Church in Roosevelt, was arrested after a 12-month investigation in which he was observed exchanging child pornography electronically and exchanging sexually explicit messages with minors. Investigators discovered over 1,300 still images and videos of children under the age of 15, some prepubescent, in sexually exploitive situations.

capabilities, suggesting that concerns of federal power and police states can only be exacerbated by relieving local governments of such responsibilities and powers.

Jurisprudential Inconsistency

Unfortunately, the Supreme Court has remained resolutely averse to deciding matters of law in the newly emerging sphere of cyberspace.

They have virtually denied cert on every computer privacy case to which individuals have appealed and have refused to determine appropriate levels of Fourth Amendment protections of individuals and computer equipment. As such, the country is remarkably divided on fundamental elements of law—establishing a legality standard of behavior in one jurisdiction which negates or supersedes the standard in another.

Extent of Victimization Experienced by American Corporations

- 25 percent of respondents detected external system penetration
- 27 percent detected denial of service
- 79 percent detected employee abuse of Internet privileges
- 85 percent detected viruses
- 19 percent suffered unauthorized use
- 19 percent reported ten or more incidents

- 35 percent reported two to five incidents
- 64 percent of those acknowledging an attack reported Web site vandalism
- 60 percent reported denial of service
- over 260 million dollars in damages were reported by those with documentation.[15]

● EXTENT OF THE PROBLEM

Many computer crimes violate both federal and state statutes. Although the federal agencies are better equipped to deal with the complexities involved with high technology crime, state agencies are also inundated by increasing requests from local agencies for assistance in the investigation and detection of computer crime. The lack of resources coupled with the array of criminal perpetrators on the Web has all but overwhelmed investigative agencies at all levels of government. Crimes committed via computer fall on a spectrum ranging from nuisance activities (spreading viruses, spamming, etc.) to computer-assisted criminal activity (stealing home addresses, maps, family information, etc.) to computer-initiated criminal activity (i.e., wire transfers, fraud). Nefarious purposes include white collar crime, economic espionage, organized crime, foreign intelligence, terrorism, sexual deviance, and technologically innovated traditional crime. Perpetrators range from suburban teenagers to disgruntled employees to incarcerated felons. To make sense of this myriad of activities, motivations, and individuals, computer crimes may be divided into three categories: (1) computer as a target; (2) computer as an instrument; and (3) computer as an incidental. While these categories often overlap, they are most useful in discussions of high technology crime.

The earliest examples of computer crime involved activities in which computers or computer components were targeted by criminals. **Phreaking**, an activity in which telecommunications systems are manipulated and ultimately compromised, was the precursor to today's hackers, while viruses and worms have become a daily concern for corporations, civic organizations, and individual users. Trojan horses and other popular hacking tools are now readily available on the Web, and the theft of data has become increasingly popular. Government entities and financial institutions, in particular, have proven especially vulnerable to data theft. While much of the activity involves recreational entertainment

for savvy computer users, implications for international security and wide-scale financial fraud are looming concerns. Additional criminal activities which target computers or their components include software piracy and trafficking in stolen goods. Organized crime groups have recognized the potential profit from the black market in computer chips, and various cases have involved organized Asian gangs trafficking in high-dollar computer chips.

Computers have also proven to be *the means* for many criminally minded individuals. Removing traditional physical boundaries and, perhaps more importantly, removing international borders, the Internet has vastly increased the potential for both traditional crimes and technology-specific activities. The appearance of anonymity creates the façade of a shield which seems to negate possible repercussions. Thus, the opportunities for embezzlement, stalking, and gambling, to name a few, have been exponentially elevated with the introduction of electronic commerce and communications. In addition, the prevalence of child pornography has skyrocketed as it has become more accessible. In fact, many individuals argue that the Internet has actually created this increase in child pornography as some individuals actually become child pornographers through experimentation—an activity which they would not have engaged in if the information had not been so accessible.

Additional crimes that have become more accessible to the masses include counterfeiting and forgery. The introduction of high-end scanners and printers has created an atmosphere ripe for the illegal reproduction of American currency and corporate or government checks. Sophisticated graphics software, popular among virtually all computer users, enable criminals to cut and paste, rearranging and transposing figures at will. Thus, computers can be the instrument in a variety of criminal activities.

Finally, computers can be containers or storage warehouses for crime unrelated to

A Sampling of Breaches of Federal Agencies[16]

Agency	Type of Breach	Potential Victims
U.S. Department of Transportation	Laptop stolen from a government vehicle in Florida	132,470
Department of Justice	Stolen laptop	80,000
U.S. Navy	Theft of two laptops	31,000
U.S. Department of Agriculture	Laptop and printouts stolen from an employee's car	350
Federal Trade Commission	Theft of laptops from an employee's car	110
U.S. Department of Agriculture	Hacker	26,000
U.S. Department of Energy	Hacker	1,502
U.S. Marines	Loss of portable drive	207,750
U.S. Department of Defense	Hacker	Unknown
U.S. Department of Veterans Affairs	Theft of laptop and hard drive from an employee's home	28,600,000
U.S. Navy	Unknown	30,000
Naval Safety Center	Employee error	Over 100,000
U.S. Navy Recruiting Offices	Office burglary	31,000
U.S. Department of Transportation	Laptop stolen from government car	132,470

technology. Drug dealers and bookies, for example, may utilize popular spreadsheet programs like Lotus or Excel to more effectively organize their records. Even burglary or homicide investigations may include evidence recovered from a computer. Indeed, as computers reach every crevice of American life, it is likely that digital evidence will be found at an increasing number of crime scenes, unrelated to computer crime. Thus, it is essential that all investigators, not just those involved in high-technology units, recognize the elevated possibility of computers as evidence receptacles.

As stated, individual actors engaged in computer crime range from suburban teenagers to disgruntled employees to incarcerated individuals, while motivations range from recreational to financial to ideological. Targets may include, but are not limited to, individuals, military or intelligence institutions, banking or financial organizations, utility or service companies, colleges or universities, and telecommunications networks. And, crimes may range from simple trespass or voyeurism to bank fraud to child pornography to international terrorism. However, one of the most common types of computer crime is unauthorized use or computer intrusion.

The figure below represents the overall distribution of cyber-security incidents and events across the six major categories identified by U.S. CERT: unauthorized access; denial of service; malicious code; improper usage; scans, probes, attempted access; and investigation.[17]

Estimates of the costs associated with computer intrusions range from $15 billion to $250 billion.[18] Estimates of the proportion of businesses attacked are just as diverse, ranging from 25 percent to almost 99 percent. Although this does not present a realistic picture, even the lowest estimates reveal the seriousness of this phenomenon. Ironically, these studies also reveal the reluctance of corporations to expend funds on data security. In fact, it is estimated that more than half of businesses spend 5 percent or less of their IT budget on security.

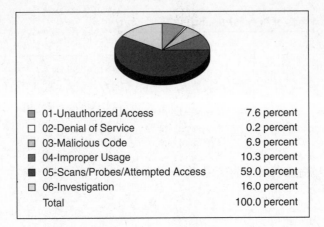

■ 01-Unauthorized Access	7.6 percent
□ 02-Denial of Service	0.2 percent
▨ 03-Malicious Code	6.9 percent
■ 04-Improper Usage	10.3 percent
■ 05-Scans/Probes/Attempted Access	59.0 percent
□ 06-Investigation	16.0 percent
Total	100.0 percent

This is reflected in the diversity of corporations which have fallen victim to computer intrusion. Nike's Web site (*www.nike.com*), for example, was hijacked and redirected to a political site in 2000. Government sites have proven equally vulnerable. In March 2000, a 19-year-old Houston cracker pled guilty to one count of conspiracy to commit teleconferencing fraud and computer cracking after hacking into various government sites, including that of the White House, and this individual was a member of GlobalHell, a notorious hacking group.

Another popular form of computer crime which often affects both government and corporate entities is the spread of computer viruses. The "Love Bug" virus, for example, affected at least 45 million computers and caused billions of dollars in damages. Victims included government agencies, educational institutions, financial corporations, and individual users alike. The systems most vulnerable to such attacks have proven to be MS Windows NT, Linux or variations, and Sun Solaris, in descending order. Recent years have also been characterized by an increase in denial of service attacks. Scott Dennis, a former computer system administrator for U.S. District Court in Alaska, launched three denial of service attacks against the U.S. District Court for the Eastern District of New York to illustrate the vulnerability of the system and prove his worth.

Perhaps the most disconcerting of all computer crime involves the visualization of the sexual exploitation of children. In a study conducted by the Department of Justice, one out of every five of the 24 million children on the Internet have received unwanted sexual solicitations. In addition, the number of online child pornography cases investigated and prosecuted has continued to grow at an exponential rate.[19] In 1998 alone, child pornography cases under investigation by the Cybersmuggling Unit of the Department of Customs in Sterling, VA, increased by 185 percent.[20] Unfortunately, this trend has continued unabated in the past decade. In 2007, Austrian authorities announced that they had busted an international child pornography ring involving almost 2,500 suspects from 77 countries. The individuals under investigation are alleged to have paid to view videos depicting young children being sexually abused—with some being gang raped and screaming in pain and fear. Approximately 600 of those under investigation were being investigated by the FBI and were located in the United States.[21] Unfortunately, this trend shows no signs of slowing as Web users increase in number daily.

THE EMERGENCE OF E-CASH: A NEW PROBLEM FOR LAW ENFORCEMENT

The past decade had witnessed an increasing proliferation of innovative payment mechanisms to facilitate e-commerce. Such innovations have utilized Internet and wireless devices, and the migration from paper to electronic payments has reached all corners of the globe. Like all other emerging technologies, the implications for e-payments are both positive and negative. Consumers have benefited, for example, from the enhanced services and efficiency offered from e-banking. In addition, the low overhead associated with online financial institutions has increased competition, resulting in lower interest rates and higher yields. On the other hand, the criminal element has embraced a variety of new payment methods which are often anonymous, involve multi-jurisdictional transactions, and exist in an environment which lacks regulation and government oversight. These characteristics facilitate money laundering and terrorist financing, and make it extremely difficult for investigators attempting to "follow the money." According to the Financial Action Task Force (FATF), these new payment methods include, but are not limited to, prepaid cards, electronic purses, mobile payments, Internet payment services, and digital precious metals.

Prepaid Cards

They are similar to debit cards in that they are attached to an account and provide access to monetary funds that are paid in advance by the cardholder. There are two primary types of prepaid card systems: limited or closed *and* multipurpose or open. **Limited purpose or closed system cards** may be used only for a finite number of purposes, and are issued by a particular merchant, telecommunications provider, or transit company. **Multipurpose or open system cards**, on the other hand, may be used for a wide range of purposes, may cross geographic boundaries, and may be used by any user. They are typically associated with a card payment network, like Visa or MasterCard, which may be attached to a particular depository account or linked to a line of credit by another merchant.

Stored Value Cards

Also known as **electronic purses**, these are cards whose value is stored electronically on the device via an integrated circuit chip. Unlike magnetic strips which only store account information, an e-purse actually stores funds on the chip. In fact, the user is literally carrying her funds with her, just as she does when places money in her purse. This method of payment is extremely convenient, as no online connection and no cardholder identification are necessary as the transaction vehicle was designed to substitute for cash. Such purses are generally reserved for micropayments, such as those used for public transportation, parking tickets, or vending machines.[22]

Mobile Payments

These payments which are made via mobile phones or other wireless communication devices. Some of these transactions are activated using voice access, text messaging protocols, or wireless application protocols.[23] This payment method is more widespread in Southeast Asia and Europe, although its use is becoming more popular in the United States. A second type of mobile payment involves the use of a telecom operator as a payment intermediary which authorizes, clears, and settles the payment. Most typically, these transactions occur when the telecom operator authorizes the consumer to charge the transactions to the phone bill.[24]

Internet Payment Services

There are two types of **Internet Payment Services** which are becoming increasingly popular in

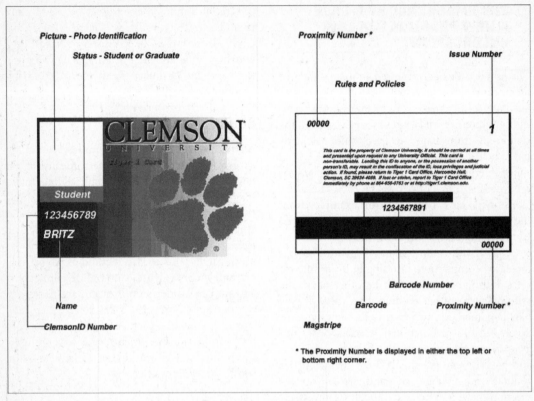

Picture - Photo Identification

Status - Student or Graduate

Proximity Number *

Issue Number

Rules and Policies

00000

1

This card is the property of Clemson University. It should be carried at all times and presented upon request to any University Official. This card is non-transferable. Lending this ID to anyone, or the possession of another person's ID, may result in the confiscation of the ID, loss privileges and judicial action. If found, please return to Tiger 1 Card Office, Harcombe Hall, Clemson, SC 29634-4059. If lost or stolen, report to Tiger 1 Card Office immediately by phone at 864-656-0763 or at http://tiger1.clemson.edu.

1234567891

00000

Student

123456789

BRITZ

CLEMSON
U N I V E R S I T Y

Tiger 1 Card

Barcode Number

Name

Barcode

Proximity Number *

ClemsonID Number

Magstripe

* The Proximity Number is displayed in either the top left or bottom right corner.

Many colleges and universities allow students to load cards with funds to eliminate the need to carry cash for incidental purchases. At Clemson University, for example, all students receive Tiger Stripes which can be used in cafeterias, restaurants, bookstores, and vending machines across campus. Students may also use them at a variety of establishments in the local community.

the United States. The first of these involve payments which rely on a bank account and use the Internet as a means of transferring funds to or from an established financial account. The second are those payments which are provided by non-bank institutions operating exclusively on the Internet that are only indirectly associated with a bank account. One of the most popular, PayPal, serves as an intermediary for individuals and organizations that wish to effect transactions via the Internet. Such intermediaries establish prepaid accounts funded from credit/ debit cards or credit transfers. Methods of fund disbursement vary among these intermediaries, with some issuing checks and others issuing credits.

Digital Precious Metals

They represent one of the newest forms of commodities trafficked on the Internet. It involves the exchange of options or the right to purchase a designated amount of precious metals at a particular price. The rationale for this type of currency involves the avoidance of currency fluctuation and foreign exchange. Unfortunately, many virtual dealers allow users to maintain anonymous accounts. This fact, coupled with the dichotomous nature of the process (i.e., the first level are the digital precious metal dealers and the second level involves a digital precious metal exchange service), exponentially increases the difficulties of criminal investigations and provides an attractive venue for money launderers.

CONCLUSIONS

Just as the introduction of the telephone gave American society the first wave of heavy breathers, telemarketers, and rapid response, the creation of the Internet has resulted in a myriad of developments, some positive, others negative. Individual users can travel all over the world at the touch of a button. They can access the latest sports scores, stock prices, and international news, while downloading their favorite music or photographs. On the surface, computers increase the independence and autonomy so prized in American society. Indeed, the ability to pack an entire briefcase on a floppy and conduct business from off-site locations like the beach or the mountains is a wondrous thing. This autonomy, however, masks an ever-increasing reliance on technology in which the masters become the slaves and the slaves become the masters. Unfortunately, this over-reliance on technology creates an extremely tenuous situation, in which computer failures can prove all but disastrous. This environment proves especially conducive to manipulation by those with nefarious intentions. Thus, an increase in antisocial and pathological behavior is all but inevitable. However, law enforcement authorities are struggling with outdated technology, a lack of significant resources, and administrative and public apathy.

DISCUSSION QUESTIONS

1. How can the intangibility of computer crime complicate investigations and subsequent prosecutions?
2. How has computer crime been characterized in the past? Do these perceptions hinder investigations? How?
3. Why are individual victims reluctant to report computer crime? What about private corporations?
4. What are some of the general costs associated with the investigation of computer crime? How do these compare with traditional investigations? What suggestions can you offer to increase the resources available for such?
5. Discuss the problems associated with the limited resources available in most police departments across the country. What can be done to alleviate some of these problems?
6. What is meant by jurisprudential inconsistency?

RECOMMENDED READING

- Baase, Sara (2002). *A Gift of Fire: Social, Legal, and Ethical Issues for Computers and the Internet.* Prentice Hall: New Jersey.
- Libicki, Martin (2007). *Conquest in Cyberspace: National Security and Information Warfare.* Cambridge University Press: Cambridge.
- Mitnick, Kevin D. and Simon, William (2003). *The Art of Deception: Controlling the Human Element of Security.* John Wiley & Sons: New Jersey.
- Stoll, Cliff (2005). *The Cuckoo's Egg: Tracking a Spy through the Maze of Computer Espionage.* Pocket Books: New York.

WEB RESOURCES

- www.ice.gov – homepage to the United States Immigration and Customs Enforcement, the largest investigative agency under the umbrella of the Department of Homeland Security. Web site provides links to activities, operations, and research conducted by the group, including those associated with terrorism, child pornography, organized crime, alien smuggling, and weapons trafficking. The site also provides links to other agencies and other resources.
- www.cybercrime.org – homepage to the U.S. Department of Justice's Computer Crime and Intellectual Property Section. The site provides links to numerous activities by the section, including, but not limited to, areas of research, enforcement, and education/outreach. In addition, the site provides news releases on current cases and provides the reader with access to emerging case law. Finally, the site includes information on "best practices" for search and seizure, and provides links to other government agencies and resources.
- www.abanet.org – the homepage of the American Bar Association. This site allows users to search for emerging issues in the enforcement, prosecution,

and defense of computer and cyber crime. It provides links to government agencies and other institutions devoted to the enforcement of computer crime statutes. In addition, it provides links to private organizations devoted to the protection and safeguard of civil liberties in areas of electronic communication and commerce.

- www.cert.org – maintained at Carnegie-Mellon University's Software Engineering Institute and home of the Computer Emergency Response Team. The site was one of the first to provide both businesses and government agencies with guidelines regarding protecting digital information and securing infrastructures. Users may access research publications and link to various public and private organizations devoted to issues associated with computer crime. The organization provides training and assistance to law enforcement personnel and others tasked with network security and computer forensics.

- www.us-cert.gov – created in 2003, the U.S. CERT is designed to be a partnership between the Department of Homeland Security and the public and private sectors. It is tasked with protection of the nation's Internet infrastructure, including the coordination of defense and response to cyber attacks in the United States. This site disseminates cyber threat warning information and provides malware analysis and recovery support, and serves as a portal of communication between the various entities concerned with the cybersecurity of the nation. The site provides links to current research and external resources.

ENDNOTES

[1]Sterling, Bruce (1994). *The Hacker Crackdown*. Available at *www.eff.orgpapers/hacker_crackdown/crack_1.html* (last accessed August 13, 2000).

[2]Ibid, p. 11.

[3]Hinduja, Sameer (2004). "Perceptions of Local and State Law Enforcement Concerning the Role of Computer Crime *Hinduja* Investigative Teams." *Policing: An International Journal of Police Strategies and Management, 27*(3): 341–357.

[4]Britz, Marjie T. (2008). *Criminal Evidence*. Allyn & Bacon: Upper Saddle River, NJ.

[5]Stambaugh, Hollis; Beupre, David S.; Baker, Richard; Cassady, Wayne; and Williams, Wayne P. (2001). "Electronic Crime Needs Assessment for State and Local Law Enforcement." DOJ # 98-DT-R-076. Washington, DC: NIJ.

[6]Hinduja(2004). Perceptions of local and state law enforcement.

[7]Ibid.

[8]Ibid.

[9]Ibid.

[10]Goroshko, Ludmila (2004). *2003 CSI/FBI Computer Crime and Security Survey*. Computer Crime Research Center, June 1, 2004. Available at *www.crime-research.org*.

[11]Center for Strategic and International Studies, Global Organized Crime Project (1998). "Cybercrime . . . Cyberterrorism . . . Cyberwarfare: Averting an Electronic Waterloo." Washington, DC.

[12]Available at *http://www.cert.org/stats/#incidents*.

[13]Spernow, Bill (2001). "A Cutting Edge Look at Enhancing Security for the Enterprise." A paper presented at the annual meetings of the Techno-Security conference, Myrtle Beach, SC, April 23, 2001.

[14]Stambaugh et al. (2001). "Electronic Crime Needs Assessment for State and Local Law Enforcement."

[15]CERT (2005). *2005 E-Crime Watch Survey*. Available at *http://www.cert.org/nav/allpubs.html*. Retrieved from the Internet on October 12, 2007.

[16]Privacy Rights Clearinghouse (2007). *Chronology of Data Breaches*. Available at *http://www.privacyrights.org/ar/chrondatabreaches.htm*. Retrieved from the Internet on October 12, 2007.

[17]US-Cert (2007). *Quarterly Trends and Analysis: September, 2007*. Available at *www.us-cert.gov*. Retrieved from the Internet on October 10, 2007.

[18]Ibid.

[19]Graves, Todd P. (2006). *Graves Announces Record Number of Child Exploitation Cases*. News Release. Office of the United States Attorney, Western District of Missouri. Available at *http://www. usdoj.gov/usao/mow/news2006/c3eNewsRelease.pdf*.

[20]Radcliff, Deborah (1998). "Crime in the 21st Century." *Infoworld, 20*(50): 65–66, December 14, 1998.

[21]CBS News (2007). *2,360 Suspects in Global Child Porn Bust: Austrian Police Announce Bust of Major Distribution Ring, FBI After 600 Suspects in U.S.* February 7, 2007. Available at *www.cbsnews.com*.

[22]FATF (2006). Report on New Payment Methods. *Financial Action Task Force Report*. October 13, 2006. Available at *www.fatf-gafi.org*.

[23]Ibid.

[24]Ibid.

CHAPTER 2

Computer Terminology and History

Chapter Outline

LEARNING OBJECTIVES

After reading this chapter, you will be able to do the following:

✓ Familiarize yourself with the basic language of computers and computer system.

✓ Explore a brief history of computer technology.

✓ Understand the pros and cons of global connectivity.

✓ Further comprehend the forms of Internet communication.

KEY TERMS & CONCEPTS

- application software
- ARPANet
- bandwith
- baud
- binary language
- bit
- bombs
- boot sequence
- byte
- bulletin boards
- buses
- cable modems
- central processing unit
- central processor
- command-line interface (CLI)
- computer forensics
- cookies
- CU-SeeMe
- data mining
- dedicated lines
- dial-up connection
- digital subscriber line (DSL)
- domains
- DNS
- droppers
- Eudora
- floppy diskettes or floppies
- forensic acquisition
- forensic authentication

- gigabytes (GB)
- graphical user interface (GUI; WIMP)
- Gopher
- hardware
- hertz
- hard disk drives
- hard drive
- host computer worms
- HTTP (hypertext transfer protocol)
- hubs
- IMAP
- Internet cache
- Internet protocol
- Internet service provider (ISP)
- keyboards
- kilobytes (KB)
- LINUX
- logic bombs
- malware
- megabytes (MB)
- microprocessors
- multiple-user systems
- modems
- Mosaic Interface
- motherboard
- network worm
- object code

- operating system
- packets
- PC cards
- PCI express bus
- Pine
- plug and play
- POP
- probe
- programs
- PUPs
- registry
- routers
- random access memory (RAM)
- scanner
- software
- source code
- TCP/IP
- trap doors
- Trojan horse
- terabytes (TB)
- time bomb
- UNIX
- UNIX OS
- URL
- universal serial bus (USB)
- virus
- World Wide Web
- worms

A BRIEF HISTORY OF COMPUTERS

If computer is defined in its simplest sense (i.e., a device used to ascertain an amount or number by calculation or reckoning), the earliest computers were invented by the Chinese over 800 years ago. These devices, known as abacuses, were unsophisticated instruments designed exclusively for mathematical computations. Comprised of rows of colored beads, abacuses were useful for only the simplest of tasks. However, the precursors of contemporary computers were not developed until the nineteenth century.

Much of today's technology may be directly attributed to ideas proposed by Londoner Charles Babbage (1822 and 1871). Babbage designed an analytical engine that could receive instructions from punch cards, make calculations with the aid of a memory bank and print out mathematical solutions. An unprecedented ideal, Babbage's device was a dismal failure due to the lack of a technological infrastructure—a necessity for any novel invention. (If such support had existed, this mechanism would have undoubtedly revealed our earliest computers.) However, the credit for today's machines is most often attributed to the work of Herman Hollerith. Indeed, Dr. Hollerith was the first to successfully introduce a device exclusively designed for data processing. This machine, developed an ocean away from Babbage, was created to tabulate the 1890 Census in the United States. Like many government employees before and since, Dr. Hollerith soon left his civil assignment (1896) and developed his own company, the Tabulating Machine Company, IBM's immediate predecessor. Although a monumental discovery, Hollerith's device bears little resemblance to the machines of today. However, his vision and foresight laid the foundation for a virtual explosion in communication, processing, and digital technology.

Subsequent developments in technology soon replaced the rather elementary machine created by Hollerith, and a virtual army of inventors has refined and perfected the rudimentary technology. Interestingly, many of these innovations have been partially, if not completely, funded by government initiatives. The first modern digital computer, for example, was built at Iowa State University by John Atanasoff, professor of physics and mathematics, and his graduate student, Clifford Berry, and was funded with federal monies. The Atanasoff–Berry Computer (ABC) had capabilities which included binary arithmetic, parallel processing, separate memory, regenerative memory, and basic computer functionality.

This technology, passed on to John W. Mauchly and John Presper Eckert, eventually resulted in the development of the Electronic Numerical Integrator and Computer (ENIAC). Built at the University of Pennsylvania's Moore School of Electrical Engineering, this device was

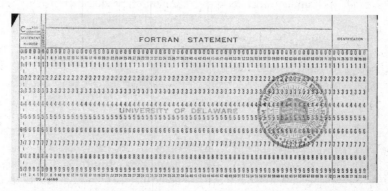

Eighty-column punch card originally used by IBM is still called the Hollerith card (*Courtesy of David L. Mills; used with permission*)

TECHNO-LINGO

A Taste of Hacking Terminology

Back door—a hole in security deliberately left within a program or software which enables non-authorized access.

Bit bucket—final destination of discarded, lost, or destroyed data.

Black hat hacker—term which refers to evil crackers.

Cracker—term originally coined by hackers which usually refers to those individuals violating secure systems for illicit purposes rather than fun. (**Hackers** claim to be motivated purely by intellectual pursuits, while "crackers" exploit systems for economic reasons or other forms of personal gain. Crackers are often referred to as "cyberpunks.")

Phreaking—art and science of cracking the phone network (i.e., making illegal phone calls).

Red hat hacker—tongue-in-cheek reference to a flavor of the Linux operating systems.

Sneaker—individual hired by a company to test its security systems by attempting to violate them.

Spaghetti or kangaroo code—complex or tangled code.

Time bomb—subspecies of logic bomb that is triggered by reaching some predetermined time or is set to go off in the event that a programmer is fired and not available to suppress action.

Trojan horse—malicious, security-breaking program designed to appear benign. Like the historical Trojan horse, these programs effectively hide something quite dangerous.

Vulcan nerve pinch—keyboard combination that forces a soft-boot or jump to ROM monitor. In many microcomputers, the combination is Ctrl-Alt-Del; sometimes called the "three-finger salute."

Wedged—often mistakenly synonymized with crashes—refers to the inability of a computer to make progress. Unlike a crash, a computer which is wedged is not totally non-functional.

Wetware—term used to refer to humans operating computers (as opposed to hardware and software).

White hat hackers—term used in the industry to designate "good" hackers.

---

responsible for calculating firing and bombing tables for the U.S. military. Fully assembled in 1945, ENIAC was composed of 30 separate units, coupled with separate power supplies and air conditioning units, and weighed 30 tons! In addition, it utilized 19,000 vacuum tubes, 1,500 relays, and required 200 kW of electrical power to operate.[1] Despite its monumental size, ENIAC was the prototype for most modern computers, mainframes, and PCs alike.

Developments in mainframe technology were accompanied by innovations in other areas of computer technology. Created around the same time as ENIAC, Colossus I was built at a secret government lab in Buckinghamshire, England, by Professor Max Newman. Unlike American innovations, Colossus I was designed exclusively for cryptanalysis. Using punched paper tape to scan and analyze 5,000 characters per second, this device proved to be invaluable in World War II as it broke the heretofore impenetrable "Enigma" codes used by the Nazi forces. This development, coupled

with the design of the ABC and the ENIAC, led to an explosion of mainframe technologies in the 1960s and 1970s, when mainframe devices came in vogue across university and corporate landscapes. Finally, the advent of PCs (originally containing operating systems like DOS and UNIX[2]) combined with the emergence of **graphical user interface** (**GUI**) platforms (like Windows™ and many Macintosh products) created a world accessible to technologically challenged individuals.

● COMPUTER LANGUAGE

Generally speaking, there are three basic components of every computer system which are designed to input, analyze, and output data: **hardware**, **software**, and firmware. (It must be noted that the following definitions are intended to simplify understanding of complex terms for undergraduates and non-computer specialists.

Known as the founder of IBM or "Big Blue," Thomas J. Watson transformed the Computer-Tabulating-Recording Company (CTR) into one of the largest conglomerates in the world. (*Getting Images, Inc.—Hulton Archive Photos*)

They are not intended to represent the sophistication and complexity of the computer world. Rather, they are intended to provide an elementary framework for informational digestion.)

Understanding Data[3]

Before a discussion of computer crime, cybercrime, and computer forensics is undertaken, it is necessary to discuss the nature of information as computers are the mechanism through which raw information (i.e., data) is processed. Although raw data may seem intimidating or complex to understand, the structure of data is actually very basic, and is based on a **binary language**. The smallest piece of data is called a **bit**. Each bit has two possible electrical states, on (1) or off (0). Thus, raw data to the naked eyes is

Storage Equivalence

Techno Terms			Visual Comparison
Nibble	= ½ a byte	= 4 bits	A single character
Byte	= 1 byte	= 8 bits	A word
	= 2 bytes	= 16 bits	
Double word	= 4 bytes	= 32 bits	
Kilobyte	= 1,024 bytes	= 2^{10} bytes	1,000 characters; one-half page of text
Megabyte	= 1,048,576 bytes	= 2^{20} bytes	Small novel; 5 MB— Shakespeare's work
Gigabyte	= 1,073,741,823 bytes	= 2^{30} bytes	Truck full of paper
Terabyte	= 1,099,511,627,776 bytes	= 2^{40} bytes	10 TB—Library of Congress

a series of 1s and 0s. Of course, raw data is difficult to interpret by users, so computers group bits together to provide identifiable meaning. The smallest such grouping occurs when eight bits are combined to form a **byte**. Each byte of data represents a letter, number, or character. For example, the raw data sequence of 01000001, appears to the user as the capital letter "A." Therefore, the author's name as it appears on a computer screen, Marjie Britz, is composed of 96 bits or 12 bytes (remember, spaces count, too). As the emphasis on stored information has increased, so has the data capacity of computers—from **kilobytes (KB)** to **megabytes (MB)** to **gigabytes (GB)**, and now, **terabytes (TB)**.[4]

To illustrate,

● COMPUTER HARDWARE

Input Devices

Hardware is composed of those components that are physical or tangible in nature. It includes common devices such as scanners, zips, modems, monitors, etc. It may be categorized as input, output, or storage devices, although these categories are not always mutually exclusive. Input devices are those mediums through which information is introduced to the computer. They include, but are not limited to, the following. **Modems** (further discussed under "Network Language") are electronic devices which connect a computer and telephone line to enable communication between computers by converting binary data to analog tones and voltages communicable over an analog communications cable and vice versa (can also be an output device). **Keyboards** are devices through which commands and information are introduced to the computer. They are, perhaps, the most recognizable of all. In fact, keyboards tend to be somewhat universal, and are usually clearly marked. Unfortunately, this type of familiarity often breeds complacence. Investigators should remember that keyboard configuration is

easily manipulated. As such, they should be aware that the suspect may have reconfigured the standard keyboard layout, creating "hot keys" which may have consequences ranging from the nuisance to the catastrophic. Any move might prove to be the case's undoing. Additionally, investigators should consider the possibility that remote users may use keyboards to manipulate a suspect system. Thus, it is extremely important that investigators recognize potential hazards posed by keyboards. The mouse (plural *mice*) is a device which moves a cursor on the screen when moved by hand. The **scanner** is a device for making a digital image of any graphic, for reproduction or processing by the computer. Other input devices, such as microphones and the like, are also commonly used.[5]

Output Devices

Output devices are those devices that produce and/or display information that has been processed by the computer for dissemination to the user. (In operation, a computer is both hardware and software. One is useless without the other. The hardware design specifies the commands it can follow, and the instructions tell it what to do.) Some of the most common of these are the following. *Monitors* were originally called cathode ray tubes (CRT). The modern monitor's precursor dates all the way back to 1895.[6] Contemporary monitors on desktop computers are usually separate from the **central processing unit** (CPU). However, some manufacturers combine CPUs and monitors. Generally speaking, computer monitors are devices that communicate to users, in a digestible format, the results of their commands. Printers are devices that create printed documents, per the computer's instructions, to reflect the results of computer commands. For investigators, printers can hold invaluable, yet often overlooked, criminal evidence. Thus, investigators should be sure to check all printers at the scene, and those computers which may be networked in remote areas (e.g., imagine yourself running to and from the

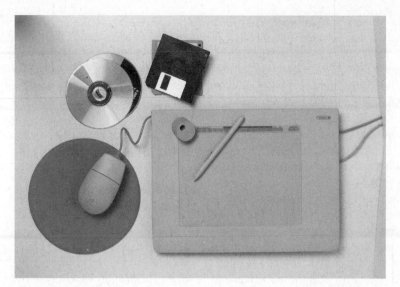

Computer systems contain various components, including, but not limited to, input and output devices. These categories are not necessarily mutually exclusive. For example, multitasking machines often incorporate input and output capabilities. (*Peter Anderson © Dorling Kindersley*)

computer, depressing the print key multiple times, desperate to have success. If the computer and its peripherals are turned off at night, and yet jobs are sent to the printer during the interim–voila–evidence).

The most important component of any computer is the **motherboard,** which is the primary circuit board of a PC to which all other elements are connected. These components include the processor memory chips, BIOS, and ROM. **PC cards** (originally *PCMCIA cards* for the organization that developed it, i.e., Personal Computer Memory Card International Association) refer to plug-in boards originally designed for laptops. Initially the size of a thick credit card, they can function as hard drives, network interfaces, flash memory cards, modems, SCSI,[7] CD-ROM, and audio drives. These may also be used in desktop computers.

Central processing unit is the single integrated circuit actually interpreting program instructions and the processing of data in a computer. (Original eight-bit processors had eight pins for accessing their external data buses. As in

other cases of technology, processor capabilities have developed at exponential rates. Intel's Pentium processors, e.g., are capable of transferring 64 bits (or 8 bytes) simultaneously!) **Buses** are multiple connections consisting of several parallel wires between chips and memory chips. These parallel electrical connections permit the transfer of several bits of data simultaneously. The first bus referred to is the processor's data bus. Determined by the age and type of the processor, the data bus is the one through which information moves from the processor to a storage device, and vice versa.[8] There are various buses available, each having its own utility. Traditionally, these devices were somewhat specific. For example, the **PCI express bus** (peripheral component interconnect express bus) is used to connect expansion cards (sound, graphic, modem, or network interface cards) to the motherboard. However, more generic buses have emerged. These buses are designed to serve as a standard connection for a variety of devices and manufacturers. The **universal serial bus (USB),** for example, is increasingly popular.

Central processors or **microprocessors**, which sit in a socket or a slot, are standardized by manufacturer and model. They are responsible for all commands executed by the computer. The speed of the processor determines the rate at which the computer performs the desired calculation. As such, they are rated by their relative speed using **hertz** (**Hz**). Also known as cycles per second, hertz measures the number of calculations the processor makes within a specific period. Initially, processor speeds ranged from 4 to 7 MHz. However, as more and more tasks became computerized, the demand for higher speeds resulted in an exponential growth of microprocessing manufacturers. This competition has proven quite beneficial to the individual consumer, and current speeds have topped 4.0 gigahertz (GHz). It is expected that the technology and the speed of processors will continue to advance.[9]

A final component found on the motherboard of a computer is the system's **random access memory** (**RAM**). RAM, which allows the computer to temporarily store information in its short-term memory, does not have any moving parts. As such, it relies on electrical impulses which read and write small pieces of data and is extremely efficient. RAM is measured by both capacity and speed. Memory chips are available to increase the system's RAM capacity, and high-end systems used for memory-dependent applications often have several gigabytes of RAM.[10] As RAM is temporary, the data stored in it will not be available once the computer is switched off. Thus, investigators should document applications which are running and screenshots prior to shutting down a suspect machine.

Hard Drives and Other Mass Storage Devices

While computer users enjoy the convenience which accompanies high-speed, high-capacity RAM, most are concerned primarily with long-term storage. (The inability for many university students to save their term papers on a lab computer's **hard drive** has led to a multitude of excuses when a system outage occurs!) **Hard disk drives** are those mass storage devices which are designed to permanently store that information which users intend to keep. As with earlier devices, hard drives are categorized by their storage capacity and are used to house both software used and information input by the user. They have advanced at a lightening pace in

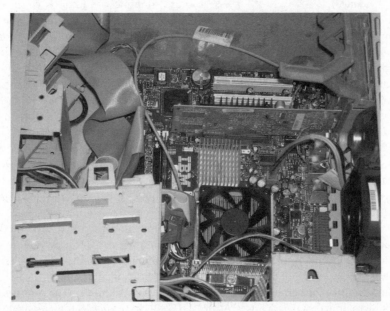

(Dr. Marjie T. Britz Ph.D)

recent years. While commercially available hard drives are most commonly measured in gigabytes,[11] the earliest devices could only hold megabytes of data! Advancements in secondary storage devices have accompanied the increase in primary hard drive capacity. In addition, a proliferation of alternative devices has emerged.

The first type of commercially available alternate storage media were known as **floppy diskettes** or **floppies**. These disks were composed of a thin, flexible magnetic storage disk encased in a square shell. Initially developed by IBM in the 1960s, floppy disks came in both 3.5" and 5.25" formats. Due to their low storage capacity and fragility, they were eventually replaced by alternate mass storage devices. Today, consumers may purchase CD/DVD, external hard drives, flash memory, or, the ever popular, thumb drives.

● COMPUTER SOFTWARE

Generally speaking, the term **computer software** refers to a series of instructions that performs a particular task. More specifically, software is the interpretation of binary byte sequences represented by a listing of instructions to the processors. Computer hardware is useless without software as it cannot move, manipulate data, or receive input. Without instructions, hardware is really just an oversized paperweight—having no known tasks, functions, or capabilities. Software is not only necessary to tell the components within a system what to do and how to act. It is also necessary to tell it how to interact with the user. There are three main types of software or instruction sets: **boot sequence** instructions; **operating system**; and **application software.**

Boot Sequence

The boot sequence of a computer refers to the series of steps taken by a computer immediately upon powering on which are necessary before it is usable. Receiving its name from "pulling itself up by its bootstraps," the boot sequence is contained in low-level data stored in a small memory chip on the motherboard, known as the CMOS. This set of instructions tells the computer in which order to access drives, and basic hardware information.

The first step in the boot sequence is commonly referred to as the POST (power-on self test) and is viewable by the user on the screen. It involves a checking of hardware operation and efficiency and memory count. A short beep usually signals the completion of this process, and then the computer moves on to loading the operating system, the user interface, and other programs designed to launch upon start-up. Users are notified that the computer is ready for input when the hard drive light stops flashing. The boot process is usually quite fast on updated systems. However, time for completion does vary based upon the number of start-up programs on a particular machine.[12]

Operating System

Perhaps the most important piece of software for any user is the operating system. Most commonly written in Assembler, C, or C++, the operating system is a piece of software that runs user applications and provides an interface to the hardware. Traditionally, almost all personal computers with the exception of Macintosh products contained some version of DOS. The original DOS pre-dated hard drives, and was contained on a floppy disk. Users would place the floppy in the drive, and load the instructions manually. As there were no graphics available at that time, DOS was simply a series of text-based instructions. Because the process was manual, users had to enter the commands exactly. One advantage to this type of **command-line interface** (**CLI**) was that computer resources expended were minimal, as the computer simply followed the input directions. However, if mistakes were made in the syntax, the computer would issue a *syntax error*—a major source of frustration for early computer users. Although some contemporary operating systems are CLI, the majority of PCs in the United States contain some form of **graphical user interface** or *GUI* (pronounced gooey) or *WIMP* (windows, icons, multitasking, and pointing device). Originally created by Xerox,™ such "point and click" technology is now the norm due to its user-friendly platform. Such advances have made computer usage far less painful for novice users, allowing them to more efficiently organize their files and data.[13] (Unfortunately, this reliance has resulted in a lack of knowledge of disk structure and underlying foundations by some individuals responsible for investigations. Hence, the disparaging terms "point and click" or "Nintendo" forensics was coined by forensic computer experts.)

Operating systems may be either single-user or multiple-user. For the most part, personal computers are just that—personal, and are designed to be used by one person at a time. This does not suggest, however, that the machines are not capable of multitasking or are exclusive to a single owner. Rather, they are not designed to be accessed my multiple users simultaneously. **Multiple-user systems**, on the other hand, such as the Windows Server family or UNIX/Linux provide for application programs to be employed by various individuals at once.

ALTERNATIVES TO DOS: POPULAR OPERATING SYSTEMS

As discussed above, DOS, originally intended for IBM personal computers, is considered to be one of the first personal computer operating systems. Based on a command-line, character-based user interface, it lost most of its early momentum when GUIs became available on personal computers. On the current market, there are a variety of products both CLI and GUI that consumers may choose from.

Microsoft Windows

Without question, Windows operating systems are the most commercially successful. Although many high-end or sophisticated computer users eschew Microsoft products completely, the average American user prefers Microsoft products due to their user friendly application.

- **Windows 1.0 (1985), Windows 2.0 (1987), Windows 3.0 (1990),** and **Windows 3.1**—As stated previously, GUIs enable us to see a visual representation of the files that are contained within a particular machine. The first GUI was developed at Xerox, a trailblazer in computer research. Both Microsoft Windows and Apple Macintosh were a result of this early framework. However, Windows 1.0, 2.0, and 3.0 proved to be notoriously unstable. Windows 3.1, an application that ran on top of DOS, was a bit more stable.

- **Windows 3.11** and **Windows NT 3.1 (1993)**—The introduction of Windows 3.11 allowed computers to network on the same segment or LAN. This was the first step in the development of a peer-to-peer network. Windows NT (New Technology) 3.1 was considered to be more secure, more efficient, and more reliable. New features included 32-bit computing, a preemptive multitasking scheduler for Windows-based applications, integrated networking, domain server security, OS/2 and POSIX subsystems, support for multiple processor architectures, and the NTFS file system.

- **Windows 95 (1995)**—Upon its debut, Windows 95 was heralded as the best thing to hit computers since the abacus. From the desktop to the architecture, the entire method of personal computing was changed. It was based on 32-bit computing, and had built-in network and Internet capability (Internet Explorer). In addition, it streamlined the software installation process, with its **plug and play** feature (i.e., the operating system itself determines appropriate settings). Finally, Windows 95 collated all of the operating system files and information into one centralized location—the **registry.**

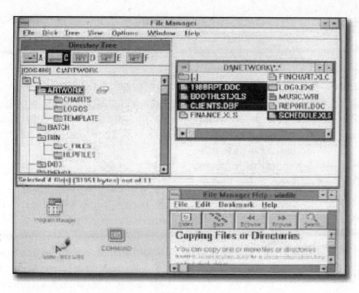

An illustration of a file manager screen in Windows 3.0.

- **Windows 98 (1998)** and **Windows 98 SE (1999)**—Windows 98, the first Microsoft product created exclusively for consumers, was widely embraced by Corporate America. It included USB support, and enhanced the multimedia and network capabilities introduced in previous Microsoft products. The inclusion of Internet Explorer 5.0 provided consumers with enhanced Web browsing and the ability to upgrade via the Internet. Finally, it automated registry checks and repairs.
- **Windows ME (2000)**—Windows ME was the last of Microsoft's products to be based on the Windows 95 code base. Designed for home computer users, it included numerous music, video, and home networking enhancements. This included a System Restore feature to allow users to roll back theirsoftware configuration to a date or time before a problem occurred.
- **Windows 2000 Professional (2000)**—Designed to replace Windows 95 and Windows 98, Windows 2000 was based on Windows NT code. As such, it is more reliable and secure. Security features include secure authentication; automatic file encryption;

A Note About NT

It is virtually impossible to talk about every product and every update by Microsoft. As with other software vendors, updates are often unforeseen and are done as problems arise. Irrespective of these types of changes, Windows products may be broadly dichotomized: Windows and Windows NT. Although they employ similar GUIs, their differences are far more pronounced. From the beginning, Windows NT was designed as a 32-bit operating system. In addition, the Windows NT kernel works in *privileged mode*. In this manner, the Windows NT operating system can isolate applications, and shut down single applications which have become unstable without affecting the rest of the system. Finally, while Windows programs are notoriously unsecure, Windows NT employs a multilayer approach which includes, but is not limited to, network share protection; auditing capabilities; use of domain controllers; file and folder access protection via permissions; and login security screens.

group policies; and Internet Protocol Security (IPSec) protocol. Ironically, many commercial users of Windows 2000 do not recognize the importance or even the existence of these security features.

- **Windows XP (2001)**—The release of Windows XP was the first time that Microsoft had merged its corporate and consumer lines around the Windows 2000 code base. Enhancements include remote control access, firewall, and increased operating system speed. To reduce the amount of counterfeit or pirated software, Microsoft included an activate feature in XP (i.e., users must contact Microsoft to obtain an activation code).

Macintosh

In 1976, Steve Jobs and Steve Wozniak released the first Apple computer. In a marked contrast to other systems, Apple machines were self-contained. Thus, Apple controlled all aspects of the computer—including the operating system, other software applications, and the hardware. This was dramatically opposed to with other systems in which countless combinations of hardware/software interfaces were employed.[14] Instead of requiring additional purchases and installation of various devices, Apple computers incorporated video, audio, and graphic into both their hardware and their software. This "hands off user!" approach proved to be popular for many individuals who were only concerned with using a computer and did not care what the mechanics entailed. Others, however, did not appreciate the total control that the Apple organization exercised.

Apple never achieved the market share that Microsoft did. Users were often dismayed at the lack of alternative software available for their machine. They also expressed dismay that while their machines contained word processing and graphics capability, their work product was not portable to other machines. Thus, for Apple users not living in an Apple world, the early convenience was eventually overshadowed by frustration. In an attempt to appease their consumer base, Apple developed technology in which both Apple and PC software could be utilized. However, their early attempts fell short. Currently, Macintosh products have resolved these issues, and a new generation of users has emerged. Newer systems are UNIX based, and are characterized by security and stability. In fact, anecdotal evidence suggests that many investigators prefer Macintosh for these reasons.

UNIX

The basis or underlying framework for many contemporary operating systems, **UNIX** was created by Bell Laboratories in 1969. It was initially designed for use by large computer systems, and was the basis for many mainframe systems employed at universities across the country. However, its inherent stability and security has encouraged many smaller organizations and corporations to adopt it. In addition, it is considered to be the backbone of the Internet, and is favored by both hackers and computer experts. While there are various versions of UNIX out there, there are two main platforms from which they derive: the Berkeley Software Distribution (BSD) and the System V Release 4 (SVR4). While some current versions of UNIX now offer a GUI-based interface, the majority of users opt for the traditional command line to maximize power. Summarily, UNIX is most appropriately characterized as a secure multiuser, multitasking operating system.

LINUX

The baby of computer operating systems, **Linux** was developed in the 1990s and has achieved a strong following in its infancy. There are a variety of reasons for its increasing popularity. First, and foremost, it's FREE. In addition, it can run on older equipment and run a multitude of hardware platforms. Finally, because it is based on the UNIX operating system, it is fast, stable, and secure.

Linux has additional benefits as well. It is easier to use than traditional CLIs, and a GUI interface has been developed for it. As it has gained

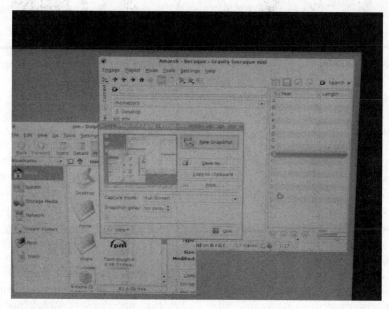

Screenshot of a Linux system employing a GUI.

popularity, software applications are emerging. For example, OpenOffice contains both word processing and spreadsheet applications. Unlike other operating systems, Linux is open source. Thus, individual users can customize the kernel so that the operating system is tailored to the specific hardware on the system.

Application Software

Application software is prepackaged instructions which allow users to perform a variety of functions, including but not limited to word processing, statistical analysis, and the like. In fact, existing software packages are all but limited to a user's imagination. Among other things, individual users can play games, create masterpieces, file taxes, and develop house plans. Semantically speaking, there are a variety of terms used to represent certain elements within the realm of software. **Programs**, for example, represent the sequence of rules through which software operates; **source code** refers to the set of instructions written in a programming language; **object code**

is what is actually executed by the computer; and so on. Collectively, any program which has been placed clandestinely on an individual's computer is referred to as a PUP (potentially unwanted program). While some **PUPs** are intended to enhance a user's Internet experience by collecting browsing information, some are much more nefarious by design.

Malware or *malicious programming code* refers to a code that causes damage to computer systems. Within this definition lies an entire subfield of terminology. **Trap doors**, for example, are codes that allow a user to enter a system without authorization (also referred to as a "back door"); a **Trojan horse**, nicknamed after the Greek myth of old, is a program that on its face has a legitimate purpose, but also has a hidden feature, such as a trap door or hidden program. Unlike viruses and worms, Trojan horses do not replicate themselves. Such programs may include those which can be triggered to cause damage or alter information; a **virus**, usually attached or inserted into a file or the boot sector of a disk, is a rogue computer program which is designed to disperse copies of itself to other computers for destructive purposes by attaching itself to programs and replicating. (A boot sector virus can also infect a hard drive, where it is much more dangerous.) They are introduced to computer systems as part of an infected COM, EXE, or boot sector program file, or through network downloads such as macros, set-up files, or e-mail attachments.[15] While most computer users are familiar with the term, many do not recognize that viruses reside on a continuum of destruction, ranging from the relatively harmless, designed to prove the superiority of its creator, to the catastrophic. In fact, some are so dangerous that they require a complete shutdown of businesses. Viruses are never accidental. They are always intentionally and deliberately designed to perform certain functions, and all are harmful in some way. For example, all consume disk space, memory, and other resources which directly affect the speed and efficiency of an individual machine, and at a minimum, their proliferation has all but required the necessity of space-draining antivirus programs.[16] They are inherently dangerous, in that they are uncontrollable. Once initiated, even the writer or creator cannot control the infestation that will result. The motivations for such creations range from boredom to retribution. **Worms** are self-contained programs (or sets of programs) which may spread functional copies of themselves or their segments to other computer systems (usually via a network connection). Although many individuals synonymize worms with viruses, they

are quite distinct. Unlike viruses, worms do not need to attach themselves to a host program nor are they designed to alter or erase files. However, system crashes may result due to their ability to infest machine space.

There are two types of worms: network worms and host computer worms. **Network worms** consist of several segments operating on different machines that use the network for several communication purposes. Once activated, these worms will scan for connections to the host node. Such vulnerabilities will enable the worm to spread throughout the network. **Host computer worms**, on the other hand, are entirely contained on the computer they run on. These worms use network connections only to copy themselves to other computers. Some variations include self-destructive programs. These "rabbit" programs terminate themselves after launching a copy on another host. Thus, at any given time, only one copy of the worm is operating on the network.

Droppers are programs that are created to avoid anti-virus detection, usually by encryption that hinders detection. Their typical function is to transport and install viruses when an infected computer performs a certain function; **bombs** are usually built into malware as an activation mechanism. Like droppers, bombs are designed to activate when a specific action occurs. **Time bombs** are those bombs that are activated at a specific time on the infected system's internal clock. For example, many individuals feared that virus

A Sampling of Forensic Terminology

Although a more comprehensive definition of forensic terminology will be discussed in later chapters, here is sample of terms commonly used in investigations involving computers.

- **Computer forensics**—the acquisition, authentication, recovery, and analysis of digital evidence.
- **Data mining**—a comprehensive analysis of large data sets designed to uncover patterns and relationships. Analysis tools include, but are not limited to, statistical models, mathematical algorithms, and artificial intelligence.

- **Forensic acquisition**—the process of making a duplicate copy of computer media.
- **Forensic authentication**—the process of proving that an acquired image is an exact copy of the suspect media. Such authentication is demonstrated when an algorithmic value calculated from the suspect media is found to be the same as that of the acquired image. This figure, which may be characterized as an electronic fingerprint, is known as an MD5 hash (message digest version 5).

writers would create bombs programmed for New Year's Eve, 1999. **Logic bombs,** on the other hand, are programs which are designed to activate upon a series of events. For example, this type of program may be activated the nineteenth time a user launches Microsoft Office. In other words, bombs are malicious scripts or scheduling programs.[17]

A BRIEF HISTORY OF THE INTERNET

In the beginning . . . there was no Internet. Yikes, those are words that are sure to frighten the staunchest of contemporary users. However, the "Internet" did not accompany the introduction of the first computers nor did Al Gore invent it as alleged. In fact, the original concept of an internet did not include commerce, global connectivity, or public usage. The initial conceptualization of such actually derived from the government suspicion and social hysteria that permeated Cold War America in the 1960s. The threat of nuclear war and mass destruction was such that government entities focused on developing electronic communication systems that would remain viable even if large portions were somehow destroyed. The beginning was a project of the *Advanced Research Project Agency Network* (**ARPANet**) sponsored in 1969 by the Department of Defense. Primarily designed to overcome threats from a blackout of communication in the event of a nuclear war, this computer network linked four universities (UCLA, Stanford, UC Santa Barbara, and the University of Utah) and was intended to facilitate communications between computers over phone lines regardless of system characteristics (Baladi, 1999). Initially used by researchers, engineers, computer experts, and the like, the system proved to be rather cumbersome (and complicated). Interactive sessions were not possible. Rather, the method of communication required users to post suggestions in papers titled "Requests for Comments" (RFC), and await responses or amendments to their

documents. The first RFC (RFC0001) was written on April 7, 1969—the closest thing to a "start date" for the Internet. There are now well over 2000 RFCs, describing every aspect of how the Internet functions.

ARPANet was opened to non-military users later in the 1970s, and early takers were the big universities—although at this stage it resembled nothing like the Internet we know today. International connections (i.e., outside America) started in 1972, but the "Internet" was still just a way for computers to talk to each other and for research into networking; there was no World Wide Web and no e-mail as we now know it. By the mid-1980s, this network was further expanded with the introduction of the NSF Net, established under the National Science Foundation by a small group of supercomputer research centers and researchers at remote academic and governmental institutions. This network was highly supported by the government, which encouraged researchers and institutions to avail themselves of this communication tool. This collaboration proved to be invaluable to the development of both online and offline computer communities, as well as the creation of a myriad of software which included **UNIX OS** (developed by Bell Laboratories); **Mosaic Interface** (a multimedia interface for information retrieval); **Eudora** (an e-mail system), contributed by the University of Illinois; **Gopher** (information retrieval tool), contributed by the University of Minnesota; **Pine** (e-mail), University of Washington; and **CU-SeeMe** (low-cost video conferencing), Cornell (Adams, 1996). Such software innovations, coupled with (and often facilitated by) government grants, created a more user-friendly cyber-world.

By the mid-1980s, the Commercial Internet Xchange (CIX) had emerged, and midlevel networks were leasing data circuits from phone companies and subleasing them to institutions (Adams, 1996). Eventually, this small network had expanded into networks of networks, until the contemporary phenomenon known as the Internet emerged. During this period, the services we use most now started appearing on the Internet. In fact, the concept of "domain names" (e.g., *www.microsoft.com*) was first introduced in 1984. Prior to this introduction, computers were simply accessed by their IP addresses (numbers). Most protocols for e-mail and other services appeared after this.

The part of the Internet most people are probably most familiar with is the World Wide Web. This is a collection of hyperlinked pages of information distributed over the Internet via a network protocol called **hypertext transfer protocol (HTTP)**. This was invented in 1989 by Tim Berners-Lee, a physicist working at CERN, the European Particle Physics Laboratory, who created the Web so that physicists could share information about their research. Thus, the Web was introduced as a restricted means of communication between scientists. Although it was originally a text-only medium, graphics were soon introduced with a browser called NCSA Mosaic. Both Microsoft's Internet Explorer and Netscape were originally based on NCSA Mosaic.

This graphical interface opened up the Internet to novice users and in 1993 its use exploded as people were allowed to "dial-in" to the Internet using their computers at home and a modem to ring up an **Internet service provider (ISP)** to get their connection to this (now huge) network. Prior to these developments, the only computers connected were at universities and other large organizations that could afford to wire cables between each other to transfer the data over. Currently, there are several quick and inexpensive ways to connect to the Internet. At the minimum, users simply need a computer, a modem, a telephone line, and intercomputer communication software. These basics allow users to connect via ISPs. New trends, however, reveal that consumers are increasingly attracted to service-oriented ISPs—sometimes referred to as "online service providers (OSPs)." These organizations provide consumers with navigational tools especially attractive to nontraditional users. Such accessibility has created unprecedented growth.

The Internet has grown exponentially in the past decade—from 300 host computers in 1981 to over 36 million in 1998.[18] Internet users have risen from 10 to 25 million in 1991, to 157 million in 1998, to over a billion in 2008; over half of households in the United States actively use the Internet. The popularity of this medium has been fueled by the diversity of information available on the Web. Users' interests range from real-time information (i.e., scores of sporting events, current stock prices, etc.) to transactional services (i.e., banking, airline reservations, etc.) to entertainment (i.e., horoscopes, movie reviews, etc.). Such popularity has also emerged due to the multitude of communications media, including e-mail, bulletin boards, newsgroups, or the most popular, the World Wide Web. The Web's popularity stems from the effortless nature of its communications. Even novice users can easily transmit audio, video, and graphic files.

NETWORK LANGUAGE

Increasingly, network language is dominating the computer landscape. While many low-end users are familiar with the acronyms, few recognize (or care) what particular terminology refers to. However, it is essential that computer investigators understand the language behind the technology.

Commonly Used Terms

Here are but a few examples of the most commonly used terms: **TCP/IP** (*Transmission Control Protocol/Internet Protocol*) refers to the suite of protocols that define the Internet. More specifically, TCP is a method of communication between programs which enables a bit-stream transfer of information. Originally proposed and designed as the standard protocol for ARPANet (the precursor of today's Internet), TCP/IP software is now available for every major kind of computer operating system, although most DOS-based systems require the purchase of additional software. To be truly on the Internet, your computer must have TCP/IP software. Luckily, it is now built into many of the most common operating systems (i.e., Microsoft Windows 95, NT, etc.).

IMAP (*Internet Message Access Protocol*) is a method of accessing electronic mail or bulletin board messages that are kept on a (possibly shared) mail server. In other words, it permits a "client" e-mail program to access remote message stores as if they were local. For example, e-mail stored on an IMAP server can be manipulated from a desktop computer at home, a workstation at the office, and a notebook computer while traveling, without the need to transfer messages or files back and forth between these computers. This technology is increasingly important as reliance on electronic messaging and use of multiple computers increase, but this functionality cannot be taken for granted: the widely used *Post Office Protocol* (**POP**) works best when one has only a single computer, since it was designed to support "off-line" message access, wherein messages are downloaded and then deleted from the mail server. This mode of access is not compatible with access from multiple computers since it tends to sprinkle messages across all of the computers used for mail access. Thus, unless all of those machines share a common file system, the off-line mode of access that POP was designed to support effectively ties the user to one computer for message storage and manipulation.

Routers are defined as special-purpose computers (or software packages) that handle the connection between two or more networks. Routers spend all their time looking at the destination addresses of the packets passing through them and deciding which route to send them on. Routers are analogous to switches found within telephone systems—the same switches that have proven irresistible to phone phreakers and their contemporary counterparts. **Hubs** are central switching devices for communications lines in a star topology. They may add nothing to the transmission (passive hub) or may contain electronics that regenerate signals to boost strength as well monitor activity (active hub, intelligent hub). Hubs may be added to bus topologies; for example, a hub can turn an Ethernet network into a star topology to improve troubleshooting.

Packets are defined as units of data exchanged between host computers. Typically, they are further distinguished as headers and data. *Packet switching* refers to the method used to move data around on the Internet. In packet switching, all the data coming out of a machine are broken up into chunks; each chunk has the address of where it came from and where it is going. This enables chunks of data from many different sources to commingle on the same lines and be sorted and directed to different routes by special machines along the way. This way, many people can use the same lines at the same time. The different headers are appended to the data portion as the packet travels through the communication layers; **cookies** are small pieces of information that an HTTP server sends to the individual browser upon the initial connection. Not all browsers support cookies. However, most popular browsers do: MS Internet Explorer 3.0 or

Sniffing for Information

As mentioned previously, certain information is considered to be a lucrative commodity to many people. Those interested include criminals and government agents alike. Information acquisition methods have evolved considerably in recent years. Electronic eavesdropping has moved from the phone lines to the Internet from electronic bugs to packet sniffers.

A packet sniffer is a program which is designed to capture data from transitory information packets across a network. To criminals, packets of interest might include usernames, passwords, account information, or proprietary data. To law enforcement officials, packets of interest might include terrorist planning, discussion of criminal activity, or child pornography. In the 1990s, the introduction of a packet sniffing program named Carnivore angered privacy advocates, who claimed that the FBI was using it to spy on the American public.

higher and Netscape Navigator 2.0 and higher. These cookies are stored on an individual hard drive for retrieval by a particular site. Theoretically, this storage is to simplify things for individual users so that their preferences and personal information do not necessarily have to be re-entered upon return access.

More succinctly, a cookie refers to a piece of information sent by a web server to a web browser that the browser software is expected to save and to send back to the server whenever the browser makes additional requests from the server. Depending on the type of cookie used, and the browser's settings, the browser may accept or not accept the cookie, and may save the cookie for either a short time or a long time. Cookies might contain information such as login or registration information, online "shopping cart" information, user preferences, etc. When a server receives a request from a browser that includes a cookie, the server is able to use the information stored in the cookie. For example, the server might customize what is sent back to the user, or keep a log of particular user's requests. Cookies are usually set to expire after a predetermined amount of time and are usually saved in memory until the browser software is closed down, at which time they may be saved to disk if their "expire time" has not been reached. Although many users naively believe that cookies are capable of reading individual hard drives and sending the user's life history to the CIA, they are simply intended to gather more information about a user than would be possible without them. Thus, cookies do not *steal* information; they simply act as storage platforms for information which a user has supplied.

Cookies operate primarily through the application of *attributes* which instruct the browser which servers to send them to. **Domains**, for example, tell browsers which host names that cookies should be returned to. A computer's **DNS** (*Domain Name System) entry* is based on a group of computers on a common network defined by a commonality of **Internet Protocol** (IP) addresses. These networks are governed by common rules and procedures and are treated as a unit. Prior to the implementation of the DNS, the translation of host names to IP addresses was done by the IP software doing a look-up in the file /etc/hosts or /etc/inet/hosts (on UNIX computers) or hosts.txt (on PCs). This system proved to be unworkable and impossible to administer with the virtual explosion of the Internet.[19] Thus, the introduction of DNS was essential for the fluidity of electronic communications. Generally speaking, DNS eases the translation of IP addresses through the utilization of hierarchical principles. Traditional top-level domain names include *com* (commercial organization), *edu* (educational institutions), *gov* (government organizations), *org* (nonprofit organizations), and *net* (Internet access providers). Foreign countries and state organizations are increasingly using two- and three-letter codes.

● REALMS OF THE CYBERWORLD

Basically speaking, there are three different levels of networked systems: *intranets, internets,* and the *Internet.* **Intranets** are small, local networks connecting computers which are within one organization and which are controlled by a common system administrator. **Internets**, on the other hand, connect several networks, and are distinguished in the literature by a lower case *i* (i.e., "internet" as opposed to "Internet"). These networks are usually located in a small geographic area, and share a common protocol (usually TCP/IP). The **Internet**, on the other hand, is the largest network in the world, an international connection of all types and sizes of computer systems and networks. It is a system of small networks of computers linked with other networks via routers and software protocols. This TCP/IP-based network links tens of millions of users, across more than 45,000 networks, in countries spanning the globe. Originally, this system was funded in large part by the U.S. government and was not available for commercial usage.

Ma Bell, the Department of Justice, and Antitrust

In 1974, the Department of Justice filed an antitrust suit against telephone monopoly AT&T. Under the terms of the suit's settlement, the company was forced to divest its local exchange service operating companies. In exchange, the company could jump into the computer business. On January 1, 1984, seven independent Regional Bell Operating Companies or "Baby Bells" were born.

In contemporary society, the Internet has become the backbone for global communications and transnational capitalism. For the most part, the explosion of such may be attributed to advances in and accessibility to inexpensive and efficient connection methods. During the Internet's infancy, users could connect only via standardized modems and telephone lines. Early service providers, like AOL, initially charged users for the period of time they spent on the Internet. As connection speeds via modems were notoriously slow, individuals racked up substantial charges. This expense was compounded by users who connected via long distance numbers. As a result, telephone companies became victimized by criminals (i.e., phreakers) seeking to avoid such charges. As competition increased with the birth of the "Baby Bells," cost to consumers began to decline.

Connections made via modem are known as **dial-up connections**. Such connections were originally categorized by the transfer rate of data using an older measure of bandwidth known as **baud.** Initially, a transfer rate of 300 baud was not uncommon. Such rates quickly evolved as market demand increased, and 1,200, 2,400, 4,800, and 9,600 baud became the standard. As these modem bandwidth rates grew, a new designation of transfer speed was developed. Currently, data transfer rates are categorized as kilobits per second (Kbps) or megabits per second (Mbps).

DATA BANDWITH TRANSFER RATES

On today's market, there are three primary varieties of high-speed, broadband connections commercially available for individuals and businesses alike: **Digital Subscriber Line (DSL), cable modems,** or **dedicated lines. DSLs** were introduced in the late 1990s and transfer data via copper telephone lines. There are a variety of different types of DSL, such as ADSL, HDSL, and RADSL. Faster than traditional cable models, DSL may transfer between 6 and 7 Mbps. Cable modems are also increasingly popular among consumers. These devices transfer data along a coaxial cable line, and provide an average data transfer rate of 1.5 Mbps (data rates will vary based on an individual cable company's mode of connection to the Internet). Although the price of the cable modem itself tends to be minimal, subscription to cable companies tend to cost consumers more than DSL offered through their local telephone provider.

While many consumers prefer cable modems or DSL connections due to their accessibility and low cost, companies often prefer to have a **dedicated line** for connection to the Internet. Such direct access is most commonly accomplished via T1. The T1 or T-1 carrier is the most commonly used digital transmission service in various countries, including the United States. It consists of channels employing pulse code modulation (PCM)

	56K Dial-up	1.5 Mbps	3.0 Mbps
1-MB file	146 seconds	5.3 seconds	2.65 seconds
100-MB file	Over 4 hours	<10 minutes	<5 minutes

signals with time-division multiplexing (TDM) to exchange data at a rate of 1.544 million bits per second. Originally comprised of copper wires, T1 lines currently include optical and wireless media. Many businesses use T1 lines to connect to an Internet access provider.

Irrespective of connection method, all have proven vulnerable to unauthorized access. Hackers have compromised countless systems, and generally employ probes to identify potential targets. A **probe** may be defined as an unusual or unauthorized attempt to gain access to or discover information about a system. Probing may be analogized to testing doorknobs to see if they are unlocked. While many probes are innocuous, opportunistic criminals use probes to identify and exploit system vulnerabilities. In addition to individual probes, some criminals employ scans (i.e., the automation of a large number of probes) to ascertain targets.

CATEGORIZING INTERNET COMMUNICATION

World Wide Web

The **World Wide Web** may be likened to an electronic marketplace where electronic storefronts of businesses, individuals, civic groups, and governments market both tangible and intangible products. Each electronic storefront established on the Internet is known as a Web site. These sites have a variety of goals. While many are profit-driven, others are developed for informational purposes only. Government agencies, public interest groups, educational institutions, and the like often use this medium as an alternative to traditional means of information dissemination that may be costly and/or labor intensive. Regardless of motivation, each Web site may be identified by its *Uniform Resource Locator* (**URL**). These URLs are used for traffic control and Web management. Appearances range from the very basic text-only sites to sophisticated visual and audio configurations. In fact, these storefronts are only limited by the proprietors' imagination. It is anticipated that this marketplace will continue to experience exponential growth at the rate of 200 percent per year. Such growth may be primarily attributed to relatively low overheads associated with cyber capitalism. Not surprisingly, the presence of criminal elements within this realm is expected to increase proportionately.

Newsgroups/Bulletin Boards (Usenet Groups)

Two of the oldest methods, and certainly the most cumbersome, of digital communications are bulletin boards and newsgroups. (Although an accurate accounting is all but impossible, estimates for the number of bulletin boards in 1990 were approximated at 30,000 within the U.S. boundaries alone. By this publication, this number could have increased tenfold.) These communications involve posting services often likened to a community bulletin board where individuals or groups post meetings, information, or the like. More succinctly, bulletin boards may be characterized as a medium of computer exchange

Would You Like Cache Back?

Comprised of high speed static ram (SRAM), a cache is a high-speed storage mechanism which is designed to enhance and expedite the loading of Internet displays. In practice, a cache folder is a collection of temporary Internet files which represent copies of Internet pages visited by the user. Cache and retrieval processes vary widely and are dependent upon settings established by the user and by the content provider. For example, individual users may increase or decrease the size of their cache based upon their security and accessibility preferences, and may manually or automatically delete the contents of the folder as desired. On the other hand, a content provider may affect how certain content is cached through site configuration.

whereby individuals may have the capability of accessing software, posting personal information and exchanging electronic mail. This medium has proven especially popular among subversive and/or racist organizations, because it is much cheaper than printed publications and because complete globalization is possible. The lack of regulations and the perception of First Amendment protection also increase the viability for criminally minded individuals. Finally, utilization of validation controls by systems operators (i.e., collection of personal and other identifying information, such as home address or telephone number) further insulates deviants from law enforcement, and makes it extremely difficult for successful infiltration or investigation.

Bulletin boards vary based on the amount of time, energy, and supervision expended by the *sysop* (i.e., an abbreviation for a system operator, who is an individual with authority to review and delete any information on the board). They also vary based on their degree of anonymity. Anonymous boards, for example, issue "handles"

to users to protect their identities. Moderate boards, on the other hand, are those in which the sysop knows (or thinks she or he knows) the true identity of the users, but members or posters do not. And, finally, known user boards are those in which role playing and pseudonymous postings are forbidden.

Bulletin boards may also be grouped by their degree of immediacy. Some boards, commonly known as chatlines, allow users to connect and "chat" simultaneously, while single-phone-line boards store messages serially in order of their posting time. Because of their reliance on the level of sysop attention and operation, others operate only during designated periods. These same characteristics determine the size and accessibility of bulletin boards. Some boards, for example, are strictly private, restricted to friends or known associates of the sysop. These boards are especially popular among criminals and deviants. Other boards are more open, and allow users access based on the operator's discretion. However, many of these boards also reserve private areas.

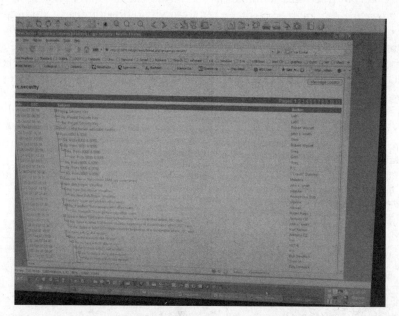

Message boards are popular media for exchanging information. Users range from sports fans to organized crime groups.

Thus, while a variety of individuals are permitted to join, they are restricted to certain portions of the board. These types of situations may also signal the presence of illicit materials or activities. Unfortunately, these types of boards may be especially problematic for law enforcement as favored individuals having unlimited access may actually serve as remote sysops, gaining control of the board via remote methods. As in previously discussed situations, this may create jurisdictional hazards for local law enforcement, particularly in those cases where the board is physically located in one jurisdiction, but is accessed, changed, or deleted remotely. These concerns are further exacerbated in situations involving national or international boards (e.g., CompuServe), which run on mainframe computers.

A final method of categorization involves the level of community found within postings, users, and system operators. Some boards are rather sterile and antiseptic, little more than software storage dumps where individuals download and/or upload software, but have no contact with other users or sysops. Other boards, however, are designed to facilitate interpersonal communications while protecting the anonymity of each poster and obscuring the contents from public dissemination, while others are designed as community affairs which emphasize public exchanges and forbid "lurkers" (i.e., those individuals who do not actively engage in communication, but simply watch those that do). Even these boards, however, may conceal nefarious activities. In fact, fringe groups abound on bulletin boards. Hackers, Satanists, anarchists, Nazis, pedophiles,

child pornographers, and the like have found homes throughout the bulletin board landscape. Many on these boards, regardless of motivation or manner, attract users through the posting of pirated software (i.e., wareZ). Purely underground boards have proven to be transient and elusive, appearing and disappearing relatively quickly.

Internet Relay Chat

Internet relay chat (IRC), most commonly characterized by online discussions in "chat rooms," is increasing exponentially. Far less expensive than telephonic conversations, IRC provides users with the opportunity to talk longer to more people. Unlike traditional telephonic communications, chat rooms allow users to interact with several others at the same time, regardless of time and space differentials. In essence, a chat room is a technologically evolved party line.

Chat rooms are structured so that users may observe and participate in real-time conversations while "identifying" the nicknames of the individuals on the channel and their corresponding IP addresses. Although some IRC rooms may be located on generic servers, for the most part these chat rooms (or channels) are facilitated by OSPs. Categorized by topic, users can visit rooms designed for a variety of individuals ranging from singles to gardeners. Similar to a social gathering, individuals then have a variety of options. They may simply choose to observe (yes, wallflowers exist even in cyberspace); they may choose to participate in

Technological Developments in Communications

- 60s—Lasers, copy machines, satellites (Echo 1, Telstar, Early Bird), fax machines.
- Early 1970s—fiber optics, videotape recorders, Intel 4004, Intel 8008.
- 1975—1980—TCP/IP spec, satellite (GPS), Apple and Microsoft developed.
- 1980s—300 baud, cell phones, IBM/PC, Macintosh.
- 1985—1990—2,400 baud, pagers, 286 processor, 9,600 baud, 386.
- 1990—2000—486, modems 28.8K baud, then 56K baud, satellites (Iridium), Pentiums I, II, III, cable modems.
- 2000—explosion of instant messaging, text messaging, DSL, Blackberrys, wireless Internet connections.

group discussions; or, they may choose to engage in a private conversation with one user—either by finding a corner of the room or stepping outside. On the surface, these rooms are provided by OSPs as a service to their customers, intended to group individuals with similar interests. In this "safe" environment, individuals may exchange ideas or information without fear of social reprisals or embarrassment. Indeed, the assurance of anonymity allows users to experiment with social (and legal) boundaries, while masking their identities and, perhaps, their intentions.

Topics in Internet chat rooms range from the innocuous to the profane. Online predators often use this medium, as it enables them to mask their identities with handles and develop relationships with unsuspecting victims. In fact, solicitations for sex are quite common in "teen" rooms.

While major OSPs facilitate this electronic dialogue, they fail to warn users of the potential for deception. In fact, most of these OSPs deny any responsibility (ethical or legal) for communications between users while promoting vacation packages and OSP social functions. (e.g., America Online encourages members to meet other users—developing singles' cruises and conventions in Vegas and the like.) Perversely, this ambiguity leads to further trust on the part of users, and provides an atmosphere conducive to criminal manipulation and sexual victimization—especially on the part of minors.

FUTURE ISSUES AND CONCLUSIONS

Advances in computer technology have increased exponentially in recent years. Ideas or visions once thought to be unattainable or fantastical are now considered to be overly simplistic or rudimentary. Simultaneously, new innovations or proposals which had originally been met with skepticism are now established mechanisms of digital communication. Indeed, technological inventions have only been slightly outpaced by their conception. The concept of cable modems, for example, was originally met with outright disbelief. However, the implementation of cable modem technology is currently sweeping the country. As in other areas of computer technology, such advances have been accompanied with significant side effects. While users delight in the speed and 24-hour connectivity of the medium, individual ne'er-do-wells have exploited stagnant IP addresses. Unlike traditional dial-ups, cable modems are characterized by individual IP addresses, independent of ISPs. Unfortunately for users, 24-hour accessibility equates to 24-hour vulnerability. This is contrary to traditional systems in which users were vulnerable only for the actual period of their online activity. In addition, Windows systems have proven to be especially vulnerable, as they provide network sharing capability. Thus, the majority of individuals who embrace contemporary technology remain blissfully unaware that these same technologies are accompanied by system vulnerabilities.

Instant Messaging and Text Messaging: The Bane of College Professors

Ask many college students their opinion of instant messaging (IMing) or text messaging (texting), and their reply is most likely to be overwhelmingly positive. Ask their professors, and their responses will be markedly different. Across campuses nationwide, students are using laptops and cell phones to communicate with friends, lovers, and family during college lectures. They are using the same technology to send peers copies or answers to exams. Although many professors forbid the use of cell phones during class time, the trend to require laptops during the same period is fraught with concerns of academic integrity. The emphasis on technologically driven courses in universities is significantly hampering the efforts of many to stop cheating. The advent of online courses has furthered the potential for cheating, as it is virtually (no pun intended) impossible to police.

DISCUSSION QUESTIONS

1. Briefly discuss the history of the Internet, including major developments and advancements.
2. How can bulletin boards be categorized? Why are they favored by some deviant subcultures?
3. Discuss the advantages and disadvantages of global connectivity.
4. List and discuss the four alternatives to the disk operating system or DOS.
5. What are some of the methods of data destruction employed by malicious users? How are they spread, and what are the implications for the future?
6. The text states that in today's society the Internet has become the backbone for global communication and transnational capitalism. Discuss the history of this transformation.

RECOMMENDED READING

- Abbate, Janet (2000). *Inventing the Internet.* MIT Press: Boston, MA.
- Chambers, Mark L. (2006). *PCs All-in-One Desk Reference for Dummies* (3rd Ed). Wiley Publishing: New Jersey.
- Ifrah, Georges (2002). *The Universal History of Computing: From the Abacus to the Quantum Computer.* Wiley Publishing: New Jersey.
- Levin, John; Levin Young, Margaret; and Baroudi, Carol (2005). *Internet for Dummies* (10th Ed). Wiley Publishing: New Jersey.
- Volonino, Linda; Anzaldua, Reynaldo; and Godwin, Jana (2007). *Computer Forensics: Principles and Practices.* Pearson Education: Upper Saddle River, NJ.

WEB RESOURCES

- http://www.ipl.org – home page of the Internet Public Library. Users may search the databases for topics of various interests. The site provides links for viewing and downloading numerous academic articles on the development of technology, the history of computers and the Internet, and the evolution of digital communication.
- http://www.isoc.org – The Internet Society (ISOC) is a professional membership society with more than 100 organization and over 20,000 individual members in over 180 countries. It provides leadership in addressing issues that confront the future of the Internet, and is the organization home for the groups responsible for Internet infrastructure standards, including the Internet Engineering Task Force (IETF) and the Internet Architecture Board (IAB).
- http://www.fcc.gov – The Federal Communications Commission (FCC) is an independent U.S. government agency, directly responsible to Congress. The FCC was established by the Communications Act of 1934 and is charged with regulating interstate and international communications by radio, television, wire, satellite, and cable. The FCC's jurisdiction covers the 50 states, the District of Columbia, and U.S. possessions.
- http://www.netlingo.com – This site contains thousands of definitions about computers, the Internet, and the online world of business, technology, and communication.

ENDNOTES

[1] Thorsen, T.; Maerkl, S.J.; and Quake, S.R. (2002). "Microfluidic Large-Scale Integration." *Science, 298:* 580–584.
[2] UNIX, created in 1969 in Bell Laboratories, was initially exclusive to large corporations and universities. Unix is especially well-suited for telecommunication systems and creates an environment particularly seductive to hackers and phreakers. Originally designed for multiuser and multitasking computers, this operating system is gaining in popularity due to its stability and inexpensiveness.
[3] For more information on data storage, please see Chapter 10.
[4] Knetzger, Michael and Muraski, Jeremy (2008). *Investigating High-Tech Crime.* Pearson Education, Inc: Upper Saddle River, NJ.
[5] Shnier, Mitchell (1998). *Computer Dictionary.* Que Corporation: Indianapolis, IN.
[6] Kovacich, Gerald L. and Boni, William C. (2000). *High-Technology Crime Investigator's Handbook: Working in the Global Information Environment.* Butterworth-Heinemann: Boston, MA.
[7] SCSI (Small Computer Interface System), which is increasingly popular, provides interfacing for up to seven peripherals (actually, as an eight-bit bus interface, but the host adapter which connects to the computer's bus also counts as a device), and allows communication between any two devices simultaneously. Relied upon for speedy transfers, wide SCSI provides up to 40 MB/sec!
[8] Knetzger and Muraski (2008). *Investigating High-Tech Crime.*
[9] Ibid.
[10] Ibid.
[11] While terabyte hard drives have been developed, they are not readily available to average consumers as of this writing. However, it is anticipated that this will change rapidly.
[12] Knetzger and Muraski (2008). *Investigating High-Tech Crime.*
[13] Ibid.
[14] Volonino, Linda; Anzaldua, Reynaldo; and Goodwin Jana (2007). *Computer Forensics: Principles and Practices.* Pearson Education: Upper Saddle River, NJ.

[15]Randall, Neil (1999). "How Viruses Work: Understanding How Viruses Work Is the First Step in Defending Against Them." *PC Magazine*, p. 1. February 9, 1999.

[16]Ibid.

[17]Ibid.

[18]Doherty, Kelly M. (1999). "*www.obscenity.com:* An Analysis of Obscenity and Indecency Regulation on the Internet."

Akron Law Review, 32(259). Available at *http://web.lexis-nexis.com* (last accessed on January 22, 2001 at 4:04 p.m.).

[19]Shnier, Mitchell (1998). *Computer Dictionary,* Que Corporation, Indianapolis, IN.

CHAPTER 3

Traditional Computer Crime: Early Hackers and Theft of Components

Chapter Outline

LEARNING OBJECTIVES

After reading this chapter, you will be able to do the following:

✓ Identify traditional problems associated with the recognition and prosecution of computer crime.

✓ Explore a history of computer crimes.

✓ Explore traditional rationales for phreakers and hackers.
✓ Explore the evolution of hacking.
✓ Learn the value of computers as marketable commodities.
✓ Explore the current state of computer crimes in the United States and abroad.

KEY TERMS AND CONCEPTS

- anonymizer
- black market dealers
- crackers
- cyber-criminal organizations
- counterfeiting
- cyberpunks

- data piracy
- gray market dealers
- hackers
- Legion of Doom
- phreaking
- shareware

- script kiddies
- software piracy
- vicinage
- wareZ

● INTRODUCTION

Like traditional areas of criminal behavior, a continuum of criminal activity, sophistication, and innovation exist among computer deviants. Ne'er-do-wells in both worlds range from novice to expert. Street criminals who leave a physical trail of evidence in their wake, for example, are no different from their technological counterparts who naively rely on the promise of anonymity posed by the vastness of cyberspace to secure them from detection by law enforcement. At the same time, individuals from both areas may hinder discovery by engaging in criminal subterfuge or traditional camouflaging techniques like the donning of ski masks or gloves. In fact, the virtuosity or tangibility of such items is the only distinction. Unfortunately, many investigators are not properly prepared to appreciate or even conceptualize such similarities, and have consequently overlooked the potentiality of criminal automation and innovation.

● TRADITIONAL PROBLEMS

As stated in previous chapters, the advent of digital communications has greatly enhanced various aspects of American life. Advances in medicine, increases in academic knowledge, and the amplification of communication

Just as Bonnie and Clyde used the newly invented automobile to flee from law enforcement authorities, today's criminals are increasingly using computer technology to thwart the police. (© Bettmann CORBIS)

technology have significantly improved the quality of life for many individuals across the country. However, these advances have not been accomplished without substantial side effects. Like their legitimate counterparts, criminal entrepreneurs have embraced this new sphere, augmenting their traditional arsenals and altering their *modus operandi* and staking a claim in this newly created world. Unfortunately, the real world has not kept pace with its virtual counterpart. Thus, the criminal justice system in general and police administrators in particular have been forced to confront contemporary problems (e.g., the lack of criminal physicality, and the intangibility and vulnerability of criminal evidence) with antiquated tools.

Traditionally, criminal statutes were predicated on the vicinage of the criminal act. Travel and location, for example, were assumed to be spatially based. Issues or concerns of jurisdiction only extended to the identification and maintenance of appropriate legal avenues and government sovereignty (e.g., state vs. federal interests). However, cyberworlds, with the potential for global connectivity, transcend traditional spatial boundaries and all but obscure legislated jurisdictions. Thus, identification of the actual **vicinage** (i.e., location of the physical act) is often quite difficult. Take, for example, an American citizen residing in the state of Tennessee who places an illegal wager on a sporting event by "purchasing" gaming software from a site located in the Canary Islands. To complicate matters, let's assume that his funds to wager and any winnings earned are withdrawn and deposited electronically at a bank in Las Vegas. While he has violated both state and federal statutes through his *possession* of an illegal gaming device (i.e., the gaming software), it is unclear whether any illegal wagering actually occurred. Thus, the lack of physicality regarding the actual wagering has created a variety of jurisdictional disputes and legal conundrums (e.g., Was criminal activity

actually committed? If so, which government agency holds jurisdictional sovereignty?). This issue is further compounded by the absence of international guidelines for cyber-activity. Indeed, many international entities have become havens for individuals or companies who intentionally circumvent the extant cyber-laws of the United States. These countries, beneficiaries of exorbitant taxes and fees from such corporations, have consistently failed to recognize the interests of the United States and others. Such government apathy has even extended to cooperation on criminal investigations in which they have no fiduciary interest. Unfortunately, a modicum of cooperation is essential even in those cases in which vicinage is firmly established. Take, for example, an individual in Washington, DC, who uses a server in Canada to send a threatening e-mail to the president of the United States. To complicate matters, let's assume that this individual utilizes an **anonymizer**[1] located in Germany, although the perpetrator and the victim are located in the same area. The cooperation of authorities in Canada and Germany may be essential to determine this "anonymous" individual. Thus, international cooperation must be created to eradicate the seduction of anonymity, which confounds even the simplest of criminal investigations.

The promise of anonymity coupled with the dearth of interjurisdictional communication creates an environment in which many individual users naively assume that their identities are safely protected, thereby encouraging deviant activity. Such seduction enhances the potentiality of criminal and nefarious activities, as both criminals and their victims are lured into a blanket of security. Online harassment, stock manipulation, and child pornography have increased exponentially as such tendencies have been intensified by the increase in anonymous e-mail accounts and re-mailers. While many individuals create cyber-identities to engage in harmless flirtations or role-playing, others hide behind handles to stalk innocents or defraud victims. Interestingly, those same individuals who create false identities for harmless entertainment fail to recognize that privacy may be a double-edged sword. Those same portals which failed to request or verify *their* subscriber information also failed to verify those with whom they are communicating.

Anonymous re-mailers also increase the susceptibility and vulnerability of naive users, and frustrate the efforts of law enforcement. These "anonymizers" are designed to strip the source-address information from e-mail messages.[2] While privacy advocates and civil libertarians argue that these resources provide a nurturing environment for the First Amendment, many re-mailers appeal to those with prurient or less than academic interests. Some even target or direct their services to those self-same individuals, claiming that their site protects users from law enforcement and intelligence agencies. Thus, the promise of anonymity and the lack of international cooperation encourage criminal activity independent of user sophistication. Unfortunately, more sophisticated approaches have been employed by those individuals who are technologically savvy.

Individuals displaying elevated levels of savoir faire have further frustrated the efforts of law enforcement via the utilization of encryption and steganography. Like other masking devices, digital encryption, the act of transforming structured data into indecipherable code, was originally intended to protect the online confidentiality of law-abiding citizens. It was employed by financial institutions, government entities, retail establishments, and the like to prevent the theft of personal and financial information. As encryption programs have become increasingly available for public consumption, however, they have been utilized by criminals to hide their activities, both on and off-line. In fact, the proliferation of encryption software, coupled with the increasing awareness of Internet security, will most likely result in even greater usage. Although the federal government has proposed legislation which would make encryption keys discoverable under court order, current investigations are often stymied by the absence of such keys. In addition, some law enforcement agencies lack adequate resources to even identify the presence of online criminal activity. Such agencies are unable to detect criminal violations until it is too late.

Unlike traditional crimes where victimization is usually obvious, detection of computer crime is often delayed due to the self-same masking devices previously discussed. Although skilled investigators can usually divine the time and location of computer crime over time, technology is changing at a rate most favorable to the criminal mind. In fact, it has always proven difficult to identify the source and destination of communications on computers (Stambaugh et al., 2001). However, the exponential increase in the multitude, diversity, and variance of telecommunication systems coupled with the advent of wireless communications has made it extremely difficult for investigators to respond within time constraints necessarily imposed by the volatility of digital evidence. (Unlike traditional communication carriers, Internet service providers are not required to maintain transmission records. Although some do, the advent of bulk billing, eliminating the need for recording transmission information, has resulted in a lack of maintenance of transactional information.) In addition, digital evidence has proven to be capable of being easily modified or deleted, and its voluminous nature has proven quite daunting for criminal investigators.

The investigation of computer crimes is often accompanied by unique obstacles. While investigators have struggled to keep abreast of recent technology, they have been hindered by a lack of judicial interest, administrative apathy, and cultural skepticism. For these reasons, a complete picture of the criminal landscape has yet to emerge. Indeed, the sheer potential of technologically supported criminal activity has yet to be realized. Although many of the obstacles appear at first glance to be insurmountable, an historical perspective of criminal behavior in general reveals similar periods of law enforcement uncertainty and criminal innovation. The introduction of the telephone, for example, allowed individuals to fine-tune their harassment of victims, plan criminal activities, and conspire across jurisdictional boundaries, while creating a plethora of law enforcement problems for authorities. In fact, early police were forced to rely on antiquated codes of behavior before the legislature passed specific legislation targeting criminal activities committed via telephone, like the Wire Act. Thus, law enforcement agencies should look to traditional statutes and federal legislation to prosecute computer crimes in the absence of technology-specific legislation.

A Short Introduction to Cryptology[3]

Jonathan C. Hoskin, Ph.D.
Division of Computing and Information Technology, Clemson University

Cryptology was initially the study of secret written messages, usually of a military or diplomatic nature, and included cryptography—the making or encrypting of secret messages—and cryptanalysis—the breaking or decrypting of secret messages. Complicating this concept is steganography, which describes secret messages hidden from normal view, although they may also be encrypted. These latter types of messages range from simplistically adding a hidden note to a word processing document, which will often go unnoticed, to manipulating an audio, graphic, or video file to include text or other information without noticeably changing its inherent visual or audio characteristics. However, with the emergence of computers, the scope of cryptology has necessarily been expanded. It now includes cryptographically strong security measures allowing for secure digital transfers of money in our Internet-based business world. Computing is in fact the most obvious dividing line in Cryptology development using new techniques developed just before computers became available and making what is believed to be unbreakable security much simpler to use.

Ignoring early history and cryptology involving mixtures of languages, it began with alphabetic manipulation most easily accomplished by sliding one alphabet relative to another. For example, the computer name "HAL" in the book and movie *2001: A Space Odyssey* can be decrypted by replacing each letter in turn with that following it, resulting in "IBM." This defines the concept of the Caesar Cipher, used by his generals, which has often been constructed by having a rotating double disk allowing the alphabet on one disk to slide relative to the other but remaining at the same place for the entire message. The algorithm or enciphering method is represented by the movable disk and the key is the number of letters displaced to encipher or decipher the message. This substitution cipher is easier to use than having one alphabet randomly jumbled, which makes the decrypting more difficult because the letters are not in alphabetic order. Numerous methods of this type of manipulation have been developed, including use of numbers and other characters.

The vast majority of all such systems noted above suffer from the same flaw—they involve simple substitution. Because each language can be characterized by the frequencies of use for each letter (in English, words typically begin with, in the order of most to least used letters, E, T, A, O, I, N, S, ...), cryptanalysis of a message is generally straightforward, simply replacing the most frequent characters in the message with the correspondingly frequent letters of the language considered. This is also true when, for example, three numbers are used to represent individual letters. Another concept of cryptography was to represent specific words with one or more characters requiring a nomenclature, which is a combination of a cipher as used above with additional codes for specific words.

(Continued)

Complexity was increased by the use of a polyalphabetic cipher, which is essentially the same Caesar Cipher discussed above, except that it changes according to the key word or phrase. For example, if the key was "abcd," then the first letter in the message would stay the same, the second letter would move one letter to the right, the third two letters to the right and the forth three letters to the right. The key would be used over and over until the entire message was encrypted. (For decryption, the letters would move to the left.) Breaking this cipher, which was at one time believed to be impossible, is not noticeably different from decrypting any Caesar Cipher; after recognizing the groups, frequency analysis is done on the four different groups of letters, of which the first, fifth, ninth etc. is the first group and the second, sixth, tenth etc. defines the second group. That same technique continues till the entire message is grouped and frequency analysis of the four groups is used to help decipher the message.

The most important cryptographic advance occurred when it was recognized that if the key used with the polyalphabetic cipher was replaced with a random string of letters (numbers), the encrypted message was inherently unbreakable. With the Caesar Cipher, a cipher disk was easy enough to give to each user, but this new cipher required a method to dispense the key or random numbers known as a "one-time pad" to each user. (As the name implies, it can be securely used for only one time.) Computers made the generation of random numbers a simple process, although they are generally referred to as pseudo-random numbers. Currently the key for message encryption/decryption needs to be 128 bits or 16 bytes long (2^{128} or 3.4×10^{38} possibilities) to be cryptographically strong. This is defined by the computational ability of state-of-the-art computers, which try all the possibilities, and this length itself might change dependent on technology.

Over a century ago, mathematics was shown to be capable of decrypting messages but even more important, in the last 40 years it has solved the problem of conveying the key or one-time pad. This involved using a key pair and relied on the difficulty of prime number factoring of very large numbers and is often called public-key cryptography. The two keys of the key pair generated are not any different except that one is public, often being made available on the Internet, and the other kept private (at least in the private email scenario). For this system to be cryptographically secure, the key is necessarily much larger, at a minimum of 1,024 bits or 128 bytes (representing 2^{1024} or 1.8×10^{308} possibilities), and is therefore much slower, a thousand times slower than the 16 byte key noted in the previous paragraph. Therefore, to increase the processing speed, only the message key is encrypted using the slower public-key cryptography, the message itself is encrypted using the faster 16-byte (random numbers) key contained in the public-key cryptographic portion.

This system works as follows. Assume I send you a message and I encrypt it with your public key, anyone can do this but only you can decrypt it with your private key. But now consider that I encrypt a message with your public key and encrypt it again with my private key. When you get that double encrypted message, you can decrypt it with my public key and then decrypt it a second time with your private key. The result is secure because only I could encrypt it with my private key and only you could decrypt it with your private key.

RECOGNIZING AND DEFINING COMPUTER CRIME

The categorization of computer crime for ease in explanation is, at best, cumbersome. However, there are three general categories of computer crime: targets, means, and incidentals. Please note that while these categories are intended to be inclusive of the myriad of computer-related crime, they are not mutually exclusive, as many computer crimes involve a multiplicity of intentions. For example, insiders may target a computer system for destruction due to perceptions of mistreatment, and, at the same time, may use the computer as a means of committing embezzlement. In hacking activities, one computer provides the means for the criminal activity, while another serves as the target. Finally, an individual may improperly gain access to a computer (i.e., unauthorized use) to steal information which resides therein. Thus, she or he would be targeting a computer, while also using it as an instrument to commit criminal activity.

It is unclear exactly when and where the first "computer crime" actually occurred. Contextually, theft of an abacus or a simple adding machine would constitute a computer crime. It is safe to assume that these types of activities occurred long before written or formal documentation was in vogue. However, the first documented instance of computer sabotage occurred in the early nineteenth century, when a textile manufacturer named Joseph Jacquard developed what would soon become the precursor to the computer card. His invention, which allowed automation of a series of steps in the weaving of special fabrics, was not popular among his workers, who feared for their continued employment. Thus, they dismantled his invention.[4] Unfortunately, such discussion does not adequately establish definitional parameters for criminal activity involving computers, nor does the literature extend clarification. In fact, not all crimes involving computers can be characterized as "computer crime." It would not be appropriate, for example, to categorize a residential burglary as a computer crime, even if a computer was among the items stolen. At the same time, the hijacking of an entire shipment of computer hard drives is more appropriately situated elsewhere. And, finally, the theft of millions of dollars via computer hacking is most properly denoted as a "cybercrime." However, in all of these situations, a forensic computer scientist may be helpful. Accordingly, this book has attempted to identify those crimes in which a computer specialist might be helpful and has used the terms *computer crime* and *computer-related crime* interchangeably.

THREE INCIDENTS

Although the threat of wide-scale criminal activity via computer has existed for decades, government officials tended to overlook the seriousness of phreaking and hacking prior to the mid-1980s. In fact, computer crime was all but ignored until a variety of cases exposed the vulnerability of data systems and outlined potential cataclysmic repercussions for national security. Unfortunately, such legislative and enforcement apathy created an environment conducive to criminal activity.

The first event to signal the potential of computer crime occurred in 1986, when an accounting error of less than one dollar was investigated by a dedicated employee at the University of California at Berkeley. This internal investigation revealed that a German hacker in the employ of the KGB had tapped into a military database and obtained sensitive (but not classified) information. Using only a personal computer and a basic modem, this individual was able to connect to Berkeley computers via an independent data carrier (i.e., Tymnet). Once connected, the hacker was able to move about the MILNET system with remarkable ease and relative impunity. The fact that such vulnerability existed within data systems was especially disconcerting to administrators because of its almost accidental discovery. In fact, without the efforts of this employee, it is highly improbable that this activity would have been uncovered. While his efforts were largely directed at accounting discrepancies, his findings resulted in the recognition of information risks associated with open systems. Governmental entities, traditionally lax in computer security, soon initiated measures to protect electronically stored information, especially military secrets. However, they continued to overlook the economic dangers associated with computer networking.

In 1988, only two years after the MILNET fiasco, legislators were forced to recognize additional threats to computer security after a program developed by a Cornell University student crippled over 6,000 computers and caused between $5 and $100 million in damages. This program, called the "Morris worm" (after its inventor, Robert Morris), was intended to attack computers via the Internet. This incident, the first of its kind, exploited security holes in the Unix operating system, infecting 10 percent of all computers connected to the Internet.[5] Such wide-scale infestation created a major stumbling block for this newly emerging medium, unforeseen by all, even its creator. (It was clear that Morris did not intend the havoc that was

Computer contaminants can cripple an entire network. They can be introduced into private systems and international ones. Robert Morris' Worm, for example, contaminated approximately 10 percent of all systems which were connected to the Internet at the time. Robert Morris is currently an associate professor at Massachusetts Institute of Technology. Although he has written numerous articles in computer security, he is still best known for the havoc he created in his youth. Ironically, Morris is the son of Robert Morris, the former chief scientist at the National Computer Security Center, a division of the National Security Agency. (*Michael J. Okoniewski/AP/World Wide Photos*)

the intended recipients as the worm had already overloaded many systems.) Morris was subsequently convicted of violating the Computer Fraud and Abuse Act (CFAA), and was sentenced to three years' probation, 400 hours of community service, and fines of more than $10,000.

The destruction caused by Morris' worm was soon overshadowed by the crash of AT&T, then America's number-one telephone provider. Although not entirely unprecedented, the magnitude of this crash, coupled with the lack of a particularized physical reason, signaled the beginning of hacking hysteria. Unfortunately, this hysteria was reminiscent of the "satanic panic" of the early 1980s in which American cities became besieged by rumors of robed worshipers slaughtering innocents. Suddenly, all technological failures were incorrectly attributed to a dark force of computer geniuses. In fact, most experts agree that the problem precipitating the crash had nothing to do with hackers at all, but was actually the responsibility of AT&T software. However, the possibility that hackers could disrupt vital services led to the persecution of several hacking groups, most notable of which was the **Legion of Doom**.

The Legion of Doom (LoD) derived its name from Superman comic books which glorified the antics of a circle of super-villains headed by criminal mastermind, Lex Luthor. Like their fictional counterparts, members of LoD relentlessly promoted themselves, boasting of their exploits on a variety of bulletin boards, including: The Legion of Doom Board, Plovernet, The Farmers

subsequently unleashed. In fact, when he recognized the possible implications of his actions, he released an anonymous message to programmers, which instructed them how to disable the worm. Unfortunately, this message did not reach many of

Three Hacker Typologies

Although hackers vary greatly in terms of sophistication and motivation, there are three general categories used to classify them. All of them are assumed to be technologically sophisticated and capable of writing code and breaching complex systems.

- **white hat hackers**—individuals who identify system vulnerabilities in the interest of promoting heightened security.

- **black hat hackers** or **crackers**—individuals who identify and exploit system vulnerabilities for nefarious purposes, including, but not limited to, destruction and theft.
- **gray hat hackers**—individuals who wear both of the preceding hats. Gray hat hackers may identify network weaknesses for system administrators, but may also provide them to black hat hackers for profit.

of Doom Board, Metal Shop, Blottoland, Atlantis, Digital Logic, and Hell Phrozen Over. In addition, individual members created boards of their own, including *Silver Spy*'s Catch-22, and *Mentor*'s Phoenix Project. Originally, members of this group were expert phreakers, not hackers. However, as technology expanded, so did the activities of LoD.

Although it is impossible to determine the number of members formally associated with LoD and to pinpoint their activities, it is clear that law enforcement incorrectly assumed that all hacking activities could be attributed to the group. While the group certainly enjoyed the infamy and notoriety associated with these assumptions, most members were not malicious or criminal minded. In fact, many of these individuals nobly proclaimed themselves as public servants, pointing out security flaws in institutional systems so that repairs would be made, while others eventually sought employment at the self-same institutions that they had victimized (e.g., longtime LoD member *Control-C* was actually hired by Michigan Bell after

victimizing them for several years. The situation proved most beneficial to Michigan Bell, because hackers were dissuaded from attacking the techno structure that their friend had been hired to protect.) Unfortunately, some members of the group did not abide by the common ethos, and did, in fact, actively exploit systems for personal gain. These individuals, namely *Fry Guy* and *The Atlanta Three* (*Prophet*, *Urvile*, and *Leftist*), were directly responsible for the downfall of the group. Ironically, *Fry Guy*, described as an LoD wannabe, had never even met the Atlanta Three.

The beginning of the end for LoD was initiated by the arrest of petty hacker and braggart extraordinaire, *Fry Guy*, following his threat that LoD would crash the national telephone network on Independence Day. Armed with criminal evidence of his manipulation of switching stations and wire fraud and credit card fraud, the Secret Service gained his cooperation, through which he revealed the "plot" by LoD to crash the phones on "a national holiday." His proclamations appeared to be on target when a blackout occurred on

A Hacking Timeline

1960s—the term "hacking" is introduced at MIT

1970s—

- phreakers emerge, costing AT&T a fortune in uncollected long-distance charges
- Phreaker John Draper (aka Cap'n Crunch) discovers a way to use toy whistles in cereal boxes to generate a 2,600-Hz sound capable of accessing AT&T's long-distance switching system

1980s—

- phreakers graduate to computer hacking
- *2600*, the first hacking magazine, is published
- hacker bulletin boards are created
- *Computer Fraud and Abuse Act of 1986* is passed by Congress
- Robert Morris' worm is released on the Internet, and he is prosecuted under the newly passed legislation

1990s—

- Operation Sundevil, a large-scale multi-jurisdictional taskforce, is created, resulting in numerous arrests and convictions of hackers across the country
- Kevin Poulsen exploits the telecom system to "win" a Porsche
- Emergence of hacking Web sites
- Kevin Mitnick arrested and prosecuted
- Release of Windows 98
- Introduction of commercially available security products

2000—present

- DoS attacks launched against various Web sites, including Yahoo!, eBay, and Microsoft
- organizations of cyber-criminals emerge
- identity theft emerges as an issue for consumers
- information becomes the leading commodity for criminals

Martin Luther King Day, 1990. (However, this failure appears to have been nothing more than an irony of coincidence.) Based on his proclamations, the Secret Service obtained pen registers on the phones of The Atlanta Three—Prophet, Urvile, and Leftist. Both Urvile and Leftist agreed to cooperate, naively, and arrogantly, believing that their activities did not constitute criminal behavior.

However, Prophet, a Unix programming expert with a criminal history, had circumvented the security measures of AT&T and downloaded and forwarded numerous copies of a document identified as *Bell South Standard Practice 660-25-104SV Control Office Administration of Enhanced 911 Services for Special Services and Major Account Center*. Copies were subsequently forwarded to the editor of *Phrack* (i.e., *Knight Lightning*), the "Phoenix Project," and a variety of

other admirers of LoD. In fact, numerous outlets carried the infamous documents, and wide-scale searches were soon initiated by the Secret Service. One such search of a sysop's computer uncovered the existence of a board called *Illuminati*—a full-service board, owned and operated by Steve Jackson Games, Inc. (SJG) which offered services ranging from electronic messaging to role-playing simulation.

The subsequent search of Steve Jackson Games, Inc. resulted in one of the first legal rulings regarding the application of the Fourth Amendment to computer systems. This seminal case, *Steve Jackson Games, Inc. v. U.S. Secret Service et al.*, 36 F. 3d 457, 463 (Fifth Cir., 1994), proved to be an embarrassment to the U.S. Secret Service. Agents were accused of Gestapo-like tactics after they seized virtually everything, including business records, private

A Sampling of Infamous Hackers

Kevin Mitnick—Arguably the most infamous of all hackers, Kevin Mitnick has been the subject of numerous books and movies. Like many hackers, Mitnick began his career with small exploits and phone phreaking. He became the target of a federal investigation after he vanished while on probation. While on the run from the authorities, Mitnick continued to engage in criminal activity, breaking into various systems and stealing a wealth of proprietary information. His downfall occurred after he hacked into the computer of fellow hacker Tsutomu Shimomura. Mitnick was arrested by the FBI in February 1995, after Tsutomu tracked him down electronically. Today, Mitnick claims to be reformed and owns a computer security firm.

cOmrade—The first teen to be incarcerated for computer hacking, Jonathan James committed his intrusions under the alias cOmrade. His targets included the Miami-Dade school system, BellSouth, and the Defense Threat Reduction Agency (DTRA), a division of the U.S. Department of Defense. The creation of a back door into DTRA provided access to usernames, passwords, and e-mail accounts of thousands of government employees.

Terminus—A Unix programmer and AT&T minicomputer expert adopted this particular handle to proclaim his hacker superiority. Although he eventually became a

telecommunications programmer, his early career included the development of the first telco scanning programs. In addition, Terminus had victimized telecommunications providers for years, pirated AT&T proprietary software, and stole electronic messages stored on their systems.

Shadowhawk—Notable for his expertise and braggadocio at hacking the AT&T system, he received a sentence of nine months and a fine of $10,000 for breaking and entering into a computer at U.S. Missile Command. While the government contended that his activities resulted in the theft of millions of dollars of data, Shadowhawk never sold or profited from the sale of any of the software illegally appropriated.

Kyrie—one of the few females achieving hacker notoriety, she specialized in abusing corporate voice mail. Unlike Terminus and Shadowhawk, Kyrie aggressively used her skills for profit, compiling a group of 150 phone freaks who paid her for her information regarding long-distance dialing codes with stolen credit card numbers. Kyrie's activities were further compounded by the fact that she included her children in her wrongdoing, denying them a legal identity and depriving them of formal education. Like those before her, Kyrie's excessive bragging led to her downfall. After phoning to taunt Assistant Attorney General Gail Thackeray, Kyrie was sentenced to 27 months for her activities.

electronic mail, the entire bulletin board, and the drafts of forthcoming games and their accompanying literature. Their arguments that the bulletin board was a medium for the exchange of hacking information was subsequently ruled as unfounded, and their execution of an *unsigned* search warrant were harshly criticized by the Court.

The legal criticisms originally levied by the Fifth Circuit were soon echoed in the private sector as well. The Electronic Frontier Foundation, hosted on "The Well," was created by Grateful Dead member David Barlow and the co-creator of Lotus 1-2-3, Mitchell Kapor. Their articulated mission was to protect the privacy of American citizens and to encourage the growth of the World Wide Web. These individuals were soon joined by several cyber-luminaries and computer entrepreneurs, including Steve Wozniak (Apple Computers) and John Gilmore (Sun Microsystems). These trailblazing efforts resulted in the creation of a variety of communication platforms designed to protect the privacy of the electronic frontier. One of the most recognizable is the Electronic Privacy Information Center (EPIC), which serves as an information clearinghouse on pending and current legislation, judicial leanings, and activities of government agencies. While it recognizes the vulnerability of sensitive information, hardware, and computer systems, this organization seeks to limit the amount of government intrusion and oversight.

● PHREAKERS: YESTERDAY'S HACKERS

As stated previously, phreakers were the precursors of today's computer hackers. Initially, the motivation was simply to break the system—a system which claimed to be impenetrable. Like their evolved counterparts, phreakers routinely held conferences in which they discussed their exploits and shared their successes. Oftentimes, these individuals would build "bridges," illegal conference calls of numerous individuals

around the world billed to someone else. However, many of these incidents were overlooked by a law enforcement population which was hopelessly overwhelmed by an increase in predatory crime and a lack of personnel, economic resources, and political assistance. Unfortunately, this situation allowed this unique population to flourish. (In 1994, e.g., it was estimated that 150,000 physical attacks on pay telephones occurred.) Thus, the 1980s and 1990s became a virtual playground for hackers and phreakers alike.

What is Phreaking?

By definition, **phreaking** involves the manipulation of telecommunications carriers to gain knowledge of telecommunications, and/or theft of applicable services. Also identified broadly as *telecommunications fraud*, phreaking includes any activity that incorporates the illegal use or manipulation of access codes, access tones, PBXs, or switches. According to accomplished phreakers, the theft of telephone access codes is the bottom rung of phone phreaking, as technical expertise is absolutely not required. By far the easiest way to steal access codes is to simply "shoulder surf," stealing the code from unsuspecting individuals while they are dialing. A more sophisticated approach, war-dialing, involves random number generators, which test numerous codes until one is successful. One of these programs running throughout the night may generate several hits, which are then compiled into a large database. The programs which enable these computerized code thefts have quickly found their way to the Internet and are readily available for downloading. Both of these techniques have proven especially popular in college dormitories, military establishments, and traveling road crews (Sterling, 1994). Unfortunately for many criminals, surveillance technology is now available to identify computerized dialing, making war-dialing for access codes rather obsolete. However, it is currently popular among Third World

Infamous Hacking and Phreaking Boards

8BBS—One of the first hacking boards, 8BBS went online in March, 1980, and became especially popular on the West Coast. This group sponsored "Susan Thunder" and perhaps, most notably, "the Condor." In fact, the Condor's activities were so self-serving that his fellow hackers turned him in to the police. (Many of his activities have reached epic proportions. Unfortunately, such propagation has all but obscured the truth of his criminal behavior.) By all accounts, this board was not developed to facilitate criminal activities. However, some individuals attracted to the board could not resist the temptation to utilize their hacking skills for illicit purposes. The board was effectively shut down after it was discovered that some of their technology had been purchased via credit card fraud.

Plovernet—East Coast hacking board Plovernet was owned and operated by a teenage hacker who was known by the handle "Quasi Moto." It was a breeding ground for hacking groups like LOD. (Lex Luthor, the LoD founder, was at one time a co-sysop.)

414 Private—A hacking group of teenagers whose antics attracted national attention (some of the first) after they hacked into the Los Alamos military computers and Sloan-Kettering Cancer Center in 1982.

ALTOS—Considered in underground circles to represent the epitome of sophisticated, international hacking, ALTOS was originally formed in Bonn, Germany.

immigrants in the United States. In addition, a slightly modified technology is now being employed by computer hackers.

Another method of defeating the telephone company—employed by such notables as Steve Jobs and Steve Wozniak, the founders of Apple Computer, Inc.—involved the invention of hardware devices (Sterling, 1994). These *blue boxes*, as they were known, were devices which "tricked" switching systems into granting free access to long-distance lines. These devices were also extremely popular among college dorms, and were considered harmless by users. However, the telephone company saw it otherwise and was directly responsible for the bankruptcy of *Ramparts*, an underground magazine which printed a do-it-yourself guide to blue-box creation. Fortunately, blue boxes have become outdated, largely ineffective since the advent of

digital switching. However, other mechanisms, devices, technologies, and *targets* of telecommunications frauds have emerged.

The War on Phreaking

By the mid-1980s, AT&T, tired of excessive losses to phone phreaking and telecom fraud, created ANI (automatic number identification) trace capability. This technology successfully dampened the spirits of many phreakers who soon found easier targets in the Baby Bells and long-distance competitors, among others. Phreakers have also infiltrated locally owned PBXs and voicemail systems, concealing themselves in hidden and unallocated places. One popular practice is to "divert" messages, thus saving the long-distance charges. This practice involves infiltrating a private branch-exchange

Seeking Revenge

Computers have proven an effective means of retaliation for terminated employees. Unlike workplace violence, the manipulation of computer systems provides a mechanism for dismantling entire corporations, leaving individual employees unharmed. Systems manager Donald Burelson, for example, employed a logic bomb which targeted the commission records for over 60,000 independent insurance agents. This logic bomb was predicated on personnel records and was activated when his employment status was changed in the system.

system, mimicking the same system, and dialing across the world. Thus, the victim actually suffers twofold: intrusion and fraud. Others simply regenerate a dial tone through a PBX or voice mail system. This strategy has been employed against such technological giants as Unisys and IBM to the tune of $300,000 and $400,000, respectively (SEARCH, 2000). While the economic benefits attract some phreakers, others are attracted to the challenge. These phreakers often wreak havoc among vulnerable systems, deleting voice mail messages and denying legitimate users access. Many companies feel so threatened by these criminals that they actually acquiesce to any demands made by them, while contemporary law enforcement authorities tend to minimize the seriousness of phreaking and even deny its very existence. Unfortunately, there is virtually no evidence to support the supposition that phreaking is outdated or decreasing in popularity. In fact, the lines between telephone phreaking and computer hacking have become increasingly blurred.

Many of the methods employed by early phreakers are now prevalent within the hacker community (many of whom started their hacking "careers" as phreakers). Patrick W. Gregory, for example, pled guilty to one count of conspiracy for teleconferencing fraud and computer cracking for his role as a founding member of a hacking ring called Global Hell.

Allegedly causing over $1.5 million in damages to various U.S. corporations and government entities, including the U.S. Army and the White House, his plea included charges of stealing telephone conferencing services from AT&T, MCI, and Latitude Communications and holding conference calls for over two years. Thus, while traditional mechanisms involving black boxes or recording devices to mimic long-distance tones have become passé, new methods involving the manipulation of PBX systems have emerged.

Innovative ways of utilizing stolen PBX codes are also being employed by individuals involved in organized crime syndicates. Known as "call-sell" operations, pre-paid calls are sold on the street using stolen access or PBX codes. These scams are highly organized and cost telecommunications providers an inestimable sum in damages. A similar scam has also been applied to recent innovations in cellular technology. This type of activity is possible due to the reprogrammable nature of cellular chips. Thus, it is relatively easy for criminals to present false caller identification to avoid billing. In addition, this activity allows criminals to avoid traditional law-enforcement wiretapping, making it especially popular among drug dealers and organized crime figures. This activity is increasing in popularity, and it is not unusual to find pirated cell phones being sold from the back of trucks across the country (Sterling, 1994).

Traditional Phreaking Tools

Red box	generates tones for free phone call
Black box	callers do not pay a charge for incoming calls
Beige box	lineman's handset
Green box	generates coin return tones
Cheese box	turns a personal phone into a pay phone
Agua box	disables government tracing

(Continued)

Blast box	phone microphone amplifier
Blotto box	shorts out all phones in your area
Blue box	generates a 2,600-Hz tone
Brown box	creates a party line
Bud box	taps into a neighbor's phone
Chatreuse box	uses electricity from phone
Chrome box	manipulates traffic signal
Color box	records phone conversations
Copper box	causes cross talk
Crimson box	acts as a hold button
Dark box	reroutes calls
Dayglo box	connects to neighbor's phone line
Diverter box	reroutes calls
Dloc box	creates a party line
Gold box	dial-out router
Infinity box	remote-activated phone
Jack box	touch-tone key pad
Light box	in-use light
Lunch box	AM transmitter
Magenta box	connects a remote phone line to another
Mauve box	phone tap without cutting a line
Neon box	external microphone
Party box	creates a party line
Pearl box	tone generator
Pink box	creates a party line
Rainbow box	kills trace

Phreaking—Making a Red Box

Various Internet sites provide tutorials of how to engage in hacking and phreaking, providing the essentials and instructing amateurs to avoid detection and prosecution—even including instructions on how to make boxes for nefarious purposes.

A "Red Box," one of the premier tools of phreaking, allows users to generate tones so that users can avoid toll charges.

Necessary Equipment

Available at local electronics retailers:

- Tone dialers
- 6.5536 MHz Crystal

Steps

- Simply open up dialer and replace the 3.579545 MHz crystal with the 6.5536 MHz one.
- Simply play the number of tones requested by the operator using the following schematic
  - $0.25—five times
  - $0.10—three times
  - $0.05—once

Other Methods

Simply buy a phreaking program like *Fear's Phreaker Tools* or *Omnibox* and record the tones from computer speakers.

● HACKING

As mentioned previously, computers may be the intended target of a criminal or may actually represent the instrumentality of the crime. Hacking activities may fall into either category. Unfortunately, the characterization and subsequent discussion of such activity may not be neatly packaged. Like more traditional criminal behaviours, the methodology employed, the motivation expressed, and the sophistication displayed are but a few characteristics which may vary drastically. Thus, hacking activities are most appropriately situated on a continuum. On the low end, there may be some individuals who take particular delight in entering systems for the sheer fun of it. Their activities may range from snooping around their neighbors' computers to searching the recesses of top-secret government databases. On the high end of the spectrum reside individuals who enter these same systems with destruction or treason in mind (discussed in more detail in Chapter 4).

Although difficult to measure, some studies have suggested that the number of computer intrusions in the United States alone number in the millions, while others suggest that the cost to the public is in excess of several billion dollars. However, hacking is a global phenomenon and is not restricted to the United States. Hackers have been found in virtually every country in which computer technology is available. Remarkably, these individuals, irrespective of national origin, display startling similarities.

Defining Hacking

The root of the term *hacking* has been claimed by the Massachusetts Institute of Technology (MIT), and dates back to the 1960s when the term was used by MIT students to refer to either the development of novel techniques to identify computer shortcuts or clever pranks. (Early examples of such pranks were not always computer related, and included placing a full-sized model of a patrol car atop the dome on Building 10.) Most probably, the term derived from the metaphor of hacking away at an object until it gave way. In the competitive culture of the MIT campus, innovative computer solutions inevitably led to even more sophisticated techniques as students attempted to outdo one another. In the 1980s, the term was popularized in the film *War Games*, and the hacker subculture exploded.

Evolution in the Hacking Community

The emergence of the term in the popular media coupled with the increase in accessibility and connectivity removed the ivory towers and dramatically increased the number of individuals engaged in hacking activity. The newcomers to the fray were often young, socially retarded males who initially became enamored of computers and computer technology through role-playing games. Such entertainment, necessitating excessive downloads, led these individuals to manipulate telephone exchanges. (Prior to the mass introduction of Internet service providers and unlimited access, calls via modem tended to be quite costly.) Common justifications for their actions included an anti-establishment ideology that inferred that corporate structures and government entities were designed to abridge individualism and discourage collective unity. (Thus, hacking organizations may be likened to Christian identity groups which believe that a government conspiracy to exploit

First Printed Example of *Hacking*

Many telephone services have been curtailed because of so-called hackers, according to Prof. Carlton Tucker, administrator of the Institute phone system. [. . .] The hackers have accomplished such things as tying up all the tie-lines between Harvard and MIT, or making long-distance calls by charging them to a local radar installation. One method involved connecting the PDP-1 computer to the phone system to search the lines until a dial tone, indicating an outside line, was found. [. . .] Because of the "hacking," the majority of the MIT phones are "trapped."[6]

American citizens is furthered by corporate assistance.) In addition, early hackers emphasized the virtuality of cyberspace, arguing that the Internet is a sphere of unreality, where nothing is concrete and everything is simulated. Finally, traditional hackers around the globe shared a sense of overwhelming empowerment in which they were the keepers of all knowledge.

Thus, the traditional hacker culture was characterized by an anti-establishment rhetoric—a feeling that was largely shared by a generation. Although the verbiage and sophistication of articulation varied, a statement made by Lloyd Blankenship (aka, the Mentor) encapsulated the angst felt by the subculture.

> This is our world now . . . the world of the electron and the switch, the beauty of the baud. We make use of a service already existing without paying for what could be dirt-cheap if it wasn't run by profiteering gluttons, and you call us criminals. We explore . . . and you call us criminals. We seek after knowledge . . . and you call us criminals. We exist without skin color, without nationality, without religious bias . . . and you call us criminals. You build atomic bombs, you wage wars, you murder, cheat, and lie to us and try to make us believe it's for our own good, yet we're the criminals.
>
> Yes, I am a criminal. My crime is that of curiosity. My crime is that of judging people by what they say and think, not what they look like. My crime is that of outsmarting you, something that you will never forgive me for.
>
> I am a hacker, and this is my manifesto. You may stop this individual, but you can't stop us all.[7]

Contemporary hacker communities have lost much of this ideological superstructure. The lure

---

List of 1980s Hacker Organizations (Compiled by *Phrack* in 1988)

The Administration; Advanced Telecommunications, Inc.; ALIAS; American Tone Travelers, Anarchy Inc.: Apple Mafia; The Association; Atlantic Pirates Guild.

Bad Ass Mother Fuckers; Bellcore; Bell Shock Force; Black Bag.

Camorra; C&M Productions; Catholics Anonymous; Chaos Computer Club; Chief Executive Officers; Circle of Death; Circle of Deneb; Club X; Coalition of Hi-Tech Pirates; Coast-To-Coast; Corrupt Computing; Cult of The Dead Cow; Custom Retaliations.

Damage Inc.; D&B Communications; The Damage Gang; Dec Hunters; Digital Gang; DPAK.

Eastern Alliance; The Elite Hackers Guild; Elite Phreakers and Hackers Club; The Elite Society of America; EPG; Executives of Crime; Extasy Elite.

4A; Farmers of Doom; The Federation; Feds R Us; First Class; Five O; Five Star; Force Hackers; The 414s.

Hack-A-Trip; Hackers of America; High Mountain Hackers; High Society; The Hitchhikers.

IBM Syndicate; The Ice Pirates; Imperial Warlords: Inner Circle I; Inner Circle II; Insanity Inc. International; Computer Underground Bandits.

Justice League of America; Kaos Inc.; Knights of Shadow; Knights of The Round Table.

League of Adepts; Legion of Doom; Legion of Hackers; Lords of Chaos; Lunatic Labs; Unlimited.

Master Hackers; MAD!; The Marauders; Md/PhD; Metal Communications, Inc.; MetalliBashers, Inc.; MBI; Metro Communications; Midwest Pirates Build.

NASA Elite; The NATO Association; Neon Knights; Nihilist Order; Order of The Rose; OSS.

Pacific Pirates Guild; Phantom Access Associates; PHido PHreakers of America; Phortune 500; Phreak Hack Delinquents; Phreak Hack Destroyers; Phreakers, Hackers, And Laundromat Employees Gang (PHALSE Gang); Phreaks Against Geeks; Phreaks Against Phreaks Against Geeks; Phreaks and Hackers of America; Phreaks Anonymous World Wide; Project Genesis; The Punk Mafia; The Racketeers; Red Dawn Text Files; Roscoe Gang.

SABRE; Secret Circle of Pirates; Secret Service; 707 Club; Shadow Brotherhood; Sharp Inc.; 65C02 Elite; Spectral Force; Star League; Stowaways; Strata-Crackers.

Team Hackers '86; Team Hackers '87; TeleComputist Newsletter Staff; Tribunal of Knowledge; Triple Entente; Turn Over and Die Syndrome (TOADS); 300 Club; 1200 Club; 2300 Club; 2600 Club; 2601 Club; 2AF; The United Soft WareZ Force; United Technical Underground. Ware Brigade; The Warelords; WASP.

of easy money, revenge, and personal notoriety have significantly tempered the righteous indignation expressed by early desktop cowboys. At the same time, traditional levels of misogyny have been reduced as more and more female code writers have emerged. This rhetorical shift and the lack of ideological consistency have resulted in an increase in hacking for profit (i.e., cracking). In addition, the proliferation of private hacking toolkits and software has spawned a generation of unskilled, financially motivated intruders (e.g., NetBus, Back Orifice, and Deep Throat). Thus, the virtual explosion of remote-access software released on the market has dramatically changed the characterization of hackers. While traditional definitions included assumptions of motivation and skill, contemporary definitions have been altered to include any individual who intentionally accesses a computer without, or in excess of, authorization irrespective of knowledge or stimulus.

Contemporary Motivation

National origin, ideology, or demographics aside, there appear to be six primary motivations for computer intrusion or theft of information in contemporary society: boredom (*informational voyeurism*), intellectual challenge (*mining for knowledge—pure hackers*), revenge (*insiders, disgruntled employees, etc.*), sexual gratification (*stalking, harassment, etc.*), economic (*criminals*), and political (*terrorists, spies, etc.*). The least destructive, but no less insidious, category of hackers are the informational voyeurs.

Like their traditional counterparts, these voyeurs are individuals whose motivations range from inquisitiveness to bravado to sensationalism. These individuals are very closely related to, but far outnumbered by, pure hackers or technological thrill seekers. Fortunately for law enforcement, these individuals are the most easily identified as they share the common affliction—braggadocio. Unlike the other categories which display a remarkable lack of consistency, pure hackers actually constitute a subculture—sharing their own jargon, rites of initiation, ethics, and lifestyles. Annual conferences, Web gatherings, and the like further solidify this marginal grouping. Traditionally, these individuals have proclaimed themselves to be seekers of knowledge, with an ethical obligation to report security holes to system administrators, and to reject any individuals who used their skills for nefarious purposes. Although some criminals have been found in their midst, history has revealed an unwillingness on the part of the hacker community to harbor these types of activities and that they actually ostracize these individuals. Self-righteous proclamations aside, their activities do pose a threat to institutional security and personal privacy. In addition, the irrepressible urge to boast of their conquests may lead others to exploit these self-same vulnerabilities, as many hackers have packaged hacking programs for novices.

Perhaps the most overlooked danger to informational security are current and former employees, commonly referred to as *insiders*. Insiders are those individuals who have authorized or legitimate access to a computer system,

Back Doors and Trojan Horses

Unfortunately, back doors and Trojan horses such as Back Orifice and NetBus are not the only mechanisms which can be utilized to view a potential target's computer files. Sometimes, "friendly" programs such as Netscape provide access for malevolent entities through program flaws.

Example—Dan Brumleve discovered problems in Netscape's implementation of Java. Naming the problem "Brown Orifice," Brumleve proved that an applet running on a Netscape browser transformed the target computer into a file server. He pointed out that these applets could be embedded in the background of any Web page, allowing viewing of a target's computer files without their knowledge. In addition, Brumleve demonstrated that the applet could be initiated through electronic mail messages read via Netscape Mail (Manjoo, 2000).

but who exceed that authorization. While some insiders intentionally circumvent security measures for personal or financial gain, the major threat posed by institutional insiders resides in the unintentional. Far more breaches of institutional security result from careless log-in practices than from targeted attacks. Employees who post passwords in conspicuous places, allow others to shoulder surf, use common names for passwords, or disclose them to strangers pose a much greater risk to informational integrity. However, intentional actions undertaken by disgruntled or former employees also pose a serious problem for corporate or institutional administrators.

It must be noted that overlooking the danger posed by disgruntled or former employees is not a new phenomenon. Many employers seldom change their locks after someone resigns or is terminated, relying on backup or secondary mechanisms. Others fail to change security codes or, more likely, patterns of codes, claiming that the expenses associated with retraining and the high rate of turnover make it impractical to change systemic practices. Many universities, for example, do not change codes for student records systems—relying on individual passwords and deleting user accounts upon termination.

Financial institutions are also responsible for inadequate security, failing to appreciate the damage that could be inflicted by someone who was formerly employed at a financial institution who knew the codes to system entries, password policies, and the intimate details of his or her former co-workers' lives. Even if this individual had been a loner, keeping to himself or herself, they would still know the number of characters required in passwords. With a little brute force, social engineering, and/or a good cracking program, their access would virtually remain the same. In addition, these individuals would have internal knowledge, such as schedules for system maintenance, etc. Even those individuals who are still employed pose a threat, as they may feel exploited. These individuals may receive personal (and financial) gratification from "getting over" on the company. In addition, these individuals might also pose a threat to their fellow employees with whom they are enamored or in competition.

FROM THE EXPERTS . . .

Social Engineering—It's Still Way Too Easy!

Introduction

For the past 20 years or so, the term "social engineering" has been a catchy term for the art-of-the-con. In most cases, it has referred to the act of getting access to or information from people or places that the social engineer should not be able to access. Much of it happens over the telephone. In my case, most of it happened while I was trying to break into an office complex. Using some natural social engineering skills and my knowledge of how things like locks, cameras, alarms, and people's minds work, I was able to retire from that line of work UNDETECTED!

How Easy Was It?

Unfortunately, it was always way too easy. I'm not a criminal, nor have I ever been arrested or convicted of any crime. I am a 100 percent white-hat good-guy. A small part of my 30 years in the technical world was spent as an inside penetration team leader for several companies over a three-year period. Companies who suspected that they had been a victim of espionage or some other intellectual property theft would hire us to attempt to find out how it might have happened. They also wanted us to recommend ways that they could prevent being a victim should they be targeted again.

(Continued)

In some ways, I always feel a little sorry for the people who don't understand how effective social engineering can be when attempting to get information or access. Obviously, I won't mention any company names, but that isn't at all necessary in order to give you an idea of how it works. Every penetration test that we were hired to conduct pretty much started the same way. After a few meetings with key people, it was decided that we would have about a 60–90-day window to conduct the test. This usually happened at the end of the final meeting at their location. None of them ever realized what we meant when we said 'Game on' (just like in paintball) as we got up from the table to leave. We always carried a briefcase to the meetings just so we would look important. Obviously, that wasn't the only reason.

They had just hired us to test their vulnerability level and their susceptibility for being victims of espionage from who knows where (could be inside or outside bad-guys). Social engineering was always my number-one weapon. As we were leaving the meeting and heading back to the elevator with our contact in the building, nature called. Three cups of coffee and a long meeting found me in need of a brief rest stop. The men's room was directly on the way to the elevator, and I said that I would be there in a minute as soon as I got rid of at least two of those cups of coffee. About three minutes later, I was standing with the others in our group by the elevator looking very relieved and much more comfortable. I was about two cups lighter, and one corporate phone directory heavier. The game was on and they had become my first social engineering victims three minutes into the project. That corporate directory would provide every bit of the information that we needed to infiltrate every one of their buildings, and convince dozens of employees that we were a part of the company as we roamed their very secure buildings off and on for over ten off-hours during the next two months.

The Little Things Matter

Little things, like what you throw in the trash, really do matter. We always found it interesting to see what people in corporations would let get out of the building. Every now and then, we would find a corporate directory in a corporate dumpster. That made it unnecessary to even get into the building to get one.

Another very important group of people in a corporation are the custodians. We would always use our social engineering skills to befriend them if we could. It's not that they are any more likely to be victims than anyone else. In some ways, they are the most important people in the building, especially at night. There is a simple reason for my saying this. They have the keys to your world. If we were able to befriend them with a good social engineering con job, we could usually get them to open certain doors for us. It wasn't that they weren't as smart or as security conscious as anyone else, they just happened to be the most important people in the building at that time for us to work on. If you don't train anyone else in your building about the potential dangers of someone coming into a building in the off-hours and asking for access to certain places, please be sure to train your cleaning crew. Establish a procedure for them to be able to quietly notify security if they encounter anyone that they don't recognize. If the person had a reason to be in the building and they are stopped by security, it would simply show that your security plan is working.

How Can You Prevent It?

As with anything else, it can't be prevented if you aren't aware of it. Security awareness training is critical if an organization wants to prevent security threats like social engineering. Employees need to know what they can do to help the organization be more secure. I suspect that in one way or another, most 'bad guys' from disgruntled employees to outside criminals to international terrorists all use some form of social engineering to gain access to places or to gain information about a potential victim. Our minds are just too trusting unless we are provided reasons not to be. As a country that is still at war, we all need to be just a little more suspicious when it comes to people calling us on the phone or walking through the front door of our buildings.

Receiving a phone call from someone that you don't know is a perfect example. The call was most likely not a social engineering attempt, but you don't know that if you don't recognize the voice on the other end. If someone calls me, I always ask who they are trying to reach. If they ask "what number is this?," I immediately ask them, "what number are you trying to reach?" Don't give them any information that they don't need to know. If the call is from someone who needs to talk to you, you can figure that out without giving them any more information than they need until their identity is verified.

More Than You Ever Wanted To Know About Social Engineering

I've provided you a brief introduction into the world of Social Engineering. I have been involved with it for so long that I decided to make it a complete chapter in our recent book *Techno Security's Guide to Managing Risks*

Stay safe out there,
Jack Wiles
The Training Company

Although the last two categories of hackers are not quite as prevalent as those previously discussed, they appear to be investigated at a much higher rate. Individuals in these categories are motivated by the potential for personal or political gain. *Criminals*, those who utilize computer technology to aggressively violate traditional criminal statutes for personal gain, are increasingly common. (Although any activity which involves unauthorized access violates federal statutes, thereby constituting a criminal act, the bulk of literature tends to separate these criminals from those individuals who violate traditional criminal statutes.)

Hierarchy of Contemporary Cyber-Criminals

Although the evolution of computers and global communications has dramatically broadened the population of cyber-criminals, the trend in categorizing them by their level of sophistication and/or their motivation has not. There are four general categories of cyber-criminals in today's society: *script kiddies*; *cyberpunks*; *hackers/crackers*; and *cyber-criminal organizations*. (While some of the categories are primarily based on sophistication and others on motivation, the categories are not necessarily mutually exclusive.)

Script kiddies, also known as *skidiots*, *skiddie*, or *Victor Skill Deficiency* (*VSD*), are the lowest life form of cyber-criminal. The term is a derogatory one used by more sophisticated computer users to refer to inexperienced hackers who employ scripts or other programs authored by others to exploit security vulnerabilities or otherwise compromise computer systems. Technologically the least sophisticated of all cyber-criminals, script kiddies are generally not capable of writing their own programs, and do not fully understand the programs which they are executing. Thus, they are not capable of targeting a specific system, but are limited to those targets which possess the identified vulnerabilities. The least advanced of this category even employ prepackaged software

like Deep Throat or DeepBus. Motivations for script kiddies can range from simple pranks, as when college students use Trojans to remotely "hide" their friends' term papers, to criminal profit, as when users capture bank account and password information to access a victim's account.

Cyberpunks is an innocuous term which has been hotly contested by First Amendment advocates but has been used by law enforcement officials to refer to individuals' intent on wreaking havoc via the Internet. The term was initially used to refer to an emerging genre which marries science fiction, information technology, and radical change in the social order. However, law enforcement authorities often use it as a category which includes vandalism, destructive programs (e.g., viruses and worms), and general mischief for no economic gain.

Sophisticated computer criminals who are capable of programming, writing code, and breaching complex systems are categorized as **hackers** or **crackers** depending on their motivation. Hackers, as previously discussed, are those individuals who identify and exploit system vulnerabilities but who lack economic motivation. Crackers, on the other hand, are those sophisticated users who employ their knowledge for personal gain. Originally known as *criminal hackers*, the term derived from a combination of the two terms.

Cyber-criminal organizations are those groups comprised of criminally minded individuals who have used the Internet to communicate, collaborate, and facilitate cyber-crime. Their motivations are never innocuous and include those activities associated with political extremism or economic gain. The sophistication of the methods employed and the technical expertise of their members range from elementary to highly complex. The term does *not* include traditional organized crime syndicates.

It is important to note that although many sources report that organized crime groups have overtaken the Web, that characterization is not entirely true. While traditional organized crime groups have certainly incorporated cyber-crime into their retinue of criminal activities, the majority of organized criminal activity that has been noted on the Web has been committed by a new type of criminal organization, one that is not necessarily involved in acts of political corruption, vice crimes, or homicide—essential components of groups categorized as "organized crime groups" or "criminal syndicates." The difference is more than a matter of simple semantics. *Organized crime* as a phenomenon has been tirelessly researched, and groups contained therein have the additional characteristics of longevity, hierarchy, protection of leaders, systems of tithing, and, most importantly, violence. As such, it is essential that the two not be discussed as one. While some researchers consistently apply the *organized crime* label to organized groups of hackers—this designation is both naive and misleading. Such groups are more appropriately called *cyber-criminal organizations*, as their structure, communication, and activity are largely contained online. This distinction will be further discussed in Chapter 6.

Criminal hackers are those who target data which is valuable on its face (e.g., trade secrets and proprietary data) or directed at data (e.g., credit card data) which may be used to further other criminal activity. Unfortunately, many users recognize the potentiality for exploitation of valuable data and include at least a modicum of security, but fail to appreciate risks associated with other forms of data. In fact, the data targeted may appear to be totally benign or innocuous. In reality, the level of intrusion and the nature of the objective may pose risks ranging from physical security to operations security.

Exploitation of data associated with the physical security of an institution may represent a precursor to a traditional burglary. Uncovering access codes for alarms in an art museum may allow a sophisticated art thief to enter a secured area undetected. This same individual may also hack into operational plans, revealing scheduling of personnel, security policies, and the like, to gather a complete working schematic of the intended target. Personnel data may also be exploited by criminal syndicates. Japan's yakuza, experts at the practice of extortion (*sokaiya*), could significantly damage, if not destroy, an entire corporation by compromising personnel information residing within its computer system.

Extortion and blackmail, cash for action or inaction, can also be committed in more traditional ways using contemporary technology. In 2000, for example, two cases involving the theft of sensitive consumer information sent shock waves through the cyber-retail community and ripples of fear through the American public. The first of these attacks was directed at a well-known cyber-store which sold audio/video materials. A hacker, known as "Maxus," gained access to over 300,000 credit card numbers and threatened to release them across the world if his demand of $100,000 was not met. Calling his bluff, CD Universe called the FBI. Unfortunately, over 25,000 credit card numbers were compromised, and "Maxus" remains at large as of this writing (Kluger, 2000). A similar case, but one which was particularly troubling, occurred in September of the same year. This incident targeted the leading money transfer agency in the World, Western Union. Over 15,000 credit and debit card numbers were captured by intruders. (Although insiders claim that the act was undertaken for purely entertainment purposes, the breach was so significant that it caused the temporary closing of the company's Web site.) Thus, the threat to sensitive information or data is more real than imagined. It must be noted that the threat posed is not exclusive to professional hackers, organized criminal syndicates, or outsiders. The introduction of previously mentioned back-door programs (i.e., NetBus, Deep Throat, Back Orifice, etc.) has also empowered novice users. (Imagine a scenario in which a prominent politician known for his conservative platform is confronted with evidence of his downloaded collection of sadomasochistic pornography.) In addition, the threat of computer contamination, which is increasingly destructive, can be used to extort money from companies with valuable data (discussed in more detail in Chapter 4).

Although many thieves are now marketing high-technology merchandise, many of their traditional storefronts are still in place. As you can see, some criminals prefer the time-tested practice of selling stolen merchandise out of the back of a van. (*Photo Courtesy of James Doyle Internet Crimes Inc.*)

● COMPUTERS AS COMMODITIES

While hacking, phreaking, and the theft of sensitive information have garnered a great deal of both national and international attention and will be further discussed in Chapter 4, the theft of computer hardware and the infringement of software copyrights have been all but overlooked. However, these activities have become quite popular as computer components become smaller and more valuable.

Hardware

Increasingly, computer components are worth more than their weight in gold (or even platinum). However, these same components tend to be less protected than even the most inexpensive of metal commodities. Computers, accessible to employees, students, and sometimes, the public at large, are extremely vulnerable to theft. In fact, many valuable computer components may be concealed in areas as small as a shirt pocket. Many computer chips worth several hundred dollars,

for example, may be hidden within a briefcase, a shirt pocket, or even a small wallet. A simple screwdriver, dress shirt, and a little know-how are the only tools needed to successfully steal thousands of dollars of material. No other criminal heist requires so little. In addition, unlike high-dollar jewelry, which may be identified by gem maps for appraisals, integrated circuits are difficult to trace. Thus, computer thieves have traditionally been able to market their stolen goods as legitimate. The increase of Internet auctions has only increased this possibility. Without the requirements imposed on traditional pawnshops, auction sites such as eBay carry no responsibility for facilitating the transfer of stolen computer components.

In its most basic sense, the term *computer components* represents a variety of equipment, but is usually reserved for the smallest portions of computer technology, like integrated circuits. Larger components, of course, are the most obvious: CPUs, storage media, computer chips, etc. Although CPUs are often not thought of as easy targets, their size, utility, and value are dependent

Although the size of CPUs and monitors often diminish their desirability for computer thieves, a sizeable black market for them still exists in many areas. (*Photo Courtesy o.f James Doyle/NYPD, ret.*)

upon demographic characteristics and local market value. (A CPU worth $1,000 in the United States might go as high as $3,000 in the UK.) Although many computers are made by large manufacturers who serialize CPUs and the subsequent components, identifying information is often superficial—capable of being manipulated quite easily (e.g., stick-on serial numbers). The sheer magnitude of computer transactions makes it virtually impossible to trace many units reported stolen. Even more profitable, however, tends to be the theft of circuitry found within computer systems in general. It is more economically advantageous, by far, to steal a CPU and sell the individual circuitry. Motherboards, ethercards, and the like tend to bring a greater return due to the inability to trace these components. In addition, integrated chips, serial ports, and drives (external and internal) prove almost impossible to trace.

The theft and resale of integrated chips has proven to be the most lucrative of component theft. Resale of such computer chips may return as much as ten times on their investment (which sure beats the stock market). One of the primary reasons that resale of this particular equipment is so lucrative is the basic law of supply and demand. While Americans have become socialized to expect a ready supply of the latest technology, other portions of the globe are not as fortunate. International residents may actually salivate at the purchase of technology that is already outdated in the United States. Thus, illegitimate global marketplaces have emerged. These marketplaces may be categorized as to their level of criminal culpability or organization.

Black market dealers are the most organized groups trafficking in stolen computer components. These individuals or groups may be likened to full-service restaurants—carefully soliciting orders and preparing merchandise as requested. Thus, their targets are selected only after they receive an order for particular merchandise. These groups actively participate in the theft itself. **Gray market dealers,** on the other hand, are often legitimate businesses with questionable, and illegal, practices. Most often, these businesses are those which specialize in made-to-order computers (i.e., non-standard or knock-offs).

They represent a major customer for thieves, being a ready outlet for their illegal wares. Buying the components at a significant discount, these companies claim ignorance. In fact, some of them resell these questionable components to other dealers. Another activity that is popular with both black market dealers and gray market dealers involves the fraudulent sale of counterfeit goods. These items, marketed and packaged as legitimate products, are often labeled as higher performance or more expensive components. Unfortunately, these types of activities are on the increase, as the profitability sharply outweighs potential risks. The sheer volume of personal computers and informal transactions coupled with legal requirements for search warrants all but negate the possibility of random identification. Thus, law-enforcement officers are forced to focus their investigations on the identification of individuals or corporations who sell an unusually high number of drives, circuits, or the like, without selling the accompanying equipment.

● THEFT OF INTELLECTUAL PROPERTY

Software

In August 2001, the FBI arrested four men and seized over $10 million worth of counterfeit Microsoft software. These arrests, the result of a 14-month investigation, revealed the increasing sophistication and organization displayed by computer criminals as many of the counterfeit items included disks with replicas of Microsoft's new hologram technology. Thus, this technology, designed exclusively to prevent software counterfeiting, is proving ineffective due to the high costs associated with obtaining licensed copies (e.g., Microsoft Office 2000 costs $599). Although highly lucrative, this activity is not as pervasive (or costly to manufacturers) as individual *piracy* (i.e., the unauthorized copying of software).

Data piracy refers to the reproduction, distribution, and use of software without the permission or authorization of the owner of copyright. Making multiple copies for personal use or distributing copies to friends or colleagues has become so commonplace that many individuals fail to appreciate, or even recognize, the illegality of their actions. The ease of replication, greatly enhanced through the advent of CD-RWs, has further exacerbated this problem as more and more users find expensive programs readily transferable. However, the greatest contributor to this activity may simply be a lack of knowledge regarding software licensing.

Most retail programs are licensed for use at just one computer site or by only one user at any time. By buying the software, an individual becomes a licensed user rather than an owner. While this individual user may be allowed to make copies of the program for backup purposes, it is against the law

---

Theft of Computer Components

- October 2006—Brothers Jimmy Luong and Danny Hung Leung were convicted of various counts of money laundering and attempted money laundering in connection with the theft of over $10 million of computer components.
- February 2001—Samuel Williams and Dion Wilson, employees of SoftBank (now ClientLogic), illegally diverted more than $700,000 of computer products to drop zones across upper New York. Although they eventually pled guilty to conspiracy to commit wire fraud and to transport stolen property, their light sentences reflect the enticing nature of this activity. (Eight to twenty-four months vs. a payout of $700,000!) Interestingly, if state statutes for larceny or theft of property had been applied, their activities would have carried heightened penalties (*www.cybercrime.gov/ williams_wilson.htm*).
- June, 2001—IBM, a perpetual target of thieves and assorted other ne'er-do-wells, was victimized when over $4 million in disk drives was stolen from their San Jose location. These drives were later recovered in Southern California.

to distribute copies to friends and colleagues. **Software piracy** is all but impossible to stop, although software companies are launching more and more lawsuits against major infractors. Originally, software companies tried to stop software piracy by copy-protecting their software. This strategy failed, however, because it was inconvenient for users and was not 100 percent foolproof. Most software now require some sort of registration, which may discourage would-be pirates, but doesn't really stop software piracy. An entirely different approach to software piracy prevention was the introduction of a new category of licensed software. Unlike expensively packaged and mass merchandised software products, **shareware** acknowledges the futility of trying to stop people from copying software and instead relies on people's honesty. Shareware publishers encourage users to give copies of programs to friends and colleagues but ask everyone who uses a program regularly to pay a registration fee to the program's author directly. Commercial programs that are made available to the public illegally are often called wareZ.

WareZ sites are extremely popular on the Internet. These sites enable visitors to download software illegally in violation of copyright protections. Unfortunately, many of these sites are created and maintained by highly sophisticated, well-educated administrators. Perhaps the earliest example of such activity was David LaMacchia, a student at MIT, who developed two bulletin boards on MIT's network named "Cynosure" and "Cynosure II." His system enabled individuals to upload popular software applications, like WordPerfect and Excel, to "Cynosure" and download those applications and more from "Cynosure II" with a valid password. Indicted for violating the Federal Wire Fraud Statute, LaMacchia was released after a court ruled that the statute did not apply to his activities. He remained at MIT, where he pursued a five-year master's program in electrical engineering and computer science. Unfortunately, LaMacchia's case was just the beginning of large-scale data piracy operations. In 2006, federal prosecutors charged 19 members of RISCISO with the piracy of software and movies totaling more than $6.5 million in copyrighted material. The group marketed their illegal wares through password-protected sites on the Internet.

Film Piracy

There are eight primary methods of film piracy: optical disc piracy; Internet piracy; videocassette piracy; theatrical print theft; signal theft; broadcast piracy; public performances; and parallel imports. Such theft is quite lucrative both in the United States and abroad. The overseas market for American films involves both new releases and old films. In the United States, the primary market is saturated with films which are not yet available on DVD or cable. The illegal copying and distribution of such films has been perpetrated by individuals and organized criminal syndicates alike. For the most part, individual criminals use less sophisticated means of data piracy, and bootlegged copies of pre-release films tend to be of low quality as they are often products of video recordings of a movie screen.

Traditional organized crime groups are more sophisticated in their approach. The Chinese Triads, for example, have developed a multilateral strategy which includes, but is not limited to *runners*; *piracy burners*, and *privacy pressers*.[8] In February 2007, members of the

---

Types of Film Piracy

1. Optical disc piracy
2. Internet piracy
3. Videocassette piracy
4. Theatrical print theft
5. Signal theft
6. Broadcast piracy
7. Public performances
8. Parallel imports

The rising cost of software coupled with the decreasing cost of CD-RWs has resulted in an explosion of counterfeit software. Unlike other areas involving stolen or compromised property, individual users are often fully aware of the nature of the merchandise as unsophisticated counterfeit copies are easily identifiable. (*Photo Courtesy of James Doyle/NYPD, ret.*)

Taiwanese Intellectual Property Rights Police and the Foundation for the Protection of Film and Video Works (FVWP) arrested several suspects on charges of digital piracy. In addition to 26 optical disc burners, authorities seized 80 DVD-R burners and 37 CD-R burners capable of producing 1,728,000 DVD-Rs and 2,664,000 CD-Rs annually. This constitutes $9 million in potential revenue.[9]

Traditionally, investigations into data piracy and counterfeit software were often difficult due to the inexperience of investigators. However, their collective experience has indicated that significant clues exist to assist them in identifications. These may include, but are not limited to,

- counterfeit hologram
- absence of original reserve label and absence of polygraphic packing
- absence of Copyright and Adjacent Rights Protection sign
- anomalies in packaging material
- absence of high quality images on the CD

● CONCLUSIONS

Increases in technology have dramatically changed contemporary society. For the most part, such changes have been positive. Increased knowledge, enhanced communication, and growth in competitive markets have all been byproducts of the information revolution. However, such advances have been accompanied by similar innovations among criminally minded individuals. Such modernization has frustrated the efforts of law enforcement agencies across the world, as they struggle with jurisdictional complications, legislative apathy, and judicial inconsistencies. Consequently, the majority of technology-savvy deviants have operated with virtual impunity, creating a landscape rich in criminal diversity.

As stated, computers may serve as the target or the means for criminals. They may be attacked for the information contained therein or as a form of retribution against an individual or organization. In addition, they may actually represent the instrumentality of the crime, serving as the proverbial smoking gun. Or, they may simply serve as a repository of criminal evidence, containing a hacker's list of stolen access codes or a bookmaker's list of customer accounts. Its advantages aside, use of computers exponentially increases the potentiality of economic loss and the magnitude of victimization. Thus, it is essential that law enforcement agencies and legislative bodies recognize the insidious nature of computer crime and allocate resources accordingly.

DISCUSSION QUESTIONS

1. Briefly discuss the lack of criminal evidence and the intangibility that law enforcement personnel traditionally have problems with in computer crime cases.
2. List and discuss the three major categories of computer crime.
3. Discuss the hindrances that criminal investigators face while dealing with the computer crime aside from the obvious struggle with the ever-changing technological world.
4. The chapter names six primary motivations for computer intrusions or theft of information in contemporary society. Name and discuss them.
5. Discuss the impact that *insiders* may have on the security of a company and the reasons that they want to participate in such acts.
6. Explain the difference between *hackers* and *crackers*.

RECOMMENDED READING

- Harris, Shon; Harper, Allen; Eagle, Chris; Ness, Jonathan; and Lester, Michael (2004). *Gray Hat Hacking: The Ethical Hacker's Handbook*. McGraw-Hill Publishing: New York.
- Kurtz, George (2006). *Hacking Exposed* (5th Ed). McGraw-Hill Publishing: New York.
- McIllwain, Jeffrey Scott (2005). "Intellectual Property Theft and Organized Crime: The Case of Film Piraxy." *Trends in Organized Crime*, 8(4): 15–39.
- Schambray, Joel; McClure, Stuart; and Kurtz, George (2000). *Hacking Exposed* (2nd Ed). McGraw-Hill Publishing: New York.
- Stoll, Cliff (2005). *The Cuckoo's Egg: Tracking a Spy Through the Maze of Computer Espionage* (Reissue Ed). Pocket Books: New York.

WEB RESOURCES

- http://www.mit.edu/hacker/hacker.html – online access to the complete text of Bruce Sterling's *The Hacker Crackdown: Law and Disorder on the Electronic Frontier*. The document is the most comprehensive account of the hacker wars of the 1980s–1990s. It includes discussion of hacking exploits and the destruction of the hacking group LoD.
- www.findlaw.com – the highest-trafficked legal Web site, which provides a comprehensive set of legal resources on the Internet for legal professionals, corporate counsel, law students, businesses, and consumers. These resources include Web search utilities, cases and codes, legal news, an online career center, and community-oriented tools, such as a secure document management utility, e-mail newsletters, and message boards.
- www.cybercrime.gov – Web site of the department responsible for implementing national strategies in combating computer and intellectual property crimes worldwide. The Computer Crime Initiative is a comprehensive program designed to combat electronic penetrations, data thefts, and cyberattacks on critical information systems. CCIPS prevents, investigates, and prosecutes computer crimes by working with other government agencies, the private sector, academic institutions, and foreign counterparts.
- www.cybersafe.gov – the Department of Justice Web site, which is linked to all forms of government information and departments specifically organized for the protection of the United States against all criminals.

ENDNOTES

[1]Anonymizers are sites which enable users to mask their IP addresses through rerouting, remailing, or deletion of header information. This successfully conceals the sender's identity.

[2]Many of these services differ in their level of security. For example, some will hold messages for a period and then send them out randomly through a multitude of other re-mailers, while others may simply strip the information and send the messages.

[3]The above represents a very limited introduction to cryptology without considering future developments. New technologies like quantum computing, having the ability to break all codes (quickly trying all possibilities), make constant vigilance a necessity for cryptographic security professionals. Similarly, quantum cryptography, based on certain random features of light, potentially makes encryption unbreakable via quantum cryptanalysis. Ramifications of these and other new technologies make cryptographic security a work in progress.

[4]United Nations (2000). "United Nations Manual on the Prevention and Control of Computer-related Criteria." *International Review of Criminal Policy*, 43 & 44. Available at *www.ifs.univie.ac.at/~pr2gq1/rev4344.html*. Retrieved from the Internet on September 9, 2007.

[5]Stambaugh, Hollis; Beupre, David S.; Baker, Richard; Cassady, Wayne; and Williams, Wayne P. (2001). "Electronic Crime Needs Assessment for State and Local Law Enforcement." DOJ # 98-DT-R-076. Washington, DC: NIJ.

[6]November 20, 1963. *The Tech*, MIT student publication.

[7]Blankenship, Lloyd (1968). Available at *http://www.mithral. com/~beberg/manifesto.html*. Retrieved from the World Wide Web on July 13, 2007.

[8]McIllwain, Jeffrey Scott (2005). "Intellectual Property Theft and Organized Crime: The Case of Film Piracy." *Trends in Organized Crime*, 8(4): 15–39.

[9]MPA (2007). *Taiwan Raids on Suspected Organized Crime Gangs Net Seizure of 117 DVD-R, CD-R Burners: Gangs Try to Eliminate Competitors by Providing Tips to Motion Picture Association Anti-Piracy Hotline.* Available at http://mpaa.org/ press_releases/taiwangangsraidfeb07.pdf.

Contemporary Computer Crime

Chapter Outline

LEARNING OBJECTIVES

After reading this chapter, you will be able to do the following:

✓ Explore the current state of Internet crimes in the United States and abroad.

✓ Identify emerging trends in Web-based crime.

✓ Develop a working knowledge of the six classifications of motive for modern computer intruders.

✓ Become familiar with more computer terms and recent laws that aid the government in cracking down on computer criminals.

✓ Gain knowledge of modern terrorists and their use of technology which is changing the face of terrorism completely

KEY TERMS AND CONCEPTS

- anonymizer
- CAN-SPAM ACT of 2003
- Classical Era
- counterfeiting
- cyberstalking
- cyberharassment
- cyberterrorism
- cybersquatting
- data diddling
- day trading
- denial of service (DoS) attack
- eco-terrorism
- erotomaniacs
- extortion
- false information
- finding

- Floppy Era
- fraud
- fraudulent instruments
- forfeiture
- forgery
- freezing
- insider trading
- Internet Era
- Internet Gambling Prohibition and Enforcement Act of 2006
- IP spoofing
- ISP-Jacking
- love-obsession stalker
- Macro Era
- macro viruses

- money laundering
- malware
- obsessional stalkers
- ransomware
- salami technique
- shoulder-surfing
- spam
- spamming
- social engineering
- stalking
- VBS worm generator
- vicinage
- vengeance
- Web-cramming
- zombies

● NEO-TRADITIONAL CRIME

While the Internet has increased the potential for interpersonal crime via computer, comparable advances in printing technologies, software capabilities, digital cameras, and the like have increased the sophistication of non-Internet criminal activity. Traditional methods of counterfeiting currency, defrauding financial institutions, viewing child pornography, and the like have all been supplanted by more advanced approaches. Techniques for manipulating stocks, exchanging radical platforms, and criminal solicitation are increasingly modified to incorporate advances in technology. These advances mirror those found in legitimate markets. The same printers, copiers, and scanners which have greatly improved the ability of illegitimate users to counterfeit stock certificates, official documents, and even currency have also been utilized to create more sophisticated security measures for American currency, making watermarks passé.

Fraud and Fraudulent Instruments

As stated previously, advancements in technology have greatly improved American life, while creating innovative opportunities for deviant members of society. **Counterfeiting** and **Forgery**, the act of creating a fraudulent document and the act of falsifying a document (including the falsification of signatures) with criminal intent, respectively, have been made far easier with the advent of high-level graphics software and hardware advances. As with other areas of computer crime, organized crime groups have aggressively utilized such advances to create new modes of illegitimate enterprise. Many of these groups have successfully used computer programs not only to create fraudulent checks but also to generate the forged signatures necessary for authentication. In Long Beach, California, for example, members of the North Vietnamese Triads used computers to forge payroll checks against major banks in excess of $20 million. Criminals have also used these techniques to perfect counterfeit currency with high-end printers and scanners. Unfortunately, this method of counterfeiting is much easier than traditional methods which required the making of printing plates. In fact, even novice computer criminals can manufacture counterfeit currency with a minimal investment of time and expense.

In addition to crimes facilitated by advancements in printing and graphics software, other traditional crimes which are being committed in the physical world are being translated into the cyber-world. Even those crimes which do not seem easily transferable are beginning to surface. For example, a ring of shoplifters were arrested by federal authorities in February 2007. These individuals had stolen merchandise from major American retailers, such as Target, Walgreens, Wal-Mart, and Safeway, and resold the products through a company called Rosemont Wholesale, who advertised their wares via *www. wholesaleramp.com*. In fact, the possibilities for Internet-facilitated criminal activity are only limited by the boundaries of imagination.

● WEB-BASED CRIMINAL ACTIVITY

In the dawning hours of the computer age, the term "computer crime" usually referred to the theft of computers or computer components. This distinction changed dramatically with the introduction of the cyberage. Increasingly, criminals have targeted a far less tangible commodity—information. At least 60 million residents of North America have online bank accounts, and at least one-third of the American workforce, or 50 million individuals, are online. In addition, big businesses and multinational corporations are increasingly relying on technology systems and the Internet for the distribution of goods and materials, communication, billing, and account management. In fact, e-commerce amounts to over $70 billion in the United States alone.[1] It should not be entirely unexpected, then, that criminals are increasingly focusing their efforts in this realm.

Just as law enforcement tended to overlook the seriousness of hacking and phreaking in the 1980s, legislative bodies have been slow to respond to the potentiality of contemporary computer crime in the twenty-first century. In fact, the strides made in electronic communications and the increasing emphasis on point-and-click platforms have enabled a variety of criminally minded individuals to expand their horizons. Traditionally, computer crime was comprised mainly of trafficking in stolen equipment or falsification of records. Although certain types of computer crime were possible prior to the introduction of cyberspace, the marriage of computer and telecommunications has resulted in an explosion of crime. The impression of anonymity has proven all but irresistible to criminally minded individuals. In fact, it may be argued that some individuals who had previously been deterred by the fear of exposure are more susceptible to the temptations posed by this type of platform. Indeed, preliminary estimates of Internet gambling, illegal in virtually every area of the country, suggest that the Web, with its promise of anonymity, has encouraged criminal activity among the masses. To wit, individuals who would never walk into an adult book store in search of photographs or videos of bestiality or child pornography, readily download those same materials in the privacy of their home. Those unwilling to walk into a bank with a gun may feel comfortable altering bank records or manipulating stock records. Those same individuals who were dissuaded from seeking revenge through traditional avenues may feel completely confident in posting embarrassing or compromising information on the Web.

Even hackers, whom many authorities believed to be a relic of the 1980s, are increasingly dangerous. Recent cases indicate that computer dependency and globalization of communication have been exploited by individual, group, and government hacking entities. A group known as Global Hell, for example, is suspected of hacking into a variety of government sites including the U.S. Department of the Interior, the United States Army, the Federal Bureau of Investigation, and the White House. Although their motivations appear to be a simple quest for notoriety as opposed to the destruction of government property, implications for national security are tremendous. Other implications of computer crime include

1. financial losses,
2. personal security (i.e., identity theft),
3. industrial espionage,
4. international security, and
5. public safety.

In fact, threats to public welfare and personal safety may surpass national security concerns.

Generally speaking, there are six categories of online crime:

- *interference with lawful use of computers*— DOS attacks, viruses, worms, other malware, cybervandalism, cyberterrorism, SPAM, etc.
- *theft of information and copyright infringement*—industrial espionage; ID theft; ID fraud, etc.
- *dissemination of contraband or offensive materials*—pornography, child pornography, online gaming, treasonous or racist material, etc.
- *threatening communications*—**extortion**, cyberstalking, cyberharassment, etc.
- *Fraud*—auction fraud, credit card fraud, theft of services, stock manipulation, etc.
- *Ancillary crimes*—money laundering, conspiracy, etc.

Interference with Lawful Use of Computers

Industrial or corporate competition has also escalated to the malicious destruction of data. This **eco-terrorism** or corporate warfare is not unique, nor is it a new concept. Traditionally, other methods of destruction included attacks on physical structures (i.e., headquarters, research laboratories, etc.) or tangible objects (i.e., file cabinets, vials of chemicals, etc.). But just as the virtuality of cyberspace has altered traditional modes of communication, education, and commerce, it has transformed the competitive arena of big business. Indeed, the interconnectivity of technological devices which have become so prized across the globe has exponentially increased the vulnerability of those self-same corporations. While the impact of a traditional mail bomb was limited to the physical area surrounding the packaging, the implications of e-mail bombs are limitless in their application and may include a complete dismantling of a company's informational infrastructure.

The Toolkit of a Cybercriminal

Although methods and mechanisms of cybercriminals vary, the majority of online victimization is perpetrated by employing one of the various tools.[2]

Bots or **zombies**—a computer which has been compromised by some form of malware which enables the criminal to remotely control that computer. For the most part, bots or zombies are employed collectively in a botnet.

Keyloggers—a software program or hardware device which records all keystrokes of a compromised computer. Depending on the device or software employed, the information is either locally stored or remotely sent to the perpetrator.

Bundlers—malware which is hidden inside what appears to be legitimate software or download. Containers often include gaming software, freeware, image or audio files, or screensavers.

DDoS—a concentrated attack on a system or service which employs botnets to disrupt or deny access to the target.

Packet Sniffers—software programs which are capable of monitoring network traffic and capturing specific data. They are often employed to "sniff" and capture passwords as they travel across the network.

Rootkits—a compilation of tools which are employed by hackers on a compromised machine. Among other things, rootkits allow criminals to maintain access, prevent detection, build in hidden backdoors, and collect information from the compromised system.

Spyware—software which covertly collects information from a compromised system. It is often bundled with legitimate software and can transmit the information collected to a designated site or user.

Scripts—short programs or lists of command which can be copied, remotely inserted, and used to attack a local computer or network.

Phishing—an e-mail or document which attempts to persuade the recipient to divulge specific information, like passwords, account numbers, etc. (It will be discussed more thoroughly in Chapter 5.)

Trojans—a general category which encompasses a variety of other cybertools. Covertly installed, these programs are designed to collect information, provide control, or distribute data.

Worms—wholly contained viruses that travel through networks, automatically duplicating and mailing themselves to other systems.

Viruses—programs or pieces of malicious code which are intended to infect or compromise random systems or machines.

Malware

As discussed in Chapter 2, **malware** or **malicious programming code** refers to code that causes damage to computer systems. This broad-based category includes *back doors, Trojan horses,* *viruses, worms,* and *DoS attacks.* All of these entities can be, and have been, employed by terrorists, hacktivists, corporate spies, criminals, and pleasure seekers. The range of their utilization includes blackmail, extortion, and espionage, while their

Malware on the Rise

According to a report compiled by McAfee, malware is increasingly popular among the criminally minded, and 85 percent of malicious programming is currently written purely for profit. Unfortunately, criminals have recognized the vulnerability of computer systems, and every month, at least 2,000 potentially malicious threats emerge. Botnets are increasingly popular to these individuals as they can be remotely controlled and are not as susceptible to anti-virus software.[3] Here are some of them:

1. W32/Sdbot.ftp
2. Exploit/Metafile
3. W32/Sober.AH.worm
4. W32/Netsky.P.worm
5. W32 Gaobot.gen.worm
6. W32/Tearec.A.worm
7. Trj/Torpig.A
8. Trj/Qhost.gen
9. W32/Alcan.A.worm
10. W32/Parite

Source: Computer Crime Research Center, 2006 (*www.crime-research.org*)

payloads in destruction range from nuisance to devastation. Some viruses, for example, may simply insert, delete, or scramble text within MS Word documents (e.g., *wm97thu* and *Anna Kournikova*). Particularly destructive viruses like *Chernobyl* may attack by erasing a portion of the hard disk that makes it impossible to access the disk, even if booting from a floppy. They may also attack the file allocation table (FAT) of the first partition, making it impossible for the disk to assemble data logically.

Viruses and Worms

Contrary to popular belief, computer viruses are not a new phenomenon. Although early mainframe users experienced anomalies, they necessarily credit such occurrences as malicious or intentional. Loss of files or misplaced lettering was attributed to programming glitches. The first recognized computer virus, *the rabbit*, appeared in the 1960s. These programs diminished the productivity of computer systems by cloning themselves and occupying system resources. These *rabbits* were strictly local phenomena, incapable of copying themselves across systems and were the result of mistakes or pranks by system programmers. The first virus attached to an executable file made its appearance in the 1970s on the Univax 1108 system.[4] *Pervading Animal* was attached to the end of an executable file and required the computer user to answer a series of questions regarding animals. Since that time, viruses have continued to evolve and are currently capable of network failure and mass destruction of data. Here is a brief timeline of some significant evolutionary developments.

Although the proliferation of viruses often makes it difficult for users to comprehend their evolution, there are four distinct eras of computer viruses. The first of these may be defined as the **Classical Era (1960s–1970s)**, in which system anomalies occurred accidentally or were a result of pranks by programmers or system administrators. The second evolutionary era, known as the **Floppy Era (1980s–1990s)**, was largely characterized by infection of DOS machines spread by removable media. During this period the spread of computer viruses was relatively limited, and the evolution of viruses was relatively slow. Due primarily to their lack of sophistication, viruses during this period were easy to detect, isolate, and eliminate. This began to change with the introduction of polymorphic viruses which emerged in the early 1990s. These viruses avoided detection by using indecipherable code, easily defeating early antivirus software which identified potential viruses by looking for segments of known virus code.

By the mid-1990s, end users became aware of the risk of viruses, and many stopped sharing programs or running executable files. At the same time, the explosion of the Internet, the electronic mail, and the Windows OS proved irresistible to virus creators. As such, macro viruses emerged, and the **Macro Era (1990s–2000s)** was born. Unlike viruses found in the first two periods, **macro viruses** infect documents and templates, not programs. Embedding the malicious code into the macro programming language found in popular Microsoft and Macintosh (e.g. Word, Excel) applications, the virus infects the system when the user opens the document. Once executed, the virus will become embedded in both current and future documents. The virus is then propagated via e-mail, networks, and the Internet. One of the first notable examples of a macro virus appeared on the Internet in March 1999. The *Melissa* virus caused more than $80 million in damages to computers across the globe. In the United States, the viruses infected 1.2 million computers of one-fifth of the nation's largest businesses. Created by David Smith, the virus was embedded in a document posted on the Internet newsgroup *Alt.sex*. Proclaiming to contain passcodes to various adult-content Web sites, users infected their computers by downloading and opening the document. The virus then propagated itself by sending e-mail to the first 50 addresses in the computer user's address book. Smith was

Year	Name	Systems Targeted	Significance
1982	Elk Cloner (created by Richard Skrenta)	Apple DOS 3.3	Released "in the wild"—not locally contained
1986	Brain (created by Basit & Amjad Frooq Alvi)	Various	First PC boot sector virus; first virus to operate in stealth mode, replacing infected sectors with clean ones.
1987	Christmas Tree	European Academic Research Network and IBM Vnet	First total epidemic of a network virus
1988	Morris Worm (created by Robert Morris)	Unix for Vax; Sun Microsystems	Picked up user passwords; focused on errors in OS
1990	Chameleon		First polymorphic virus. Defeated traditional platforms for virus detection
1990	Murphy Nomenclatura Best		Creation of Bulgarian "virus production factory" and first BBS devoted to virus making
1992	Michelangelo	Windows	Causes boom in antivirus software
1996	Win.Tentacle	Windows 3.x	First Windows epidemic
1997	Linux.bliss	Linux	First virus for Linux
1997	Homer		First network worm virus using FTP to propagate
1997	mIRC worms	Windows	Virus scripts are transmitted along Windows IRC channels
1998	Win32.HLLP.DeTroie	Windows	Capable of transmitting information from the infected computer to the owner
1998	Back Orifice	Various	Introduction of clandestine installation of Trojans, enabling remote access to infected computers
1998	VBScript.Rabbit	Windows	Creation of HTML virus—employing the MS Windows and Office options, infection of remote computers and Web servers, replication via e-mail
2000	LoveLetter	Windows	First widely distributed virus making use of the VBS extension. Considered the costliest virus, as system administrators were unprepared for it.[5]

(Continued)

Year	Name	Systems Targeted	Significance
2000–2001	Nimda, CodeRed, Sircam	Windows	Re-emergence of the worm. Replication via e-mail and scans and infects Web servers. Capable of infecting computers by simply viewing of subject line in Outlook. Originally touted as having the capacity to bring down the Internet.
2000	Liberty	Palm OS	First harmful Trojan to target Palm Pilot operating systems.[6]
2003	Slammer	Windows/Internet	First fileless or "flash" worm. Caused several segments of the Internet to crash. Did not copy itself but remained in memory.
2003	Lovesan	Windows/Internet	Exploited weakness in Windows 2000/XP
2003	Sobig	Windows/Internet	Widespread DoS attack on selected sites designed to facilitate spam attacks.[7]
2003	Mimail	Windows/Internet	Exploited latest vulnerability in Internet Explorer which allowed binary code to be extracted from HTML files and executed.[8]
2004	Various (Sasser, MyDoom, NetSky, etc.)	Windows/Internet	Proliferation of viruses dedicated to facilitating mass spam attacks.

subsequently sentenced to 20 months in federal prison, three years of supervised release, 100 hours of community service, and a fine of $5,000. In addition, he was prohibited from accessing a computer of any kind.[9]

In the wake of the *Melissa* virus and the prosecution of David Smith, investigators recognized that the transmission of viruses was continuing to evolve. In mid-2000, two viruses heralded a new period in virus sophistication and distribution. The **Internet Era (2000–present)** began with the introduction of a group of publicized infections: *CodeRed*, *SirCam*, and *w32/Nimbda.A-mm*. One of the group's methods of propagation was similar to *Melissa*'s exploitation of Microsoft Outlook. All were capable of using an infected system's address book to infect other computers. However, this new group demonstrated a variety of alternative methods of replication that were not found in previous viruses. *CodeRed*, for example, scanned the Internet for vulnerable machines, then infected them; while *Nimda* ("admin" spelled backwards) infected computers even when the infected e-mail was simply viewed through MS Outlook's preview window.[10] Unfortunately, the re-emergence of network worms continues to plague users and system administrators alike. An increasing proliferation of such worms is continuing to cause untold damages, and worms are increasingly utilized to perpetrate large-scale DoS attacks. While the motivations for their creation vary, more and more are being unleashed for economic gain.

Public Apathy and Increased Vulnerability

Especially popular among hackers in the 1980s, the threat of malicious programming code created near hysteria among early computer users and spawned an entire industry. However, the creation of antivirus and firewall programs has almost negated the unease experienced nearly two decades ago. Unfortunately, they have also led to a false sense of security among the American public, resulting in an apathetic approach to data security. In fact, malicious attacks or information theft are so dangerous that even computer giants like Apple and IBM have not been immune.

Regardless of the level of scrutiny afforded to computer viruses or other contaminants, their threat remains genuine. In fact, virus creation and dissemination has become more pronounced with the inception of made-to-order virus and worm tool kits readily available via the Internet. The **VBS**

Worm Generator (VBSWG 1.50b), for example, allows *script kiddies* (i.e., novice users with malicious intentions) to create viruses quickly and painlessly. Reportedly created in Buenos Aires, Argentina, VBSWG 1.50b creates VBS worms that infect Windows systems with MS VBS runtimes or Windows Scripting Host 5.0. Unfortunately, this includes Windows 95 SE, 98, and 98 SE. Although other toolkits exist (including Satanic Brain Virus Tools, 1.0; the Instant Virus Production Kit, and Ye Olde Funky Virus Generator), this particular one has been directly responsible for a variety of recent viruses, including the popular *Anna Kournikova* virus, and is so specialized that users may name their own virus and select from a variety of payloads. It even allows users to choose the manner of virus activation (i.e., timed, immediate, etc.).

DoS (Denial of Service) and DDoS (Distributed Denial of Service) Attacks

The primary objective in a **denial of service (DoS) attack** is to disable a large system without necessarily gaining access to it. Traditionally, the most common DoS attack involved mail-bombing (e.g., jamming a system's server with voluminous e-mail). Other traditional methods included the time-proven method of manipulation of phone switches or the more sophisticated method of low-level data transmission. These attacks were directed at some of the Web's most popular portals, including *www.amazon.com*, *www.eBay.com*,

and *www.Yahoo.com*. Motivations varied from personal to organizational to political. During this period, national infrastructures remained relatively unscathed, and attacking packets originated from a single address or network.[11]

Enter Botnets and Zombie Armies

Since their inception, criminals have now recognized and developed a new methodology for DoS attacks. Known as DDoS (distributed denial of service) attacks, this emerging technology employed zombie or robot (aka bot) machines to increase the effectiveness and efficiency of their

Contemporary Computer Viruses: Old Wine in New Bottles

Computer viruses can serve a variety of illegitimate purposes. Motivations can range from simple boredom to international terrorism, while payloads can be configured to be systemically destructive or act as covert information servers. The potential hazards of computer viruses have national security implications as informational warfare and global espionage are increasingly conducted via electronic media.

An evaluation of recent viruses reveals that we are not learning from our mistakes. In fact, many

contemporary viruses are actually variants of the same source code with similar methodology and payload. Security experts suggest that this phenomenon may be attributed to an inadequate inoculation period, where users experience a heightened (but brief) awareness of data vulnerability. Thus, administrators must develop innovative training programs while continuously updating their virus protection.

payload. **Zombies** or **bots** are compromised computers attached to the Internet which are often used to remotely perform malicious or criminal tasks. They are often used in large batches (i.e., *zombie armies* or *botnets*), and the majority of owners of zombie computers are unaware of their usage. Their use is increasingly common as they effectively camouflage the perpetrator and decrease the operating costs of their criminal operation associated with bandwidth. Zombie computers have been used in a variety of highly publicized DDoS attacks, such as the SPEWS service in 2003 and the Blue Frog service in 2006. Unfortunately, botnets employing zombie computers are difficult to identify and shut down and require the disassembly and tracing of an individual bot to identify the perpetrator.

In 1999, the first known DDoS attacks occurred, with tools known as *Trinoo* and *Tribe Flood Network* (TFN). Since that time, such attacks have become commonplace and have been employed by a variety of individuals or groups, such as extortionists, business competitors, and terrorists. In fact, many businesses and corporations are so fearful of the potential economic loss caused by such an attack, that they often acquiesce to the demands of cyberextortionists, even before an attack has been launched. It is not uncommon, for example, for extortionists to threaten online gambling sites with a DDoS attack in the days immediately preceding a popular sporting event.

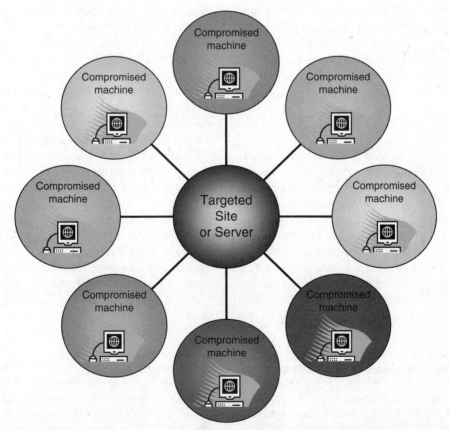

Diagram of how DDoS attacks operate via compromised machines, remotely controlled by the perpetrator.

> *Cyber-extortion*—the use or the implicit threat of use of technological means to cause harm to the physical being, reputation, or property of an individual, organization, or company as a means to obtain the consensual exchange of property from that individual, organization, or company.

Even the mafia has not proven immune to such strong arming tactics. In 2006, members of New York's Bonanno crime family were forced to pay "protection" money and beef up online security for their online gaming site *www.playwithal.com*.

In June 2007, the Department of Justice and the FBI announced that an ongoing cybercrime initiative, *Operation Bot Roast*, had identified over one million compromised computer IP addresses. Recognizing that the majority of victims remained unaware of their computer's victimization, the FBI announced that they would join with industry leaders and other government agencies (including Microsoft and the Botnet Task Force) to inform and educate computer users of their vulnerability.[12] Botnets and the use of zombie armies are increasingly popular and pose significant risk to individual users, businesses, and national security.

Spam

Although the term *spam* has long been a part of American language, its contemporary meaning bears little resemblance to its original etymology. In today's verbiage, the term **spamming** may be defined as the abuse of electronic messaging systems to randomly or indiscriminately send unsolicited bulk messages. While spam may be found in a myriad of electronic communications (i.e., instant messaging, Usenet newsgroup, blogs, mobile phones, etc.), most users are familiar with the term as it applies to e-mail. In fact, it seems unlikely that

any regular user of e-mail has escaped victimization. It is increasingly employed by some advertisers to reduce operating costs and escape accountability. In addition, it can be employed by criminals launching DDoS attacks irrespective of primary motivation. While many end users view spam as little more than a nuisance, some of the direct effects associated with the practice of spamming include the cost in human time of reading or deleting the messages; reduced productivity due to reduction of focus; purchase of anti-spam software; and, the consumption of computer and network resources. The exact costs of spam are difficult to determine; a 2005 study conducted by the University of Maryland estimated that spam resulted in almost $22 billion in lost productivity alone! They calculated this figure by multiplying the average time which workers spent deleting spam each day (i.e., three minutes) by the number of online adults by the average wage.[13] The study further revealed that 11 percent of individuals receive at least 40 such messages daily.

Traditionally, electronic spam was most commonly used by advertisers or by businesses themselves. Not all of the spam was innocuous, and it was popularly employed by pornography sites. Currently, an anti-spam backlash has significantly reduced the viability for legitimate companies to employ the practice, and most have abandoned it altogether. However, the amount of spam continues to increase, and is currently used to spread viruses; deliver Trojans or other malware; initiate DDoS attacks; commit identity

Smurfing, Fraggling, and DDoS Attacks

To avoid detection by authorities, some criminals are using two distinct methods of DDoS attacks. The first, known as *smurfing*, occurs when a perpetrator utilizes ICMP echo (ping) traffic at IP broadcast addresses from spoofed source addresses. The second, known as *fraggling*, utilizes UDP echo packets instead of ICMP. In both cases, the providers or machines which are most likely to be victimized are IRC servers and their providers.

Although Hollywood depictions often portray hackers as super sleuths who conduct their invasions under the cover of darkness, today's hackers are more likely to commit such violations in open areas like computer stores or university centers. (*Michael Newman/PhotoEdit Inc.*)

theft; facilitate Internet fraud; promote political extremism; and, further a variety of other online crime, like extortion and blackmail.

In 2003, Congress created the **CAN-SPAM ACT of 2003** (Controlling the Assault of Non-Solicited Pornography and Market Act). The law became effective on January 1, 2004, and established criminal penalties for individuals or entities violating any of the Act's provisions. The most important elements of the Act are:

- *Prohibition of false or misleading header information*—i.e. routing information, domain name, and sender must accurately identify the message's sender
- *Prohibition of deceptive subject lines*—i.e. subject line cannot mislead the recipient about the message's content
- *Requirement of opt-out method*—i.e. recipient must be informed of and have access to a mechanism for opting out of future communications.
- *Requirement of notification of advertisement and physical postal address of sender.*

- *Enhances penalties for individuals using dictionary attacks to develop mailing lists.*
- *Provides penalties for individuals who gain unauthorized access to a computer for the purpose of sending spam.*[14]

In 2006, Daniel J. Lin became the first person convicted of violating the Can-Spam Act and was sentenced to three years in federal prison and imposed a $10K fine. Lin, along with his partners, distributed millions of e-mail messages advertising various products, including weight loss patches and "generic" Viagra. To increase sales and to advertise his wares, Lin sent bulk e-mails with fraudulent header information through a variety of zombie computers.[15]

In addition to the Can-Spam Act, the federal government has employed other contemporary legislation to prosecute spammers. In May 2007, for example, Robert Soloway was indicted by a federal grand jury on various charges, including multiple counts of mail fraud, wire fraud, e-mail fraud, aggravated identity theft, and money laundering. Dubbed the "Spam King" by federal authorities,

Soloway operated numerous Web sites and domains which hid spam tools inside software marketed as legitimate. Allegations also include the creation of a botnet of more than 2000 proxy computers. The indictment was a culmination of a joint operation conducted by the U.S. Postal Inspection Service, the DOJ's Computer Hacking and Intellectual Property unit; the Internal Revenue Service; and the FBI.[16]

Ransomware and the Kidnapping of Information

In recent years, *ransomware*, a new type of malware, has come to the attention of law enforcement authorities. Although it originally surfaced in late 1989 with the *PC CYBORG/AIDS Information Trojan*, it remained largely under the surface to both criminals and law enforcement until 2005.[17] **Ransomware** may be defined as a malware program which encrypts or otherwise renders computer or digital resources inoperable or inaccessible in furtherance of the illegal compulsion of an action or exchange. Unlike the majority of malware, whose survival is almost entirely contingent upon concealment, ransomware proclaims its existence at inception. Ransomware is solely designed to further criminal interests and is used most often to extort money from its victims.

The success of ransomware hinges on a variety of factors, including, but not limited to user education, sophistication of product, victim urgency, and secure method of payment.

- **User education**—Ransomware is most successful when the applicable victim lacks knowledge of or is apatetic to system security. For example, users may protect themselves from potential extortion efforts simply by employing good backup policies or by implementing system restoration software.
- **Sophistication of product**—Ransomware is most successful when the level of data destruction caused by sabotage is not recoverable using commercially available software or simple backup practices. For example, ransomware which incorporates itself into a machine's operating system would require payment by the victim.
- **Victim urgency**—In order for ransomware to be successful, the compromised data must have some worth to the victim. For example, a victim may be unwilling to pay a ransom for the return of vacation photos, but may be willing to pay a small fortune for the return of tax-related documents on April 14.
- **Secure method of payment**—The ultimate goal of ransomware (i.e., the collection of ransom) can only be realized in situations where a secure method of payment is available. Necessarily, such a method must be both readily accessible to the victim and the perpetrators and disguisable from authorities. Herein lies the proverbial rub for many ransomware developers. Although payment aggregators, like PayPal, have been successfully employed by cyber criminals, they may only be utilized by account holders. As victims may not have access to such sites, alternative methods like e-cash, wire transfers, and such, might be more viable. At the same time, each of these methods inherently contains some risk of discovery. Thus, new forms of payment have emerged.

Just as with traditional ransoms, the greatest risk of discovery in ransomware cases always concerns the transfer of money. Due to these risks, some developers are devising complex schemes to facilitate their economic windfall. Some of these perpetrators, for example, will funnel illegal funds through legitimate companies, thereby hiding the criminal act and laundering the funds at the same time. These companies may be either willing accomplices or secondary victims. Sophisticated criminals may develop multiple levels of concealment through the development of e-shell companies. To further insulate themselves from detection and prosecution, some ransomware developers will not accept a direct

Ransomware—Notable Examples

- *PC CYBORG/AIDS Information Trojan*—this Trojan was distributed through the U.S. Postal Service in a socially engineered package which contained a seemingly innocuous floppy. Once installed, the Trojan operated by replacing the autoexec.bat file. Upon the 90th reboot of the machine, directories were hidden and file names encrypted. At the same time, the victim was informed of the action and prompted to pay a $378 renewal of license fee to recover the data.
- *GPCoder*—Although this Trojan originally surfaced in May 2005, updated versions have consistently appeared.

These updated versions of GPCoder, distributed via e-mail, employed complex RSA encryption to predetermined file extensions. Upon execution, victims were instructed to visit a particular site to purchase a decoder.
- *CryZip*—Surfacing in March 2006, CryZip attached itself to all running processes in the form of a DLL file. It was similar to GPCoder, except that it collected all affected files into a password protected zip file and utilized an E-Gold account for ransom collection.

---

payment to themselves under any circumstances. Instead, they may direct the victim to a legitimate online merchant with whom they have established a referral-based system of commissions.[18]

Theft of Information, Data Manipulation, and Web Encroachment

While most American scholars (and citizens) recognize the impact of the Industrial Revolution on American culture, norms, and means of production, they seem resolutely opposed to embracing the concept of the Information Revolution. Without question, the introduction of global communications, digital automation, and transnational commerce has brought profound changes to every facet of American life. In this new age, traditional physical objects have been transformed into virtual concepts, and tangible commodities have been replaced by things far less concrete. In this new age, information has become the black market's platinum currency. In this section, we will discuss the criminal theft of information or data manipulation. However, the crime of identity theft will be discussed in detail in the following chapter.

Traditional Methods of Proprietary Information Theft

Whether the motivation is personal, economic, or political, the method of theft of information has remained remarkably unchanged over the past several decades. While many individuals struggle to understand, for example, how President Clinton's e-mail was compromised at least twice during his presidency, security experts point to White House employees as the likely culprit. Criminals usually prey on systemic vulnerabilities or employee weaknesses to steal or gain unauthorized access to privileged information. While the first may seem the first line of attack, research indicates that uninformed or careless employees pose the greatest threat. In fact, research indicates that data security and adequate training of personnel is a low priority for *all* levels of institutions, including government entities. Unfortunately, the lack of prioritization enables criminals to steal passwords and enter even the most complex systems almost at will.

Perhaps the easiest, and therefore the most popular, method for stealing passwords involves **social engineering**. Using deceptive practices, criminals employ traditional confidence scams to gain access to company computers or telephone systems. Most commonly acting as representatives for a vendor's security system or the company's IT section, criminals persuade employees to volunteer their user names, passwords, or both! Information thieves may also gather personal information about an employee from the employee themselves or their co-workers, as many, many individuals personalize their passwords despite the advice of their supervisor or IT security administrator. Hometowns, birthdates, anniversaries, alma maters, school mascots, nicknames, social security numbers and maiden, children's, spouse's, or pets' names are commonly used as passwords. (So, if Ellen Burnstein is single with two cats, chances are her password won't be hard to figure out.)

Either of these approaches has little danger of exposure and allows criminals to begin attempts at breaching security measures immediately. Remember: employees (even honest ones) are a company's biggest liability in terms of data security. Even if institutional security measures preclude personalized passwords, employees still pose a risk to data and system security due to their lack of regard (often due to naiveté) for its importance. Failing to appreciate the value of the data in their control, many employees will often post their passwords in conspicuous places— sometimes taping them to their computer monitors! (Ironically, this may be most common in situations where system administrators are attempting to tighten system security by routinely changing passwords, requiring multiple or multi-level passwords, or preventing their personalization.) In other cases, employees will be susceptible to **shoulder-surfing** (i.e., literally watching over someone's shoulder as he or she inputs a password).

Employees who fail to follow proper security procedures for disposing of personal correspondence and company paperwork also pose a security risk to an institution's digital technology. Just as criminals of old would search trash containers for discarded credit card receipts, payroll records, and the like, hackers often resort to diving through corporate trash sites. Unfortunately, unwitting administrators and employees routinely dump sensitive information into the nearest trash receptacle. Information such as old technical manuals, internal phone lists, and organizational charts and correspondence provide a wealth of information for the malicious hacker.

Recent studies indicated that the emergence of private e-mail accounts, removable media and instant messaging are increasingly responsible for theft of information or breaches in digital security. In fact, many businesses have or are beginning to institute policies concerning the use of instant messaging and e-mail, and many have prohibited the use of removable media, like thumb drives.[19] These policies have become increasingly necessary due to the increase in insider theft of proprietary information and destruction of data, both in the United States and abroad. The below figure represents the current state of compromised data in the United Kingdom. It includes statistics from both large companies exclusively and all companies collectively.[20]

More sophisticated approaches to gaining unauthorized access to "secured" data may be employed by computer hackers. One approach involves systemic vulnerabilities created by vendors in which remote access is allowed to perform routine maintenance, such as updating, on their systems. Hackers may target these backdoors in an attempt to gain superstar privileges. In addition, some successful hacking attacks may be attributed to a system administrator's negligence. Some system administrators, for example, never

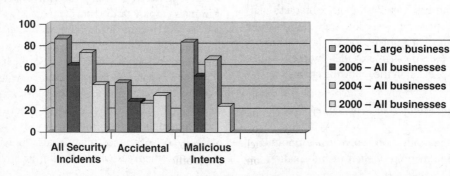

change the defaults in their networks once they are installed! By utilizing lists of default passwords, readily available on the Net, unauthorized users are able to gain root access by simply using traditional network defaults.

Trade Secrets and Copyrights

The increasing commercialization of knowledge has exponentially increased the theft and trafficking of proprietary information. While some criminals have chosen to actively extort money from an organization by compromising their data, others have recognized the value inherent in the sale of such information. Such perpetrators have ranged from corporate insiders to crackers to organized cyber-gangs. For example, one employee at Gillette Company in Boston was caught using company equipment to solicit bids for the design specifications for Gillette's Mach-3 razor.[21] However, such practices are not limited to common criminals or corporate insiders. It can also be committed by industry competitors or even government entities! Such government agencies (and agents) engage in such behavior for personal gain and/or use patriotic arguments to justify their behavior. For example, the former head of the French Secret Service admitted on American television that his organization had planted electronic eavesdropping devices on Air France flights from New York to Paris. Information collected was then forwarded to the French corporation French Mirage. This information enabled the company to undercut the bid of an American corporation. This multimillion dollar contract was directly attributed to the actions of their state-run intelligence service! This type of behavior, he argued, was necessary for smaller countries who wished to compete in today's global economy.[22]

Political Espionage

Technology has also escalated the potential for sophisticated attacks on a country's national security and public infrastructure. The most obvious, but not the most insidious, of such attacks continues to be the theft of information.

Like their corporate counterparts, government entities have not invested adequate resources to protect secrets technologically stored or created. In fact, many would argue that national security issues in general have become all but obscured since the end of the Cold War. Unfortunately, there appears to be no such apathy on the part of foreign governments. Indeed, the FBI estimates that at least 120 foreign governments are actively working on intelligence operations currently targeting the United States.[23] At the same time, the United States has seen an increase in trusted government agents charged with espionage (e.g., Robert Hansen). These threats are not only real, but are also increasingly sophisticated.

In 1998, while Benjamin Netanyahu was Israel's Prime Minister, intelligence agents infiltrated Telrad (subcontracted by Nortel, an American telecommunications conglomerate). By installing undetectable chips during the manufacturing process, agents were granted access to top secret and otherwise classified information. Such data included communications between President Clinton and senior staff officials within the National Security Council. This arrangement, which included weekly reports to Tel Aviv, was made possible due to a multimillion-dollar contract to replace communications equipment between Nortel, Telrad, and the Israeli Air Force. Curiously, contract specifications granted access to manufacturing areas by members of the Israeli Air Force *to protect government secrets!* As disconcerting as these activities may be, they are by no means the most insidious. In fact, a simpler, far more popular, method of technological espionage involves the physical theft of data storage containers (i.e., CPUs, diskettes, etc.).

Like most inventions created to increase the efficiency and effectiveness of corporate and government employees, the introduction of laptop computers was heralded as the solution to employee angst. Designed to facilitate home-based work environments, laptops were intended to empower overburdened workers, enabling them to work at home, on vacation, or at the dentist's office. However, their introduction has not been accomplished without a myriad of associated problems. In fact, their sheer portability, often seen as their greatest strength, is also their greatest weakness, making them prime targets for the burgeoning data black market. Neither corporate nor government entities have been unscathed, and all areas of the globe have experienced this pattern of criminal activity. In London, for example, two government laptops filled with top secret or classified information were stolen from the same railway station over a period of two months. During the Gulf War, American officials were forced to tighten security measures after a laptop containing secrets of the Allies' war plans was stolen from an official car while the Wing Commander it was assigned to was car shopping. In fact, a variety of laptops have been stolen in recent times, usually as a result of employee carelessness (one was left in a taxi after a night of heavy drinking!). One location which has proven to be particularly popular among thieves is airports—a new variant of the classic briefcase switch. Simply replacing the targeted laptop with one of their own, thieves often escape detection and leave few clues for investigators. Another method which has proven successful involves a pair or team of thieves. While one thief stands at the end of the electronic scanner located at security checkpoints, another intentionally creates a diversion in front of the owner after the laptop has been placed on the moving belt. This method, however, poses greater risk to the perpetrator as the likelihood of detection increases. Regardless, both of these methods are only possible through an individual victim's carelessness. Thus, employers must address the vulnerability and subsequent security of laptops during training. Unfortunately, other incidents are a result of systemic vulnerabilities. These thefts, while just as costly, are more preventable once identified, as traditional methods of physical security may be employed. This lesson was recently learned by the State Department after an inventory search was initiated due to the theft of a laptop containing top-secret arms control data. This inventory revealed that more than 15 additional

laptops were unaccounted for! Since this embarrassment and public relations disaster, the State Department has reportedly tightened security measures and established firm parameters of accountability for laptop users.

Data Manipulation—Political Terrorism

Recent events have forced the realization and recognition of the country's physical vulnerability to religious and/or political zealots. In the wake of the events of September 11, 2001, American citizens clamored for immediate retaliation against shadow targets. Unfortunately, such shadows have proven to be extremely elusive, and undeterred in their fanaticism. However, the disaster did awaken the American public and its corresponding government institutions to the dangers posed by terrorism—a danger long recognized by leaders from other areas of the globe. In fact, such hazards from extremists have existed for centuries.

Traditionally, terrorist actions involved physical actions directed at physical or human targets. Intending to create chaos, public disorder, and, ultimately, government instability, terrorist factions have long fantasized upon striking a mortal blow to their targets—temporarily shutting down the entire society and causing widespread fear. With the possible exception of the World Trade Center/Pentagon attacks of 2001, however, these sorts of "successes" have proven unobtainable, especially in First World countries. In fact, many individuals, academics, and institutions alike have declared that the positive environment (i.e., the rebirth of patriotism, community solidarity, and government resolve) born in the wake of the 9/11 tragedy has all but negated any victory which Bin Laden's group may have originally claimed. Such American resiliency has astounded residents across the globe, but several experts have suggested that the phenomenon may be attributed primarily to the magnitude of human loss *and* the broadcasting of the entire event, including clean-up and rescue. They suggest that a pattern of smaller attacks may have been more successful in disrupting the targeted society, as the sheer magnitude of destruction all but anesthetized the American public, releasing a collective rage at those responsible. Thus, it may be argued that traditional notions (and methods) of terrorism, focusing on mass mayhem and physical destruction may be supplanted by a more sophisticated, subtler approach.

Similar to their counterparts involved in organized criminal activity, international terrorist groups are increasingly using advances in technology to increase their effectiveness and efficiency. They are using the Internet, for example, to formulate plans, spread propaganda, elicit funding, communicate, and terrorize their intended target. The Internet, in particular, is a wonderful tool for creating fear because the potential for victimization increases. In addition, the threat feels more real to individuals who were not directly involved than in a traditional attack. The wide-scale, sustained panic that has resulted from a variety of recent computer viruses, for example, had far more impact on daily behavior and individual awareness than the events of September 11, 2001. Thus, a new day of terrorism which involves the theft or manipulation of data has dawned.

Cyberterrorism may be defined as a deliberate, politically or religiously motivated attack against data compilations, computer programs, and/or information systems which is intended to disrupt and/or deny service or acquire information which disrupts the social, physical, or political infrastructure of a target. This general definition encompasses the complex myriad of possibilities involving the implementation of computer technology in terrorist activities. Like other activities involving the theft or manipulation of data, computers may be incidental to the activity or serve as the target or the instrument or all of the above. It is anticipated that most cyberterrorist acts will employ technology to target information systems, data, or the like. Thus, in this sort of activity, computers will be both targets and weapons. Such instrumentality is necessary to facilitate the acquisition of sensitive data, while the targeted device acts at best as an information server and, at worst, as a self-imploding weapon of mass destruction.

Such implementation may take various forms, including, but not limited to, hacking, denial of service attacks, and viruses or worms. Any of these forms could be successfully directed at critical national and/or international infrastructures, causing electric blackouts, disrupted communications, and the like. While not nearly as sensational as traditional weapons of mass destruction, these targeted strikes could actually pose a greater danger to the American public, due to the interconnectivity and ultimate reliance on public switch telecommunications. Think of the devastation that could result from a simple (but sustained) electric blackout in Los Angeles. Water purification systems, telecommunications, 911 emergency and central dispatch systems, fuel outlets, financial institutions, public GPS systems, etc. could all become useless, creating an untenable situation for public safety officials and health providers and destroying public trust and social integrity.

Web of Hate and Destruction

One month after the Oklahoma City bombing, the Antiterrorism and Effective Death Penalty Act of 1996 (AEDPA), providing for the study of terrorist-type information, was enacted. Subsequent research conducted by the Department of Justice (1997) revealed a virtual plethora of bomb-making information in both traditional publishing venues (e.g., *Guerilla's Arsenal: Advanced Techniques for Making Explosives and Time Delay Bombs; Deadly Brew: Advanced Improvised Explosives; The Anarchist Cook-*book; *The Anarchist Arsenal,* etc.) and electronic media. The proliferation of electronically accessible information is especially troubling, as the sheer availability and affordability (i.e., *free*) creates a broader, less traditional audience, which includes disgruntled teens and incarcerated felons. This information includes, but is not limited to, instructional sites for a variety of bombs (thermite, pipe, mail, etc.), and newsgroups and BBSs for exchanging information and soliciting advice.

Imagine the loss of life that could result if hackers successfully penetrated and manipulated data sets located at major research centers or the Centers for Disease Control. Surreptitiously altering a small portion of a formula for a vaccination, changing the labeling instructions for biological contaminants, or systematically removing years of priceless research or patient records could result in tens of thousands of deaths. The introduction of a computer virus or worm could also wreak unforeseen havoc on public health, as officials across the globe have recently discovered. In Britain and Italy, for example, computer viruses wiped out vital information from lengthy hematology studies and one year's worth of AIDS research. While in the United States, one large hospital in the Northeast lost over 40 percent of its patient records due to a particularly destructive virus.

In addition to these highly focused attacks, terrorist organizations across the world are increasing in strength by propagandizing their radical rhetoric to a global audience. Like many domestic groups (e.g., Aryan Nations, White Aryan Resistance (WAR), Nation of Islam, etc.), international organizations have found a safe, virtual platform where they can spew their venomous dogma without fear of physical discovery or attack. These groups have also effectively used the Internet to solicit funds and recruit new members—streamlining the hate industry and reducing propaganda expenditures. In addition, groups such as Osama bin Laden's al Qaeda, Hezbollah, and Hamas are actively exchanging e-mail and utilizing strong encryption algorithms to support their organizations.[24] (In fact, Ramzi Yousef, one of the designers of the first World Trade Center bombing, stored detailed plans to destroy U.S. airliners on encrypted files on his laptop computer.) Other approaches include the launching of massive denial of service attacks and defacement of Web sites against foreign governments.[25]

These attacks are perpetrated by amateurs and professionals alike. The "Internet Black Tigers," a group allegedly affiliated with the Tamil Tigers, have repeatedly attacked official sites of numerous governments, while a variety of Chinese hacktivists announced their intention to launch massive DoS attacks against American financial and government sites in the wake of a crash involving a U.S. surveillance plane and a Chinese fighter. While American hackers vowed to fight back, the long-term effects of such activity are often trivialized by officials, who claim that tightened site security will eliminate the successes of such actors. They fail to recognize the international conflicts or nuclear implications which may arise from the actions of cyberpunks. Unfortunately, hacking activities appear to be gaining in popularity as how-to information is freely distributed via the Internet (discussed in detail in Chapter 6).

Web Encroachment

Cyber-squatting is another form of criminal activity which is specific to the technological age, although many question the justification for its illegality. Basically, **cyber-squatting** may be defined as the practice of infringing on trademarked property via electronic means. The first method of cyber-squatting involves the purchase of domain names consistent with the names of established companies or businesses (e.g., *www. toysrus.com* or *www.thegap.com*). The second includes the purchase of domain names which are the same as such businesses but with common misspellings or typographical errors in them (e.g., *www.toysareus.com* or *www.tgegap.com*). Specifically outlawed by the Anti-Cybersquatting Consumer Protection Act of 1997, this type of activity has been characterized as the epitome of techno-capitalism by some, but branded criminal by government authorities. Characterization notwithstanding, this Act has been utilized against individuals like John Zuccarini, who purchased thousands of domain names which represented common misspellings of popular businesses and *mousetrapped* accidental visitors (e.g., opening advertising boxes which require users to click on, and therefore look at, the advertisements to make them go away).

Dissemination of Contraband or Offensive Materials

Perhaps one of the most common, and certainly the most disturbing, criminal activities facilitated through cyberspace is the sexual exploitation of children. From the onset of electronic bulletin boards, pedophiles and child pornographers flourished with relative immunity in the virtual world. The introduction of the World Wide Web has only increased the prevalence of such activity, and a virtual explosion of child pornography has resulted. While traditional mechanisms for enforcement against such persons included federal and state regulations, the virtual nature of cyberspace has protected peddlers from traditional measures and has raised questions regarding the legality of prohibitions. In addition, it has hampered law enforcement efforts by insulating those inclined from enforcement by negating traditional methods of distribution which exposed perpetrators to third parties.

Child Pornography

As stated previously, the Web's advantages of increased knowledge, potential for self-education, and global connectivity have been accompanied by significant disadvantages as well, and an atmosphere most conducive to criminal networking has

been a byproduct. Where else could pedophiles or child pornography peddlers meet and exchange information with little or no threat of prosecution? Many individuals with deviant tendencies have found others similarly stimulated via posting services or electronic bulletin boards, and they are protected under the umbrella of the First Amendment because of their capability of performing "common carrier" functions—like the telephone company or the post office. Such judicial perception, coupled with the increase in Internet communications, has resulted in an explosion of child pornography and the exploitation of children. In fact, this apathy has all but encouraged the development of associations dedicated to the exploitation of children. NAMBLA (the National Association of Men and Boy Lovers of America), for example, is an organization which proudly proclaims that its mission is to forge relationships between men who love boys! Sponsoring a Web site, this organization is no longer forced underground, but has an established presence on the Web. Unfortunately, they are not alone. Numerous bulletin boards, newsgroups, Web sites, and chat rooms are dedicated to this type of behavior, and remain hidden behind the First Amendment.

The possession or distribution of child pornography is jurisdictionally illegal in all 50 states and in all territories under the umbrella of

Nambla—North American Man/Boy Love Association

During the heyday of gay rights organizations, many advocates argued that the age of sexual consent be either lowered or completely eradicated, as they argued that homosexual youths were being unfairly targeted by law enforcement and society. In 1978, Tom Reeves convened a meeting entitled "Man/Boy Love and the Age of Consent." At that time, David Thorstad and over two dozen men and boys formed an organization known as the North American Man/Boy Love Association. While other groups associated with gay rights originally championed the group's efforts, they eventually abandoned NAMBLA when it became clear that the organization's stated

agenda tended to portray all homosexuals as child predators. (Harry Hay, a leader and pioneer of the gay rights' movement, originally protested the group's exclusion from various gay rights marches and platforms.) In fact, by the 1980s NAMBLA supporters had disappeared, and many, gay rights organizations openly rejected them and their platform.

Today, NAMBLA openly declares itself as a group dedicated to ending *the oppression of men and boys who have freely chosen mutually consensual relationships*.[26] The group has consistently challenged privacy and other constitutional issues and have met with only marginal success. In

(Continued)

the most recent case, *U.S.* v. *Mayer*, 06-50481 (9th Cir., 2007), the Court dismissed First, Fourth, and Fifth Amendment challenges, arguing that an FBI agent acted unfairly in investigating the organization.

In 2001, an undercover FBI agent joined the organization. Over a period of several years, the agent met with various members and attended organizational gatherings. During the course of the investigation, FBI agent Robert Hamer had various conversations with members involving the illegal exploitation of minors, including some with the defendant regarding the development of a travel agency which catered to trips to facilitate the sexual contact between NAMBLA members and minors. Defendant Mayer was subsequently convicted of travel with intent to engage in illicit sexual conduct in violation of 18 U.S.C. § 2423(b). On appeal, Mayer argued that the investigation was initiated based upon his membership in NAMBLA—an action that violated his First Amendment right to free speech and association. In addition, Mayer argued that the agent's undercover persona and subsequent actions violated his Fourth and Fifth Amendment rights. Although the Ninth Circuit has a reputation of being "liberal," they ruled that his claims were without merit.

the United States. Apart from state statutes, it is also illegal on the federal law, although the Supreme Court ruled that the Child Pornography Prevention Act was unconstitutional. (As evidenced by the text box "Federal Efforts: A Couple of Examples", traditional federal statutes may still be utilized to combat the growing problem.) To address the increasing proliferation of online child pornography, the federal government has created the CyberTipline (*www.cybertipline. com*), which is operated by the National Center for Missing and Exploited Children, and the *Innocent Images* project which is coordinated by the Federal Bureau of Investigation. It has also provided funding for collaborative efforts at the local level. However, the definitions and parameters of child pornography legislation varies across definition.

Under Title 18, child pornography is defined as any "visual depiction . . . of sexually explicit conduct" involving a minor. Such conduct includes acts such as intercourse, bestiality, and masturbation, as well as *lascivious exhibition of the genitals or pubic area*. However, such designations have not been consistently incorporated into state law. In addition, disparity among the states exist as to the definition of a "minor" child. While federal (and some state) law extends protection to all children under the age of 18, others place the age of exploitation much lower. Maine, for example, only protects children under the age of 14!

According to the Office of Juvenile Justice and Delinquency Prevention (OJJDP) and the National Center for Missing and Exploited Children (NCMEC), almost all possessors of child pornography are white males who are older than 25. The vast majority of them (83 percent) had images of prepubescent children in a situation depicting sexual penetration. More than one-fifth of these images depicted sexual violence to children, including bondage, torture, and rape. In addition, more than 50 percent of the cases investigated by law enforcement were a result of third party information. While the possession of child pornography cases mainly originated from state and local agencies (60 percent), others were initiated by federal and international authorities. Most frightening, however, is the fact that 40 percent of those arrested for child pornography were considered to be "dual offenders" who had also sexually victimized children, and an additional 15 percent had *attempted* to sexually victimize children by soliciting undercover investigators who had posed online as minors.[27] Unfortunately, the statistics revealed in the *National Juvenile Online Victimization Study* are but the tip of the iceberg. It is important to remember that they were based solely on those *arrested* for possession of child pornography. Statistics which reveal the true extent of the online victimization and exploitation of children via the Internet are all but impossible to estimate.

Motivations for child pornography possession vary widely, ranging from sexual gratification to economic gain. For the most part, however, the

International Efforts to Control Online Child Pornography

Among other things, the U.S. Constitution and Bill of Rights protect American citizens from unreasonable searches and seizures and grants them the ability to freely express their thoughts, ideas, and expressions. Without question, these guarantees provide Americans with the highest degree of freedom without hindering quality of life aspirations. However, these same protections allow many online criminals to advertise and sell illicit materials, as it is virtually impossible for American authorities to monitor electronic communications within these parameters. Other countries have successfully combated child pornography through the passage of legislation which censors online content.

In 2007, Swedish authorities announced that Picsearch, a popular Internet search engine, would delete all current and future links to sites containing child pornography. In addition, the company agreed to provide a listing of sites to law enforcement authorities. Swedish authorities believe that a reduction in accessibility to such sites will reduce the proliferation of child pornography and reduce physical child exploitation.

---

literature reveals four primary motivations for such possession:

- *pedophilia* or *hebephilia*—possession is designed to satisfy sexual fantasies or provide gratification for those individuals who are sexually interested in prepubescent children or adolescents
- *sexual miscreants*—possession is designed to satisfy a desire for new and different sexual stimuli
- *curiosity seekers*—possession is undertaken to satisfy a peculiar curiosity
- *criminal opportunists*—possession, and subsequent distribution, is designed for economic profit.

Although all child pornography possessors are a concern for society in general, and law enforce-

ment in particular, those posing the greatest immediate threat to the physical safety of children are those motivated by *pedophilia* or *hebephilia*. Fortunately, these individuals may be the easiest to catch for law enforcement as they often find it necessary to maintain trophies or visual stimuli of their victims and may graphically articulate elaborate fantasies through writings or such.

Child Enticement/Exploitation

Child pornography is insidious on its face, as a relationship between the possession of child pornography and child molestation has been well documented both in the academic literature and judicial opinions. In fact, almost 40 percent of arrested offenders who met victims online possessed child pornography.[28] It is used as both a tool for sexual gratification, and, more

---

Federal Efforts: A Couple of Examples

- Federal Bureau of Investigation (FBI)—Innocent Images
  - In 2001, the FBI launched *Operation Candyman*, a sting operation targeting three child pornography rings. Deriving its name from one of the suspects, the operation revealed over 7,000 registered users of a site dedicated to child exploitation. At the current time, the operation is continuing and further arrests are anticipated.
- U.S. Immigration and Customs Enforcement (ICE)
  - *Operation Predator* is part of ICE's expanded interior immigration enforcement strategy, which focuses on identifying and removing criminal aliens, immigration fugitives, and other immigration violators from the United States. The agency's top priority is arresting and removing foreign nationals who pose a threat to public safety or national security.
  - In 2007, the agency concluded an 18-month investigation in which almost 5,000 individuals were arrested on various charges relating to child pornography. The investigation was actually initiated by evidence uncovered in a case of money laundering.

disturbingly, as a means to seduce or groom (i.e., overcome inhibitions about sexual activity) potential victims. Just as the Web has streamlined the availability of and accessibility to such materials, it has provided a social environment in which predators scan the landscape for potential targets. Their typical prey includes those individuals who express frustration with parental controls or who appear particularly naïve or vulnerable. These include children who are confused about their own sexuality or

In 2002, David Westerfield was charged with the murder of seven-year-old Danielle Van Dam. During the trial, prosecutors introduced evidence from Westerfield's computer of images of female children being raped. Westerfield was found guilty and sentenced to death by a California judge. The case made headlines across the country. Unfortunately, the significance of Westerfield's predilection for child pornography was largely overlooked by the popular media who focused on the lifestyle of the victim's parents, avowed swingers who were engaging in sexual activity with strangers the night of the child's disappearance . (Pool Photo/Getty Images, Inc.—Getty News.)

who express feelings of ostracism. Typically, the victims are youngsters who enjoy access to unsupervised computer communications. While many of them are actively seeking associations with adult suitors, others are unsuspectingly lured into fictional relationships which encourage dangerous liaisons. Such was the case with a Connecticut teen who was raped by Francis Kufrovich, a California man posing as a teenager. Unfortunately, it is anticipated that this type of behavior will increase in pace with the availability of Internet communications. However, proactive law-enforcement initiatives may result in the identification and prosecution of offenders.

Although many pedophiles searching the Internet for victims usually practice with the expectation of limited enforcement, proactive, cursory investigations may allow investigators to surprise the unsuspecting predators. Fortunately for law enforcement, many of these perpetrators assume that (1) the individuals to whom they are communicating are accurately representing themselves, and (2) their behavior is hidden behind a Web of anonymity. In fact, these perceptions have proven to be shortsighted as even non-criminals mask their identity, and the First Amendment does not protect anonymous communications. These characteristics may be exploited by proactive law enforcement agencies like the San Jose Police Department, who may create fictitious organizations or identities to seduce the seducer. (In addition, law-enforcement agencies may find evidentiary support in the forensic analysis of seized media from the suspect's home as most child pornographers keep their collections within arm's reach.)

Online Pharmacies

The emergence of a worldwide marketplace and the lack of applicable regulations have resulted in an explosion of questionable capitalist enterprises. Online pharmacies, for example, benefit consumers by encouraging competitive pricing with non-cyber outlets, but offer little protection against fraud. Virtually all of the available online pharmacies claim legitimacy, arguing that transactions require valid prescriptions. However, many of these

Federal Statutes: Child Pornography and Exploitation

Section	Prohibits	Mandatory Minimum	Maximum Penalty
18 U.S.C. § 2251(a)	Employing, using, or enticing a minor to engage in sexually explicit conduct for the purpose of producing a visual depiction of that conduct	15 years—1st offense 25 years—2nd offense 35 years—3rd offense	30 years—1st offense 50 years—2nd offense Life—3rd offense
18 U.S.C. 2251 (b)	Parent or guardian permitting a minor to engage in sexually explicit conduct for the purpose of producing a visual depiction of that conduct	Same as above	Same as above
18 U.S.C. § 2251(c)	Employing, using, or enticing a minor to engage in sexually explicit conduct outside the U.S. to produce a visual depiction of that conduct for the purpose of transporting it to the U.S.	Same as above	Same as above
18 U.S.C. § 2251(d)	Advertising to receive, trade, buy, or distribute a visual depiction of a minor engaging in sexually explicit conduct or to participate in any act of sexually explicit conduct with a minor for the purpose of producing a visual depiction of that conduct	Same as above	Same as above
18 U.S.C. § 2251A(a)	Parent or guardian selling or transferring custody of a minor knowing or intending that the minor will be portrayed in a visual depiction of sexually explicit conduct, or offering to do so	30 years	Life
18 U.S.C. § 2251A(b)	Purchasing or obtaining custody of a minor, knowing or intending that the minor will be portrayed in a visual depiction of sexually explicit conduct, or offering to do so	Same as above	Same as above
18 U.S.C. § 2252(a)(1)	Transporting a visual depiction of a minor engaging in sexually explicit conduct	5 years—1st offense 15 years—2nd offense	20 years—1st offense 40 years—2nd offense
18 U.S.C. § 2252(a)(2)	Receiving or distributing a visual depiction of a minor engaging in sexually explicit conduct	Same as above	Same as above

(Continued)

Federal Statutes: Child Pornography and Exploitation (*Continued*)

Section	Prohibits	Mandatory Minimum	Maximum Penalty
18 U.S.C. § 2252(a)(3)	Selling, or possessing with intent to sell, a visual depiction of a minor engaging in sexually explicit conduct	Same as above	Same as above
18 U.S.C. § 2252(a)(4)	Possessing a visual depiction of a minor engaging in sexually explicit conduct	None—1st offense 10 years—2nd offense	10 years—1st offense 20 years—2nd offense
18 U.S.C. § 2252A(a)(1)	Transporting child pornography	5 years—1st offense 15 years—2nd offense	20 years—1st offense 40 years—2nd offense
18 U.S.C. § 2252A(a)(2)	Receiving or distributing child pornography	Same as above	Same as above
18 U.S.C. § 2252A(a)(3)	Reproducing child pornography for distribution, or advertising material as an obscene visual depiction of a minor engaging in sexually explicit conduct or as a visual depiction engaging in sexually explicit conduct	Same as above	Same as above
18 U.S.C. § 2252A(a)(4)	Selling, or possessing with intent to sell, child pornography	Same as above	Same as above
18 U.S.C. § 2252A(a)(5)	Possessing child pornography	None—1st offense 10 years—2nd offense	10 years—1st offense 20 years—2nd offense

sites operate illegally, maintaining no license at all or dispensing medicines in states in which they are not licensed. Some do not even require a valid prescription, prescribing medicine to individuals who complete short questionnaires, while others simply dispense medicine upon demand.

Like other areas of traditional commerce which have been impacted by the emergence of the Internet, the sale of pharmaceutical drugs is changing dramatically. Although many Americans shop at local drugstores for convenience in the processing of insurance claims, many argue that there are a variety of reasons why they prefer the online sites. These include

- the privacy and convenience of ordering medications from their homes
- greater availability of drugs for shut-in people or those who live far from the pharmacy

- the ease of comparative shopping among many sites to find the best prices
- greater convenience and variety of products
- easier access to written product information and references to other sources than in traditional storefront pharmacies.[29]

Although many legitimate, non-cyber pharmacies have used the Internet to enhance customer convenience, others exist solely in cyberspace (some offering drugs that have been banned by the FDA). To see one such Web site, go to *www.onlinepharmacy.com*. Unfortunately, enforcement on online illegal drug transactions has proven to be extremely difficult due to the fact that pharmacies are licensed by individual states and are largely exempt from FDA regulations. However, recent collaborative efforts between agencies have proven to be marginally successful.

In 2005, a multi-agency task force which included the Drug Enforcement Administration and the Federal Bureau of Investigation arrested individuals in Canada, India, and 11 American cites for operating a fraudulent online pharmacy that sold $20 million worth of controlled drugs to individuals across the globe. Physically located in India, the Internet ring supplied drugs for 200 Web sites. Authorities involved in *Operation Cyber Chase* seized $7 million from various banks and over 7 million doses of drugs. The pharmacy, which did not require a prescription, sold Schedule II–V pharmaceutically controlled substances, including anabolic steroids, amphetamines, and the painkiller Vicodin.

In another highly publicized case, Clyde L. Moore II, owner of Louisiana-based Advanced Healthcare Pharmacy (ADVACOR), was arrested for running an illegal online pharmacy. The company was primarily involved with the receipt of processing fees for the facilitation of customer purchases of pharmaceutical drugs from foreign pharmacies. In addition, ADVACOR contracted physicians to prescribe drugs without a face-to-face interaction between the patient and the doctor—a clear violation of federal law. In spite of these recent successes, specific legislation is still necessary to solidify enforcement efforts and establish clear jurisdictional boundaries.

Online Gambling

American society has had a perverse relationship with gambling since the colonial period. While some colonies, like the Puritan-led Massachusetts Bay Colony, treated it as a tool of the devil; others viewed it as a harmless diversion. As such, early laws regarding gambling were inconsistent, both in substance and application. However, even those colonies which outlawed gaming relied on state-sponsored lotteries to raise revenue. (In fact, lottery revenues are directly responsible for the development of some of the nation's most prestigious universities, including Harvard and Yale.) Eventually, even state-sponsored gambling became largely illegal as lottery scandals and a religious zealotry swept the nation.[30] Thus began the nation's love/hate relationship with the activity.

By the 1920s, state attitudes toward gambling had become entrenched. While some states, especially those in the South, outlawed the activity in its entirety; other states developed more selective approaches to prohibition, allowing parimutuel wagering in horse racing or church-run bingo. Casinos, slot machines, and table games were prohibited in most areas, and organized crime groups quickly stepped in to fill the public's demand. Since that time, organized crime has found a way to insinuate itself into all types of gaming and all geographic areas, even those outside the United States.

In 1995, Internet Casinos, Inc. (ICI), launched the first online casino with 18 games. Since that time, Internet gaming has been increasing exponentially, fueled in part by the increasing visibility and idolatry of international poker stars. In 2005, one study estimated that the revenues from online gambling were close to $10 billion dollars,[31] and that figure is expected to quadruple by 2010. There are several factors which make online gaming attractive to consumers. These are the same factors which may increase the dangers of addiction, bankruptcy, and crime. These include, but are not limited to,

- The *lack of physicality and geographical location* makes online casinos accessible to any user with a computer, PDA, or cell phone. Users can access a gambling site from home, hotel rooms, libraries, sporting events—anywhere.
- The *continuous operation* of online casinos makes them accessible 24 hours a day.
- The *accessibility to minors* increases the consumer base for online gambling, as proper age verification is not attempted.
- The *increase in e-banking* allows users to access and add funds without ever leaving their chair. This lack of a cooling off period is exacerbated by the psychological intangibility of e-cash, and encourages customers to overspend.

Combating Illegal Online Gambling through Denial of Financing

Long before the passage of the IGPEA, eight of the largest banks had implemented policies to deny payment authorization of Internet gambling transactions.[32] While such strategies were initially successful, gaming operators developed mechanisms for avoiding blockages—some legal, some not.

- **Fraudulent methods:** miscoding of transactions; development of third party companies; submission through non-gambling merchants; and so on.
- **Legal methods:** online payment aggregators, wire transfers, online debit cards, and e-cash.

In addition to the dangers to individuals, online gambling is also detrimental to American society as a whole as they fail to create jobs or other revenue, and provide avenues for money laundering.

Early federal attempts to regulate the industry and to enforce anti-gambling laws proved largely ineffective, as inconsistency in the federal courts left a patchwork of legalized gambling with one exception. The courts have consistently ruled that online sports betting is prohibited by the Act. However, it is still uncertain as to whether the Act has any enforcement powers in non-sports wagers. This is primarily attributed to the antiquated language of the Wire Act (1961), which specifically forbade any sports wagers AND those wagers placed over a "wire." As a result, various federal and state statutes have been enacted which more clearly articulate the prohibited methods of transmission and the types of wagering involved.

The most comprehensive of the federal efforts has focused primarily on the reduction of demand. The *Internet Gambling Prohibition and Enforcement Act of 2006* (IGPEA) sought to reduce the flow of money to online gambling sites by regulating payment systems. This enforcement effort came in the wake of decisions made by various government entities which concluded that online gambling debts incurred on credit cards were unenforceable. In essence, this shifted the burden of oversight and regulation to individual banks and credit-issuing institutions, which have a vested interest in denying such charges. However, site operators soon devised ways to circumvent the efforts of financial information.

Thus, the IGPEA created statutes which formally regulated payment systems.

In addition to decreasing the ready availability of funding to online gamblers, the IGPEA also authorized state and federal law enforcement to seek injunctions against persons or entities which facilitated illegal Internet gambling. As a result, the U.S. Department of Justice has increasingly targeted those associations, sites, or media which advertise online gambling. In this regard, they are having some success among media giants. For example, Clear Channel Communications, Infinity Broadcasting, Discovery Networks, Yahoo!, and Google have all stopped carrying gambling advertisements.[33]

Although some pro-gambling advocates argued that the Act violated various constitutional provisions, including dual-sovereignty and the First Amendment, the first indictment under the Act came a mere one month after its passage. In August 2006, James Giordano, a professional poker player alleged to be the reputed kingpin of an international online sports betting ring, was indicted after investigators cloned his hard drive and installed a recording device while he was attending a family wedding. It is estimated that the amount of wagers placed during the investigation exceeded $3.3 billion. Others indicted in the scheme were various mob members associated with the Luchese crime family and a scout for the Washington Nationals. The indictments signaled a successful end to an investigation which was initiated based on evidence discovered in a prescription drug resale scheme linked to the Bonanno crime family. Ironically, the site *www.playwithal.com* had been targeted

Early Attempts at Prosecuting Online Casinos

Legal questions notwithstanding, both local and federal enforcement authorities have identified and prosecuted individuals for Internet gambling via traditional fraud statutes. Missouri Attorney General Jay Nixon, for example, obtained a civil injunction and damages totaling over $65,000 against Interactive Gaming and Communications, Inc., while Minnesota Attorney General Hubert Humphrey III has pursued Las Vegas-based Granit Gate Resorts for false advertisement, as it led citizens to believe that Internet gambling was entirely legal. In addition, both the Wire Act and the Crime Control Act have been used to pursue individual bookmaking organizations. (Jay Cohen was the first defendant convicted of illegally operating a sports betting business which accepted wagers on sporting events via Internet.

However, many more cases are pending.) However, the absence of regulatory oversight encourages dishonest or criminal practices. It is entirely possible, for example, for a virtual casino to simply roll up the proverbial carpet if enforcement efforts become intense or if their net-to-debt ratio becomes unfavorable to the owners. In fact, individual gamblers gamble simply by providing their credit card information to unknown entities. The Internet Gambling Prohibition and Enforcement Act of 1996 is designed to reduce the availability of financing for online gamblers. While proponents of the Act expect to see a reduction in online gambling, detractors argue that it will simply create a situation in which individuals seek less legitimate means of financing and greater victimization of American citizens.

for a DDoS attack by Russian mobsters, forcing Giordano and his mob associates to beef up Web security.[34]

Despite government efforts to reduce the desirability of online casino operation, more gambling sites appear regularly. Without exception, American consumers spend more money on recreational activities, including gambling, than any other country in the world. As such, online casinos cater to American consumers, offering traditional games and advertising in areas focusing on American consumption. In addition, new legislation passed by the federal government has little effect on entities located outside the United States, and international cooperation seems unlikely, as many foreign nations embrace offshore casinos. In fact, these governments often court site operators as they often pay elevated taxes in impoverished countries. Such problems in international cooperation are evidenced by the recent position of the World Trade Organization.

Lack of International Cooperation and the WTO

The World Trade Organization (WTO) is largely recognized as the trade arbitrator in the new global economy. The organization is designed to settle disputes between nations, while maintaining a variety of multilateral agreements. Of significant importance is the General Agreement on

Trade in Services (GATS), a compilation of multinational agreements which bind all members to treat the services and service suppliers equally and as favorably as the nation member itself. This component is critical in terms of online gambling.

Recently, the governments of Antigua and Barbuda initiated a complaint with the WTO against the United States for the increasingly restrictive measures against online gambling. Their primary argument rested on the fact that there was an array of gambling and betting services commercially available with the United States, but federal prohibitions against international gambling (e.g., the Wire Act, the Travel Act, and the Illegal Gambling Business Act). They collectively argued that such prohibitions were leading causes of the decline of the Internet gaming industry in Antigua. More specifically, they alleged that America's prosecution of Cohen and the World Sports Exchange significantly reduced the desirability of operating online casinos in Antigua—a fact which has directly harmed the nation's economy.

While the WTO recognized that a long history of prohibition of gambling existed in the United States, they appeared to hold the United States to specific verbiage and argued that their omission of a commitment to gambling and betting could not be construed as a commitment to prohibit it under international agreements. They rejected the contention that the Wire Act, the Travel Act, and the Illegal Gambling Business Act were necessary to promote morality within the country's boundaries. Despite the legitimate American interest in the prevention of money laundering, organized crime, fraud, risks to children, and to public healthy, they concluded that the country's refusal to engage in dialogue with Antigua to mitigate these concerns rendered them moot as a continuing commitment to discourse was a foundational requirement. Consequently, the final ruling of the panel suggests that the United States must give foreign suppliers the right to provide online gaming, even though domestic suppliers do not share that right. In effect, it demanded that the United States repeal historical federal statutes which have been in existence longer than the GATS itself. Currently, the case is under appeal, and the final impact has yet to be determined. However, it is apparent that an affirmation of the ruling would place the American government in the unenviable position of accepting (and even promoting) foreign gambling operators, while denying American businesses the right to compete.

Threatening and Harassing Communications

Irrespective of motivation, the proliferation of Internet communications has provided criminals with a safer, more effective environment in which to threaten their victims. Perceived anonymity and the convenience of online communication have resulted in a virtual explosion of online victimization. While many of the criminals involved in such activity have simply altered their method of exploitation or harassment, the increase in the same suggests that the medium has created an entirely new breed of perpetrators. In either category, aggressors are engaged in activities which promote fear and insecurity among those targeted.

Victims of harassment and stalking are overwhelmingly females or children, while most stalkers are white males between the ages of 18 and 35.[35] Although motivations of individual stalkers vary, there are four general categories. The first, and most common, are known as **obsessional stalkers**. On average, these individuals seek to reestablish a relationship with an unwilling partner and are considered to be the most dangerous of stalkers. In fact, their pattern of intimidation, coercion, and harassment are almost parallel to that of the perpetrators of domestic violence. The second most common category involves individuals who have low self-esteem and target a victim whom they hold in high regard. An example of this **love-obsession stalker** is John Hinkley, Jr.—who shot President Reagan to gain the attention of actress Jodie Foster. The third category of stalkers is referred to as **erotomaniacs**. These stalkers are delusional, and believe that their victim is in love with them or has had a previous relationship with them. When arrested, these individuals often garner much media attention, as their intended targets are often celebrities or high profile people. Perhaps the best example of this type of stalker was Margaret Mary Ray, a middle-aged mother who repeatedly broke into David Letterman's home. Ray, a diagnosed schizophrenic, told investigators and responding officers that Letterman was her husband. While it is not clear what motivates this particular group of stalkers, academics suggest that mental illness or tragic events precipitate this sort of behavior. (Ray eventually ended her own life by placing herself in front of a locomotive.) The final category of stalkers is the newest and most unique. Unlike the previous categories, the **vengeance** or **terrorist stalker** does not seek or fantasize about a personal relationship with the victim. Rather, these individuals are motivated by either economic gain or revenge.[36]

Cyberstalking and Harassment

In addition to increasing the viability of vice crimes to assorted individuals, computers have also provided the means for many individuals to more effectively stalk and harass their targeted victims. Just as its real-world counterpart, the insidious nature of this type of activity has

Stalking: Some Sobering Statistics

- More than 1 million women and almost 400,000 men are stalked annually in the United States.
- 78 percent of victims are female, while 87 percent of perpetrators are male.
- 69 percent of females and 81 percent of males having a protective order experienced repeated contact.
- 81 percent of females stalked by a domestic partner or husband were physically assaulted, and 31 percent were sexually assaulted.
- 2/3 of stalkers pursue their victims at least once a week.[37]

remained unrecognized. In fact, individuals were free to verbally, physically, and sexually harass and terrorize objects of their attentions. However, Congress enacted legislation in 1994 which prohibited this type of behavior, due primarily to the attention garnered in the wake of the stalking and murdering of actress Rebecca Shaeffer in 1990. In the most general sense, **stalking** may be defined as the willful, malicious, and repeated following and/or harassing another person in an effort to inflict or cause fear of actual harm through words or deeds. By extension, **cyberstalking** is the same form of activity committed via electronic communications. **Cyberharassment**, on the other hand, focuses on actual harm suffered, including defacement of character, and the like. In fact, the distinctions between the two are subtle at best. In a general sense, the primary differences between the two involve actual harm suffered. Cyberstalking statutes, for example, are directed at activities which *may* be threatening or *may* result in injury. Cyberharassment statutes, on the other hand, involve activities which are threatening, harassing, or injurious on their face. Due to the lobbying of many Hollywood heavyweights, stalking is often treated more harshly, and is usually treated as a felony. Fortunately, federal authorities and many state legislators have passed anti-stalking legislation. However, both have failed to fully incorporate all of the activities which may be committed in this increasingly sophisticated age. For example, the Interstate Stalking Punishment and Prevention Act of 1996 (18 U.S.C. § 2261A) made it a federal offense to

travel across a State line or within the special maritime and territorial jurisdiction of the United States with intent to injure or harass another person, and in the course of, or as a result of, such travel places that person in reasonable fear of, or serious bodily injury to . . . that person or a member of that person's immediate family shall be punished as provided in section 2261 of this title.

Although this has been used successfully, other federal legislation directly targeting online stalking have not passed Congressional muster (two bills, introduced in the 103rd and 104th Congress, died in committee). These bills would have amended the Federal Telephone Harassing Statute to include communications by modem or other two-way wire, and would have forbidden anonymous interstate or foreign communications made *with the intent to annoy, abuse, threaten, or harass any person at the called number.*

In the past several years, most states have attempted to modernize traditional statutes, and 44 states specifically incorporate electronic communications in their stalking and harassment statutes.[38] In addition, other states have passed legislation or rendered traditional statutes technology-neutral. However, there appears to be a lack of consensus regarding the insidious nature of harassment and stalking activities overall, and third-party harassment and/or stalking has not been addressed. Thus, new legislation at all levels is desperately needed as online stalking will almost certainly outpace offline stalking due to the perceptions of confidentiality and the empowerment of anonymity.

Many individuals, including both law enforcement and civilians, continue to perceive that cyberstalking is less dangerous than physical stalking. However, cyberstalking has the potential to be far more insidious and pervasive as the popularity of remailers, anonymizers, ease of access, mass distribution capability, and the like increase. As with other crimes, individuals who may not be tempted to engage in physical retribution or stalking of a particular victim may be lured into cyberstalking. In addition, such activities may lead to physical or real-world stalking activities.

Eight percent of women and 2 percent of men in America are stalked each year. In the general public, these numbers would represent over 1 million women and 370, 990 men in the United States every year.[39] However, the LAPD District Attorney's Office and NYPD's estimates of cases that include physical stalking predicated on previous electronic communications are 20 percent to 40 percent, respectively. (In Great Britain, the figures were 58 percent of men and 41 percent of women as victims.) Generally speaking, empirical evidence indicates that cyberstalkers mirror their offline counterparts. They are usually male, the majority of their attentions are focused on women, and they are usually known to their victims. In addition, their motivations appear to be remarkably similar. Some pursue these criminal activities out of obsession, jealousy, anger, or a desire to control (Packard, 2000).

The actual process of cyberstalking may take many forms, including tracking the victim's online activity or sending them a barrage of threatening e-mails, while cyberharassment activity may include abusive e-mails or the posting of fictitious or slanderous information in a public forum. In the late 1990s, for example, an image of Jeanne Mentavolos, one of the first female cadets at a traditionally male institution, was distributed across the world via the Internet. The image involved an altered photograph of the victim in which she appeared to have male genitalia. Oftentimes, the motivation behind harassment is one of retaliation, as in the case of Gary Dellapenta. Dellapenta, a former security guard, actually solicited the rape of a woman who had rejected his advances by posting rape fantasies on a variety of pages while impersonating the victim. He even provided her address, and methods of bypassing the victim's security system. However, the courts have been reluctant to establish electronic boundaries of the First Amendment, and have narrowly interpreted cyberstalking and cyberharassment legislation.

As stated, the courts have been reluctant to identify certain communications as threatening, arguing that a strict scrutiny of individual cases is necessary to protect constitutional provisions. For example, in 1995, Jake Baker (aka Abraham Jacob Alkhabaz), a University of Michigan student, electronically communicated with an individual in Ontario, Canada, plans to abduct, torture, rape, murder, and other assorted actions. He also posted a story about his classmate in which he and a friend torture, rape, and sodomize her with a curling iron before setting her on fire. *Jerry continues to maul at her breasts. He pulls them as far away as they'll go away from her body, twisting them to cause even more pain . . . Jane howls out loud. It's not even a human sound. Her eyes glaze over from the pain and torture* (*Alkhabaz*, 104 F.3d at 1498). Upon a consensual search, investigators also found e-mails between Baker and Arthur Gonda of Ontario, Canada, which fantasized about the abduction, bondage, torture, humiliation, mutilation, rape, sodomy, murder, and necrophilia of a variety of individuals—including generalized teens and one individual from Baker's hometown—which stated:

> *I would love to do a 13 or 14 year old. I think you are rights . . . not only their innocence but their young bodies would really be fun to hurt. As far as being [sic] easier to control . . . you may be right, however you can control any bitch with rape and a gag.* (Alkhabaz, 104 F.3d at 1499)

Initially the pair were charged with 18 U.S.C. § 875(c), which prohibits the interstate communication of threats to injure or kidnap another person and a superseding indictment charging them with an additional five counts. However, a lower court quashed the superseding indictment, arguing that

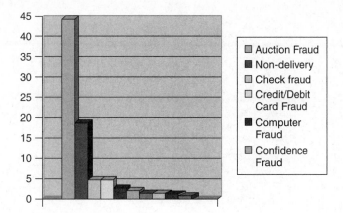

the e-mails were not "true threats" under the First Amendment as they were communicated to a third party. The Sixth Circuit upheld the ruling.[40] In essence, the court ruled that their communications did not constitute a "threat" under the provisions of the act as the fantasies were not specifically communicated to the alleged victims. More specifically, the court argued that fantasies or musings, regardless of nature, were not criminal activities absent a specific expression of intent. To wit, their e-mail communications could refer to any 13- or 14-year-old, and was thus too indeterminate to satisfy *Kelner*'s specificity requirement. Unfortunately, the requirement of specific intent nullified this action, as well as many future actions.

Online Fraud

Like telemarketing fraud, the amount of money consumers are losing to Internet fraud is increasing dramatically. More specifically, American consumers reported $198.44 million in losses, with a median dollar loss of $724 per complaint. Over 200,000 complaints were filed with the Internet Crime Complaint Center (IC3). An analysis of the data revealed that Internet auction fraud was the most reported offense, comprising 44.9 percent of all referred complaints. The non-delivery of merchandise and/or payment accounted for 19 percent of complaints, while 5 percent of complaints involved check fraud.[41]

Among perpetrators, more than three-fourths were male and approximately half were located in one of the following seven states: California, New York, Florida, Texas, Illinois, Pennsylvania, and Tennessee. Although a significant number of fraudsters were located in foreign countries like the UK, Nigeria, Canada, Romania, and Italy, the majority of perpetrators resided in the United States. Not only were males more likely to be complainants, they also lost more money than their female counterparts. The vast majority of reported victimization was initiated via electronic mail or Web pages. Unfortunately, such statistics represent only *reported* crime and victimization.[42] Thus, the actual number of total victims and dollars loss is sure to be exponentially higher.

Most Common Types of Fraud Complaints

1. Auction fraud
2. Non-delivery of merchandise and/or payment
3. Check fraud
4. Credit/Debit card fraud
5. Computer fraud
6. Confidence fraud
7. Financial institution fraud

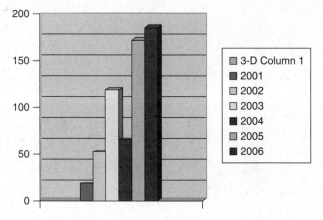

Yearly dollar losses (in millions) of referred complaints.

Web-Cramming/ISP Jacking

Web-cramming is most often accomplished when criminals develop new Web pages for small businesses and non-profit groups for little or no expense. While advertising their service as free, these criminals actually engage in unauthorized phone charges on their victim's accounts. The most common scam involves the use of "rebate checks." These checks, when cashed, transferred the consumer's ISP, placing monthly service charges on their telephone bill. Web-cramming is possible because telephone companies contract to provide billing and collection services for other companies that sell telecommunications-related services.

ISP-jacking, on the other hand, involves disconnecting individual users from their selected Internet service providers and redirecting them to illegitimate servers. In these cases, users are lured into downloading software which surreptitiously disconnects their chosen Internet service provider, silences their modem, and reconnects them to a remote server. Increasingly common, this type of scam has traditionally been overlooked by law enforcement authorities. However, the creation and implementation of computer crime units has helped somewhat. In 1999, the Royal Canadian Mounted Police, for example, uncovered a complicated scam in which Canadian users were rerouted through Moldova (a republic in the former Soviet Union) and other international locations to Dallas, Texas—resulting

in thousands of dollars in long distance charges. As a result of their investigation, at least two Web sites (*www.sexygirls.com* and *www.erotica2000.com*) were shut down. Unlike other scams which tend to focus on customers of pay-for-porn scams, this particular type of scam does not require the posting of credit card information, and therefore, is more insidious as even the most cautious users are snared. Unfortunately, telecommunications fraud is often given a low priority among local and state authorities, and as a result techno-cowboys remain relatively free to wreak havoc on unsuspecting victims. Such is the case in the burgeoning marketplace of Internet scams, where auction fraud, credit card fraud, get-rich-quick schemes, and "work at home" scams are common occurrences.

While Internet scams have taken on a variety of appearances and may appear quite innovative to the untrained investigator, many of them are simply new tricks from an old dog. Get-rich-quick and work-at-home schemes have simply found a new home on the information superhighway. Job, scholarship, and loved-one searches requiring advance fees have replaced the sometimes nefarious gumshoes of the past. In fact, individuals and entities which have traditionally preyed on the vulnerable within society have simply developed new, more sophisticated modes of operation. Such is the case with the *Nigerian found money* and *advance fee* scams (discussed in Chapter 6).

Complaint Type	Percentage of Reported Total Dollar Loss	Media $ Loss (rounded)
Nigerian letter fraud	1.7	5,100
Check fraud	11.1	3,744
Investment fraud	4.0	2,694
Confidence fraud	4.5	2,400
Auction fraud	33	603
Non delivery	28.1	585
Credit/Debit card fraud	3.6	428

Fraud via Data Manipulation

Non-traditional methods of fraud are also emerging due to the advances in technology. **Data diddling**, for example, is becoming increasingly popular, and can be committed by anyone having access to an input device. Generally speaking, *data diddling* refers to any method of fraud via computer manipulation. More succinctly, data diddling usually refers to the deliberate manipulation of an existing program to redirect or reroute data representing monies or economic exchanges. This level of criminal activity is more sophisticated than the average counterfeiting scheme and is extremely hard to recognize. With few exceptions, it is committed by company or government insiders who exceed their authorization or by outsiders utilizing Trojan horses. One of the most notorious cases of data diddling involved the **salami technique** or the redirection of thin slices of accounts into a designated location. In this case, an individual preying on a systemic flaw which kept track of money to the 1/100 of a penny redirected this infinitesimal amount into his personal bank account to the tune of several million dollars! Even government entities have not proven immune to economically motivated electronic fraud. The Veterans Affairs Administration, for example, was swindled for close to $50K by an employee who directed funds to fictitious corporations which he had established just for this purpose[43] and in Marin County, California, Fire Chief Richard Mollenkopf electronically embezzled three-quarters of a million dollars.

Similar type of activities which do not require insider status or a comparable level of sophistication have also increased due to the growth of electronic banking (i.e., money transfers, direct deposit, electronic billing, etc.). Unlike traditional methods of remote banking, electronic banking relies on the electronic verification of personal identification without exception. Electronic thieves may use traditional techniques of fraudulent identification (i.e., routing phone calls to the suspect's house) or the new method of *IP spoofing* to gain control of a targeted account.

IP spoofing involves the manipulation of packets (i.e., messages that are exchanged between computers). These communications are indirectly routed across varying systems. Addresses attached to these messages verify the sender and the recipient organization, respectively. Necessary for the synchronization of transmissions, this also enables technology-savvy individuals to more successfully mimic an innocent victim, as many electronic authentication platforms rely exclusively on IP verification. Thus, criminals may gain access to large amounts of money simply by disguising their computers. IP spoofing may also be used to redirect Internet traffic. *Domain Name Hijacking* is especially popular among political hacktivists and petty vandals, and is committed when individuals change domain name ownership by *spoofing* messages to domain name registrars like *Network Solutions.*™ This approach has been used to attack several corporate giants. *Nike,*™ for example, was successfully targeted in June 2000 when visitors to the company's site were redirected to the environmentally conscious *www.s11.org* (who denied any connection to the rerouting). It has also been employed by individuals involved in stock manipulation.

Securities Fraud and Stock Manipulation

While the emergence of the "information superhighway" has exponentially increased knowledge among many users, it has also created a false sense of empowerment in others. This is especially true among *day traders*. Although **day trading** (the process of buying and selling highly speculative stocks within one trading day) has existed since the creation of the New York Stock Exchange (NYSE), it was mainly reserved for brokers. In fact, for many years, brokers or licensed traders were the only individuals with the capability of accessing real-time trading information. However, the Internet has made it possible for untutored individuals to *instantly* access stock values and statistics. So there has been a marked increase in the number of individuals engaging in day trading. Unfortunately, many of these individuals do not fully understand the securities in which they are investing or the market conditions which bear upon stock prices. As such they are extremely vulnerable, as many found out when the bottom fell out of tech stocks. This susceptibility has proven disastrous in many cases and has even resulted in violence.

Though not all day traders lose their life savings and become homicidal, many are seduced by bulletin boards or Web pages which claim to provide expert investment advice. While the majority of these pages are created by and subscribed to by stock novices seeking their fortune, some are actually created by criminals. One criminal fraud involves the creation of Web pages to solicit money for unfounded investment advice. In early 2000, for example, the Securities and Exchange Commission (SEC) filed charges against "Tokyo Joe" (Yun Soo Oh Park) and his company "Tokyo Joe's Societe Anonyme." Together, this scam netted $1.1 million in fees from members in exchange for investment advice, daily stock picks, and membership to a private chat room. Unfortunately for investors, he only promoted stocks in which he held an interest.

False information is another method in which unwitting investors are parted from their money. The first identified case of this type of Internet stock manipulation involved an individual who circulated false information regarding PairGain. By posting fraudulent information regarding the takeover of the company by an Israeli company and by providing a link to a fraudulent Web site which appeared to be a legitimate news server, this individual caused the stock to increase in price by 30 percent, with trades totaling seven times the average volume! Unfortunately, those investors who bought the stock at the inflated price suffered significant losses. The perpetrator was subsequently found guilty of securities fraud and sentenced to five years of probation, five months of home detention, and over $90,000 in restitution to his victims. An additional example of false information involved the manipulation of Emulex. Mark Simeon Jakob, 23, was charged with nine counts of securities fraud and two counts of wire fraud after he falsely posted information on Internet Wire, Inc., his former employer. Jakob made over $200,000 by selling Emulex stock short after disseminating information which claimed:

1. Emulex was under investigation by the SEC.
2. Emulex's CEO was resigning.
3. That the company's revised earnings showed a loss.

Tragedy in Atlanta

In the last several years, fortunes have been gambled and lost on the increasingly volatile stock market. For the most part, these losses are strictly financial. However, one tragic case in Atlanta involved an individual who lost his life savings on highly speculative stocks, killed his wife and children, and then targeted employees at a financial firm.

Misinformation and Widespread Panic

Many individuals assume that information contained on the Web is valid and reliable. Unfortunately, such naivete can often have catastrophic consequences. A 14-year-old boy in Hong Kong created a Web site which circulated false stories regarding the SARS epidemic. He predicted a governmental action that would make Hong Kong a closed port. As a result, widespread panic caused chaos at local markets, which were overrun by citizens stocking up on essentials to carry them through the quarantine. He was subsequently arrested and placed under welfare control for 12 months.[44]

This information caused the stock to tumble from $110 to $43 in less than one hour, and temporarily cost the company $2 billion in market value. Although the company's stock is now secure and their financial situation is soundly framed, many individual investors, some of whom sold their shares at a 50 percent loss, did not recover.

Insider trading is also increasing due to the proliferation of day trading activity. In March 2000, 19 people were arrested in a massive insider trading scheme. This scheme was predicated on the advice of one "insider" who solicited interested individuals in chat rooms, offering them inside advice for a percentage of their profits. Over a 2½-year period, this individual communicated insider information via chat rooms and instant messages, netting a profit of $170,000 for himself and $500,000 for his partners. Although authorities subsequently identified and prosecuted some of the individuals involved in this scheme, there are an indeterminate number remaining. (The North American Securities Administrators Association estimates that Internet-related stock fraud costs investors approximately $10 billion per year or $1 million per hour!) While most of this fraud is conducted electronically, some schemes actually involve threats of violence.

Organized crime groups have manipulated stocks and exchanges by employing traditional strong-arm tactics outside the realm of cyberspace. Japanese crime groups, in particular, have been quite successful at extorting money, securities, and/or insider information through the art of *Sokaiya*, a process where individuals are threatened with violence or loss of reputation. In fact, many authors attribute much of Tokyo's bubble economy to the Yakuza's grip on the Japanese stock exchange.[45] Russian and Italian groups have also made inroads into the market. Although the vast majority of their involvement has been via traditional (i.e., non-electronic) means, it is anticipated that their emergence in the techno-world is a foregone conclusion.

● ANCILLARY CRIMES

Money Laundering

Metaphorically speaking, the term **money laundering** refers to the cleansing or cleaning of money. Legally speaking, the term is a bit more precise, and refers to an enterprise or practice of engaging in deliberate financial transactions to conceal the identity, source, and/or destination of income. Traditionally, the term was used specifically to encompass illicit transactions by criminal syndicates. Contemporary definitions recognize all financial transactions designed to generate an asset to conceal illegal activity. This considerably broadens the traditional definition, and includes activities ranging from, but not limited to: tax evasion, fraudulent accounting, securities fraud, and narcotics trafficking. In practice, the broadened definition also encompasses illegal concealment of illicit profits by individuals, small businesses, corporation, criminal syndicates, corrupt officials, and even corrupt governments. It is increasingly considered to be the backbone of both domestic and international black markets and underground economies. Unfortunately, the Internet has exponentially increased

Prosecuting Money Laundering in the United States

While there are various state and federal statutes which may be used to prosecute money launderers, the most comprehensive statute by far is the Currency and Foreign Transactions Reporting Act (aka Bank Secrecy Act). This congressional statute requires all financial institutions to submit five types of reports to the government:

- IRS Form 4789–Currency Transaction Report (CTR)
- U.S. Customs Form 4790–Report of International Transportation of Currency or Monetary Instruments (CMIR)

- Department of the Treasury Form 90-22.1–Report of Foreign Bank and Financial Accounts (FBAR)
- Treasury Department Form 90-22.47/OCC Form 8010-9, 8010-1–Suspicious Activty Report (SAR)
- Treasury Department Form 90-22.53–Designation of Exempt Person Form

both the amount of the revenue concealed and the ease in transaction subterfuge.

Although money laundering has historically been a foundational element for both organized crime and international terrorism, the enormous profits associated with illegal narcotics have necessitated an increasing reliance on alternative methods. Modest estimates place the figure in the trillions of dollars. In fact, one study indicated that as much as $1.8 trillion a year was laundered in the illegal drug trade alone—a figure representing between 2 percent and 5 percent of the world's gross domestic product! This number is only compounded by the fact that the globalization of communication and commerce has led to an increase in sophisticated, transnational financial crime.

A Brief History of Money Laundering

Throughout the history of American organized crime, money laundering has been employed by various individuals and criminal syndicates to provide a legitimate source of income for large sums of illegally earned money. As the IRS did not zealously pursue tax evaders prior to Prohibition, the practice was not necessary for ne'er-do-wells until the 1920s. However, the inability to successfully prosecute organized crime figures led to a series of high profile cases of tax evasion for notable gangsters like Al Capone. As criminals recognized their vulnerability, they sought to develop methods to legitimize both their incomes and their lifestyles. (e.g., Meyer Lansky, considered to be one of the fathers or American organized crime, engaged in what was known as "capital flight," in which large transfers of American capital were diverted to offshore accounts.)

Irrespective of the first known example of money laundering, it is most likely that the term itself was actually coined by another notable Chicago gangster, Murray "the Camel" Humphries. Considered to be one of the most successful figures in Chicago organized crime, Humphries purchased a string of Laundromats and actively controlled the Chicago Laundry Owner's Association. However, the first time the term appeared in print was during the Watergate scandal when it was discovered that Nixon's "Committee to Re-elect the President" routed illegal campaign contributions through Mexico.

Internationally, an increased recognition gathered steam through the 1980s and 1990s. During this period, the Vienna Convention and the European Union both required members to criminalize the practice. In addition, the Financial Actions Task Force was created by the G-7 Summit in Paris in 1989. Although originally directed at stemming the flow of transnational crime, international awareness was further heightened in the wake of 9/11, when it was alleged that Clearstream, a Luxembourg clearing house for banks practicing "financial clearing" (i.e., centralizing debit and credit operations for hundreds of banks), was a major player in the underground economy through its system of unpublished accounts. Of most concern were purported links to the Bahrain International Bank, an institution owned by Osama bin Laden.

Process of Money Laundering
Whether technological or traditional, the process of money laundering occurs in three stages: placement, layering, integration.

- **Placement**—the initial point of entry for illicit funds;
- **Layering**—the development and maintenance of complex networks of transactions designed to obscure the process and the source of illegal funds. This involves the "layering" of financial and commercial transactions and/or assets. More specifically, "layering of funds" is accomplished by conducting multiple transactions or by developing complex hierarchies of assets aimed toward distancing origination from laundered assets.
- **Integration**—the return of funds into the legitimate economy.

For a variety of reasons, most of which are associated with decreased detection and prosecution, criminals are increasingly turning to the Internet to facilitate money laundering. First, the lack of physicality and bulk associated with e-money or e-funds eliminates the need for the identification and maintenance of physical structures to store or otherwise conceal large amounts of cash (i.e., the materiality of physical money greatly enhances the potential of discovery by law enforcement officials). Second, the risk of detection is further reduced as criminals no longer have to physically possess the illegal "goods." With a simple click, they can move their money without ever touching it. And, finally, e-money provides criminals with a higher degree of anonymity—as no serial numbers or identifying marks are present. In fact, the adoption of encryption techniques and the facility of remote transfer exponentially increase the anonymity of e-money.[46]

Although the methods, instruments, and resources used in online money laundering are distinct, the process itself remains the same. First, the placement of the funds involves the establishment of e-money accounts. Such accounts enable them to exchange digital currency without physical interaction. Second, the online launderers electronically "layer" their money. This may be accomplished through the transfer of funds between a network of offshore companies or accounts; the purchasing of foreign currency; or the purchase of high-end merchandise for resale. While this stage of the process is the most attractive to criminals, it is the most troublesome for authorities. In the quest to increase consumer interest and customer convenience, many e-banking sites now allow individuals to open accounts with no physical interaction or without a link to a pre-existing, traditionally established account.[47]

Traditional Methods of Money Laundering

- **Gambling**—There are a variety of ways in which criminals can launder money through gambling, but all involve a showing of "winnings." In this way, the money launderer can report the winnings as earnings. For example, Joe Bettor goes to the local horse-track where the odds of winning the trifecta or superfecta are substantial. While he doesn't buy a ticket of his own, he identifies the winner of the prize, and pays them a bit more than the face value of their winnings in exchange for the ticket. He then takes the winning ticket to the window and cashes it in. Such cash prizes often amount to more than $100,000. As such, he can now declare that sum as legitimate income.
- **Real Estate**—In this method, the launderer presents legitimate bank instruments and funds to purchase a piece of real estate at a publicly recorded price, far below market value. Behind the scenes, the balance of the purchase is paid with illegal funds. The property is then sold at full market value—voila—washed money.
- **Irregular Funding**—Laundering of money through irregular funding occurs when an individual or entity

(Continued)

gives money or funds to an individual or entity who legitimately receives large sums of money. This intermediary then deposits the funds into a legitimate account, takes a percentage of the deposit, and returns the remainder to the launderer in the form of a cheque.

- **Corruption Officials and/or Non-Profit Organizations**—Similar to money which is laundered through irregular funding, some funds are washed by corrupt officials or non-profit organizations. This occurs when the organization transfers funds between trusted organizations to mask donations from illicit sources.
- **Captive Businesses**—The method involves the creation of a business with unregulated cash flow, so that small amounts of illicit funds can be channeled through the business and taxes paid. Many such businesses are those that deal directly with the public in a service-related activity or those that are labor intensive. As

cash-flow businesses are hard to monitor in terms of the influx of capital, anonymity and the lack of direct accountability make them especially attractive to those seeking to legitimize assets. These include, but are not limited to, bars, restaurants, hair salons, contractors, electrical trades, plumbing companies, and the like. Unfortunately, it is not possible, or even reasonable, to assume that government entities could require a direct accounting of all consumer identities in these types of businesses. Nor is it possible to create systems of government monitoring and supervision of such. Thus, a record of transaction amounts has traditionally been accepted as *prima facie* evidence of actual financial activity. (This is not to suggest, however, that this type of money laundering is always successful. Forensic accountants can often discover money laundering by the absence of purchasing records for parts or materials.)

The final phase in money laundering, of course, is the reintroduction of the money into the legitimate economy. This can be accomplished in a variety of ways, including the production of false invoices for goods and services. Online launderers commonly use companies or corporations that ostensibly provide Internet service or which operate entirely in the virtual world. By developing individual or company bank accounts, criminals can generate payment from that account to their own online casino or betting service. Thus, it appears that the company is legitimate, although no services are actually provided. Unlike similar practices in the

physical environment, such transactions do not require additional documentation evidencing delivery of goods or the purchase of raw materials.

Fighting Money Laundering

The prosecution of e-laundering must follow traditional methods which incorporate the 3F's—**finding, freezing,** and **forfeiture**. Such methods have proven successful in combating traditional money laundering. Such efforts must be both an international and community effort. International forums must communicate with and provide education to consumers, e-merchants, banks, and

---

Why Is Online Laundering Increasing?

In addition to the lack of physical interaction and the perception of anonymity, online laundering proves more efficient to those seeking to wash illicit funds. Complex audit trails can be constructed in a matter of keystrokes by electronically transferring funds between numerous accounts. Due to jurisdictional disputes and the vicinage requirement for warrants, criminals can successfully create sophisticated, and legally frustrating, trails through countless jurisdictions, further obscuring his/her footprints.

Summarily, traditional methods of money laundering are being replaced by those associated with the Internet.

This trend is expected to continue due to the following characteristics of online laundering.

- less overhead
- less paperwork
- ease of transaction
- lack of physical interaction
- reduction of risk
- harder to identify
- harder to prosecute.

Internet service providers. In addition, emerging legislation should include accountability provisions for all such actors. For example, the Financial Action Task Force has suggested the following requirements for Internet service providers:

- maintenance of reliable subscriber registers with appropriate identification information;
- establishment and maintenance of log files with traffic data relating Internet-protocol number to subscriber and to telephone number used in the connections;
- assurances that the information will be maintained for a reasonable period of time AND that it will be made available to law enforcement authorities during criminal investigations.

In addition to ISPs, money laundering can only be controlled with the assistance of financial institutions. Accountability provisions should be incorporated into statutes which would hold those institutions with inadequate security measures responsible for facilitating money laundering. The refrain "know your customer" is a common one among those in bank security. To assist American banks in this endeavor, the U.S. Office of the Comptroller of the Currency has released a handbook on Internet banking which encourages banks to create systems to identify unusual or suspicious activities, much of which focuses on authenticating the identity of both private and corporate consumers. Authentication of identity is considered critical in the fight against both money laundering and identity theft. Banks are strongly encouraged to develop security measures such as PIN codes, digital certificates using a public key infrastructure (PKI), physical devices such as smart cards, USB plug-ins or other types of "token," transaction profile scripts, biometric identification where available, etc. In addition, it is recommended that banks engage in a threefold authentication process which involves the verification of something the person knows, something they have, and something they are (i.e., a biometric characteristic).

The recommendations from the USOCC also included monitoring procedures for online transactions in which the following situations should evoke greater scrutiny:

- unusual requests, timing of transactions or e-mail formats
- anomalies in types, volumes, or values of transactions
- incomplete online applications accompanied by a refusal for additional information or cooperation
- inconsistencies or conflicts of information on online applications, such as physical address and location of e-mail address
- multiple online applications
- multiple online transactions involving inter-bank wire transfers between multiple accounts.

As stated, money laundering is the backbone of the illicit economy. Fortunately, the international community has recognized the need for the prosecution and incarceration of those who are involved in facilitating criminal activity. Such recognition has been primarily based on a collective awareness of the impact of the extraction of capital from the legitimate economy and the increasing infiltration of criminal syndicates and terrorist organizations in legitimate business due to the reduction of competition caused by the influx of illicit funds. In the past decade, various international bodies have been created to increase communication and cooperation between agencies and countries (discussed more thoroughly in Chapter 7).

CONCLUSIONS

If we had your skills in the 60s, the 80s would have never happened.

—Winn Schwartau, *Electrohippies*

Corporate and national security are becoming increasingly vulnerable to criminal acts. While computers have been instrumental in the creation of sophisticated defense and security mechanisms, they have also created unprecedented risks to national security on a variety of levels. First, computers act as the technical equivalent of storage warehouses—stockpiling information ranging from satellite locations to troop deployment to personal information of government personnel. Traditionally secure from all but the most dedicated of professionals, this information has long been an extremely valuable commodity. Their current vulnerability has not led to market devaluation. In fact, it is this very vulnerability that has proven irresistible to espionage agents, common criminals, and computer hackers alike.

Second, the increasing connectivity and interdependence of government and poorly regulated public infrastructures is creating a technological house of cards, in which the failure of one critical system could upset the precarious balancing of the entire techno-driven society. Third, the technical expertise necessary for information warfare has significantly declined due to the ready availability of instructional guidelines on the information superhighway. Fourth, the number of threat groups with sophisticated methodologies and advanced technology systems has exponentially increased. And, finally, there is the lack of recognition and government apathy which has been displayed toward protecting digital systems. Thus, the theft or manipulation of data may also lead to a new style of terrorism both here and abroad.

The costs associated with computer crime are difficult to estimate. Measurable costs include lost productivity, damage to systems, law enforcement resources, and security software and updates. However, the dollar amounts associated with these characteristics do not begin to address the potential harm experienced by the general global economy, and the U.S. economy, in particular. In fact, the loss of consumer confidence may disrupt or even destroy the position enjoyed by the United States in the global marketplace. Since many of these activities are facilitated through the use of botnets, government authorities must hold servers accountable. The imposition of monetary fines for operators running SMTP servers with open relays or unrestricted, anonymous-access FTP servers should hinder the efforts of many computer criminals. Similar accountability statutes should be developed and enforced against ISPs, hosts, or other e-businesses which facilitate illegal activity. Emerging statutes should include provisions for asset forfeiture and all should be aggressively pursued and enforced. It must be noted that while the United States should take the lead in these efforts, they cannot disadvantage American consumers, businesses, or corporations by enacting laws inconsistent with global practices (i.e., if we force American companies to require transparency while others do not—consumers will flock to non-American e-businesses, harming our economy and encouraging black market or illicit activities.)

DISCUSSION QUESTIONS

1. What is software piracy? How pervasive is it, and how can it be eliminated?
2. How do contemporary hackers vary from their predecessors?
3. Discuss the six classifications of motive for contemporary computer intruders.
4. What does the term "theft of information" mean? Discuss the implications of such in terms of national security.
5. How has technology changed the face of terrorism? How could it be utilized in the future?
6. Discuss the evolution of criminal behavior in the United States, including in your answer the utilization of technological advances.
7. What are anonymizers, and what is their relevance to computer crime and investigations?
8. What events precipitated the development of enhanced data security measures taken by the federal government?
9. What are the three categories of computer crime? What are some of the individual crimes included in each?
10. How have organized crime syndicates utilized computer technologies to further their criminal interests? What are the implications for the future?
11. What are some of the laws which have specifically targeted online criminal behavior? Have they been employed effectively? Why or why not?

RECOMMENDED READING

- Ferraro, Monique and Casey, Eoghan (2004). *Investigating Child Exploitation and Pornography: The Internet, Law and Forensic Science*. Academic Press: New York.
- National Center for Missing and Exploited Children. *http://www.missingkids.com/en_US/publications/NC144.pdf*.
- Skoudis, Edward and Liston, Tom (2005). *Counter Hack Reloaded: A Step-by-step Guide to Computer Attacks and Effective Defenses* (2nd Ed). Pearson Education: Upper Saddle River, NJ.
- Wolak, Jani; Finkelhor, David; and Mitchell, Kimberly J. (2005). *Child-Pornography Possesors Arrested in Internet-Related Crimes*.

WEB RESOURCES

- www.virtualglobaltaskforce.com – a compilation of law enforcement agencies dedicated to eradicating child exploitation via the Internet. Member organizations include the Australian High Tech Crime Centre, the Child Exploitation and Online Protection Center (UK), the Royal Canadian Mounted Patrol, US Department of Homeland Security, and Interpol.
- http://www.fbi.gov/innocent.htm – homepage of the FBI's *Innocent Images* project. The site provides links to assorted facts and publications regarding the exploitation of children via the Internet. In addition, it provides information and links to other sources which look at the current laws and cases.
- www.nw3c.org – homepage of the National White Collar Crime Center, a congressionally funded, nonprofit organization which compiles information and provides education on all topics surrounding white-collar crime. Although the organization's primary mission is to provide a nationwide support system for agendas involved in the prevention, investigation, and prosecution of economic and high-tech crimes, it also includes various resources on the investigation of computer-related crime and Internet fraud.
- www.viruslist.com – site provides numerous articles on the state of malware in contemporary society. In addition, it contains links to international news sources focusing on computer crime. Finally, it provides a comprehensive glossary of terms for the computer novice.
- www.missingkids.com – home page to the National Center for Missing and Exploited Children. The site provides links to various academic articles addressing the exploitation of minors via the Internet. In addition, it provides information regarding current case law and evolving legislation.
- www.fincen.gov – homepage of the Financial Crimes Enforcement Network, an organization created by the U.S. Department of the Treasury. Includes links for both private consumers and state agencies. Information contained includes statistics on the state of financial crime and money laundering as well as current law enforcement initiatives and pending legislation.
- http://www.law.cornell.edu/uscode/ – A direct link to the United States Code which is maintained by Cornell University. Allows users to directly access specific portions of the code, and to search the code by key terms.
- http://www.occ.treas.gov/handbook/bsa.pdf – maintained by the Office of the Comptroller of Currency, Administrator of National Banks, U.S. Department of the Treasury. It is a direct link to the Bank Secrecy Act.
- www.unodc.org – official homepage of the United Nations Office of Drug Control—includes links to numerous articles and government documents relating to computer crime, terrorism, and money laundering.

ENDNOTES

[1] Lewis, James A. (2006). *McAfee Virtual Criminology Report: North American Study into Organized Crime and the Internet.* McAfee: *http://www.mcafee.com/us/threat_center/white_paper.html*. Retrieved from the Internet on June 30, 2007.

[2] McAfee (2005). *McAfee Virtual Criminology Report: North American Study into Organized Crime and the Internet.* Available at: *www.macafee.com*.

[3] Ibid.

[4] Kapersky, Eugene (2004). *The History of Computer Viruses.* Available at *http://www.virus-scan-software.com/virus-scan-help/answers/the-history-of-computer-viruses.shtml*. Retrieved from the web on August 7, 2007.

[5] Kuo, Chengi Jimmy (2005). *Stay Safe Online Campaign's AntiVirus Presentation.* Available at *http://www.ftc.gov/bcp/workshops/security/comments/chengijimmykuo.pdf*. Retrieved from the Internet on August 7, 2007.

[6] Kapersky, Eugene (2004). *History of Malware: 2000.* Available at *http://www.networkworld.com/news/2001/0918admindll.html*. Retrieved from the Internet on August 7, 2007.

[7] Kapersky, Eugene (2004). *History of Malware: 2003.* Available at *http://www.viruslist.com/en/viruses/encyclopedia?chapter=153311316*. Retrieved from the Internet of August 7, 2007.

[8] Ibid.

[9] Cleary, Robert (1999). *United States of America v. David Smith*, Criminal no. 99–18 U.S.C. § 1030(a)(5)A-Information. Available at *http://www.usdoj.gov/criminal/*

cybercrime/meliinfo.htm. Retrieved from the Internet on August 7, 2007.

[10]Kapersky, Eugene (2004). *History of Malware: 2001*. Available at *http://www.viruslist.com/en/viruses/encyclopedia?chapter=1533 11184*. Retrieved from the Internet on August 7, 2007.

[11]Kessler, Gary C. (2000). *Defenses Against Distributed Denial of Service Attacks*. Retrieved from the Internet on July 18, 2007.

[12]FBI (2007). *Over 1 Million Potential Victims of Botnet Cyber Crime*. Available at *www.fbi.gov*. Retrieved from the Internet on June 17, 2007.

[13]Claburn, Thomas (February 3, 2005). Spam Costs Billions: The Cost of Spam in Terms of Lost Productivity has Reached $21.58 Billion Annually. *Information Week*. Available at *http://www. informationweek.com/story/showArticle.jhtml?articleID=5930 0834*. Retrieved from the Internet on July 22, 23, 2007.

[14]Available at *http://www.ftc.gov/bcp/conline/pubs/buspubs/ canspam.shtm*.

[15]United States Department of Justice (2006). *First Man Charged Under U.S. "CAN-SPAM" Act Sentenced to Three Years in Prison*. Available at: *http://www.usdoj.gov/usao/mie/ press/Sep_2006.pdf*.

[16]United States Department of Justice (2007). *Seattle Spammer Indicted for Mail and Wire Fraud, Aggravated Identity Theft and Money Laundering: Man Sold Spamming Software and Spamming Services Impacting Millions of Computers*. Available at *http://www.usdoj.gov/usao/waw/press/ 2007/may/soloway.html*.

[17]Giri, Babu Nath and Jyoti, Nitin (2006). *The Emergence of Ransomware*. A paper presented at the AVAR International Conference. Available at *www.mcafee.com/us/local_content/ white_papers/threat_center/wp_avar_ransomware.pdf*.

[18]Ibid.

[19]DTI (2006). *Information Security Breaches Survey 2006: Technical Report*. Available at *www.dti.gov.uk/files/file28343. pdf*. Retrieved from the Internet on July 20, 2007.

[20]Ibid.

[21]Andreano, Frank P. (1999). "The Evolution of Federal Computer Crime Policy: The Ad Hoc Approach to an Ever-Changing Problem." *American Journal of Criminal Law*, 27(81).

[22]Ibid.

[23]SEARCH (2000). *The Investigation of Computer Crime*. The National Consortium for Justice Information and Statistics: Sacramento, CA.

[24]Kerr, Donald M. (September 6, 2000). Statement for the Record on *Carnivore Diagnostic Tool* before the United States Senate: The Committee on the Judiciary. Washington, DC. Available at *www.fbi.gov/pressrm/congress/congressoo/ kerr090600.htm*; Kluger, Jeffrey (June 24, 2000). "Extortion on the Internet." *Time* 155(3): 56.

[25]Kerr, Donald M. (July 4, 2000). Statement for the Record on *Internet and Data Interception Capabilities Developed by FBI* before the United States House of Representatives: The Committee on the Judiciary Subcommittee on the Constitution. Washington, DC. Available at *www.fbi.gov/pressrm/congress/ congressoo/kerr072400.htm*. (last accessed February 12, 2001).

[26]Available at *www.nambla.org*.

[27]Wolak, Janis; Finkelhor, David; and Mitchell, Kimberly J. (2005). *Child-Pornography Possessors Arrested in Internet-Related Crimes: Findings from the National Juvenile Online Victimization Study*. National Center for Missing and Exploited Children. Available at *www.missingkids.com*. Retrieved from the Internet on August 17, 2007.

[28]Ibid.

[29]Henkel, John (2000). Buying Drugs Online: It's Convenient and Private, but Beware of Rogue Sites. *FDA Consumer Magazine*. Available at *http://www.fda.gov/fdac/features/2000/ 100_online.html*. Retrieved from the Internet on July 20, 2007.

[30]Barker, Tom and Britz, Marjie T. (2000). *Joker's Wild: Gambling in the United States*. Praeger Publishing: Connecticut.

[31]Lindner, Anne (2006). "First Amendment as Last Resort: The Internet Gambling Industry's Bid to Advertise in the United States." *Saint Louis University Law Journal*, 50(1289). Available at *www.lexisnexis.com*.

[32]Weinberg, J. (2006). "Everyone's a Winner: Regulating, not Prohibiting, Internet Gambling." *Southwestern University Law Review*. 35(2): 293–326.

[33]Lindner, Anne (2006). "First Amendment as Last Resort: The Internet Gambling Industry's Bid to Advertise in the United States." *Saint Louis University Law Journal*, 50(1289). Available at *www.lexisnexis.com*.

[34]Venezia, Todd; Martinez, Erika; and Livingston, Ikimulisa (2006). *$3.3 Billion Casino Royale*. Newsday: Long Island.

[35]Tjaden, P. and Theonnes, N. (1998). *Stalking in America: Findings from the National Violence Against Women Survey*. Washington, DC: U.S. Department of Justice, National Institute of Justice.

[36]Office of Victims of Crime (2002). National Victim Assistance Academy, Washington, DC: Office of Justice Programs. Available at *http://www.ojp.usdoj.gov/ovc/assist/ mvaa2002/chapter22_2sup.html*.

[37]NCVC (2007). *Stalking Center: Comprehensive Statistics*. National Center for Victims of Crime.

[38]National Conference of State Legislatures (2007). *State Computer Harassment or "Cyberstalking Laws"*. Available at: *http://www.ncsl.org/programs/lis/cip/stalk99.htm*.

[39]Packard, Ashley (2000). Does Proposed Federal Cyberstalking Legislation Meet Constitutional Requirements? *Communications Law and Policy*, 5(505). Available at *www. lexis-nexis.com*. Retrieved from the Internet on July 7, 2007.

[40]*U.S.* v. *Alkhabaz* 104 F.3d at 1499.

[41]National White Collar Crime Center and the Federal Bureau of Investigation (2007). *Internet Crime Report—2006*. Available at: *www.ic3.gov/media/annualreport/2006_ic3report.pdf*.

[42]Ibid.

[43]Andreano (1999). The Evolution of Federal Computer Crime Policy.

[44]Broadhurst, Roderic (2006). "Developments in the Global Law Enforcement of Cyber-Crime." *Policing: An International Journal of Police Strategies and Management*, 29(3): 408–433.

[45]Grennan, Sean and Britz, Marjie T. (2007). *Organized Crime: A Worldwide Perspective*. Prentice Hall: Upper Saddle River, NJ.

[46]Ping, He (2004). "New Trends in Money Laundering—From the Real World to Cyberspace." *Journal of Money Laundering Control*, 8(1): 48–55.

[47]Phillippsohn, Steven (2001). "The Dangers of New Technology—Laundering on the Internet." *Journal of Money Laundering Control*, 5(1): 87–95.

CHAPTER 5

Identity Theft and Identity Fraud

Chapter Outline

LEARNING OBJECTIVES

After reading this chapter, you will be able to do the following:

✓ Gain a quick clarification of terms related to identity theft and fraud.

✓ Understand the difference between identity theft and identity fraud.

✓ Explore the five types of identity theft/fraud.

✓ Investigate the virtual and Internet methods in which computer criminals steal an identity.

✓ Develop a knowledge of the crimes that are committed due to identity theft/fraud and also the process in which they are committed.

KEY TERMS AND CONCEPTS

- assumption of identity
- breeder documents
- credit identity theft/fraud
- identifying information
- identity fraud
- identity theft
- immigration benefit fraud

- keyloggers
- popcorning
- pharming
- phishing
- reverse criminal record identity theft
- skimmers

- spoofing
- virtual identity theft/fraud

But he that filches from me my good name Robs me of that which not enriches him And makes me poor indeed

(Shakespeare, *Othello*, Act iii., Section 3, as cited by DOJ, 2006[1])

⬤ INTRODUCTION

According to the U.S. Federal Trade Commission, approximately 10 million Americans are affected by identity fraud each year due to computer theft, loss of backups, or compromised information systems.[2] Such fraud is usually undertaken for economic gain. However, it may also be used to gain access to secure or privileged areas. In this area, minors may attempt to purchase alcohol or gain access to night clubs or gambling establishments. More insidious uses may involve foreigners seeking border entry or terrorists desiring concealment. In fact, personal identification information has become a marketable commodity, one whose worth is increasing steadily.

Information Procurement and Breeder Documents

In order to complete the process of identity theft/fraud, perpetrators must first obtain personal identification information. Once this information is in their possession, a "breeder document" is created or accessed. As the name suggests, breeder documents are then utilized to procure additional fraudulent documents. Breeder documents include passports, birth certificates, drivers' licenses, social security cards, military identification, and the like. Such documents are either entirely contrived or obtained through fraudulent means, most often through the corruption of authority, the black market, or, increasingly, the Internet. For example, birth certificates are extremely easy to access through a variety of Internet sites with little more information than the date and county of birth and parents' names.

Traditionally, the generic term *identity theft* has been utilized to describe any use of stolen personal information. However, such characterization fails to provide a comprehensive picture of the totality of possibilities surrounding that construct known as *identity*. **Identity fraud,** which encompasses identity theft within its purview, may be defined as the use of a vast array of illegal activities based on fraudulent use of *identifying information* of a real or fictitious person. Thus, it provides for the creation of fictitious identities. Initiated from a single "breeder" document (i.e., fictitious or stolen identifiers), identity fraud is committed when a credible identity is created by accessing others' credit cards, financial or employment records, secure facilities, computer systems, or such. Upon development of the credible identity, the criminal possibilities are endless. Small-time criminals, for example, simply engage in several counts of credit card fraud by ordering merchandise for their personal use. More sophisticated criminals may use such information to create additional lines of credit and separate bank accounts to maximize the profitability of theft. And, terrorists may aggressively exploit the information to conceal their own identity, hide from authorities, gain access to sensitive data, and further their ideological philosophy. The information necessary to perpetrate such activities may come from a variety of sources, including, but not limited to, names, addresses, dates of birth, social security numbers, taxpayer identification numbers, alien registration numbers, passport numbers, historical information (e.g., city of birth or mother's maiden name), and/or biometric information (e.g., fingerprints, voice prints, and retinal images).

Individuals involved in the theft and utilization of personal identification information and fictitious identities may prey upon private citizens, company employees, corporate executives, and government workers. At the same time, identity theft/fraud may be perpetrated by individuals, loose social or business networks, terrorist groups, and criminal organizations. It may be used for personal gain, corporate interests, or to facilitate the globalization of crime by terrorists and organized crime groups. The criminal acts which may be engaged in by such entities include, but are not limited to, money laundering, drug trafficking, alien smuggling, weapons smuggling, extortion, misappropriation of funds, embezzlement, and other financial crimes. Thus, all American citizens and corporations may be targeted and victimized. More importantly, identity theft/fraud has significant national security implications in the areas of border crossings and immigration, airlines and other modes of public transportation, flight and other specialized training, and personal, commercial, or Hazmat licenses.[3] Unfortunately, successful procurement of one foundational document of identification enables its holder to secure a variety of others. Coupled with the boundless nature of the Internet, the task of eradicating identity

---

Distinguishing Between Identity Theft and Identity Fraud

Although many sources fail to distinguish between identity theft and identity fraud, a comprehensive definition of the utilization of fraudulent or stolen identification is necessary if legislation, enforcement, and prosecution are to be effective.

- **Identity theft**—the illegal use or transfer of a third party's personal identification information with unlawful intent.

- **Identity fraud**—a vast array of illegal activities based on fraudulent use of identifying information of a real or fictitious person.

Irrespective of the method of deception, both may utilize personal information, such as name, address, date of birth, social security or taxpayer identification number, alien registration or passport number, historical information, and/or biometric information.

fraud/theft for American law enforcement and government officials seems almost impossible.

TYPOLOGIES OF INTERNET THEFT/FRAUD

Contrary to popular belief, identity theft is not a new phenomenon. In fact, the first recorded example of identity theft may be found in the Old Testament, in the book of Genesis. In the tale of Esau and Jacob, Jacob steals Esau's identity to receive his father's blessing. With the assistance of his mother, Jacob successfully disguises himself as Esau and manipulates his father. Although such trickery seems rather unsophisticated by today's standards, identity thieves may employ similar, albeit technological, strategies to achieve their objectives.

In contemporary society, identity theft/fraud is typically categorized by the intention or motivation of the offender. In the most general sense, identity theft/fraud may be dichotomized as either financial or non-financial. Under this broad umbrella, there are five main types of identity theft/fraud occurring in the United States:

- assumption of identity
- theft for employment and/or border entry
- criminal record identity theft/fraud
- virtual identity theft/fraud
- credit or financial theft

Assumption of Identity

This is the rarest form of identity theft/fraud and occurs when an individual simply assumes the identity of their victim, including all aspects of their lives. It must be noted that this type of activity is atypical as it is significantly more difficult to accomplish. Even if a thief could identically duplicate the physical characteristics and appearance of their intended target, the likelihood of mastering personal histories, intimate relationships, and communication nuances is extremely remote.

Theft for Employment and/or Border Entry

This type of identity theft/fraud is increasingly common due to the growth of illegal immigration and alien smuggling. It involves the fraudulent use of stolen or fictitious personal information to obtain employment or to gain entry into the United States. In an early study, the General Accounting Office reported that INS officials seized fraudulent

---

Assumption of Identity: The Case of the Murderous Twin

In November 1996, Jeen "Jeena" Young Han recruited two teenage boys to murder her identical twin, Sunny, to start a new life, free of her troubled past. At the time of the plot, Jeena had failed to return to jail after she had received a five-hour furlough from her 180-day sentence for burglary, grand larceny, and forgery. Witnesses at Jeena's trial testified that the siblings had had a long contentious history, including physical altercations, theft of property, and police reports. In fact, Jeena contended that she never intended to kill her sister, but simply hired the boys to accompany her to Sunny's apartment to reclaim some personal belongings. She further testified that she did not know that the boys had a gun.

During the trial, both boys indicated that they attempted to gain entrance to the apartment by posing as magazine salesmen. They further indicated that Jeena had provided the guns and paid for the duct tape, twine, gloves, and various magazines to be used as a prop. Fortunately for Sunny, she was in the bathroom and was able to call authorities when the pair forced their way into the apartment. Although Sunny and her roommate were bound and forced into the bathtub, the plot was thwarted by the arrival of the police. Immediately freeing the girls, the boys asked the girls to tell the police that it was just a prank.

Attorneys for all three defendants claimed that the actions of their clients amounted to nothing more than a bad joke. However, prosecutors successfully argued that Jeena had intended to kill her sister to assume her identity. All three were convicted and sentenced to lengthy prison terms.

documents by the tens of thousands. The documents most frequently intercepted by officials included alien registration cards, nonimmigrant visas, passports and citizenship documents, and border crossing cards. These documents were presented by aliens who were attempting to enter the United States in search of employment or other immigration benefits, like naturalization or permanent residency status.[4] The study further indicated that large-scale counterfeiting of employment eligibility documents (e.g., social security cards) attributed to the rising tide of fraudulent documents.

Criminal Record Identity Theft/Fraud

This type is often overlooked in discussions of identity theft, perhaps because it is not as common or because the immediate financial repercussions are not significant. It has been used historically by individuals attempting to evade capture or criminal prosecution. *Reverse criminal record identity theft* occurs when a criminal uses a victim's identity not to engage in criminal activity but to seek gainful employment. Unfortunately, criminal record identity theft/fraud is especially insidious as it often remains undiscovered until the victim is pulled over for a routine traffic violation. Unlike other types of identity

fraud, in this case many victims are horrified to discover that they have been victimized by a friend or relative. In 1995, Joshua Sours was informed by a department store that he owed them money in restitution for theft of items. A subsequent investigation into the happenings revealed that Sours had been the victim of identity theft. In addition to the shoplifting charges, Sours's criminal record also showed charges of possession of marijuana. The perpetrator in this case, a high school friend of the victim, had intentionally stolen his identity to protect himself from a criminal record.[5]

Like all victims of identity theft, an individual who has been the victim of criminal record identity theft faces legal obstacles to his/her identity rehabilitation. First, victims must prove that they were not the individual who was involved in the criminal incident in question. Second, they must obtain a judge's order to amend, clear, or expunge the record. (Although they may sympathize with a victim's plight, clerks in the criminal records division do not have the authority to change records without a court order.) With the proper documentation, it appears that judges are amendable to amending court records. However, there is no fast track into the system, and victims have to

The Doctor's Wife and the Symbionese Liberation Army

In 1999, residents of St. Paul, Minnesota, were shocked to learn that an unassuming doctor's wife had been on the FBI's Most Wanted list for a variety of terrorist acts committed in the 1960s. It appears that Kathleen Soliah, a 1960s radical, had been moonlighting as a suburban housewife for over 23 years. Soliah had been on the run since 1976, when a grand jury indicted her for her participation in a failed pipe bombing attack on a Los Angeles police officer. Although the evidence against her in that case was not remarkably strong, the testimony of Patricia Hearst placed her at the scene of the famed Crocker National Bank robbery in 1975, in which a young woman was killed. According to Hearst, Soliah was an active participant in the robbery, and actually kicked a pregnant bank employee, resulting in a miscarriage. Soliah was captured after her

case was displayed for the second time on *America's Most Wanted*. Although she pled guilty, her new community rallied around the woman they knew as Sara Jones Olsen. While many refused to accept the fact that there had been a prominent woman with a fraudulent identity living in their midst, others simply indicated that her past crimes should be forgiven as her assumed life had been lived beyond reproach. Soliah even formally changed her name to match her assumed identity during the legal proceedings. After several legal appeals and controversies, it appears that Ms. Soliah or Mrs. Olson (whichever you prefer) will be eligible for parole or release less than ten years from the date of her incarceration. Not bad for someone who admitted to engaging in an armed robbery with a terrorist group and participation in an attempted bombing of an LAPD squad car.

stand in line with everyone else. Thus, it can often take months or years to correct their record.

The financial burden associated with such activity can be quite significant. As criminal violations and some traffic offenses remain on an individual record indefinitely, victims are often forced to hire an attorney to document their victimization petition to the court, and act as an intermediary between themselves and law enforcement. Thus, victims bear both the legal and financial burden of clearing their record. Victims who do not have the financial means to engage in the clearing process may face continuing challenges.

Virtual Identity Theft/Fraud

A relatively new phenomenon, by definition, it involves the use of personal, professional, or other dimensions of identity toward the development of a fraudulent virtual personality. As in the previous types, motivations can range from the relatively innocuous to extreme malevolence. Unlike physical identities which are tied to social networks, legal documentation, and biological characteristics, virtual identities are, for the most part, personally constructed. Indeed, many individuals develop a virtual identity which is antithetical to their physical one—making themselves taller, richer, younger, more charismatic, and so on. In other words, virtual identities are often far removed from reality. As such, they are inherently less veracious and less trustworthy. They are often used for online dating, role playing, and accessing deviant sites or locations containing questionable content. Although many individuals create virtual identities to explore forbidden areas or satisfy

their curiosity behind a veil of anonymity, most do not cross the line between the legal and the illegal worlds. Criminals, however, employ them as a shield from prosecution, secure in the knowledge that the borderless environment is difficult to police.

Deviant activities associated with this type of identity theft/fraud run the gamut of deviant/illegal behavior. Some individuals may assume a virtual identity to engage in online flirtation or facilitate an extramarital affair. Others may do such to deceive others into revealing personal information to further harassment or stalking or to facilitate financial fraud. Others may actually encourage or solicit a criminal act.

Credit Identity Theft/Fraud

This is by far the most common type of identity theft/fraud. It is also the most feared by the American public. Credit identity theft/fraud may be defined as the use of stolen personal and financial information to facilitate the creation of fraudulent accounts. This definition, specific by design, requires the affirmative act of securing additional credit. It does not include traditional activities like the illegal use of a stolen credit card, as that activity is more appropriately situated under statutes concerning credit card fraud. It is also not defined under identity theft, as the primary incentive is instant gratification. As credit cards are treated as cash by consumers and merchants alike, the use of a stolen one may be likened to purse snatching or pick-pocketing without physical contact. Once the "cash" is gone (either by reaching the card limit or through notification to

Physical vs. Virtual Identity Theft and Verification of Identity

Although the consequences may be the same, physical and virtual identity theft are not synonymous. In the physical world, an individual's identity is inherently tangible—supported by social networks, legal documentation, and biology. Virtual identities, however, are—supported solely through digital input. In either event, identities are typically verified in one of three ways: presentation of identification documents; verification of secret knowledge; or satisfaction of physical recognition. Thus, identity crime can only be accomplished through deception or the circumvention of such safeguards.

Computer Forensics and the Search for Virtual Adultery

By Steven M. Abrams, M.S.

While not computer crime *per se,* investigations of marital infidelity often take on the trappings of a criminal investigation. The private detectives who conduct marital investigations have long borrowed the tools and procedures of law enforcement. Similarly, the computer forensic tools and methods employed by computer crime investigators found their way into domestic relations investigations.

Pornography has been a prominent feature of Western society since prehistoric times. Archeologists in Germany have found prehistoric pornography in the form of 7,200-year-old erotic clay figurines of a man and a woman sculpted so as to fit together in a manner depicting sexual intercourse. The word "pornography" comes from ancient Greece, where it referred to the short erotic graffiti left by prostitutes to advertise their services. The Greeks were also known to have produced erotic paintings more than 3,000 years ago. Thus, pornography has been a constant feature of Western society since its inception and has continually adapted itself to technological advances.

Adultery also has ancient roots, dating back as far as monogamy itself. Socio-biologists have theorized, based upon available archeological evidence, that our ancient hominid ancestors were "basically promiscuous . . . constantly in pursuit of sex, following the dictates of their rampant hormones." (Metthais Schultz, *Sex in the Stone Age: Pornography in Clay, http://service.spiegel.de/cache/international/spiegel/ 0,1518,350042,00.html.*) The Western concept of monogamous relationships, recognized ultimately by the formal institution of marriage, furthers the economic and social stability of society by imposing a moral code of conduct that aims to subvert the hormonal dictates of modern humans.

For as long as society has imposed these moral codes, there have been individuals who, especially when given sufficient anonymity, have given in to the dictates of their rampant hormones; hence the perpetual allure of "sin cities"—from the ancient Sodom and Gomorrah to the present-day Las Vegas. ("What happens in Vegas, stays in Vegas.") The anonymity afforded by these sin cities allows individuals, so inclined, to follow the dictates of their hormones free from the watchful gaze of society, which otherwise acts to keep such urges in check, lest the transgressor be subjected to public humiliation. Throughout time, public humiliation has taken many forms, from being forced to wear the scarlet letter "A" to being placed in the stocks in the village square. Societal pressure to adhere to the moral code has decreased substantially since the middle of the last century. Consequentially, adultery is a widespread phenomenon in our society today. According to *The Janus Report on Sexual Behavior,* more than a third of men and a quarter of women admit to having had at least one extramarital sexual experience (*Probe Ministries—Adultery, www.probe. org/content/view/13/72/*).

Today the Internet allows individuals to view and share pornography and sexually charged correspondences from the anonymity and safety of one's home, seemingly free from the watchful gaze of one's community. No longer kept in check by the fear of public humiliation, Internet users have created hedonistic cybercommunities (virtual sin cities), where they are free to act out their every fantasy. Unfortunately, this sexual freedom enjoyed on the Internet is for many people addictive and all-encompassing and leads to the disruption of their marriages.

With the rise in the popularity and availability of high-speed Internet service in the home, the number of marriages disrupted by spousal Internet extramarital sexual activity has risen proportionately. In 2004, nearly 75 percent of households in the United States had access to the Internet and 54 percent had broadband Internet services, and that number is growing steadily as the competition between phone companies and cable service providers drives down the cost of broadband Internet access. Among households with incomes of $100,000 or greater, 95 percent have computers and 92 percent have broadband access to the Internet. High speed Internet access allows for nearly real-time multimedia content, such as music and video. The Internet with its vast multimedia content has become the primary milieu of Western popular culture, so it is natural that pornography and sex trade have migrated from traditional print, movies, and red light districts to the Internet.

There are three major categories of Web sites that figure prominently in domestic relations investigations. Traditional pornography sites are basically the adaptation of pornographic print media and motion pictures to the Internet. These sites offer static content, generally in the form of digital photographs and digital movies. Pornography sites, based upon the nature of their content, range from relatively

(Continued)

tame photographic sites, hosted by the publishers of traditional gentlemen's magazines (e.g., *Playboy*, *Penthouse*, and *Hustler*), to extremely hardcore video sites featuring every imaginable form of video content created expressly to appeal to the various prurient sexual interests of the viewers.

Interactive pornography sites are an adaptation of the red light district peep show to the Net using webcams and interactive video conferencing software to allow pornographic models to perform a personalized sex show for Internet viewers who direct the interactive performance by sending messages to the models in real time. As with traditional peep shows, viewers pay a fee for these performances based on how long they watch. In both types of pornography Web sites, there is no expectation that the viewer will actually meet or form a relationship with the models. Payment is made solely to view the content for an immediate voyeuristic experience. Use of these pornographic Web sites will generally leave numerous pornographic images and HTML files containing obscene sexual language on the viewer's hard drive.

In the third type of sexual Web site, often referred to as Internet Dating Web sites, the goal is to meet with potential sexual partners online with the possibility of continuing the relationship in the real world. These Web sites are generally based around a database containing the personal profiles and photographs of the members of the Web site's cybercommunity. Members can use the Web site's database to search for potential mates based on various physical and psychosexual characteristics and their geographical location. These Web sites allow members to anonymously contact and correspond with the potential mates located with the help of the database search. These correspondences can take the form of anonymous e-mails, instant messages, or chats within online chat rooms hosted by the dating Web site. There are a myriad of dating sites on the Internet, varying by the nature of the relationship desired. eHarmony.com, True.com, Adultfriendfinder.com, and Match.com are generally aimed at those looking for serious dating relationships, although unscrupulous users will frequently use these sites with the hopes of finding casual sex partners. All of these "relationship" dating Web sites will leave large numbers of member photos on the hard drive. These photos are generally easy-to-spot thumbnail-sized "head and shoulder" shots. Often HTML files containing the e-mails and chats associated with the use of these Web sites can be found on the users' hard drives. Alt.com is a dating Web site aimed at those looking for S&M, B&D (sadism and masochism, bondage and discipline), and fetish-type sexual experiences. The member photos on Alt.com tend to be more explicit and kinky than those found on the "relationship" dating Web sites. Other dating Web sites, such as HorneyMatches.com and SexMatch.com, are aimed specifically at those wanting casual, often "discrete," sexual liaisons. Generally, anyone whose profile on any of the dating sites states that they are looking for a "discrete" sexual relationship is married and cheating.

"Cybersex" is sex performed in real time using digital medium. In its simplest form, cybersex can be a typed sexual dialog sent between two or more people using instant messages or a chat room. Often this erotic messaging is accompanied by masturbation. Similar sexual activity can be accomplished using a telephone as the means of communications, in which case the activity is called phone sex. With the advent of broadband Internet, video teleconferencing is widely available over the Internet using a personal computer and inexpensive webcams. Many of the dating Web sites now feature the ability to use Webcams to interact with (e.g., see and hear) potential mates in real time. Other webcam video conferencing Web sites and software intended for business applications are being co-opted for the purpose of interactive Internet sexual activity. The Web sites include paltalk.com, CUseeMe.com, and the video chat features in AIM, MSN and Yahoo Instant Messenger. Thus cybersex is no longer confined to the realm of text messages. Another recent development pushing the envelope of interactive sexual activity on the Internet called teledildonics has introduced the use of remotely controlled sex toys into cybersex. One such device named a "sinulator" includes a transmitter, a dildo vibrator, and a receiver. The transmitter connects to the USB port of the computer. The receiver connects to the vibrator. Commands from the cybersex partner are sent via the Internet to the sinulator-equipped computer where (via USB) the transmitter relays the commands via the receiver to the vibrator. The vibrators are controlled using a Web browser and a dashboard-like control panel at the Sinulator.com Web site. There is also a sex toy for men called a fleshlight that can act as a remote controller (in lieu of the dashboard) for the woman's sinulator via the Internet. Thus both cybersex partners can interactively exchange direct genital stimulation via the Internet.

Psychologists have long reported on the emotional damage done to the marriage bond by cybersex. Even when just textual in form, the physiological and emotional effects of cybersex can mimic that of real sex, and cybersex has been cited during divorce trials as the reason for the breakdown of

(Continued)

marriages. This phenomenon has been dubbed in the media as cyberadultery, the new infidelity, and virtual adultery. The courts thus far have just begun to come to terms with cybersex and virtual adultery. In *Yohey* v. *Yohey*, the husband's cybersex encounters with "over a hundred" women, and his admitted sexual affair with a woman he met in an Internet chat room figured prominently in the trial court's award to the wife of what amounted to 86 percent of the marital property. *Yohey* v. *Yohey*, 890 So.2d 160, 163 (Ala. Civ. App., 2004). The division of marital property, even in equitable distribution states, does not necessarily need to be even, as long as it is equitable. Courts look to factors including the length of the marriage, the age and health of the parties, the future earning prospects of the parties, the standard of living that each party is accustomed to, and the fault of the parties contributing to the breakup of the marriage. (See *Golden* v. *Golden*, 681 So.2d 605,608 (Ala. Civ. App. 1996)). The case is increasingly being made in family courts and law school classrooms across the country that cybersex and virtual adultery should be considered as a fault ground for divorce. In her article entitled, "The New Politics of Adultery," Brenda Cossman argues that "the legal definition and the underlying harm of adultery have changed considerably over time, from a narrow concern of illegitimate offspring to a much broader violation of marital emotional intimacy" (Brenda Cossman, *The New Politics of Adultery*, 15 Colum. J. Gender & L. 274, 277). In this new understanding of adultery as a violation of marital intimacy and exclusivity, "[t]he category of infidelity has thus been expanded to include a broad range of both sexual and non-sexual encounters. No longer restricted to 'natural heterosexual intercourse' . . . infidelity is now framed as a violation of the emotional intimacy of marriage" (*Id.* at 281). The new debate is focused squarely on "whether viewing Internet pornography and participating in cybersex constitutes adultery" (*Id.* at 280). Psychologists are now coming forward to warn that cybersex and watching Internet pornography is disrespectful of one's spouse and can cause emotional harm to the marriage. But is that "adultery"? At least one court while declining to equate cybersex with adultery, did find that the shock to one spouse upon discovering the cybersex messages left by the other spouse, whether intentionally left where the other spouse could find them or not, constituted cruelty, another fault ground for divorce in that jurisdiction. The court awarded a disproportionate share of the marital estate to the innocent spouse, thus penalizing the spouse who had engaged in cybersex.

Clearly, in the current legal climate, it is advantageous in any jurisdiction which considers the fault of the parties in determining the division of marital property to employ computer forensics to search for and secure evidence of Internet pornography and cybersexual activity as part of discovery in domestic relations matters.

the card issuer), the theft is completed. Credit identity theft, on the other hand, is limitless and not bound by the amount of cash or credit which is immediately available. Rather, it allows criminals to create additional sources of revenue through the establishment of multiple accounts. As such, this type of criminal activity is increasingly popular. In 2006, the FTC reported that the personal information of 3.2 million Americans was used to open new accounts or loans.[6]

● PREVALENCE AND VICTIMOLOGY

Like other areas of criminal behavior, estimates on the prevalence of identity theft/fraud vary widely. Historically, academics have struggled to develop a valid system of crime measurement. Unfortunately, there are a variety of factors which negatively affect a true measure of crime. These traditional obstacles have included lack of reporting victimization by the public (often attributed to perceptions of apathy), lack of reporting by police to federal agencies, jurisdictional discrepancies in crime measurement, and selective enforcement based on community standards and departmental resources. These characteristics have also been found to affect reporting of identity theft/fraud.

An accounting of the prevalence of identity theft/fraud has been further confounded by additional factors, including:

- delayed notification or awareness of victimization
- the vested interest of private companies to exploit consumer fear
- the lack of mandatory reporting and inconsistent application by federal agencies
- Lack of national standards in measurement

Currently, there are four primary sources of information on identity theft/fraud data: credit reporting agencies; software companies; popular and trade media; and government agencies. The veracity of such sources is intrinsically related to the motivation of the same. Both credit reporting agencies and software companies have a vested interest in the prevalence and danger of identity theft, as both offer products marketed to fearful consumers. As such, it is in their best interests to exaggerate the phenomenon. Government entities, on the other hand, rely on accurate measures to allocate resources, investigate cases, and educate the public. However, the nature and structure of such agencies often thwart the efforts of individual actors and researchers. In fact, exact government figures and statistics are not available due primarily to a lack of mandatory reporting and the criminal multiplicity of the phenomenon. While federal agencies report all crimes by section, they do not report them by their subsection. For example, while the amendments made by the Identity Theft Act are included as subsections (a – (i) f section 1028, Title 18 of the U.S. Code, accounting agencies do not have comprehensive statistics on offenses charged specifically under that subsection.[7] In addition, identity theft is usually a component of another crime. Thus, reporting of that criminal act may be housed under a different section altogether. However, recent years have seen various attempts at encapsulating the general prevalence, methods, and victims of identity theft/fraud.

The first and most comprehensive study of identity theft was completed by the U.S. General Accounting Office (GAO) in 2002. The study was based on two primary sources of data. The first involved data collected from three national consumer reporting agencies and two payment card associations (i.e., MasterCard and VISA). The second involved information for original interview data from a variety of law enforcement agencies, including, but not limited to, the U.S. Federal Bureau of Investigation, the U.S. Internal Revenue Service, the U.S. Social Security Administration, the U.S. Secret Service, the U.S. Postal Inspection Service, and the Federal Trade Commission. The study revealed that identity theft/fraud was dramatically increasing and was the number-one consumer complaint to the Federal Trade Commission (FTC). More specifically, two credit reporting agencies indicated a 36 percent and 53 percent increase in fraud alerts. (Such alerts, designed to warn creditors that a consumer's personal information may be fraudulently used, encourage creditors to seek additional identity verification.) In addition, calls to the Identity Theft Clearinghouse increased over 500 percent in two years, and losses incurred by MasterCard and Visa increased by 43 percent. Ironically, the study did not find a comparable loss of consumer confidence, as online shopping increased during the study period.

Since GAO's seminal study, other research projects by government agencies have been conducted. In 2004, the Federal Trade Commission released a report that indicated that nearly 5 percent of all respondents had been victims of identity theft in the past year, and 6 percent of Americans had been victimized by thieves misusing their existing credit cards or card numbers. (This amounted to almost 15 million American citizens.) In addition, 12.7 percent of survey participants reported that they had discovered the misuse of their personal information in the past five years. The most common consumer complaint was identity theft. According to victim reports,

- 42 percent involved cases where stolen identity facilitated credit card fraud
- 20 percent involved cases of unauthorized telecommunications or utility services
- 13 percent involved cases of bank fraud
- 9 percent involved cases in which personal information was used for employment purposes
- 7 percent involved cases of fraudulent loans
- 6 percent involved cases involving the procurement of government documents or benefits;
- 19 percent involved other types of identity theft
- 20 percent involved cases where multiple crimes were committed.[8]

They also indicated that identity theft was the most common consumer complaint. They estimated that the total annual cost to individual victims was approximately $5 billion, and the cost to businesses and financial institutions amounted to an additional $47 billion. The cost to law enforcement ranged from $15,000 to $25,000 per case.[9]

It is anticipated that the trends espoused in the FTC's report will continue and that instances of technologically facilitated identity theft will increase both here and abroad. As consumer demand for online banking, communication, and shopping increases, so shall their risk of victimization. Indeed, this move toward a "one-click" society has significant implications for online criminal activity.

Victims and the Costs Associated with Victimization

Just as it is hard to effectively measure the prevalence of identity theft/fraud, it is equally difficult to measure the costs incurred by such criminal activity. Online schemes are particularly insidious as the costs associated with them go far beyond the dollar amount of the actual fraud. Costs are incurred by both the individual victim and the financial institution or lender extending money or credit based on fraudulent identity. Additionally, the loss of consumer confidence may have rippling effects which are immeasurable. Individual victims, for example, may come to doubt the veracity of any unsolicited e-mail, even those that are entirely legitimate or may be unwilling to conduct any future business online. Such doubts may force some organizations to return to traditional methods of communication, including both mass and individual mailings. With the rising costs of postage, this could cost companies millions.

Additional difficulties in estimating costs associated with identity theft/fraud are more direct and may be attributed to the delayed awareness of the victim, a general lack of reporting, the delayed awareness of the victim, and a trend toward statistical aggregation by reporting agencies. Several studies have suggested that the average time between the occurrence of the crime and the victim becoming aware of being victimized was 12 to 14 months.[10] Even in those cases where victims identified their victimization, many victims indicate a reluctance to report their victimization due to a perception that investigative agencies would be apathetic to or are incapable of prosecuting their victimization. Others display a general ignorance as to the identity of the appropriate or applicable agency. Finally, reporting agencies often aggregate their data, reporting them as national trends or statistics. As an example, one report indicated that costs to the American economy in 2007 topped $50 billion, while costs in Britain and Australia were aggregately reported as $3.2 and between $1 and $3 billion, respectively.[11] While such reporting is valuable in certain respects, it often overlooks the costs associated with individual victimization.

Although exact figures of identity theft are impossible, a general profile of the individual victims has been consistent in a variety of studies. Across the globe, Americans are most likely to be targeted and victimized by identity thieves. This has been largely attributed to the fact that Americans are perceived to be wealthier and less suspicious than others, have greater access to the Internet, and are increasingly conducting more personal business online. In addition, the lack of regulation by authorities has left American consumers more vulnerable. Within the United States, white males in their early 40s who lived in metropolitan areas were most likely to be victimized.[12] Seniors were least likely to be victims of identity theft, but were often targeted with specific financial scams. African-Americans were more likely to suffer from non–credit card identity theft, especially theft of telephone and other utility services, and check fraud.[13]

In most cases, the victim did not know or was not acquainted with the perpetrator.[14] On average, individual victims spent $550 and between 30 and 40 hours to repair the immediate harm inflicted.[15] (It must be noted that financial institutions and merchants often bear the brunt of identity theft, as consumers are not responsible for more than $50 in fraudulent credit card charges.) However, the indirect and ongoing costs associated with victimization far surpass those quantifiable. Many victims may experience long-term repercussions, including, but not limited to, harassment from debt collectors, banking problems, loan rejection, utility cutoffs, and maybe even arrest for the perpetrator's other crimes. Thus, the disruption of their daily lives and psychological damages dramatically exceed any financial loss. According to the Identity Theft Resource Center, victims spend an average of 600 hours attempting to remedy the long-term repercussions of identity theft/fraud due to the absence of universal police report![16]

Victims have repeatedly reported difficulty in obtaining a police report which documents that their identity has been compromised or stolen. Such documentation is essential for victims seeking to reclaim their lives and recover their personal and economic stability. Unfortunately, some local agencies are simply too overwhelmed, while others negate the seriousness of the victimization. To combat this, a standardized or universal police report which enables individuals to document their victimization should be developed. This would further enable local law enforcement to file a report and enter the complaint information into the centralized FTC's Identity Theft Data Clearinghouse.

Future Increases

It is anticipated that instance of identity theft/fraud will continue to increase as the globalization of communication and commerce continues. Criminals have successfully thwarted law enforcement initiatives and safety precautions. Fraud alerts placed upon credit reports, for example, are often ignored, and numerous incidents have occurred where additional fraudulent activity is noted even after alerts were in place. Repeat or continuous victimization is made possible due to the lack of cooperation by lenders and consumer reporting agencies. In fact, a U.S. Senate Committee noted that lenders persist in attributing the fraudulent activity to the victims, and credit bureaus are notoriously uncooperative.[17]

As stated, both lenders and the credit industry have often confounded law enforcement by their reluctance to join in the efforts to combat identity theft/fraud. While both have different justifications, they are singularly motivated by capitalism. Although lenders bear the brunt of the financial costs associated with identity theft/fraud, they seem willing to absorb the costs because of the benefits that flow from easily available credit. With lenders competing for consumer dollars, they are unlikely to implement programs which inconvenience or somehow offend potential customers. On the other hand, credit bureaus do not have a consumer base to alienate, as consumers are largely at their mercy. Emerging trends suggest that credit bureaus actually have a disincentive to reduce the damages caused by identity theft/fraud. Some have already created revenue-generating programs designed to "protect" consumers from fraudulent or incorrect entries on their reports. Consumers may purchase such protection for additional fees, and the creation of such services has provided a source of needed revenue, which may offset the losses incurred by the passage of the Fair and Accurate Credit Transactions Act (FACTA) which requires credit reporting agencies to provide free reports to consumers. A further detriment to their cooperation is the fact that existing law does not provide a cause of action against consumer reporting agencies or creditors for reporting erroneous information *unless* it can be demonstrated that the agency or lender acted negligently.

The prevalence of identity theft/fraud is also expected to increase in pace with the increase in the outsourcing of information and services. American and European companies, in particular, are increasingly moving data-keeping operations out of their respective companies due to cheap labor offered in foreign countries. One of the biggest beneficiaries of this trend appears to be India. In the absence of international standards, such practices are inherently risky. In 2006, almost half a million dollars were stolen out of bank accounts at Britain's HSBC. The theft was made possible through the actions of one employee who illegally transferred information to fellow conspirators. American citizens banking at Citibank were similarly victimized to the tune of $350K. Unless a prohibition of foreign outsourcing is passed, the victimization of Americans is expected to continue.

● PHYSICAL METHODS OF IDENTITY THEFT

Now that we know the prevalence and victimology of identity theft/fraud, it is important to discuss how it is committed. Although the methodology employed by criminals is limited only to their individual imagination, there are two broad categories of techniques: physical and virtual. Irrespective of media hype, the vast majority of identity theft/fraud is perpetrated via traditional, non-Internet methods. In fact, estimates indicate that only 9 percent to 11 percent of identity theft/fraud is attributable to Internet usage. However, that number is expected to significantly increase as the United States moves to a paperless society.

As stated, the majority of identity theft/fraud is facilitated by the theft or requisition of information through traditional methods. In fact, many individuals are cautious to protect themselves from victimization by avoiding Internet banking or online shopping, yet avoid taking similar precautions in the physical world. Anyone can be a victim of identity theft, even if they have never used a computer. The theft of information is not always accomplished through the physical theft or removal of its container. Individuals who have been granted a position or level of trust by an individual or entity (e.g., babysitters, friends, and maids) may have legitimate access to premises housing such information. Other non-technical methods include theft, social engineering, and shoulder surfing. (Some of these methods were discussed in the previous chapter. Thus, they will not be included here.)

Mail Theft

Although it is hard to identify which method of identity theft/fraud is most commonly employed, the theft of information from physical mailboxes is certainly one of the most common. Unfortunately, numerous documents containing personal and financial information is deposited in unlocked containers on the side of the road until it is retrieved. Often times, such retrieval is conducted by someone other than the intended recipient and is used to generate illicit profit or to facilitate criminal activities. Physical mailboxes can contain a plethora of valuable information. Even as the government cautions citizens to take measures to protect their personal and financial information, they themselves are delivering government identification documents through U.S. Mail. Many times, they even mail breeder documents. This includes, but is not limited to, driver's licenses, passports, and financial statements from the U.S. Social Security Administration—one of the very agencies tasked with the investigation and prosecution of identity theft!! Nongovernment-issued valuable documents include credit card applications, bank statements, insurance cards, tax information, and so on. Birth certificates and death records ordered online might also be delivered in this way.

Although some thieves randomly target mail boxes, others target those whose red flag signals outgoing mail. This technique, known as **popcorning**, often scores credit card numbers and banking information. Ironically, credit card companies are no longer including the entire card number on statements, but consumers are providing the number on their payment. Thus, a thief can obtain a credit card number, checking information and other personal information from an outgoing payment. This is often sufficient for them to get started. However, thieves who are more patient may continue to monitor the box for additional information. Accordingly, the U.S. Postal Service and security experts suggest that outgoing mail should be taken directly to the post office or placed in U.S. Postal Service

Some Instances of Compromised Data

Date	Institution	Type of Breach	Number of Victims
2/2005	Choicepoint	Bogus accounts by ID thieves	145,000
4/2005	Ameritrade	Loss of tapes	200,000
5/2005	Time Warner	Loss of tapes	600,000
6/2005	Citifinancial	Loss of tapes	3,900,000
6/2005	CardSystem Solutions	Hacking	40,000,000
4/2005	Wachovia, Bank of America, PNC Financial Services Group	Dishonest insiders	676,000
4/2005	Georgia DMV	Dishonest insiders	465,000
5/2006	American Red Cross	Dishonest insider	1,000,000
5/2006	Equifax	Theft of laptop from private car	2,500
6/2006	ING	Theft of laptop from private home	13,000
6/2006	Union Pacific	Theft of laptop	30,000
6/2006	AIG	Theft of computer server	930,000
6/2006	Denver Election Containing voter records	Theft of a 500 pound cabinet	150,000
6/2006	Ernst & Young	Theft of laptop from private car	243,000
5/2006	Vystar Credit Union	Hacker	34,400

Source: www.privacyrights.org/ar/ChronDataBreaches.htm.

depositories. In addition, many experts urge consumers to invest in a post office box.

Dumpster Diving

As the name implies, dumpster diving is the practice of sifting through commercial or residential trash or waste for information deemed valuable. Such information ranges widely, but may include account numbers, social security or tax payer identification numbers, and passwords. It may be located on discarded computer media or in paper form and may be housed in personnel records, accounting spreadsheets, receipts, invoices, or the like. Fortunately, both consumers and businesses have increasingly taken measures to prevent the

Case in Point—Mail Theft

Three individuals, including two Navy sailors, were charged in an identity theft scheme in which they stole credit card statements, checks, and other personal documents from mail receptacles in Norfolk. Using the information they collected, the men manipulated bank employees, transferring and withdrawing cash from the victims' accounts.

Both seamen were naturalized citizens from Sierra Leone and Nigeria misuse of discarded information. Many now employ paper shredders and disk-wiping software. However, many do not.

Diving for information has been practiced by criminals and law enforcement alike. Early hackers found the trash to be especially helpful toward their exploitation of computer vulnerabilities. Passwords, computer systems, and software could be located there. In addition, company directories or personnel records facilitated further information collection via social engineering. Law enforcement authorities have also engaged in the practice to identify evidence of criminal behavior, both to further the development of probable cause and for courtroom introduction. In fact, trash depositories have yielded a plethora of criminal evidence over the years, both circumstantial and direct. Murder weapons, corpses, incriminating correspondence, bookmaking spreadsheets, and even narcotics have all been found by dumpster diving. (Historically, government agents routinely searched the trash of organized crime figures. However, the practice is no longer effective as criminal syndicates often exchange their trash with private citizens.) Government agents have also covertly employed the practice to gather intelligence on both foreign and domestic enemies. While some individuals suggest that dumpster diving is becoming obsolete, there is no evidence to support that.

Although many individuals are becoming more aware of it and employing preventive measures, there are still millions who do not.

Theft of Computers

Physical theft of computers is among the most common techniques employed by identity thieves, as it alleviates the need to analyze and organize voluminous paper documents. As the majority of individuals necessarily store personal information on their computer, identity fraudsters are all but guaranteed a score. Even those individuals without technical expertise recognize that the computer as a warehouse of information has significant value on the black market, even if they themselves are incapable of retrieving the data. Areas vulnerable to such activity are limited only by the criminal mind. In fact, a careful recounting of all thefts in history is not necessary to note that few, if any, locations have proven impregnable to a determined criminal. Areas particularly vulnerable to theft of computers, however, have included private residences or buildings, public transit or commercial transport (especially airports), lodging, recreation centers, and government offices. Unfortunately, there have been numerous cases in which computers have been stolen from government employees and others employed in capacities involving storage of personal information.

Case in Point—Dumpster Diving

In December of 2006, David Dright was arrested and charged with 27 counts of identity theft. He obtained the personal information used in his fraud from dumpster diving in a variety of locations, focusing on the trash receptacles of large businesses. Files found at his home contained personal information on a variety of individuals, including 91 players of Major League Baseball (MLB).[18] He had stolen the player information from trash receptacles located outside the offices of Illinois-based SFX Baseball, Inc. Documents included financial statements, investment portfolios, credit reports, and other personal information. Apparently, he was not a baseball fan and did not have an understanding of the value of his find, completely overlooking the significance of NY Mets outfielder Moises Alou and Chicago Cubs Juan Pierre. Instead, he focused on records of deceased children and the elderly. His scam was uncovered when a senior citizen notified the police that he had received a confirmation of credit from a company unknown to him. It remains unclear as to why SFX Baseball, Inc., did not employ commercial shredders to protect their clientele.[19]

Government sources indicate an increase in the numbers of citizens who have had their laptops stolen while traveling. Whether for leisure or business, traveling significantly decreases the level of personal security available to citizens. As such, the criminal element has exploited these vulnerabilities, developing schemes to steal laptops from security conveyor belts, hotel rooms, and restrooms. (They have also used similar tactics to steal or copy government and business and personal identification documents.)

Bag Operations

Another tactic historically utilized by intelligence agents which is currently used by identity thieves and fraudsters is known as a "bag operation," and it involves the surreptitious entry into hotel rooms to steal, photograph, or photocopy documents; steal or copy magnetic media; or download information from laptop computers. Almost routine in many countries, bag operations are typically conducted by the host government's security or intelligence services, frequently with

---

Case in Point—Computer Theft

Private Residences

In late 2006, teenagers Christian Brian Montano and Jesus Alex Pineda were arrested and charged with theft and conspiracy to commit burglary for breaking into a private residence and stealing a variety of items, including a government-issued laptop. Ironically, the theft was random and the defendants did not realize the value of the laptops, until the U.S. Department of Veterans Affairs (VA) publicly announced that it contained personal information on 26.5 million veterans. The laptop was subsequently returned to the VA by an informant after a $50,000 reward was established. According to the VA, the analyst had been taking work home with him on an unauthorized basis for several years.[20]

Motor Vehicles

In December 2006, the personal identification information of 30,000 North Carolina residents was stolen from the private vehicle of an employee for the North Carolina Department of Revenue. Fortunately, the taxpayers were immediately notified in accordance with a newly minted notification law. This was not the case in Florida, when a laptop computer from the Inspector General's Office at the Department of Transportation was stolen out of a government vehicle. The computer contained the unencrypted names, social security numbers, birth dates, and addresses of nearly 133,000 Florida residents.

Business Offices

In November 2006, thieves broke into the Wilkes-Barre Driver License Center in Hanover Township, Pennsylvania, and removed equipment used in the production of driver's licenses and computers containing personal information of

over 11,000 individuals. No arrests have been made, and the investigation is ongoing.

University Buildings

In November 2006, three desktop computers were stolen from the University of Idaho's fundraising office. The information contained on the computers included the social security numbers, names, and addresses of approximately 70,000 students, employees, alumni, and donors.

Airports

Airport security at Brussels International Airport reported that two thieves exploited a contrived delay around the security x-ray machines. The first thief preceded the traveler through the security checkpoint and then loitered around the area where security examines carry-on luggage. When the traveler placed his laptop computer onto the conveyer belt of the x-ray machine, the second thief stepped in front of the traveler and set off the metal detector. With the traveler now delayed, the first thief removed the traveler's laptop from the conveyer belt just after it passed through the x-ray machine and disappeared.[21]

Hotel Rooms

In September 2006, industrial giant General Electric reported that a laptop containing personal information of 50,000 current and former employees had been stolen from a locked hotel room. Although the company suggested that the computer had not been stolen for the information contained therein, they quietly informed affected employees and provided free credit monitoring.[22]

the cooperation of the hotel staff. They are most often committed when guests leave their room. However, there have been cases in which individuals have collected the information while the occupants were sleeping. In most cases, victims remain unaware of their victimization as the scheme is designed to steal information while leaving the physical item in place. Hotel safes and vaults do not enhance the security for individuals, as they are accessible to the foreign intelligence officer through collusion with the hotel.

The advent of mass storage removable media has significantly increased the efficiency of bag operations which target computers. Entire hard drives can be copied while their owner takes a dip in the hotel pool or works out in the hotel gym. Thus, public and private employers are cautioning employees to maintain physical possession of sensitive data at all times during their travels—either by keeping such data on removable media or by simply leaving their laptops at home.[23]

Child Identity Theft

Increasingly, law enforcement authorities are reporting startling numbers of parents stealing their children's identities. Unfortunately, this type of identity theft or fraud is especially difficult to recognize and prosecute. The primary problem, of course, is the delayed identification of the victimization, as credit reports are usually not generated until the first application for credit, which usually occurs after the individual reaches the age of 18. Second, the theft itself is not characterized as either child abuse or exploitation, so the primary investigative agency for children (i.e., child protective or social services) does not maintain regulatory compliance within their purview. And finally, judges do not normally require family perpetrators to provide copies of their children's credit reports to probation or parole officers, so criminals may create alternate identities for themselves for employment, evasion of authorities, and financial gain.

Insiders

Many authorities suggest that corporate and government insiders pose the greatest risk to identity theft. As in other areas of computer crime, motivations vary and the facilitation of fraud is not always intentional. In fact, careless employees account for a large amount of the identity theft in the United States. Such negligence has been committed by both individual employees and corporate divisions. In 2005, for example, Bank of America reported that the personal information of 1.2 million U.S. government employees, including U.S. senators, had been compromised when tapes were lost during shipment. In the same year, CitiGroup reported that UPS had lost the personal financial information of nearly 4 million Citigroup customers.

In addition to lost data, some corporations (and even more individuals) have failed to properly destroy data on discarded equipment. In one notable example, researchers from the Glamorgan University in Wales discovered passwords and user names of various business executives on used drives purchased on a popular auction site. This included sensitive information from companies like financial services firm Skandia; food biotechnology company Monsanto; and Scottish & Newcastle's pub division.[24]

Fraudulent or Fictitious Companies

Recently, a more sophisticated method of identity theft/fraud involves the creation of shell companies. Almost always conducted by an organized

Disgruntled or Former Employees

Disgruntled or former employees have also sought revenge or additional revenue by selling sensitive information to the highest bidder. In 2005, for example, a former AOL employee pleaded guilty to selling 92 million user names and passwords to a spammer.

A Sampling of Breaches at Universities in 2005

Date	Institution	Type of Breach	Possible Number of Victims
3/2005	UC Berkeley	Stolen laptop	98,400
3/2005	Northwestern	Hacker	21,000
4/2005	Tufts University	Hacker	106,000
4/2005	Michigan State	Hacker	40,000
3/2005	Boston College	Hacker	120,000
6/2005	University of Hawaii	Dishonest insiders	150,000
3/2006	Georgia Tech. Authority	Hacker	573,000
4/2006	Ohio University	Hacker	300,000
4/2005	Oklahoma State	Missing laptop	37,000
5/2005	University of Iowa	Hacking	30,000
5/2005	Valdosta State	Hacking	40,000
5/2005	Duke University	Hacking	5,500
6/2005	Kent State	Stolen laptop	1,400
6/2005	UCONN	Hacking	72,000
7/2005	Michigan State	Hacking	27,000
7/2005	USC	Hacking	270,000
7/2005	University of Colorado	Hacking	36,000
8/2005	Sonoma State	Hacking	61,709
8/2005	University of Utah	Hacking	100,000
8/2005	University of North Texas	Hacking	39,000
9/2005	Kent State	Stolen computers	100,000
9/2005	Miami University	Exposed online	21,762
10/2005	Montclair State University	Exposed online	9,100
11/2005	Georgia Tech	Stolen computer	13,000
12/2005	University of San Diego	Hacking	7,800
12/2005	Cornell University	Hacking	900
12/2005	Colorado Tech	Erroneous e-mail containing SSNs and other personal information	1,200

Note: In 2006, breaches were discovered in a variety of educational institutions including, but not limited to, Notre Dame; Old Dominion; University of Northern Iowa; Georgetown University; Vermont State Colleges; University of South Carolina; University of Alaska—Fairbanks; Ohio University (multiple incidents); University of Texas; Purdue; University of Delaware; Sacred Heart University; Florida International University; Miami University; University of Kentucky (multiple incidents); University of Texas—El Paso; Western Illinois University; University of Alabama—Birmingham; San Francisco State University; University of Tennessee; Northwestern; University of Iowa; California Polytechnic State University; Belhaven College; Wichita State University.

ring of criminals, fake companies are established which are engaged in the processing or collection of personal financial information. These fictitious businesses range from debt collection to insurance agents. In a highly visible case, over 145,000 consumers were put at risk by Choicepoint, an Atlanta-based company, which is one of the largest data aggregators and resellers in the country. Among other things, it compiles, stores, and sells information on the vast majority of American adults with over 19 billion records. Their consumer accounts included employers, debt collectors, loan officers, media organizations, law offices, and law enforcement agencies. Through the development of fictitious companies, the thieves hit the Fort Knox of personal information. It is expected that these sorts of practices will increase as data aggregators increase and the demand for information explodes.

Card Skimming and ATM Manipulation and Fraudulent Machines

A more sophisticated method of data theft involves the reading and recording of personal information encoded on the magnetic strip of an ATM or credit card. Once stored, the stolen data is re-coded onto the magnetic strip of a secondary or dummy card. This process, known as card skimming, results in a dummy card, which is a full service credit or debit card indistinguishable from the original while purchasing. While card skimming was traditionally reserved to facilitate credit card fraud, it is increasingly being employed with the collection of other

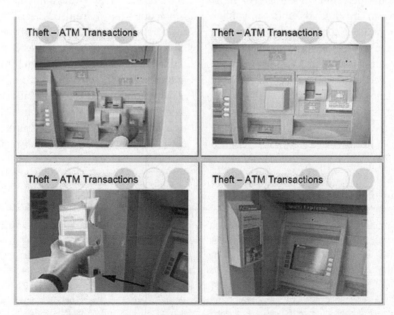

Preparing an ATM for identity theft with a card copier (top photos) and camera (bottom photos)—(*Courtesy of University of Texas at Austin Police Department*).

personal information to create additional accounts. Card *skimmers* come in a variety of shapes and sizes (most often miniaturized cameras or copiers and can be mounted on retail and automated teller machines (ATMs)). In some cases, thieves have actually developed fraudulent ATMs. Thus, consumers are strongly encouraged to only use those machines that are maintained by financial institutions, and to be alert for any suspicious equipment or appendage.

VIRTUAL OR INTERNET FACILITATED METHODS

The majority of identity theft/fraud is still committed via traditional or non-technological methods. However, American consumers still express greater fear of the theft of identifying information via the Internet. This fear has been exacerbated by reports in the media and the prevalence of unsolicited, information-seeking e-mails. It is anticipated that instances of Internet-facilitated identity theft will increase due to the increasing outsourcing of information, increase in consumer shopping and online banking, and increase in commercial globalization.

Although the Internet is currently available to even the most unsophisticated computer user, the structure of the medium is inherently vulnerable. In fact, online identity theft is largely facilitated by weaknesses in a range of Internet standard protocols created before the implications of cybercrime were revealed. Such protocols, like SMTP, were designed in an environment of trust in which early users were like members of a technological elite club. In fact, the World Wide Web was designed not for security but efficiency; protocols like SMTP make validation extremely difficult. However, the masses have trampled traditional gates and barriers, and the perception of trust is no more.[25] Thus, many identity thieves are changing their modus operandi of information collection. Instead of sorting through garbage or discarded documents, thieves may use a variety of hacking methods to collect identification information. Potential targets of such intrusion include both personal computers and information databases, such as those maintained by financial institutions, consumer research groups, government entities, or private corporations. While hacking an individual computer is often the easiest, unauthorized intrusions into large databases provide greater opportunity for exploitation.

Additional benefits deriving from these more sophisticated methods include the reduction of risk, a cloak of anonymity, and a global pool of potential victims. In addition, victimizing someone from another state or even another country may delay both detection and the potential for successful prosecution. So we can see that although identity theft/fraud was present long before the globalization of communication and commerce, the increase in online banking and personal data storage has dramatically affected the prevalence of such criminal activity. Other methods of virtual identity theft are by deceiving naïve users, using malicious software, data repository theft (i.e., government databases), data resellers, and network impersonation.

Case in Point—One Hacker's Success

Although stereotypes of lone hackers downplay their potential dangerousness, the largest case of compromised data suggests otherwise. In September 2004, a hacker employed an SQL injection attack on CardSystems Solutions' Web application and Web site to install hacking programs on computers attached to their network. The programs were designed to collect and transmit magnetic stripe data stored on the network to computers located outside the network every four days. As a result, the hacker obtained unauthorized access to magnetic stripe data (i.e., customer name, card number and expiration date, a security code used to electronically verify that the card was genuine, and other personal information) of over 40 million individuals. As a result, the Federal Trade Commission filed a complaint against the credit authorization firm, alleging violations of the Federal Trade Commission Act.[26]

Phishing

Perhaps the most commonly recognized method of online identity theft/fraud is *phishing*. Phishing means the solicitation of information via e-mail or the culling of individuals to fake Web sites (i.e., those designed to look like a legitimate firm). Phishing often occurs when a potential victim receives a cautioning e-mail from a fraudster which impersonates an Internet service provider, merchant, and/or a financial institution. Such messages contain solicitations for account or personal information. Normally alarming in some manner, requests are made to "update or service an account" or to provide additional information. Between 2004 and 2005, 73 million Americans received an average of 50 fraudulent e-mail messages. Of these, 57 million adults in the United States indicated that they believed that they had received a phishing attack e-mail, while 2.4 million online consumers reported losing money directly because of these attacks.[27]

Phishing is effective because such scams employ scare tactics to encourage quick compliance with the directives contained therein. They inform the victim that an action is necessary to avoid disruption of service. To expedite recipient compliance, they provide a link within the e-mail. Unfortunately, people engaging in phishing are also extremely difficult to prosecute as phishing sites are almost always temporary, and victims are often unaware of their vulnerability and subsequent victimization for years.

Although phishing attacks vary based on characteristics of intended targets, they may be grouped into several broad categories.

- **Spoofing** involves the spoofing of e-mails or Web sites by using company trademarks and logos to appear to represent a legitimate financial institution or Internet service provider (ISP). Such scams use banks and online shopping sites almost exclusively. One study indicated that 30 percent are linked to eBay or Pay-Pal, while approximately 60 percent target U.S. Bank or Citibank.[28]
- **Pharming** is an advanced form of phishing which redirects the connection between an IP address (i.e., consumer seeking legitimate site) and its target serve (i.e., legitimate site). It can be accomplished at the DNS server through either cache poisoning or social engineering; or through the local machine through a Trojan which modifies the host file. This is accomplished when the link is altered so that consumers are unwittingly redirected to a mirror site.[29]
- **Redirectors** are malicious programs which redirect users' network traffic to undesired

---

Case in Point—Fishing and the IRS

In recent years, phishing scams have become increasingly creative as consumers become more cautious. As such, citizens have been inundated with communications appearing to be sent by financial institutions, high schools, and even the Internal Revenue Service (IRS). One phishing fraud has attempted to seduce Americans by suggesting that the IRS has good news for them. After all, who wouldn't click on an IRS link to expedite their refund or, even better, receive an unexpected refund? Two other scams request the submission of specific forms.

- Bogus IRS letter and Form W-8BEN (Certificate of Foreign Status of Beneficial Owner for United States

Tax Withholding) asked non-residents to provide personal information such as account numbers, PINs, mother's maiden name, and passport number. The legitimate IRS Form W-8BEN, which is used by financial institutions to establish appropriate tax withholding for foreign individuals, does not ask for any of this information.
- Form W-9095 (also known as W-8888), an entirely fictitious form, informs the recipient that they have a short period of time to respond in full or will risk losing certain exemptions.

sites. According to the Anti-Phishing Working Group, utilization of traffic redirectors and phishing-based keyloggers is on the increase. They further report that the most common form of malicious code is designed to modify DNS server setting or host files so that either specific or all DNS lookups are directed to a fraudulent server, which replies with "good" answers for most domains.[30]

- **Advance-fee fraud or 419 fraud**—some individuals will willingly divulge personal and financial information to strangers if they believe that a large financial windfall will soon follow. Discussed in more detail in Chapter 6, this fraud is accomplished when an e-mail message is distributed to a victim which asks the recipient for their assistance in claiming "found" money. It comes in a variety of forms and was traditionally committed via the U.S. Postal Service.

- **Phishing Trojans and spyware**—Traditionally, Trojans and other forms of spyware were delivered as executable files attached to e-mails. However, Trojans have become increasingly sophisticated in recent years. (Discussed in more detail below.)

- **Floating windows**—Phishers may place floating windows over the address bars in Web browsers. Although the site appears to be legitimate, it is actually a site designed to steal personal information. Traditionally, potential victims could protect themselves by identifying URL anomalies. However, phishers have become more sophisticated and have developed Javascript replicas that appear to be variations of the legitimate URLs.

Phishing is particularly insidious as the costs associated with phishing scams go far beyond the dollar amount of the eventual fraud. Costs are incurred by both the individual victim and the financial institution or lender extending money or credit based on fraudulent identity. However, the loss of consumer confidence may have rippling effects which are immeasurable. Victims, in particular, may doubt the veracity of any unsolicited e-mail, even those that are entirely legitimate, or may be unwilling to conduct any future business online. Such doubts may force organizations to return to traditional methods of communication, including both mass and individual mailings. With the rising costs of postage, this could cost companies millions.

Spyware—Generally

Consumers often precipitate their own victimization by opening file attachments, downloading free software, screensavers, and songs, or by downloading video clips or images from adult Web sites, unwittingly infecting their computer with spyware. In addition, malicious Active X pop-up dialog boxes are also employed so that criminals can install spyware, adware, or Trojans. In a report prepared by Earthlink and Webroot Software, almost 55 million instances of spyware were identified. Over 26 percent of these were adware and adware cookies, and an additional 20 percent involved Trojans.[31] One particularly nasty form of adware, *CoolWebSearch,* is capable of hijacking homepages, triggering massive pop-ups, changes to browser settings, and self-modification.[32]

Trojans

Trojans and other forms of malware are often referred to as PUPS (potentially unwanted programs), as they are often housed with commercial utilities designed for worthwhile goals like parental control, but which are diverted from their original purpose to commit criminal acts.[33] Trojans come in a variety of forms and include, but are not limited to, keyloggers, backdoors, and password stealers. In fact, discussions of the various forms often overlap as many data-gathering programs are often categorized by their delivery. Originally, most Trojans were delivered via an attachment to an e-mail in the form of an executable file. However, contemporary Trojans are much more insidious as they can be remotely triggered.

Overall Results	Month of March	Month of April	Total (January 1–April 30, 2004)
SpyAudit scans	237,199	420,761	1,483,517
Spyware instances found	7,086,770	11,305,471	40,846,089
Instances of spyware per scanned PC	29.9	26.9	27.5
Spyware Installations on Scanned PCs by Category			
Adware	1,262,078	2,298,201	7,642,556
Adware cookie	5,750,392	8,873,555	32,700,340
System monitor	35,915	60,873	245,432
Trojans	38,385	72,842	257,761[34]

One such Trojan (Backdoor-BAC) was originally released in 2003 by Russian hacker "Corpse." Increasingly sophisticated variants of the Trojan may be purchased online for prices ranging from $200 to $500. While all variants include the creation toolkit, prices increase depending on specifications. With this Trojan, malware authors without much technical knowledge can create their own settings before recompiling the code. The centralized server is called a "blind drop." It usually involves a singular hosting machine with a basic directory structure, which receives the data via a PHP file and then outputs it into log files.[35] Programs of this type attack vulnerabilities in Microsoft's Internet Explorer. Trojans on infected machines capture network information and logins, and wait for the user to browse a Web site that requires authentication. Upon initiation of such activity, the Trojan collects transaction data, such as username and password, and then sends the stolen data to a dedicated host that enters the stolen data into incremental log files.[36]

Keyloggers and Password Stealers

By definition, *keyloggers* are devices or software programs which record the input activity of a computer or system via keystrokes. Depending on the device or software employed, the captured information is either locally stored or remotely sent to the perpetrator. Such devices are designed to capture passwords and other private information.[37] Contemporary keyloggers allow users to view screenshots in addition to keylogging activity. According to a white paper published by McAfee, the number of alerts listed by the Anti-Phishing Working Group multiplied by 100 between January 2004 and May 2006. At the same time, the number of keyloggers has increased by 250 percent since 2004. Although there are various types and brands

Phishing Detection

There are some commercially available programs directed at phishing detection.

- Some ISPs, like Earthlink, offer a downloadable toolbar that alerts a user before they visit a fraudulent site by comparing the URL against the toolbar's list of known fraudulent sites and by analyzing unknown sites for fraudulent tactics.

- Internet security firm WholeSecurity has developed software which detects fraudulent sites by analyzing Web addresses and domain name registration.
- Microsoft's SenderID is a program which validates the sender's server IP address.[38]

Case in Point—Trojans

In May 2006—an international group of cyber-criminals installed Trojans on computers in public places, like cyber-cafés. The unwitting victims, many of whom were American, English, and Canadian tourists, provided the criminals with their banking information. The theft was later uncovered by Standard Bank, who alerted the international banking community.

of keyloggers, they may be dichotomized by their physical composition as either software or hardware devices. Both types are relatively inexpensive for general users, with prices ranging between $20 and $300, depending on specifications. Traditionally, hardware keyloggers were tiny keystroke-recording devices, which were inserted into or attached to the keyboard cable. Currently, USB keyloggers, which closely resemble a typical thumb drive, can be easily attached and removed. Physical keyloggers are undetectable by software, but are visible to knowledgeable individuals—both physically and through the machine's operating system. Software programs, on the other hand, may be detectable by software, but are invisible to victims.

In March 2005, British authorities foiled a scheme to steal over $400 million from the London offices of the Japanese bank Sumitomo Mitsui. Britain's National Hi-Tech Crime Unit (NHTCU) unraveled the scheme when the bank discovered that hackers had compromised their network and installed keyloggers. Yeron Bolondi, an Israeli native, was arrested after he attempted to transfer over $25 million into an Israeli account. It remains unclear as to how the keyloggers were actually installed.[39]

CRIMES FACILITATED BY IDENTITY THEFT/FRAUD

Although the theft of personal data is extremely profitable, its value often lies in the criminal activity facilitated by the data and not in the theft itself. Identity theft is the foundational element on which some criminals and terrorists build illegitimate complex structures. The possession of the commodity in question enables such individuals or entities to remain anonymous, enter private areas, avoid detection and enforcement, and transfer resources (Gordon and Willox, 2003). Criminal activity facilitated by identity theft/fraud is largely a four-phase process:

1. procurement of stolen identifiers
2. a breeder document (e.g., passport, birth certificate, driver's license, and social security card) is created or obtained
3. the breeder document is used to create additional fraudulent documents and solidify an identity
4. the fraudulent identity is employed in the commission of a criminal act

Software Keyloggers	Hardware Devices
Popular programs: Guardian, RemoteSpy, PC Spy, PC Pandora	**Popular brands**: KeyGhost, Keelogger, KeyloggerHRD, SpyBuddy
Cost: Range between $20 and $150	**Cost**: Range between $20 and $300
Advantages: Allows for remote surveillance by e-mailing reports, screen shots, and contextual viewing	**Advantages**: Records every keystroke, including BIOS passwords; undetectable by software
Disadvantages: May be detected by software; initiates after start-up	**Disadvantages**: attached to a local machine; usually reserved for desktops

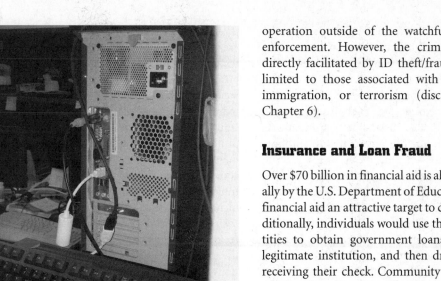

Keyloggers are mechanisms which capture information from installed keylogging devices. Software keyloggers also provide screen-capture features, which users can utilize to view screenshot images of victim activity. Hardware and software keyloggers have varying advantages and disadvantages. Hardware keyloggers can be easily installed and removed. The above photo contains two such devices. One is plugged into the USB port and the other connects the keyboard to the CPU. Both devices were generously donated by KeyGhost (*Dr. Marjie T. Britz Ph.D*).

Crimes facilitated by identity theft/fraud include, but are not limited to, student loan fraud, immigration fraud, social security fraud, insurance fraud, credit card fraud, tax fraud, and various telemarketing and/or Internet scams. They can also indirectly include traditional crimes ranging from auto theft to narcotics/weapons trafficking and organized crime. In fact, criminals can successfully utilize fictitious or fraudulent identities to escape detection or avoid prosecution in almost any criminal activity. Career criminals, for example, also use them to relocate their criminal enterprises or to establish a new base of

operation outside of the watchful eye of law enforcement. However, the crimes which are directly facilitated by ID theft/fraud are largely limited to those associated with fraud, illegal immigration, or terrorism (discussed in the Chapter 6).

Insurance and Loan Fraud

Over $70 billion in financial aid is allocated annually by the U.S. Department of Education, making financial aid an attractive target to criminals. Traditionally, individuals would use their own identities to obtain government loans, enroll in a legitimate institution, and then drop out upon receiving their check. Community colleges were often preferred as the upfront cost of registration and enrollment was generally cheaper—leaving the fraudster with more money. The introduction of distance education or online courses is making this fraud even easier as individuals do not have to physically appear on campus, and they may intentionally enroll in programs out of state to minimize their risks of being exposed. Although direct costs are not available, indirect costs are immeasurable as every penny allocated to fraudsters is money lost to those in need. In fact, every taxpayer is victimized as the monies are rarely recovered. Additional costs associated with those fraudulent loans facilitated by identity theft are borne by the individual victims in terms of loss of time and wages, legal costs to repair their credit (and credibility), and psychological suffering.

College students may be particularly vulnerable to identity theft as a national survey revealed that almost one-half of all college students kept personal financial information in their dorm room, and 31 percent said that their room or a room in their building had been burglarized. In addition, college students are consistently inundated with "pre-approved" credit applications, as lenders attempt to create longstanding relationships with potential consumers as soon as they are legally responsible.[40] In 2003, John Christensen was arrested for using 43 stolen identities to fraudulently obtain $316K in student loans.

Insurance fraud is another area which has been characterized by an increase in scams facilitated by identity theft/fraud. On the low end of the spectrum, some individuals procure a victim's personal information to obtain "free" (i.e., billed to another) medical care. Such fraud is often practiced by illegal aliens and petty criminals. As it does not bring significant economic gratification, sophisticated criminals employ the practice for other reasons. Their scams require the collusion of others, usually insiders. These thieves fraudulently obtain medical identification numbers to submit claims for "phantom" (i.e., nonexistent) treatment. Such information is often obtained by dumpster diving, burglary, hacking, or the corruption of employees. The costs to victims include insurmountable medical bills, damage to credit, elimination of health benefits, increased premiums, denial of health coverage or life insurance due to fraudulent medical history, and improper treatment.

Immigration Fraud and Border Crossings

Immigration fraud varies by dynamics, methods, and motivations. It may be conducted by either individuals or criminal organizations to secure border crossing, obtain immigration benefits, or further terrorist activity. Irrespective of type or motivation, immigration fraud poses a severe threat to national security because it inherently creates a vulnerability that enables criminals and terrorists to gain entry into and remain within the borders of the United States. Immigration fraud facilitated by identity theft is a component of many immigration-related issues such as human smuggling and trafficking, critical infrastructure protection, worksite and compliance enforcement, and national security investigations. Such activity is often commingled with other types of fraud involving government-issued licenses and identification, state-issued public assistance, and social security fraud. The federal government has created the Identity and Benefit Fraud Unit under the umbrella of the U.S. Customs and Immigration Enforcement Agency to coordinate the efforts of other federal agencies investigating this type of activity.[41]

Immigration benefit fraud involves the willful misrepresentation of material fact on a petition or application to secure an immigration benefit. It may prove quite lucrative to perpetrators and often involves sophisticated schemes with multiple co-conspirators. Fraudulent documents which have been used to obtain immigration benefits include traditional breeder documents, work permits, documentation of residency, green cards, etc. Such documentation was traditionally precipitated by the trafficking of lost or stolen passports. However, the most recent surge in immigration-benefit fraud may be partially

---

Case in Point—Insurance Fraud, Evading Justice, and a Burning Corpse

In 2005, investigators in Texas notified Molly Daniels that her husband had been killed in a single car accident. Remarkably calm, Daniels was proudly introducing a new live-in boyfriend to friends and family immediately after the accident. Although family members expressed dismay at the widow's behavior, they grudgingly accepted her new arrangement. Investigators, on the other hand, were not so accepting. Conducting DNA analysis on the burnt corpse, they were not entirely surprised to find that the deceased victim was not Clayton Wayne Daniels. In a subsequent search of the Daniels' home computer, investigators discovered a complicated scheme to create a new identity for Clayton, complete with the creation of a fraudulent birth certificate and drivers' license for Molly's new boyfriend, Jacob Alexander Gregg. Apparently, the couple thought that the $110,000 death benefit from an insurance policy would allow them to start a new life where Clayton would not have to face charges of sexual assault. Unfortunately for them, the insurance policy never paid out, Clayton went to jail anyway, and Molly is serving 20 years in a Texas prison.

Case in Point—Immigration Fraud

In December 2006, agents from U.S. Immigration and Customs Enforcement executed search warrants on meatpacking plants in six states. The raids came after an 11-month investigation into misuse of social security numbers and benefit fraud. Activities culminated in the arrest of almost 300 employees of Swift & Company, the world's second largest meat processing plant. Initial charges included false representation of social security number, aggravated identity theft, fraud of immigration documentation, and false representation of U.S. citizenship. In addition, some of the individuals were charged with illegal re-entry after deportation. In January 2007, 53 of the individuals were indicted by federal grand jury on various counts of aggravated identity theft. The remaining 242 individuals were deported. (Only the most serious offenders were indicted due to system considerations.)

attributed to the Visa Waiver Pilot Program (VWPP), which eliminates the traditional requirement of passports for nationals from selected countries. The surge may also be attributed to an emerging method (i.e., the fraudulent representation of U.S. employment for aliens). Characterized as the new wave in alien smuggling, successful criminal entrepreneurs are enhancing and streamlining their illicit services through the creation of fictitious companies for which aliens ostensibly work.[42] Unfortunately, due to its multilayered nature and multi-jurisdictional approach, it is extremely difficult to investigate and prosecute.

Although the false representation of U.S. citizenship for immigration benefits costs the federal government countless dollars, there are far more serious possibilities. It has been well documented that at least seven of the hijackers in the terror attacks of 9/11 had obtained state-issued (Virginia) identification documents through the use of fraudulent breeder documents. Such documents were used to enter the country, board the aircraft, and clear airport security. Unfortunately, recent studies indicate that our borders remain largely unsecured (see below).

Fraudulent identification used to facilitate terrorist activity plagues other members of the international community. According to the French Minister of Justice, the most frequent terrorist offenses encountered in French legal investigations include the falsification of administrative documents, forgery, transport and

How Successful Are We in Identifying Fraudulent Documents at Border Crossings

On August 2, 2006, Gregory D. Kutz, managing director of Forensics Audits and Special Investigations for the U.S. Government Accountability Office testified before Congress regarding the state of border security. His statement, which follows, indicates that the United States continues to have significant weaknesses in border screenings.

To perform our 2006 follow-up investigation, we created a fictitious driver's license and birth certificate with the same name that we used in the tests conducted for the work we did in 2003. We also created another fictitious license and birth certificate. To create all these documents, we used commercial software that is available to the public. As agreed with your offices, we chose to test a no-representative selection of nine land crossings at both the northern and southern borders . . . We conducted our work from February 2006 through June 2006 in accordance with the President's Council on Integrity and Efficiency Quality Standards for Investigations. Agents successfully entered the United States using fictitious driver's licenses and other bogus documentation through nine land ports of entry on the northern and southern borders. CBP officers never questioned the authenticity of the counterfeit documents presented at any of the nine crossings. On three occasions . . . agents crossed the border on foot. At two of these locations . . . CBP allowed the agents entry into the United States without asking for or inspecting any identification documents.[43]

concealment of counterfeit stamps, and the trafficking in stolen passports.[44] A further study commissioned by the French Senate reported that professional forgers were supplying both the criminal community and terrorist networks with fake or fraudulent identity documents. One case study included in the report involved individuals who were convicted of criminal conspiracy in relation to a terrorist group, concealment of administrative documents, possession of false administrative documents, and concealment of counterfeit stamps. At the time of their arrest, the pair had 30 French passports, 60 revenue stamps, and 60 laminated films bearing the initials "RF" (for *Republique Francaise* or the French Republic) in their possession. Subsequent investigation revealed that their logistical activities were linked to a radical Islamic faction, and the documents were intended for groups in Afghanistan and Pakistan. Thus, document fraud provides the mechanism for terrorist activity across the globe. It is anticipated that this sort of behavior will increase in pace with online identity theft.

CONCLUSIONS AND RECOMMENDATIONS

As the globalization of commerce and communication increases, it is anticipated that the methodology of identity theft will become increasingly sophisticated. This could pose significant challenges to law enforcement authorities and signal increased public vulnerability. First, identity theft is often characterized by either excessive delays or the entire absence of detection. In fact, many victims do not realize that they have been victimized until they are denied credit, receive court summons, or, in extreme cases, arrested. Second, law enforcement agencies have historically lacked the resources necessary for the continuous training and equipment upgrades required to effectively investigate computer-related criminal activity. As non-violent crimes are not perceived as

seriously as those that are violent, administrators have demonstrated reluctance to allocate funds toward this end. Third, even in those rare agencies where resources and administrator apathy are not a problem, jurisdictional questions often confound local authorities. Because online identity theft is inherently multi-jurisdictional, local authorities (and community residents) often believe that they are powerless. Fourth, there is currently no centralized information system that provides for specific tracking of identity theft cases. This is exacerbated by the absence of mandatory reporting, and the myriad of criminal codes applicable to activities facilitated by identity theft (i.e., crimes committed via the theft of information may be classified and prosecuted under traditional statutes like fraud, terrorism, etc.). Fifth, American citizens often prove easy targets due to our reliance on social security numbers as a sole or primary means of identity authentication. Such ubiquitous use makes them widely available. Finally, and perhaps most importantly, both investigators and citizens are adversely affected by the lack of cooperation displayed by financial institutions. Thus, future legislation must address each of these concerns independently and comprehensively.

In the past decade, state and federal authorities have passed numerous laws directed at identity theft and the crimes associated with it. By 2006, for example, 25 state laws were passed, and 34 bills were introduced in the U.S. Congress that specifically targeted this sort of criminal behavior. However, the content and scope of such legislation varies widely. While some laws include civil remedies for victims, others do not. While some laws include penalty enhancements for multiple victims, others do not. Such disparities further complicate jurisdictional questions and decrease the effectiveness of legislation. Thus, it is essential that standardized legislation which effectively delineates jurisdiction and reduces the amount of vulnerable data be enacted. It must be noted that increased government regulation and oversight has proven to be controversial and criticized by

Educating the Public—Protect Yourself

Although it is virtually impossible to completely safeguard belongings and identity from dedicated criminals, educating the community on the following precautionary measures results in a more secure community and enhanced public perception. As a general rule, consumers should be encouraged to engage in privacy self-defense, taking precautions to safeguard their most valuable asset—their identity.

- **Physical World**
  - Use common sense.
  - Guard personal information and mail. Do not divulge any personal information with businesses unless it is absolutely necessary. Do not complete warranty registrations, consumer surveys, and so on. If possible, avoid retailers which require a "loyalty card" for discounts.
  - Whenever possible, pay in cash
  - Regularly monitor your credit and financial accounts
  - Reduce unnecessary personal information in your belongings (i.e., only carry essentials documentation)
  - Shred, shred, shred—good mantra to live by—you can never shred too much.
  - Minimize unsolicited credit offers by choosing to opt out
  - Register phone numbers with the FTC's Do-Not-Call Registry.
- **Online World**
  - Don't take the bait! Ignore the fancy bait, and stay away from phishers.
  - Never use links included in e-mails. Type the address yourself.
  - Install and regularly update security software, including anti-virus, anti-spyware, and firewalls.
  - Know your buddies—never IM, text, or e-mail a stranger.
  - Wipe or destroy drives completely before disposal.
  - Use strong passwords.
  - Refrain from sharing personal information via technology.

the business community. However, future legislation aimed at the reduction of identity theft/fraud should, at a minimum,

1. Expand the definition of personal identifying information to include both general information (i.e., name, address, SSN, etc.) AND unique biometric data (inclusion of the latter would assure the statute's continuing legal viability as technology evolves)
2. Establish a central repository of vital statistics (i.e., drivers' licenses, birth and death records, property and tax information, etc.)
3. Develop alternate means of identity authentication
4. Prohibit the exportation of personal information to foreign countries
5. Provide victims with the ability to petition the court for a finding of factual innocence
6. Provide for consumer-initiated credit "freezes" or "blocks"
7. Restrict access to or publication of social security numbers
8. Ban the sale of social security numbers
9. Require the oversight of data-selling companies
10. Require enhanced identity authentication practices
11. Develop a standardized police report
12. Develop civil remedies and criminal penalties directly proportionate to the loss suffered
13. Provide civil remedies for victims
14. Develop incentives for businesses, financial institutions, and consumer reporting agencies
15. Hold credit reporting agencies and lenders responsible for their mistakes (i.e., make lenders who choose to eschew identity verification policies financially accountable to individual victims (including all costs associated with the victimization))
16. Provide for ongoing funding for research, enforcement, and public education ID theft/fraud

17. Mandate incident report
18. Create a centralized incident database

The creation of appropriate legislation is essential to reduce the occurrences of identity theft/fraud. Without international cooperation, however, its effectiveness will be severely curtailed. Development and compliance of international standards and cooperation must be sought. Coupled with public education and the creation of alternate means of identity authentication, these methods could significantly alter the technological criminal landscape.

DISCUSSION QUESTIONS

1. Name and briefly discuss the broad categories that phishing is split into.
2. Criminal activity facilitated by identity theft/fraud is largely a four-phase process. Discuss and give examples of each.
3. Bring out the contrast between identity theft and identity fraud
4. Briefly describe each of the physical methods of identity theft.
5. Identity theft and fraud attract many different kinds of crime. Discuss the crimes that are included in the text and list anymore that you can think of.
6. The text describes the difficulty in estimating the cost of victimization of identity theft/fraud; explore these causes and discuss the lack of reporting issue in depth.

RECOMMENDED READING

- Lynch, Jennifer (2005). "Identity Theft in Cyberspace: Crime Control Methods and Their Effectiveness in Combating Phishing Attacks." *Berkeley Technology Law Journal, 20*(1): 259.
- President's Identity Theft Task Force (2007). *Combating Identity Theft: A Strategic Plan.* Available at *http://www.idtheft.gov/reports/StrategicPlan.pdf.*

WEB RESOURCES

- www.irs.gov – the homepage of the Internal Revenue Service. By utilizing the site's search tool, users may access multiple documents, publications, and resources regarding various identity theft topics,

including current scams, consumer alerts, reporting, prevalence, and the like.
- www.earthlink.net/spyaudit/press – a complete report of the state of spyware.
- www.antiphishing.org – Homepage of the Anti-Phishing Working Group, the global pan-industrial and law enforcement association focused on eliminating the fraud and identity theft that result from phishing, pharming, and e-mail spoofing of all types. The site provides links to various reports on identity theft, phishing, pharming, organized crime, and so on.
- www.consumer.gov/idtheft – Maintained by the Federal Trade Commission, the Web site serves as a one-stop national resource to learn about the crime of identity theft. The site provides consumers and businesses with detailed information necessary to deter, detect, and defend against identity theft. Provides links to other government agencies, resources, and publications.
- www.mcafee.com – official homepage of McAfee, the leading manufacturer of security and anti-virus software. The site provides access to various articles on emerging trends in computer crime, malware, and enforcement efforts. The site also provides information on current virus alerts and provides links to other organizations and agencies involved in computer security.
- www.antiphishing.org – official homepage of the Anti-Phishing Working Group, which is an international effort which unites pan-industrial and law enforcement interests in a forum accessible and digestible to the public. It publishes monthly reports on phishing and other topics.

ENDNOTES

[1] DOJ (2006). *Fact Sheet: The Work of the President's Identity Theft Task Force.* September 19, 2006. Available at *www.usdoj.gov.*
[2] Paget, Francois (2007). "Identity Theft." *White Paper,* January. McAfee. Available at *www.mcafee.com/us/local_content/white_papers/wp_id_theft_en.pdf.* Retrieved from the Internet on August 8, 2007.
[3] Gordon, Gary R. and Willox, Norman A. (2003). *Identity Fraud: A Critical National and Global Threat: A Joint Project of the Economic Crime Institute of Utica College and LexisNexis, a Division of Reed Elsevier Inc.* Utica, NY: Economic Crime Institute.
[4] GAO (2002). *Identity Fraud: Prevalence and Links to Alien Illegal Activities.* Before the Subcommittee on Crime, Terrorism and Homeland Security and the Subcommittee on Immigration, Border Security, and Claims, Committee on the Judiciary, House of Representatives. United States General

Accounting Office. Available at *http://www.consumer.gov/ idtheft/pdf/gao-d02830t.pdf* (last accessed on May 5, 2007).

[5]Perl, Michael W. (2003). "It's Not Always about the Money: Why the State Identity Theft Laws Fail to Adequately Address Criminal Record Identity Theft." *Journal of Criminal Law and Criminology, 94*(1): 169–208.

[6]FTC (2007). Available at *http://www.ftc.gov/bcp/edu/ microsites/idtheft/reference-desk/reports-2006–2007.html.* Retrieved from the Internet on August 21, 2007.

[7]GAO (2002). *Identity Theft: Prevalence and Cost Appear to be Growing.* Report to Congressional Requesters. United States General Accounting Office. Available at *http://www.gao.gov/ new.items/d02363.pdf.* Retrieved from the Internet on August 18, 2007.

[8]Gordon. and Willox (2003). *Identity Fraud.*

[9]Newman, Graeme R. (2004). "Identity Theft." Problem-Oriented Guides for Police: Problem Specific Guides Series, 25. Available at *www.cops.usdoj.gov.*

[10]Allison, Stuart F.H.; Schuck, Amie M.; and Lersch, Kim Michelle (2004). "Exploring the Crime of Identity Theft: Prevalence, Clearance Rates, and Victim/Offender Characteristics." *Journal of Criminal Justice, 33*(19–29).

[11]Paget (2007). "Identity Theft."

[12]Newman (2004). "Identity Theft."

[13]Federal Trade Commission (2003). *Identity Theft Report.* Available at *www.ftc.gov/reports/index.htm.* Retrieved from the Internet on August 9, 2007.

[14]Allison et al. (2004). Exploring the Crime of Identity Theft.

[15]Ibid.

[16]Newman (2004). "Identity Theft."

[17]Sovern, Jeff (2004). "Stopping Identity Theft." *The Journal of Consumer Affairs, 38*(2): 233–243.

[18]Main, Frank (2006). Major League Dumpster Diver: Man Stole Players' Financial Data from Dumpster. *Chicago Sun-Times,* December 21, 2006. Available at *http://findarticles.com/ p/articles/mi_qn4155/is_20061221/ai_n17073966.* Retrieved from the Internet on 22 August 2007.

[19]Wischnowsky, Dave (2006). ID Theft Hits Big Leagues. *Chicago Sun-Times,* December 21, 2006. Available at *http://www.chicagotribune.com/news/nationworld/chi-0612210 120dec21,1,2056825.story?coll = chi-newsnationworld-hed.* Retrieved from the Internet on August 21, 2007.

[20]Ferguson, Scott (2006). Two Men Charged with Theft of VA Laptop. *eWeek.com.* Available at *http://www.eweek.com/ article2/0,1895,2000006,00.asp.* Retrieved from the Internet on August 22, 2007.

[21]USDA (2007). *Theft While Traveling.* Available at *http://www.usda.gov/da/pdsd/Security%20Guide/T4travel/ Theft.htm.* Retrieved from the Internet on August 22, 2007.

[22]Consumeraffairs.com (2007). *GE Loses Laptop Left in Hotel Room: 50,000 Employees and Retirees Records at Risk.* Available at

http://www.consumeraffairs.com/news04/2006/09/ge_laptop. html. Retrieved from the Internet on August 22, 2007.

[23]USDA (2007). *Theft While Traveling.*

[24]Hinde, Stephen (2006). "Identity Theft: Theft, Loss and Giveaways." Computer Fraud & Security, May: 18–20.

[25]Marshall, Angus M. and Tompsett, Brian C. (2005). "Identity Theft in an Online World." *Computer Law and Security Report, 21:* 128–137.

[26]United States of America Federal Trade Commission Complaint. *In re the Matter of CardSystems Solutions, Inc., a corporation.* Docket No. C-052–3148. Available at *http://www.ftc.gov/os/caselist/0523148/0523148complaint.pdf.*

[27]Paget (2007). "Identity Theft."

[28]Lynch, Jennifer (2005). "Identity Theft in Cyberspace: Crime Control Methods and Their Effectiveness in Combating Phishing Attacks." *Berkeley Technology Law Journal, 20*(1): 259.

[29]Paget (2007). "Identity Theft."

[30]Ibid.

[31]Earthlink (2004). *Earthlink and Webroot Release Second SpyAudit Report.* Available at *www.earthlink.net/abour/press/ pr_spyAuditReport/.* Retrieved from the Internet on September 5, 2007.

[32]Hinde (2006). "Identity Theft."

[33]Paget (2007). "Identity Theft."

[34]Earthlink (2004). *Earthlink and Webroot Release Second SpyAudit Report.*

[35]Lynch (2005). "Identity Theft in Cyberspace."

[36]Ibid, p. 8.

[37]Ibid.

[38]Ibid.

[39]Keizer, Gregg (2005). Keyloggers Foiled in Attempted $423 Million Bank Heist. *TechWeb.* Available at *http://www.techweb. com/wire/security/159901593.* Retrieved from the Internet on September 15, 2007.

[40]Bradshaw, Jim (2003). *Students Urged to Protect Their Identity.* U.S. Department of Education Press Release, December 11, 2003. Available at *http://www.ed.gov/news/ pressreleases/2003/12/12112003.html.*

[41]ICE (2007). *Protecting National Security and Upholding Public Safety.* Available at *http://www.ice.gov/partners/idbenfraud/ index.htm.*

[42]Gordon and Willox (2003). *Identity Fraud.*

[43]Kutz, Gregory D. (2006). Border Security: Continued Weaknesses in Screening Entrants into the United States. Testimony before the Committee of Finance, U.S. Senate, August 2, 2006. Available at http://finance.senate.gov/hearings/testimony/2005test/080206gk.pdf (last accessed on May 15, 2007).

[44]Paget (2007). Identity Theft.

CHAPTER 6

Terrorism and Organized Crime

Chapter Outline

LEARNING OBJECTIVES

After reading this chapter, you will be able to do the following:

✓ Fully understand the concept of terrorism
✓ Learn the impact of the Internet on terrorism and organized crime
✓ Develop a working knowledge of organized crime
✓ Gain insight into the future direction of organized crime
✓ Recognize and understand the contemporary characteristics of organized crime

KEY TERMS AND CONCEPTS

- carding
- critical data
- critical data threat
- cybergangs
- cyberterrorism
- electronic dead drops
- environmental terrorism

- global jihad movement
- individual terrorism
- labor racketeering
- money laundering
- narcoterrorism
- nationalistic terrorism
- online social networking site

- physical infrastructure
- political-social terrorism
- religious terrorism
- skimming
- state-sponsored terrorism
- terrorism
- tyrannicide

For the United States of America, there will be no forgetting September the 11th. We will remember the fire and ash, the last phone calls, the funerals of the children, and the people of my country will remember those who have plotted against us. We are learning their names. We are coming to know their faces. There is no corner of the Earth, distant or dark enough, to protect them. However long it takes, their hour of justice will come.[1]

In the wake of the 9/11 terror attacks, the government and the American public articulated a resolve to immediately seek out and destroy those enemies, both foreign and domestic, who sought to bring down the fabric of American society. Unfortunately, good intentions, even those attended with dedication and resources, are not always realized so quickly, if at all. In fact, terrorist organizations have increasingly targeted American interests and have maximized their efficiency and effectiveness through online mechanisms. Organized crime groups have employed similar strategies and have become transnational entities. Separately, the heightened sophistication of the groups poses significant challenges to the international law enforcement community. Collaboratively, those challenges may prove insurmountable as relationships between them emerge.

TERRORISM

Terrorism is not a new phenomenon. On the contrary, terrorism has existed since the beginning of civilization. Attacks on legitimate structures have been perpetrated by individuals or groups of all cultures throughout history. Social reactions to such attacks have varied from horror to

In 2001, Osama bin Laden orchestrated the worst recorded terrorist attack committed on American soil. His organization used advanced technology to plan the events and to communicate with the participants. (*[Photographer]/Agence France Presse/Getty Images*)

complacence to support depending upon the perceived legitimacy of such acts. While some terrorists have been publicly executed, others have been deified. In fact, the concept is quite complex and not easily defined. Most often, characterizations and designations of acts against the government vary across the population.

Defining Terrorism

The word "terror" comes from the Latin term *terrere,* which is defined as "to arouse fear." Although individuals and organizations sought to arouse fear in ancient civilizations, the current etymology of the term is probably traced to Robespierre's "the Terror," which immediately followed the French Revolution.[2] Etymological origins aside, no universal definition of terrorism exists. Rather, individual and social definitions are influenced by a variety of characteristics, including individual

politics, ideologies, national original, theology, or organizational agenda. As a result, definitions may vary by region, state, or nation.

According to the United Nations Office on Drugs and Crime, there is no international definition for terrorism.. Although attempted a number of times, consensus among all member states has not been achieved. Below is a sampling of traditional definitions:

- **Government Definitions**
  - **League of Nations Convention** (1937)— *all criminal acts directed against a State and intended or calculated to create a state of terror in the minds of particular persons or a group of persons or the general public.*[3]
  - **UN Resolution Language** (1994)— *criminal acts intended or calculated to provoke a state of terror in the general public, a group of persons or particular persons for political purposes are in any circumstance unjustifiable, whatever the considerations of a political, philosophical, ideological, racial, ethnic, religious or other nature that may be invoked to justify them.*[4]
  - **U.S. Department of Defense** (2007)— *the calculated use of unlawful violence or threat of unlawful violence to inculcate fear; intended to coerce or to intimidate governments or societies in the pursuit of goals that are generally political, religious, or ideological.*[5]
- **Academic Definition**
  - Schmid and Jongman (1998)—*Terrorism is an anxiety-inspiring method of repeated violent action, employed by (semi-) clandestine individual, group or state actors, for idiosyncratic, criminal or political reasons, whereby—in contrast to assassination—the direct targets of violence are not the main targets. The immediate human victims of violence are generally chosen randomly (targets of opportunity) or selectively (representative or symbolic targets) from a target population, and serve as message generators. Threat- and violence-based communication*

processes between terrorist (organization), victims, and main targets are used to manipulate the main target (audience(s)), turning it into a target of terror, a target of demands, or a target of attention, depending on whether intimidation, coercion, or propaganda is primarily sought[6]

○ Tsfati and Weimann (2002)—*an attempt to communicate messages through the use of orchestrated violence*[7]

Perhaps it is not the definitions of terrorism which are lacking, but the approach taken by individuals or entities driven to reduce the phenomena to a concise, flowing statement. Like organized crime, terrorism is too complex to be so nicely packaged. Rather, encapsulation of the phenomena requires a listing approach. Thus, **terrorism** is a sum of the following components:

- an act of violence
- the victimization of innocents
- methodical or serial operations
- advance planning
- criminal character
- absence of moral restraints
- political demands
- attempts to garner attention
- performed for an audience
- unpredictability or unexpectedness
- intended to instill fear

Perhaps it is the last characteristic which most clearly sets terrorist acts apart. The incitation of fear is pivotal to the impact or importance of any given action. In other words, it is the defining component by which we distinguish terrorist acts from those which are simply criminal.

Classification Through Motivation

Terrorists and terrorist groups vary widely in their longevity, methodology, sophistication, and commitment. While some groups have shown

Between 1978 and 1995, three people were killed and over 20 were injured in a series of mail bombings targeting universities and airlines. The perpetrator, known as the Unabomber (a shortened version of University–Airline bomber), published a 35,000-word manifesto in the *Washington Post* and the *New York Times*. His diatribe targeted technology, arguing that modern science had ruined the human race. Ironically, the perpetrator, Ted Kaczynski, was a brilliant mathematician who had begun his studies at Harvard in his mid-teens. (*Michael Gallacher/Missoulian/Getty Images, Inc-Liaison*)

great resiliency, others have been extinguished as quickly as they were ignited. Thus, it is impossible to discuss all groups which are, have been, or will be engaging in terrorists acts. Rather, it is more appropriate to discuss the groups collectively by their motivation: **individual, nationalistic, religious, political-social, environmental,** and **state-sponsored.**

- **Individual terrorism**—Individual terrorism is often overlooked in discussions of the phenomenon as there is a collective perception that such individuals have limited impact and do not constitute a significant threat. Such individuals act independently and typically eschew group involvement. Their motivations are as disparate as the individual actor themselves but are largely directed as a discontentment with society in general. Theodore "Ted" Kaczynski (aka the Unabomber) is an example of an individual terrorist.
- **Political-social terrorism**—This type of terrorism is often the most ambiguous as the actors are often characterized by the success of their operations. Theoretically speaking, political-social terrorism is perpetrated by groups which are attempting to accomplish an articulable political agenda. Most often, these groups engage in behavior to overthrow the established order in order to replace it with their own. Depending upon the emergent government, groups which are successful are referred to as *patriots, revolutionaries, heroes, freedom fighters,* or *regimes.* An example of the former might include the early American colonists, while an example of the latter would include Castro's 26th of July Movement. Thus, yesterday's terrorists who are successful are often portrayed as today's heroes. After all, history is written by the victor.
- **Nationalist terrorism**—Nationalistic terrorism is characterized by groups which share a collective perception of oppression or persecution. Generally, these groups maintain some social commonality or group identification (i.e., ethnicity, race, culture, language, or religion). Historically, nationalist groups maintain large memberships and significant longevity due to their ability to recruit on platforms of persecution. These groups include many prominent Arab Palestinian terrorists groups, like HAMAS (Islamic Resistance Movement), Hezbollah, Palestine Islamin Jihad (PIJ), and Palestine Liberation Front (PLF). It also includes the Irish Republican Army (IRA) and the Spanish Basque separatists, Euzkadi Ta Askatasuna (ETA).
- **Environmental terrorism**—Commonly known as *ecoterrorism,* environmental terrorist groups base their ideology on the conservation of natural resources. Some groups also focus on animal rights. In the United States, the first group to engage in violent acts (i.e., arson) was *Earth First!.* However, their actions pale in comparison to later groups, such as the Earth Liberation Front (ELF), which has set fire to commercial properties and private vehicles. One of the most prominent animal rights groups, the Animal Liberation front (ALF), has directed similar efforts at university research centers or industries which engage in activities which exploit or harm animals.
- **State-sponsored terrorism**—Like political terrorism, state-sponsored terrorism is defined by the established order. In today's world, it contains two broad groups of actors: (1) those governments that engage in acts of terror against their own citizens (i.e., Nazi Germany, Bosnia, etc.); (2) those governments who support or carry out terrorist acts against other governments. According to the United States, the governments of Cambodia, Rwanda, and Bosnia are currently engaging in acts of terror against their own citizens, while Cuba, Syria, and Iran

continue to support international terrorist acts against other countries.

- **Religious terrorism**—Perhaps the most prevalent, and certainly the most dangerous, groups of terrorists are motivated by religious ideologies. Historically, these groups have displayed the highest degree of longevity, devotion, and success. Empowered by God and justified by scripture, these groups have waged war and slaughtered innocents—all in the name of religion. Their zealotry blinds them to human suffering, and even the most horrific acts are seen as glorious. Such ideologies are not limited to one particular faith or denomination. Although Islamic groups have garnered the most attention in the past decade, Christian and Jewish groups remain. Some of the groups that are most actively engaged in acts of terror include:
  - **Christian:** Army of God, God's Army, Nagaland Rebels, Phineas Priesthood, National Democratic Front of Bodoland
  - **Judaic:** Kahane Chai, Kach
  - **Islamic:** al Qaeda, HAMAS, Jihad Rite, Turkish Hezbollah, Palestinian Islamic Jihad

Roots of Contemporary Terrorism

Although particularly identifying one group or one act as the first example of terrorism is debatable, it suffices to say that documented cases date back at least as far as the ancient Greek and Roman republics. As contemporary society perceives the murder or assassination of a head of state as an act of terrorism, the murder of Julius Caesar (44 *bc*) might be seen as one of the first documented terrorist acts. However, group terrorism became more common in the Middle Ages. It is believed that the word *assassin,* as a derivative of the Arabic term "hashashin" (i.e., "hash eater"), has its roots in the period when a sectarian group of Muslims were employed to *spread terror in the form of murder and destruction among religious enemies, including women and children.*[8] Early accounts suggest that this group of assassins was particularly feared and were perceived to be more dangerous due to their predilection for hashish. Their legacy impacts the region even today and is evident by the high rate of **narcoterrorism** in the area. (Current groups involved in narcoterrorism include, Revolutionary Armed Forces (FARC) in Columbia, Maoist Sendero Luminoso (Shining Path) in Peru, the Palestinian Liberation Organizations (PLO), Chechens in Russia, Popular Front for the Liberation of Palestine (PFLP) and Hamas, Hezbollah, and the Islamic Jihad.)

Assassination as a concept gained both acceptance and ideological support in areas around the world, especially when political leaders were targeted. *Tyrannicide* became a common practice in Renaissance Italy and was widely advocated in Spain and France during the Age of Absolutism.[9] Its acceptance was largely due to the writings of a Spanish Jesuit scholar, Juan de Mariana. According to the Jesuit, the legitimacy of a ruler was in the hands of the people, not in divine ordination. Indeed, the right of selection lay not with the ruler but with those who are ruled. Thus, the public possessed both the right of rebellion and the remedy of assassination.[10] Since that time, the murders of many political figures has been justified in this manner. In fact, the notion that such actions were unconscionable did not become *en vogue* until after the remaining monarchies had been toppled in the twentieth century.

Contemporary American society has become largely desensitized to violent crime. Some might even argue that the nation is tolerant of violence which is economically motivated or between acquaintances or family. However, it still recoils from random acts of violence and finds attacks on government officials to be abhorrent. Quite simply, American citizens find it difficult to grasp a concept that is alien to a culture in which cash is king. It is this very aspect which makes the United States such a desirable target for terrorists. We are, after all, the best audience for this sort of drama.

Terrorist Groups Designated by the United States Department of State

Abu Nidal Organization (ANO)	Liberation Tigers of Tamil Eelam (LTTE)*
Abu Sayyaf Group (ASG)	Libyan Islamic Fighting Group (LIFG)
Al-Aqsa Martyrs Brigade	Moroccan Islamic Combatant Group (GICM)
Ansar al-Sunna (AS)	Mujahedin-e Khalq Organization (MEK)
Armed Islamic Group (GIA)	Columbian National Liberation Army (ELN)*
Asbat al-Ansar	Palestine Liberation Front (PLF)
Aum Shinrikyo (Aum)	Palestinian Islamic Jihad (PIJ)*
Basque Fatherland and Liberty (ETA)*	Popular Front for the Liberation of Palestine (PFLP)*
Communist Party of Philippines/New People's Army (CPP/NPA)	Popular Front for the Liberation of Palestine-General Command (PFLP-GC)
Continuity Irish Republican Army (CIRA)	Al-Qaeda (AQ)*
Gama'a al-Islamiyya (IG)*	Al-Qaeda in Iraq (AQI)*
HAMAS*	Al-Qaeda in the Islamic Maghreb (AQIM) [Formerly Salafist
Harakat ul-Mujahedin (HUM)	Group for Call and Combat (GSPC)]*
Hezbollah*	Real IRA (RIRA)*
Islamic Jihad Union (IJU)	Revolutionary Armed Forces of Colombia (FARC)
Islamic Movement of Uzbekistan (IMU)	Revolutionary Nuclei (RN)
Jaish-e-Mohammed (JEM)	Revolutionary Organization 17 November
Jemaah Islamiya Organization (JI)	Revolutionary People's Liberation Party/Front (DHKP/C)*
Al-Jihad (AJ)	Shining Path (SL)*
Kahane Chai (Kach)*	United Self-Defense Forces of Colombia (AUC)
Kongra-Gel (KGK/PKK)	
Lashkar e-Tayyiba (LT)	*Note:* *designates an official Web presence
Lashkar i Jhangvi (LJ)	

Terrorism as a Stage

Terrorist attacks are often carefully choreographed to attract the attention of the electronic media and the international press. Taking and holding hostages increases the drama. The hostages themselves often mean nothing to the terrorists. Terrorism is aimed at the people watching, not at the actual victims. Terrorism is a theater. (Jenkins, 1975: 4)

Many theorists argue that terrorism may be characterized as theater—a stage in which the audience is far more important than the actors.[11] Analogizing terrorist acts as stage productions is helpful in discussing the phenomenon. Preplanning activities are consistent with those found in the theater. These include: script preparation, cast selection, set creation, prop development, and stage management.

Producers of the terrorist drama are meticulous in every detail. Once a script has been prepared, the selection of the cast commences. Lead actors are carefully chosen for their fit and their fortitude. Understudies are available for those whose performance is lacking. To ensure the success of the production, dress rehearsals are conducted prior to opening night, and promotion of the event is undertaken. In fact, those orchestrating the final drama are more essential to its success than the actors on the stage. This includes public relations personnel who are tasked with identifying appropriate media outlets (domestic and international), promotion, and serving as a pseudo-liaison between the press and the organization once the production is over. In most cases, Western media is the preferred outlet for postproduction publicity as it is perceived to be more international in scope. Summarily, the physicality of terror is far less important than the emotional or psychological repercussions resulting from the act. This concept is especially important in discussions of the danger of cyberterrorism.

Cyberterrorism as a Concept

Although the 9/11 attacks demonstrated both the hatred directed at and the damage that could be exacted from the United States, scholars and practitioners alike eschew the notion that terrorist acts as a phenomena can be perpetrated via the Internet. Many argue that terrorism requires a display of physical catastrophe or suffering. However, terrorism may be philosophically viewed as a simple act of communication. Like all communications, a terrorist act contains a transmitter, a recipient, a message, and a reaction. The terrorist, serving as the transmitter, communicates a message to his/her target and awaits a reaction. To a terrorist, selection of the recipient of the message is extremely important. It is the audience to the act, not the actual victim, who is the intended recipient, and whose reaction is most critical. The notion that today's generation, largely desensitized to images of mass destruction, would be unaffected by attacks on that medium which is central to their lives is both naive and absurd. In fact, the contemporary prioritization of values is vastly different from that of yesterday. Our entire culture is shifting from the physical to the virtual. Whereas industrialization emphasized physical attributes, the technological world has rejected that. Thus, while twentieth-century terrorism focused on physical violence, a new age might be dawning.

In the rare occurrence when the potential was recognized, traditional definitions of cyberterrorism have concentrated solely on the use of the Internet as an attack mechanism. Only activities such as dissemination of malicious programs or direct attacks on critical structures were included. These definitions grossly misrepresent the reality and potentiality of technology. Contemporary definitions of cyberterrorism must address the totality of the phenomenon, incorporating *any* utilization of Internet-based technology into traditional definitions of terrorism. As such, **cyberterrorism** may be defined as the premeditated, methodological, and ideologically motivated dissemination of information, facilitation of communication, or attack against digital information, computer systems, and/or computer programs which requires advanced planning and is intended to result in social, financial, physical, or psychological harm to noncombatant targets and audiences; or any dissemination of information which is designed to facilitate such actions. In the past decade, the Internet has been employed in a variety of ways

A Note About Hacktivism

A new form of civil disobedience which marries sophisticated hacking methods and the social consciousness of the political activists is known as **hacktivism** or electronic civil disobedience (ECD). This political activism may be likened to traditional sit-ins. It does not include violent or destructive acts. Rather, it involves the peaceful and/or nonviolent breaking of unjust laws. Increasingly, it involves acts which are more symbolic than active.[12] By definition, **hacktivism** is the act of computer trespass to achieve or advance political causes.

Hacktivist groups do not aim to destroy data. Rather, their activities are designed to temporarily block access so that attention is directed to a particular issue. The primary difference between hacking and hacktivism is that hacktivism has a specific purpose which is both ethical and ideological. It is not financially motivated nor is it intended to cause physical harm, severe economic loss, or destruction of critical infrastructures. For the most part, such actions are either motivated by the commodification of the Internet at the hands of corporate engineers or violations of human rights by oppressive governments. Groups which have been involved in such activities include Electronic Disturbance Theater, Cult of the Dead Cow, and the Hong Kong Blondes.

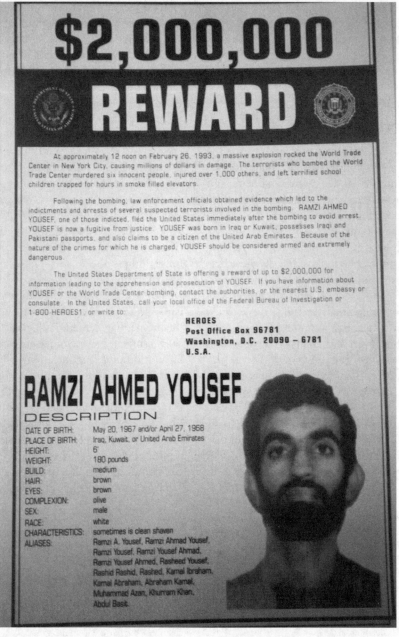

Computers are employed by terrorists in a variety of ways. When Ramzi Yousef was arrested for terrorist activities including the 1993 bombing of the World Trade Center, investigators discovered plans to fly domestic aircrafts into American targets on his laptop. (© Jeffrey Markowitz/Sygma/Corbis)

by terrorist organizations. Such use includes, but is not limited to,

- propaganda, information dissemination, recruiting, and fundraising
- training
- communication
- research and planning
- criminal activities and money laundering
- attack mechanism

TERROR ONLINE

Although achieving a global designation for "terrorist sites" is near impossible, a recent study of official homepages of terrorist organizations and their supporters indicate that terrorist sites have increased both in quantity and in global representation. The past decade has seen a virtual explosion in such sites, from less than 100 to more than 4,800.[13] These numbers, of course, only include obvious sites and do not include the thousands of other sites that are carefully hidden within the vastness of cyberspace. Remember that some groups are reluctant to proclaim a site as their own but will use supporter sites to communicate messages and propagandize rhetoric. Thus, the volume of terrorist-related sites is simply staggering.

According to Tsfati and Weimann, a resurgence in terrorist rhetoric in Europe has led to a marked increase in both the development of European-based terrorist groups and their presence on the Web. These groups have joined traditional groups with roots in South America, East Asia, and the Middle East. Despite geographic origination, it was noted that those groups with an online presence could be characterized as national, revolutionary, or religious movements. Those with criminal or psychotic motives were noticeably absent. It was further noted that the most common content on such sites was general information including organizational history and biographies of group luminaries.[14] Additionally, the majority of sites contained the group's ideology and goals, and the members cast themselves as victims by citing examples of oppressive government actions, the restriction of liberties, and the need for political activism. For example, the Colombian EIN site focuses on the limitations imposed on the freedom of expression and of the press; while groups like FARC argue that citizens are politically detained by oppressive governments.

Propaganda, Information Dissemination, Recruiting, and Fundraising

Terrorists employ the Internet in a variety of ways—both visibly and covertly. While much of the communication, training, planning, and execution of their designs are conducted behind the cloak of invisibility, terrorists also employ the Internet as a tool for propagandizing their ideology. This effectively enables them to spread their rhetoric and recruit members from a global community. For the most part, most political terrorists deliberately avoid flagrant displays of physical attacks or assertions of superiority. Instead, they focus on rationales and justifications for aggressive tactics and characterize themselves as patriots, protectors, or even victims. Thus, propaganda strategies employed by political terrorists seeking broad appeal often fall into one of four categories of justification:

1. **"No choice" justifications**

   In casting themselves as victims, these groups present the government as unjust at best, or evil, at worst. They present themselves as amenable to peaceful solutions and appeal to the masses by arguing that their violent actions are reactionary— the last resort in their campaign for universal principles and humanity. In this way, these groups can justify their actions and appeal to marginalized community members, even those who would abhor violence in any other context. Ironically, many of these groups cite sources like the UN Universal Declaration of Human Rights— a document which attempts to ensure equality for all and eradicate terrorist groups. Thus, their actions may be deemed legitimate, and supporters need not be chagrined or shamed by their contributions.

2. Demonizing and Delegitimization Justifications

In this scenario, organizational members are presented as proverbial dragon slayers or an army of warriors sanctified to serve as protectors of the commoners. Vilifying the government, the organizational rhetoric appeals to the multitude of peasants who are powerless against the faceless monster. For example, Hezbollah sites portray the Israelis as terrorists.

3. Emphasis of Weakness

Similar to previous justifications, some groups justify their actions by arguing that the only weapon available to the weak is terror. Again, online terror sites concentrate on recruitment and propaganda platforms which deny their strength and their violence. Instead, the groups emphasize their own weakness and the vulnerability of the community. While not openly stated, this approach implies that terrorist actions are all that is available in their depleted arsenal.

4. Peaceful, NonViolent Rhetoric

Although few groups employ this online strategy, the Basques and the ELN present themselves as peaceful entities. They superficially proclaim an abhorrence of violence and stress the urgency for a peaceful solution, diplomatic settlement, or internationally induced arrangement.

To further widen their appeal, most political terrorist groups present their online material in various languages. Downplaying the results of their violent acts and making their rhetoric and propaganda available in multiple languages increases the potential for cooperation between multinational individuals and appeals to the international bystander.

Unlike political terrorists, those motivated by religious ideology often openly embrace and promote human suffering. Depicting themselves not as victims but as martyrs, these groups glorify violence as divine ordination. For example, various al Qaeda sites contain images of roadside bombings, the decapitation of American hostage Nick Berg, and the bombing of the World Trade Center. In this way, they are appealing to true believers. While they seek to expand their membership, their recruiting efforts are most often concentrated on inciting religious fanaticism. Such imagery appeals to those seduced into waging *jihad* and reinforces feelings of righteousness. Young people are desensitized to the horror through the use of rap videos and electronic games which glorify the murder of American soldiers.[15] Unfortunately, these groups have also exploited contemporary culture's voyeuristic appetite, successfully utilizing mainstream Web sites like *www.YouTube.com* to showcase their handiwork. It must be noted that such activities and products are not limited to groups from the Middle East. Propaganda videos have also been made by organizations in Chechnya and Bosnia.

Both political and religious terrorists groups use the Internet to raise money for their activities. Monetary contributions are usually facilitated by payment aggregators. Those sites not accepting contributions directly will often direct interested parties to links to "legitimate" (i.e., puppet) organizations accepting donations for the group. Some of these secondary organizations even have online gift shops where individuals can purchase a variety of merchandise from the organization. This online exposure serves to primary purposes. First, it allows the organization to create legitimate sources of revenue. Second, it appeals to arm-chair warriors (i.e., those individuals who never display physical participation in terrorist groups but who feel as if the purchase of political merchandise is equivalent to activism).

Training

In addition to using the Internet to promote their ideologies and rhetoric, terrorist groups are actively using the medium as a training platform. In fact, the possibilities are endless. Just as corporations and organizations with legitimate goals have turned to Web-based training to offset corporate downsizing, terrorist organizations are increasingly utilizing the Web to offer online tutorials.[16] Topics of such Web-based learning may include both traditional and emerging training modules. They are most often presented in the form of films, but training documents, outlines, and checklists are also popular. Traditional topics of such Web-based learning may include bomb building, use of surface-to-air missiles, border jumping, and creating fraudulent identification. One video offered a step-by-step guide in creating a suicide vest and showed the detonation effects associated with it, while others provided instructions on the creation of Claymore mines and other forms of explosive devices. In fact, online training materials are only limited by the imagination of a terrorist organization. If they can think it, they can post it. Some sites even have experts available online to answer questions.

Research and Planning

In addition to disseminating information and training programs to believers, the Internet may also be utilized to *gain* knowledge or information. Critical information such as satellites, military deployments, engineering schematics, and the like are readily available to those knowing where to look. It is entirely possible that the 9/11 terrorists found information including floor plans and design characteristics of the World Trade Center or techniques employed by demolition experts to progressively collapse large structures. Computers seized in Afghanistan have revealed that al Qaeda collected intelligence and sent encrypted messages on targeted locations,[17] and the detailed plans for flying commercial airplanes into American buildings were located in encrypted files on Ramzi

Yousef's computer. A further example of such usage was the discovery by British Army Intelligence of printouts from Google Earth in the possession of insurgents, who used them to pinpoint attacks. Terrorists can also choose from a selection of "how-to" manuals, ranging from bomb-making, to virus creation, to mass poisoning, etc. When French authorities arrested Kaci Warab, they discovered that he had been trained in sophisticated detonation devices at Abu Musab al Zarqawi's camp. One of the designs uncovered involved the use of Web-capable cell phones which could be remotely activated (i.e., detonated) via a Web site. Thus, the possibilities associated with data mining have not been overlooked by terrorist organizations. By mining the billions of online pages, terrorists can collect all information necessary to execute a successful attack of a designated target. Blueprints, executive personnel, schedules, and maintenance information can all be located online. Aerial photographs, vacation videos, and satellite images are all there. In fact, terrorists can obtain more information online than they could if they had visited the site themselves, and the risk of exposure is almost entirely eliminated.

Information necessary for planning purposes may also be collected by data theft or unauthorized access. Personal computers and databases are often equivalent to a digital Fort Knox—a repository of priceless information. Unfortunately, a brief sampling of data breaches reveals that appropriate measures of security are not in place.

Juba: Fact or Fiction?

In 2005, a video depicting the sniper killings of American soldiers surfaced on the Internet. The video opens with a brief narration in which the alleged sniper vows to kill American soldiers because of his hatred of George W. Bush. The video then appears to show the sniper leaving his vehicle and shooting his identified targets. Since that time, other Juba videos have surfaced, each depicting sniper attacks, and some which include footage of a sniper training camp. One of the videos depicts a shadowy figure who is ostensibly returning from a successful attack. He is shown marking a tally of kills, before he sits down to record a diary entry. The voice on the video reports that coalition forces are terrified of his prowess and suggests that there are dozens of other snipers out there. The authenticity of the videos has been widely questioned. In 2006, Iraqi authorities declared that they had caught the Baghdad sniper. Irrespective of truth, terrorist organizations have used the controversy to spread uncertainty and fear.

Communication

The increasing employment of technology is making terrorist networks much more resilient to law enforcement actions, as time and space have been conquered by the Internet. These characteristics have made the Web especially popular to terrorists in the wake of September 11, who are increasingly turning to the medium to reduce their physical vulnerability. Perhaps the greatest benefit of the Internet enjoyed by terrorists is the reduction of risk associated with communications. Online dialogue is cheaper, international in scope, more widely accessible, and poses far less risk than traditional methods—a fact that was recognized by Osama bin Laden. Biographer Hamid Mir reported that members of al Qaeda carried laptops into hiding and exile in the wake of September 11. Unlike the Taliban, which forbade any modern innovations, including toothbrushes and televisions, bin Laden's al Qaeda embraced technology. In fact, bin Laden proved to be a visionary in this regard, employing emerging technology long before American intelligence agencies recognized the potential repercussions.[18] It is not coincidental, for example, that cyber-cafés proliferate in the remote Afghan–Pakistan border and the town of Chitral, a summer hideout for bin Laden which is hardly accessible by land or air.[19]

Traditionally, intelligence analysts targeted terrorists when they were most vulnerable (i.e., while congregating at mosques, crossing borders, or moving encampments). American intelligence sources routinely identified and arrested terrorists as they traveled to distant places like the Sudan, Yemen, or Afghanistan to train individuals. Now, such actors are not traveling, creating a situation in which law enforcement authorities find it difficult to operate. Even in those situations requiring physical

A Sampling of Breaches of Federal Agencies[20]

Agency	Type of Breach	Number Affected
U.S. Department of Transportation	Laptop stolen from a government vehicle in Florida	132,470
Department of Justice	Stolen Laptop	80,000
U.S. Navy	Theft of two laptops	31,000
U.S. Department of Agriculture	Laptop and printouts stolen from an employee's car	350
Federal Trade Commission	Theft of laptops from an employee's car	110
U.S. Department of Agriculture	Hacker	26,000
U.S. Department of Energy	Hacker	1,502
U.S. Marines	Loss of portable drive	207,750
U.S. Department of Defense	Hacker	unknown
U.S. Department of Veterans Affairs	Theft of laptop and hard drive from an employee's home	28,600,000
U.S. Department of Agriculture	Hacker	26,000
U.S. Navy	Unknown	30,000
Naval Safety Center	Employee error	over 100,000
U.S. Navy Recruiting Offices	Office burglary	31,000
U.S. Department of Transportation	Laptop stolen from government car	132,470
U.S. Department of Energy	Hacker	1,502

travel, operatives are no longer required to carry incriminating information or evidence, as schematics, blueprints, and formulae are globally accessible at the touch of a button.

Terrorists use a variety of online communication methods. To avoid detection through packet sniffers, terrorist groups routinely use **electronic dead drops** to communicate. This is accomplished when a constructed e-mail is not transmitted but saved in the drafts folder where multiple individuals have access through the use of passwords. For example, Muhammad Siddique Khan coordinated the 2005 London bombings by leaving communiqués regarding plan operations and rendezvous points in the "draft" folder of a Yahoo! account which was accessible to all conspirators who knew the username and password associated with the account. This method is increasingly popular as both American and British authorities are prohibited by law from hacking into mail servers. The use of *dead drops* has a variety of advantages. Most importantly, they may be utilized to facilitate asynchronous, anonymous communications.[22]

Terrorists are also using **online social networking sites**, which allow users to create personal profiles and associate with those communities in which shared interests are noted. One of the most popular among terrorists is *Orkut*. Established by Google employee Orkut Büyükkökten, the invitation-only social network service is similar to MySpace and FaceBook, and has over 13 million members. The site allows the creation of online communities and includes various groups comprised of al Qaeda sympathizers. Information available to members includes videos of terror attacks, photos of deceased American soldiers, recruitment solicitations, and propaganda materials.

To further confound investigators, operatives often employ codes. When Kamel Daoudi, an al Qaeda computer engineer, was arrested, authorities seized a codebook which allowed Western intelligence services to decrypt thousands of e-mails and telephone conversations which had previously been impossible to decipher. Unfortunately, such finds are not the norm, and terrorist organizations change their coding strategies on a regular basis. When, and if, authorities are successful in cracking the code, it is usually too late.

Perhaps most frightening is the notion that terrorists are currently employing steganography to communicate via the Internet. This includes the hiding of maps and photographs of terrorist targets and posting instructions for terrorist activities on sports chat rooms, pornographic bulletin boards, and other Web sites.[23] The exchange of these hidden messages can be facilitated through electronic dead drops or online postings. For example, a terrorist could open an account with an online auction site or download site and hide messages within photographs of items they post for sale or audios posted for exchange. Such deceptive tactics were employed by terrorists in the failed plot to bomb the American embassy in Paris.

Attack Mechanism

The Internet has provided numerous advantages to modern society. Individuals now have access to worldwide communications and resources, and the globalization of commerce has been realized. However, the same complexity and interconnectivity which produces such benefits creates systems in which small or minor disruptions may have cataclysmic consequences. Such vulnerability

Terrorist 007

In 2005, London authorities arrested Younes Tsouli, a Moroccan-born student whose online screen name, *Irhabi 007*, translated to "Terrorist 007." Computer forensics revealed that Tsouli was connected to a variety of seemingly unrelated terrorist activities across the globe. In addition to promoting terrorism and participating in terrorist training, Tsouli enlisted two American students who filmed potential targets, like the U.S. Capitol.[21]

Systemic Vulnerability

On August 14, 2003, a massive blackout in the Northeast caused the shutdown of nuclear plants, airports, and various other industries. It also affected over 50 million consumers in Connecticut, Massachusetts, Michigan, New Jersey, New York, Ohio, Pennsylvania, and Southeastern Canada. Although an outdated power grid, and not terrorism, was to blame, the ramifications of future or more massive outages and the potentiality of targeted attacks were soon realized.

was recognized by the President's Commission as early as 1997, long before September 11 and the blackout on the Eastern seaboard. The tight coupling and feedback loops which characterize the architecture of the Web result in an unsound infrastructure. Although an electronic Pearl Harbor has not yet occurred, the potentiality of such is frightening.

Terrorists focus on those critical complex networks which define and sustain a given society. In American society, that includes financial markets, commerce and capitalism, transportation, and communications. The selection of the World Trade Center in September of 2001 was both deliberate and methodical. It hit at two targets central to American culture—capitalism and security. Because many of the country's financial firms had previously establishing contingency plans, the attack was not successful in crippling the American economy. The existence of alternate facilities for data, information, and computer equipment minimized the damage to financial markets. Such contingency plans have been further enhanced in the wake of the attacks, and the physical security of obvious targets (i.e., water sources and food supplies) has been greatly improved. Digital attacks, however, have not been properly addressed. On the contrary, terrorists might employ digital weapons of mass disruption in future attacks.

Generally speaking, there are two types of cyber-terrorist threats: (1) those associated with the **physical infrastructure**; and (2) those associated with **critical data**. Digital threats to the physical infrastructure would involve the compromise of a critical system which severely affected critical physical infrastructures. This would include, but is not limited to, power grids, water and sewer systems, dams, hospitals, communications, GPS, air traffic systems, pipelines, and network with the potential of death. A **critical data threat** would involve the compromise of a critical computer system to alter, manipulate, or destroy critical data with the potential of death, destruction, and/or economic turmoil. This would include targeted attacks of databases like Social Security, Centers for Disease Control, the Department of Defense; etc.[24]

● TERRORISM AND CRIME

Criminal activities committed by terrorists range from acts of mass destruction to nonviolent financial crimes to support their operations and mission. As discussed in the previous chapter, terrorists utilize identity fraud to further a variety of interests, including, but not limited to, concealing their activities and obscuring their physical location from investigative authorities, hiding their whereabouts, funding of terrorist activities, and gaining unauthorized access to sensitive areas. In addition, terrorist groups are actively engaged in both narcoterrorism and money laundering.

Criminal Activities

Identity theft has been a focus of both public and private interest for the last several years. However, the events of September 11 had a profound effect on the urgency expressed by such individuals and institutions toward identity fraud. The awakening that theft of identifying information could be used for more than credit card fraud was chilling to the American public, in general, and worrisome to law enforcement authorities, in particular. In fact, all acts of recent terrorist activity directed at the United States have been facilitated in some way by stolen or fraudulent forms of identification. For example, each of the suicide bombers involved in the 9/11 attacks had established fraudulent identities. This included driver's licenses, stolen credit cards, fictitious or temporary addresses, social security numbers, and passports or other fraudulent travel documentation. This was most likely facilitated by the al Qaeda training manual, which specifically instructs members on the process of obtaining fraudulent identification.

Terrorist groups are actively involved in identity theft/fraud for a multitude of reasons. Terrorist groups may use compromised information to gain access to private or secure data or locations. The ability to assume the identity of another has enabled terrorists to gain access to top secret information and facilities. They have also been used to evade the attention of law enforcement and defeated government watch lists. This enables them to travel on commercial transportation. As discussed in Chapter 4, the assumption of identity can be utilized in both the physical and virtual world in a variety of ways. The use of fraudulent identification hampers law enforcement in that it makes it extremely difficult to identify and track the physical location of a known terrorist. It also allows the same individuals to expand their recruitment in new territories without the knowledge of law enforcement. At the same time, terrorists may use stolen credit card information and fraudulent identities to fund the operational costs of running a terror network. To further insulate themselves from identification and prosecution, terrorists may also employ electronic banking.

Criminalizing Terrorist Acts

If terrorism is characterized as a theatric production, then the American public is the targeted audience. Coupled with our cultural naiveté, Western nations are increasingly attractive due to their tendency to concentrate vital assets and critical infrastructures in small geographic clusters. In addition, the growing complexity and interconnectedness of modern society and the geographic concentration of wealth, human capital, communications, and knowledge renders the United States irresistible to foreign terrorists. As an example, in 90 minutes of a bright fall day almost 3,000 lives were lost, a building which took seven years to construct was destroyed, and at least $30 billion in direct costs were realized. (Indirect costs are still continuing.)

Prior to September 11, 2001, terrorism in the United States was not a top concern among overburdened law enforcement agencies. In fact, the most common forms of terrorists act formally charged in the United States prior to that day were kidnapping, murder, and hostage-taking. (After the attacks, a marked increase in charges involving fraud has been noted. However, it is important to remember that fraudulent documentation has only been recently categorized under terrorist statutes.) In the wake of the 9/11 attacks, both state and federal statutes significantly broadened the scope of terrorist acts which may be prosecuted in criminal courts. At the current time, there are four primary categories of terrorist activities which may be prosecuted under federal law.[25]

Government Efforts

In 2002, the *Homeland Security Act* expanded provisions housed within the *U.S. Patriot Act,* which required that all information gathered during a criminal investigation which related to foreign or counterintelligence information be shared with other federal agencies. The Act was intended to facilitate inter-agency communication and the coordination of agency efforts through the creation of the Department of Homeland Security (DHS).

Upon inception, DHS assumed control of approximately 180,000 employees from various federal agencies and offices and became responsible for the coordination and maintenance of a variety of databases. These watch lists included:

- Department of State—*Consular Lookout and Support System*—designed to support visa and passport issuance.
- Department of State—*TIPOFF Database*— a pure terrorist watch list, it involves interagency cooperation with Consular Lookout and Support System; Interagency Border Inspection System; National Automated Immigration Lookout System; and international governments.

- Federal Bureau of Investigation—*Violent Gang and Terrorist Organization File*— intended to manage information on organized crime activities, including those associated with domestic terrorist activities.
- Immigration and Customs Enforcement— *Border Inspection System*—intended to facilitate border crossing inspections. The system includes information on potential terrorists and people suspected of narcotics trafficking or other law enforcement violations.

Type	Description
International Terrorism	International terrorism incidents which impact on the United States. Involves acts of an international nature, including threats or conspiracies to engage in such acts, which are violent or otherwise dangerous to human life and which appear motivated by an intent to coerce, intimidate, or retaliate against a government or a civilian population ("terrorist motive"). The conduct is of an international nature if it occurs primarily outside the United States or transcends national boundaries, or involves a foreign terrorist organization.
	Statutory violations which, when accompanied by a terrorist motive, constitute federal crimes of terrorism include, but are not limited to, 18 U.S.C. 32, 37, 81, 175, 175b, 229, 351, 831, 842(m)&(n), 844(f)&(i), 930(c), 956, 1114, 1116, 1203, 1362, 1363, 1366(a), 1751, 1992, 1993, 2155, 2280, 2281, 2332, 2332a, 2332b, 2339, & 2340A; 42 U.S.C. 2284; or 49 U.S.C. 46504, 46505(b)(3), 46506, & 60123(b). See 18 U.S.C. 2332b(g)(5). (National Priority (N).)
Domestic Terrorism	Involves acts, including threats or conspiracies to engage in such acts, which are violent or otherwise dangerous to human life, which appear to be motivated by an intent to coerce, intimidate, or retaliate against a government or a civilian population ("terrorist motive") and which occur primarily within the United States and do not involve a foreign terrorist organization.
	Statutory violations which, when accompanied by a terrorist motive, constitute federal crimes of terrorism include, but are not limited to, those listed under the Program Category of International Terrorism. (National Priority (N).)
Terrorist Financing	Involves instances in which an individual or group of individuals subject to the jurisdiction of the United States knowingly provide material support or resources, directly or indirectly, to a foreign terrorist organization or to support the carrying out of a terrorist act. This includes violations brought under 18 U.S.C. 2339A and 2339B (providing material support to terrorists), 1956 (where the money laundering or transfers involve specified unlawful activity of a terrorist nature), and any other federal criminal violation where the intention is to provide material support to terrorists or to conceal the provision of such support. (National Priority (N).)

Type	Description
AntiTerrorism	Any matter or case where the underlying purpose or object of the investigation is antiterrorism related (domestic or international). This program category is meant to capture United States Attorney Office activity intended to prevent or disrupt potential or actual terrorist threats where the offense conducted is not obviously a federal crime of terrorism. To the extent evidence or information exists, in any form, reasonably relating the case to terrorism or the prevention of terrorism (domestic or international), the matter should be considered "antiterrorism." For example, a case involving offenses such as immigration violations, document fraud, or drug trafficking, where the subject or target is reasonably linked to terrorist activity, should be considered an "antiterrorism" matter or case. Similarly, a case of identity theft and document fraud where the defendant's motivation is to obtain access to and damage sensitive government facilities should be considered "antiterrorism." (National Priority (N).) Sub-classes of AntiTerrorism are: • AntiTerrorism/Environmental • AntiTerrorism/Identity Theft • AntiTerrorism/Immigration • AntiTerrorism/OCDETF Drugs • AntiTerrorism/Non-OCDETF Drugs • AntiTerrorism/Violent Crimes • AntiTerrorism/All Others

Conclusions

The Internet was originally designed to be a citadel—an impregnable bastion that would operate even if large sectors were lost in the event of a nuclear war. However, the increasing complexity, interconnectivity, and diversity of the Internet may have weakened its security due to a subsequent increase in routers and root servers. The compromise of routers, interdependent components of a

Online Domestic Terrorism

Although many Americans are most fearful of terrorist acts perpetrated by foreign groups, domestic terrorists have been quite active in online attacks.

• **Animal rights**–In March 2006, six defendants associated with Stop Huntingdon Animal Cruelty (SHAC) were convicted under the federal Animal Enterprise Terrorism Act. The group targeted Huntingdon Life Sciences, Britain's largest animal testing facility, which has a branch in New Jersey. Among other acts, those convicted were responsible for inciting various threats and acts of vandalism against Huntingdon employees and their children after they posted personal information about them on their Web page. In addition, the group was responsible for mass e-mailing companies doing business with HLS. Some of those targeted severed their ties with HLS.[26]

• **Pro-life**–Throughout the 1990s, numerous abortion doctors were attacked or murdered by antiabortion extremists. Many of these doctors were listed in the notorious Nuremberg Files, a list of abortion doctors. The document, created by the American Coalition of Life Activists (ACLA), was posted on the Internet in 1997 by Neal Horsley. The Web site also includes personal information about over 200 abortion providers, including names, family members, addresses, and photographs. While the site's creator argued that such promotion was protected under the First Amendment, a federal appellate court disagreed. The site was officially shut down in 2002.

vast network which direct packets of information, could create a synergistic disruption. Unfortunately, the recognition for the potentiality of the facilitation of terrorist activities is minimized by law enforcement. As a result, significant threats to the nation's infrastructure exist. In fact, the increasing virtual nature of terrorist networks is making them much more resilient. Online terrorist sites focus on propaganda and recruitment, while the physical activities of the same groups are designed to create chaos and terror. The audiences to which the two play are completing different – thereby broadening their appeal and constituency.

Like other netizens, political extremists and terrorists can find an online community just for them. Continuous online contact enables geographically dispersed individuals with intense passions or beliefs to congregate, exchange information and ideas, and define themselves. In effect, the Web may be characterized as a rainbow coalition of jihadists—transcending international and physical boundaries and providing a panacea for ideologues and political extremists. Terrorist groups have successfully used the Internet to plan, communicate, and propagandize their exploits. They have increasingly recognized the power of the mass media. Without question, it is far more effective than obscure activities in the bush. Western media, in particular, is targeted as it is more international in scope. Remember, the physicality of terror is less important than the emotional or psychological repercussions resulting from the act.

It is difficult to develop strategies to deal with terrorist Web sites. If they are identified and shut down, intelligence gathering capabilities from that site are eliminated. Thus, the best strategy may be to simply monitor them. In fact, a campaign of misinformation might be our best bet. The creation of government-operated fraudulent sites could lead to a wealth of intelligence and enable officers to lure terrorists into the open. Some authors have even suggested the use of faulty bomb-making tutorials which would actually cause the death of the terrorist.[27]

Increases in interconnectivity have resulted in a subsequent increase in vulnerability. The global community, in general, and the United States, in particular, must decentralize the digital infrastructure. However, this may be counter to a national conscience that demands greater efficiency, convenience, and low prices. This pervasive Wal-Mart mentality has decreased our ability to protect ourselves. At a minimum, the nation should explore local energy production and alternative energy sources to liberate individual users from the electricity grid. In addition, local and regional food production networks should be explored.

Irrespective of the method employed, combating the growing online presence of terrorists can only be accomplished after a globally accepted definition of cyberterrorism is developed and empirical research is conducted. While definitions of cyberterrorism should incorporate all the elements included in this chapter, empirical analysis should be conducted to fully encapsulate:

- the nature of the rhetoric
- the means and methods of communication between members
- the means and methods of information dissemination and propaganda
- the means and methods of nonideological, criminal activity committed by terror groups to facilitate ideological missions

● ORGANIZED CRIME

Some scholars posit that transnational organized crime will be one of the defining issues in the twenty-first century—like the Cold War was for the twentieth century and colonialism was for the nineteenth century.[28] It has been noted that the scale of such activity poses a significant threat to national security in a variety of ways, including, but not limited to trafficking in nuclear materials, sophisticated weaponry, and human smuggling. The illegal laundering of massive profits through

Web-based financial transactions may indirectly result in the destabilization of national financial systems and world markets. The most catastrophic destabilizations will occur in transitional states but have the potential to dramatically affect even major economies like Japan and Italy, as evidenced in the 1990s.[29] In fact, economies transitioning to democracy face the likelihood of the entrenchment of organized crime in both their political and economic systems. Such has occurred in the wake of the collapse of the Soviet Union, and in other Eastern European countries. Even China is confronting an increased organization of domestic crime groups.[30]

Like terrorist organizations, organized crime groups are increasingly turning to technology to enhance the complexity and profitability of their criminal pursuits. Unfortunately, these transnational activities pose significant challenges to law enforcement authorities due to corrupt political systems, lax international banking laws, lack of mutual legal assistance treaties, and most importantly, a lack of international consensus and global definitions.

Defining Organized Crime

As noted previously, all *organized crime groups* began as criminal gangs. Organized crime (OC) groups do not appear spontaneously. In fact, all OC groups discussed in this text were traditionally treated as street gangs. For the most part, the vast majority of organized crime groups originated as a result of perceived oppression and discrimination or perceptions of restrictive governments. Throughout history, the emergence of criminal groups and subsequent violence has been greatest during periods of economic depression. The deprivation experienced in the mid-1800s, for example, was characterized by a dramatic increase in gang affiliation in New York City.[31] However, economic deprivation is not the sole determinant in gang development. Indeed, the convergence of a variety of variables bears greater weight than any single causative agent and may enhance the

potentiality for organization within street gangs. A cultural emphasis on masculinity, historical territorial rivalries, and the advent of mass unemployment all serve to increase the primacy of group affiliation and decrease the likelihood of antigang maturation of members. Thus, the evolution of common street gangs into organized criminal syndicates involves a variety of factors. However, the majority of definitions associated with both fail to address this issue. In fact, definitions of *organized crime* are as diverse, as inaccurate, and as numerous as those traditionally associated with criminal gangs. Law enforcement gatherings, senatorial committees, academic consortiums, and even Hollywood studios have created definitions based largely on anecdotal recounts of mob informants. For the most part, these definitions have focused primarily on Italian organized crime—denying the existence of criminal syndicates among other ethnicities.[32]

The first attempts to formally define *organized crime* were undertaken by two different government commissions. While both of them uncovered a network of sophisticated, multi-jurisdictional criminal entrepreneurs, they proved to be largely ineffectual at the time. The first definition of organized crime in the United States was created in 1915 by the Chicago Crime Commission. In an attempt to define what they considered *institutionalized crime,* the commission was the first of its kind to recognize differences between traditional crimes and criminals and the emerging pattern of criminal behavior perpetrated by organized criminal groups. They found that such entities were unique in that they resembled an independent society of sorts, with systemized tasks and practices, unique traditions and rituals, and distinctive jargon. These findings were expanded upon by the Wickersham Commission of 1929. This commission, designed to evaluate the impact of prohibition, found that the organization of criminal activity surrounding prohibition was actually created by it. (Unfortunately, the structure that was created during and flourished throughout the period did not end with the repeal of the Eighteenth Amendment, as profits from bootlegging had been utilized to create additional criminal markets.) As with the recommendations of its predecessor, the admonitions put forth by the Wickersham Commission were largely ignored until the 1950s, and organized crime continued on its path of organizational sophistication and criminal maturation.

In 1957, a string of gangland murders and the discovery of a meeting of top echelon underworld figures in Apalachin, New York, propelled the Italian mafia into the national spotlight. Such events served as an impetus for government scrutiny and law enforcement activity. At that time, the Kefauver Committee, which had been in existence since 1950, increased their efforts to evaluate the connection of organized crime to gambling. In addition, the Committee expanded their original focus to include a plethora of other organized criminal activities. Headed by Senator Estes Kefauver, the Committee transfixed the American public as they televised the testimony of over 600 witnesses. The national appeal was twofold: (1) the invention of the television was relatively new; and (2) witnesses included movie stars, politicians, and prominent OC figures. The Committee concluded that an international conspiracy to traffic narcotics and other contraband had deep roots in immigrant communities across the United States, and that an organized criminal syndicate with a sophisticated hierarchy was directly responsible for the proliferation of vice-related activities. Unfortunately, their assertions were largely predicated on assumptions and hyperbole, as virtually no testimony alluded to a vast criminal network. Although an historical evaluation indicates that their statements were largely accurate, their overstatements and generalizations distanced the very audience they intended to impress.[33]

The McClellan Committee formed in the early 1960s proved to be more successful in proving the existence of the Italian mafia. The Committee, formally known as the Senate Permanent Subcommittee on Investigations, was largely assisted by the testimony of mob turncoat Joe Valachi. For the first time, the government had access to an organizational insider privy to the group's structure, customs, and criminal activities.[34] Confessions from Valachi, like most anecdotal accounts of life in the mob, indicated that the majority of his youth was spent in various street gangs (including the "Minute Men") where he engaged in a variety of disorganized criminal activities like burglary, fencing stolen goods, etc. He testified that he and others of his street gang joined an organized group of criminals called La Cosa Nostra (LCN), which when literally translated means "this thing of ours." He outlined the organization structure of the entity, identifying layers of leadership and the roles and responsibilities of each. He additionally testified as to the existence of a formal commission of leaders and the identities of current players in OC. Finally, he fully discussed methods of racketeering and the infiltration of legitimate marketplaces by Italian organized crime. Although the Committee failed to outline a specific definition of organized crime, Valachi's testimony added the element of racketeering, previously absent in articulated models of organized crime.

In 1967, the President's Commission on Law Enforcement and the Administration of Justice offered an extremely vague, overly inclusive definition of the phenomenon, stating that OC involved: *a society that seeks to operate outside the control of the American people and their government. It involves thousands of criminals, working within structures as large as those of any corporation.* Under this definition, other ethnic groups which were heavily involved in syndicated criminal activity were excluded. However, the Omnibus Crime Control and Safe Streets Act of 1968 remedied this oversight, declaring that OC included:

> . . . the unlawful activities of the members of a highly organized, disciplined association engaged in supplying illegal goods and services including, but not limited to gambling, prostitution, loan-sharking, narcotics, **labor racketeering**, and other lawful activities.

Although the Act's definition proved to be more inclusive than its predecessors, it failed to address issues of political corruption—a variable

Peter Gotti, pictured here, presided over the Gambino crime family in New York City. Like other organized crime groups, the Italians are increasingly involved in computer-related crime. (*AP/ Wide World Photos*)

necessary for the continuation of criminal groups. Perhaps by design, the language included therein excluded individuals who were not card-carrying members of an organized crime family. In addition, it disregarded the motivation behind such activities, making no mention of pecuniary gain. In fact, these two characteristics of OC were not addressed until 1980, when the Pennsylvania Crime Commission focusing primarily on organized crime activities in Philadelphia and Pittsburgh, expanded the definition put forth by the Omnibus Crime Control and Safe Streets Act of 1968, stating that organized crime is:

> The unlawful activity of an association trafficking in illegal goods or services, including but not limited to gambling, prostitution, loansharking, controlled substances, labor racketeering, or other unlawful activities or any continuing criminal conspiracy or other unlawful practice which has as its objective large economic gain through the fraudulent or coercive practices or improper governmental influence.

Covering all the bases, the Commission also directly expanded upon the original definition put forth by the President's Commission on Law Enforcement and the Administration of Justice, characterizing organized crime as:

> A society that seeks to operate outside the control of the American people and their governments. It involves thousands of individuals working within structures as complex as any large corporation, subject to laws more rigidly enforced than those of legitimate governments. Its actions are not impulsive but rather the result of intricate conspiracies, carried on over many years and aimed at gaining control of whole fields of activity in order to amass huge profits.[35]

Although the definition set forth by the Pennsylvania Crime Commission was the most comprehensive of the period, it omitted territoriality and monopolization. Contemporary definitions of organized crime must include the following characteristics:

1. **Structure and hierarchy**—Virtually all organized crime groups are characterized by recognition of responsibility, task assignment, and leadership. Whether

formally appointed or elected, each organized crime groups has a system of interrelated positions specifically designed to facilitate task accomplishment. Such officials, recognized by organizational members, assign responsibilities, dictate policy and procedures, and ensure compliance. However, contemporary groups are not as hierarchical as their predecessors and are characterized by loose networks.

2. **Violence**—The utilization of violence and the threat thereof is necessary for both task efficacy and organizational longevity. It is an essential component of criminal activities such as extortion, loansharking, and racketeering. It is also important in maintaining control over organizational members. Ironically, the potentiality for violence may be more important than the actual violence itself as reputations for violence often negate the need to employ it.

3. **Recognizability**—Organized crime groups are recognized not only by law enforcement authorities, but by their communities as well. This is necessary for the extortion of funds, as they rely on the specter of a mass, criminal organization to intimidate potential victims. It is also necessary for the corruption of political figures. Such recognizability may be likened to the threat of violence that is not employed in which targets realize their own vulnerability against an army of criminals.

4. **Longevity**—Whether guided by religious zeal or motivated by pecuniary gain, organizational goals must include its preservation. Members must recognize the continuity of group ideology and the organization itself. Such recognition necessarily includes their own impermanency and vulnerability.

5. **Recruitment**—To further ensure organizational longevity, criminal groups must maintain the ability to replenish their ranks as positions become available. Traditionally, ethnically based organized crime groups recruited youngsters from the neighborhood—evaluating their criminal prowess and organizational loyalty by assigning small tasks. While recent immigrant criminal groups have continued this practice, traditional groups like LCN are increasingly forced to replenish their personnel with family members or longtime associates. (Throughout the text, the author will discuss the various methods of recruitment employed by individual organizations.)

6. **Innovative and entrepreneurial and opportunistic**—All organized crime groups are characterized by elevated levels of entrepreneurial criminal activity. Such innovation is necessary as changes in legislation and law enforcement efforts combine to reduce the cost-benefit ratio of various activities. The repeal of the Eighteenth Amendment, for example, forced organized crime groups to develop new markets to replace revenue lost by the legalization of alcohol. In the twentieth century, many groups turned to narcotics to refill depleted coffers. In the twenty-first century, the same groups have increasingly utilized nonmember hackers.

7. **Exclusive membership**—Entrance into the criminal group requires some commonality with organizational members. As Asbury (1928) discovered in his evaluation of criminal gangs in turn-of-the-century New York, those groups that came together for the sole purpose of committing criminal activity, lacking ethnic solidarity also lacked organizational longevity. Culture, shared experiences, traditions, and religion often play a role in the solidification of norms and expectations of the group prior to criminal activity. Such commonalities may include, but are not limited to, race, ethnicity, criminal background, or ideology.

However, such common traits do not ensure organizational admittance. Just as money is not the sole factor in entrance to exclusive country clubs, incumbent members closely scrutinize a potential member's background. In fact, the level of inspection employed by these groups is often greater than that found in law enforcement agencies. Organizational fit, individual loyalty, and criminal ability are but a few of the factors which determine an individual's acceptance.

8. **Strict rules and regulations**—Organized crime groups are characterized by elevated levels of rules and restrictions. Paramount in each is the rule of silence. Individuals violating organizational secrecy are almost always killed. While rules vary between individual groups, all are established to ensure organizational longevity and task efficacy. Rules of conduct between members, for example, are necessary to negate potential friction within the group. Noncompliance results in organizational discipline ranging from loss of respect to loss of life.

9. **Ritualistic**—Just like noncriminal societies, aberrant groups also display a tendency for ritualism. Induction ceremonies, organizational meetings, and the like, are all characterized by ceremonial trappings. The development of jargon and customary displays of respect solidify members and further sanctifie the organization itself.

10. **Profitability**—All members of organized crime syndicates are expected to enhance organizational coffers through criminal enterprise. The practice of tithing to organizational leaders or elders furthers the interests of the organization in the form of political bribery or, in some cases, the support of criminal defense. Even ideologically based groups must maintain a positive cash flow to support their dogmatic platform.

11. **Racketeering and infiltration of legitimate business**—Although traditionally associated with LCN, the practice of racketeering and the infiltration of legitimate businesses has permeated all corners of organized crime. With the increasing amount of legislation designed to identify illegal profits, the laundering of money through legitimate sources has become increasingly common. In addition, a façade of legitimacy furthers organizational goals and increases organizational longevity, as the business of crime becomes more palatable to an American public desensitized to white collar crime.

12. **Corruption of political officials**—The organized corruption of political officials, including police officers, politicians, and jurists has a long history in the United States. Criminal gangs have colluded with these entities beginning with Tammany Hall in the early 1800s. In fact, early systems of policing, which included the practice of appointments by Alderman and then the Board of Police Commissioners in New York City, established an incestuous relationship among politicians, police, and criminal gangs (i.e., the police owed the politicians that appointed them, the politicians owed the criminal gangs which fixed their elections, and the criminal gangs owed them both).

13. **Monopolistic**—Like their legitimate counterparts, organized crime groups enhance their profitability through monopolization. Such efforts are not solely restricted to criminal activities like narcotics, gambling, and prostitution. Indeed, criminal groups seek to monopolize legitimate industries as well. In New York and Atlantic City, for example, the Italian mafia's involvement in organized labor resulted in a construction monopoly, where builders were forced to pay a street tax for every building erected. In addition, the garbage industry in New York was long controlled by LCN, who received

monies from every "independent" collector in the city. Such monopolies are possible through their use of violence and labor racketeering.

14. **Criminal activity**—It goes without saying that all organized crime groups engage in criminal activity. Such activity ranges from the relative simplistic crimes of gambling, prostitution, loan-sharking, extortion, burglary, murder, assault, and arson to more complex endeavors like racketeering, stock fraud, narcotics trafficking, alien smuggling, money laundering, and casino skimming. The level of each is largely determined by organizational culture and individual capability. While some groups may specialize in one type of criminal activity, like narcotics, others engage in a variety.

Currently, there are a variety of organized crime groups actively operating in the United States. Those with a physical presence based on a social commonality include, *La Cosa Nostra*, 1%'s or Outlaw Bikers; Eastern Europeans, Vietnamese and Korean street gangs, Chinese Triads, Nigerians, Jamaican Posses, Israelis, Puerto Ricans, Mexicans, Cubans, Colombians, Dominicans, El Salvadorans, prison gangs, and the People and Folk Nations.

Distinguishing Organized Crime from Cybergangs

In 2004, a joint investigation by American and Canadian authorities resulted in the arrest of almost 30 people. Those arrested in *Operation Firewall* included individuals from Eastern Europe, Russia, and the United States. Many published accounts heralded the arrival of organized crime in cyberspace. Well . . . not exactly.

The characterization of a coordinated criminal effort by multiple hackers as *organized crime* is not now, nor was it ever, accurate. By definition, *organized crime* is a recognizable entity containing characteristics exclusive to the phenomenon. Familiarity, commonality, corruption of political authority, and most importantly, violence are essential components for definitional and enforcement purposes. While criminal conspiracies committed by a collection of virtual strangers may result in an organized criminal activity, the absence of traditional elements necessarily negates notions of constancy and longevity. Rather than forcing these emergent groups into traditional definitions, it is essential that both practitioners and academics recognize the individuality of such and develop terminology unique to the phenomenon. A differentiation between organized criminal syndicates and *cybergangs/cyber-criminal organizations* must be maintained. Thus, the following definitions are proposed:

- **organized crime**—*A recognizable, monopolistic, self-perpetuating, hierarchical organization willing to use violence and the corruption of public officials to engage in both traditional vice related activities and complex criminal enterprises, which ensures organizational longevity through physical interaction, ritualistic practices,, rules and regulations, organizational tithing, and investment in legitimate businesses.*[36]
- **cybergangs/cyber-criminal organizations** —*Groups of individuals brought together through the medium of the Internet which conspire and/or commit non-violent criminal acts facilitated by the exploitation of networked or interconnected systems.*

It is important to note that the intentional demarcation of the two groups does not suggest that one is not actively engaged in computer-related crime. On the contrary, traditional organized crime groups, like the Italian and Russian mafias, have aggressively exploited advancements in technology, and are currently employing nonmembers for their technical or sophisticated knowledge. In addition, organized crime groups are increasingly collaborating with cybergangs, either contractually or through the purchase of compromised data, to facilitate

Criminal Activities and Cybergangs: A Case in Point

Carding is a new type of fraud, which uses account numbers and counterfeit identity documents to complete identity theft and defraud banks and retailers. Victims of *carding* include both financial institutions who often absorb the cost of fraudulent transactions, and individuals who suffer damages relating to their credit histories.[38]

In 2004, a joint investigation by U.S. and Canadian authorities resulted in numerous arrests of individuals belonging to underground criminal groups, including *Shadowcrew*, *Carderplanet*, and *Darkprofits*. These groups were responsible for the development of *carder* sites in which information was readily available for sale or for sharing. This information included social security numbers of deceased individuals, how-to manual on committing fraud, and how-to manual on collecting numbers. Methods of payment for services varied from monthly subscriptions to charge-per-download.

- **carderplanet.com**—Established by Dmitro Ivanovich Golubov (aka Script), the site had over 7,000 members and compromised data from millions of bank accounts across the globe. Highly structured, the enterprise was managed by a variety of individuals who called themselves "The Family." Dallas native Douglas Cade Havard called himself "Capo dei Capi," a spoof on a term used in Italian organized crime to mean "boss of bosses."

- **Shadowcrew.com**—Managed by a Russian and two Americans, the site had approximately 4,000 members and was dedicated to facilitating malicious computer hacking and the dissemination of stolen credit card, debit card, bank account numbers, and counterfeit identification documents (i.e., drivers' licenses, passports, and social security cards). According to the Department of Justice, Shadowcrew members trafficked in at least 1.7 million stolen credit card numbers and caused losses in excess of $4 million.[39]

online theft, extortion, and fraud. For example, some of New York's mafia families purchased calling card numbers from the cybergang *Phonemasters*.[37]

ORGANIZED CRIME AND TECHNOLOGY

By definition, organized crime groups are opportunistic. Thus, their activities have run the gamut of criminal statutes and are limited only by their imaginations. Such innovation and entrepreneurialism has allowed them to flourish despite concerted government efforts and the evolution of market demands. Indeed, traditional organized crime groups have embraced technological advancements and adapted the modality of their operations. While the parameters of this text preclude an exhaustive discussion of all criminal activities and the criminogenic environment which produced them, the table below lists some examples of traditional crimes and their contemporary counterparts.

Thus, organized crime groups have aggressively exploited technological advancements. For the most part, these groups have simply incorporated such developments into traditional methods, greatly enhancing the efficiency and effectiveness of their criminal schemes.

Extortion

Extortion has long been considered to be the backbone of organized crime. Every American group has been actively involved in protection rackets and has insinuated itself into legitimate businesses by force. While traditional methods vary, most involve the threat of physical violence, destruction of property, or the disclosure of sensitive (i.e., embarrassing) information. Due to the prevalence of organized crime, business owners are often forced to seek protection from the very organization that is strong-arming them. Currently, that trend has extended to the Internet. In 2004, Eastern European organized crime syndicates threatened various online gambling sites in the days leading up to Great Britain's largest horse race of the year. The

Traditional Criminal Enterprises	Computer-Related Crime
Extortion/protection rackets—threat of personal harm, destruction of property, or loss of reputation.	**Extortion/protection rackets**—threat of denial of service Attack, site defacement, or disclosure of damaging information.
Cargo heists—traditional targets included, but were not limited to, cigarettes, clothing, perishables, liquor, toiletries, furniture, electronics, etc.	**Cargo heists**—contemporary targets include computer components and personal information.
Credit card fraud—traditionally facilitated through theft and the exploitation of reporting systems	**Credit card fraud**—contemporary methods include the use of "skimmers" which record personal information contained on magnetic strips, the use of data compromised by fraudulent sites, phishing, and through the black market purchase of financial identities or personal information.
Fraud—involves the misrepresentation of circumstances. Traditional methods required physical interaction.	**Fraud**—Contemporary schemes include online auction and stock fraud.
Gambling—traditional methods involved street policy rackets and sports wagering.	**Online gambling**—contemporary methods include online casinos and Internet sports wagering.
Money laundering—traditional methods included real estate transactions, straw purchases, and casinos.	**Money laundering**—contemporary methods include electronic layering, international commodities, and online businesses.
Theft of property—traditional targets included any physical item with monetary value.	**Theft of property**—contemporary targets include identification documentation, personal data, and proprietary secrets.
Sex and pornography—traditionally involved in the ownership of strip clubs and brothels and the distribution of pornographic films.	**Sex and pornography**—contemporary methods include the ownership of pornography sites and online "escort" services. In addition, the creation of such businesses is often used to further other criminal activity like credit card fraud and money laundering.
Confidence scams—traditional methods involved physical interactions or mail solicitations.	**Confidence scams**—contemporary methods are facilitated via the Internet and electronic mail.
Trafficking in criminal contraband and fencing of stolen property—traditional methods relied upon storefront operations or physical merchandising	**Trafficking in criminal contraband and fencing of stolen property**—contemporary methods include online auction sites, online storefronts, and the like.
Counterfeiting of currency—traditional methods relied upon the creation of plates and printing presses and targeted physical currency, especially denominations of the American dollar	**Counterfeiting of currency**—contemporary operations include a variety of methods involving high-end printers and graphics software. In addition, the introduction of e-currency has resulted in a new breed of counterfeiting, which is also employed to launder money.
Manufacture and sale of counterfeit goods—traditional items included high-end luxury items like designer handbags, jewelry, or garments.	**Manufacture and sale of counterfeit goods**—contemporary items include software, computer components, DVDs, etc.
Illegal substances—beginning with alcohol and graduating to narcotics, the trafficking of illegal substances is the backbone of many organized crime groups.	**Illegal substances**—contemporary practices include the development of online pharmacies and international partnerships facilitated through the Internet.
Human smuggling—traditional methods of human smuggling involved unsecured border crossing via the use of private transportation.	**Human smuggling**—contemporary practices include both traditional means and the production of fraudulent identification documents for illegals.

Grand National Web site operators were threatened with concentrated distributed denial of service attacks (DDoS) if they failed to pay the requisite protection fee. The subsequent series of attacks took several online betting sites offline, including Hollywood Sportsbook, Pinnacle, and BCBets. Ironically, another extortion scheme targeting online betting sites forced operators of *www.play-withal.com* to hire security specialists. The site was operated by a professional gambler with ties to the Lucchese crime family.

Cargo Heists and Armed Robbery

Traditional organized crime groups have long displayed a proclivity to "boosting" merchandise. Hijackings of commercial cargo have largely been characterized as nonviolent "lay downs" by victims which are facilitated by inside information or assistance. Examples of targeted cargo include cigarettes, perishables, and clothing. However, some heists have demonstrated the ruthlessness that can be displayed by members of organized crime. Perhaps the most infamous cargo heist in history was immortalized in the film *Good Fellas*. The 1978 crime involved the robbery of a Lufthansa storage vault located at Kennedy Airport. Acting on information provided by Lufthansa employee, Louis Werner, the gang of thieves was able to circumvent sophisticated security practices and leave with millions of dollars worth of currency and jewels. Although the heist itself involved little violence, at least 13 of the co-conspirators were killed in the weeks and months following the score. Jimmy Burke, the leader of the crew, and Paul Vario, a Lucchese capo, were sentenced to prison for their involvement.

It is estimated that global losses associated with cargo crimes account for $50 billion a year, half of which is committed within the United States.[40] Increasingly, organized crime groups are focusing on high-tech cargo as it is more lucrative and largely untraceable. This trend was noted as early as 1996, when it was calculated that over 500 heists by organized criminals totaled over $1.4 million of computer components.[41] Groups which have been actively involved in such activities include, but are not limited to, La Cosa Nostra, Chinese Triads, Vietnamese street gangs, and assorted South American organizations.

Fraud

Although estimates vary, profits from fraudulent schemes total in the billions of dollars. This figure is a direct result of the exponential growth of computer-related fraud. However, its sheer prevalence makes it to calculate the amount of fraud which is directly attributable to organized crime.

Bank Fraud—The emergence of the Internet and the increasing prevalence of online banking and automated services has resulted in a subsequent increase in victimization associated with these conveniences. Organized crime groups across the globe have actively exploited security holes to perpetrate various forms of bank fraud. In addition, European authorities have warned that members of organized crime groups are infiltrating banks through employment. Below are but a few examples:

- In 1999, hundreds of thousands of dollars from local banks in South Africa were lost when an organized crime group used the Internet and bank-by-telephone services to hack into financial institutions.[42]
- In 2000, Russian organized crime groups attempted to steal more than $10 million form a U.S. bank by making approximately 40 wire transfers to accounts around the world.[43]
- In 2000, various members of Sicily's Cosa Nuova created a clone of the Bank of Sicily's online banking. The group intended to divert $400 million allocated by the European Union to regional projects in Sicily. To accomplish the scheme, the money was to be laundered through the Vatican Bank and various financial institutions in

Switzerland and Portugal. Fortunately, the plan was thwarted by an informant.[44]

ATM/Credit Card Fraud—Traditional methods of ATM/Credit Card Fraud were largely successful due to the lack of computerized databases and lax security measures. Criminals in possession of stolen cards could remain under the radar by immediate usage and multiple low-dollar purchases. As security measures and computerized databases were developed to combat the problem, organized crime groups adapted new methods of operations. The most popular of these methods is *skimming*. By definition, "skimming" is the illegal duplication of credit cards achieved by running the card through a reader that captures information stored in the magnetic strip on the back. These devices are increasingly sophisticated, and may be attached to a belt, affixed to the underside of a counter, etc. In 2002, Canadian authorities identified eight counterfeit card factories which were receiving information from 116 retail locations across North America.

Stock Fraud—Within the last two decades, organized crime groups have been involved in the manipulation and corruption of stocks and securities. In 2001, members of four of the five New York mafia families were convicted of various counts of stock fraud in "pump and dump" scams. Millions of dollars were generated for the families through the corruption and development of brokerage houses which "specialized" in a handful of stocks. These stocks, largely worthless, were sold to investors after mob associates created a demand for them by cold-calling victims and promoting their value. Of course, the mob dumped them when the stocks' values were inflated. Organized crime groups have continued this sort of criminal enterprise through the use of mass spamming, employing botnets to inundate potential victims.

Money Laundering

Money laundering may be defined as the introduction of illegally obtained funds into the legitimate financial marketplace. In 2003, the United States Drug Enforcement Agency estimated that the amount of money laundered for illicit purposes surpassed $600 billion per year. Global estimates suggest that laundered money accounts for 2 percent – 5 percent of the world's gross domestic product.[45] Historically, the practice was employed to "wash" the countless billions of dollars in money earned through drug trafficking. However, the globalization of commerce has led to an increase in international complicity between organized criminal syndicates, which has resulted in a virtual explosion of money laundering for a variety of other enterprises.

Money laundering is a necessary element of the longevity and continued viability of organized crime. Both federal and international laws require a demonstration of taxable income consistent with the corresponding quality of life displayed by a criminal suspect. Thus, criminals must develop methods to legitimize their criminal proceeds. Traditionally, this was accomplished through real estate transactions, gambling venues, or legitimate fronts. While successful, these approaches were both risky and cumbersome. The introduction of e-commerce, e-banking, and online gambling has significantly reduced the risk of prosecution and streamlined the money laundering process.

In 2007, Jose Miguel Battle, Jr., one of the bosses of *La Corporacion* (aka The Corporation or the Cuban Mafia), was ordered to forfeit $642 million and serve over 15 years in prison for his part in an illegal gambling operation which prospered through the use of violence and intimidation. The acts included in the indictment also included money laundering and multiple murders.[46] In a plea agreement, Battle admitted to laundering funds through electronic transfers from corporation-owned businesses in both the United States and foreign countries to banks in Spain and the United States.

The Sex Trade

Like extortion and narcotics, all organized crime groups operating in the United States have been, at some level, involved in the sex trade. Traditionally, organized crime groups owned and operated both legitimate and illegitimate establishments in this regard. Strip clubs, massage parlors, brothels, and escort services are but a few examples of such endeavors. In addition, organized crime groups have been involved in the manufacturing and distribution of pornography. (Some international groups have also been involved in the exploitation of minors and child pornography.) In recent years, such groups have vastly expanded the availability and marketability of their "goods" and "services" through the development of online storefronts. While online pornography sites are not within the exclusive purview of organized crime, those operated by criminal syndicates often collect more than money from their customers. In fact, these sites are often used to facilitate additional criminal activities.

In the waning days of the twentieth century, Richard Martino and investors in his company made billions of dollars in the online pornography market. Although not remarkable in the product for sale in the legitimate marketplace, Martino's company was unique in that it had ties to organized crime and committed numerous counts of credit card fraud. The $230 million online fraud, the largest in history, resulted in guilty pleas by six members of the Gambino crime family. Martino, a reputed soldier in the family, allegedly paid capo Salvatore Locascio at least $40 million.

The scheme was relatively simple. Individual visitors to the adult site were asked for credit card information ostensibly for age verification. The group then used the information to make unauthorized charges on the victims' accounts. The money laundering scheme that followed, however, was quite sophisticated and involved transferring money between various corporations to avoid detection. These companies included: Mical Properties, Dynamic Telecommunications, Inc., and Westford Telecommunications, Inc.

Confidence Scams

These scams are highly organized and are perpetrated by individuals involved in the Nigerian organized crime syndicate. Long a mainstay of this group, these types of scams have emerged in the techno-landscape with a vengeance, rendering traditional investigative methods and prosecutorial avenues moot. More succinctly, gang members have simply changed the mode of communication from traditional postal operations to electronic platforms. Unfortunately, the scams appear to be just as successful in this arena, as their scams have enabled them to defraud individuals and businesses without the complication of oral or personal communication.

Nigerian Advance Fee Scheme: Known internationally as "4–1–9", the section of the Nigerian penal code which addresses fraud schemes. This scam is usually directed at small- and medium-sized businesses or charities. Quite elementary in nature and execution, the *4–1–9 scam* has six primary steps:

1. Victims are identified and targeted through sources ranging from trade journals, professional directories, newspapers, etc.
2. Individual or company receives e-mail from a "government or agency official" (such as a senior civil servant in one of the Nigerian ministries, like the Nigerian National Petroleum Corporation).
3. The e-mail informs recipient that this government or agency is willing to transfer millions of dollars in "over-invoiced contracts" if recipient provides blank copies of letterhead, banking account information, and telephone/fax information.
4. As the scam involves cultivating the trust of the recipient, more official documentation is received from the "government or agency" (i.e., authentication letters with official-looking stamps, government seals, or logos which support the claims).
5. Once trust is obtained, up-front fees are requested for taxes, government bribes, attorney fees, or the like.[47]

Of course, there is no money, but these scams remain wildly successful due primarily to

American and European greed. Designed to delude the victim into thinking that he or she had been singled out or is extremely lucky to be the beneficiary of such grandiosity, these scams are also successful because victims are loathe to report their sheer gullibility. Unfortunately, individuals and corporations have been divested of millions of dollars before they realize the error of their ways. Such individuals, wishing to make a quick buck (in this case, several million), fall victim to these hoaxes even though warning signs are all around. Some even fall victim to a secondary scam known as the *Nigerian recompensation scam.* Just like the original scam, this fraud is initiated through an unsolicited electronic communication in which the perpetrators claim to be members of the Nigerian government's recompensation unit—a unit designed to make restitution to victims of Nigerian scams. Once again relying on official-looking documents and titles, victims are asked to forward sums of money to cover administrative costs. Amazingly, many of those previously victimized are easy prey for this secondary assault!

In addition to the 4–1–9 scams, there are six additional patterns of Nigerian fraud:

1. disbursement of money from wills,
2. transfer of funds from over-invoiced contracts,
3. conversion of hard currency,
4. purchase of real estate,
5. contract fraud (COD of goods or services), and
6. sale of crude oil at below-market prices.

Unfortunately, each pattern of criminal activity shares similar characteristics which ensure their success and profitability. First, each of the scams has an aura of urgency and the ephemeral in which the victims are encouraged to work with utmost haste before this lucrative (albeit slightly illegal) opportunity evaporates. Second, targets precipitate their future victimization (i.e., the victim becomes the aggressor), in which they become willing to expend

greater funds if the deal is threatened. Third, victims are seduced into silence—reluctant to share their "good fortune" with others. Finally, victims are dazzled by documents in which inferences of corrupt government officials or corporate officers support their very authenticity—remember, many of these forms are actually byproducts of previous scams.[48]

Collectively, these scams cost American corporations and private citizens millions of dollars. The problem has become so pervasive that the United States Secret Service has established *Operation 4–1–9.* This effort receives approximately 100 calls and 300 to 500 pieces of related correspondence per day![49] In fact, the U.S. Secret Service has even established a presence at the American Embassy in Lagos in an attempt to improve the efficiency and effectiveness of their investigations and countermeasures. Unfortunately, the lack of international cooperation and the lack of adequate prosecutorial avenues (i.e., federal laws specifically prohibiting mail fraud do not apply to electronic communications) have made it extremely difficult for law enforcement authorities.

Fencing of Stolen Property

In order to profit from their various criminal schemes, organized crime groups must transform commodities into cash. This activity, known as *fencing,* has traditionally been conducted via physical storefronts, pawn shops, word of mouth, and, of course, out of the back of a truck. The introduction of the Internet has enabled criminals to conduct their operations in a virtual space, largely free from law enforcement surveillance and physical vulnerability. According to a 2007 survey conducted by the National Retail Federation, 71 percent of retailers recovered goods from e-Fencing operations.[50] For the most part, such activities involved the use of online auction sites. Organized crime groups can also utilize these sites to identify merchandise in demand. In this way, they can target specific commodities for theft.

Below is an actual copy of an e-mail received from one of the author's students. Although these scams are anything but new, the method for distribution is changing. Note the misspellings and grammatical errors.

From: "DON CYRIL" <don_cyrilcc@email.com>
To: xxxxxxxxxxxx@hotmail.com
Subject: URGENT AND CONFIDENTAIL
Date: Thu, 31 Oct 2002 01:22:07-0500

3/5 RIDER HAGGARD CLOSE,
JOHANNESBURG,
SOUTH AFRICA.
Phone: 874762864167
Fax: 874762864168

SUBJECT: {URGENT TRANSACTION PROPOSAL} RE: TRANSFER OF $126,000,000.00USD. {ONE HUNDRED AND TWENTY SIX MILLION UNITED STATES DOLLAR}.

With due respect and humility, I write to you this business transaction proposal. I am Mr. DON CYRIL, the auditor General of a bank in South Africa. During the course of our auditing, I discovered a floating fund in an account opened in the bank in 1990 and since 1993, nobody has operated on this account again. After going through some old files in the records, I discovered that the owner of the account died without a heir/next of kin or any close relation. I am writing following the impressive information about you through one of my friends who run a consultancy firm in your country.

The owner of this account is Mr. Gordon G. Scott, a foreigner, and a sailor. He died in 1993 in a road accident and no other person knows about this account or anything concerning it. The account has no other beneficiary and my investigation proved to me as well that Mr. Gordon G. Scott until his death was the manager Diamond Safari Company (pty) South Africa.

According to our Banking policies and guideline here which stipulates that if such money remained unclaimed after five years, the money will automatically be transfered into the Bank treasury as unclaimed fund. The request of foreigner as next of kin in this business transaction is occasioned by the fact that the customer was a foreigner and a citizen of south Africa cannot stand as next of kin to a foreigner.

We will start the first transfer with twenty six million {$26,000,000.00usd}. Upon successful conclussion without any disappointment from your side, he shall re-apply for the payment of the remaining amount to your account. The amount involved is {USD126M} One hundred and twenty six million United States Dollars. Only I want to first transfer $26,000,000.00 {twenty six million United States Dollar} from this money into a safe foreigner's account abroad before the rest, but I don't know any foreigner, I am only contacting you as a foreigner because this fund cannot be approved to a local account for the deseased owner is a foregner. It can only be approved into a foreign a/c.

The management of the bank is ready to release this fund to any person who has the correct information about the account. With my influence and the position of the bank officials, we can transfer this money to any foreigner's reliable account which you can provide with assurance that this money will be intact pending our physical arrival in your country for sharing. The bank officials will destroy all documents of transaction immediately we receive this money leaving no trace of the fund to any place. Two of us will fly >to your country immediately after the fund is remmited into your account.

I will apply for annual leave to get visa immediately I hear from you that you are ready to act and receive this fund in your account. I will use my position and influence to obtain all legal approvals for onward transfer of this money to your account with appropriate clearance from the relevant ministries and foreign exchange departments.

At the conclusion of this transaction, you will be given 35% of the total amount, as a foreign partner, in respect to the provision of a foreign account, 60% will be for me, while 5% will be for reimbursement of any expenses incured during the curse of the transaction.

Therefore to enable the immediate transfer of this fund to you as arranged, you must apply first to the bank as relation or next of kin of the deceased, indicating your bank name, your bank account number and location where the fund will be remitted.

Upon the receipt of your reply, I will send to you by fax or email the text of the application. I will not fail to bring to your notice that this transaction is hitch free and that you should not entertain any atom of fear as all required arrangements have been made for the transfer. You should contact me immediately as soon as you receive this letter. Trusting to hear from you immediately through this very email address.

DON_CYRIL10@LYCOS.COM
Thanks and best regards,
DON CYRIL

Data Piracy and Counterfeit Goods

Organized crime groups are increasingly involved in the theft of intellectual property and the manufacturing and distribution of counterfeit software, DVDs, and videos. As discussed in Chapter 4, there are eight distinct areas of film piracy:

- Optical disc piracy
- Internet piracy
- Videocassette piracy
- Theatrical print theft
- Signal theft
- Broadcast piracy
- Public performances
- Parallel imports

Contemporary syndicates have been especially active in optical disc and Internet piracy. In London, for example, members of the Chinese Triads flooded the city with pirated James Bond and Harry Potter DVDs before their scheduled release. While such activity is not generally perceived as serious by either local law enforcement or the American public, the organized crime groups that are involved in these activities are often involved in far more violent and insidious crimes.

In 2005, almost 40 members and associates of the Yi Ging Organization were indicted in New York City for various offenses, ranging from trafficking in counterfeit DVDs and CDs to traditional organized crime activities like racketeering, extortion, usery, witness tampering, money laundering, and narcotics trafficking. The indictment alleged that illegal gambling parlors profited approximately $50,000 per night, while millions more were generated from digital piracy. The indictment alleged that members routinely traveled to China to obtain illegal copies of American and Chinese DVDs, then smuggled them into the United States. The organization then mass produced the discs and sold them at various store locations throughout New York City.[51]

Human Smuggling

Illegal immigration to the United States is not a new phenomenon. The promise of personal freedom, civil liberties, and economic opportunities has long prompted non-Americans to seek residency within the nation's borders. While countless individuals have endured the labor intensive process of legal entry, others have chosen to enter the country through illegal means. As a result, American authorities created the United States Border Patrol in 1924. Historically housed under Immigration and Naturalization Services, the U.S. Border Patrol and the U.S. Customs Service are now under the large umbrella of the Department of Homeland Security.

Traditional methods of smuggling included, but were not limited to, organized border jumping, and by using planes, trains, and automobiles. However, methods involving illegal immigration and naturalization fraud are increasing dramatically. These sophisticated measures often include the use of fraudulent identification and fraudulent representation of U.S. employment. The use of high-end printers, the availability of personal information via the Web, and sophisticated graphics programs have made the creation of fraudulent passports and other identification relatively easy. This same technology has enabled large scale smugglers to create fictitious companies which sell verification of false employment to individuals seeking illegal entrance. Such usage was discovered in 90 percent of L-1 visa petitions.[52]

The increase in immigration fraud committed by organized crime groups may be attributed to a variety of reasons. First, the number of lost or stolen American passports has risen as more and more Americans travel abroad. Second, various countries have eliminated visa policies. And, finally, the *Visa Waiver Pilot Program* originally articulated in the *Immigration Reform and Control Act* allows qualifying foreign nationals to enter the United States for 90 days for business or for pleasure without a nonimmigrant visa.

Sale and Distribution of Counterfeit Identity Documents: A Case in Point

In 2005, a joint task force of investigators from the ICE, IRS, SSA, and the U.S. Postal Service arrested various members of the Castorena Crime Family in Denver, Colorado. Led by Pedro Castorena-Aba.rra and his brothers, the organization was involved in the large-scale manufacturing and distribution of counterfeit identity document throughout the United States. Documents available from the group included: social security cards, work authorization documents, proof of vehicle insurance cards, temporary vehicle registration documents, and utility bills. Among items seized in the investigation were several hundred counterfeit identity documents and devices and tools for the production of same. Silk-screen printing templates, document laminators with security seals and holograms, and 20 computerized laboratories were also seized by authorities. Criminal proceeds of the group were laundered through legitimate fronts, various bank accounts, and money wire remitters.[53]

CONFRONTING CONTEMPORARY ORGANIZED CRIME

Organized crime groups are characterized by both innovation and longevity. A brief survey of criminal syndicates reveals a pervasiveness and tenacity which has remained resilient to even the most concentrated enforcement efforts. The introduction of technology has vastly expanded the potentiality of such groups and enhanced their methods of operation. However, academics and practitioners have failed to recognize the distinction between organized criminal activities and organized crime as an entity. As a result, current law enforcement endeavors have been largely ineffectual. Such efforts can only be successful if the following measures are taken:

- Recognition of the diversity among emerging groups.
- Recognition of the economic motivation between hacking and cyberattacks by organized crime groups (i.e., the problem is not hacking, *per se*, but online extortion via DOS, disruptions of service, and Web site defacement).
- Incorporation of the KYC (know your customer) requirement in banking to high-tech industry to prevent infiltration by illicit operators. In addition, KYP (know your partner) requirements should be included. Such incorporation would necessarily mandate background checks and corporate accountability. This would minimize the potential for the entrenchment of criminal syndicates into the largest global industry, such as what happened in the Russian banking and energy systems.
- Recognition that traditional hacking methods employed by organized crime groups are innovative.
- Recognition of the convergence (and sometimes interdependency) of transnational organized crime and terrorism.
- Global harmonization of regulation and the development of mutual legal assistance treaties, which include legislation on banking and securities laws and guidelines for police action
- Combination of bilateral and multilateral efforts
- Development of specific strategies for individual groups (strategies must vary as criminal organizations are quite diverse).
- Empowerment of local government through the increase in resources.
- Education and increased accountability for e-banking vendors and companies.

THE INTERSECTION OF ORGANIZED CRIME AND TERRORISM

The Internet has significantly changed the operational landscape of both organized crime groups and terrorist organizations. Just as American society has embraced the globalization of commerce and communications, these deviant groups have aggressively exploited the technology to further their criminal designs. Ironically, such utilization has been remarkably similar. Both entities use the medium to communicate with co-conspirators, to identify and research potential targets, and as a mechanism of attack. Even organizational and operational structures are increasingly similar as emerging OC groups are largely characterized by fluid networks. As a result, both groups have the potential to contribute to, facilitate, and even orchestrate acts of mass destruction.

Both entities exist in environments of minimal government controls, weak enforcement of law, and open borders. Terrorists and OC groups, alike, actively exploit geographic locales which are far removed from control centers of government authority. For example, the Russian Far East has been employed as a haven for both due to its distal proximity from Moscow. This is also true in areas adjoining the Golden Triangle, as terrorist groups of Myanmar can operate with impunity and finance their radical rhetoric through narcotics trafficking.[54] Countries experiencing transitional governments are also targeted by illicit organizations as they are most often characterized by the absence of state control, weakened law enforcement, and erosion of cohesive culture.

Although terrorists are more likely to use charities, both entities commingle resources and engage in legitimate markets—making it difficult to distinguish licit and illicit funds. This is further complicated by both groups' involvement in the laundering of funds, often characterized by the same methodologies, networks, and operators. Both groups are also involved in sophisticated criminal activities like identity theft, corruption of authority, DDoS attacks, hacking, credit card fraud, and narcotics trafficking. Toward these ends, they have armed themselves with the latest technological advancements, including cellular and satellite phones, encryption and steganography software, and global positioning systems.

Contemporary demarcation between organized crime groups and terrorist organizations is blurred as terrorists are increasingly engaged in organized crime activity to finance their rhetoric, propaganda, recruitment, and acts of terror. In fact, operational structures of the two often intersect, allowing terrorists to conceal themselves within criminal syndicates. Fortunately, the methods of identification and prosecution of individuals involved in both sorts of organizations are also remarkably similar. Protection of borders, following the money, and the freezing of assets have all proven effective in combating organized crime and terrorist groups.

DISCUSSION QUESTIONS

1. List and describe the methods of online communication among terrorists.
2. Explain the different classifications of motivations of terrorism.
3. Discuss bin Laden's role in incorporating the Internet in his terrorist group.
4. How are terrorist groups and organized crime groups similar in their modality and criminal operations?
5. How has technology changed the face of organized crime?
6. List the contemporary characteristics of organized crime groups.

RECOMMENDED READING

- Combs, Cindy C. (2007). *Terrorism in the Twenty-First Century* (4th Ed). Prentice Hall: Upper Saddle River, NJ.
- Grennan, Sean and Britz, Marjie T. (2007). *Organized Crime: A Worldwide Perspective*. Prentice-Hall: New Jersey.
- Kaplan, Eben (2006). *Terrorists and the Internet*. Council on Foreign Relations. Available at: *www.cfr.org/publication/10005* (last accessed December 31, 2006).
- Lewis, James A. (2002). "Assessing the Risks of Cyber Terrorism, Cyber War and Other Cyber Threats." Center for Strategic and International Studies. Washington, DC.
- McAfee (2005). *McAfee Virtual Criminology Report: North American Study into Organized Crime and the Internet*. Available at: *www.mcafee.com*.

- Rider, Barry (2001). Cyber-Organized Crime: The Impact of Information Technology on Organized Crime. *Journal of Financial Crime, 8*(4): 332–347.
- Tsfati, Yariv and Weimann, Gabriel (2002)."Terror on the Internet." *Studies in Conflict and Terrorism, 25:* 317–332. Available at: *www.terrorism.com.*
- Weimann, Gabriel (2006). *Terror on the Internet: The New Arena, the New Challenges.* United States Institute of Peace Press: Washington, DC.
- Williams, Phil (2004). Department of Homeland Security, Office of Inspector General, Office of Information Technology. *DHS Challenges in Consolidating Terrorist Watch List Information.*

WEB RESOURCES

- http://www.lib.msu.edu/harris23/crimjust/orgcrime. htm – maintained by Michigan State University Library, this site contains links to numerous articles, government publications, and academic resources on organized crime.
- http://policy-traccc.gmu.edu – homepage of the Terrorism, Transnational Crime and Corruption Center, a research center at George Mason University. This site provides links to national and international agencies, academic publications, and assorted other resources on terrorism and organized crime.
- http://www.yorku.ca/nathanson/default.htm – homepage to the Nathanson Centre of Transnational Human Rights, Crime and Security, located at York University, the site contains active links to numerous academic articles, government resources, and informational sites. In addition, the site provides a comprehensive outline of the structure of organized crimes, groups currently engaged, and the nexus of organized crime and terrorism.
- http://www.cisc.gc.ca/ – homepage of Canada's Criminal Intelligence Network, the site provides access to group publications, including annual reports on the status of organized crime in Canada. In addition, the site provides active links to assorted government resources and online articles.
- http://www.soca.gov.uk/ – homepage to the United Kingdom's Serious Organized Crime Agency, the site provides an updated image of organized crime in the United Kingdom.
- http://www.fbi.gov/research.htm – maintained by the Federal Bureau of Investigation, the site provides access to assorted research publication and FBI reports. In addition, it includes links to other agencies and resources on various topics.
- http://www.state.gov/s/ct/rls/crt/2006/82738.htm – sponsored by the U.S. Department of State, this site provides a comprehensive listing and history of those organizations or groups designated as Foreign Terrorist Organizations by the United States.
- http://www.ojp.usdoj.gov/nij/international/programs/ terro_research_share.html#tp – link to the National Institute of Justice's International Center for Terrorism Research Activity. The site provides links to various scholarly publications and provides information and applications for external support for research in terrorism.

ENDNOTES

[1] President George W. Bush, November 1, 2001, in his address to the UN General Assembly.

[2] Tsfati, Yariv and Weimann, Gabriel (2002). "www.terrorism. com: Terror on the Internet." *Studies in Conflict and Terrorism, 25:* 317–332.

[3] UNODC (2007). *Definitions of Terrorism.* Available at *http://www.unodc.org/unodc/terrorism_definitions.html.* Retrieved from the Internet on October 15, 2007.

[4] United Nations (1994). General Assembly, 84th Plenary Meeting, December 9, 1994. Available at *http://www.un.org/documents/ga/res/49/a49r060.htm.* Retrieved from Internet on October 15, 2007.

[5] UNODC (2007). *Definitions of Terrorism.*

[6] Schmid, Alex P., and Albert J. Jongman, et al. (1988). *Political Terrorism: A New Guide to Actors, Authors, Concepts, DATA Bases, Theories and Literature* (2nd Ed.). North-Holland Publishing: Amsterdam.

[7] Tsfati and Weimann (2002). "*www.terrorism.com*".

[8] Combs, Cindy C. (2007). *Terrorism in the Twenty-First Century* (4th Ed). Prentice Hall: Upper Saddle River, NJ.

[9] Ibid.

[10] Ibid.

[11] Jenkins, B. (1975) *International Terrorism.* Los Angeles, CA: Crescent Publication; Tsfati, and Weimann (2002). "*www.terrorism.com*".

[12] Manion, Mark and Goodrum, Abby (2000). "Terrorism and Civil Disobedience: Toward a Hactivist Ethic." *Computers and Society* (June): 14–19.

[13] Weimann, Gabriel (2006). *Terror on the Internet: The New Arena, the New Challenges.* United States Institute of Peace Press: Washington, DC.

[14] Tsfati and Weimann (2002). "*www.terrorism.com*"

[15] Kaplan, Eben (2006). *Terrorists and the Internet.* Council on Foreign Relations. Available at *www.cfr.org/publiction/10005* (last accessed December 31, 2006).

[16] Ibid.

[17] Thomas, Timothy (2003). "Al Qaeda and the Internet: The Danger of "Cyberplanning." *Parameters* (Spring): 112–123.

[18]Some of the first commercial satellite telephones were used by bin Laden while he was hiding in Afghanistan, and he produced some of the first propaganda videos with hand-held cameras.

[19]Debat, Alexis (2006). "Al Qaeda's Web of Terror." *ABC News.* March 10, 2006.

[20]Available at *http://www.privacyrights.org/ar/ChronData Breaches.htm.*

[21]ZDNet (2007). "FBI Reveals London Student's Online Terrorist Links." *Security Threats Toolkit.* October 1, 2007. Available at *http://news.zdnet.co.uk/security/0,1000000189,392 89731,00.htm.* Retrieved from the Internet on October 17, 2007.

[22]Schneier, Bruce (2001). "Terrorists and Steganography." *Crypto-Gram Newsletter.* September 30, 2001. Available at *www.schneier.com.* Retrieved from the Internet on October 17, 2007.

[23]Ibid.

[24]Berinator, Scott (2002). "The Truth About Cyberterrorism." *CIO Magazine.* Available at *www.cio.com/archive/031502/ truth.html.*

[25]Available at *www.doj.gov.*

[26]Woolcock, Nicola (2006). *Animal Rights Activists Convicted in the US of Terrorizing British Lab: The Americans Waged a Campaign Against Huntindon Life Science.* Available at *http://www.timesonline.co.uk/tol/news/world/us_and_americas/ article737247.ece.* Retrieved from the Internet on October 17, 2007.

[27]Kaplan (2006). *Terrorists and the Internet.*

[28]Shelley, Louise (1997). *Threat from International Organized Crime and Terrorism.* Congressional Testimony before the House Committee on International Relations. (October 1, 1997).

[29]Grennan, Sean and Britz, Marjie (2007). *Organized Crime: A Worldwide Perspective.* Prentice-Hall: Upper Saddle River, NJ.

[30]Ibid.

[31]Asbury, Herbert (1927). *Gangs of New York.* Harper Collins: New York.

[32]Grennan and Britz (2007). *Organized Crime.*

[33]Ibid.

[34]It must be noted that Valachi's testimony has been discredited by various sources due to its self-serving nature. In addition, Valachi's account is peppered with inaccuracies promoted by the popular media of the time. Thus, it is unclear as to which portions of his testimony actually reflect his independent recollections, and which are patently false.

[35]Grennan and Britz (2007). *Organized Crime.*

[36]Britz, Marjie T. (2006). *The Emerging Face of Organized Crime.* A paper presented at the 2006 Cybercrime Summit, Kennesaw State University.

[37]Power, Richard (2000). *Tangled Web: Tales of Digital Crime for the Shadows of Cyberspace.* Que Publishing: New York.

[38]DOJ (2004). *Nineteen Individuals Indicted in Internet "Carding" Conspiracy: Shadowcrew Organization Called 'One-Stop Online Marketplace for Identity Theft'.* Press Release. October 28, 2004. Available at *http://www.usdoj.gov/opa/pr/ 2004/October/04_crm_726.htm.* Retrieved from on October 15, 2007.

[39]Ibid.

[40]FIA (2001). *Contraband, Organized Crime and the Threat to the Transportation and Supply Chain Function.* Available at *http://www.cargosecurity.com/ncsc/images/contraband.pdf.* Retrieved from the Internet on October 7, 2007.

[41]Ibid.

[42]Britz (2006). *The Emerging Face of Organized Crime.*

[43]Ibid.

[44]Williams, Phil (2001). "Organized Crime and Cybercrime: Synergies, Trends, and Responses." *Transnational Crime: Global Issues.* Available at *http://usinfo.state.gov/journals/ itgic/0801/ijge/gj07.htm.* Retrieved from the Internet on October 7, 2007.

[45]Gordon, Gary R. and Willox, Norman A. (2003). *Identity Fraud: A Critical National and Global Threat.* Electronic Crime Institute and Lexis Nexis: New York: NY.

[46]Acosta, R. Alexander (2007). *Judge Orders Organized Crime Leader to Forfeith Hundreds of Millions of Dollars.* Available at *http://www.state.gov/m/ds/rls/81906.htm.* Retrieved from the Internet on October 7, 2007.

[47]Grennan, Sean; Britz, Marjie; Rush, Jeff; and Barker, Tom (2000). *Gangs: An International Approach.* Prentice-Hall: Upper Saddle River, NJ.

[48]Ibid.

[49]Grennan and Britz (2007). *Organized Crime.*

[50]National Retail Federation (2007). *2007 Organized Retail Crime Survey Results.* Available at *www.nrf.com.* Retrieved from the Internet on October 12, 2007.

[51]ICE (2005). *U.S. Indicts 39 Members and Associates of Violent Criminal Organization in New York City.* Available at *www.ice. gov/pi/news/newsreleases/articles/050909newyork.htm.* Retrieved from the Internet on October 9, 2007.

[52]Gordon and Willox (2003). *Identity Fraud.*

[53]ICE (2006). *Investigative Background on Castorena Family Organization.* Available at *www.ice.gov/pi/news/newsreleases/ articles/060619_dc_bkg.htm.* Retrieved from the Internet on September 9, 2007.

[54]Shelley, Louise (2000). "The Nexus of Organized Criminals and Terrorists." *International Annals of Criminology, 40*(1–2): 85–91.

CHAPTER 7

Avenues for Prosecution and Government Efforts

LEARNING OBJECTIVES

After reading this chapter, you will be able to do the following:

✓ Have knowledge of traditional statutes that also apply to current problems with computer crime.

✓ Discover recent federal government legislation on online behavior.

✓ Gain knowledge of investigative tools used by the government to reduce the risk of modern technology.

✓ Develop an awareness of data mining and the programs imbedded in it.

✓ Have an idea of the international attempt to solve the problem of computer crime.

KEY TERMS AND CONCEPTS

- aggravated identity theft
- business community
- Carnivore
- Child Pornography Protection Act
- civil liberty/non-profit advocacy organizations
- Computer Fraud and Abuse Act

- data mining
- federal interest computer
- Financial Modernization Act of 1999
- government entities
- hacking statute
- HTCIA
- IACIS

- Identity Theft and Assumption Deterrence Act
- Infragard
- Innocent Images
- National Infrastructure Protection Center (NIPC)
- packet sniffing

● INTRODUCTION

As stated previously, the advent of computer crime has resulted in a myriad of problems for law enforcement administrators. The lack of resources available to small agencies, the traditional apathy toward nonviolent crime, and the reluctance of legislative action have enabled many computer criminals to act with virtual impunity. While it is anticipated that an increase in technology-specific legislation and the modification of extant statutes is forthcoming, lawmakers should evaluate existing federal and state law for prosecutorial avenues currently available. This would empower local agencies and reduce demands on federal agencies.

Traditionally, state and local officials have been forced to rely exclusively on the expertise of better-trained, better-funded federal agencies. Unfortunately, these agencies are incapable of addressing every call for assistance. In addition, they are often unwilling to expend resources on crimes which do not constitute threats to institutional security, the economic infrastructure, the exploitation of children, individual safety, or violation of federal law. (It is unlikely, for example, that a federal agency would assist law enforcement in cases constituting misdemeanor offenses or those offenses which appear to be minor in nature—e.g., installation of Back Orifice on a personal computer, a currently contained virus which destroyed

Local Trailblazers

Although federal efforts have been attacked as overly intrusive, local efforts which include less invasive measures have been commended. (Unfortunately, such commendations have not resulted in job security.) As in other areas of computer investigations, Chicago and Phoenix were two of the first local jurisdictions to actively pursue computer criminals. (Many of these enforcement efforts mimicked their criminal counterparts, springing up virtually overnight in an ad hoc manner.) Chicago was quite effective but dipped off the radar screen after the scandals associated with the LoD crackdown. Phoenix, under the guidance of the ably equipped Gail Thack-eray, gained notoriety among the hacker community. In May 1990, Operation SunDevil was launched. This operation included 150 Secret Service agents, 40 seized computers, and 12 cities (Cincinnati, Los Angeles, Miami, Detroit, Tucson, Phoenix, Newark, San Diego, Richmond, San Francisco, Pittsburgh, and San Jose). Other cities like New York City and Chicago were also included in the sting. Because the thrust of the operation was computer seizure and not arrest, the hacker community was taken completely unaware. Unlike previous activities, the hacker community was taken aback completely. Luckily, this trend is continuing.

two computers.) Law enforcement administrators should carefully evaluate state statutes. When used creatively, many can be directly applied to criminal activity involving computers. Remember, the method of execution is not an essential element in criminal law. Intent, action, and illegality are inherent in every case of larceny, for example. The method is irrelevant. Thus, an individual who utilizes a computer to steal money from a bank is just as culpable as the individual who resorts to physical theft. At the same time, criminal mischief or vandalism statutes may be utilized to prosecute an individual who remotely alters data. Investigators and administrators must be encouraged to look for the obvious! While there are a variety of statutes which have been enacted to specifically address technological crime, traditional statutes should be utilized where the former are lacking.

TRADITIONAL STATUTES

Title 18 of the United States Code has long been characterized as an invaluable resource for state and local legislators in development of state codes. As such, it can be used as a guideline for investigators seeking to apply non–technology-specific prohibitions generically to computer crime. In addition, Titles 15 and 17 may be useful.

Although the above is not intended to serve as an exhaustive listing of all available statues, it is illustrative of the typologies of statutes applicable to criminal activity involving computers. Administrators and investigators should peruse their own state codes and avail themselves of existing prosecutorial avenues. (Virtually all state resources, for example, prohibit the interception of electronic communications. These statutes could be used to creatively prosecute individuals who are utilizing Trojans to access other machines.) In addition, administrators must petition legislatures for relief and familiarize themselves with computer-specific statutes which are emerging.

THE EVOLUTION OF COMPUTER-SPECIFIC STATUTES

While many state legislatures have been slow to enact computer-specific statutes, the United U.S Congress has reacted more quickly. Thus, measures enabling the prosecution of electronic fraud, hacking, and the theft of intellectual property may be found at the federal level. Unfortunately, this legislation has been buffeted by a variety of legal challenges, the language characterized by jurists as vague and ambiguous. Such efforts can be traced back to 1977, when Senator Abraham Ribicoff (Connecticut) introduced the Federal Computer Systems Protection Act (FSCPA). Although the Act was eventually defeated, it created a climate ripe for future legislation.

Criminal Activity Statute	Applicable
Fraud and Embezzlement	
18 U.S.C. § 2314	Applies to goods known to be stolen or fraudulently obtained and worth more than $5,000 transported in interstate commerce.
18 U.S.C. § 641	Embezzlement or theft of public money, property, or records.
18 U.S.C. § 2071	Prohibits concealment, removal, or mutilation of public records.
18 U.S.C. § 1005	Prohibits concealment, removal, or mutilation of the records of banks or credit institutions. (Remote alteration or the like would clearly fall within these provisions.)
18 U.S.C. § 1006	Prohibits false, fictitious, or fraudulent statements to a department or agency concerning a matter within the jurisdiction of the same *when something of value is involved.* (May be utilized if individuals misrepresent themselves to gain access to programs or pages.)
Terrorism or Espionage	
18 U.S.C. § 1905	Prohibits the disclosure of confidential information by a government employee.
18 U.S.C. §§ 793, 794, 795	Prohibits the gathering, transmission, or loss of defense information; prohibits the transmission or delivery of national defense information to a foreign government or agent; prohibits the sketching or photographing of defense installations. (May be utilized if individuals attach live feeds of military bases or the like or upload pictures or maps onto the Internet.)
Child Seduction	
18 U.S.C. § 2421	Prohibits the interstate transportation of minors for sexual activity.
Child Exploitation	
18 U.S.C. § 2251	Prohibits the sexual exploitation and other abuse of children.
Stalking	
18 U.S.C. § 2261	This amendment to Title 18 makes it a federal crime to engage in repeated harassing or threatening behavior that places the victim in reasonable fear of death or bodily injury. Summarily stated, any person who travels (or causes to), uses (or causes to) the mail or any facility in interstate or foreign commerce, or enters or leaves (or causes to) Indian country is guilty of stalking if they place an individual in reasonable fear of death or harm to a loved one.
18 U.S.C. § 875(c)—The Hobbs Act	Whoever transmits in interstate or foreign commerce any communication containing any threat to kidnap any person or any threat to injure the person of another, shall be fined under this title or imprisoned not more than five years, or both.
Forgery and Counter-feiting 18 U.S.C. §§ 471–509	
Credit Card Fraud	
15 U.S.C. 41 § 1644	Prohibits the use, attempt, or conspiracy to fraudulently use credit cards in interstate or foreign commerce. In addition, it prohibits the transportation of such cards, and receipt or concealment of goods and tickets purchased and money received through card transactions. (This statute could be used on individuals posting credit card numbers on BBSs or on "carding"—hackers who use stolen credit card information to purchase goods or services.)

(Continued)

Criminal Activity Statute	Applicable
Extortion	
18 U.S.C. § 1951	
Copyright Infringement	
17 U.S.C. §§ 102, 103	Provides definitional guidelines for protected information or material. In particular, it offers protection for idea(s), procedure, process, system, method of operation, concept, principle, or discovery, regardless of the form in which it is described, explained, illustrated, or embodied in such work.
17 U.S.C. § 506	Prohibits the reproduction, preparation, distribution, or public release of copyrighted material. This includes art, photographs, writings, etc. Probably one of the most common forms of theft on the Internet—where ideas are routinely misrepresented.
Software Piracy	
15 U.S.C. § 1114	Prohibits the manufacturing of counterfeit products (may include software or hardware).
RICO	
18 U.S.C. §§ 1961–1968	Provides for the prosecution of individuals involved in a pattern of racketeering. It also provides for the punishment of offenders and the seizures of their assets.
Access Device Fraud	
18 U.S.C. § 1029	Individuals may be prosecuted under this statute if they knowingly and with intent to defraud, produce, use, trafficking, or in some cases simply possess counterfeit and/or unauthorized access devices or device-making equipment. Such devices are broadly defined as cards, plates, codes, account numbers, electronic serial numbers, mobile identification number, personal identification number, or other means (Soma et al., 1996). Although this statute was not directed toward computer-facilitated fraud, the courts have ruled that it may be used in cases where computer passwords are fraudulently obtained to steal things of value (*U.S.* v. *Fernandez*, No. 92 CR. 563 (RO), 1993 WL 88197 (S.D.N.Y. March 25, 1993.)) In addition, this statute could be used to prosecute phreakers using illegal boxes or electronic passwords used to access financial accounts, and the like. This section, never mentioning the word "computer," has been utilized by the Secret Service to prosecute those individuals who have stolen information or software from computers.
Illegal Wiretapping	
18 U.S.C. § 119	A variety of laws at the state and federal level make it illegal for individuals to unlawfully intercept electronic communications. This would include utilization of keyloggers or other functions included in back-door programs like NetBus or Back Orifice (since these programs also grant access to them). These would include provisions under Title 18 (18 U.S.C. § 2511). In addition, 18 U.S.C. § 2701 prohibits the intentional acquisition of or alteration or destruction of stored communications. Thus, those individuals who intentionally access e-mail accounts not belonging to them may be prosecuted under this statute.

Murphy's Law

Ribicoff's actions stemmed from a computer scam conducted by Ian Murphy, the computer consultant for Universal Studios theatrical release *Sneakers* and a world-class thief. Murphy began his consulting "career" as a thief who created dummy corporations to facilitate the transfer of thousands of dollars in computer equipment. Upon his conviction, his mother promptly petitioned Congressman Larry Coughlin to investigate the *leniency* of his sentence. (Apparently, she was outraged that her son was not being adequately punished.) Coughlin's response was to introduce legislation which eventually became known as the Counterfeit Access Device and Computer Fraud and Abuse Act of 1984 (Baker, 1993).

Computer Fraud and Abuse Act of 1986

Originally known as the Counterfeit Access Device and Computer Fraud and Abuse Act of 1986, Section 1030 of Title 18 of the United States Code, quickly became the federal government's main weapon in fighting computer crime. Known as the **hacking statute**, the act in its original form was very narrow in scope, making it a felony to knowingly

Access a computer without authorization, or in excess of authorization, in order to obtain classified United States defense or foreign relations information with the intent or reason to believe that such information would be used to harm the United States or to advantage a foreign nation. Second, the 1984 Act made it a misdemeanor knowingly to access a computer without authorization, in excess of authorization, in order to obtain information contained in a financial record of a financial institution or in a consumer file of a consumer reporting agency. Third, the 1984 Act made it a misdemeanor knowingly to access a computer without authorization, or in excess of authorization, in order to use, modify, destroy, or disclose information in, or prevent authorized use of, a computer operated for or on behalf of the United States if such conduct would affect the government's use of the computer. The 1984 Act also made it a crime to attempt or to conspire to commit any of the three acts described above (Andreano, 1999).

This legislation proved to be largely ineffective due to the ambiguity of the statutory language and an overemphasis on financial information. (Only one person was successfully prosecuted under the original provisions.) However, Congress strengthened the Act in 1986, taking great pains to clarify terms originally characterized as vague. **Federal Interest Computer**, for example, was expanded to include any computer *which is used in interstate or foreign commerce or communications*. This enabled federal authorities to assume jurisdiction if a crime was committed via computer in a distant state. It also expanded the original language, broadening its scope to include all financial records, not just those institutions and records found within the Right to Financial Privacy Act of 1978. In addition, the revisions expanded the criminal intent requirement from *knowingly* to *intentionally*. Thus, inadvertent intrusions would not be prosecutable. More succinctly, the new Act made it a misdemeanor to gain unauthorized access to financial information from any financial institution or credit reporting agency, any information in the possession of the government, or any private information where the defendant's conduct involved interstate or foreign commerce; and, a felony if the activity involved an expectation of gain or if the offense was in the furtherance of another crime. Finally, the 1986 revisions specifically targeted hackers by criminalizing password trafficking.

As stated, these revisions proved to be invaluable to the investigation and prosecution of computer crime. Generally speaking, the current version of the Act (several subsequent revisions have taken place) protects computer(s) which are utilized in interstate commerce or communication, computers which involve the federal interest, and any government computers. Actions included in this statute include theft, destruction, or corruption of sensitive information, including, but not limited to, defense secrets, financial records, and passwords. In addition, the statute reduces traditional standards of *mens rea*, allowing the prosecution of individuals who behave with reckless disregard. (This would include the spread of computer viruses and back-door programs like NetBus and Back Orifice.)

Ironically, one of the first individuals to be charged with a felony under this statute was Robert Morris, the infamous creator of the "Morris Worm," and son of the former chief scientist at the National Computer Security Center. The Act was also used to prosecute Herbert Zinn (aka Shadowhawk) and Kevin Mitnick. "Shadowhawk" was an 18-year-old high school dropout and hacker extraordinaire. Herbert Zinn, considered a juvenile at the time of his arrest, was sentenced to nine months and fined $10,000 for breaking into computers ranging

Perhaps the most infamous of hackers is Kevin Mitnick, a poster child for the Electronic Frontier Foundation and other libertarian groups. (*AP/World Wide Photos*)

from NATO to the U.S. Air Force. In addition, Zinn stole 52 AT&T programs valued at over $1 million. Provisions under the Act could have resulted in a prison term of 20 years for an adult charged with the same range of offenses. Unlike Zinn, Kevin Mitnick, one of the most infamous hackers in history, had a criminal history the length of which rivals that of many organized crime figures. His successful conviction under this Act was a result of his theft of programs valued at more than $1 million from Digital Equipment Corporation and the illegal manipulation of MCI service codes.

The *Computer Fraud and Abuse Act* has also been successfully used against employees who have exceeded their authorized access. In fact, the constitutionality of the Act has been affirmed in cases ranging from hackers to government employees. Perhaps the first (or best known) was *United States* v. *Rice,* in which an IRS employee accessed Service records to determine the scope the Service's case against his friend. As he was not in the criminal investigation decisions, Rice's actions constituted unauthorized access. His subsequent conviction was affirmed on appeal.

National Information Infrastructure Protection Act of 1996 (NIIPA)

As stated, the *Computer Fraud and Abuse Act* has been successfully utilized to prosecute hackers. However, the Act does have significant limitations in that it only involves those cases in which computer data is a target. It does not include other offenses committed via or in conjunction with computer technology nor did it include non-interest computers. To remedy this, Congress passed the *National Information Infrastructure Protection Act of 1996.*[1] This extended the protections, traditionally afforded to federal interest computers, to any computer attached to the Internet even if all of the computers were located in one state. In addition, the Act identified broad areas of computer-related crime which involve either accessing computer systems without/or in excess of authorization or

Computer Fraud and Abuse Act—18 U.S.C. § 1030

- Section 1030 expands the power of the Secret Service by specifying that "the United States Secret Service shall, in addition to any other agency having such authority, have the authority to investigate offenses under this section." However, due to Congress' refusal to remedy jurisdictional turf battles between the USSS and the FBI, authority is somewhat unclear.
- Section 1030 also prohibits simple access of full or part-time governmental computers—no damage must be done in order for this act to be violated.
- Section 1030(a)(4)—punishes those who use computers in schemes to defraud victims of property of more than $5,000.
- Section 1030(a)(5)—creates three separate offenses, two felonies and one misdemeanor (depends on intent and authority of the actor)—criminalizes the transmission of a program, information, code, or command, and as a result of such conduct, intentionally causes damage without authorization to a protected computer (felony); damage may include the availability or integrity of data, program, system or information that (1) causes loss of more than $5,000 within a year to one or more persons; (2) modifies or impairs, or potentially modifies or impairs, the

- medical examination, diagnosis, treatment, or care of one or more persons; (3) causes physical injury to a person; or, (4) threatens public health 1030(e)(8).
- Section 1030(a)(5)—generally governs access without authority (outsiders).
- Section 1030(a)(5)(B)—individual who intentionally accesses a protected computer and, as a result of such conduct, recklessly causes damage is guilty of a felony.
- Section 1030(a)(5)(C)—individual who intentionally accesses a protected computer and, as a result of such conduct, causes damage is guilty of a misdemeanor when it cannot be shown that the damage caused was either intentional or reckless.
- Section 1030(a)(6)—prohibits trafficking in passwords, information, or devices through which unauthorized access may result, if such trafficking affects interstate or foreign commerce or is a government computer—*aimed primarily at hackers, and underground hacking boards.*
- Section 1030(a)(7)—involves extortion through threats to damage a protected computer (this has been utilized against a variety of individuals who have threatened to exploit holes in security systems if their demands are not met).

causing damage to computers. To wit, the subcategories criminalize the following acts:

- **18 U.S.C. § 1030(a)(1)**—transmitting classified government information;
- **18 U.S.C. § 1030(a)(2)**—obtaining information from financial institutions, private sector computers, and U.S. government
- **18 U.S.C. § 1030(a)(3)**—affecting the government's use of a U.S. department or agency nonpublic computer
- **18 U.S.C. § 1030(a)(4)**—fraud
- **18 U.S.C. § 1030(a)(5)**—hacking and malicious programming. This section criminalizes damaging protected computers via hacking or malware *even if* the damage was not intentional
- **18 U.S.C. § 1030(a)(6)**—intent to or trafficking in passwords
- **18 U.S.C. § 1030(a)(7)**—extortion or communication of threats

These modifications have served to close numerous loopholes in original legislation. By extending protection to all computers connected to the Internet, NIIPA provides for the prosecution of hacker attacks on both intrastate government and financial institution computers. In addition, by removing the trespass requirement and adding an intent or recklessness element, NIIPA provides for the prosecution of insiders who intentionally damage computers.[2] The Act further provides for the prosecution of individuals trafficking in passwords or those who attempted to extort money or values from an individual or entity by threatening computer harm. Finally, and perhaps more importantly, NIIPA successfully eliminates several defenses predicated on intent, implied authorization, or value of access. More specifically, NIIPA requires only an intent to access not an intent to cause damage. Thus, individuals attempting to access a protected computer may be prosecuted even if their motivation was not fiduciary.

EVOLVING CHILD PORNOGRAPHY STATUTES

Although a variety of laws have been enacted to combat the increase in technological crime, none are more emotionally charged than those dealing with child pornography. Beginning in 1977, Congress has attempted to eliminate child pornography. Originally criminalized at the federal level with the Protection of Children against Sexual Exploitation Act of 1977 (PCSE), Congress has periodically revised legislation to protect children from sexual exploitation in keeping with emerging legal doctrine. However, lower courts have remained divided on new legislation, and the Supreme Court has denied *cert* on the majority of cases. Traditionally, evaluations of child pornography statutes relied primarily on two Supreme Court decisions, whose interpretation of and application to emerging laws have been diverse.

In 1982, the Supreme Court evaluated freespeech challenges to child pornography and found them wanting (*New York* v. *Ferber*, 458 U.S. 747). Uncharacteristically emphatic, the Court ruled that child pornography was outside the scope of the First Amendment, and allowed states to enact blanket prohibitions against visualizations of children engaged in sexual situations. The Child Protection Act of 1984 (CPA) incorporated this decision. Although the Act lacked technological specificity, it was widely used against online offenders until the emergence of the Child Protection and Obscenity Act of 1988. While this Act officially prohibited the use of computers to transport, distribute, or receive such materials, it, and its successor, has been widely criticized by freespeech advocates. At the same time, the Court has remained resolutely silent.

Prior to the passage of the **Child Pornography Protection Act** (CPPA) in 1996, definitions of child pornography appeared to be nationally, if not universally, accepted. However,

the incorporation of technology-specific language resulted in a slew of constitutional challenges, and lower courts displayed sharp disagreement. Perhaps the most controversial, and certainly the most attacked, provision of the revised Act involved the use of electronically altered photographs in depicting child pornography. Noting technological advancements, Congress recognized the possibility of creating child pornography out of innocent images. To prevent this, Congress expanded the definition of child pornography to include altered pictures of identifiable children, and depictions of what "appears to be" or "conveys the impression of" minors engaged in sexually explicit situations. (The latter includes wholly artificial images, entirely created through virtual, as opposed to actual, children.) Unfortunately, the Supreme Court ruled that the inclusion of such provisions rendered the Act unconstitutional as the potential for *virtual* rather than *actual* victimization abridged the guarantees set forth by the First Amendment.

In the wake of the *Ashcroft* decision, Congress passed the *Prosecutorial Remedies and Other Tools to End the Exploitation of Children Today* (PROTECT)*Act*. Although it sought to reinstate the original provisions housed within the CPPA, it also included a variety of other measures designed to protect children both on- and off-line. The most important of these included:

- mandatory life sentences for offenders involved in a sex offense against a minor if such offender has had a prior conviction of abuse against a minor;
- the establishment of a program to obtain criminal history/background checks for volunteer organizations;
- authorization for electronic eavesdropping in cases related to child abuse or kidnapping;
- prohibition against the pretrial release of persons charged with specific offenses against children;
- elimination of the statutes of limitation for child abduction or child abuse;

- prohibition against the pretrial release of persons charged with specific offenses against children;
- provided for the appointment of a national AMBER Alert Coordinator
- elimination of waiting periods for missing persons cases involving victims between the ages of 18 and 21;
- avenues for reporting missing persons between the ages of 18 and 21 to NCIC;
- prohibition against computer-generated child pornography;
- application of the *Miller* standard of obscenity in drawings, sculptures, and pictures of such, which depict minors in obscene situations or engaged in sexual activity.
- Enhancement of sentences for the possession and distribution of obscene images of minors
- Authorization of fines and imprisonment of up to 30 years for U.S. citizens or residents engaging in illicit sexual conduct abroad

IDENTITY THEFT AND FINANCIAL PRIVACY STATUTES

Identity theft/fraud has become the defining crime of the information age. It is estimated that at least 10 million incidents occur each year. However, this figure does not approach the numbers imagined by the general public. Although traditional statutes contain some provisions which may be applied to crime associated with the theft and misuse of personal information, statutes specifically addressing identity theft and financial privacy were not created until the waning days of the twentieth century. Such statutes have often been hastily prepared by individuals attempting to assuage constituent fear. Ironically, privacy advocates have often criticized the emerging legislation.

Identity Theft and Assumption Deterrence Act of 1998 (Appendix A)

In October 1998, the *Identity Theft and Assumption Deterrence Act* was passed by Congress. It was the first act to make the possession of another's personal identifying information a crime, punishable by up to 20 years in prison. More specifically, the Act stated that it is unlawful if an individual:

> Knowingly transfers or uses, without lawful authority, a means of identification of another person with the intent to commit, or to aid or abet, any unlawful activity that constitutes a violation of Federal law, or that constitutes a felony under any applicable State or local law.

In addition, the law expanded the traditional definition of "means of identification" to include:

(A) name, social security number, date of birth, official State or government issued driver's license or identification number, alien registration number, government passport number, employer or taxpayer identification number;

(B) unique biometric data, such as fingerprint, voice print, retina or iris image, or other unique physical representation;

(C) unique electronic identification number, address, or routing code; or

(D) telecommunication identifying information or access device

The Act was extremely significant for a variety of reasons. First, the Act criminalized the use of both public and non-public information. Second, it provided expansive definitions to fully clarify the phenomenon. Third, it designated the United States Sentencing Commission to incorporate identity fraud and identity theft into the Sentencing Guidelines, and specifically provided for a system of victim restitution, including attorney's fees, lost time at work, and denial of credit. It further provided a formula for sentence enhancements if aggravating factors were present. As a result, considerations for sentencing include, but are not limited to, the amount of loss, the sophistication of the scheme, the amount of planning, the number of victims, and the susceptibility and status of the victims.[3] Finally, the Act officially designated the Federal Trade Commission (FTC) as the repository for consumer complaints and as the agent of information dissemination for consumers, credit reporting agencies, and law enforcement.

The Financial Modernization Act of 1999 (Appendix B)

While the *Identity Theft and Assumption Deterrence Act of 1998* was primarily enacted to provide criminal penalties for the theft and misuse of personal identifying information, the *Financial Modernization Act of 1999* was enacted to promote greater accountability of and provide civil remedies against corporate America. Also known as the *Gramm-Leach-Bliley Act* or *GLB* for short, the Act includes provisions to protect consumers' personal financial information held by financial institutions. In addition, the *GLB* grants authority for administration and enforcement to the states and eight federal agencies. There are three principal parts to the privacy requirements: the *Financial Privacy Rule,* the *Safeguards Rule,* and pretexting provisions.

The regulations contained within the *Financial Privacy Rule* and the *Safeguards Rule* apply to various financial institutions and companies who receive personal financial information. Under the provisions of the *Financial Privacy Rule,* such entities must provide individuals with a clear, conspicuous, and accurate statement of the company's privacy practices. It also mandates an "opt-out" option, where consumers and customers can prohibit the disclosure of certain personal information. Consumers are further protected by provisions of the *Safeguards Rule,* which requires companies to develop and implement a comprehensive security plan to safeguard personal consumer information. Additionally, the GLB contains provisions which protect consumers from individuals and companies that obtain personal financial information under false pretenses (i.e., "pretexting"). Finally, the Act limits when financial institutions may disclose personal information, including social security numbers, to nonaffiliated third parties.

Fair and Accurate Credit Transactions Act of 2003 (FACTA)

In 2003, Congress amended the *Fair Credit Reporting Act* (15 U.S.C. §1861). The resulting law, known as the *Fair and Accurate Credit Transactions Act of 2003* (FACTA), included a variety of changes which generally addressed consumer rights and specifically targeted identity theft. While many of the provisions contained therein remain unrealized, FACTA remains the most comprehensive approach to combat the growing problem.

Major Provisions to FACTA

- **Free Credit Report**—Consumers may avail themselves of one free credit report from each of three largest credit reporting agencies (Equifax, Experian, TransUnion). This provision encourages consumers to regularly monitor their credit reports, therefore allowing the discovery of unlawful activity much more quickly. Initially, the provision was ineffective, as the process was not streamlined. Consumers may now request their free copies through *www.annualcreditreport.com.* However, it is not recommended to request and access individual reports online. Ironically, the FTC has filed at least one suit against, and issued several warnings to, various imposter sites designed to steal your personal information.

- **Fraud Alerts**—Consumers have the right to create alerts on their credit files, indicating that they have been the victim of identity theft and that some information included in the report may be based on the victimization. Such alerts must be attached to the credit file and provided to all entities requesting data. In addition, credit reporting agencies must exclude such accounts from those used for marketing purposes by third parties and provide additional free credit reports to consumers who have initiated the alert process. In files containing alerts, businesses seeking to extend credit are required to contact the consumer directly or to take other reasonable steps to authenticate the applicant. These actions are designed to minimize the potential costs associated with the theft by hampering the acquisition of additional credit and by encouraging verification of identity by potential creditors.

- **Active Duty Alerts**—FACTA also contains special provisions for individuals actively performing military duty. Requires credit reporting agencies to place an active duty alert within a credit file of an individual actively serving in the military. In addition, it also provides for an automatic two-year "opt out" from lists provided to third parties.

- **Truncation of Credit/Debit Account Numbers**—FACTA prohibits merchants from putting any but the last five digits of a credit card number on customer receipts. This is designed to minimize the effectiveness of dumpster diving by limiting the amount of information printed on a receipt. As a result, many dumpster divers have modified their *modus operandi* to focus exclusively on manually imprinted receipts which are often used by small businesses or roadside merchants.

- **Truncation of Social Security Numbers**—Like the previous provision, FACTA requires credit reporting agencies to exclude the first five digits of consumer social security numbers from their disclosures upon request.

- **One-Call Fraud Alerts and Enhanced Victims' Resolution Process**—Creation of a national system of fraud detection and alerts to increase the ease of incident reporting and protection of credit standings. Known as "one-call fraud alerts", the system allows consumers to generate a nationwide fraud alert with one phone call.

- **Mandates to Card Issuers to Investigate Changes of Address and Requests for New or Additional Cards**—Requires all creditors to send notification of changes to both the old and new addresses. It is intended to quickly alert victims.

- **Blocking or Elimination of Fraudulent Information**—Allows consumers to file "no fault letters" with police authorities to eliminate the release of fraudulent information. It also requires credit reporting agencies to block those entities which supplied fraudulent information from further submitting information on the credit report.

- **Fraud Alert Requirements by Credit Reporting Agencies**—Provides for the inclusion of a fraud alert upon request by a consumer which states that some information included in the report may be based on identity theft. Such alerts must be attached to the credit file and provided to all who request data.

- **Requirement of Credit Reporting Agencies to Divulge Consumer Credit Scores**—This measure is designed to increase the probability of discovery of victimization.

- **Limits the Commingling of Medical and Financial Information**—In order to decrease the possibility of identity theft/fraud which is perpetrated through dumpster diving or breaches of security of health providers, the Act significantly limits the commingling of medical and financial information.

- **Debt Collectors**—In situations where consumers notify debt collectors that the debt is unknown to them or may be a product of identity theft, FACTA requires debt collectors to inform their third-party employers that the alleged debt may be the result of identity theft. They must also provide the affected consumer with information regarding their rights and the handling of disputes. In addition, they must provide the consumer with all information regarding the debt, including applications, statements, etc. Upon notification that the debt is the result of theft or fraud, the creditor is prohibited from placing the debt in collection or selling the debt to a third party.

- **Civil Action**—The Act provides for a civil action to be brought when violations occur. However, such suit must be brought within two years of the discovery of the violation *or* five years after the date of the violation itself, whichever is earlier.

Credit Bureaus and Free Credit Reports

The Fair and Accurate Credit Transactions Act of 2003 (FACTA) allows consumers to obtain a free credit report from each of the big three credit bureaus each year, and to place a fraud alert in their file. In addition, consumers may obtain additional reports for a fee.

Free credit report—*www.annualcreditreport.com*
To order your report by phone, call: (877) 322-8228
To order your report by mail: Annual Credit Report Request Service, P.O. Box 105281, Atlanta, GA 30348-5281

Equifax—*www.equifax.com*
To order your report by phone, call: (800) 685-1111
To order your report or report fraud by mail: P.O. Box 740241, Atlanta, GA 30374-0241
To report fraud by phone, call (800) 525-6285

Experian—*www.experian.com*
To order your report or report fraud by phone, call: (888) 397-3742
To order your report by mail: P.O. Box 2104, Allen TX 75013
To report fraud by mail: P.O. Box 9532, Allen, TX 75013

TransUnion—*www.tuc.com*
To order your report by phone, call: (800) 916-8800
To order your report by mail: P.O. Box 1000, Chester, PA 19022
To report fraud by phone, call: (800) 680-7289
To report fraud by mail: Fraud Victim Assistance Division, P.O. Box 6790, Fullerton, CA 92834

Identity Theft Penalty Enhancement Act of 2004

In addition to the provisions found within the *Identity Theft and Assumption Deterrence Act of 1998* and the *Fair and Accurate Credit Transactions Act of 2003,* Congress has enacted legislation specifically articulating enhanced criminal penalties. By creating a new category of crime known as **aggravated identity theft**, the *Identity Theft Penalty Enhancement Act of 2004* increases sentences and potential punishments for individuals who use a stolen or fraudulent identity to commit additional crime. It additionally provides for mandatory prison sentences for employees or individuals in a position of trust who steal data to further identity theft. More specifically, the Act includes a mandatory two-year sentence for identity theft in addition to any penalties for any related crime, and an additional five-year prison term for aggravated identity theft to commit an act of terrorism. This is in addition to the penalties for the act of terrorism itself and any punishments that proceed from the identity theft.

Additional Efforts to Protect Personal Information

Social security numbers are especially attractive to identity thieves, as they are permanently assigned to American citizens. Traditionally, they could be easily obtained through perusal of public records, where they are prominently displayed on various documents like bankruptcies, tax liens, civil judgments, real estate transactions, voter registrations, and the like. In recent years, Congress and state legislatures have attempted to limit their availability in a variety of ways. Such legislation applies to both public and private sector entities. For example, both Arkansas and Colorado prohibit the use of SSNs as student identification numbers, while South Dakota prohibits their display on drivers' licenses. Federal actions have been housed in identity theft legislation like the *Identity Theft and Assumption Deterrence Act of 1998* and the *Gramm-Leach-Bliley Act.* Congress has enacted laws which protect the personal information of licensed drivers and medical patients.

- *Drivers Privacy Protection Act*—prohibits the disclosure of SSNs and other personal information from a motor vehicle record in any situation not expressly permitted under the law. Permissible purposes include:
  1. the use by a government agency in carrying out its function;
  2. in connection with motor vehicle or driver safety and theft (i.e., emissions, alterations, recalls, advisories, and research activities);

State Laws

Beginning with Arizona in 1996, 48 states have enacted legislation within the past decade to protect the privacy of their residents. As the personal impact and methodology of identity theft has evolved, so have state statutes. California has proven to be the leader and standard bearer of legal evolution in this area. In the wake of the data breach of the state government payroll database, the state enacted the *Database Breach Notification Act* (California Code Sections 1798.29, 1798.82, and 1798.84). The Act required that any government agency or private organization inform any consumer which could potentially be affected by a breach of computer security *unless* the compromised data was encrypted or the notification has the potential to jeopardize a law enforcement investigation. The protected private data includes social security numbers, drivers' licenses, and/or financial account number plus password. Most state statutes have not incorporated mandatory consumer notification due to resistance by corporations who fear the loss of consumer confidence. However, the California law does have national implications as it refers to all California residents. Thus, corporations in other states are still obligated to notify California residents or face civil penalties. California law also created a database of victims for law enforcement, and provided victims with mechanisms for credit repair. California law does not provide for affirmative defenses. (New York is the only state in the country whose identity theft statutes contain three affirmative defenses for identity theft or illegal possession of personal identification information. More specifically, the New York statute allows individuals to challenge charges if personal identification information was used to illegally purchase alcohol or tobacco or gain entrance to an establishment with age restrictions).

3. The use in the normal course of business to prevent fraud and verify the accuracy of information submitted or in the recovery of a debt;
4. the use in legal or arbitral proceedings;
5. any other use specifically authorized by state laws in regard to the operation of a motor vehicle or public safety.

- *Health Insurance Portability and Accountability Act*—protects the privacy of social security numbers and health information that identifies an individual and restricts health care organizations from disclosing such information to others without the patient's consent. In addition, it requires medical offices or any other company that maintains health records to provide appropriate levels of computer security to ensure their safety.

FEDERALLY FUNDED INITIATIVES AND COLLABORATIONS

While the courts have continued to interpret computer-specific legislation arbitrarily, government efforts have continued to create working groups and governmental committees to address emerging issues in technology. One of the first of these, the President's Working Group on Unlawful Conduct on the Internet, chaired by Attorney General Janet Reno, brought together individuals from all levels of the community, including representatives from the **business community** (Internet Alliance, the Computer Systems, the Computer Systems Policy Project, the Business Software Alliance), **government entities** (National Association of Attorneys General, the National District Attorneys Association, the National Association of Boards of Pharmacies, and the National League of Cities), and **civil liberty/non-profit advocacy organizations** (including the National Center for Missing and Exploited Children, the Center for Democracy and Technology and the Electronic Privacy Information Center).

This group was originally tasked with providing an analysis of legal and policy issues involving the Internet for criminal behavior. More specifically, they were charged to evaluate:

1. the extent to which existing federal laws are sufficient to address unlawful conduct via the Internet (provide a framework for analyzing policy and legal responses);

2. the extent to which new technologies or legal authorities may be needed to investigate and prosecute Internet crime (i.e., the development of new tools and formulating training strategies);

3. the utility of education and "empowerment tools" to minimize the risks associated with this behavior (i.e., give teachers and parents the ability to teach their children proper usages) (DOJ, 2000).

Generally, the group developed a three-tiered approach:

1. **regulation** of Internet criminal activity in the spirit of traditional criminal law (i.e., consistent with statutory and constitutional mandates), stressing that technological crime should be treated the same as criminal activity which is not technologically advanced, ensuring privacy and protection of civil liberties;

2. **recognition** of special needs and challenges of investigating and prosecuting such activity, while emphasizing the need for tool development, enhanced training, and interagency (and international) cooperation;

3. **development** of specialized curricula including cyber-ethics and support for leadership within the private sector.

The group postulated that enhanced training of average users would decrease the risk that they would become involved in unlawful activity.

In addition, the group found that there were some laws in place which adequately addressed certain types of criminal activities, noting that traditional statutes which criminalize credit card fraud, gambling, identity theft, and the like may be used to address online or offline behavior. However, the group also recommended that many of these should be amended to specifically identify developing technologies and additional statutes or legislation should be enacted to address those activities peculiar to the Internet and computers. In particular, the group argued that mechanisms for tracing (and tracking) online offenders must be developed as the lack of current regulations allows ISPs to discard records at will, making it virtually impossible to identify originating information on dated activities or multi-jurisdictional cases. More specifically, they suggested that requirements attached to traditional telecommunications providers be applied to ISPs. (Imagine the chaos that would result if a bomb threat received via telephone was untraceable because the records were only kept for six hours.) As procedural guidelines require judicial oversight and articulated probable cause, digital evidence is often destroyed before judicial approval can be granted.

Finally, the group encouraged local agencies to establish a presence on the Net, introducing the community to the department and enabling citizens to make comments, suggestions, and (too often) complaints. Superficially, this presents an appearance of technological competence, to residents and criminals alike. More importantly, this establishes a link between the community and department, opening valuable lines of communication which could lead to an increase in anonymous tips, and ultimately improving organizational efficiency and effectiveness. (Remember: The same anonymity that draws criminals to the Web provides a level of comfort for tipsters who wish to remain anonymous.)

Unlike the President's Working Group on Unlawful Conduct on the Internet, which focused on individual online crime, Presidential Decision Directive 63 (PDD63) was more global in scope, calling for a strategic plan to defend the nation against cyberattacks. This directive called for an investment of $1.46 billion in 2000 to defend the nation's critical infrastructures (i.e., power generation systems, banking and financial institutions, transportation networks, emergency services and telecommunications). In addition, the directive articulates the goal for a reliable, interconnected, and secure information system infrastructure by 2003. This directive was also the centerpiece for the National Infrastructure Protection Center, a national agency which brings private industry and government resources together.

In 1995, a satchel of dynamite, a truckload of fertilizer, and disel fuel killed 168 people in Oklahoma city. Six years later, terrorists used American airliners to maximize both fear and the loss of life. Today, the right command sent over a network to a power generation station's control computer could be just as devastating as a backpack full of explosives or airliners. In addition, the perpetrator would be more difficult to identify and apprehend. (*Neville Elder/Corbis/Sygma.*)

The **National Infrastructure Protection Center** (NIPC) is also responsible for the development of **Infragard**, an organization which attempts to bring local community leaders, corporate executives, and law enforcement agencies together to discuss potential threats. Other articulated objectives of the group include protecting computer systems; education and training on vulnerabilities; access to an Alert Network with encryption furnished by the NIPC to report voluntarily actual or attempted illegal intrusions, disruptions, and vulnerabilities of information systems; and, finally, access to a secure information Web site reporting recent intrusions, research related to infrastructure protection, and the capability to communicate securely with other members. Unfortunately, many insiders report that Infragard has not lived up to expectations. Anecdotal evidence suggests that the traditional distrust of the FBI by private industry may

be interfering with the group's mission. However, other initiatives undertaken by the federal government promise a variety of benefits to local agencies. For example, the designation of a prosecutor in each U.S. Attorney's Office to serve as a computer and telecommunications coordinator for that district has reduced the likelihood of duplicative efforts. In addition, *LawNet* (if implemented as designed) will further coordinate anti-cybercrime efforts between state and federal agencies. Designed to be available 24 hours a day/7 days a week, LawNet attempts to articulate jurisdictional boundaries and procedures for multijurisdictional cases, which is especially problematic in online child pornography cases. (This effort has also been criticized for the ambiguity surrounding funding and allegations of federal totalitarianism.)

Perhaps the most successful, and certainly the least controversial, of all federally funded

Other Government Initiatives

Mid-80s—FCIC (Federal Computer Investigations Committee) comprised of local officers, state officials, and federal agents. However, some claim this is a shadow group, which has no membership role, no official place of residence, and no formal funding.

1989—CERT (Computer Emergency Response Team) was created in response to the Morris Worm. It is located at Carnegie Mellon University's Software Engineering Institute in Pittsburgh. CERT acts as an informational clearinghouse for public and private computer networks and assists entities which have been victimized.

1991—National Computer Crime Squad (FBI)—located in Tysons Corner, VA, part of the Washington Metro Field Office of the FBI.

1995—DOJ: computer/telecommunications coordinator program which designates at least one Assistant U.S. Attorney—each of the 93 U.S. Attorney's offices have an in-house, high-tech expert.

October, 1996—Computer Crime Unit was removed from the General Litigation Section and elevated to a higher level, renamed Computer Crime and Intellectual Property Section.

November, 1997—Computer Crime Unit created within the General Litigation Section of the Justice Department (CCU).

March, 2000—The National Institute of Justice Office of Science and Technology (NIJ/OST) established the Cyber-Science laboratory.

February, 2004—The Federal Bureau of Investigation unveiled a new laboratory and training center in New Haven, CT, designed to serve as a training ground for investigators and provide a state-of-the-art computer forensics laboratory.

initiatives is **Innocent Images**. This initiative, founded in 1995, had investigated over 800 cases in which adults had traveled interstate to meet minors for illicit purposes, and more than 1,850 cases of child pornography in a five-year period. Adequately funded, this project receives more than $10 million a year in federal funds.

LAW ENFORCEMENT OPERATIONS AND TOOLS IN THE UNITED STATES

Although computer crimes date back several decades, criminal investigations and prosecutions started more slowly. Historically, such investigations focused almost exclusively on bulletin boards, the communication medium of choice for early computer criminals. Since that time, methodologies of both computer communication and criminal investigations have changed dramatically. Criminals, not bound by considerations of law and cultural norms, have employed various methods to perpetrate their nefarious schemes. In response, law enforcement agencies have had to employ similar tactics to identify and thwart their endeavors. Such proactive approaches, however, have not always been embraced by privacy advocates. The debate between privacy and protection is a long one and will not be resolved here. Suffice to say that privacy advocates and law enforcement authorities are almost always at odds. In recent years, packet sniffing and data mining programs have proven to be favorite targets of organizations like EPIC and the ACLU.

Packet Sniffers and Key Loggers

Perhaps the most controversial tool in the FBI's investigative arsenal is the sniffing program **Carnivore**. This program, designed to run in a Windows platform, claims to be a knockoff of commercial software and proprietary source code developed by the FBI. It is designed to "sniff" or "filter" e-mail on a particular network via a network card, routing evidence to a

Carnivore According to the FBI

In the face of sharp criticism by privacy advocates, the FBI has vehemently denied that Carnivore is designed to target innocent citizens. As a response, the FBI issued a formal statement to the U.S. House of Representatives, which stated that:

> [Carnivore is] a very specialized network analyzer or "sniffer" which runs as an application program on a normal personal computer under the Microsoft Windows operating system. It works by "sniffing" the proper portions of network packets and copying and storing only those packets which match a finely defined filter set programmed in conformity with the court order. This filter set can be extremely complex,

and this provides the FBI with an ability to collect transmissions which comply with pen register court orders, trap and trace court order, Title III interceptions orders, etc.

Carnivore does not search through the contents of every message and collect those that contain certain key words like "bomb" or "drugs." It selects messages based on criteria expressly set out in the court order, for example, messages transmitted to or from a particular account or to or from a particular user. If the device is placed at some point on the network where it cannot discriminate messages as set out in the court order, it simply lets all such messages pass by unrecorded.[4]

removable disk. According to the FBI, it is seldom used and is designed to be used in very rare instances where it is possible to demonstrate probable cause and state with particularity and specificity: (1) the offense; (2) place (telecommunications facility) where interception is to occur; (3) a description of the communications targeted for interception; and (4) the identities of the perpetrators. Legally, the application must also include an explanation as to why this is necessary (i.e., other attempts to collect that type of evidence) and how other tools have proven inadequate. Thus, the FBI states that it is not an intelligence-gathering tool. Rather, it is designed to be a mechanism for evidence collection. Court orders are limited to 30 days, and termination of interception must take place once the objective is achieved. Court orders are often contingent upon weekly reports on the status of the investigation.

Although the media has focused exclusively on Carnivore, the program is but one piece of a covert surveillance triad known as "DragonWare Suite." This suite is capable of "reconstructing the Web-surfing trail of someone under investigation." This suite also includes "Packeteer" and "Coolminer." In actuality, Carnivore is actually the end result of an evolution in **packet-sniffing** software. The common link in this evolution was initially called Omnivore, inarguably a more benign label. This original platform, designed as a sniffer of e-mail streams, had the capability to print out targeted e-mails and store other data on a removable drive. In fact, the FBI assured citizens that Carnivore represented a more efficient and strategic weapon, designed to surgically identify and intercept those communications specified by court order; it would ignore those which fell outside these specifications. Unfortunately, the government has acknowledged that these ideals are, as yet, unrealized and privacy advocates remain unsatisfied.

In 2001, the FBI introduced the *Cyber Knight* project. Among the new tools included in the program was the keylogger *Magic Lantern*.[5] This software was designed to defeat encryption software by recording the keystrokes and mouseclicks of a suspect who deliberately scrambled computer files. Such devices are necessary as some encryption programs have made it impossible for officials to descramble files containing criminal evidence. Because the software could be installed remotely without the need for physical entry into personal offices or private residences, it was argued that a search warrant was not required. However, many civil libertarians argue that the action is far more intrusive, deceptive, and dangerous. After all,

Able Danger

One of the first data mining activities by the federal government was actually developed to combat transnational terrorism prior to the 9/11 attacks in 2001. In 1999–2000, the U.S. Army's Land Information Warfare Agency, acted on a request by the U.S. Special Operations Command (SOCOM). Although little information is known about the specifics of the program, the Department of Defense has indicated that Able Danger was a demonstration project which employed link analysis to identify underlying relationships and connections between individuals who did not appear to be associated. The data included in the study was a combination of open source and classified information. Such data has since been destroyed according to U.S. Army regulations. However, significant controversy surrounds the program, and it has been alleged that the analysis had identified Mohammed Atta, one of the 9/11 hijackers prior to the attacks.

Magic Lantern is, by definition, a Trojan. Privacy advocates have objected strenuously to the government's use of malware. As a result, civil liability remains a concern, as privacy groups like EPIC continue to pursue litigation involving packet sniffers, keyloggers, and increasingly, data mining.

Data Mining

Data mining may be defined as a comprehensive analysis of large data sets designed to uncover patterns and relationships. Analysis tools include, but are not limited to: statistical models, mathematical algorithms, and artificial intelligence. It can be performed on most data formats, including not only those that are quantitative in nature but also those which are represented in textual or multimedia forms. Analysis parameters can include:

- **association** (i.e., patterns where events are connected, such as the purchase of a high-end printer and graphics software);
- **sequence of path analysis** (i.e., patterns where events are sequential, such as the death of an individual and the filing of a life insurance claim);
- **classification** (i.e., identification of new patterns, such as the purchase of massive quantities of fertilizer and the renting of a truck);
- **clustering** (i.e., finding and visually documenting groups of previously unknown facts, such as voting and alcohol consumption);
- **forecasting** (i.e., patterns which enable the development of predictions of future activities, such as the prediction that incoming college freshmen might establish bank accounts).

As opposed to traditional statistical analysis of hypothesis testing, data mining allows users to examine several multidimensional data relationships simultaneously, identifying those that are unique or frequently represented.[6] As such, data mining is increasingly popular in both the private and public sectors.

Data mining practices have exploded over the past several years. This marked increase may be attributed to a variety of factors, including the increased availability of information, decreased storage costs, the growth of computer networks, the increasing centralization of data, and, of course, the development of neural networks and advanced algorithms. It has been employed in the private sector to survey customer information, reducing fraud and waste. It has greatly enhanced medical and academic research capabilities and led to the development of more complex research questions. It has been used in the public sector to appropriately allocate resources and streamline services. And, it has been used by criminals and terrorists to identify patterns and vulnerabilities.

Data mining has been increasingly employed by law enforcement agencies in a variety of ways. As expected, privacy advocates have criticized the practice, and litigation has commenced. Perhaps the most controversial use of data mining involves programs established by the Department of Homeland Security (DHS). Even public support for many of the programs created in the immediate aftermath of the 9/11 attacks of 2001 has significantly eroded or been totally eviscerated.

Terrorism Information Awareness Program (TIA) and Secure Flight

In the days immediately following September 11, 2001, government resources were allocated to enhance the nation's intelligence tools and capabilities. As a result, the Information Awareness Office (IAO) was created at the Defense Advanced Research Projects Agency (DARPA) in January 2002. Originally, the role of this office was in part to bring together, under the leadership of one technical office director, several existing DARPA programs focused on applying information technology to combat terrorist threats. It was intended that such programs would counter asymmetric threats by achieving *total information awareness* useful for preemption, national security warning, and national security decision making.[7] A more comprehensive articulation of interest and organizational goals revealed the following three research topics:

> language translation, data search with pattern recognition and privacy protection, and advanced collaborative and decision support tools. Language translation technology would enable the rapid analysis of foreign languages, both spoken and written, and allow analysists to quickly search the translated materials for clues about emerging threats. The data search, pattern recognition, and privacy protection technologies would permit analysts to search vast quantities of data for patterns that suggest terrorist activity while at the same time controlling access to the data, enforcing

laws and policies, and ensuring detection of misuse of the information obtained. The collaborative reasoning and decision support technologies would allow analysts from different agencies to share data.[8]

More succinctly, the program was designed to improve the data mining capabilities of various agencies. It provided for automated rapid language translation and improved search and pattern recognition. The incorporation of such technologies greatly enhanced the government's ability to evaluate patterns of communication, association, and relationships between English and non-English texts. However, the implementation of the program received harsh criticism which was exacerbated, or even fueled, by a questionable administrative appointment and a controversial logo. Critics argued that the appoint of Dr. John M. Poindexter, a prominent figure in the Iran-Contra affair, coupled with the depiction of an all-seeing eye viewing the globe, represented a nefarious scheme by the government to compromise individual privacy. As a result, the Omnibus Appropriations Act for Fiscal Year 2003 and the Department of Defense Appropriations Act of 2004 sounded a death knell for the fledgling program.

Computer-Assisted Passenger Prescreening System (CAPPS II)

Like the TIA, the *Computer-Assisted Passenger Prescreening System* (CAPPS II) emerged in the days following the 9/11 attacks. Slightly more palatable to the general public, CAPPS II was designed to enhance security measures on commercial airlines originally introduced in 1996. In its current form, such security measures utilize a rule-based system which identifies those passengers which require additional security screening. Described by the Transportation Security Administration (TSA) as *an enhanced system to confirm the identities of passengers and to identify foreign terrorists or*

The selection of this logo for the Office of Information Awareness enabled privacy advocates to create paranoia about the Office's activities. Conspiracy theorists envisioned an omnipotent government whose primary goal was to spy on American citizens.

persons with terrorist connections before they can board U.S. aircraft,[9] the program included verification of information within the passengers name record (i.e., full name, address, phone number, data of birth, etc.) through comparison with commercially collected data. Such comparison, conducted by commercial data providers, employed traffic light designations of GREEN (normal screening), YELLOW (additional screening), and, RED (denial of boarding and law enforcement scrutiny).

Implementation of CAPPS II encountered serious problems almost from inception. Privacy advocates vociferously boycotted Delta Airlines and threatened other commercial airlines with similar actions once it was revealed that Delta was cooperating with authorities. Further media leaks, reporting that personal information had been shared with law enforcement authorities, resulted in the targeting of JetBlue and NorthWest Airlines. Concerns of data creep further compounded privacy concerns when it was reported that CAPPS II may be used to identify individuals with outstanding state or federal arrest warrants, domestic terrorists, and illegal aliens. As a result, CAPPS II was cancelled and replaced with a new system called Secure Flight.[10]

Although Secure Flight performs the same function and collects the same information as its predecessor, it emphasizes passenger privacy and includes a passenger redress process. It attempts to drastically reduce misidentifications, and collects less personal information from consumers. The *Traveler Redress Inquiry Program* streamlines the redress process for misidentified individuals. However, privacy advocates continue to cry foul, and law enforcement authorities have complained that it hampers their efforts to identify terrorists and potential threats.

Multi-State Anti-Terrorism Information Exchange Pilot Project (MATRIX)

The *Multi-State Anti-Terrorism Information Exchange Pilot Project* (MATRIX) was initially developed by Seisint to facilitate collaborative information sharing and factual data analysis. MATRIX developed a list of over 100,000 names of suspicious individuals based on a mathematical formula which they called High Terrorist Factor (HTF). This number was calculated after

Secure Flight Process

Passenger		All Airlines		Secure Flight
Required data: - Full name - Itinerary	Reservation → ← Boarding Pass	Sends required passenger information to Secure Flight	Passenger Information (Secure) → ← Boarding Pass Instructions (Secure)	Performs watch list matching
Optional data: - Date of birth - Gender - Redress number				Resolves possible No-Fly matches

(U.S. Government Office)

analysis of information which included age, gender, social security anomalies, credit history, ethnicity, possession of or links to a pilot's license, and proximity to suspect locations. In an attempt to develop baseline data, the MATRIX pilot program utilized an application known as FACTS (Factual Analysis Criminal Threat Solution). This application was designed to provide for query-based searches of nearly 4 billion records from both private and public sources. Information compiled included that which was found on documents of record, and included, but were not limited to, government-issued professional licenses (i.e., private investigators, constables, etc.); government-issued privilege licenses (i.e., drivers', fishing, concealed weapons, etc.); probate records (i.e., birth, death, marriage, and divorce records); criminal histories; bankruptcy filings; motor vehicle registrations; telemarketing and direct call lists; airline or travel reservations or records; magazine subscriptions; telephone logs; credit histories; and banking records (i.e., account information, payment history, and credit accounts).

Once again critics were given ammunition when it was revealed that the founder of Seisint, Hank Asher, had a criminal history involving drug smuggling. Although he was never charged due to his cooperation, law enforcement authorities report that he was the pilot in several drug smuggling cases.[11] In fact, both the Drug Enforcement Administration and the Federal Bureau of Investigation had previously cancelled contracts with another Asher company. Other concerns included the receipt of millions of dollars in federal funding for a state-based information sharing initiative. And, finally, privacy advocates criticized an approach in which private companies created mathematical algorithms and analytical criteria without public or legislative input.

According to the FDLE, the MATRIX program was an unqualified success. Unfortunately, the cessation of federal funding resulted in an abandonment of the pilot study. However, Florida and other participating states indicated that they would seek to continue use of the FACTS application.

Automated Targeting System (ATS)

The *Automated Targeting System* (ATS) was developed by the Department of Homeland Security within the *Treasury Enforcement Communications System*. It was designed to screen travelers entering the United States by automobile, airplane, or rail. Housed within the Bureau of Customs and Border Protection (CBP), ATS assesses risks for cargo, conveyances, and travelers. There are six categories, or modules, of activity:

- ATS-Inbound—inbound cargo and conveyances (rail, truck, ship, and air)
- ATS-Outbound—outbound cargo and conveyances (rail, truck, ship, and air)
- ATS-Passenger—travelers and conveyances (air, ship, and rail)
- ATS-Land—private vehicles arriving by land
- ATS-International—cargo targeting for CBP's collaboration with foreign customs authorities
- ATS-Trend Analysis and Analytical Selectivity Program (ATS-TAP)—analytical module

Like other data mining practices by law enforcement, ATS has been harshly criticized by privacy advocates. In 2006, a suit was filed to suspend the systems as it applied to individuals; or, in the alternative, fully apply all Privacy Act safeguards to any person subjected to the system.

Although it was originally designed to enhance customer service in the private sector through customizing profiles of individual shoppers, it has increasingly been employed by criminals and law enforcement alike.

Terrorist Surveillance Program

First disclosed to the public in December 2005 via news report, the *Terrorist Surveillance*

The Funding of Data Mining and Emerging Investigative Tools

The *National Intelligence from Massive Data Program* (NIDM) actively supports the development of new technology and data management techniques through the funding of grants allocated by the Advanced Research Development Activity (ARDA). The ARDA supports research which leads to advances in intelligence gathering or analysis. Some of their recent areas of interest have included Advanced Information Assurance, Novel Intelligence from Massive Data Information Exploitation, Quantum Information Science, and Global Infosystems Access. The NIMD is a program dedicated to the mining and analysis of large data. Such tools are increasingly necessary as data becomes more voluminous.

Program has been employed by the National Security Agency (NSA) since 2002. Among other things, the program includes the domestic collection, analysis, and sharing of telephone call information. According to statements issued by the President and the Department of Justice, the program is reserved for international calls with links to al Qaeda or related terrorist groups, and requires review and reauthorization every 45 days. Privacy advocates have repeatedly expressed concerns over the potential for abuses. Recently, such concerns were validated when it was revealed that the NSA had contracted with AT&T, Verizon, and BellSouth to collect information about domestic telephone calls. Although the content of such disclosures is not entirely clear, the compromise of privacy expectations and a subsequent erosion of public trust occurred.[12]

Collaborations and Professional Associations

Although still hopelessly underfunded, many local jurisdictions have taken their cue from the early efforts in Phoenix and Chicago. In fact, roughly 2/3 of all agencies surveyed in an NIJ research project reported that they were involved in a federal, state, or local interagency task force. As expected, these task forces were most common in the Western region of the United States where the presence of high-tech corporations is much *en vogue*. (In fact, over half of the task forces identified were in this area.) Not surprisingly, the lowest number of such task forces was found in the Southeast, where local budgets and technological resources seem to be disproportionately low. Fortunately, new partnerships are emerging due primarily to the efforts of individual investigators.

Operation WebSnare

In 2004, the federal government launched a collaborative law-enforcement operation to identify and prosecute perpetrators involved in online fraud, identity theft, and other computer-related crime. Operation WebSnare resulted in 160 investigations in which more than 150,000 victims lost more than $215 million. At its conclusion, there were 103 arrests and 53 convictions.

WebSnare's Collaborating Agencies

36 US Attorney's Offices
Criminal Division of the Justice Department

37 of the 56 FBI field divisions
13 of the 18 Postal Inspection Service field divisions
Federal Trade Commission
U.S. Secret Service
Bureau of Immigration and Customs Enforcement of the
    Department of Homeland Security.

In March 2000, the CyberScience Laboratory (CSL) was established through the partnership of the New York Electronic Crimes Task Force and the National Institute of Justice Office of Science and Technology (NIJ/OST). Championed by law enforcement, the mission of the CSL is to

- implement cyber-security training seminars/workshops/expos nationwide in order to build capacity at the state and local law enforcement levels

- develop a consortium of government, industry, and academic resources to address technical issues
- share forensic tool knowledge base from government and industry with the National Law Enforcement and Corrections Technology Centers (NLECTCs) and state and local agencies
- heighten national awareness
- facilitate and provide technological assistance

CSL works closely with both public and private agencies, and a coalition which shares forensic knowledge with all levels of law enforcement has emerged. Coalition members include:

- Air Force Research Laboratory/ Information Directorate
- Connecticut State Police Crime Laboratory
- Dolphin Technology, Inc.
- GHI, Inc.
- Griffiss Institute
- High Tech Crime Investigation Association (HTCIA)
- International Association of Computer Investigative Specialists (IACIS)
- Joint Council on Information Age Crime (JCIAC)
- L-3 Communications, Analytics Corporation

- Nassau County Police Department
- National CyberCrime Training Partnership (NCTP)

- National Institute of Justice—Office of Science and Technology
- National White Collar Crime Center (NW3C)
- New Jersey State Police
- New York State District Attorney Association
- New York State Office of the Attorney General (NYSOAG)

- New York State Police

- Regional Computer Forensics Laboratory— Western NY (RCFL-WNY)

- RJ O'Leary Computer Consulting Services LLC
- United States Secret Service Electronic Crimes Task Forces: Charlotte, Chicago, Houston, Los Angeles, Miami, New England, New York, San Francisco, and the Washington Field Office
- University of Dayton: Institute on Law, Technology & Security
- WetStone Technologies, Inc.

Thus, a variety of professional associations have become the premier method of knowledge dissemination among computer investigators. One of the most popular, the High Tech Computer Investigators Association (HTCIA) has regional chapters which come together annually. These regional chapters are bound by the same rules and covenants, but vary in expertise, personnel, and training. Members include representatives from law enforcement as well as from security communities, vendors, and some academics. Sponsorship is a prerequisite and defense attorneys or experts need not apply. **HTCIA** is a non-profit organization and is designed exclusively for training and informational purposes. Unfortunately, other professional associations have been developed or have evolved into self-serving entities.

The International Association for Computer Investigation Specialists (**IACIS**) has marketed itself as a non-profit, professional organization aimed at serving the law enforcement community. However, its training platform and emphasis on accreditation has perverted the traditional goals, and many practitioners have become disillusioned. Unlike HTCIA, this organization offers a "certification" program, in which individuals are certified as "computer forensic experts." Although their training is not required for such certification, fees are required for the actual testing. Thus, individuals who are recognized across the country as computer forensic specialists are not formally recognized as such by IACIS. Unfortunately, the lack of nationally established criteria for expert certification undermines the credibility of such testing practices.

While a variety of other associations exist, IACIS and HTCIA are by far the most recognized and respected. Both have proven resilient to both criticism and skepticism. They have proven that a lack of resources, governmental interest, and public apathy may be overcome through determination and dedication. They have created an opportunity for professional training and practitioner communication and have provided a platform for political grandstanding and financial grubstaking. In addition, they have incorporated law-enforcement ethics and coordinated international efforts.

● INTERNATIONAL EFFORTS

We need to reach a consensus as to which computer and technology related activities should be criminalized, and then commit to taking appropriate domestic actions.

—Attorney General Janet Reno, January 21, 1997.

Although the 1990s have been characterized in the United States as the "Information Age," law enforcement communities have been slow to respond to the potential for cyber-criminality. However, an increasing recognition of the insidious nature of computer crime has reached global proportions. Both Japan and Britain, for example,

have incorporated computer crime statutes into extant legislation. While Hong Kong has expanded their Telecommunications Ordinance to generally address cybercrime, Britain has created technology-specific initiatives targeting technological crime. The Regulation of Investigatory Powers Act (RIP), all but negating traditional notions of privacy in the United Kingdom, has allowed law-enforcement agencies to monitor and intercept Internet communications. It has also allowed government agencies free access to encryption keys, a much disputed issue in the United States. While these actions have been widely acclaimed as proactive measures to newly emerging criminal behavior, most countries have enacted reactionary laws. Cybercrime laws in the Philippines, for example, were created only after the creator of the Love Bug Virus walked free as a direct result of a deficit in technology-specific legislation.

OECD and the Select Committee of Experts on Computer-Related Crime of the Council of Europe

Perhaps the first comprehensive international effort to combat criminal behavior created via computer began between 1983 and 1985 when an ad hoc committee discussed the *international harmonization of criminal laws in order to fight computer-related economic crime.*[13] This committee, sponsored by OECD, also made suggestions as to a listing of offenses to which all member countries should agree. These suggestions included the criminalization of:

1. Any manipulation of data which is intended to commit illegal transfer of funds or other valuables.
2. Any manipulation of data intended to commit forgery.
3. Any manipulation intended to interfere with the functioning of a computer or other telecommunications system.
4. Any incident of software theft or software piracy.

5. Any unauthorized access or interception of another's computer with malicious intent.

In addition, the Select Committee of Experts on Computer-Related Crime of the Council of Europe, established after the OECD, included two lists. The first, proposing a number of items whose criminalization were optional, was overshadowed only by the second, which mandated the criminalization of other behavior. The first list, including optional revisions, included the criminalization of:

1. **The alteration of computer data or computer programs**—the alteration of computer data or computer programs without rights.
2. **The practice of computer espionage**—the acquisition by improper means or the disclosure, transfer, or use of a trade or commercial secret without right or any other legal justification, with intent either to cause economic loss to the person entitled to the secret or to obtain an unlawful economic advantage for oneself or a third person.
3. **The unauthorized use of a computer**—the use of a computer system or network without right that either (i) is made with the acceptance of significant risk of loss being caused to the person entitled to use the system or harm to the system or its functioning, or (ii) is made with the intent to cause loss to the person entitled to use the system or harm to the system or its functioning, or (iii) causes loss to the person entitled to use the system or harm to the system or its functioning.
4. **The unauthorized use of a protected computer program**—the use without the right of a computer program which is protected by law and which has been reproduced without right, with the intent either to procure an unlawful economic gain for himself or for another person or to cause harm to the holder of the right.[14]

The second list included mandatory offenses which should be criminalized by all participating countries. Their categories, more broad in nature, included:

1. **Computer fraud**—the input, alteration, erasure, or suppression of computer data or computer programs, or other interference with the course of data processing that influences the result of data processing, thereby causing economic or possessory loss of property of another person with the intent of procuring an unlawful economic gain for himself or for another person.
2. **Computer forgery**—the input, alteration, erasure, or suppression of computer data or computer programs, or other interference with the course of data processing in a manner or under such conditions, as prescribed by national law, that it would constitute the offense of forgery if it had been committed with respect to a traditional object of such an offense.
3. **Damage to computer data or computer programs**—the erasure, damaging, deterioration, or suppression of computer data or computer programs without right.
4. **Computer sabotage**—the input, alteration, erasure, or suppression of computer data or computer programs, or other interference with computer systems, with the intent to hinder the functioning of a computer or a telecommunications system.
5. **Unauthorized access**—the access without right to a computer system or network by infringing security measures.
6. **Unauthorized interception**—the interception, made without right and by technical means, or communications to, from and within a computer system or network.
7. **Unauthorized reproduction of a protected computer program**—the reproduction, distribution, or communication to the public without right of a computer program which is protected by law.

8. **Unauthorized reproduction of a topography**—the reproduction without right of topography protected by law, of a semiconductor product, or the commercial exploitation or the importation for that purpose, done without right, of a topography or of a semiconductor product manufactured by using the topography.[15]

The group is currently comprised of 30 member states, and it continues to promote economic and social welfare of less developed nations through the coordination of efforts of member states. To reduce political corruption and to further human rights, the group has established a working group on bribery. They have been especially active in the areas of cyber-crime and online security—devoting much emphasis to encryption technology. More recently, the group has developed guidelines aimed at cyber-terrorism, computer viruses, and hacking.

Council of Europe's (CoE) Cybercrime Conventions

The Council of Europe was originally founded in 1949, and is comprised of 45 countries, including members of the EU and nonmember countries from Central and Eastern Europe. Originally designed to address common concerns which have economic, social, cultural, legal, and administrative impacts, they are also tasked with implementing measures aimed at international crime. In 1996, the Council established the Cybercrime Convention.[16] Their primary mission was threefold: (1) the establishment of universal definitions of central criminal offenses; (2) identification of appropriate investigative powers tailored to information technology; and (3) the development of international treaties and cooperative agreements.

The Convention established four broad categories of computer-related criminal offenses.

- **Title I**
  - Includes offenses which violate the confidentiality, integrity, or availability of data.

This includes, but is not limited to, unauthorized access; interception of non-public transmissions of data; interference with data or computer systems; misuses of computer-related devices (i.e., hacker tools).

- **Title II**
  - Broad category of offenses which include the traditional crimes of fraud and forgery via computers.
- **Title III**
  - Broad category of content related offenses which involve the possession, creation, or distribution of criminal contraband. Originally, this category of offenses was limited to images of the sexual exploitation of children but has now been expanded to include racist or xenophobic material.
- **Title IV**
  - Broad category of offenses related to copyright infringement committed via a computer system on a commercial scale.

In addition to the categorization of criminal activity, the initiative serves to strengthen Mutual Legal Assistance (MLA) treaties, and provides for the establishment of an international computer crime assistance network. The language also provides comprehensive powers to member states to expedite preservation of digital evidence and interception of electronic data. Unfortunately, anticipations of wide ratifications have been largely unrealized.

Financial Action Task Force

The Financial Action Task Force was established by the G-7 Summit in July 1989 to combat the growing problem of money laundering. Since that time, the mission has been extended to include the identification and eradication of terrorist financing. Toward this end, the FATF has developed policies and promoted training to encourage the development of streamlined legislation and regulatory reforms to address both money laundering and terrorist financing.

Financial Action Task Force Members

Argentina, Australia, Austria, Belgium, Brazil, Canada, Denmark, Finland, France, Germany, Greece, Hong Kong, China, Iceland, Ireland, Italy, Japan, Luxembourg, Mexico, the Kingdom of the Netherlands, New Zealand, Norway, Portugal, the Russian Federation, Singapore, South Africa, Spain, Sweden, Switzerland, Turkey, the United Kingdom, the United States, the European Commission, and the Gulf Cooperation Council.

Currently, the FATF is comprised of 33 members: 31 member jurisdictions from six continents and the European Commission and the Gulf Cooperation Council.

The Financial Action Task Force has continued to reevaluate approaches to the problems of money laundering and terrorist financing. In 1990, they established international standards in the form of the *Forty Recommendations*, which explicitly delineated strategies to disrupt money laundering methods and markets. These recommendations were revised in both 1996 and in October 2001, following the terror attacks in the United States. In the 2001 revisions, they issued *Eight Special Recommendations* which specifically addressed issues relating to terrorist financing. The initiatives of the FATF have resulted in a comprehensive framework for governments to develop domestic efforts against money laundering and terrorist financing. Their most recent directive, The *40 + 9 Recommendations* (Appendix C), have been endorsed by over 150 jurisdictions across the globe, and by the Boards of the International Monetary Fund (IMF) and the World Bank.

The *Recommendations* issued by the FATF focus on three primary areas: law enforcement systems and prosecution of offenses; regulation and financial systems; and, international cooperation.

- **Law Enforcement Systems and Prosecution of Offenses**—The FATF encourages all countries to develop criminal statutes and avenues for prosecution for both money laundering and the financing of terrorism. Such actions should clearly identify what behaviors are prohibited and provide for the confiscation of assets.
- **Regulation and Financial Systems**—the FATF encourages all countries to regulate financial institutions within their borders to incorporate anti–money laundering practices. Such requirements of due diligence would include, but not be limited to, the report of suspicious activity, "know your customer" policies, and the strengthening of customer identification measures in international and domestic wire transfers.
- **International Cooperation**—the FATF encourages all governments to coordinate and cooperate with one another in the investigation and prosecution of those involved in money laundering and terrorist financing. This includes the development of mutual legal assistance treaties and information sharing.

Summarily, the FATF encourages national governments to develop and enforce laws specifically aimed at money laundering and terrorist financing, and to hold financial institutions accountable for noncompliance which facilitates either. At the same time, they encourage cooperation between countries and the development of mutual legal assistance treaties.

Interpol

Consisting of over 180 member states, the International Criminal Police Organization (aka Interpol) is designed to provide support for law enforcement agencies across the globe by facilitating communication, cooperation, and the exchange of information; coordination of joint operational activities of member states; and, by developing and disseminating best practices in training and investigations. In addition, the organization maintains the Universal Classification System for Counterfeit Payment Cards which provides timely information on trends and techniques involving forgery of payment cards. In terms of cyber-crime, Interpol has advocated the development of regional working groups of experts to develop and disseminate best practices for computer-related investigations. They have also developed and implemented training platforms, as nearly half of Interpol's members do not have the infrastructure for online communications. Interpol has listed finance and high-technology within its top two priorities.

Virtual Global Taskforce (VGT)

In 2003, the *Virtual Global Taskforce* was created as a collaborative effort between the Australian High Tech Crime Centre, the Child Exploitation and Online Protection Centre (UK), the Royal Canadian Mounted Police, the U.S. Department of Homeland Security, and Interpol. It is designed to deliver low-cost, high-impact initiatives that deter pedophiles and prevent the online exploitation of children. By reducing the confidence of potential perpetrators through the removal of perceptions of anonymity, the group aims to deter online misconduct. Their most notable initiative is know as *Operation Pin*. This program involves a Web site which claims to contain images of child exploitation and pornography. Visitors to the site who attempt to download images are confronted by an online law enforcement presence and informed that they have committed a criminal offense and that information about them has been forwarded by appropriate authorities.

United Nations Convention against Transnational Organized Crime (UNCATOC) and Association of Southeast Asian Nations (ASEAN)

Originally introduced in Palermo, Italy, in late 2000, the *United Nations Convention against Transnational Organized Crime* was signed by 147 states and 110 parties by 2003.[17] Like FATF, the Convention developed mutual legal assistance between states and established broad categories of criminal offenses. Unlike FATF, these categorizations focused exclusively on the activities of criminal syndicates. They included participation in an organized criminal group; money laundering, corruption and the obstruction of justice; illicit manufacturing and trafficking in firearms; and, the smuggling of migrants. Within these provisions, however, the Convention expressly outlined methods for enforcing and prosecuting the misuse of computers and telecommunications networks; provisions for training and materials; and, placing obligations on states. Although the Convention only addressed serious crimes committed by criminal groups, their definition of "transnational" crime provides some framework for a new paradigm of organized crime, one more focused on criminal networks and less bound by structural characteristics. This is similar to ideas originally espoused by ASEAN.

The Association of Southeast Asian Nations (ASEAN) was developed in 1967, and is now composed of the following countries: Indonesia, Malaysia, Philippines, Singapore, Thailand, Brunei Darussalam, Vietnam, Lao PDR, Myanmar, and Cambodia. Since inception, the group had two primary objectives: (1) to increase economic growth, social progress, and cultural development; and (2) to promote regional peace and stability through abiding respect for justice and the rule of law in the relationship among countries in the region. Increasingly, the group has redirected its original focus to computer-related rime, and has encouraged increased cooperation with both Interpol and the United Nations. Such efforts are remarkably similar to that of the *Asian Pacific Economic Council* (APEC), a group founded in 1989 to promote economic growth among member states. Like the other international coalitions previously discussed, the mission of the group had expanded to include criminal legislation, police training, and international collaboration. They have recently focused on the recognition of global terrorism and the protection of global infrastructures, and have established working groups between experts toward this end.

CONCLUSIONS

Although recognition of the insidious nature of computer crime is increasing, much work remains to be completed on all levels of government. Legislation and the codification of computer criminality must keep abreast of emerging technology. Until such a time, investigators should look to traditional statutes to prosecute individuals committing traditional crimes via electronic means. In the United States, local agencies may find provisions under Title 18 particularly useful. Both local and federal agencies should also implement traditional investigative methods until the constitutionality of emerging technologies is tested. Pen registers (used to identify outgoing numbers from a phone) and trap and trace devices (used to identify originating numbers of wire or electronic communications) combined with a solid investigation may be used successfully to identify harassing behavior without actually compromising the sanctity of the content of the communication.

Even in areas where state, local, and federal government agencies have enacted regulations to specifically address online criminal behavior, some activity is sure to be overlooked. Thus, law enforcement officials must continue to evaluate the applicability of traditional legislation. The Federal Wire Fraud Act, for example, enables prosecutors to pursue individuals illegally transferring funds, accessing bank computers, and the like. While most computer-specific legislation has tended to be enacted on the federal level, state and local agencies may be able to implement generic statutes of enforcement. For example, although many states have not formally encoded electronic vandalism statutes, innovative departments may still pursue individuals responsible for computer worms or viruses through criminal mischief and destruction of property codes. In fact, local and state law enforcement officials should carefully evaluate local regulations and identify applicable statutes.

International entities have also been at odds regarding the level of privacy afforded certain types of data. Constitutional provisions in the United States, for example, apply elevated levels of security to those transmissions that include publishable material. The range of such protections may be characterized as a continuum, with totalitarian governments affording no protection to electronic communications, democratic societies providing security in compliance with strict due process, and libertarian societies affording blanket protections to personal communications. However, virtually (no pun intended) all countries have recently passed guidelines on electronic monitoring of computer communications. Recent legislation in the United States regarding the use of electronic surveillance devices (i.e., ECPA) has extended protections originally reserved for aural communications to digital transmissions. (It must be noted that the FBI claims that traditional methods of electronic surveillance have been responsible for securing convictions of more than 25,000 individuals in 13 years.[18]) Similar efforts have also been undertaken in Denmark and Germany.[19]

Compounding the traditional problems associated with computer crime is the reluctance of some countries to react to international mandates. Citing jurisdictional sovereignty and fear of American imperialism, member states of international consortiums have failed to enact the very agreements that they have helped to create. Thus, sovereignty and levels of privacy must be identified and understandings of socio-legal interests achieved. Such efforts should not create an environment that impedes economic growth or stifles individual expression. In fact, the government must be ever-vigilant to the interests of society while taking measures to encourage economic growth consistent with an increasingly global marketplace.

DISCUSSION QUESTIONS

1. What actions has the federal government taken to legislate online behavior? How have these mandates evolved over time?
2. How may traditional statutes be applied to the contemporary phenomenon of computer crime?
3. What are some suggestions that you would make to local agencies?
4. Briefly describe the recent additions in Europe's CoE.
5. Discuss and describe the most recent statute in relation to identity theft, showing why it is significant and how it aids the cause to slow identity theft.
6. How is the partnership of professional associations useful?

RECOMMENDED READING

- Seifert, Jeffrey W. (2007). Data Mining and Homeland Security: An Overview. *CRS Report for Congress.* Order Code RL 31798. January 18, 2007.
- Transportation Security Administration. March 11, 2003. *TSA's CAPPS II Gives Equal Weight to Privacy, Security.* Press Release. Available at *www.tsa.gov* (last accessed on May 15, 2007).
- Wagner, David. (Summer 2007)."A Comprehensive Approach to Security." *MIT Sloan Management Review,* 48(4): 8. *Expanded Academic ASAP.* Gale. Clemson University. September 25, 2007. Available at *http://find.galegroup.com/itx/start.do?prodId = EAIM.*

WEB RESOURCES

- www.eff.org – homepage for the Electronic Frontier Foundation. The site provides access to various cases and legal filings regarding privacy violations by law enforcement or government

actions. As the EFF is often the plaintiff in civil actions filed against authorities, the site provides access to breaking news in the debate between privacy and protection.
- www.cybersciencelab.com – The CyberScience Laboratory (CSL) provides the CyberSecurity community with the necessary tools and training to combat electronic crime and build capacity at the state and local levels nationwide.
- http://www.aseansec.org/ – homepage of the Association of Southeast Asian Nations. The site provides a comprehensive history of the organization, including the group's mission. In addition, the site provides links to various publications and resources on organized crime and the Internet.
- www.interpol.int – the homepage of Interpol, the world's largest international police organization with over 180 member countries. It is designed to facilitate international police co-operation even where diplomatic relations do not exist between particular countries. Available in several languages, the site provides access to breaking news about international crime trends, criminal syndicates, and computer crime.
- http://www.virtualglobaltaskforce.com – the homepage of the Virtual Global Taskforce. The group, dedicated to the prevention and prosecution of online child abuse, provides access to the latest news regarding online predators and law enforcement successes.

ENDNOTES

[1]18 U.S.C. § 1030.
[2]Nicholson, Laura J.; Shebar, Tom F.; and Weinberg, Meredith R. (2000). "Computer Crimes: Annual White Collar Crime Survey." *American Criminal Law Review, 37*(2). Available at *http://www. accessmylibrary.com/coms2/summary_0286–28748235_ITM.* Retrieved from the Internet on August 10, 2007.
[3]Pastrikos, Catherine (2004). "Identity Theft Statutes: Which Will Protect Americans the Most?" *Albany Law Review, 67*(4): 1137–1157.
[4]Kerr, Donald M. (September 6, 2000b). Statement for the Record on *Carnivore Diagnostic Tool* before the United States Sentate: The Committee on the Judiciary, Washington, DC. Available at *www.fbi.gov/pressrm/congress/congressoo/kerr090600.htm.*
[5]Stevens, Gina and Doyle, Charles (2003). Privacy: An Overview of Federal Statutes Governing Wiretapping and Electronic Eavesdropping. Report for Congress: #98-326. Available at *http://www.epic.org/privacy/wiretap/98-326.pdf.* Retrieved from the Internet on October 7, 2007.
[6]Seifert, Jeffrey W. (2007). *Data Mining and Homeland Security: An Overview.* CRS Report for Congress. Order Code RL 31798 (January 18, 2007).

[7]Department of Defense. (May 20, 2003). *Report to Congress Regarding the Terrorism Informational Awareness Program, Detailed Information.* Available at *http://wyden.senate.gov/leg_issues/reports/darpa_tia_summary.pdf* (last accessed May 15, 2007).

[8]Ibid.

[9]Transportation Security Administration. (March 11, 2003). *TSA's CAPPS II Gives Equal Weight to Privacy, Security.* Press Release. Available at *www.tsa.gov* (last accessed on May 15, 2007).

[10]Seifert (2007). *Data Mining and Homeland Security.*

[11]Ibid.

[12]Ibid.

[13]Available at *www.ifs.univie.ac.at/~pr2gq1/rev4344.html.*

[14]United Nations (2000). "United Nations Manual on the Prevention and Control of Computer-Related Criteria." International Review of Criminal Policy, 43 & 44. Available at *www.ifs.univie.ac.at/~pr2gq1/rev4344.html (last accessed May 31, 2006).*

[15]Ibid.

[16]Broadhurst, Roderic (2006). "Developments in the Global Law Enforcement of Cyber-Crime." *Policing: An International Journal of Police Strategies and Management, 29*(3): 408–433.

[17]Ibid.

[18]Available at *www.fbi.gov/programs/carnivore/carnivore2.htm.*

[19]United Nations (2000). "United Nations Manual on the prevention and Control of Computer-related Criteria."

CHAPTER 8

Applying the First Amendment to Computer-Related Crime

Chapter Outline

LEARNING OBJECTIVES

After reading this chapter, you will be able to do the following:

- ✓ Obtain information concerning the legal perception of indecency and obscenity.
- ✓ Overcome the difficulty in defining child pornography.
- ✓ Learn of the contradictions in the court system on the topic of child pornography.
- ✓ Gain knowledge of legislation that is geared directly toward technology and the Internet.
- ✓ Discuss in full detail the subject of Internet gambling

KEY TERMS AND CONCEPTS

- child pornography
- *Child Pornography Prevention Act*
- *Child Protection Act*
- *FCC* v. *Pacifica Foundation*
- indecency
- *Miller* v. *California*

- *New York* v. *Ferber*
- obscenity
- *Osborne* v. *Ohio*
- *Protection of Children Against Sexual Exploitation Act of 1977*
- *Roth* v. *United States*

- *Regina* v. *Hicklin*
- *Telecommunications Reform Act of 1996*

INTRODUCTION AND GENERAL PRINCIPLES

As stated previously, the most common judicial challenges facing computer crime investigators include inconsistent interpretations and applications of the First, Fourth, and Fourteenth Amendments to emerging advancements in technology. Constitutional challenges have been issued, for example, in cases where traditional, non-technology-specific statutes have been utilized to combat the lethargy of legislative entities within a particular jurisdiction. Subsequent appellate decisions, based largely on non-technology-specific case law, have also come under attack, with some displaying favoritism for law enforcement, others for civil rights, and still others, drifting aimlessly with no apparent consistency in rationale or legality (e.g., Ninth Circuit). Unfortunately, such legal capriciousness has not been alleviated even in those jurisdictions which have attempted to incorporate technological innovations into traditional criminal statutes, due to the lack of responsiveness of the Supreme Court. Thus, the very legislation which has been enacted to assist and guide law enforcement in the murky world of technology where all traditional boundaries of legality, reality, geography, and criminality are blurred has been all but negated by appellate courts unequipped for the sheer novelty of their language and the resulting ambiguities surrounding technological advancements. The resolute silence of the Supreme Court has exacerbated the problem, leaving the country rudderless, with lower courts floundering—contradicting one another and creating a patchwork of constitutionality unintended by the framers.

Perhaps the most controversial legal issues involving the utilization of computer communication and technological innovations concern the First Amendment. As one of the most precious freedoms guaranteed to Americans, the provisions of the First Amendment have been zealously guarded by the Supreme Court. As such, the Court has consistently ruled that any statute seeking to abridge the Freedom of Speech must be narrowly constructed as to regulate the smallest amount of speech.[1] Originally such distinctions were considered to be outside the scope or daily routines of patrol officers, who were primarily concerned with issues arising from the Fourth and Fourteenth Amendments. First Amendment challenges have kept pace with technological advancements—providing no easy answers, while presenting a myriad of legal conundrums. Such challenges include the inviolability of electronically published materials, the sanctity of electronic communications, the intersection of obscenity and community standards, and the necessary level of particularity and specificity in emerging legislative acts. While lower courts have tended toward consistency on the first two issues by reaffirming traditional case law, they have not even reached a semblance of consensus on the latter two.

OBSCENITY IN GENERAL

Defining obscenity has long been a concern among civilized societies. In the most generic sense, it is something not easily defined, but recognizable on sight, irrespective of medium. Traditionally, the Supreme Court has been the standard bearer for the line of demarcation between something simply perverse and that which is obscene—often making direct statements about specific materials, and sometimes, generalized proclamations about indecency. Although rare, such broad proclamations encompass a myriad of situations, and provide legal justification and academic rationale for their existence. For example, broad laws which prohibited depictions of minors in explicit or sexual situations were upheld due to the sheer indecency of such portrayals, *and* the increased potential for future victimization of generalized children due to their existence. However, the advent of electronic communications and sophisticated graphical programs has muddied the waters—making it possible for child pornographers to argue that computer-generated images (or *virtual* children)

Defining Obscenity

The Court has always grappled with the rather elusive or intangible concept of obscenity. As one frustrated justice put it in holding that *Roth*[2] protected all obscenity except "hard core pornography":

> I shall not today attempt further to define the kinds of material I understand to be embraced with that shorthand description; and perhaps I could never succeed in intelligibly doing so. But I know it when I see it.[3]

lack the requisite specified victim. Although few would agree that this argument has merit and most would willingly apply blanket prohibitions to any image, real or created, which exploited children, many challenges to recently emerging prohibitions have found a receptive audience among the judiciary. Thus, concrete notions of decency and pornography have not withheld the intangibility and virtuality of computer technology, and the Supreme Court remains resolutely mute.

● TRADITIONAL NOTIONS OF DECENCY

Prior to the 1950s, traditional notions of decency and obscenity were governed by an obscenity statute originally developed in 1868 in *Regina* v. *Hicklin*.[4] This statute developed a level of obscenity which evaluated the alleged immorality of Catholic priests. To wit, it evaluated "whether the tendency of the matter charged . . . is to deprave and corrupt those whose minds are open to such immoral influences and into whose hands a publication of this sort may fall."[5] The vagueness and obscurity of this antiquated language remained largely in effect until 1957 when *Roth* v. *United States*[6] determined that obscene material was not constitutionally protected by the First Amendment. In its purest sense, *Roth* coupled the reasonable man with the community standard doctrine. Unfortunately, when abstractly applied, it appeared to cement a concept of national morality—creating a doctrine as unworkable as its predecessor.

The Supreme Court revisited the issue in 1973, establishing a three-pronged analysis of questionable materials and clarifying the sanctity of jurisdictional morality. While recognizing the difficult balance between the state's interest in protecting the *sensibilities of unwilling recipients* from exposure to pornographic materials and the *dangers of censorship inherent in unabashedly content-based laws*, the Court held that a work is obscene and not covered under the protections of the First Amendment, if (1) an average person who is capable of applying contemporary community standards (2) determines that a work "depicts or describes, in a patently offensive way, sexual conduct specifically defined by the applicable state law" and (3) "taken as a whole, lacks serious literary, artistic, political, or scientific value."[7] Thus, the Court recognized the jurisdictional variability in standards of morality and banished the notion of universal decency. However, the Court also reiterated premises originally specified in *Ginsberg* v. *New York*,[8] which recognized distinctions between certain categories of individuals. While stressing the need for individual consideration and cautioning against generalized or overbroad statutes, the Court ruled that minors and adults must be treated differently when definitions of constitutionally protected materials are at issue (i.e., minors' rights do not reach the standard of adults in questions of obscenity). Most importantly, the Court ruled that the state has a *compelling interest* in protecting the welfare of children, ruling that material which would not be considered for adults may still be considered as such by minors. Such interest is so compelling, in fact, that its consideration has affected all subsequent obscenity rulings by the Court, irrespective of medium.

Since *Miller*, the Supreme Court has been forced to consider technological advancements in media of communication and their applicability to First Amendment protection, as well as to distinguish between *obscenity*, *indecency*, and *profanity*. Beginning with **FCC v. Pacifica Foundation**,[9] the Court has ruled that new media of communication must be scrutinized as they are developed and that varying media result in varying protections. In *Pacifica*, for example, the Court basically diluted traditional First Amendment protections enjoyed by the print media and established new boundaries for free speech via television and radio broadcasts. In addition, it distinguished between obscene speech and indecent speech, ruling that "indecent" speech, even if it does not reach the level of obscenity, cannot be broadcast during times when children may be presumed to be part of an audience. It further ruled that the broad-based nature of radio communication mandated a greater level of scrutiny because (1) it was more accessible to children; (2) broadcasting invaded the home of individual citizens, thus creating a constant risk of exposure; and (3) the scarcity of frequencies allowed government regulation. Thus, George Carlin's broadcast monologue, *Filthy*, which included references to excretory and sexual activities in an offensive manner, violated 18 U.S.C. 1464 and was not entitled to First Amendment protection, because of the content of the communication, the pervasiveness of the selected medium, and the subsequent accessibility to children.

The Court further reiterated these premises in *Sable Communications, Inc.* v. *FCC*[10] and *Turner Broadcasting System, Inc.* v. *FCC*[11] when it held that telephone communications and cable broadcasts, respectively, are afforded different degrees of First Amendment protection, comparable to their disparate accessibility to children. While reaffirming that obscene material is not sheltered by constitutional mandate, the Court held that telephone communications and cable television

enjoy heightened levels of protection because they are not as pervasive or accessible as they require affirmative actions and do not reach captive audiences. The Court further afforded dial-up media greater First Amendment protection than their cable broadcast counterparts. However, the Court failed to establish an unequivocal standard of protection afforded to either medium. It simply ruled that protections afforded to cable communications were similar to those enjoyed by traditional print media. Finally, the Court restated the *compelling interest* in protecting children, but argued that a comprehensive ban of *indecent* communications would constitute an unacceptable infringement of free speech. As such, they upheld the constitutionality of the traditional statutes (see box), but cautioned against generalizing them. Unfortunately, these seminal rulings have not assisted contemporary law enforcement, as hoped. In fact, the application of traditional obscenity statutes remains convoluted and inconsistent at best, while emerging legislation has been largely ignored by the Supreme Court.

● EMERGING STATUTES AND THE AVAILABILITY OF OBSCENE MATERIAL TO CHILDREN

As discussed, traditional statutes of obscenity, profanity, and indecency have been widely challenged by civil libertarians with varying results. Generally speaking, the court and government entities have recognized varying degrees of jurisdictional tolerance for questionable materials, and considered disparate standards of community morality. However, all actors have unilaterally dismissed readily available obscene material *and* child pornography from active consideration of First Amendment challenges, recognizing both a compelling government interest in protecting children from harm[12] and a subsequent interest in prosecuting those individuals who promote the sexual exploitation of children.[13] As such, federal and state bodies have acted consistently to supplant traditional

Traditional Statutes

18 U.S.C. § 1460—crime to possess obscene material with intent to distribute

18 U.S.C. § 1462—crime to distribute or receive obscene material through a common carrier in interstate or foreign commerce

18 U.S.C. § 1464—crime to broadcast obscene, profane, or indecent language

18 U.S.C. §§ 1465 and 1466—crime to knowingly transport or engage in the business of selling obscene, lewd, or filthy material through interstate commerce. (This statute was first successfully applied to the Internet in *U.S.* v. *Thomas*[14]—which held that using a computer to transmit pornographic material violated this statute.)

standards and formally encode those interests in legislation which would withstand the onslaught of emerging technologies.

The first act specifically aimed at protecting families and children from online sexually explicit materials was incorporated into the **Telecommunications Reform Act of 1996**. Introduced by Senator James Exon (D-Neb), it was *designed to regulate the previously untamed frontier of cyberspace.* Criminalizing the harassment, stalking, annoyance, or abuse of any individual in an electronic medium, the act further criminalized any obscene communication to a minor recipient or the transmission of any communication that depicted or described sexual or excretory activities or organs that were *prima facially* offensive. Touted by law enforcement officials as a valuable weapon in the protection of children, the act was quickly dealt a mortal blow in jurisprudential circles. Challenged by a diverse grouping of non-profit organizations, educational societies, and business communities, the act was immediately struck down by the U.S. District Court for the Eastern District of Pennsylvania. Applying a strict scrutiny analysis, the court invalidated the law on two grounds: overbreadth and vagueness. Essentially, the court ruled that the breadth of the law would unconstitutionally abridge adult expression of free speech *and* that the law failed to establish a line of demarcation separating valuable materials and those criminal in nature. This decision was affirmed by the Supreme Court, which invalidated sections 47 U.S. C. 223(a) and 223(d) and held that *the interest in encouraging freedom of expression in a democratic society outweighs any theoretical but unproven benefit of censorship* (at 2346–2347). The Supreme Court further likened the Internet to a marketplace of ideas and suggested that it was entitled to the highest level of First Amendment protections so that the free flow of ideas and the exchange of information would continue undeterred. Arguing that an absolute right to free speech is a noble idea worth pursuing, but one which is not necessarily possible, the Court compared Internet communications to traditional notions of telephonic communications, in which individuals must take affirmative actions to access obscene material via the Net. Emphasizing that their research revealed a minimal risk to children of exposure to obscene material by simply *surfing the Net*, the Court upheld the District Court's ruling, applying the highest standard of First Amendment protection to the Internet. In essence, they ruled that although the government's interest was legitimate, the means taken (i.e., the Communicat Decency Act) threatened to *torch a large segment of the Internet community*[15] and that the characteristics of scarcity and invasiveness which are predicates of standards applied to broadcast media are lacking in Internet communications. The Court based their ruling on the reasoning that the Internet did not invade an individual's home, have a history of extensive government regulation, and has no scarcity of available frequencies. Thus, the limitations on broadcast media do not apply to the Internet even though commercial speech is not as protected, and communications media like radio and television enjoy far less protection than their print media counterparts. In addition, it ruled that the compelling government interest in protecting children was outweighed by the broadness and vagueness of the CDA as it suppressed an overbroad area of protected speech when a less restrictive area or provision could have been enacted. Finally, the Court ruled that the statute should have incorporated or addressed all three prongs of *Miller*, instead of just one.

DEFINING CHILD PORNOGRAPHY

Like issues relating to the accessibility of obscenity to children on the Internet, depictions of **child pornography** or the exploitation of children have been hotly debated by civil libertarians and law enforcement officials. Unlike debates regarding accessibility or pervasiveness of obscenity, however, traditional classifications of child pornography have remained virtually absolute in most cases. Forsaking court categorizations of **obscenity**, **indecency**, or *profanity*, the majority of legislative and judicial entities have upheld even the vaguest or most obscure of all child pornography definitions, citing the potential harm to children. However, a minority of courts have tended to be more liberal in their application of the First Amendment, and even the most nobly designed statutes have been successfully challenged.

Beginning with the ***Protection of Children Against Sexual Exploitation Act of 1977***,[16] communities have attempted to prohibit visual depictions of child pornography, while lower courts have grappled with the constitutionality of such legislation. As a result, the intersection of legislative intent and jurisprudential interpretation has resulted in continuous renovations of extant laws, whereby prohibitive statutes have been revamped in keeping with the current judicial climate. The *Protection of Children Against Sexual Exploitation Act of 1977*, for example, was directly guided by the principles originally established in *Miller*.

Applying the three-pronged obscenity test, the act expressly prohibited those explicit depictions of children which did not have redeeming social value. In keeping with *Miller*, it also did not require scienter on the part of the violator as to the age of the individuals depicted. This omission proved to be the act's Achilles heel, as the Ninth Circuit ruled, and the Supreme Court upheld, that "the First Amendment mandates that a statute prohibiting the distribution, shipping or receipt of child pornography require knowledge of the minority of the performers as an element of the crime it defines."[17] Thus, the act, in and of itself, was invalidated. As a result of these deficiencies and the Supreme Court's ruling in *Ferber*, Congress enacted the ***Child Protection Act of 1984***.[18] This act eliminated the obscenity requirement established in *Miller*. However, the Court did recognize a specific state interest in enacting legislation prohibiting child pornography.

APPLYING CASE LAW TO CHILD PORNOGRAPHY STATUTES

As stated, child pornography definitions have been the result of the intersection of jurisdictional mandates and constitutional interpretations. While the Court has been loath to issue blanket prohibitions involving child pornography at the federal level, it has upheld such prohibitions at the state level. Thus, law-enforcement officials may find more success in combating child pornography with state resources. Without question, the single most important decision regarding state prohibitions of child pornography may be found in ***New York* v. *Ferber***.[19] In *Ferber*, a bookstore proprietor, convicted for selling films depicting young boys masturbating, argued that a New York statute prohibiting the promotion of sexual performances by children under the age of 16 through the distribution of materials depicting such activity was unconstitutionally overbroad. Ferber argued that because the statute also prohibited the distribution of materials, such as medical and/or educational books, which *deal with adolescent sex in a realistic but non-obscene manner*,[20] it failed to establish a level of obscenity consistent with *Miller*. The Supreme Court, however, held that states are granted more leeway in the regulation of pornographic depictions of children than in the regulation of obscenity (756) because:

1. the use of children as subjects of pornographic materials is harmful to the physiological, emotional, and mental health of the child;

2. the standard of *Miller* v. *California*[21] for determining what is legally obscene is not a satisfactory solution to the child pornography problem;

3. the advertising and selling of child pornography provide an economic motive for and are thus an integral part of the production of such materials, an activity illegal throughout the nation;

4. the value of permitting live performances and photographic reproductions of children engaged in lewd exhibitions is exceedingly modest, if not de minimis;

5. recognizing and classifying child pornography as a category of material outside the First Amendment's protection is not incompatible with this Court's decisions dealing with what speech is unprotected. When a definable class of material, such as that covered by [458 U.S. 747, 748] the New York statute, bears so heavily and

pervasively on the welfare of children engaged in its production, the balance of competing interests in clearly struck, and it is permissible to consider these materials as without the First Amendment's protection (pp. 756–764).

In a clear departure from normal procedure, the Court specifically relied on statistics and opinions gathered from sources ranging from scholars to law-enforcement practitioners to child psychologists. Noting that the federal government and 47 states had enacted statutes to prohibit the production of child pornography, the Court emphatically stated that child pornography was a national problem. Through the extrapolation of the potential harm to real children resulting from virtual images, the Court squarely placed child pornography outside the umbrella of free speech guaranteed by the Constitution, noting that any literary, artistic, political, scientific value of child porn does not ameliorate potential harm to children. However, the Court also cautioned against overgeneralization of their ruling, unwittingly setting the scene for a new round of challenges.

There is no serious contention that the legislature was unjustified in believing that it is difficult, if [458 U.S. 747, 760] not impossible, to halt the exploitation of children by pursuing only those who produce the photographs and movies. While the production of pornographic materials is a low-profile, clandestine industry, the need to market the resulting products requires a visible apparatus of distribution.

Notable Quotes from *Ferber*

The prevention of sexual exploitation and abuse of children constitutes a government objective of surpassing importance.

The legislative judgment, as well as the judgment found in the relevant literature, is that the use of children as subjects of pornographic materials is harmful to the physiological, emotional, and mental health of the child.

The distribution of photographs and films depicting sexual activity by juveniles is intrinsically related to the sexual abuse of children in at least two ways. First, the materials produced are a permanent record of the children's participation and the harm to the child is exacerbated by their circulation. Second, the distribution network for child pornography must be closed if the production of material which requires the sexual exploitation of children is to be effectively controlled . . .

The most expeditious if not the only practical method of law enforcement may be to dry up the market for this material by imposing severe criminal penalties on persons selling, advertising, or otherwise promoting the product.

The *Miller* Standard, like all general definitions of what may be banned as obscene, does not reflect the State's particular and more compelling interest in prosecuting those who promote the sexual exploitation of children. Thus, the question under the *Miller* test of whether a work, taken as a whole, appeals to the prurient interest of the average person bears no connection to the issue of whether a child has been physically or psychologically harmed in the production of the work.

It is irrelevant to the child who has been abused whether or not the material

> has a literary, artistic, political or social value. It is not rare that a content-based classification of speech has been accepted because it may be appropriately generalized that within the confines of the given classification, the evil to be restricted so overwhelmingly outweighs [458 U.S. 747, 764] the expressive interests, if any, at stake, that no process of case-by-case adjudication is required. When a definable class of material, such as that covered (in this case) bears so heavily and pervasively on the welfare of children engaged in its production, we think the balance of competing interests is clearly struck and that it is permissible to consider these materials as without the protection of the First Amendment.

In an effort to balance the interests of children and the Constitution, the Court suggested alternatives to child involvement in the production and distribution of child pornography. To wit, *if it were necessary for literary or artistic value, a person over the statutory age who perhaps looked younger could be utilized. **Simulation outside of the prohibition of the statute could provide another alternative**.* (Unfortunately, this language has become the focal point in current debates involving simulated child pornography.) In addition, the Court argued that any legislation must be evaluated independently, as the First Amendment does require specificity in an elemental application. Thus, it ruled that the behavior proscribed and the level of scienter must be clearly articulated, although it failed to provide thresholds for each. In fact, no formal level of scienter existed until 1990.

In ***Osborne* v. *Ohio*,**[22] the Court finally established a standard of scienter that had been lacking in *Ferber*. More specifically, the Court stated that traditional definitions of *recklessness plainly satisfied the requirement laid down in* Ferber. This important demarcation was once again supported by the potential harm to children generated by the existence of child pornography. The Supreme Court reiterated premises originally articulated in *Ferber*, and declared that Ohio may constitutionally proscribe "the possession and viewing of child pornography as it was enacted on the basis of its compelling interests in protecting the physical and psychological well-being of minors and in destroying the market for the exploitative use of children by penalizing those who possess and view the offending materials." In addition, the Court noted that the Ohio statute "encourages possessors to destroy such materials, which permanently record the victim's abuse and thus may haunt him for years to come . . . and which, available evidence suggests, may be used by pedophiles to seduce other children." Although the Court did vacate *Osborne*'s conviction on a legal technicality, it was a major victory for law enforcement as it failed to strike down the statute in question, noting that the constitutionality of statutes determined to be overbroad is still upheld if a court restricts its application and the court's interpretation is known to practitioners. In addition, it rejected the petitioner's interpretation and application of *Stanley* v. *Georgia*[23] which prohibited a state from limiting the *private* possession of obscene material, arguing that later decisions like *Ferber* had spoken to the narrowness of *Stanley* (i.e., that child pornography is not the same as traditional materials deemed to be obscene). To wit, "the difference here is obvious: The state does not rely on a paternalistic interest in regulating Osborne's mind. Rather, Ohio has enacted 2907.323(A)(3) in order to protect the

MySpace, Accountability, and the Law

In recent years, individuals have flocked to virtual meeting rooms across the globe. Unfortunately, the lack of restrictions on some of these sites often provides an area ripe for child exploitation and victimization. While some would argue that such companies should be held liable for the sexual assault of a minor which was facilitated by their site, a Texas court has disagreed. In *Doe v. MySpace, Inc.*, the court ruled that the CDA provided MySpace with immunity from tort liability even if MySpace was aware of the risk of sexual assault and took no precautions. The court declined to extend the duty of premises owners to "virtual premises." In addition, the court ruled that claims of negligence and gross negligence failed under common law as MySpace had no duty to protect the victim from sexual assault, even if the attack was foreseeable.[24]

victims of child pornography; it hopes to destroy a market for the exploitative use of children."

Once again recognizing the potential harm, the Court ruled that the legislative judgment, as well as the judgment found in relevant literature, is that the use of children as subjects of pornographic materials is harmful to the physiological, emotional, and mental health of the child.

> That judgment, we think, easily passes muster under the First Amendment (Ferber, 458 U.S. at 756–758). It is also surely reasonable for the State to conclude that it will decrease the production of child pornography if it penalizes those who possess and view the product (495 U.S. 103,110), thereby decreasing demand. In Ferber, where we upheld a New York statute outlawing the distribution of child pornography, we found a similar argument persuasive: "the advertising and selling of child pornography provide an economic motive for and are thus an integral part of the production of such materials, an activity illegal throughout the Nation. 'It rarely has been suggested that the constitutional freedom for speech and press extends its immunity to speech or writing used an integral part of conduct in violation of a valid criminal statute.'
>
> Id., at 761–762, quoting Giboney v. Empire Storage & Ice Co., 336 U.S. 490, 498 (1949)

Thus, both *Ferber* and *Osborne* recognized the state's compelling interest in protecting children from harm. While even the most commonsensical application of technology-specific legislation would appear to be constitutionally supported in light of these rulings, lower courts have failed to reach consensus on emerging legislation at both the state and federal levels.

TECHNOLOGY-SPECIFIC LEGISLATION—CONTENTION IN THE COURTS

In an effort to tighten prohibitions of child pornography on the federal level, Congress replaced the *Protection of Children Against Sexual Exploitation of 1977* with the *Child Protection Act of 1984* (CPA). Dismissing the traditional obscenity standard found in *Ferber*, the Court also dismissed the requirement that the production or distribution of the material be for the purpose of sale, thereby formally recognizing that a large portion of pornographic trafficking was for sexual gratification. This act was also amended to include prohibitions of:

1. the production or use of advertisements for child pornography (*Child Sexual Abuse and Pornography Act of 1986*, Public Law No. 99–628, 100 Stat. 3510 (1986) codified as amended at 18 U.S.C. § 2251);
2. the use of a computer to transport, distribute, or receive child pornography (*Child Protection and Obscenity Enforcement Act of 1988*, Public Law No. 100–690, 102 Stat. 4181 (1988) codified as amended at 18 U.S.C. §§ 2251A–2252)); and,
3. the possession of three or more pieces of child pornography (*Child Protection Restoration and Penalties Enhancement Act of 1990*, Public Law No. 101–647, § 301, 104 Stat. 4789 (1990) codified as amended at 18 U.S.C. S 2252(a)(4)).

In fact, there have been more than a handful of amendments made to the original Act banning child pornography. However, all of these amendments have concentrated on the utilization of real children in the production and distribution of such materials.

In 1996, Congress, anticipating an explosion of explicit material on emerging media like the Internet, again revisited the problem of child pornography. The **Child Pornography Prevention Act** of 1996, departing from traditional legal reasoning, was enacted to prohibit virtual child pornography, arguing in part that the very existence of child pornography, real or not, increases child molestation and pedophilia. To wit, the law specifically forbade "any visual depiction, including any photography, film, video, picture, or computer or computer-generated image or picture, whether made or produced by electronic, mechanical, or other means, of sexually explicit conduct." This verbiage, considered by many to be vague and ambiguous, has resulted in a myriad of constitutional challenges across the country.

Generally speaking, the *Child Pornography Prevention Act of 1996* (CPPA) expanded the Child Pornography Act to include the production and distribution of computer-generated or other mechanically altered images of minors engaging in explicit conduct. Unlike the original CPA and the preceding amendments, which were drafted after definitive ruling by the Court, the CPPA *preceded* any discussion of simulated child pornography. Rather, relying on the extrapolation of potential harm to children by pedophiles aroused by such images, the act assumed that the lack of an actual victim is irrelevant as actual or real victimization may occur via a communication of no social significance and which fails to further the interest of free thinking. Indeed, it would appear to many that the risk of child victimization is not diminished by the fact that no actual children were victimized as the viewer is largely unaware of the true nature of the scene depicted. At issue among the lower courts was the generalized language of the CPPA which prohibited material that *appears to be* or *conveys the impression of* child pornography. While the First,

Fourth, and Eleventh Circuits upheld the constitutionality of the act, denying it was overbroad or vague,[25] the Ninth Circuit (California) ruled conversely.[26]

In *United States* v. *Mento*,[27] the Petitioner argued that the act was unconstitutional as it unfairly abridged the First Amendment as it is aimed at inhibiting the expression of child pornography itself as opposed to the secondary effect of such expression. While the Fourth Circuit agreed that the act's ban of child pornography *unquestionably constitutes a content-based regulation* which is not rendered content-neutral by its intent to control the secondary effects of the material in question, it ruled that those same regulations withstand strict scrutiny because they are narrowly tailored to serve a compelling government interest. To wit, "Mento interprets *Ferber* too narrowly. *Ferber* necessarily dealt only with depictions of actual children long before virtual pornography became an issue . . . [it] in no way stands for the proposition that permissible governmental interests in the realm of child pornography would be forever restricted to the harm suffered by identifiable children participating in its production." In addition, the court ruled that the Court's earlier decisions in *Ferber* and *Osborne* clearly stated a compelling government interest in protecting *all* children from potential exploitation resulting from child pornography— *not* just those involved in the actual production. Finally, the court ruled that there is no difference between the harm posed by actual vs. virtual child pornography, arguing that child molesters viewing images of child pornography receive sexual gratification if those images *appear to be* minors. Thus, no compelling government interest would be served with the removal of the words "appears to be" as without them, proof of age of those individuals presented would be required to overcome reasonable doubt. The Ninth Circuit did not agree.

In 1997, the Ninth Circuit, in keeping with their traditional zealousness in matters relating to the First Amendment, struck down the bulk of the Child Pornography Prevention Act.[28]

More specifically, the court held that the CPPA was unconstitutional "to the extent that it proscribe[d] computer images that [did not] involve the use of real children in their production or dissemination [4]". Thus, sections 2556(8)(B) and 2556(8)(D) were deemed unconstitutional by the court, who reasoned that content-based restrictions on free speech are presumptively unconstitutional in the absence of a *compelling interest* by the government in prohibiting images of non-real children. The court denied the adequacy of the extant literature in establishing the potential harm posed by this sort of material. In addition, the court declared the language of the act vague, arguing that it did "not give the person of ordinary intelligence a reasonable opportunity to know what [was] prohibited, and fail[ed] to provide explicit standards for those who must apply it, with the attendant dangers of arbitrary and discriminatory application [12]". Finally, the court rejected the notion of generalized victims in keeping with earlier decisions.[29]

In *Boos*, the court reasoned that individual victims were more salient than societal interests. Interestingly, Boos, a child pornographer who exchanged pornographic images and erotic fantasies of children via the Internet, argued that his sentencing was inaccurate as his crimes represented the victimization of society, not of the individuals depicted ruling that Congress intended to protect *real* children from *actual*, not expected, exploitation, the court denied his claim, and affirmed the upward sentencing departure based on the number of images found. Thus, the Ninth Circuit clearly established a standard of evaluation which protects large portions of child pornography activities, in direct contradiction to other circuits across the country. In 2002, Supreme Court ruled in favor of the Ninth Circuit's interpretation and struck down the CPPA, stating that "the prospect of crime . . . by itself does not justify laws suppressing protected speech."[30]

While many critics of the decision suggest that their decision directly contradicted the protections housed with *Ferber* and *Osborne*, the court used neither to justify their decision.

Instead, the court relied upon obscenity standards originally articulated in *Miller*. Such standards require proof that the "work" in question, when taken as a whole, appeals to *prurient interests, is patently offensive in light of community standards,* and *lacks serious literary, artistic, political or scientific value.* According to the court, the "CPPA prohibits speech despite its serious literary, artistic, political, or scientific value. The statute proscribes the visual depiction of an idea—that of teenagers engaging in sexual activity—that is a fact of modern society and has been a theme in art and literature throughout the ages."[31]

The court argued that both teenage sexual activity and the sexual abuse of children had inspired countless literary works, including that of William Shakespeare and contemporary movies. In addition, they noted that case law prohibits the evaluation of the artistic merit of a work based on a single explicit scene. As such, they ruled that the CPPA violated the First Amendment because it "lacks the required link between its prohibitions and the affront to community standards prohibited by the definition of obscenity."[32]

The court angered both law enforcement authorities and parental groups by suggesting that law enforcement efforts could eradicate the proliferation of child pornography. Apparently unfamiliar with academic research regarding punishment and criminal behavior, the court noted that

> If virtual images were identical to illegal child pornography, the illegal images would be driven from the market by the indistinguishable substitutes. Few pornographers would risk prosecution by abusing real children if fictional, computerized images would suffice.

Thus, the Court ruled that virtual or simulated pornography was not prohibited under *Ferber*, but the depiction of real or actual children was. This ruling makes it possible for predators to surreptitiously take photographs of real children and use graphics software to create pornographic images in the likenesses of those real children.

By making virtual pornography legal, the *Ashcroft* decision threatens children in a variety

Is This legal?

Chester Mo Lester, a convicted pedophile, sits at a corner table of a local pizzeria that caters to children of all ages. Appearing entranced by the text messaging function of his cell phone, Chester quietly snaps photographs of the innocent children at play. Then, in the privacy of his home office, Chester "morphs" the images by obscuring the actual children's faces and creating sexually explicit photos. Chester utilizes the morphed images for his own gratification, and then sells them online to other pedophiles. Has he committed a federal crime?

of ways. It may be argued that the legality itself might lead to a new population of child pornographers and/or pedophiles as even computer novices can develop morphed photographs. Such pornography may be used by pedophiles to sexually seduce minors. It may be used to create a perception that such behavior is fun or exciting. Peer pressure or the desire to be like others in their cohort may increase their vulnerability and, ultimately, their victimization. It is also possible that pedophiles may actually blackmail their potential targets by creating morphed images depicting the victim and threatening to release them to family or friends if they do not acquiesce to their demands. However, the greatest threat posed by the *Ashcroft* decision is the inability to prosecute sexual predators. It may be argued, for example, that heightened numbers of child pornographers will lead to an increase in child molestation—as graphic images may whet the appetite and desires of pedophiles.

Ashcroft makes it extremely difficult to prosecute child pornography even in cases where real or actual children are victimized as the burden of proof soundly rests with the state. Proving that the images are NOT computer generated will become increasingly difficult as graphics programs continue to advance. In essence, the specific recognition that computer-generated images of child pornography are not illegal creates an automatic defense against criminal charges. It can be argued that such "virtual pornography defense" creates *prima facie* reasonable doubt unless an actual victim is identified and is available to testify regarding their victimization.

Impact of *Ashcroft* Decision on State and Local Prosecutors' Offices

Since the *Ashcroft* Decision, Prosecutors' Office	Prosecutors (%)
Has had cases involving virtual-image defense	40
Has had such cases gone to trial	5
Is prosecuting fewer CP cases	4
Is not pursuing some cases it would have previously purchased	9
Has been affected by fudges' decisions interpreting *Free Speech*	15
Respondent has received training about prosecuting Internet crimes	75
Is using these tactics for dealing with *Free Speech* decision:	
consulting with federal agencies to identify children	64
consulting with other sources to identify children	56
using obscenity laws to prosecute CP cases	25
using experts to testify that images are not computer generated	30
letting the jury decide	11

Strategies to the Virtual Pornography Defense

In the days immediately following the *Free Speech Coalition*, many law enforcement authorities and scholars alike worried about the potential impact of subsequent child pornography cases. Anecdotal evidence suggests that the decision is having an effect on federal cases, and that perpetrators are less likely to plead guilty. However, state and local cases have fared better. This is especially true of jurisdictions where the state law does not contain the same verbiage as the original Child Pornography Prevention Act. In those cases in which the *virtual-images defense*

is invoked, the following prosecutorial strategies have proven successful:

- having a federal law enforcement agent testify as to the origins of the images
- having a forensics expert compare CP images to virtual images and testify that the CP images were not virtual
- presenting a doctor's affidavit that the children were real and having the jury decide whether the pictures depicted real children

In the wake of *Ashcroft* v. *Free Speech Coaltion*, Congress changed the original language of the CPPA to include any digital image "that is or **is indistinguishable from** that of a minor engaging in a sexually explicit" conduct. To further strengthen federal law, they also passed the *Prosecutorial Remedies and Other Tools to End the Exploitation of Children Today Act* (ACT). By specifically incorporating the *Miller* test of obscenity, the PROTECT Act was designed to overcome the constitutional challenges of overbreadth and vagueness that had been at issue in *Ashcroft*. More specifically, Congress forbade the possession or distribution of computer-generated pornography or images, drawings, or sculptures depicting children in sexual activity or other *obscene* situations as defined by *Miller*. As the same time, Congress reiterated traditional prohibitions against behavior in which children were targets and provided for enhanced punishments for sexual predators. Congress specifically noted that the *Ashcroft* decision made it virtually (no pun intended) impossible to prosecute existing statutes as virtual and real images depicting child pornography are indistinguishable without identification of a specific victim. The PROTECT Act, designed to overcome the deficiencies of the CPPA, has already been challenged in the courts. In 2006, the Eleventh Circuit ruled that the "pandering provision" of the Act violated the First Amendment.

● INTERNET GAMBLING

Just as Congress has attempted to eliminate child pornography in the United States, Internet gambling has increasingly been targeted. In an attempt to combat the growing problem, the government has focused on the reduction of financing and the elimination of promotion. By targeting those associations, sites, or media which advertise online gambling, it is anticipated that the number of available sites will be reduced. Unlike earlier efforts, the *Internet Gambling Prohibition and Enforcement Act* authorizes state and federal law enforcement to seek injunctions against persons or entities which facilitate illegal Internet gambling. Although in its infancy, the Act is displaying some success among media giants as Clear Channel Communications, Infinity Broadcasting, Discovery Networks, Yahoo!, and Google have all stopped carrying gambling advertisements.[33] As expected, civil libertarians have argued that the provisions contained within the Act are unconstitutional.

Gambling operators and some gaming presses have argued that placing restriction or prohibitions on advertising is a clear violation of the First Amendment. In a preemptive strike, Casino City, Inc., filed a motion for declaratory judgment against the Department of Justice on First Amendment grounds.[34] Although the government's subsequent Motion to Dismiss was successful, the case is currently on appeal. The Court's position on future challenges to prohibitions against gambling advertisements is uncertain. An analysis of a variety of cases may shed some light on the future direction of the Court.

- **Central Hudson Gas and Electric v. Public Service Commission of New York**[35]—One of the most important decisions evaluating the application of the First Amendment to commercial speech, *Central Hudson Gas and Electric* created a four-prong test which has become the standard. The Court set forth four questions:
  - ○ Is the commercial speech concerning *lawful activity and not misleading*?
  - ○ Is the government's interest in restricting the speech in question *substantial*?
  - ○ Does *the regulation directly advance the governmental interest asserted*?
  - ○ Is the prohibition *more extensive than is necessary to serve that interest*?[36]
- **Posadas de Puerto Rico Associates v. Tourism Co. Of Puerto Rico**[37]—In the most basic sense, the Court in *Posadas* upheld a statute prohibiting the advertisement of gambling to Puerto Rican residents. Applying the four-prong test developed in *Central Hudson Gas and Electric*, they noted that the government had a belief that:

  > . . . excessive casino gambling among local residents . . . would produce serious harmful effects on the health, safety and welfare of the Puerto Rican citizens, such as the disruption of moral and cultural patterns, the increase in local crime, the fostering of prostitution, the development of corruption, and the infiltration of organized crime.
  >
  > These are some of the very same concerns, of course, that have motivated the vast majority of the 50 States to prohibit casino gambling. We have no difficulty in concluding that the Puerto Rico Legislature's interest in the health, safety, and welfare of its citizens constitutes a "substantial" governmental interest.

- **44 Liquormart, Inc. v. Rhode Island**[38]—Although the decision in *Posadas* seemed to reflect the Court's recognition in state sovereignty in the protection of its citizen. Gambling operators have been heartened by the Court's ruling in *44 Liquormart, Inc.* In this case, the Court noted that

  > The First Amendment directs us to be especially skeptical of regulations that seek to keep people in the dark for what the government perceives to be their own good. That teaching applies equally to state attempts to deprive consumers of accurate information about their chosen products.

However, the implications of the Court's ruling are unclear. While the Court firmly placed the heaviest burden on the government, the advertisement in question focused on a *legal* activity. Any assurance or confidence on the part of the gaming industry may be misplaced, as the behavior or activity advertised in their case is still illegal.

At the current time, it remains illegal for any broadcast or online media to advertise online gambling. By definition, such advertisement equates to the aiding and abetting of a criminal act. The threshold for conviction is relatively low. Knowledge of the illegality of such action is not a requirement for prosecution. Simple demonstration of intent to advertise is sufficient to sustain a criminal conviction. For now, operators may be charged and convicted. However, the constitutionality of anti-gambling legislation and prohibitions on certain types of commercial speech remains questionable. It is expected that legislation and subsequent case law will evolve as technology continues to advance.

CONCLUSIONS

Technology-specific legislation, enacted to combat the growing problem of computer-related criminal behavior, has been greeted with a myriad of legal challenges. Although many legal issues have emerged, a large majority of such cases involve the First, Fourth, and Fourteenth Amendments, and virtually all of the challenges to child pornography legislation have questioned the parameters of the First Amendment. In the most basic sense, the First Amendment protects an individual's right to free expression from interference from government entities. More succinctly, any content-based restriction of the free flow of information is expressly prohibited, and when regulation of speech is necessary, it must be accomplished in the least restrictive manner possible. While few would argue that the guarantees found within the Amendment warrant substantial lessening, many may support some sort of blanket prohibition of materials which might be threatening to children.

The Supreme Court has repeatedly recognized a compelling government interest in the protection of children (e.g., *New York* v. *Ferber, Osborne* v. *Ohio, FCC* v. *Pacifica, Globe Newspaper Co.* v. *Superior Court,* 457 U.S. 596, 607), stating that "a democratic society rests, for its continuance, upon the healthy, well-rounded growth of young people into full maturity as citizens".[39] In addition, it has recognized the insidious nature of child pornography and held that such material is outside the scope of protections provided by the First Amendment. However, the introduction of emerging legislation which attempts to address technologically generated or altered images has come under fire by civil libertarians, and the Supreme Court has not yet ruled on the constitutionality of such prohibitions. As a result, jurisdictional application of federal legislation is contradictory.

DISCUSSION QUESTIONS

1. Provide a historical analysis of the legal concepts of *indecency* and *obscenity* within the United States. You should pay particular attention to the decisions rendered in *Ferber* and *Osborne*. What is the current climate of the Court, and what are your predictions for the future of indecency and obscenity in cyberspace?
2. Fully discuss the jurisprudential inconsistency in the application of child pornography laws across the country. What are the advantages and the disadvantages to a conservative application of the law? To a liberal application? Which is most consistent with your own view?
3. What appears to be the primary issue debated in the application of the Child Pornography Prevention Act of 1996? What is the latest ruling by the Supreme Court regarding this matter?
4. Briefly discuss the growing problem of the advertisement of gambling sites.
5. Discuss the notion that the *Ashcroft* decision has made children more vulnerable, while also focusing on the ways in which they become more vulnerable.

RECOMMENDED READING

- Lindner, Anne (2006). "First Amendment as Last Resort: The Internet Gambling Industry's Bid to Advertise in the United States." *Saint Louis University Law Journal, 50* (1289) . Available at *www.lexisnexis.com.*
- Shiffrin, Steve H. and Jesse H. Choper. 2007. First Amendment, Cases, Comments & Questions, 4th (Casebook) Supplement. Thomson West.

WEB RESOURCES

- www.epic.org – homepage of the Electronic Privacy Information Center. The site provides links to breaking news and case law involving technology and the First Amendment.
- www.cybercrime.gov – the homepage of the Computer Crime and Intellectual Property Section of the United States Department of Justice. The site provides links to breaking news and cases involving technology and constitutional questions. In addition, it provides access to Congressional testimony and manuals and guidelines used by DOJ.
- www.ecpat.net – the homepage of ECPAT (End Child Prostitution, Child Pornography and Trafficking of Children for Sexual Purposes), an international network of organizations and individuals working to eradicate child exploitation across the globe. The site provides links to international law enforcement efforts, research initiatives, and both scholarly and government publications.

ENDNOTES

[1]*Broadrick* v. *Oklahoma*, 413 U.S. 601 (1973).
[2]*Roth* v. *United States*, 354 U.S. 476 (1957).

[3]*Jacobellis* v. *Ohio*, 378 U.S. 184 (1964), Stewart concurring.

[4]*Regina* v. *Hicklin*, 1868 L.R. 3 Q. B. 360 (1857).

[5]*United States* v. *Kennerley*, 209 F. 119, 120 (S.D.N.Y. 1913).

[6]*Roth* v. *United States*, 354 U.S. 476 (1957).

[7]*Miller* v. *California*, 413 U.S. 15 (1973).

[8]*Ginsberg* v. *New York*, 390 U.S. 629 (1968).

[9]*FCC* v. *Pacifica Foundation*, 438 U.S. 726 (1978).

[10]*Sable Communications, Inc.* v. *FCC*, 492 U.S. 115 (1989).

[11]*Turner Broadcasting System, Inc.* v. *FCC*, 518 U.S. 727 (1996).

[12]*Ginsberg* v. *New York*, 390 U.S. 629, 639 (1968); *FCC* v. *Pacifica Found*, 438 U.S. 726, 749–750 (1978); *Santosky* v. *Kramer*, 455 U.S. 745, 766 (1982).

[13]*New York* v. *Ferber*, 458 U.S. 761 (1982); and *Osborne* v. *Ohio*, 495 U.S. 13, 109–111 (1990).

[14]*United States* v. *Thomas*, 74 F.3d. 701 (1996).

[15]*Reno* v. *ACLU*, 117 S.Ct. at 2336.

[16]Protection of Children Against Sexual Exploitation Act of 1977 (Pub. L. No. 95-225, 92 Stat. 7 (1977) (codified as amended at 18 U.S.C.SS 2251–2253).

[17]*United States* v. *Thomas*, 893 F.2d 1066 (Ninth Cir.), cert denied, 498 U.S. 826, 111 S.Ct 80 (1990); *United States* v. *X-Citement Video, Inc.* (982 F.2d 1285, Ninth Cir., 1992).

[18]Child Protection Act of 1984 (Pub. L. No. 98-292, 98 Stat. 204 (1984)—codified as amended at 18 U.S.C. §§ 2251–2253).

[19]*New York* v. *Ferber*, 458 U.S. 747 (1982).

[20][458 U.S. 747, 753].

[21]*Miller* v. *California*, 413 U.S. 15 (1973).

[22]*Osborne* v. *Ohio*, 495 U.S. 103 (1990).

[23]*Stanley* v. *Georgia*, 394 U.S. 557 (1969).

[24]*Doe* v. *MySpace, Inc.*, No. A-06-CA-983-SS (W.D. Tex. 2007).

[25]*United States* v. *Hilton*, 167 F.3d 61 (First Cir., 1999); and *United States* v. *Mento*, #99-4813 (Fourth Cir., 2000); *United States* v. *Acheson*, 195 F.3d 645 (Eleventh Cir., 1999).

[26]*Free Speech Coalition* v. *Reno* (Ninth Cir., 1999)—(198 F.3d 1083, Ninth Cir., 1999) #97-16536.

[27]*United States* v. *Mento*, #99-4813 (Fourth Cir., 2000).

[28]*Free Speech Coalition* v. *Reno*, #97-16536.Available at *www.findlaw.com*. Retrieved from the Internet on April 10, 2007.

[29]*United States* v. *Boos*, #96-50404. Available at *www.findlaw.com*. Retrieved from the Internet on April 10, 2007.

[30]*Ashcroft* v. *Free Speech Coalition*, 535 U.S. 234 (2002).

[31]Ibid.

[32]Ibid.

[33]Lindner, Anne (2006). "First Amendment as Last Resort: The Internet Gambling Industry's Bid to Advertise in the United States." *Saint Louis University Law Journal*, *50* (1289). Available at *www.lexisnexis.com*.

[34]*Casino City, Inc.* v. *U.S. Department of Justice*, No. 04–557-B-M3 (M.D. La. August 7, 2004). Available at: *http://ww2.casinocitypress. com/complaintfiledon8-9-04.pdf*.

[35]*Central Hudson Gas and Electric* v. *Public Service Commission of New York*, 447 U.S. 557 (1980).

[36]Ibid.

[37]*Posadas de Puerto Rico Associates* v. *Tourism Co. Of Puerto Rico*, 478 U.S. 328 (1986).

[38]*44 Liquormart, Inc.* v. *Rhode Island*, 517 U.S. 484 (1996).

[39]*Prince* v. *Massachusetts*, 321 U.S. 158, 168 (1944).

CHAPTER 9

The Fourth Amendment and Other Legal Issues

Chapter Outline

LEARNING OBJECTIVES

After reading this chapter, you will be able to do the following:

✓ Develop substantive knowledge on the Fourth Amendment.
✓ Learn the difference between warranted and warrantless searches and how they relate to computer-related searches.
✓ Explore the controversies surrounding the U.S. Patriot Act.
✓ Increase their knowledge on privacy as it relates to technology today.
✓ Examine the application of the Fourth Amendment to both public and private employees
✓ Discuss the evolution of the expectation of privacy.
✓ Become very familiar with the various privacy acts that have been developed over the past two decades.

KEY TERMS AND CONCEPTS

- consent
- ECPA
- exclusionary rule
- expectation of privacy
- incident to arrest
- National Security Letters (NSLs)

- *Ortega* doctrine
- overbreadth
- particularity
- plain view
- probable cause
- seizure
- secondary warrant

- specificity
- *Steve Jackson Games*
- Stored Communications Act
- third party origination
- totality of the circumstances
- territorial privacy

● INTRODUCTION

Possibly excepting the First Amendment, the Fourth Amendment has been considered to include the most important constitutional protection against governmental intrusion into personal matters. Generally speaking, the Fourth Amendment provides protection against unreasonable searches and seizures conducted by government officials. As such, searches must be predicated on

probable cause—a legal term used to denote that a reasonable person would conclude that (1) a crime has been committed, (2) evidence of that crime exists, and (3) evidence presently exists at the place to be searched. Only in extreme situations is this determination made by individuals other than magistrates.

The Fourth Amendment protects people, not places. It protects both tangible and intangible items, extending even to oral communications.

Thus, physical intrusion is not necessary to establish a constitutional violation.[1] Thus, a judicial order must be obtained to conduct limited electronic surveillance. The Fourth Amendment only applies to government searches and seizures. It does not apply to searches and seizures conducted by private parties unless they are acting with the knowledge of and under the supervision or direction of law enforcement.

HISTORY OF THE FOURTH AMENDMENT

Fearful of the tyranny inherent in England's system, the forefathers of the United States saw fit to introduce checks and balances in the American judicial system. The division of federal powers into three distinct branches: executive, judicial, and legislative. The Constitution itself, specifically providing for the sovereignty of individual states, proved to be the most resilient. In fact, the first ten amendments to the document (the Bill of Rights) added the specificity that the original Constitution failed to articulate. Such amendments were necessary to solidify the sanctity and security of the American home and the privacy of its citizens, one of the greatest concerns, due to the abuses of power practiced by government officials in England where it was common practice to invade and search a home without any semblance of due process.

One of the greatest debates surrounding the Constitution involves the role of the Fourth Amendment. On the one hand, conservative approaches, fearing that those government officials least responsible to the electorate would become too powerful, hesitate to view the Constitution as a living document. The notion that judges who are granted lifetime tenure will create policies or make decisions based upon individual notions of constitutional scope make these individuals uncomfortable. Those on the opposing side make the argument that the Constitution is designed to serve as a guide for limiting government powers, not a limitation.

An evaluation of the past century reveals that the second notion has taken root in the rulings of the Supreme Court. While many of these decisions have undermined the ability of the government to control the decisions of individual citizens (*Griswold* v. *Connecticut* struck down a prohibition on contraceptives; *Roe* v. *Wade* struck down a prohibition of abortions), others have seemed to increase the ability of government to intrude upon the personal privacy afforded to those same individuals. More specifically, the same justices who upheld reproductive rights have expanded the rights of government officials to electronically monitor American citizens. Beginning with *Olmstead* v. *U.S.*,[2] the Supreme Court has evaluated the level of protection afforded to individuals in electronic communications.

The *Olmstead* decision ruled that the sanctity afforded to a private home did not include telephone communications made within that home. Their implication was clear—the Fourth Amendment protected places, not people. Almost four decades later, a different court would reverse the decision in its entirety.[3] Indeed, the *Katz* ruling appeared to grant American citizens more protection under the Fourth Amendment than ever before. *Katz* ruled that "the Fourth Amendment protects people, not places . . . what [a person] seeks to preserve as private, even in an area accessible to the public, may be constitutionally protected." Thus, those communications which are held on public telephones may be granted protection if individuals have a reasonable expectation of privacy or take measures to make their communication private. The court further ordered that future wiretaps be granted only after adequate judicial review is undertaken and approval granted. Consequently, all federal and state domestic wiretaps require a court order predicated on an articulation of probable cause. Since these seminal rulings, advances in technology have far outpaced legislative proceedings and judicial rulings. In fact, the sluggish nature of the judicial system is all but antithetical to the activity surrounding computer, wireless, and communication technology. Thus, the rule of law must be found in emerging case law and in the general principles of the exclusionary rule.

First enunciated in *Weeks* v. *U.S.*,[4] the **exclusionary rule** stated that if government agents engage in unlawful searches or seizures, then all fruits of that action could not be used in subsequent prosecutions. Such "fruits of the poisonous tree" not only included evidence collected in tainted searches, but *any* information or evidence obtained in later activities if such were predicated on the original search. In essence, this rule was necessary because the self-restraint of the police did not provide adequate protection against violations of the Fourth Amendment. It was intended to prevent governmental abuse of search and seizure powers. As such, the courts have traditionally excluded any evidence seized in violation of the Fourth Amendment. However, more recent case law has limited the exclusionary rule to those actions that deter *future* constitutional violations, not to punish past actions.[5] Unfortunately, the Supreme Court has remained resolutely silent on issues of digital evidence and the amount of privacy afforded to wireless communications. Therefore, the exclusionary rule has been used sparingly in computer crime cases, and the most pressing consideration is the legislative and judicial articulation of the limitations of the **expectation of privacy** in cyberspace.

THE EXPECTATION OF PRIVACY AND ELECTRONIC SURVEILLANCE

Although not specifically verbalized in the text of the U.S. Constitution, legislative bodies have attempted to extend an "expectation of privacy" to American citizens in specific situations (see box "Legislating Privacy"). Virtually all of these statutes, however, have been challenged, and the Supreme Court has been left to establish objective measures of privacy. Generally speaking, they have ruled that the Fourth Amendment,

prohibiting unreasonable searches and **seizures**, cannot be translated into a general constitutional right to privacy. In fact, they have noted that other provisions of the Constitution protect personal privacy from other forms of governmental invasion, such as the First Amendment's imposing limitations upon governmental abridgment of freedom to associate and privacy in one's association, the Third Amendment's prohibitions on the nonconsensual peacetime quartering of soldiers, and to some extent, the Fifth Amendment's reflection of the Constitution's concern for the right of each individual to a private enclave where he may lead a private life, whereas the protection of a person's general right to privacy is, like the protection of his property and of his very life, left largely to the law of the individual states. This "right" to privacy is moderated only by the expectation of such privacy, which is not a generalized notion but based on case characteristics.

Certain characteristics may erode expectations of privacy. For example, those things knowingly divulged to third parties are not subject to Fourth amendment protection,[6] but those things he/she seeks to keep private, even in an area accessible to the public, may be.[7] Unfortunately, the issue of what constitutes disclosure is all but unclear. For example, a bank depositor has no claim under the Fourth Amendment because *the depositor takes the risk in revealing his affairs to another, that the information will be conveyed by that person to that government*".[8]

Many people are concerned that with the advent of information-driven technology that even the limited expectation of privacy currently recognized will be eroded. They argue that the degree of information that is necessary to live in cyber-worlds will all but negate privacy in the United States if it is not protected in some fashion. Medical records, financial information, and personal details disclosed under a façade of anonymity or confidentiality via emerging communication mediums, for example, may be surveyed by government officials. Thus, characteristics and the constancy

Legislating Privacy

Federal Wiretap Act, 18 U.S.C. § 2511 and the Stored Communications Act—derivatives of the original Wiretap Act enacted in 1968. Both were included in the **Electronic Communications Privacy Act of 1986** and sought to establish federal privacy protections and standards in light of advances in computer and telecommunications technologies.

Wiretap Act—protects against unauthorized "interception" of electronic communications (18 U.S.C. § 2511).

Stored Communications Act—protects against unauthorized access to electronic communications while in electronic storage (18 U.S.C. § 2701).

CALEA (Communications Assistance for Law Enforcement Act of 1994) also known as Digital Telephony Act (47 U.S.C. 1002)—1994 Amendments to the Federal Wiretap Act extended protection to cordless and cellular calls. Mandates that new technology does not interfere with and does not impede some law enforcement interception. Prohibited telephone carriers from developing technology which impedes law enforcement investigations (i.e., electronic interception). In addition, Congress required carriers to configure their systems to ensure the privacy and security of communications not authorized to be intercepted.

Title III of the Omnibus Crime Control and Safe Streets Act of 1968—was enacted by Congress in response to the rulings by the Supreme Court. It delineated specific requirements for wiretapping. It stated that wiretaps were only permissible if issued upon a ruling of probable cause by a court official. It also required that all other investigative techniques were exhausted and that precautions were taken to ensure that "innocent" conversations were excluded from analysis. It further outlined punishments for violations, and required disclosure of such surveillance upon cessation of activity.

Foreign Intelligence Surveillance Act (FISA–1978)—Congressional act which regulated wiretapping in national security cases. Much broader than Title III, it allows more invasive searches with a lower probable-cause threshold. The most important differences include (1) no requirements to disclose the contents of or even the presence of the surveillance, unless the government seeks to introduce them in a criminal prosecution; (2) affords no protection for individuals who are not permanent residents or citizens of the United States; (3) does not necessarily require *criminal* activity—rather, it allows surveillance for individuals who are believed to be engaged in clandestine intelligence activities on behalf of a foreign power.

Comprehensive Crime Control Act (1984)—Congress extends to the United States Secret Service jurisdictional powers over credit card fraud and computer crime.

---

of interpretation vary, especially in regard to electronic surveillance.

Types of Recognized Privacy

As a legal concept, privacy is both fluid and complex due to a myriad of competing interests. Generally speaking, however, the concept of privacy may be divided into distinct categories: physical, communications, information, and territorial. Protections or extensions of privacy in each may be found in different areas. Without exception, the Court has extended the highest expectation of privacy to the physical self, and has used the Fourth Amendment as justification. Privacy afforded to communications, on the other hand, is usually linked to the First Amendment's freedom of speech and association in which the government may not interfere with the flow of communication between citizens.

The Court has extended protection to information via the Fourteenth Amendment's guarantee of due process. It was judicially created in a series of "right to privacy" cases, including *Griswold* and *Roe* v. *Wade*.[9] However, it is the last category of privacy which is often the most difficult to define. In fact, **territorial privacy** in cyberspace is all but intangible as it has traditionally been defined by established boundaries on the intrusion into a specific space or locale.[10]

⬤ ELECTRONIC SURVEILLANCE AND THE RIGHT TO PRIVACY

Due to the resolute silence of the Supreme Court, the issue of electronic surveillance and the application of traditional statutes have been somewhat haphazard. Like conventional wiretap standards, the legality of this issue has been tested much more in the private sector, where employers routinely attempt to control the activities of their employees.

Certain companies routinely place employees under electronic surveillance, arguing that it is necessary to improve efficiency and productivity. It has been reported that airline personnel are instructed (and their performance evaluated) to complete reservations within two minutes, while directory assistance operators are expected to maintain a 29-second average call length (Tuerkheimer, 1993). Interestingly, private wiretaps are prohibited, but not extended to restraints on private interception of e-mail and network communications. Recent court decisions do not indicate that individual privacy protections are likely to emerge. In fact, there has been a tendency by courts to imply that the expectation of privacy is more limited with the introduction of computers and cyberspace. Thus, employers and law enforcement have been granted greater leeway in monitoring electronic communications. Systems administrators, in particular, are increasingly authorized to monitor employee communications. Such authorization has increased the reliance of law enforcement on workplace surveillance.

⬤ PRIVATE V. PUBLIC-SECTOR SEARCHES

Traditional expectations of privacy within the work area have varied based on contextual elements of each case. However, public employers are much more limited in their actions than are their private counterparts. Generally speaking, purely personal items which have no connection to the employment relationship are not subject to standards for a workplace search. However, other factors which are considered include:

1. whether the items or areas to be searched have been set aside for the employee's exclusive or personal use;
2. whether the employee has been given permission to store personal information within the area;
3. whether the employee has been advised that the system may be accessed by others;
4. whether there has been a history of searches or inspections of the area; and,
5. whether there is a clearly articulated policy which identifies common areas vs. private areas[11]

Public employers are directly bound by the rulings originally articulated in *Ortega*. This three-pronged approach determines:

1. whether the employee's expectation of privacy was consistent with the operational realities of the workplace (i.e., the exclusivity of the workspace, accessibility to workplace by others, nature of employee's duties, knowledge of search procedures or practices, and reason for search);
2. whether the invasion of the employee's Fourth Amendment protections was reasonable when balanced against governmental interest in the intrusion (reasonable suspicion is sufficient in investigations involving work-related employee misconduct); and,
3. whether the search was reasonable at inception, and was the subsequent scope of the search related to the original justification of the search.[12]

In essence, *Ortega* ruled that while employees may have a reasonable expectation of privacy against workplace intrusions by law enforcement personnel, when supervisory personnel are responsible for the intrusion, "operational realities of the workplace . . . may make some employees' expectations of privacy unreasonable" (*Ortega*). Thus, *Ortega* may be characterized as a scale that weighs the individual employee's expectation of privacy against government interest (i.e., supervision, control, and efficient operation of the workplace). Under these general considerations articulated in the **Ortega doctrine**, employers who fail to warn employees of systems monitoring or allow employees access to electronic mail for personal reasons as well may lose some of their monitoring powers over employees due to an elevated expectation of privacy.

APPLICATION OF *ORTEGA* TO E-MAIL: THE CASES OF *SIMONS* AND *MONROE*

Although the legal landscape is far from clear, two cases appear to apply the *Ortega* doctrine to electronic mail. In *U.S.* v. *Simons*, an employee of the Foreign Bureau of Information Services (branch of the CIA) was indicted for violation of child pornography statutes after a systems administrator discovered that over 1,000 pornographic images had been downloaded. During trial, Simons moved to suppress, arguing that he had a reasonable expectation of privacy on his individual workstation. Court disagreed, stating that the systems administrator was simply monitoring usage of network resources by employees and used the word "sex" to identify inappropriate activity. The Court further stated that even if the employee had an expectation of privacy, the system administrator's actions including viewing the employee's workstation computer and copying the hard drive were both justified at their inception and reasonable in scope. Thus, systems administrators may scan networks to identify non-work-related activity.

A further case, *United States* v. *Monroe*,[13] allowed administrators to search non-delivered messages stored on an employee server for system maintenance. This particular case involved a

system administrator who opened several messages stored on the server prior to their arrival at the destination mailbox (messages were placed here indefinitely if they were too large or were defective). The system administrator opened several of these messages because of the amount of storage that these messages required and the danger that they posed to the stability of the system. Upon discovering that they were addressed to the accused and were from newsgroups with sexually explicit names, the administrator accessed the accused's e-mail account, searching through messages sent from the user to the originator of the 59 e-mail messages. Deciding that these messages were not sent to the user inadvertently, and, in fact, represented a consensual exchange, administrators then released the information to the commander, and copied the image files and printouts of two e-mail messages from the accused to the newsgroup. They also copied to disk a memo from themselves for the record detailing their discovery of the files. This information was used by the Air Force Office of Special Investigations (AFOSI) to obtain search authorization for searching and seizing all computer-related items. Defendant argued that he had an expectation of privacy and that while he consented to monitoring, he did not **consent** to being investigated. Court disagreed, stating that he had no reasonable expectation of privacy in files lodged in the government server. They further noted that there was no reasonable expectation of privacy in the e-mail box in regard to supervisory oversight, as the system was properly bannered with a warning indicating that use of the system conferred consent to monitoring. Thus, employers may protect themselves through warning banners, negating future contentions of privacy.

Both *Simons* and *Monroe* indicated the court's reluctance to extend rights of privacy to proprietary government equipment. In each case, it was determined that systems administrators may monitor employee communications and actually search computers attached to networks, as there is no expectation of privacy. Indeed, both courts likened these types of maintenance searches to private searches and, therefore, permissible. Summarily, government employees using government computers have no expectation of privacy from systems administrators acting within the scope of their duties. (These duties may include maintaining security through routine systems protection monitoring, system management, prevention of unauthorized access, verification of security procedures, survivability and operational security. To maintain security, these individuals routinely engage in systems protection monitoring.) This is not to suggest, however, that other forms of privacy are not constitutionally protected, but must be tested by the degree to which they exceed the scope of the private search.

While systems-protection monitoring may constitute a legitimate workplace search, monitoring electronic mail by law enforcement must be based on consent of one or more parties to the communication *or* authorized by court order, warrant, or special probable cause circumstances.[14] Thus, law enforcement has traditionally relied on system administrators to report unlawful intrusion and other sorts of criminal activity. However, system administrators may not gather the amount of information necessary for a criminal prosecution, as they are not necessarily concerned with the content of the suspect communication. As such, law enforcement has looked to (and prayed for) broad interpretations of the ECPA, PPA, CALEA, and the Fourth Amendment.

THE ELECTRONIC COMMUNICATIONS PRIVACY ACT AND THE PRIVACY PROTECTION ACT OF 1980

In order to provide a framework for the protection and privacy of electronic data, legislators have passed several pieces of legislation including the Privacy Protection Act, the Electronic Communications Privacy Act, and the Communications Assistance for Law Enforcement Act.

Coupled with the Fourth Amendment, this legislation has also attempted to address the issues of searching and seizing digital evidence. Although the court has not specifically ruled upon limitations surrounding these issues or expectations of privacy within computer systems or products, lower courts have afforded some insight (albeit contradictory) into the application of legal doctrines to electronic communications. On its surface, the Electronic Communications Privacy Act (**ECPA**) applies specifically to computer searches, while the Privacy Protection Act attaches the same significance to electronic bulletin boards and other online computer systems. Both statutes broaden traditional constitutional protections found within the Fourth Amendment.

Electronic Communications Privacy Act of 1986

The Electronic Communications Privacy Act (1986) extended provisions originally found in Title III of the Omnibus Crime Control and Safe Streets Act of 1968 to include non-aural electronic communications, including electronic mail. It also extended Title III to wireless communications. Theoretically, it was designed to ensure the privacy of American citizens, as Congress argued that privacy may be inadvertently eroded with the advent of technology. They argued that lack of privacy within technological exchanges would deter further development: a situation they wished to avoid as it would impede electronic commerce. However, they also identified the potential for criminal activity. Thus, they provided penalties for individuals who knowingly intercepted wireless and electronic communications, while providing avenues of surveillance for law enforcement officials.[15] Unlike protections provided by the Fourth Amendment, these statutory prohibitions apply to all individuals, not just those acting on behalf of the government.[16] Theoretically, then, the ECPA was formulated in such a way that it necessarily conferred an expectation of privacy to emerging mediums of communication and stored messages.

Three Titles Under ECPA

Although the first two are the most relevant to forensic computer investigations, there are three titles found under the Electronic Communications Privacy Act. The first updated Title III of the Omnibus Crime Control and Safe Streets Act of 1968; the second provided protection for stored electronic communications (limited to systems affecting interstate or foreign commerce); and the third governs the use of trap and trace devices. Generally speaking, the ECPA is most applicable to unread electronic mail. Once the communication has been fully transmitted, the Fourth Amendment applies.[17] These titles, designed to work together, are actually somewhat vague and ambiguous. Theoretically modeled after the Federal Wiretap Act, the ECPA is a congressional attempt to broaden expectations of privacy with emerging technologies while providing avenues for interceptions. In essence, the ECPA protects against unauthorized access, disclosure or interception by the government, individuals, and third parties while providing potentially harsh civil penalties.

Title I of the Act outlines statutory procedures for intercepting wire, oral, and electronic communications. Prior to the passage of the ECPA, only those audio communications sent by a common carrier which could be heard and understood by the human ear were protected by traditional wiretap statutes. In effect, the ECPA extended these protections to inaudible, digital, and other electronic communications (i.e., those transmitted through copper wire, coaxial or fiber optic cables, microwave, or radio transmissions). In addition, the ECPA removed the common carrier requirement, while providing protection for nontraditional forms of communication (i.e., video, text, computer data, etc.). However, there

are several ambiguities found within the statute that give some scholars pause.

One failing of the ECPA for law enforcement purposes is one that has not yet been heard by the courts. The ECPA's statutory protections are only extended to those communications which affect interstate or foreign commerce. While the Internet appears to fall squarely within this realm, other types of systems may not. Thus, questions arise in cases involving company intranets or other systems which do not physically cross state lines. An additional failing involves the omission of an articulated exclusionary rule for evidence collected in violation of the statute. While the ECPA provides monetary compensation to those who are violated, it does not specifically provide for the suppression of the fruits of the violation. However, attorneys may rely on traditional mechanisms for relief. First, many violations of the ECPA also constitute violations of the Fourth Amendment. As such, the exclusionary rule may apply. In addition, attorneys may petition for "declaratory relief" in the form of a suppression order, as provided by the ECPA. (Interestingly, an automatic exclusion is provided in traditional wire-tap statutes. It is unclear why this omission exists.)

This statute also prohibits the manufacturing, possessing, or selling of interception devices (including software)—with one important exception. Government agents are exempt from this provision, although they must secure a court order to intercept the contents of a communication. However, they are not prohibited from identifying the *existence* or *presence* of such communication. Thus, law enforcement officers may identify connections between computers and monitor the recipients and sources of an individual's electronic mail. In laymen's terms, investigators can covertly survey Joe Public, but they cannot listen to his conversation. An additional exception, applicable to system administrators, enables sysops to take actions necessary to maintain or manage an electronic mail system. This does not, however, grant them the authority to read e-mails or communications. Rather, it has been interpreted to mean that routine communications which do not pose a threat to the system are private. At the same time, the court has upheld the admissibility of criminal evidence which was obtained when system administrators monitored messages which were excessive in size, slowing the system. Other exceptions have been made when one of the parties to the communication issued consent and when banners which informed users of the possibility of monitoring were included on systems.

Title II—often referred to as the **Stored Communications Act**—provides protection to stored communications. In essence, this is designed to protect those communications not in transmission which have been stored or saved in some way. More specifically, this title prohibits access to a facility through which an electronic communication service is provided, to obtain, alter, or restrict or prevent authorized access to a communication held in electronic storage. This rule also prohibits electronic communication providers from disclosing the contents of a communication held in such storage and also prohibits said providers from disclosing any contextual information included in a message carried or maintained by the provider. As in all things, however, there are some exceptions that may be helpful to law enforcement. The first allows such disclosure if permission is granted by any party to the communication or the subscriber. The second allows disclosure of such information to law enforcement if it inadvertently comes to the attention of the system administrator and if it pertains to the commission of a crime. (On its face, it would

---

The Reins on Electronic Surveillance

1. **Title III and ECPA**—provide law enforcement with the capability of electronically monitoring targeted communications:

   a. **By design**—electronic surveillance should be used judiciously, and only in those situations where they are deemed necessary.

   b. **Authorization**—can only be made by a federal district court judge, *not* federal magistrates like traditional search warrant applications. Very important—is supposed to elevate the judicial oversight and the privacy protections afforded American citizens.

2. **Requirements under TITLE III**

   a. Must be authorized by a Federal District Court Judge.

   b. Must demonstrate probable cause which specifies, with particularity, the offenses being committed, the telecommunications facility (or place) from which the targeted communication is to be intercepted, a description of those communications, and the identities of the perpetrators.

   c. Must identify previous attempts at evidence collection, and articulate why less intrusive methods have proven unsuccessful. This may include unacceptable levels of danger.

   d. Generally limited to 30 days, although extensions may be granted.

   e. Progress Reports issued on a regular basis (7–10 days).

   f. Surveillance must be terminated if the objectives are met prior to the 30-day period.

   g. Must be recorded for evidence integrity, and sealed under the supervision of a Federal district judge.

   h. Upon surveillance termination, targeted subjects must be notified of the previous surveillance and given an inventory of the communications catalogued.

   i. Service providers must cooperate with authorities with valid court orders. However, they are also bound by the same provisions as law enforcement. That is, they may be held liable for violations of this Act.

   j. **Emergency provisions**—Attorney General, Deputy or the Associate Attorney General may, if authorized, initiate electronic surveillance of wire or electronic communications without a court order, if an application for such order is made within 48 hours of surveillance initiation.[18]

3. **Punishments available under TITLE III**—any party to an illegal interception may be charged with a federal offense punishable by imprisonment up to 5 years, a fine, or both. Also, those individual victims may seek compensation through civil proceedings.

appear that those communications that are stored on a server prior to downloading by the recipient would be protected. The courts, however, have handed down rulings inconsistent with this supposition.) Finally, **Title III** addresses pen registers and trap and trace devices.

These titles, designed to work together, are actually somewhat vague and ambiguous. Theoretically modeled after the Federal Wiretap Act, the ECPA is a congressional attempt to broaden expectations of privacy with emerging technologies while providing avenues for interceptions. In essence, the ECPA protects against unauthorized access, disclosure, or interception by the government, individuals, and third parties while providing potentially harsh civil penalties. It also provides for the backup preservation of electronic files when notice to the subscriber would cause destruction.[19] More specifically, the act requires a subpoena or court order compelling the system administrator to make copies. It further stipulates that due notice be given to the subscriber (i.e., suspect) within three days of copying. The suspect then has 14 days to file a motion to suppress or to vacate the court order before the government can access said copies.

Privacy Protection Act

The Privacy Protection Act of 1980 (PPA), codified under 42 U.S.C. § 2000, made it unlawful for local, state, or federal law enforcement authorities to search or seize those materials which may be publishable. In essence, it attempted to expand the scope of the 1968 wiretap act to include electronic bulletin boards, specifically protecting "work product" (i.e., mental impressions, conclusions, opinions, or theories of the person who prepared, produced, authored, or created such material) and "documentary materials" (i.e., materials upon which information is recorded, and includes mechanically, magnetically, or electronically recorded cards, tapes, or discs). However, it has been criticized by various courts and numerous citizen groups for its vagueness, ambiguity, and the overbroad scope of its content.

Important Definitions Found Within the ECPA

1. "Wire communication"—any aural transfer made in whole or in part through the use of facilities for the transmission of communications by the aid of wire, cable, or other like connection between the point of origin and the point of reception (including the use of such connection in a switching station) furnished or operated by any person engaged in providing or operating such facilities for the transmission of interstate or foreign communications or communications affecting interstate or foreign commerce and *such term includes any electronic storage of such communication.*

4. "Intercept"—the aural or other acquisition of the contents of any wire, electronic, or oral communication through the use of any electronic, mechanical, or other device.

8. "Contents"—when used with respect to any wire, oral, or electronic communications, includes any information concerning the substance, purport, or meaning of that communication.

12. "Electronic communication"—means any transfer of signs, signals, writing, images, sounds, data, or intelligence of any nature transmitted in whole or in part by a wire, radio, electromagnetic, photo-electronic, or photo-optical system that affects interstate or foreign commerce, but does not include:

    a. any wire or oral communications
    b. any communication made through a tone-only paging device;
    c. any communication from a tracking device
    d. electronic funds transfer information stored by a financial institution in a communications system used for the electronic storage and transfer of funds

14. electronic communications system—means any wire, radio, electromagnetic, photo-optical, or photo-electronic facilities for the transmission of electronic communications, and any computer facilities or related electronic equipment for the electronic storage of such communication.

Interestingly, the PPA does not preclude admitting evidence seized in violation of this act. Rather, it specifically provides civil remedies for victims of government abuse.[20]

Victims may include publishers, authors, editors, newspapers, or individuals/companies involved in the dissemination of information. This includes those individuals who act as system operators for electronic bulletin boards or newsgroups. Under this statute, all information which is compiled for purposes of public distribution may not be seized without probable cause. This does not suggest, however, that officers are prohibited from evaluating this type of information. Rather, investigators *may* prevent allegations of abuse if drives are imaged and returned or if subpoenas are issued upon probable cause. In other cases, departmental policy may dictate on-site searches (not recommended) or rapid investigation and subsequent return. In addition, this material may be seized if there is reason to believe that advance notice would result in destruction, alteration, or concealment of such materials or if the documents have not been produced as required by a court order. Summarily, higher levels of scrutiny are afforded to computers which are operating electronic bulletin boards or are part of a network. However, the messages

which are transmitted and received from BBS communications are afforded virtually (no pun intended) no protection. Reasoning that messages are posted in **plain view**, courts have ruled that expectations of privacy are all but nonexistent. Thus, investigators may monitor or actively survey an activity occurring in these cyber-exchanges with one important exception. Private bulletin boards or those not accessible to the general public do carry an elevated expectation of privacy.

Much like traditional vice investigations, officers may develop pseudonyms and alter-identities to engage in online exchanges. When done so through legitimate venues and when other investigative techniques would not be productive, investigators may act as observers without necessarily revealing themselves. (Remember: individuals who intentionally disclose information to unknown parties (as individuals on bulletin boards most assuredly are) run the risk of encountering law-enforcement officers.) However, the sanctity of the messages themselves must be maintained. This applies not only to sysops, but to individual users as well. Thus, law-enforcement officers must exercise due care when searching computers due to the relative ease with which a BBS can be created and operated. As additional privacy has been afforded

The Case of Steve Jackson Games, Inc.

Perhaps the most notorious of all court cases involved a small company in Texas which produced game-playing software and published game-playing manuals. They also ran a bulletin board system in which numerous members posted messages and sent and received electronic mail. SJG came to the attention of the Secret Service when it became known that the co-sysop had illegally downloaded a sensitive 911 document by hacking into a Bell South computer. Arguing that the easy accessibility threatened emergency communications, the Secret Service raided SJG and seized three computers, 300 disks, and a variety of other equipment.

Illuminati, SJG's BBS, was effectively shut down. The Secret Service then read messages stored on the board, and deleted others at will. SJG argued that the government had violated provisions found within the Federal Wiretap Act and Title I of the ECPA. In a seminal ruling, the court ruled

that e-mails are only subject to interception during actual transmission and the Federal Wiretap Act did not apply to e-mail in electronic storage. In addition, the court ruled that Title I of the ECPA is not applicable to the unauthorized access of electronic messages stored in a service provider computer.

However, the court did find that the Secret Service had violated the requirements of Title II of the ECPA (18 U.S.C. § 2703). The court also declined to extend a "good faith" defense for the agents' reliance on the warrants. This case proved to be a public relations disaster for the U.S. Secret Service. Long characterized as the most professional of the federal agencies, the USSS has long been immune from the scandals which have plagued other agencies. However, the fallout of this particular case includes an increasingly suspicious and hostile audience of computer users.

to them, investigators should endeavor to identify any potential BBS operated by the suspect or maintained on a targeted system.

Defining Interception Under ECPA and the PPA

Like traditional wiretap statutes, the ECPA and the PPA both hinge on the actual *interception* of a communication. Under the original Wiretap Act, a communication was "intercepted" if the acquisition of the communication was contemporaneous with the transmission of information from sender to recipient. This is consistent with the current meaning, yet some privacy advocates question the applicability of traditional standards. Currently, acquisition must occur "before arrival." Some argue that messages in storage which have been sent but not yet opened by the recipient have not been "received". Thus, looking at these stored communications would represent an interception. However, the courts have not agreed, interpreting *interception* to include any act which allows individuals to view an electronic message while it is in actual transmission.[21] Privacy advocates have expressed hope that this trend may change, as a recent case winding its way through the courts directly contradicts this.[22]

Communications Assistance for Law Enforcement Act

In an attempt to further articulate the need for greater latitude in electronic surveillance and to incorporate wireless communication and emerging communications media, the federal government developed an initiative known as the Communications Assistance for Law Enforcement Act (CALEA). This act, also debated in the appellate court system, required that the manufacturers of telecommunications equipment and service providers develop systems which provide the capability for surveillance of telephone and cellular communications, advanced paging, satellite-based systems, and specialized mobile radio. The act also required the delivery of "packet-mode communications" by these providers to law enforcement without a warrant.

Theoretically, this Act amended certain provisions found within the ECPA to *heighten* privacy protection. (Remember: the ECPA attempted to balance three competing interests: law enforcement needs, privacy, and technological innovation).[23] With the CALEA, Congress explicitly declared that the surveillance requirements of the Act should be narrowly interpreted, and not expand, but maintain, traditional levels of government surveillance. In addition, they required carriers to develop secure systems which ensured the privacy of communications not authorized to be intercepted. They further prohibited the government in general, and the FBI in particular, from dictating network or equipment design standards. In fact, the FBI initially supported the Act and its relevant limitations for law enforcement. In August 1994, Director Louis Freeh assured Congress, and the American people, that CALEA was not intended to further erode privacy expectations, declaring:

> Without question . . . court-authorized electronic surveillance is a critical law enforcement and public safety tool. I think we have reached a remarkable compromise and achievement in preserving that tool as it has existed since 1968 . . . We believe that the legislation, as introduced this past Tuesday, offers the strongest investigative assurances that the authority which Congress gave us in 1968 will continue unimpeded by technology (Digital Telephony Hearings, supra note 9, at 112–113).

However, Freeh's earlier statements, made on behalf of the FBI, are not consistent with recent actions by the Bureau. In fact, the FBI has consistently argued that they, in addition to the entire law-enforcement community, are unfairly restricted by the provisions established by Congress. In particular, they argue that CALEA requires cellular phone companies and other wireless providers to have location tracking capability built into their configurations. They have loosely interpreted CALEA's provisions, and argued that interception of conference calls which include judicially approved, targeted communications may continue even if the target is no longer a party to the communication.

Finally, the government has argued that mere pen register orders sufficiently provide the authority to obtain signaling information and communication content. They argue that the delivery of the entire communication is necessary because of the difficulties associated with distinguishing signal and content in communications which involve packet switching protocols.[24] In addition, the Bureau has argued that carriers should be required to ensure that encrypted communications be decipherable even if the individual user holds the key. Once again, this directly contradicts the act's original provisions.

Challenges to the CALEA

In direct contravention of their earlier assurances before Congress, the FBI, claiming to represent the entire law enforcement community, has attempted to extend the original provisions established under the Federal Wiretap Act. Once zealously guarded by the Court and Congress, these privacy protections have been slowly eroded. The Clinton administration, for example, in its proposed anti-terrorism statute, asked Congress to permit roving wiretaps, lessening the sanctions on illegal wiretaps, and creating exemptions to the Foreign Intelligence Surveillance Act, which eliminated much of the privacy protection originally included. Although they were largely defeated in this effort, the Justice Department has been successful in challenges to the CALEA and the ECPA. In cooperation with the FCC, for example, requirements that cellular phones be traceable and that information on digits dialed during a communication (i.e., account numbers, credit card numbers, etc.) be recoverable have been established, directly contradicting those provisions in the CALEA which extended privacy to cellular communications and prohibited the government from interfering with the development of technology. In addition, the Justice Department's effort to require disclosure of communication content along with addressing or signaling data from telecommunication

providers using "packet switching" technology has all but negated the original provisions established by the Federal Wiretap Act.

Applying the Wiretap Act to E-mail Interceptions—*U.S. v. Councilman*[25]

In 2004, the Vice-President of Interloc, a subsidiary of Alibris, instructed employees to develop code which would intercept, copy, and store all incoming messages from *www.amazon.com* prior to their delivery to the member's e-mail. Thus, the e-mail was read by someone other than the intended recipient prior to its delivery. Count one of the indictment against VP Councilman charged the defendant with a violation of 18 U.S.C. § 371 for conspiracy to violate 18 U.S.C. § 2511. It was alleged that the defendant

> Allegedly conspired to intercept the electronic communications, to intentionally disclose the contents of the intercepted communications . . . and to use the contents of the unlawfully obtained electronic communication . . . Finally, the government alleged that defendant had conspired to cause a person to divulge the content of the communications while in transmission to persons other than the addresses of the communications.

The object of such conspiracy was to exploit the information to achieve a commercial advantage for Alibris and Interloc.

Defendant moved to dismiss the indictment for failure to state an offense under the Wiretap Act, as the e-mail interceptions at issue were in *electronic storage* as defined in 18 U.S.C. § 2510(17) and could not be intercepted as a matter of law. In their ruling, the court differentiated the circumstances of this case from *Steve Jackson Games*, where messages were retrieved from storage in a computer, and they noted that the network system itself created a system of storage by using an MTA (Message Transfer Agent)—a system, which collects the mails, transfers it to other MTA's until reaching its destination. Although the messages were clearly intercepted prior to reaching their final destination, the provisions housed within the Wiretap Act do not attach as they do not protect stored messages. To wit:

> The Wiretap Act's purpose was, and continues to be, to protect the privacy of communications. We believe that the language of the statute makes clear that Congress meant to give lesser protection to electronic communications than wire and oral communications. Moreover, at this juncture, much of the protection may have been eviscerated by the realities of modern technology. . . . the language may be out of step with the technological realities of computer crimes. However, it is not the province of this court to graft meaning onto the statute where Congress has spoken plainly[26]

⬤ THE PATRIOT ACT

Prior to the passage of the *Uniting and Strengthening America by Providing Appropriate Tools Required to Intercept and Obstruct Terrorism Act* *of 2001* (USA Patriot Act), courts were inconsistent in their rulings of applicability of ECPA to computer network communications.[27] However, the introduction of the Patriot Act was heralded by law enforcement authorities as the most effective tool in the arsenal to fight terrorism and computer crime alike. As constructed, many of the Act's provisions were to *sunset* (i.e., expire) on the last day of 2005. However, in the months preceding the sunset date, a push by supporters made 14 provisions permanent and placed four-year sunsets on the other two in March 2006.[28] Although the Act was passed with much support and little fanfare in the immediate aftermath of the 9/11 attacks, attacks on the legislation have increased as the horror of 9/11 recedes into the background of the American conscience.

The Patriot Act is comprised of ten distinct titles with corresponding subsections. For the most part, each title represents a modification of

---

A Summary of the U.S. Patriot Act

1. **Title I—Enhancing Domestic Security Against Terrorism**

   The six sections of *Title I* of the Patriot Act include the development of a counterterrorism fund; a condemnation of discrimination against Arab and Muslim Americans; increased funding for the technical support center of the FBI; requests for military assistance to enforce prohibition in certain emergencies; expansion of National Electronic Crime Task Force Initiative; and, specification of presidential authority. With the exception of *Section* 106, the provisions housed within *Title I* are generally considered to be uncontroversial.

2. **Title II—Enhanced Surveillance Procedures**

   Of all of the titles included in the Patriot Act, none have been as hotly debated as provisions housed within *Title II*. Containing 25 sections, Title II amends numerous acts, including, but not limited to: the *Foreign Intelligence Surveillance Act of 1978* (FISA), the *National Security Act of 1947*, and the *Electronic Communications Privacy Act of 1986* (ECPA). The title addresses various issues including trade sanctions against governments supporting terrorism, and provisions for redress and compensation of affected individuals. Most significantly, the title greatly broadens federal powers in the interception of telephonic and electronic communications, and amends rules associated with computer crime investigations.

3. **Title III—International Money Laundering Abatement and Anti-Terrorist Financing Act of 2001**

   Generally speaking, Title III focuses on the prevention, detection, and prosecution of international money laundering and the financing of terrorism. Title III amends both the *Money Laundering Control Act of 1986* and the *Bank Secrecy Act of 1970*. The three subtitles of Title III strengthen banking rules regarding international money laundering; increases record keeping

(Continued)

and reporting requirements; encourages communication and collaboration among law enforcement and the financial community; and, penalty enhancements for counterfeiting and the smuggling of currency.

4. **Title IV—Protecting the Border**

Title IV attempts to identify, prevent, and eradicate terrorism within the United States by strengthening immigration policies. In includes amendments to the *Immigration and Nationality Act.* The title has three subtitles: Protecting the Northern Border; Enhanced Immigration Provisions; and, Preservation of Immigration Benefits for Victims of Terrorism. In addition, the Act provides additional resources for federal agencies. It has been harshly criticized by civil libertarians.

5. **Title V—Removing obstacles to investigating terrorism**

Like the previous titles, Title V contains a variety of provisions and amends a number of previous Acts,

including the *State Department Basic Authorities Act of 1956;* the *DNA Analysis Backlog Elimination Act of 2000;* the *General Education Provisions Act;* the *National Education Statistics Act of 1995;* the *Right to Financial Privacy Act of 1978;* the *Fair Credit Reporting Act;* and, FISA.

6. **Title VI—Providing for victims of terrorism, public safety officers and their families**

7. **Title VII—Increased information sharing for critical infrastructure protection**

8. **Title VIII—Strengthening the criminal laws against terrorism**

9. **Title IX—Improved Intelligence**

10. **Title X—Miscellaneous**

previous statutes (e.g., The *National Information Infrastructure Protection Act, Cable Act, Foreign Intelligence Surveillance Act,* etc.) that incorporate technology-specific language. While some of the titles address traditional law enforcement activities involving physical space, others specifically address electronic communications and digital media. Close scrutiny of the Act has been accompanied by large-scale protests and allegations of constitutional violations. The Act in its entirety may be retrieved online at http://www.govtrack. us/congress/billtext.xpd?bill=h107-3162.

Enhanced Presidential Authority

Section 106 amended the *International Emergency Economic Powers Act* (50 U.S.C.1702)[29] and significantly expanded the discretionary power of the President. To wit:

...when the United States is engaged in armed hostilities or has been attacked by a foreign country or foreign nationals, confiscate any property, subject to the jurisdiction of the United States, of any foreign person, foreign organization, or foreign

country that he determines has planned, authorized, aided, or engaged in such hostilities or attacks against the United States; and all right, title, and interest in any property so confiscated shall vest, when, as, and upon the terms directed by the President, in such agency or person as the President may designate from time to time, and upon such terms and conditions as the President may prescribe, such interest or property shall be held, used, administered, liquidated, sold, or otherwise dealt with in the interest of and for the benefit of the United States, and such designated agency or person may perform any and all acts incident to the accomplishment or furtherance of these purposes.

Thus, the President or his/her designee can seize and liquidate property within the United States of any foreign individual, entity, or county who is suspected of planning, authorizing, aiding, or engageing in an attack. The section additionally permits the government to present classified information *ex parte* and *in camera* (i.e., secretly) to support the forfeiture if the decision is subjected to judicial review. Although affected individuals may file a challenge to confiscation under *Section 306* through the use of an *affirmative defense*, civil libertarians argue that due process is violated as the burden of proof automatically shifts to a defendant issuing an affirmative defense. In addition, challenge proceedings permit the inclusion of evidence that would be otherwise inadmissible under the *Federal Rules of Evidence*. Thus, civil libertarians argue that the very fabric of constitutional presumptions of innocence and requirements of evidence veracity is destroyed.

Electronic Surveillance and Criminal Investigations

American society has always been characterized by a zealous pursuit of personal freedom and protection of liberties. As such, both the Court and Congress have attempted to identify and articulate the appropriate balance between individual privacy and community interests. Beginning with *Katz* v. *United States*,[30] the Court specifically extended an expectation of privacy to electronic communications in a phone booth without a warrant. The following year, Congress passed the *Omnibus Crime Control and Safe Streets Act of 1968*[31] to provide protection for most conversations, while recognizing specific situations in which electronic surveillance could be employed by law enforcement authorities. This multilayer protection has been reinforced repeatedly throughout the subsequent decades. Privacy advocates argue that the U.S. Patriot Act has significantly decreased, if not obliterated, such protections. At the same time, supporters of the Act argue that the Act contains significant privacy protections which were not incorporated in earlier legislation. Thus, the debate continues.

Title II and Electronic Surveillance

Title II of the U.S. Patriot Act addresses parameters and procedures for electronic surveillance, and has been criticized most often by privacy advocates. Many of the provisions contained therein reduced privacy afforded to telephone communications to those afford to electronic communications. (Prior to the passage of the Patriot Act, law enforcement had access to stored electronic communications (i.e., e-mail) but not stored wire communications (i.e., voice-mail)). The following is a brief summary of the important changes in this regard.

- **Sections 201** and **202**—expanded the authority to intercept wire, oral, and electronic communications to crimes of terrorism and computer crimes.
- **Section 203**—allows the sharing of information between law enforcement agencies, specifically between federal agencies. It also provides for the disclosure of information to state agencies.
- **Section 206**—amended FISA to provide for *roving surveillance* in situations where the actions of the target may thwart the investigation or identification of persons.
- **Section 207**—amended the *Foreign Intelligence Surveillance Act* to expand the duration of FISA surveillance of non-United States persons from 45 to 90 days
- **Section 208**—amended the *Foreign Intelligence Surveillance Act* to increase the number of district court judges tasked with surveillance oversight from 7 to 11 judges
- **Section 209**—streamlined the process of tapping of electronic communications by recognizing that the advent of MIME (Multipurpose Internet Mail Extensions) has resulted in a myriad of attachments ranging from aural to video.
- **Section 210**—amended previous legislation to force compulsory disclosure of service provider records. While the traditional law provided a very narrow scope of information (i.e., name, address, length of communication, and means of payment), the Patriot Act included records of session times and durations and temporarily assigned network addresses. This significantly enhanced the process of identifying computers and tracing Internet communications. In addition, it incorporated technology-specific verbiage

to expand traditional authorities to non-telephone communications.

- **Section 211**—provided for the compulsory disclosure of financial and transactional records of cable subscribers. The implications housed within this section are far-reaching as cable companies are now providing Internet and telephone services, along with cable television programming. However, the amendments specifically preclude the disclosure of cable subscriber selection of video programming.

- **Section 212**—provided for the voluntary disclosure of customer communications or records by providers in cases in which they believe there is an emergency involving immediate danger of death or serious physical injury to someone.

- **Section 213**—expanded powers of search and seizure of law enforcement to include provisions for "sneak and peek" warrants or surreptitious searches (i.e., those without the knowledge or consent of the owner). Hotly contested by privacy advocates, Section 213 amended 18 U.S.C. 3103(a) to allow the issuance of warrants which may be executed without notification in cases in which the following conditions might result:

  1. endangering the life or physical safety of an individual;
  2. flight from prosecution
  3. destruction or tampering with evidence
  4. intimidation of potential witnesses
  5. otherwise seriously jeopardizing an investigation or unduly delaying a trial

- **Sections 214** and **215**—reiterated pen register and trap and trace authority and expanded records which could be accessed under FISA. The provisions have been targeted by privacy advocates who claim that the verbiage eliminates traditional requirements that the government prove that the target is an agent of foreign power. Prior to the passage of the Patriot Act,

authorities could only examine library records in cases where evidence amounted to probable cause that a crime had been committed.

- **Section 216**—amended ECPA to clarify that the pen/trap statute applies to a broad variety of communications technologies (i.e., e-mails and Internet Protocol addresses). In addition, the Act gave federal courts the authority to compel assistance from any provider of communication services in the United States whose assistance is appropriate to effectuate the order. Finally, Sections 210, 211, and 212 increased both the content and compulsion of subscriber records.

- **Section 217**—allows authorities to intercept wire or electronic communications of a computer trespasser if they obtain permission from the owner; or if they are engaged in an investigation; or, if authorities have *reasonable grounds* to believe that the contents of the communications are relevant to the investigation. Privacy advocates argue that the provision is an ill-concealed attempt by law enforcement to erode the privacy afforded to American citizens. They claim that the provision is irrelevant to terrorism.

- **Sections 219** and **220**—amended the *Federal Rules of Criminal Procedure* to provide for single-jurisdictional search warrants. This allows authorities to obtain national search warrants.

- **Section 222**—specifically notes no other provision of obligatory assistance from wire or electronic communication providers except as expressly articulated in the act. In addition, it specifically notes that expenses incurred by such providers shall be reasonably compensated.

- **Section 223**—provides for civil liability and redress of grievances for unauthorized disclosures. It includes provision for potential administrative discipline and civil action against the U.S. government.

Fully discussed in previous sections, it is sufficient to say that the pen register and trap and trace law prior to the passage of the Patriot Act only provided for the collection and/or recording of numbers dialed. In fact, contents of communications were specifically precluded by previous legislation. Title II of the Act specifically provides for the disclosure of communication content, reduces traditional requirements of probable cause, and equates telephone and Internet communications. Privacy advocates argue that telephone dialing and computer networking are inherently different animals. They argue that Internet connections necessarily reveal some contextual information not included in the original language of pen register law. Internet addresses may contain, for example, search terms; concepts; and business, school, or organizational names. Such information far exceeds the numeric information included in both ECPA and the *Omnibus Crime Control and Safe Streets Act*.[32]

National Security Letters and Other Fourth Amendment Issues

Privacy advocates also attack provisions of the Act not included in Title II. In particular, they argue that the increased used of **National Security Letters (NSLs)** is evidence of the Act's potential danger. Originally conceptualized in 1986, NSLs were originally authorized by high ranking federal officials in the pursuit of an agent of foreign power. The Patriot Act expanded these provisions to include the issuance of such letters if a local agent can certify that the information sought is relevant to an international terrorism or foreign intelligence investigation. In addition, the Patriot Act significantly increased the types of information which may be requested. Such information includes, but is not limited to:

- driver's licenses and government records
- assorted commercial records, including hotel bills, apartment leases, and storage rental agreements.
- Cash deposits, money transfers (both wire and digital), and casino credit records.
- Medical bills and health information
- Student records

In addition, the Act expanded the list of financial institutions required to file *suspicious activity reports*. Traditionally, such institutions were limited to banks and credit agencies. However, the Patriot Act extended such responsibilities to include

---

Privacy, Electronic Surveillance, and the First Amendment

Without question, the Patriot Act greatly expanded the 1978 Foreign Intelligence Surveillance Act (FISA)—which provided for the creation of secret courts to review applications for domestic wiretaps and searches in the interest of national security. This standard has been significantly lessened in the wording of the Patriot Act. In fact, provisions housed within allow for analysis of library records and library Internet usage with a simple argument that such analysis is relevant to an ongoing terrorist investigation, irrespective of the presence of an actual crime or probable cause. In addition, the Act specifically prohibits library employees from revealing the presence of government suspicion or government scrutiny to patrons. In response, some libraries are reducing or eliminating log-in registers, sign-up sheets, and unnecessary logs. Others are posting warning signs to patrons, indicating that the federal government might be monitoring their activity.

The modification of FISA has created concerns among academics as well. They argue that free speech and intellectual freedom is significantly harnessed by the potentiality of electronic surveillance (McClintick, 2005). As Internet-based research becomes more popular due to the increasing accessibility of academic sources and dissemination of international knowledge, the significance of electronic monitoring of Web sites rises accordingly. As a result, academics exploring areas which could be loosely construed as "suspicious" must choose between academic inquiry and governmental intrusion. Thus, those academics conducting research on subversive groups, political extremism, or even, alternative lifestyles might be discouraged from pursuing such inquiry on the Web. Privacy advocates argue that such constraints unconstitutionally abridge intellectual freedom, and point to case law for support (McClintick, 2005).

money-transfer businesses. As a result, such *suspicious activity reports* jumped from under 200,000 in 2000 to almost 1 million in 2005.[33] Finally, the Act eased restrictions on foreign intelligence gathering within domestic borders and expanded the traditional definition of terrorism to include *domestic terrorism*, significantly increasing the number of activities to which the expanded surveillance and law enforcement powers can attach.

● CURRENT STATE OF PRIVACY

Although law-enforcement officials are quick to point out that wiretapping and electronic surveillance are reserved for the most serious of cases, statistics suggest otherwise. Between 1968 and 2006, the list of offenses for which wiretapping is permitted has more than tripled. In addition, the number of federal, state, and local law-enforcement wiretaps is steadily increasing, and unsuccessful wiretap applications are all but nonexistent.[34] In 2006, for example, out of 2,181 applications presented for approval, only one FISA application was rejected.[35] Finally, the short duration requirement first articulated in *Katz* has been so eroded as to become defunct. Wiretaps are routinely issued for far longer than originally specified. In fact, wiretaps lasting in excess of 400 days are no longer entirely unusual.

Challenges to Warranted Searches

In the most general sense, the Fourth Amendment to the U.S. Constitution requires that all warrants particularly describe the place to be searched, the items to be seized, and applicable justifications to prevent *general, exploratory rummaging in a person's belonging.*[36] Although courts have responded differently, the current climate indicates that warrants must be adequately narrow so that individual officers may reasonably infer the limits of the search. In addition, this **particularity** must be so specified that unrelated items remain immune from search and/or seizure. Unfortunately, the particularity requirement may prove somewhat burdensome for

officers investigating computer-related crime due to characteristics unique to computers.

Unlike traditional cases in which warrants are issued for very specific items in very specific locations, computer searches involve potentially voluminous amounts of criminal evidence. Conversely, they may contain very small amounts of evidence hidden within a virtual warehouse of information. Thus, they may be characterized as the proverbial needle in a haystack. In addition, enhancements in technology allow suspects to hide criminal evidence in plain sight much more effectively than they once did. Although many legal analysts have likened these types of searches to file-cabinet searches, this analogy is sorely lacking. Investigators looking for child pornography in a file cabinet, for example, may simply glance through files, quickly dismissing text documents. Unfortunately, such practices are not adequate in computer searches. Suspects may change file extensions, use steganography or encryption programs, or employ a variety of other simple methods to hide incriminating information from investigators. Thus, a debate on the particularity and **specificity** necessary for voluminous computer searches rages on.

Particularity

Traditional case law has established that the Fourth Amendment expressly prohibits exploratory searches, requiring searches to be "tailored to its justifications".[37] Thus, search warrants that include searches for "all records" have generally been considered to lack particularity.[38] However, court decisions regarding computer searches have varied not only across jurisdiction, but within them as well. The Ninth Circuit, notoriously unfriendly to law enforcement, have uncharacteristically supported law enforcement interests by suggesting that computer searches may not be held to the same standard of specificity demanded in traditional cases;[39] and by upholding the seizure of an entire computer system (hardware, software, and storage media) because "the affidavit in the case established probable cause to believe Lacy's entire computer system was likely to evidence criminal activity."[40] These views were supported in large part by two rulings in the Tenth Circuit which ruled that the sheer volume and variety of stored information precludes specificity. In other words, warrants can "not be expected to describe with exactitude the precise form the records might take".[41] The Tenth Circuit reiterated this perspective in *U.S. v. Simpson*,[42] where they argued that warrants authorized broad searches of computers and computer equipment including individual files, so **secondary warrants** were not necessary, and in *U.S. v. Campos*—upheld a warrant which authorized the seizure of computer equipment:

> which may be, or [is] used to visually depict child pornography, child erotica, information pertaining to the sexual activity with children or the distribution, possession, or receipt of child pornography, child erotica, or information pertaining to an interest in child pornography or child erotica.

It further affirmed the government's original contention that child pornographers often hide contraband, stating that:

> . . . he often stores it in random order with deceptive file names. This requires searching authorities to examine all the stored data to determine whether it is included in the warrant. This sorting process can take weeks or months, depending on the volume of data stored, and it would be impractical to attempt this kind of data search on site. . . searching computer systems for criminal evidence is a highly technical process requiring expert skill and a properly controlled environment . . . it is difficult to know before a search which expert should analyze the system and its data . . . the controlled environment of a laboratory is essential to its complete analysis.

All of these rulings seemed to trumpet victory for the law enforcement community. However, both the Ninth and the Tenth Circuit have issued rulings which appear to be diametrically opposed to these cases.

In 1995, the Ninth Circuit ruled invalid a warrant which allowed the seizure of *virtually every document and computer file*. The court further ruled that the warrant failed to separate criminal vs. non-criminal documents and to specify how they related to specific criminal activity.[43] Although this would appear to directly contradict their earlier rulings, it is consistent with the inconstancy found within juridical circuits. The Tenth Circuit has also issued rulings which contravene previous holdings. In *U.S. v. Carey*,[44] the Tenth Circuit denied a general warrant that was directed at drug paraphernalia, in which officers searched JPEG files and found child pornography— although government claimed that their finds were "inadvertent" and therefore legal under the "plain view" doctrine, the court ruled that the contents of the file were not in plain view.

Although the courts have been anything but consistent, most courts have granted greater latitude in computer searches and seizures. *U.S. v. Hay*[45] upheld the seizure expressly stating that digital evidence can be stored virtually anywhere. Thus, it is necessary to look at all of the possibilities. They also ruled that it was proper and necessary to seize the computer system, as forensic analysis is not always possible at the scene. This ruling is consistent with *United States v. Kufrovich*,[46] which argued that criminal evidence may be hidden or outside the practicality of on-site searches. The issue before the court involved the validity of a broad-based warrant accompanied with an appendix suggesting that on-site searches are not practical and may sacrifice the effectiveness of data recovery. They have also consistently ruled that when the computer is actually an instrument of the crime, warrants require less particularity. *Davis v. Gracey*,[47] and *U.S. v. Kimbrough*,[48] for example, ruled that the seizure of a computer and all of its associated storage, printing, and viewing devices in a child pornography case was permissible as those items represented an instrumentality of the crime.

The courts have also been willing to accept broad seizures of storage media. *U.S. v. Sassani*,[49] upheld the seizure of 382 floppies. In addition, the courts have consistently upheld that individual items on a diskette may be counted singularly. This is extremely important to child pornography cases in which sentencing is based on number of images. Thus, defendants who argue that the diskettes, not the actual graphics files, should be counted as containers will be unsuccessful.[50] In addition, *U.S. v. Lyons*[51] held that there was no expectation of privacy on a stolen computer (this involved a case where an employee had stolen a computer from his employer, Unisys, and also software programs. FBI agents located the stolen computer through a valid warrant. Subsequent warrantless search of the stolen computer revealed the proprietary software. He argued that the search was not permissible.) Thus, when possible, investigators should attempt to seize entire computer systems so that adequate investigation may occur. Supporting documentation such as the appendix in *Kufrovich* is also highly recommended until the Supreme Court hears a similar case. However, in cases where seizure of an entire computer is not possible or legally impermissible, proper imaging of drives will enable investigators to conduct a thorough investigation. In addition, investigators should seek secondary warrants whenever they are in doubt as to the scope of the original warrant so as to avoid challenges based on **overbreadth**.

Seizure of Evidence

For purposes of the Fourth Amendment, the reasonable actions that are less intrusive than a traditional arrest depends on a balance between the public interest and the individual's right to personal security free from arbitrary interference by law officers, and consideration of the constitutionality of such seizures involves a weighing of the gravity of the public concerns served by the seizure, the degree to which the seizure advances the public interest, and the severity of the interference with individual liberty.[52]

The Fourth Amendment's mandate of reasonableness does not require the agent to spend days at the site viewing the computer screens to determine precisely which documents may be copied within the scope of the warrant, so long as a review procedure promptly after seizure safeguards against the government's retention and use of computer-generated documents known to lie beyond a reasonable interpretation of the warrant's scope.[53]

Similar to the rulings regarding particularity challenges, the courts have been reluctant to rule adversely to police interests on challenges of overbreadth of equipment seizure. In cases in two different districts, courts have ruled that officers may search any container which they reasonably believed could contain criminal evidence.[54] *Sissler*, more importantly, argued that officers were not required to give deference to descriptive labels and that items could be seized and transported to a place where careful analysis could be conducted. Basically, the Court has ruled that "the requirement that warrants shall particularly describe the things to be seized makes general searches under (¨13) then impossible and prevents the seizure of one thing under a warrant describing another. As to what is to be taken, nothing is left to the discretion of the officer executing the warrant."[55] This holding was applied to technology-specific warrants in *Center Art Galleries— Hawaii, Inc. v. U.S.*,[56] where they invalidated a warrant as "overbroad because it allowed virtually unrestricted seizure of items without describing the specific crimes suspected." Finally, *U.S. v. Tamura*[57] cautioned investigators to obtain secondary warrants when specified and unspecified documents were seized wholesale, specifically ruling that further approval of a magistrate is necessary. In addition, the search and search and seizure of *encrypted* files may only be acceptable if the warrant specifies such. (In consent searches, encrypted or otherwise protected files may heighten expectations of privacy.) If encrypted files are seizable, but are not accessible due to unknown keys or passwords, investigators may wish to seek a subpoena to compel individuals to reveal the same. When seeking such action, investigators should liken the situation to traditional investigations where a key was necessary to search items which were included in a warrant (i.e., safes, etc.). In addition, courts have upheld the search and seizure of deleted or erased files, likening them to pieces of a shredded ransom note.[58]

Another consideration often discussed in challenges to seizing evidence includes the intermingling (often called "commingling") of personal or irrelevant information with potential evidence. These challenges have often been predicated on voluminous searches of text or database documents which include nonevidentiary materials. Although the courts have not ruled on this specific issue in computer cases, investigators may avoid challenges by using software which searches for specific text or keywords within documents. By carefully documenting the software packages used and the keywords searched for, investigators can argue that they acted with due regard for the privacy of the individual. Another safeguard may include securing an additional warrant (which specifically addresses the documents in question) to search for this information. It is absolutely critical for investigators to be cognizant of the potential hazards involved in these types of cases and plan their strategies accordingly. For example, preliminary warrants should specifically include all materials which may include criminal evidence that are to be seized. Investigators may argue that removal of all computer media is necessary to prevent contamination and destruction of potential evidence. Once in the custody of law enforcement, application for an additional warrant can only strengthen the case against judicial challenges. Indeed, the broadness traditionally afforded to computer searches may be extremely curtailed once exigent dangers are removed.

Due to the lack of specificity contained within current statutes and criminal codes, emerging legal dogma has consistently included storage devices such as diskettes—floppies, zips, etc. Several cases have been consistent with *United States* v. *Ross*.[59] In *New York* v. *Loone*[60] the court ruled that agents did not require a second warrant for computer media. According to the court, the initial warrant, clearly specifying the search and seizure of "any and all computers, keyboards, Central Processing Units, external drives and/or internal drives, external and internal storage devices such as magnetic tapes and/or disks or diskettes"[61] was sufficient to search the information included within the computer media. More specifically, the court ruled that *Ross* allows officers to search the entire area in which criminal

evidence may reasonably be found even if various points of entry emerge.

Third Party Origination

While the scope of the Fourth Amendment is unclear in searches conducted by law enforcement, no protection exists for those searches conducted by third parties acting independently absent direction from the government. This issue is increasingly common as more and more cases are brought to the attention of law enforcement via computer repair technicians and network administrators. As always, the admissibility of information collected in an investigation by a third party hinges on whether the third party was constructively acting as an agent of the government. Courts have repeatedly ruled that files which are open to the public negate any expectation of privacy and that relinquishing computers to a third party reduces or eliminates an expectation of privacy. This includes computer hardware and any communications or shared files.

In *United States* v. *Pervaz*[62] the court evaluated the admissibility of information gathered by a cellular telephone company after being alerted by authorities that they were being victimized. The court ruled that "the extent of the government's role in instigating or participating in the search, its intent and the degree of control it exercises over the search and the private party, and the extent to which the private party aims primarily to help the government or to serve its own interests" (at 6). In this case, the court ruled that the company's actions were primarily motivated by its wish to identify those individuals guilty of defrauding their consumers, as opposed to helping the government. In addition, the fact that the government was not informed of the company's intention to undertake action to ascertain the culprits' identities was indicative of the lack of control exercised by the government in this situation. Clearly, this case involved individuals or entities that were acting independently of government instruction. Such was not the case, however, in *United States* v. *Hall*,[63] where a computer technician copied files from a computer he was repairing under the direction of law enforcement. In this particular case, the technician inadvertently discovered several images of child pornography, phoned the authorities, and copied the files which they specified. Although the court recognized that the authorities acted inappropriately, they upheld the conviction on the grounds that the actual warrant was predicated on items found prior to law enforcement instruction. In this case, the court also evaluated the argument that the ruse to allow time for warrant preparation perpetrated by said repairman under the direction of law enforcement was violative of the Fourth Amendment. The court ruled that the one-day delay was not unreasonable because it was brief and based on adequate suspicion.[64]

Other Arguments Used in Warranted Searches

Particularity and overbreadth are not the only challenges that have been levied against law enforcement searches. Traditional challenges like staleness of evidence and insufficient probable cause have also found their way into this new realm. However, the courts have not issued generalized rulings. Rather, they have tailored their interpretations to case characteristics. In *U.S. v. Hay*,[65] the court upheld the search and seizure of an entire computer system which was predicated on information that was several months old. The defendant argued that the warrant was stale as it was based on a transfer of child pornography six months previously. The Court disagreed, citing *Lacy*. The court affirmed the expert (i.e., police) opinion that collectors of child porn tend to keep images for an extended period and that computer depictions, in particular, are easily stored. Thus, it was reasonable to believe that the images were still there. (Lacy's affidavit was predicated on a transfer of data that was ten months old.)

In *U.S. v. Lacy*,[66] an individual downloaded six image files from a Danish bulletin board known for trafficking in child pornography. Although the defendant argued that this activity was not sufficient to establish probable cause that he received and possessed computerized visual depictions of child pornography, the court disagreed. However, the Ninth Circuit had previously ruled that a

warrant application (supported through affidavit) predicated on assumptions as to how "child molesters," "pedophiles," and "child pornography collectors" behave did not establish probable cause to search for items other than the specific photographs ordered by the defendant in a sting operation. Thus, the legal waters remain murky.

Warrantless Searches

Regardless of case characteristics, there are certain categorical situations in which the courts have ruled that no warrant is required. As in non-computer cases, circumstances which may indicate potential harm to human life, the destruction of relevant evidence, and other characteristics which may frustrate legitimate law enforcement efforts may allow officers to seize evidence in the absence of a warrant. While some of these "warrantless searches" are deemed necessary for the protection of human life and criminal evidence, others are based on an independent waiver of the Fourth Amendment.

Consent

Some searches may involve individuals who have voluntarily waived their Fourth Amendment rights. Consent searches are admissible without a warrant if consent is given voluntarily by an individual who has the proper authority over the area to be searched and is legally capable of granting such access.[67] Under these guidelines, consent may be given by a third party if that third party has a shared interest or authority over the equipment.[68] However, the subsequent search must be limited to that area of the consenting third party's common authority.[69] In computer cases, the presence of encryption or security mechanisms may negate the concept of common authority unless that person giving consent had previously been given the unlocking capability by the owner. Networked computers may also be immune from consent searches, as system operators may have access to most, but not all, files. The same is true with family members. Thus, the most important characteristics in determining the validity (and legality) of consent are physical control and limited access. In other words, if a computer is shared by family members, and the suspect member has taken pains to prevent common access (i.e., encryption, steganography, etc.), others may not be able to give consent. Investigators must also evaluate the totality of the circumstances in any particular situation to determine the validity and the *scope* of the consent being offered.

In legal terms, the **totality of the circumstances** would include a compilation of age, education, intelligence, physical, and mental conditions of the person granting consent. It also includes whether the individual was incarcerated and had been notified of his or her right regarding consent. If a child's computer is the intended search target, parents may give consent if the child is under 18. Over the age of 18, the totality of the circumstances would include factors such as the dependency of the child, the location of the computer, and the like. The *scope of consent* also hinges on the totality of the circumstances. It is rarely holistic and all-encompassing. Rather, it hinges on the breadth of the reasonable understanding of the grantor. *Government agents may not obtain consent to search on the representation that they intend to look only for certain specified items and subsequently use that consent as a license to conduct a general exploratory search.*[70] Finally, the courts have made it clear that the burden to prove that the search was within the scope of the consent lies with the government.[71]

Exigent Circumstances and Emergency Situations

The courts have ruled that actions which are undertaken to protect or preserve human life are acceptable even if they would not be so in non-emergency situations.[72] Thus, officers are not precluded from making warrantless entries if they reasonably believe that an individual(s) is in need of immediate aid. Upon entry, contraband or criminal evidence which is in plain view may be seized. Keep in mind that reasonable seizures do not automatically warrant subsequent searches. In other words, officers may (and should) seize a computer where evidence is at risk, but should seek judicial approval before undertaking a search of its contents.[73]

A Case for Consent—A Caution for Investigators

U.S. v. *Turner*[74]—suppressed evidence of child pornography after it was found in a consensual search by an individual who was identified as a suspect in the sexual assault of his neighbor.

Facts of the case—Defendant was charged with one count of child pornography after officers found child porn on his computer. At the time, the investigators were investigating the sexual assault of his neighbor. Upon noticing blood on his window sill and throughout the house, investigators suspected Turner and obtained his permission to search his house for items involving the sexual assault of his neighbor. Subsequently, the defendant waited outside while the investigators initiated a comprehensive search. Upon seeing a screen saver on his computer screen of a naked woman that resembled the victim, the investigator searched his hard drive for last documents accessed and picture files. He found photographs of adult women in bondage-type situations. After phoning the district attorney, the officer copied adult pornography over to a floppy. In addition, the officer extended his search to "My Computer" and opened files which had names that suggested child pornography (e.g., "G-Images", "young with breasts," etc.). The officer subsequently found images which appeared to be child pornography. The district court suppressed the evidence saying that names suggesting child pornography were unrelated to the charges. The Circuit Court affirmed, yet expanded.

Rulings

1. Although the defendant agreed to a general search for evidence of the assault, it was not reasonable to assume that the investigators would look in places where evidence of the assault could not be contained.

(Continued)

Thus, the search was exploratory—which is not permissible. Citing *Florida* v. *Jimeno*[75] the court argued that "the scope of a [consensual] search is generally defined by its expressed object."

2. Officers exceed the scope of the consent search. His consent was based on the understanding that they were looking for "any signs the suspect had been inside [the apartment] . . . " "any signs a suspect had left behind." The court stated that "it obviously would have been impossible to abandon physical evidence of this sort in

a personal computer hard drive, and bizarre to suppose—nor has the government suggested—that the suspected intruder stopped to enter incriminating evidence into the Turner computer."

3. Also "an objective observer, witnessing in context the pre-consent exchange between Turner and the investigating detectives, reasonably would construe 'evidence of the assault itself' to mean physical evidence linked to the crime scene, rather than documentary or photographic evidence."

Once again, the totality of the circumstances will determine the presence and duration of exigent searches and seizures. In determination of the applicability, the courts have found several factors which should be evaluated. These include:

1. the degree of urgency involved;
2. the amount of time necessary to obtain a warrant;
3. whether the evidence is about to be removed or destroyed;
4. the danger or possibility thereof at the site;
5. information which suggests that the possessors of said material are aware of the officer's intention to secure it;
6. the ready destructability of said contraband.

These characteristics may prove especially salient in situations in which computers are involved as digital evidence is particularly fragile. Remember: warrantless seizure is limited to the length of the exigency. Once the urgency is passed, warrants must be obtained.

When specifically applied to computer cases, the courts have ruled that seizure of computer hardware may be conducted under this doctrine, but the subsequent search of hardware may necessitate a warrant. In *U.S.* v. *David*,[76] the court held that while the officer's seizure of suspect's computer memo book was reasonable in light of the defendant's action of deleting files, the subsequent search and re-access was not reasonable as there was adequate time to secure a search warrant. In this case, the court analogized the computer with a

container arguing that the authorization for a warrantless seizure does not necessarily grant authorization for a search of such item.[77] One of the determining factors, of course, would be the ever-resilient "expectation of privacy." If, for example, the circumstance surrounding such computer suggests security, a warrant will be required.

Incident to Arrest

Traditionally, those situations in which an officer's safety may be compromised allow for searches without a warrant. The search of an individual and his/her immediate vicinity upon arrest has been determined reasonable as it is necessary to ensure the safety of the officer and those around him/her.[78] While this includes the seizure of those items within the arrestee's possession and immediately within reach, it may not include further search of these items. Thus, the search of a laptop, palmtop, or electronic organizer for data is prohibited by the Electronic Communications Privacy Act of 1986. Thus, investigators should secure a warrant before proceeding. Although originally intended to protect officers from armed suspects, *Robinson* has been applied to pagers, and the courts have consistently ruled that investigators may access the memory at the time of arrest.[79] This permission has not been extended to personal computers, laptops, and personal digital assistants (PDA). However, the court did validate the seizure of a zip disk found in the car of an arrested suspect but failed to rule on the constitutionality of the subsequent search.[80] Once again, investigators must be cautioned that issues of search and seizure are separate! Thus, the subsequent search of items seized may not be justified, irrespective of the legality of the seizure.

Plain View

Things which are obviously evidence of a crime can be collected when the officer is acting in a lawful manner; items which are unobstructed may be seized. In addition, those things which are criminal contraband may be seized. *However,* investigators *cannot* broaden the scope of the original search based on new evidence. Instead, investigators should obtain a secondary warrant prior to further investigation.[81] However, the courts have been reluctant to extend plain view to the contents of an entire computer citing *Coolidge,* which argued that "the plain view doctrine may not be used to extend a general exploratory search from one object to another until something incriminating at last emerges."[82]

The most notable computer-specific case involving plain view, *U.S. v. Carey,*[83] was extremely narrow in scope and was not intended to be the final word on the matter. The facts of the case preclude any such generalization. In this case, the original thrust of the search specifically targeted evidence of drug trafficking. While searching through computer files, the investigator, by his own admission, noticed a large number of JPEG files containing sexually explicit names. He then opened a variety of these images and ascertained that they were child pornography. Once the first image was viewed, the detective changed the direction of his search to include child pornography, thus, subsequent "findings" were not inadvertent, but intentional. He then opened a variety of these images, ascertained that they were child pornography, and "changed the focus of his search." Government likened the search to a file cabinet, but the court rejected this, stating that it was the content of the files, not the files themselves which were seized. In addition, the Court pointed out that the files were not in "plain view" as they were closed. However, the Court was quick to point out that this ruling did not address the particularity necessary in all computer cases—just this one. In addition, in the concurring opinion, a justice points out that the defendant's testimony made it impossible to uphold an argument of plain view. Indeed, had the officer not made his intentions clear, the evidence may not have been dismissed (i.e., it is reasonable that criminals hide evidence, and it may be necessary to ascertain the contents).

Since *Carey,* courts have upheld plain view discoveries on the computer when stating that the actions of the agent were consistent with the terms of the original warrant. The court ruled against an argument by the defendant that the searching of JPEGs was not consistent with searching for hacking activities. The Court ruled that the officer's practice of systematically searching documents without regard to file names or suffixes was reasonable, as potential evidence could be hidden anywhere in the defendant's files (i.e., the officer does not have to assume that file extensions adequately characterize the contents of the file).[84] Thus, law enforcement should take note:

1. Focus on the original search warrant. If contraband is found in pursuit of items covered under the original warrant, get a secondary warrant!
2. Automated or SOP which are conducted in every case (i.e., text string, thumbnail of graphics, viewing of subdirectories, etc.) may support an officer's contention that files outside the scope of the original warrant were inadvertently discovered during routine procedures.

Border Searches

The Supreme Court has recognized a special exception to the warrant requirement for searches occurring at the country's international borders, ruling that warrantless searches at the border are acceptable on their face.[85] Probable cause and reasonable suspicion are not necessary for routine searches. However, reasonable suspicion must be present for more intrusive searches. The Court has ruled that borders may be less tangible than traditionally thought—extending the power of border searches to include areas several miles from the actual border.[86] While case law applying this doctrine to cyberspace boundaries is not yet available, we can certainly anticipate future occurrences.

Other Warrantless Searches

Traditionally, automobiles, field interrogations, and inventory searches have also been areas in which searches were conducted without the necessity of a warrant. However, they are not exactly applicable to computer-related evidence. Inventory searches, for example, are designed to protect the rights of the arrestee by detailing his or her personal property. As computer files are not discoverable under plain view, the presence of a floppy in a detainee's shirt pocket is all but meaningless without specific probable cause. The same applies to automobiles and field interrogations.

● OTHER LEGAL CONSIDERATIONS

Vicinage

Although the courts have not ruled specifically on questions of jurisdiction and sovereignty, past Supreme Court cases may indicate an issue which may arise. (i.e., contemporary crimes transcend traditional boundaries). In *Johnson* v. *U.S.*,[87] the Court ruled that the "requirement of venue states the public policy that fixes the situs of the trial in the vicinage of the crime, rather than the residence of the accused". This premise was reaffirmed by *Travis* v. *U.S.*[88] which ruled that the locality of the offense, not the personal presence of the offender, is the constitutional basis for venue. If this premise is not revisited (and reversed), then prosecution of computer crime committed on the Internet will be all but impossible.

Undercover Techniques

Although the courts have issued contradictory rulings in many areas, most are in agreement regarding the appropriateness of traditional investigative techniques. In *United States* v. *Charbonneau*,[89] the court ruled that real-time, online conversations observed by an agent in a chat room did not require a warrant as there is no expectation of privacy in virtual areas where others visit. They argued that people conversing in chat rooms run the risk of talking to an undercover agent. Elaborating on *Hoffa* v. *U.S.*[90] the court ruled that senders of electronic mail run the same risk as those using the Postal Service in that they might be mailing it to an undercover agent. Thus, there is no Fourth Amendment protection which applies to chat room conversations.

Sentencing Guidelines

Although a variety of cases have involved departures from sentencing guidelines, most involve the definition of "items." This is increasingly important as child pornography statutes are specifically tied to the number of items. Unfortunately, courts have proven no more consistent in this area than others we have previously discussed. While some courts have ruled that individual diskettes represent one item, others have ruled that "a graphic file is the container used for compiling and storing visual depictions in a computer qualifies as an item."[91] And *U.S.* v. *Hall*,[92] rejected an argument that a computer disk regardless of disk content should be counted singularly, further ruling that computer files are the equivalent of items under sentencing guidelines. Courts have also ruled that hard disks do not constitute a singular item under the sentencing guidelines.[93]

A two-level sentencing enhancement for using a computer to obtain or possess child pornography was added to the Sentencing Guidelines in U.S.S.G. § 2G2 4(b)(3) primarily as a deterrent against the presumed anonymity of the Internet. It also recognized the particular difficulties of detection and prosecution of cyberspace child porn. Unfortunately, the trend across the judicial landscape is to depart downward! Thus, many child pornographers receive sentences far less than those which are provided for under law. Curiously, the courts have granted such departures for reasons ranging from the lack of a direct impact on the supply of child pornography on the Web to good behavior on the part of a child pornographer who failed to further act out sexual deviations.

CONCLUSIONS

Because the Supreme Court has remained resolutely mute on the convergence of technology and the expectation of privacy, no constitutional framework has been established. Thus, a lack of uniformity in legal application of constitutional standards exists. Many of these concerns focus almost exclusively on the Fourth Amendment, while others involve the Exclusionary Rule. The introduction of the Patriot Act in 2002 has dramatically changed the legal landscape, and electronic surveillance has increased significantly. While law enforcement proponents embrace emerging legislation, privacy advocates have expressed concern, arguing that constitutional protections have been significantly reduced or completely eradicated.

The lack of physicality of data origination poses jurisdictional questions and the lack of cooperation among local and federal agencies further compounds the issue. The lack of a clear ruling by the Court on computer warrants further leads to an over-reliance on federal resources, which leads to claims of imperialism and loss of state sovereignty. Thus, it is essential that the Court issue clear edicts on the issues discussed throughout this chapter. Otherwise, claims of disproportionate or jurisdictional inconsistency are well founded.

DISCUSSION QUESTIONS

1. Briefly discuss the evolution of the Fourth Amendment in regard to physical searches.
2. What do you believe is a good balance of individual privacy and governmental interest?
3. How has electronic surveillance changed since the 1950s? Have technological advancements lessened or increased expectations of privacy? Why or why not?
4. How has *Ortega* been applied to electronic mail?
5. What is the ECPA and why was it designed?
6. Why are traditional definitions of "interception" problematic when applying them to electronic communications?
7. What are some examples of warrantless searches and in what circumstances may they be conducted?

RECOMMENDED READING

- Bellia, Patricia L.; Berman, Paul Schiff; and Post, David G. (2006). *Cyberlaw: Problems of Policy and Jurisprudence in the Information Age*. Thomson/West: Connecticut.
- Cook R. Stephen (2004, July). "United States v. Bach and the Fourth Amendment in Cyberspace." *Criminal Law Bulletin*, 40(4), 410–414.
- Ferrera, Gerald (2004). *Cyberlaw: Text and Cases*. Thomson/West: Connecticut.
- Doyle, Charles (2002). *The USA Patriot Act: A Legal Analysis*. CRS Report for Congress. Available at: *http://www.fas.org/irp/crs/RL31377.pdf*.
- Penney, Steven (2007). "Reasonable Expectations of Privacy and Novel Search Technologies: An Economic Approach." *Journal of Criminal Law & Criminology*, 97(2), 477–529.
- Schwarzenegger, Christian and Summers, Sarah (2007). *The Emergence of EU Criminal Law: Cyber Crime and the Regulation of the Information Society*. Hart Publishing: United Kingdom.

WEB RESOURCES

- http://cyberlaw.standford.edu – the homepage of the Center for Internet and Society at Stanford Law School. The site provides links to various resources on breaking news and case law involving the Fourth Amendment and computers. In addition, the site provides links to publications of Stanford Law School.
- http://cyber.law.harvard.edu/home/ – the homepage of the Berklman Center for Internet and Society at Harvard Law School. The site explores a variety of issues involving technology and society, including legal, social, and international issues.
- http://www.catalaw.com – a comprehensive catalog of both national and international law. Provides access to legal codes, legislation, law articles, and breaking news on legal issues. Allows the user to search by topic and geographical location.

- http://library.albany.edu/subject/guides/law.htm –
an exhaustive listing of all legal search engines. Users
can link to national and international codes; academic journals; discussion groups; law libraries; law
reviews; news; and dictionaries.

ENDNOTES

[1]*Warden* v. *Hayden*, 387 U.S. 294 (1967); *Katz* v. *United States*,
389 U.S. 347 (1967).

[2]*Olmstead* v. *United States*, 277 U.S. 438 (1928).

[3]*Katz* v. *United States*, 389 U.S. 347 (1967).

[4]*Weeks* v. *United States*, 232 U.S. 383 (1914).

[5]Britz, Marjie T. (2008). *Criminal Evidence*. Allyn & Bacon:
New York.

[6]*Lewis* v. *United States*, 385 U.S. 206 (1980); *United States* v.
Lee, 274 U.S. 559 (1982).

[7]*Rios* v. *United States*, 364 U.S. 253 (1960); *Ex parte Jackson*, 96
U.S. 727 (1877).

[8]*United States* v. *Miller*, 425 U.S. 435 (1976).

[9]381 U.S. 479 (1965); 410 U.S. 113 (1973).

[10]Benoliel, Daniel (2005). "Law, Geography and Cyberspace:
The Case of On-Line Territorial Privacy." *Cardozo Arts
and Entertainment Law Journal*, 23(125). Available at
www.LexisNexis.com.

[11]Britz (2008). *Criminal Evidence*.

[12]Ibid.

[13]*United States* v. *Monroe*, 50 M.J. 550 (A.F.C.C.A. 1999).

[14]Coacher, LeEllen (1999). "Permitting Systems Protection
Monitoring: When the Government Can Look and What It
Can See." *Air Force Law Review*, 46(155).

[15]Dempsey, James X. (1997). "Communications Privacy in the
Digital Age: Revitalizing the Federal Wiretap Laws to Enhance
Privacy." *Albany Law Journal of Science and Technology*, 8(1).
Available at *www.cdt.org/publications/lawreview/1997albany.
shtml* (last accessed on 10 August 2007).

[16]Winick, Raphael (1994). "Searches and Seizures of
Computers and Computer Data." *Harvard Journal of Law and
Technology*, 8(1): 75–128.

[17]Soma, John T., Banker, Elizabeth A., and Smith, Alexander R.
(1996). "Computer Crime: Substantive Statutes & Technical &
Search Considerations." *The Air Force Law Review*, 39(225).
Available at *www.lexisnexis.com*. Retrieved from the Internet
on August 13, 2007.

[18]Kerr, Donald M. (September 6, 2000b). Statement for the
Record on *Carnivore Diagnostic Tool* before the United States
Sentate: The Committee on the Judiciary, Washington, DC.
Available at *www.fbi.gov/pressrm/congress/congressoo/kerr090600
.htm*.

[19]Ibid.

[20]Winick (1994). "Searches and Seizures of Computers and
Computer Data."

[21]*United States* v. *Meriwether*, 917 F.2d 955, 960 (Sixth Cir.,
1990); *Steve Jackson Games, Inc.* v. *U.S. Secret Service et al.*, 36
F.3d 457, 463 (Fifth Cir., 1994); *U.S.* v. *Reyes*, 922 F.2d Supp.
818, 836 (S.D.N.Y. 1996).

[22]*Fraser* v. *Nationwide Mutual Insurance* (decided March,
2001) United States District Court for the Eastern District of
Pennsylvania. # 98-CV-6726—has suggested otherwise;

*the meaning of interception does not change when the com-
munication is indirect, passing through storage in the course
of transmission for sender to recipient . . . in an e-mail
communication system, as in a voice-mail communication
system, a message passes through intermediate storage in
the course of transmission . . . retrieval of a message from
storage while it is in the course of transmission is "interception" under the Wiretap Act: retrieval of a message from
storage after transmission is complete is not "interception"
under the Act.* (p. 8 of 21, *www.paed.uscourts.gov/docu-
ments/opinions/01D0255P.HTM*).

[23]Ibid.

[24]Ibid.

[25]*United States* v. *Councilman* (First Cir., 2004) No. 03–1383.

[26]Ibid.

[27]McClintick, James (2005). "Web-Surfing in Chilly Waters:
How the Patiot Act's Amendments to the Pen Register Statute
Burden Freedom of Inquiry." *American University Journal of
Gender, Social Policy and the Law*, 13(353). Available at *www.
lexisnexis.com*.

[28]DOJ (2006). *Fact Sheet: USA Patriot Act Improvement and
Reauthorization Act of 2005*. March 2, 2006. Available at *http://
www.usdoj.gov/opa/pr/2006/March/06_opa_113.html*.
Retrieved from the Internet on September 15, 2007.

[29]The *International Emergency Economic Powers Act* (50 U.S.C.
1702) was passed in 1977 to replace the *Trading with
the Enemy Act of 1917*. While maintaining the original
thrust of the 1917 Act, the new Act specifically provided
for increased due process in response to concerns by civil
libertarians.

[30]*Katz* v. *United States*, 389 U.S. 347 (1967).

[31]18 U.S.C. 2510–2522.

[32]McClintick (2005). Web-Surfing in Chilly Waters.

[33]U.S. Treasury Report (2006).

[34]Ibid.

[35]Available at *http://epic.org/privacy/wiretap/stats/fisa_stats.
html*.

[36]*Coolidge* v. *New Hampshire*, 403 U.S. 443 (1971).

[37]*Maryland* v. *Garrison*, 480 U.S. 79 (1987).

[38]*Naugle* v. *Witney*, 755 F. Supp. 1504.

[39]*United States* v. *Gomez-Soto*, 723 F.2d 649 (Ninth Cir.,
1984)

[40]*United States* v. *Lacy*, 119 F.3d 742, 745 (Ninth Cir., 1997).

[41]798 F.2d 380, 383 (Tenth Cir., 1986).

[42]*United States* v. *Simpson*, 152 F.3d 1241 (Tenth Cir., 1998).

[43]*United States* v. *Kow*, F.3d 423, 427 (Ninth Cir., 1995).

[44]*United States* v. *Carey*, 172 F.3d 1268. (Tenth Cir., 1999

[45]*United States* v. *Hay*, 2000 WL 1576880 (Ninth Cir, 2000).

[46]*United States* v. *Kufrovich*, 997 F. Supp. 246 (1997).

[47]*Davis* v. *Gracey*, 111 F.3d 1472, 1480 (Tenth Cir., 1997).

[48]*United States* v. *Kimbrough*, 69 F.3d 723, 727 (Fifth Cir., 1995).

[49]*United States* v. *Sassani*, 1998 WL 98875 (Fourth Cir.,
March 4) (Per curium) (unpublished decision), cert. denied,
119 S.Ct. 276 (1998).

[50]*United States* v. *Perreault*, #9930087 (Ninth Cir., 1999).

[51]*United States* v. *Lyons*, 992 F.2d 1029 (Tenth Cir., 1993).

[52]*Rawlings* v. *Kentucky*, 448 U.S. 98 (1980).

[53]*United States* v. *Gawrysiak*, 972 F. Supp. 853, 866 (D.N.J. 1997).

[54]*United States* v. *Musson*, 650 F. Supp. 525 (D.Colo. 1986) and
United States v. *Sissler*, 966 F.2d 1455 (W.D. Mich 1991).

[55]*Marron* v. *United States*, 275 U.S. 192 (1927).

[56]*Center Art Galleries—Hawaii, Inc.* v. *United States* 875 F.2d 747 (Ninth Cir., 1989).

[57]*United States* v. *Tamura,* 694 F.2d 591, 595–596 (Ninth Cir., 1982).

[58]*United States* v. *Upham,* 168 F.3d 535.

[59]*United States* v. *Ross,* 456 U.S. 798, 820–822 (1992).

[60]*New York* v. *Loone,* 630 N.Y. S.2d 483 (Monroe Cty. Ct. 1995).

[61]Ibid.

[62]*United States* v. *Pervaz,* 118 F.3d 1 (First Cir, 1997).

[63]*United States* v. *Hall,* 142 F.3d 988 (Seventh Cir., 1998).

[64]*United States* v. *Mayomi,* 873 F.2d 1049 (Seventh Cir., 1989).

[65]*United States* v. *Hay,* 2000 WL 1576880 (Ninth Cir. Wash.).

[66]*United States* v. *Lacy,* 119 F.3d 742 (Ninth Cir., 1997).

[67]*Schneckloth* v. *Bustamonte,* 412 U.S. 218 (1973).

[68]*United States* v. *Matlock,* 415 U.S. 164 (1974).

[69]*United States* v. *Block,* 590 F.2d 5335 (Fourth Cir., 1978).

[70]*United States* v. *Dichiarinte,* 445 F.2d 126 (Seventh Cir., 1971).

[71]*United States* v. *Schaefer,* 87 F.3d 562, 569 (First Cir., 1996).

[72]*Mincey* v. *Arizona,* 437 U.S. 385, 392–393 (1978); *United States* v. *Doe,* 61 F.3d 107, 110–111 (First Cir., 1995).

[73]Levin, Robert B. (1995). "The Virtual Fourth Amendment: Searches and Seizures in Cyberspace." *Maryland Bar Journal,* *XXVII*(3): 2–5.

[74]*United States* v. *Turner,* 98–1258 (First Circuit, 1999).

[75]*Florida* v. *Jimeno,* 500 U.S. 248 (1991).

[76]*United States* v. *David,* 756 F. Supp. 1385, 1392 (D.Nev., 1991).

[77]*Texas* v. *Brown,* 460 U.S. 730, 750 (1983).

[78]*United States* v. *Robinson,* 414 U.S. 218, 234–236 (1973).

[79]*United States* v. *Reyes,* 922 F. Supp. 818, 833 (S.D.N.Y. 1996).

[80]*Cf. United* v. *Tank,* 200 F.3d 627, 632 (Ninth Cir., 2000).

[81]*United States* v. *Carey,* 172 F.3d 1268, 1273 (Tenth Cir., 1999).

[82]*Coolidge* v. *New Hampshire,* 403 U.S. 443, 465; 29 L.Ed. 2d 564, 91 S.Ct. 2022 (1971).

[83]*United States* v. *Carey,* 172 F.3d 1268.

[84]*United States* v. *Gray,* 78 F. Supp. 2d 524 (D. VA, 1999).

[85]*United States* v. *Ramsey,* 431 U.S. 606 (1977).

[86]*Almeida-Sanchez* v. *United States,* 413 U.S. 266 (1973).

[87]*Johnson* v. *United States,* 351 U.S. 215, 219–221 (1956).

[88]*Travis* v. *United States,* 346 U.S. 631, 633–634 (1961).

[89]*United States* v. *Charbonneau,* 979 F. Supp. 1177 (S.D. Ohio, 1997).

[90]*Hoffa* v. *United States,* 385 U.S. 293 (1966).

[91]*United States* v. *Wind,* 128 F.3d 1276 (Eighth Cir., 1997).

[92]*United States* v. *Hall,* 142 F.3d 988 (Seventh Cir. 1998).

[93]*United States* v. *Fellows,* 157 F.3d 1197 (Ninth Cir., 1998).

CHAPTER 10

Forensic Terminology and Developing Forensic Science Capabilities

Chapter Outline

LEARNING OBJECTIVES

After reading this chapter, you will be able to do the following:

- ✓ Learn some of the problems associated with computer investigation.
- ✓ Gain insight on how computer disks are structured.
- ✓ Be able to discuss the means in which computers store data.
- ✓ Explore the types of data recovery methods which agencies use today.
- ✓ Develop a working knowledge of FAT and its importance to computer investigation.
- ✓ Learn the five categories of software that can be used in computer investigation.

KEY TERMS AND CONCEPTS

- active files
- application analysis
- ASCII
- Basic Input/Output System (BIOS)
- binary system
- bits
- bootstrap loader
- boot disk
- boot sector
- CD-ROM
- CD-RW
- clusters
- compressed files
- computer
- computer storage
- cyclical redundancy check-sum (CRC)
- cylinder
- data preservation
- data verification tools
- deleted files

- encryption
- File Allocation Table (FAT)
- file allocation units
- file slack
- file viewers
- floppy disks
- graphical user interface (GUI)
- hard/fixed disks
- HashKeeper
- head
- hexadecimal system
- hidden files
- imaging
- indexing
- logical drives
- logical extraction phase
- logical file size
- Maresware
- master boot record (MBR)
- MD5-Hash
- overt files
- partition

- partition table
- password crackers
- password–protected files
- physical drive
- physical extraction phase
- physical file size
- primary storage
- power-on self-test (POST)
- read-only memory (ROM)
- secondary storage
- sectors
- semi-permanent storage
- static memory
- standard operating procedure (SOP)
- steganography
- text searching
- time frame analysis
- tracks
- unallocated file space
- volatile memory
- write-blocking

FORENSIC COMPUTER SCIENCE—AN EMERGING DISCIPLINE

As stated, the introduction of computer technology has heralded the approach of a new wave of illegitimate behavior and multiplied the avenues of criminal procurement. The utilization of technology has also changed the investigative playing field and necessitated the development of contemporary forensic techniques. More succinctly, the digitalization of information and the increasing interconnectivity of society require a corresponding ability to retrieve inadvertently lost data, as well as that which has been intentionally misplaced. While such abilities clearly serve the law enforcement mission, they may also be utilized by corporate entities and individual citizens to ensure the continuity of public services, private interests, and government stability.

Private interests aside, forensic computer science is critical to the successful disposition of computer-related cases. Empirical methodologies serve a variety of law enforcement functions and provide the accountability necessary in a democratic society. In the most general sense, computer forensics provides a mechanism for the investigation of computer-related criminal activity consistent with constitutional mandates. To wit, privileged information is protected and the integrity of potential evidence is maintained by (1) maintaining a chain of custody; (2) ensuring that viruses are not introduced to a suspect machine during analysis; and (3) ensuring that evidence or potential evidence remains in an unaltered state (i.e., not destroyed, damaged, or otherwise manipulated during the investigative process). In addition, it enhances the likelihood of timely processing—necessary to protect departments from civil litigation claiming unreasonable interruption of business operations. More specifically, it establishes procedures for the recovery, preservation, and analysis of digital evidence.

Computer forensic science protects digital evidence from possible alterations, damage, data corruption, or infection by design or carelessness. By providing mechanisms for evidence duplication, it enables the creation of forensically sound images useful for data analysis. As such, it prevents allegations of corruption or misconduct on the part of investigators, all but guaranteeing evidentiary introduction in court. It also uncovers all relevant files on suspect systems, including overt, hidden, password-protected, slack, swap, encrypted, and some deleted files. In addition, computer forensics assists in information dissemination as printouts may illustrate an overall analysis of the subject computer such as system layout, file structures, data and authorship information, documentation of any data manipulation, and any other relevant computer system information manipulation.

TRADITIONAL PROBLEMS IN COMPUTER INVESTIGATIONS

The ability to retrieve electronic data is increasingly important in both criminal and civil investigations. Electronic data recovery should not be

---

Who Benefits from Forensic Computer Science?

Prosecutors—a variety of crime where incriminating documents can be found, ranging from homicide to financial fraud to child pornography.

Civil litigators—personal and business records which relate to fraud, divorce, discrimination, and harassment.

Insurance companies—mitigate costs by using discovered computer evidence of possible fraud in accident, arson, and workman's comp cases.

Corporations—ascertain evidence relating to sexual harassment, embezzlement, theft, or misappropriation of trade secrets and other internal/confidential information.

Law enforcement officials—for pre-search warrant preparations and post-seizure handling of computer equipment.

Individuals—support of claims of wrongful termination, sexual harassment, or age discrimination.

Encryption—A New Nightmare for Investigators

Recent paranoia about government intrusion fanned by civil libertarians has increased many computer users' awareness of data security. As such, many are now employing **encryption** technology, both manual and automated. The possibilities for manual encryption are virtually endless. For example, users can encrypt their own data by simply adding or subtracting a constant in hexadecimal mode or by switching nibbles (i.e., splitting bytes down the middle and transposing the two). Luckily, most users are either unaware of such potential or are too lazy. Thus, they often rely on encryption options found within many popular software packages, such as WordPerfect™, Excel™, Lotus™, Microsoft Word™ and PKZIP™ files. Subsequent files, relying on algorithmic computations, *may* be defeated with forensic packages. However, some users employ more sophisticated encryption strategies, such as *BestCrypt*™ and *PGP*™, which may store passwords of up to 128 characters!

BestCrypt™, a popular program among pornographers, uses Blowfish, Twofish, and Gost2814789 encryption (256 bit) to encrypt the entire drive and may prove impenetrable through traditional methods. In addition, this program, and others like it, also has a variety of options quite detrimental to computer investigations, including: (1) hot keys—all virtual drives automatically close if hot key combination is pressed; (2) timeout option—all virtual drives close automatically after a specified period of inactivity; and (3) container guard—prevents the users from accidentally deleting encrypted containers. In addition, this particular program allows users to employ their own encryption algorithms, making it virtually impossible for investigators to manually crack.

reserved for instances where the instrumentality of computer technology has been demonstrated. In fact, digital evidence has been utilized in cases ranging from homicide to software piracy. However, the importance of computer forensic capabilities has not been universally recognized, and is, in fact, in debate in departments across the country. Traditionally, this reluctance was attributed to *cyberphobia*, or the fear of new technology. Such fear of innovation is consistent with, but not unique to, the police subculture or its administration. Indeed, administrators across the world experience sedentary apathy (i.e., atrophy), and are hesitant to employ new technologies. In addition, law enforcement administrators, grappling with the emerging socio-legal culture of political correctness and multiculturalism, express dissatisfaction with the changing nature of police work and perceive computer forensics as unnecessary constraints on budgets already stretched to the limit.

Inadequate Resources

The lack of adequate resources necessary for the procurement of forensic software and training is not alien to state and local agencies. Long characterized by dwindling budgets and increased responsibilities, local police agencies have been forced to compete amongst themselves for the proverbial scraps thrown from state and federal tables. As expected, small or rural agencies lack the competitive edge present in larger, more sophisticated agencies, which often have individuals or units assigned exclusively to grant writing. Although not equivalent to rocket science, the successful preparation and submission of grant proposals does require a certain knack. Such idiosyncrasies are often discussed at annual meetings which small agencies fail to attend due to lack of resources. Thus, the vicious cycle continues whereby the least equipped agencies are the least able to secure external funding for necessary equipment or training. Even those agencies currently favored by funding entities struggle to justify the exponential costs associated with computer forensics.

As the forensic analysis of computer technology becomes *en vogue* across the country, training programs have increasingly targeted large, well-funded corporate entities. Although most reserve a selected number of seats and offer "discounts" to law enforcement officers, many are still priced outside the resources of the law enforcement community, routinely garnishing as much as $2,000 per person (e.g., NTI—New Technologies, Inc.; Litton/TASC; etc.) and providing individualized, renewable licenses. In an effort to combat disproportionate opportunities and the rising cost of training, federal agencies such as the Federal Bureau of Investigation (FBI) and the Federal Law Enforcement Training Center (FLETC) have developed similar courses. Ostensibly, these courses are "free" to qualified law enforcement personnel. However, the number of attendees is limited, and certain organizations appear to receive preferential treatment. Even those programs which do not display bureaucratic nepotism often lack significant representation of smaller agencies. In fact, many agencies are unable to avail themselves of the "free" training often found at the federal level as they cannot afford the loss of personnel (e.g., one person from a ten-person

With funds generated from state and federal grants. South Carolina's State Law Enforcement Division (SLED) was able to secure a new facility for their computer crime unit and purchase new equipment. Unfortunately, this is not the norm in many agencies. (*Courtesy of SLED*)

department represents 10 percent of their entire organization!). However, the creation of non-profit training and research centers (e.g., the National White Collar Crime Center (NW3C)) is a step in the right direction.

Lack of Communication and Cooperation among Agencies

Because of the competition inherent among local governments, law enforcement has long been typified by a lack of cooperation and communication between bordering agencies. Although agencies have often been forced to develop formal partnerships by legislative entities threatening to withhold allocated financing, such shotgun alliances have not been characterized by spirited collaboration. Rather, these relationships may be likened to arranged marriages, with neither party entirely fulfilled but both sedated with counterproductive complacency. Fortunately, computer forensic professionals have overcome jurisdictional competition, developing listservs and practitioner associations (e.g., HTCIA, IACIS, etc.) which share information and encourage cooperation among investigators.

Overreliance on Automated Programs and Self-Proclaimed Experts

The lack of resources and the flux of technology coupled with technological ignorance have resulted in an overemphasis on automated recovery programs and self-proclaimed experts. As we will discuss later, automated forensic programs are essential tools in a computer crime fighter's toolbox and are extremely useful in routine investigations. However, they are not the end-all, be-all to computer forensic science. In fact, the familiarity and utilization of automated programs may result in a situation where investigators know just enough to make them potentially hazardous to the very investigation to which they are dedicated. Couple this with their informal anointment as "departmental computer expert" and a situation dangerous to litigation erupts. Fortunately for law enforcement, defense attorneys have accepted such "expertise" at face value, but this trend is sure to evaporate.

Lack of Reporting

Although rarely impeached in judicial proceedings, the expertise of law enforcement personnel is often challenged privately. Perceived largely as incompetent, law enforcement officials have unsuccessfully encouraged victims of computer-related crime to report their victimization. Such perceptions have only been exacerbated by corporate advisors who routinely discourage formal notification. Rosenblatt,[1] for example, argues that "victims should not report a case to law enforcement unless they are willing to cooperate in subsequent prosecution" and advises clients to contact local authorities prior to invoking federal powers as they are more malleable. Strongly suggesting that local agencies are more appropriately situated to investigate business computer cases, he warns that federal entities "will not investigate cases which do not involve large losses."[2] Unfortunately, such advice is speculative at best. Anecdotal evidence suggests that local law enforcement is grossly lacking in adequate resources. Thus, even the most dedicated of agencies may lack the necessary wherewithal to properly conduct such investigations. Further admonitions contained therein suggest that Rosenblatt's book is only appropriate for self-serving corporate interests and may, in fact, be counterproductive, if not blatantly detrimental, to formal criminal inquiries.

Evidence Corruption

As a result of the problems discussed above, many computer investigations have been conducted in a less than perfect manner. Often relying on officers versed in popular software programs being identified as "departmental computer experts" or non-sworn computer "experts" whose primary role is to identify all obvious files on a hard drive, many

cases have been lost before they even got to court. Unfortunately, these investigators do not adequately understand computer structure, and the civilian "experts" do not understand nor appreciate the legal complexities of evidence preservation and custodial documentation (i.e., investigators are evidence-oriented and computer specialists are computer-oriented).

Thus, evidence is often overlooked, corrupted, or destroyed entirely. Some networked computers, for example, have been seized and simply disconnected without saving dialogue or documenting configuration, resulting in an inability by the investigator to reconfigure a seized system in court (may overcome this by using a "fox and hound" cable locator). Other cases have been lost by a failure to search hidden files or slack space. Thus, it is essential that recognized standards of forensic computer science be developed through the interaction of LE and the corporate community. In the interim, all investigations should be conducted in keeping with the three cardinal rules of computer forensic science: (1) always work from an image; (2) document, document, document; and (3) maintain the chain of custody.

● COMPUTER FORENSIC SCIENCE AND DISK STRUCTURE

Traditional problems associated with the investigation of computer-related crime notwithstanding, computer forensic science can only be initiated by individuals with at least a basic understanding of computer structure.[3] Although few users intellectualize the contents and layout of their computer system, investigators must be aware of both the physical and the logical

---

Three Cardinal Rules of Computer Investigations

1. Always work from an image, leaving the original intact.

2. Document, document, document.

3. Maintain the chain of custody.

Tracks, Cylinders, and Sectors

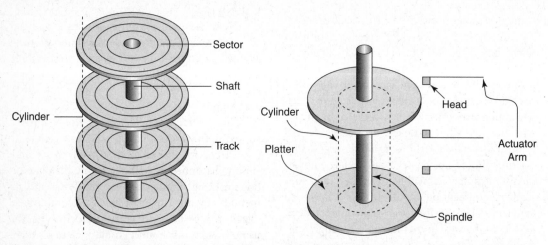

Illustration of a Cylinder: Physically, a drive is usually composed of a number of rotating platters. Each platter is divided concentrically into tracks. In turn, tracks are divided into sectors, which are further divided into bytes. Finally, read/write heads are contained on either side of the platters.

Head—Each platter has one head per side. These heads are very close to the surface of the platter, and allow reading of and writing to the platter. Heads are numbered sequentially from zero.

Tracks—the concentric bands dividing each platter. Tracks are numbered sequentially beginning with zero.

Cylinder—the set of tracks located in the same position on every platter in the same head position. Unlike physical disk units, cylinders are intangible units. Simply put, they are a cross-section of a disk. (Imagine using a hole puncher on a perfectly positioned stack of paper. The resulting hole would be a visible representation of an empty sector.) Each double-sided floppy has two tracks. The same track is on all stacked platters. The set of corresponding tracks on a magnetic disk that lie the same distance from the disk's edge. Taken together, these tracks from a cylindrical shape. For a hard drive, a cylinder usually includes several tracks on each side of each disk platter.

structure, disk management, and memory storage. In a most basic sense, computers are comprised of three primary components: hardware, software, and firmware.[4]

A *computer* may be defined as a device capable of storing, transmitting, or manipulating data through mathematical and logical processes or operations.[5] *Static memory* is that area on hard and/or floppy disks in which data and programs are stored, while *volatile memory* is that area of a computer which holds data during processing and is erased when power is shut down. *Semi-permanent storage* refers to that area of a disk that is not dependent upon a power source for its continued maintenance and which may be changed under the appropriate operating conditions (i.e., storage devices, floppy and fixed disks, magnetic tapes, etc.). This area is where the majority of the work and storage is conducted and where most processed data is stored. Thus, it is extremely important in computer forensics. *Computer storage* is the holding of data in an electromagnetic form for access by a computer processor. *Primary storage* is data in RAM and other built-in devices. *Secondary storage* is data on hard disks, tapes, and other external devices. *Floppy disks* or *diskettes* are single circular disks with concentric tracks that are turned by spindles under one or more heads. *CD-ROMs* have a single track, spiraling from the disk edge toward the center, which may only be written to once (CDs write data from the *center* out, and music from the *outside* in), while *CD-RWs* act as traditional disk drives which may be written to more than once. *Hard/fixed disks* are one or more disks comprised of one or more heads which are often fixed inside a sealed enclosure (may have

Ram vs. Rom—Computer Memory

Random Access Memory (RAM) is that volatile memory which is used to store programs and data that are being accessed by the user. Also referred to as *main memory*, data contained in RAM is lost when computers are powered down. Traditionally reserved for hard drives, RAM is now found in other computer hardware like printers to allow storage and formatting of pages queued for printing so that other computer functions are not delayed.

Read-Only Memory (ROM) is that memory built into the operating system which can be accessed, but not altered, such as that which contains programs necessary for the booting process.

more than two sides if the disk consists of more than one platter).

Disk Structure and Data Storage

On all disks in DOS-based systems, certain structural rules exist in which physical drives are loaded first, logical drives second, and drivers third. **Physical drives** refer to devices and data at the electronic or machine level, while **logical drives** (most important in computer forensics) are allocated parts of a physical drive that are designated and managed as independent units.

The smallest forms of data storage are represented by *binary digits* or **bits**. Based on a principle of two, bits may be likened to on/off switches. Collections of bits are interpreted by the computer and are reported to users as characters, words, etc. and are basically transformed into a format most appropriate for non-mechanical, human consumption. In essence, this process identifies a standard association between particular binary patterns and characters so that compatibility between systems and system components are ensured. The most common set of associations is the *American Standard Code for Information Interchange* or ***ASCII***. This code defines characters for the first 128 binary values (i.e., 0 to 127). The first 32 of these are used as non-printing control characters that are designed to control data communications equipment and computer printers and displays.[6] Extended ASCII code has since been developed by IBM and provides particular character symbols to binary values 128 through 255.[7]

Computers interpret data in a variety of ways. In a **binary system**, interpretative rules are associated with a base of two with integers represented by zeroes and ones. In a **hexadecimal system**, on the other hand, interpretative rules are associated with a base of 16 with integers ranging from 0 to 9 and A to F. In a binary system, the range of whole numbers that can be represented by a single byte is 0 to 255.

Storage Equivalence

Techno Terms			Visual Comparison
Nibble	= 1/2 a byte	= 4 bits	A single character
Byte	= 1 byte	= 8 bits	
	= 2 bytes	= 16 bits	A word
Double Word	= 4 bytes	= 32 bits	
Kilobyte	= 1,024 bytes	= 2^{10} bytes	1,000 characters; One-half page of text
Megabyte	= 1,048,576 bytes	= 2^{20} bytes	Small novel; 5 MB— Shakespeare's work
Gigabyte	= 1,073,741,823 bytes	= 2^{30} bytes	Truck full of paper
Terabyte	= 1,099,511,627,776 bytes	= 2^{40} bytes	10 TB—Library of Congress

Thus, it is often necessary to use two bytes to represent whole numbers, and four bytes where *greater* levels of precision are required.[8] Hexadecimal interpretations provide data analysts with a more compact method of listing and evaluating long binary sequences, as the interpretative scheme has a base of 16 and 16 digit symbols. Investigators should routinely evaluate files with a hexadecimal viewer, as some programs (Microsoft products, in particular) reuse memory blocks without modification. Although this does not allow viewing of these blocks in normal mode, hexadecimal views may reveal the content of these blocks.

Irrespective of interpretative scheme, data is stored in disks in fixed units. *Sectors,* the smallest physical storage unit on a disk, are arc-shaped portions of one of the disk tracks. Although the operating system determines the size of each sector, magnetic disks formatted for U.S. versions of Windows contain a standard 512 bytes. Beginning at 1, sectors are numbered sequentially on a track-by-track basis. *Clusters,* also known as *file allocation units,* are comprised of one or more adjacent sectors and represent the basic allocation units of magnetic disk storage. Although size varies with disk size, clusters represent the minimum space allocated to an individual *file* in DOS. Basically,

clusters make it easier for operating systems to manage files, although some allocated space remains unused in most cases. (Remember: space is allocated to files in specified units. Thus, a file will always be allocated at least one cluster even if it is only nine bytes.) Files, composed of one or more clusters, are the smallest unit that enables distinguishing one set of data from another and may be looked at logically or physically for forensic purposes. The *logical file size,* for example, refers to the exact size of a file in bytes. In contrast, the *physical file size* refers to the actual amount of space that the file occupies on a disk. Such distinction is necessary in comprehensive investigations as it allows for the discovery of information found within that portion of unused space between the *logical end of a file* and the *physical end of a cluster* (i.e., file slack). (Although this concept may seem complex, it may be likened to a table in a restaurant in which a couple is seated at a table for four. Although the extra two chairs are empty, they constructively belong to those individuals until they are finished with their meal.) For example, two clusters will be allocated for a physical file of 2016 bytes. The excess space, or file slack,[9] may contain the remnants of older files or other evidence, including passwords, old directory structures, or miscellaneous information

Base Casting

Spindle

Slider (and Head)

Actuator Arm

Actuator Axis

Actuator

Cover Mounting Holes (Cover not shown)

Case Mounting Holes

Platters

Ribbon Cable (attaches heads to Logic Board)

SCSI Interface Connector

Jumper Pins

Jumper

Power Connector

Tape Seal

(Pearson education/PH College)

stored in memory. (This is extremely important for investigative purposes, as most individuals who intentionally delete files in the hopes of hiding them from investigators do not realize that these remnants may include critical evidence.) *Compressed files* are those files which have been algorithmically compressed to save space.

The next level of data storage on a hard drive is known as a *partition*. Disk partitions are portions of fixed disks that the operating system identifies as a single unit (maximum of four). Letter designations are given to these entities that can be formatted for different file and operating systems. To increase the system's fault tolerance or speed file access, Windows NT and other operating systems may treat multiple partitions on different physical disk drives as a single disk volume (identified by a single drive letter). Every bootable hard disk includes one disk partition for any operating system it stores that may be used to start the computer. To allow the operating system to treat a single hard disk as multiple logical disks, the hard disk may have an "extended partition" that can be subdivided into a maximum of 23 additional logical disks. In other words, every hard disk drive has a primary partition or extended partitions, with one requirement. The partition of the "boot" drive where the operating system resides *must* be bootable. (Programs like Microsoft's FDISK or Norton's GDISK prepare a hard disk for use by creating partitions and logical disks. Partitioning creates a master boot record and **partition table** for the hard disk. Floppy disks do not require partitioning.)

Data Location

Once investigators can articulate the structure of fixed disk and identify the units of data, it is necessary to understand how to locate specific data contained therein for forensic purposes. On DOS-based systems, *File Allocation Tables* (**FAT**) are especially important in this respect as they provide the mechanism for data configuration on a given medium. (This is not the same housekeeping strategy as NTFS under NT.) Generally speaking, the FAT is the system used to identify and locate files on a disk. The 12-, 16-, and 32-bit designations used by DOS indicate how many bits the FAT uses to identify where on the disk (appropriate cluster numbers) a file resides. Literally speaking, every number contained within the FAT identifies a particular cluster. Information contained therein identifies: if the cluster is "bad" or available; if the end of a file is contained within; and points to the next cluster attached to a file. Originally created to manage space on floppies (FAT12), the system was later extended to manage fixed/hard disks with FAT16 and was employed in DOS and older Windows systems. However, the system proved to be cumbersome and failed to manage data economically. (As an example, if a partition size was 2GB, each cluster would be 32KB. Thus, a file requiring 4KB would result in 28KB of slack space (32KB − 4KB = 28KB)). To remedy this waste, FAT32 was developed. Currently in use by most Microsoft products, except Windows NTFS, FAT32 is a more robust system which manages space more efficiently by utilizing smaller cluster sizes. Thus, less space is wasted, making data management faster and more efficient. (Unfortunately, this is bad news for investigators, because it reduces the slack space in which evidence is often found.) Generally speaking, the emergence of FAT32 is advantageous to users in two primary areas: (1) FAT32 systems can reallocate and change the size of the root directory; (2) FAT32 drives contain a copy of the boot record(s), which may make the system less prone to failure. There is no limit as to how large the root directory can be or where it can be located.

Partition Table

Like the FAT, the partition table describes every logical volume on a disk. In addition, it identifies corresponding locations, indicates which partition is bootable (only one partition may be bootable at a time), and contains the MBR. Traditionally standard, newly improved software packages (e.g., Partition Magic, etc.) enable the manipulation of partition by even the least sophisticated user. This knowledge is extremely important in forensic

Master Boot Sector/Record/Parition Table[10]

Master Boot Record (MBR)[11]

When you turn on your PC, the processor has to begin processing. However, your system memory is empty, and the processor doesn't have anything to execute or really even know where it is. To ensure that the PC can always boot regardless of which BIOS is in the machine, chip makers and BIOS manufacturers arrange so that the processor, once turned on, always starts executing at the same place, FFFF0h.

In a similar manner, every hard disk must have a consistent "starting point" where key information is stored about the disk, such as how many partitions it has, what sort of partitions they are, etc. There also needs to be somewhere that the BIOS can load the *initial boot program* that starts the process of loading the operating system. The place where this information is stored is called the **master boot record (MBR)**. It is also sometimes called the *master boot sector* or even just the boot sector. (The master boot sector should not be confused with *volume boot sectors*, which are different.)

The master boot record is always located at cylinder 0, head 0, and sector 1, the first sector on the disk. This is the consistent "starting point" that the disk always uses. When the BIOS boots the machine, it will look here for instructions and information on how to boot the disk and load the operating system. The MBR contains the following structures:

Master Partition Table: This small table contains the descriptions of the partitions that are contained on the hard disk. There is only room in the master partition table for the information describing four partitions. Therefore, a hard disk can have only four true partitions, also called primary partitions. Any additional partitions are logical partitions that are linked to one of the primary partitions. One of the partitions is marked as active, indicating that it is the one that the computer should use for booting up.

Master Boot Code: The MBR contains the small initial boot program that the BIOS loads and executes to start the boot process. This program eventually transfers control to the boot program stored on whichever partition is used for booting the PC.

investigations, as it enables users to hide entire partitions. Investigators unaware of this fact may be confused to see that the logical drive size is contrary to identified characteristics. Partition data is stored at physical cylinder = 0; head = 0; sector = 1.

Data Management—Operating Instructions

The **boot sector** of a computer is located at the very first sector of the physical disk or *absolute sector 0*. (Under WIN98, there are actually three boot sectors making up the entity.) It contains code that enables the computer to find the partition table and the operating system (Similarly, the first sector of every partition is referred to as the *partition boot sector*.) The **Basic Input/Output System (BIOS)** is a number of machine code routines stored in ROM which includes various commands including those necessary for reading physical disks by sector. These commands are executed upon system booting. The first of these to be executed is referred to as the *bootstrap loader*.

Boot Up Sequence of a Computer (Ibm Clone)

1. ROM/BIOS
2. POST
3. Switches or CMOS data
4. Pathway or drive specifications—normally A: then C:
5. Master Boot Record ({Cyl = 0, Head = 0, Sec = 1)
6. Bootable Partition
7. Boot Record
8. Io.sys
9. DBLSPACE.BIN
10. MSDOS.SYS
11. CONFIG.SYS (optional)
12. COMMAND.COM (shell command in config.sys may change this)
13. *AUTOEXEC.*BAT (optional)

Data Integrity

Files may also be identified by a computer-generated (i.e., calculated) value known as a **cyclical redundancy checksum (CRC)**. This is especially important for forensic investigators as images may be validated by comparing the original CRC value with the imaged files. This process, initiated when data has been transmitted between computers, involves computer calculation on the data transmitted. Upon receipt of the data, an identical computation by the receiving computer is conducted. If the calculations reach different conclusions, the receiving computer will request the retransmission of data. This process may also be utilized on all storage media on which compressed data is stored. This verification process is especially important in criminal cases where validity of evidence is contestable.

MD5 Hash—Like the CRC discussed above, the MD5 Hash is a verification tool which may be employed in computer investigations. Developed by RSA, this 128-bit number is an identifier which acts as the equivalent of digital DNA. The odds that two different files have the same value are 2^{128}. Some forensic tools have utilities which search for particular files by hashes. **HashKeeper**™, a program developed by the NDIC (National Drug Intelligence Center), keeps a listing of various known files. Investigators should develop their own hash files for their toolboxes. Keep in mind, investigators are usually interested most in the *unknown*. Thus, any mechanism which allows

investigators to reduce the number of files for evaluation is a godsend.

● DEVELOPING COMPUTER FORENSIC SCIENCE CAPABILITIES

Now that we have identified some of the very basic components and terms associated with disk structure, we must now identify the procedures, policies, and practices that constitute the development of an effective forensic computer science unit within a department. Like other units found within law enforcement agencies, the development and regular review of **standard operating procedures** (SOP) are essential as technology changes. As recommended by the IOCE (International Organization on Digital Evidence), these SOP should be reviewed annually due to the changing nature of technology. This ensures that personnel, training, equipment, and procedures continue to be appropriate and effective. In addition, these SOP should be consistent with current scientific knowledge in order to emphasize validity and reliability.

The IOCE also suggests that these SOP should be clearly articulated and readily available. They include recommendations for discussing appropriate software, hardware, and specific investigative procedures. However, some experts argue that such formalization may

---

MD5 Hash as a Verification Tool

Although there are an infinite number of files which may be created and stored on any given system, there are only a finite number of hash values available. Thus, it has been argued by some defense attorneys that the dawning of increasingly sophisticated machines will eventually lead to the creation of two disparate files with the same generated hash value. However, Brian Deering (NDIC) analogizes the chance of randomly generated matching hash values to hitting the Pennsylvania Lottery Super 6, 5.582×10^{41} (or 558,205 billion, billion, billion, billion) times before this will occur. Thus, it does seem *computationally infeasible to produce two messages having the same message digest.*

Source: http://theory.lcs.mit.edu/~rivest/Rivest-MD5.txt.

be dangerous and that written procedures may be subpoenaed and thus hazardous to law enforcement investigations. Therefore, administrators must exercise caution in the preparation of such procedures. Every conceivable deviation or such should be documented—and language should be as flexible as possible. (Remember: Every crime scene and criminal investigator is different. Thus, data recovery tools, data capture tools, data duplication tools, and data analysis tools may vary for every investigation.) Such a plan should address the development of a computer laboratory, pre-search routines, crime-scene procedures, and evidence analysis. Although most departments do not have the resources to assemble state-of-the-art facilities and a full-time investigative team, a "barebones" laboratory with the appropriate computer hardware, software, and storage capabilities should be developed as soon as possible, as it is literally impossible to successfully prosecute computer-related crime without proper analysis and custodial accountability. However, such development is often overlooked, because many departments have tended to focus on quick fixes, collecting digital evidence with no consideration of analysis capabilities or legal ramifications surrounding improperly handled data.

While perfect departments in perfect worlds would immediately assemble the best

(and most expensive) equipment and a library of software to rival Microsoft, law enforcement agencies across the United States are not privileged with this luxury. As such, the following categories are not intended to be concrete—in fact, they are intended to represent the minimum requirements for an effective and efficient computer crime unit. In the software section, for example, readers should be aware that there are various other tools available to computer crime investigators. Those discussed in the text are those that have been widely accepted in the field unless otherwise noted. Such discussion is not intended to serve as an endorsement for particular products. In fact, investigators should test all equipment and software for themselves, as they will be required to testify as to their validity and reliability in court.

The importance of such validation cannot be overstated as past experience reveals that many investigators do not know the entire functionality of the software that they employ to recover data, proving immediately fatal to courtroom examination. In addition, the software programs discussed in this text are primarily reserved for forensic analysis of hard drives or removable media. Network analysis is outside the scope of this text. (It must be noted that complete forensic laboratories should also include a multitude of network-specific software for

Choosing Appropriate Tools

Unfortunately, there is no magic formula for success in computer forensics. Information contained within affidavits, warrant parameters, number of personnel, and investigative tools will vary widely based on case characteristics. As such, forensic toolkits should be specifically tailored to individual searches or seizures. At a minimum, the following factors must be considered in the development of investigative approaches:

- Type of suspect device
- Type of suspect operating system

- Type of software applications employed by suspect device
- Type of hardware platforms characterizing suspect device
- Application of appropriate domestic and international law
- Potential negative repercussions (i.e., liability, public concern, or bad publicity).

ongoing investigations. Such software should be capable of tracing connections, identifying ISPs, pinging specific IP addresses, and the like.)

MINIMUM HOUSING REQUIREMENTS

The first step in the development of computer forensic capabilities is the construction of a computer laboratory. As with other areas in which forensic analysis is conducted, the allocation of private space that is forensically friendly is extremely important. Investigators should attempt to identify (and articulate) an environment that is comfortable to investigators, equipment, and evidence, alike. Once identified, investigators then face the daunting task of acquiring such space from chief executives. Investigators should concentrate their justifications on the necessity of protecting the expensive nature of the materials to be housed therein and emphasize the vulnerability of electronic equipment. As always, justification arguments should concentrate on areas most important to the chief. One investigator, for example, successfully received the necessary space by arguing that the nature of the work (i.e., pornography, child exploitation, etc.) required privacy to preclude the possibility of litigious activity by coworkers offended (or possibly "sexually harassed") by such exposure. (It appears that the chief in this particular case did not want to knowingly create a potentially "hostile" work environment.) By focusing on the bottom line, like the potential expenses associated with replacing damaged components and defending sexual harassment cases, arguments may prove more persuasive to chiefs concerned with dwindling resources.

Investigators should identify the minimum spatial requirements for evidence storage as well as analysis, bearing in mind the sluggish nature of the criminal justice system. Such space should be privately contained and environmentally appropriate, free from dust, debris, corrosive materials, electronic hazards, and extreme temperatures. (Remember: the evidentiary value of computers in traditional evidence rooms has been inadvertently destroyed by carelessness, dust, or unhealthy climatic conditions.) Cipher combination locks should be obtained to properly secure the area, as the absence of controlled entry may result in chain-of-custody challenges. Evidence storage areas should be additionally secured and include fireproof housing. Both areas should include heavy construction metal shelving for the placement of evidence and bookshelves for the number of manuals and documentary evidence associated with computer-related crime. As in traditional laboratories, appropriate work areas should be established with well-built tables and ergonomically designed adjustable chairs. (This is critical in forensic computer laboratories as the vast majority of analysis is conducted from a seated position.) In addition, all areas of containment should be climate-controlled for temperature and moisture, providing a comfortable workspace for investigators and non-destructive environment for evidence.

Minimum Housing Requirements

1. Cipher combination locks
2. High-security combination safe
3. Heavy construction metal shelving for evidence
4. Bookshelves
5. Work areas including tables
6. Ergonomically designed adjustable-height chair
7. Long-term storage capability
8. Environmentally controlled work and storage space

Like other sorts of criminal evidence, computer components and data should be kept under lock and key to maintain the integrity of the evidence in question. Such locks, like the one pictured here, prevent unauthorized access and may negate chain of custody challenges. (*Courtesy of SLED*)

MINIMUM HARDWARE REQUIREMENTS

Although the acquisition of computer hardware has become more reasonable in recent years, investigators should bear in mind that technology is changing at an alarming rate. Thus, any purchase could become obsolete in a relatively short period of time. As such, the acquisition of said equipment should be characterized by both parsimony and prescience, reserving some funds (whenever feasible) for the future. At the same time, lab architects should acquire as much forensic equipment as possible. As most local agencies will have to focus on widely available and most digestible (i.e., translatable across diverse backgrounds of personnel) software, they are all based on Windows.[12] Below

are some examples of various systems, ranging from the bare bones to the ideal[13]:

Basic Lab System (bare bones laboratory sufficient for small work loads but not preferred)

- **Processor Speed:**   3 GHz
- **Memory:**   1 GB
- **Network:**   Gigabit Network Card
- **I/O Interfaces:**   USB 2.0, Serial, Parallel
- **Flash Media Readers:**   Multi-Reader
- **Optical Drive:**   Dual Layer DVD +/− RW Drive
- **OS Drive:**   ATA 7200 RPM

- **SCSI card:** Adaptec 2940 UW
- **Evidence Storage Drive:** ATA 7200 RPM
- **Operating System:** Windows XP Professional
- **Display:** Single 17" or 19" CRT or LCD
- **Uninterruptible Power Supply:** 650 VA
- **Write Blocker:** None (Use DOS or LinEn)
- **Scanner:** None
- **Printer:** Monochrome Laser Printer
- **Evidence Backup:** Blank DVDs

Better Lab System (a step-up from bare bones, but still only designed for single-tasking workloads)

- **Processor Speed:** 3.8 GHz Hyper-Threading/Dual Core
- **Memory:** 2 GB
- **Network:** Gigabit Network Card
- **I/O Interfaces:** Firewire (400 & 800), USB 2.0, Parallel, Serial
- **Flash Media Readers:** Multi-Reader
- **Optical Drive:** Dual Layer DVD +/– RW Drive
- **OS Drive:** SATA 10k RPM
- **SCSI Card:** Adaptec 29160
- **Evidence Storage Drive:** ATA RAID 7200/10k RPM
- **Operating System:** Windows XP Professional or Windows 2003 Server
- **Display:** Single or Dual 19" CRT or LCD
- **Uninterruptible Power Supply:** 1000 VA
- **Write Blocker:** FastBloc2 LE and FastBloc SE

- **Scanner:** none
- **Printer:** Monochrome Laser Printer
- **Evidence Backup:** Western Digital Caviar RE Hard Drives

Power Lab System (capable of handling larger workloads simultaneously)

- **Processor Speed:** Dual EM64T Xeon or Dual Core Athalon 64 × 2
- **Memory:** 3 GB (With 3/GB Switch in boot.ini)
- **Network:** Gigabit Network Card
- **I/O Interfaces:** Firewire (400 & 800), USB 2.0, Parallel
- **Flash Media Readers:** Multi-Reader
- **Optical Drive:** Dual Layer DVD +/– RW Drive
- **OS Drive:** U320 LVD SCSI 15k RPM
- **SCSI Card:** Adaptec 29160
- **Evidence Storage Drive:** ATA/SATA RAID-5 Array, 7200 RPM
- **Operating System:** Windows 2003 Server
- **Display:** Dual 19" LCD or CRT
- **Uninterruptible Power Supply:** 1000 VA
- **Write Blocker:** FastBloc2 LE, FastBloc 2 FE & Adaptor Kit, FastBloc SE
- **Scanner:** Color Scanner
- **Printer:** Color Laser Printer
- **Evidence Backup:** LTO Tape Backup

Dream Lab System:

- **Processor Speed:** Quad Xeon or Quad, Dual-Core Opterons
- **Memory:** 4+ GB
- **Network:** Gigabit Network Card
- **I/O Interfaces:** Firewire (400 & 800), USB 2.0, parallel
- **Flash Media Readers:** multi-reader
- **Optical Drive:** Dual Layer DVD +/– RW
- **OS Drive:** U320 LVD SCSI 15k RPM
- **Page file Drive:** Separate U320 LVD SCSI 15k RPM
- **SCSI Card:** Adaptec 39160
- **Evidence Storage Drive:** SCSI RAID-5 Array comprised of 10k or 15k RPM SCSI Drives
- **Operating System:** Windows 2003 Enterprise Edition
- **Display:** Triple 19" LCD or single 42" Plasma
- **Uninterruptible Power Supply:** 1500 VA
- **Write Blocker:** FastBloc2 LE, FastBloc 2 FE & Adaptor Kit, FastBloc SE
- **Scanner:** Color Scanner
- **Printer:** Color Laser Printer
- **Evidence Backup:** SDLT Tape Backup
- **Optical Autoloader:** Rimage DVD creation system

Basic Field System (sufficient for small workloads)

- **Type of Computer:** laptop
- **Processor Speed:** 2 GHz "Mobile" Processor
- **Memory:** 2 GB+
- **Network:** Gigabit Network Card
- **I/O Interfaces:** Firewire (400 & 800), USB 2.0, Parallel
- **Optical Drive:** CD+/– RW Drive
- **OS and Data Drive:** ATA 5400 RPM
- **Operating System:** Windows XP Professional
- **Write Blocker:** FastBloc2 FE & Adaptor Kit, FastBloc SE Wiebetech Forensic SCSIDock

Dream Field System (sufficient for very large workloads)

- **Type of Computer:** laptop
- **Processor Speed:** 3.8 GHz+
- **Memory:** 2 GB+
- **Network:** Gigabit Network Card
- **I/O Interfaces:** Firewire (400 & 800), USB 2.0, Parallel
- **Optical Drive:** Dual Layer DVD +/– RW Drive
- **OS Drive:** SATA 7200RPM
- **Evidence Storage Drive:** Lacie External 1TB Firewire 800 Enclosure
- **Operating System:** Windows XP Professional or Windows 2003 Server

- **Write Blocker:** FastBloc2 FE & Adaptor Kit, FastBloc SE Wiebetech Forensic SCSI Dock
- **Battery:** High Capacity Spare Battery

EXTRA SUPPLIES

2.5" ←> 3.5" laptop hard drive adapters
1.8" ←> 3.5" micro hard drive adapters
68 pin ←> 50 pin SCSI adapters
80 pin SCA ←> 68 pin SCSI adapters
IDE ←> SATA adapters
Molex Power ←> SATA drive power adapters
IDE Zip Drive
Blank media for archival purposes
Tool kits
Spare 400-wire and 80-wire HDD cables
Spare SATA HDD cables
Spare computer power supplies
Spare computer fans

Whenever possible, investigators should secure funding for digital cameras. (*Courtesy of SLED*)

Spare, wiped hard drives (various sizes and manufacturers)
Spare fastbloc
Spare crossover cables
Spare laptop batteries
Spare PCMCIA/PC Card NIC's

● MINIMUM SOFTWARE REQUIREMENTS[14]

As mentioned previously, the identification and analysis of digital evidence poses unique challenges to traditional investigators. Discovery of such information is extremely important for successful case disposition. Although hardware provides the necessary framework for data acquisition and analysis, it is ineffective without corresponding forensic software. (Remember: individual investigators should test all software which they employ to enhance their credibility in court and to ensure that there will be no surprises.) Generally speaking, there are five broad categories of software tools necessary to equip a barebones laboratory:

1. **Data preservation**, duplication, and **verification** tools
2. Data recovery/extraction tools
3. Data analysis tools
4. Data reporting tools
5. Network utilities

Data Preservation, Duplication, and Verification Tools

Traditionally, suspect drives and disks were copied at the directory level. In fact, this practice is still utilized in the private sector by some IT personnel. However, this procedure lacks forensic robustness, as it only captures recognized files, ignoring fragments of information that may be found in deleted files and slack space. **Imaging** programs are designed to correct this fault by providing a bitstream image of the suspect drive,

Boot Disks

Literally speaking, **booting a computer** simply means to pull a computer up by its bootstraps or more succinctly to load a computer's operating system (OS). Prior to loading the operating system, a computer is largely unusable by most people. The operating system provides the medium for users and application software to communicate or interact. Most users do not know that a **power-on self-test** (**POST**), initiated when the power supply is activated, is located in the read-only memory (ROM) of every computer. This test, which is relatively quick on most computers (increasingly so as computer capabilities are enhanced), ascertains the peripherals attached to a given system. These peripherals include all drives (floppy and hard), video hardware, memory, keyboard, mouse, modem, scanners, printers, etc. Once completed, this program informs the computer where to load the operating system from. Depending on system configuration, the computer then "looks" for the OS (aka *boot sequence*). On many systems, the computer first checks the floppy drive for this information. If not found, the computer then looks for it on the hard drive.

Many computers allow users to change the boot sequence, enabling users to specify the hard drive or CD-ROM, bypassing the floppy. This is especially popular with computer-savvy criminals. Knowing that information contained in the swap file is only changed when traditional booting occurs, they may intentionally reconfigure their system, making it harder to boot from a floppy. In addition, such individuals may manipulate *command.com* in order to circumvent investigations. Traditionally, this type of information was critical in the prevention of data destruction. However, automated programs with Windows platforms have made boot disks largely obsolete. They are still used in non-Windows environments.

bit-for-bit, byte-for-byte. It enables investigators to perfectly duplicate a suspect drive onto a form of removable media (type of media will vary based on the spatial characteristics of the suspect drive). This is essential for courtroom purposes. Investigators should *always* work from an image, preserving the original evidence. This counters many defense challenges and negates the possibility of data destruction or manipulation (both accidental and intentional). (Remember: preservation of the original enables investigators to make additional images at their leisure.)

Mobile forensic machines like those employed by South Carolina's State Law Enforcement Division (SLED) enable investigators to image suspect media and analyze data on-site. (*Courtesy of SLED*)

Raw vs. Proprietary Image Formats

While some programs provide raw data images, others are proprietary in nature. Although many debates rage in computer forensics, this is not one of them. Rather, investigators agree that raw images files are the best. In fact, the only detractors to this idea appear to be the manufacturers of such programs. Without question, proprietary file formats are both restrictive and more costly. At a minimum, their usage requires permanent licensing commitments. As the wheels of justice are notoriously slow, the preservation of electronic evidence can be extremely expensive. The use of proprietary formats may force agencies to update software licenses or lose company support. In addition, the newer version may lack backward compatibility, making it necessary to restore the image back out and reacquire using the new version. This process can be extremely time consuming and can be avoided entirely by using raw formats.

There are a variety of imaging products readily available for law enforcement. Investigators should carefully select at least two that they are most comfortable with. As with all forensic tools, it is essential that multiple tools are available, as the tool that investigators most rely on will be the one that fails when they least expect it. When selecting imaging tools, investigators should choose the ones that have been accepted by the forensic community and which are efficient in both speed and compression. In addition, it is HIGHLY recommended that investigators choose tools which are capable of writing image files in a raw data format. By nature, these images have both longevity and transferability. Unlike proprietary image formats, raw image files may be accessed and interpreted by all popular forensic packages and do not have backward compatibility issues. Such portability is essential in criminal investigations and significantly reduces the costs associated with the maintenance of forensic laboratories and software libraries.

According to the National Institute of Standards and Technology (NIST), forensic imaging programs must meet the following requirements:

- The tool must be capable of making a bit-stream duplicate or an image of an original disk or partition onto fixed or removable media.
- The tool must not alter the original disk.
- The tool must be able to access both IDE and SCSI disks.
- The tool must be able to verify the integrity of a disk image file.
- The tool must log I/O errors.
- The tool must provide substantial documentation.

Contemporary forensic investigators have a variety of imaging tools to choose from. While traditional practices required stand-alone imaging programs, most integrated packages now have both imaging and verification capabilities.

Verification Programs

In addition to imaging programs, Investigators should consider the utilization of both independent verification programs and those that are included within imaging packages.[15]

Verification programs are those programs which read disks a track a time, beginning with head 0 and progressing to the last head, calculating an algorithmic signature represented by unique file identifiers. While comparisons focusing on *Cyclical Redundancy Checksums* (CRCs) have traditionally withstood courtroom challenges, investigators should consider the utilization of programs capable of comparing MD5 Hashes, as they issue 128-bit identifiers.

Hardware imaging solutions, provide an audit trail for investigators which may be introduced in court. (*Photo Courtesy of James Doyle/NYPD, ret.*)

Data Recovery/Extraction Utilities

Once verified images have been obtained, it will be necessary for analysts to recover digital information. Fortunately, much criminal evidence is obvious to even novice investigators. However, investigators should remember that unobvious places may also contain critical data. As such, forensic laboratories must have software capable of revealing obscure information. Like other areas of forensic software, investigators should employ both manual and automated programs to reveal hidden and deleted files, unlock encrypted files, and detect steganograpy. Traditionally, disk managers like *Norton Utilities*™ were employed toward most of these ends. Such basic management programs allowed users to automatically or manually recover erased files

(*Unerase*™); view and edit the entire contents of a disk or floppy in text, hexadecimal, or directory mode (*Diskedit*™); evaluate file slack (*Diskedit*™) and search for identified text. Contemporary programs provide enhanced capabilities, and most were specifically created as forensic tools as opposed to disk managers.

Data may be hidden or manipulated in a variety of ways and in various locations. In preparation for data analysis, files must be restored and made available. Thus, all forensic laboratories must maintain software which can extract hidden or manipulated data. Generally speaking, there are two types of extraction: physical and logical. The **physical extraction phase** identifies and records data across the entire physical drive without regard to file system, while the **logical extraction phase** identifies and recovers files and data based on the installed operating system(s), file system (s), and/or application(s).[16]

Methods of physical extraction include:

- **keyword searching**—this may be useful as it allows the examiner to extract data that may not be accounted for by the operating system and file system. Keyword search tools may be purchased as stand-alone tools, but they are also included in many integrated packages.
- **file carving**—processed across the physical drive, data carving may assist in recovering and extracting useable files and data that may not be accounted for by the operating system and file system. File or data carving tools are often incorporated into integrated forensic packages.
- **extraction of the partition table and unused space on the physical drive**—Evaluation of the partition table and unused space may identify the file systems present and determine if the entire physical size of the hard disk is accounted for.[17]

Methods of logical extraction are based on the file system present on the drive and may include data from such areas as **active files**,

deleted files, **file slack**, and **unallocated file space.** Steps may include:

- Extraction of the file system information to reveal characteristics such as directory structure, file attributes, file names, data and time stamps, file size, and file locations.
- Data reduction to identify and eliminate known files through the comparison of calculated hash values to authenticated hash values.
- Extraction of files pertinent to the examination. Methods to accomplish this may be

based on file name and extension, file header, file content, and location on the drive.
- Recovery of deleted files.
- Extraction of password-protected, encrypted, and compressed data.
- Extraction of file slack.
- Extraction of the unallocated space.[18]

Data Analysis Software

Only after data recovery and restoration may analysts turn to the arduous task of data analysis. As with other areas of computer forensics, both

Uncovering Digital Evidence

Like other types of criminals, individuals engaged in computer related criminal activity often attempt to obscure evidence of their involvement. Investigators should remember that their activities are consistent with their nontechnological counterparts and search for clues underneath objects just as they would at a traditional crime scene. Luckily for investigators, computer criminals often lack criminal sophistication and are unable to destroy the remnants of their activities. Below is a list of files which may be found in a criminal investigation in which forensic analysis may prove critical.

- **Overt files**—Those things which are not hidden, deleted, encrypted, or intentionally or unintentionally covert.
- **Hidden files**—Files which are manipulated (often intentionally) to cover the contents of the original file. Traditional practices used by suspect users included the alteration of file extensions. Fortunately, most forensic packages compare file headers and established file extensions, thereby rendering this type of concealment ineffective.
- **Slack space, free or unallocated space, and swap files**—Valuable information and criminal evidence may be located in areas of the disk largely free from manipulation. *Free space* is that part of the disk which the computer has not yet overwritten with data (i.e., space that is currently unused but a possible repository of previous data). *Slack space* is the area of the disk located between the end of the current file data and the end of the last assigned disk cluster of that file. *Swap files* include those which are temporarily placed on the computer when applications run out of space. Forensic packages restore these areas and provide investigators with the ability to analyze information contained therein.

- **Password-protected files**—Files which are protected from nonauthorized users with password programs. Ranging from the elementary to the sophisticated, basic password programs make the contents unreadable without the proper key.
- **Compressed files**—Popular compression software enables users to maximize disk space and is often used to increase the efficiency of file transmission across networks. Typically, compressed files are not readable by any software other than the compression utility employed to compress them. Additionally, most compression software allows users to install passwords. Contemporary forensic packages include tools for the identification and examination of compressed files.
- **Encrypted files**—Encrypted files have long been used by government officials to protect national security. As far as computers are concerned, many private citizens have utilized encryption programs to protect their own sensitive information. In its most basic form, encryption refers to the process of converting a message from its original form ("plaintext") into an indecipherable or scrambled form ("cipertext"). Most encryption programs use an algorithm to mathematically transform data, decipherable only to those individuals or entities holding an access key. This access key acts as a password. The security of encryption programs varies with the strength of the algorithm and the key.
- **Steganography**—Like encryption, steganography involves the securing of information through the manipulation of data. Unlike encryption, which prevents access to specified data through the use of ciphertext, steganography is actually designed to hide the data from view.

automated and manual products are available for evidence analysis. Generally speaking, automated analysis tools are designed to be useful to virtually anyone, including unskilled investigators. Case characteristics and situational variables will dictate the level and sophistication of the search necessary. Certainly, cases involving threats to national security are such that an exhaustive examination of all available materials is all but mandated. Simple cases involving 40 counts of child pornography in which the criminal evidence clearly resides on a suspect's desktop may not require such detail. Unfortunately, many investigators have become too reliant upon such tools and fail to comprehend the nature of their operations, leaving them susceptible to courtroom impeachment. Thus, it is essential that analysts understand the process of the software selected.

Regardless of approach, data analysis tools may be grouped in five general categories: **indexing, text searching, viewers**, **time frame analysis**, and **application analysis**. Contemporary forensic packages have incorporated the majority of these into their automated programs. Both of the most popular forensic packages, Guidance Software's EnCase and Access Data's Forensic Toolkit, automatically create an exhaustive index of the acquired drive. Although the process is quite time consuming, it is necessary for courtroom testimony of evidence integrity and provide investigators (and jurors) with a roadmap to the suspect drive. Software which provides for the analysis of applications and file structures further creates a picture of the suspect drive, revealing the level of user sophistication. Such analysis should include:

- reviewing the file names for relevance and patterns
- identifying the number and type of operating systems
- correlating the files to the installed applications
- considering relationships between files, such as e-mails and file attachments
- identifying unknown file types to determine their value to the investigation

- examining the users' default storage location for applications and the file structure of the drive to determine if files have been stored in their default or an alternate location
- examining user-configuration settings
- analyzing file metadata, the content of the user-created file containing data additional to that presented to the user, typically viewed through the application that created it (i.e., files created by word processing applications include authorship, last time edited, number of edits, etc.)

File viewers and text searching software significantly increase the efficiency of computer investigations. **File viewers**, often used in child pornography cases, allow front-page viewing of multiple files (including those that are archived), thus enabling investigators to quickly identify questionable graphics files. **Text** searching software, another critical forensic tool, allows investigators to search for specific words, phrases, and strings appropriate to individual cases. Traditionally, investigators used individual programs for viewing files and searching text.

Reporting Software

Forensic laboratories must also maintain utilities for the proper documentation and reporting of findings. Once again, it is important to note that integrated forensic packages have incorporated such utilities into their platforms. However, if nonintegrated or manual software is employed, forensic laboratories should be equipped with utilizes, such as word processing or spreadsheet programs, to create professional reports consistent with court expectations.

Miscellaneous Software

Once analysis has been completed, investigators must develop mechanisms for interpreting and relaying highly technical information to lay persons without losing robustness of evidence. While many automated programs present information in a digestible format, investigators should also have presentation-specific software

Digital Evidence and Demonstration of Legal Elements

Once data extraction is complete, analysis of the evidence can begin. In a nutshell, analysis refers to the process through which a relationship between digital evidence and case specifics is established. This includes identification and demonstration of any evidence that speaks to the elementation of a criminal act. Although elements vary across statute, certain universals exist in criminal codes. In cases involving computers, evidence may be located which addresses the following elements:

- *Actus reus*—evidence of the act may be located through text searching, data carving, evaluation of images, network analysis, etc.
- *Mens Rea*—evidence of the suspect's guilty mind or intent may be demonstrated by the use of data hiding techniques, deletion or wiping of drives, composition of passwords, etc.
- *Concurrence* and *Causation*—evidence of the relationships between the act, the intention, and the harm may be demonstrated through timeframe analysis.
- *Harm*—evidence of the actual harm suffered may be demonstrated through identification of child pornography, videos of criminal behavior, etc.
- *Ownership*—evidence of the ownership of the questioned data may be demonstrated through timeframe analysis, evaluation of password, and application or file analysis.

Thus, forensic laboratories must be equipped with software which addresses or uncovers evidence necessary to sustain a criminal conviction.

(e.g., *PowerPoint*™) available for nontraditional or unique cases, as well as a collection of popular applications (e.g., *MSWord*™, *Excel*™, etc.). In addition, forensic laboratories should be equipped with *wiping software*: (1) so that criminal contraband can be permanently removed from suspect machines (after final disposition) and (2) so that confidential, classified, or sensitive material can be permanently removed from departmental equipment prior to disposal through sale or recycling. Programs meeting the Department of Defense standards regarding declassification of hard disks and cleansing of floppies which are available include, but are not limited to, Maresware's™ *DECLASFY*™,

Tech Assist's™ *ByteBack*™, and Access Data's™ *WipeDrive*™.

Antivirus software is also essential in a forensic laboratory, as it protects both evidentiary matter and departmental equipment from destruction. Relatively inexpensive, programs like *McAfee's Virus Scanner*™ catch traditional viruses and provide users with timely updates as new threats emerge. Finally, it is recommended that forensic laboratories employ anti-theft software on their equipment, as the replacement of such equipment is often outside the limits of departmental resources. Programs like Maresware's™ *BRANDIT*™ enable the branding of a physical hard drive with up to five lines of identifying information.

Digital Forensics at the National Institute of Standards and Technology

James R. Lyle
Douglas R. White
Richard P. Ayers

Overview

There are three digital forensic science projects currently providing resources for the digital investigator underway at the National Institute of Standards and Technology (NIST). These projects are supported by the U.S. Department of Justice's National Institute of Justice (NIJ), federal, state, and local law enforcement, and the National Institute of Standards and Technology Office of Law Enforcement Standards (OLES) to promote efficient and effective use of computer technology in the investigation of crimes involving computers. Numerous

(Continued)

other sponsoring organizations from law enforcement, government, and industry are also providing resources to accomplish these goals. The three projects are the following:

- National Software Reference Library (NSRL)
- Computer Forensic Tool Testing (CFTT)
- Computer Forensic Reference Data Sets (CFReDS)

NSRL

The NSRL project collects software from various sources and incorporates file profiles computed from this software into a Reference Data Set (RDS) including hashes of known files created when software is installed on a computer. The law enforcement community approached NIST requesting a software library and signature database that meets four criteria:

- The organizations involved in the implementation of the filter must be unbiased and neutral.
- Control over the quality of data provided by the database must be maintained.
- A repository of original software must be made available, from which data can be reproduced.
- The database must provide a wide range of capabilities with respect to the information that can be obtained from file systems under investigation.

The primary focus of the NSRL is to aid computer forensics examiners in their investigations of computer systems. The majority of stakeholders are in federal, state, and local law enforcement in the United States and internationally. These enforcement organizations typically use the NSRL data to aid in criminal investigations. Other stakeholders include businesses and other government agencies use the NSRL as a referential extension of their routine IT operations.

The NSRL has three components:

- A large collection of original software packages.
- A database containing detailed information about the files in those software packages.
- A public NSRL Reference Data Set (RDS) which contains a subset of the metadata held in the database. The RDS is published and updated quarterly, as NIST Special Database 28.

The collection of original software allows NIST to investigate file metadata that may be called into question

or apply future algorithms against the files. The NSRL includes virtually any type of software available, such as operating systems, database management systems, utilities, graphics images, component libraries, etc., in many different versions.

The NSRL database contains metadata on computer files that can be used to uniquely identify a file and its provenance. For each file in the NSRL collection, the following data are published:

- Cryptographic hash values (MD5 and SHA-1) of the file's content. These uniquely identify the file even if, for example, it has been renamed.
- Data about the file's origin, including the software package(s) containing the file and the manufacturer of the package.
- Other data about the file, including its original name and size.

Law enforcement, government, and industry organizations use the RDS to review files on a computer by matching file profiles. The data is used to rapidly identify files on computer systems, based solely on the content of the files.

In most cases, NSRL file data content helps eliminate known files, such as operating system and application files, during criminal forensic investigations. This process increases efficiency by reducing the number of files that must be manually examined during an investigation.

The RDS is a collection of digital signatures of known, traceable software applications. Currently, the RDS contains metadata and hash values for over 40 million software files. There are software applications in the NSRL that are considered malicious code, i.e., steganography tools and hacking scripts. The intent of the RDS is as a filter of *known* file signatures, not exclusively limited to safe *applications*. There are no instances of illicit data, e.g., child abuse images. Further details are available at http://www.nsrl.nist.gov.

CFTT

The goal of the CFTT project is to establish a standard or concise methodology for testing computer forensic software tools by development of general tool specifications, test procedures, test criteria, test sets, and test hardware. The results provide the information necessary for toolmakers to improve their tools, for users to make better-informed choices about acquiring and using computer forensics tools, and for interested parties to understand the tools capabilities.

(Continued)

The testing methodology developed by NIST is functionality driven. The activities of forensic investigations are separated into discrete functions, such as hard disk write protection, disk imaging, string searching, etc. A test methodology is then developed for each referenced category. After a test methodology is developed, tested, and approved it is posted to the Web where it can be used by anyone to test a tool's specified functional implementation as designed into a given computer forensic tool. The specifications and test plans can be found at *http://www.cftt.nist.gov*.

After a tool category is selected, the development process is as follows:

1. NIST staff and law enforcement representatives develop a specification document that sets forth requirements that the forensic tool should meet.
2. The specification is posted to the Web for peer review by members of the computer forensics community and for public comment by other interested parties.
3. Relevant comments and feedback are incorporated into the specification.
4. A test methodology is developed and an assertions and test plan document is produced that specifies how to implement the test methodology.
5. The test plan document is posted to the Web for peer review by members of the computer forensics community and for public comment by other interested parties.
6. Relevant comments and feedback are incorporated into the specification.
7. A test environment with support software is designed and implemented for the test plan.
8. NIST posts support software to the Web.

Once a tool is selected for testing, the test process is as follows:

1. NIST acquires the tool to be tested.
2. NIST reviews the tool documentation.
3. NIST selects relevant test cases depending on features supported by the tool.
4. NIST develops test strategy.
5. NIST executes test cases.
6. NIST produces test report.
7. Steering Committee reviews test report.
8. Tool vendor reviews test report.
9. NIJ posts test report to Web. (*http://www.ojp.usdoj. gov/nij/topics/ecrime/cftt.htm*)

NIJ has published test reports on several forensic imaging tools, several software write block tools, and a variety of hardware write block devices. Currently specifications and test methodologies for deleted file recovery and string searching tools are in development. In addition to forensic tools for acquisition and analysis of digital data on desktop and laptop computers, CFTT is also developing test methodologies for mobile devices.

Data acquisition performed on cellular devices operating over Global System for Mobile Communications (GSM) and non-GSM networks has proven not only frustrating but extremely tedious due to the rapid rate of new cellular devices available on the market. Software vendors specializing in cellular forensics are forced to continuously provide updates to software and associated hardware in order to maintain support and provide examiners with solutions for the latest technologies. Mobile device forensic research performed in the Computer Security Division of the Information Technology Laboratory (ITL) at NIST produces numerous reports on tools capable of acquiring data from Personal Digital Assistants (PDAs), smart phones, and cellular devices operating over GSM and non-GSM networks.

NIST forensic science researchers take part in numerous conferences worldwide, providing software vendors, forensic specialists, incident response teams, and law enforcement personnel with prescribed overviews of the current capabilities and limitations of forensic applications that acquire data from cellular devices as well as suggestions on preservation and handling of digital data. Research conducted over the past two years has produced the following publications:

- NISTIR 7250 Cell Phone Forensic Tools: An Overview and Analysis (*http://csrc.nist.gov/publications/nistir/ nistir-7250.pdf*)
- SP800–101 Guidelines on Cell Phone Forensics (*http:// csrc. nist.gov/publications/nistpubs/800–72/sp800–72.pdf*),
- NISTIR 7387 Cell Phone Forensic Tools: An Overview and Analysis Update (*http://csrc.nist.gov/publications/ nistir/nistir-7387.pdf*),
- Forensic Software Tools for Cell Phone Subscriber Identity Modules (*http://csrc.nist.gov/mobilesecurity/ Publications/JDFSL-proceedings2006-fin.pdf*).

In addition to the NIST reports and conference articles produced, our research has provided extensive involvement

(*Continued*)

with software engineers from various manufacturers troubleshooting potential issues, providing suggestions on product improvement and overall dependability, which have played a key role in the evolution of cellular forensics software. Research conducted and shared materials have shown to be invaluable insofar as providing academia with a starting point for education materials, informing law enforcement and forensic examiners of expectations of the interaction between numerous devices and tools, and informing vendors of anomalies while providing a baseline for software improvement.

CFReDS

The **Computer Forensic Reference Data Sets (CFReDS)** provide to an investigator documented sets of simulated digital evidence for examination. Since CFReDS has documented contents, such as target search strings seeded in known locations, investigators can compare the results of searches for the target strings with the known placement of the strings. Investigators can use CFReDS in several ways including validating the software tools used in their investigations, equipment check-out, training investigators, and proficiency testing of investigators as part of laboratory accreditation. The CFReDS site is a repository of images. Some images are produced by NIST, often from the CFTT (tool testing) project, and some are contributed by other organizations. In addition to test images, the CFReDS site contains resources to aid in creating test images. These creation aids are in the form of interesting data files, useful software tools, and procedures for specific tasks. The CFReDS Web site is *http://www.cfteds.nist.gov.*

● A SAMPLING OF POPULAR FORENSIC SOFTWARE

Maresware

Maresware is a set of command line programs that can be used for computer forensics, data analysis, secure wiping, and imaging hard drives. Originally designed to assist law enforcement in the analysis and processing of computer-related evidence, over the years, Maresware has evolved to also be an excellent e-discovery tool. Maresware, written entirely in 'C', was designed to handle extremely large amounts of data at maximum speed. It can process the raw multimegabytes of data generated by both computer forensic examiners and forensic auditors. The efficiency of Maresware software is further enhanced by the fact that each of the programs performs only one specific task, one-program one-task. This design feature not only maximizes processing speed by reducing overhead from unnecessary internal program overhead, but also allows the user to build and configure and modify scripts to perform as needed. This gives the user ultimate control. It also makes "outside the box" processes possible. But you must be able and willing to think outside the box. (An auditor once developed a 1,000-line batch file using Maresware. Set it and forget it.)

Maresware may also be used for simultaneous drive wiping. Some federal agencies have adopted the software to wipe multiple drives at the same time. This significantly reduces the amount of time traditionally expended in wiping forensic drives for reuse. Other forensic utilities include, string searching, hashing, imaging, file cataloging, and header matching. Although Maresware remains a command-line application, investigators may combine programs to case specifications. Finally, e-discovery and redaction are supported by programs that provide automated, forensically sound file copying and deleting from multiple locations with multiple names. For example, one investigator employed Maresware to copy 8,000 files and tree structure from multiple locations AND delete the originals. Summarily, Maresware offers a variety of tools for forensic investigators and may be tailored for individual cases. It may be employed in both pubic and private sectors.

Guidance Software

EnCase™ Forensic, by Guidance Software, is a fully automated program touted for its user-friendly (some say idiot-proof) nature. A comprehensive package, *EnCase™* includes mechanized imaging, verification, and analysis capabilities, all within a graphical user interface (GUI) environment. In addition, it automatically identifies and displays all graphical image files in gallery format, unzips and searches zip files, and provides a tree-like view of the registry. Newer versions provide for the integration of other programs, like **password crackers**, and enables hexadecimal viewing. (It must be noted, however, that while it provides for integration, agencies must purchase these additional software programs independently.) One of the first of its kind, *EnCase™* remains one of the most popular programs found in local agencies due to its familiarity. Without question, *EnCase™* is useful in the majority of routine investigations. Guidance Software also provides links and resources to court decisions and law articles on topics relating to computer forensics. Like other forensic packages, however, it is quite costly to law enforcement, and the price of upgrades is significant. In addition, it has been criticized for being too user-friendly and for providing a false sense of security to unskilled investigators. Currently, it is facing competition from other vendors which are providing additional tools and offering competitive bundling packages. Its price has not been published.

Guidance Software also manufactures an imaging/verification hardware device. According to the manufacturers, *FastBloc™* allows for direct data acquisition from Windows at speeds up to 2–3 times the speed of native DOS acquisitions. It allows for noninvasive Windows acquisitions and subsequent verification, as opposed to the more technical DOS environment. Finally, it allows for previewing information through a direct IDE connection and enables the reading of IDE hard drives with a fast, flexible SCSI interface. However, images obtained with *FastBloc™* are only compatible with the *EnCase™* forensic software. **Vendor site:** *www.guidancesoftware.com*.

Ultimate Toolkit

The *Ultimate Toolkit™* (UTK™), by Access Data, is a GUI, automated program which bundles a variety of stand-alone programs by Access Data. Each of the programs contained within the suite can be purchased individually and are compatible with a variety of other packages, including *Encase™*, *Snapback™*, and *Safeback™*. Among other utilities, the program provides hashing verification, known file filtering, encrypted file identification, deleted file recover, and INSO viewing (full and thumbnail). Without question, the incorporation of password crackers, imaging software, registry viewers, wiping and network software has significantly increased the popularity and utility of this software. In addition, the software includes utilities for the automated production of professional reports. While EnCase contains many of the same capabilities, Access Data's product is considered to be more intuitive and less proprietary. For example, FTK contains an e-mail feature which is capable of automatically searching for and displaying of e-mails in a readily digestible format. At the same time, the products are capable of importing images created with other imaging programs. *Price*: $1,949. *Vendor site*: www.accessdata.com.

The following programs are included in the Ultimate Toolkit bundle but may also be purchased individually.

- **Forensic Toolkit®(FTK^{TM})**—a comprehensive tool for forensic examination, FTK provides for full text indexing, advanced search, deleted file recovery, and e-mail graphics analysis. In addition, it contains a utility for data carving, providing for contextual analysis of suspect files. *Price:* $1,095.
- **FTK Imager**—this program allows for the acquisition of physical device images, the creation of simultaneous multiple images from a single source, and provides ready access to CDFS and DVD file systems. *Price:* $89.
- **Registry Viewer^{TM}**—a utility which enables users to view Windows registry files and generate reports. As with the other programs contained herein, it integrates seamlessly with **FTK**. *Price:* $149.
- **Password Recovery Toolkit^{TM} (PRTK^{TM})**—this program provides for the discovery and identification of encrypted files on handheld,

desktop, and server computer systems. This program provides locksmithing tools for a variety of popular software, including: Microsoft Word™, Excel™, Lotus 1–2–3™, Paradox™, Symantec Q&A™, Quattro Pro™, AmiPro™, Approach™, QuickBooks™, ACT™, WinZip™, Professional Write™, DataPerfect™, Microsoft Access™, CCMail™, MicrosoftMail™, Quicken™, Dbase™, Ascend™, Lotus Organizer™, Microsoft BOB™, PKZip™, PGP™, Microsoft Scheduler™, VersaCheck™, Symphony™, Word Pro™, Microsoft Money™, BestCrypt™, Microsoft Outlook/Exchange™, Norton's Diskreet™, TaxWise™, Novell NetWare™, and WindowsNT™. The program may be used independently or integrated with other forensic software. In addition, it allows for the importation of specialized word lists and also provides for the exportation of word lists, enabling investigators to use a suspect drive against itself (i.e., by creating a dictionary comprised of every word on the suspect machine including passwords).

- **Distributed Network Attack (DNA)—50 Client**—this program extends decryption capabilities beyond a single computer by using the distributed power of multiple computers across a network to decrypt files and recover passwords. *Price*: $1,495.
- **WipeDrive™ 3.0**—this program is designed to forensically wipe drives. It may be used to remove criminal contraband or employed to wipe drives for reuse.

Other Forensic Utilities

As mentioned previously, integrated forensic tools are increasingly popular among law enforcement agencies due to the universality of application and user friendly approach. Although it is not recommended that forensic laboratories rely exclusively on such packages, cost and personnel considerations have significantly reduced the popularity of stand-alone or command-line programs. As the text is not intended to provide an exhaustive examination of forensic practices, descriptions, and explanations of all available tools will not be undertaken here. However, a brief discussion of some of them may be helpful to illuminate other practices in the field.

- **Imaging and Verification**—Historically, two of the most popular stand- alone imaging utilities employed for forensic investigators were *ByteBack*™ and *Safeback*™. Although their popularity as forensic tools has diminished as agencies increasingly choose integrated platforms, they bear mentioning here.
  1. **ByteBack**—ByteBack™ is a program created by Tech Assist and is currently available at *www.toolsthatwork.com*. In addition to providing bitstream images, *Byteback*™ is capable of addressing damaged media, scanning for physical flaws and reporting all bad sectors, and automatically reconstructing partition tables and boot records (i.e., will read physically damaged drive. If you command it to do zero retries, it will skip over damaged heads, sectors, etc. However, the user must invoke the reporting command, so it reports the action of skipping.) Because the program works in physical sector mode, it also supports multiple formats, including Linux, Unix, NFTS, Fat16, and Fat32 and enables investigators to determine file formats and read partial sectors. It may be utilized in cases requiring onsite analysis. The program allows direct access and includes a four-terabyte limit, enabling investigators to bypass the BIOS and image everything together, respectively. Finally, it incorporates the MD5 standard into most program operations and allows for verification at every step. One disadvantage to the program is that it will not write to streaming media (i.e., tape). However,

this criticism is becoming increasingly passé, as alternative media become more efficient.

2. **Safeback**—By far, *Safeback*™ is the most popular stand-alone imaging program utilized by investigative agencies. Created exclusively for forensic investigations, this package was not created as a disk manager. Like *ByteBack*™, this program copies both the physical hard drive and logical partition tables, as well as providing MD5 verification. Unlike *Byteback*™, this program will write to streaming media. However, this program, now owned by New Technologies, Inc. (NTI), is expensive, and only individual licenses are issued. (Unlike most forensic software companies which issue more generalized licenses, NTI reserves software for individual officers as opposed to agencies or machines.)

- **Wiping Programs**—In order to reduce evidence processing costs, agencies may wish to reuse hard drives. To ensure that cross contamination of data does not occur, investigators must thoroughly scrub or "wipe" the drive. Wiping programs vary in both security and cost, but forensic laboratories must demonstrate that the wiping process employed meets that of the rigorous standards established by the Department of Defense (DOD). Currently, there are a variety of wiping programs on the commercial market which meet these standards. A DOD-approved wipe is one in which the original information is overwritten with ones, zeros, and random characters at least seven times. While most forensic packages include a wiping program in their platforms, Maresware's™ *DECLASFY*™, Tech Assist's™ *ByteBack*™, and Access Data's™ *WipeDrive*™ may be purchased separately and have proven popular in law enforcement agencies.

- **Unix**—Although the majority of computer forensics laboratories at the local level specifically address Windows platforms, UNIX tools should be procured by local agencies, as they are free and do not add to the often exorbitant costs associated with the development of forensic labs.

1. **Data Dumper** (**dd**)—A free utility for UNIX which is capable of making exact copies of disks for forensic analysis, Data Dumper is a command-line tool which requires a comprehensive understanding of command syntax to function properly.

2. **Grep**—A standard program on UNIX systems, the **Grep** application allows searches containing a particular sequence of characters. Through the utilization of metacharacters, the program provides for wider search parameters than traditional programs' text-searching utilities.

3. **The Coroner's Toolkit**—A collection of free tools for the forensic analysis of UNIX machines, The Coroner's Toolkit is specifically designed to be used in the investigation of a computer intrusion. Applications contained in the kit may be employed to reconstruct the activities of an intruder through the examination of recorded times of file access. It may also be used to recover deleted files.

CONCLUSIONS

The investigation of computer-related crime is increasingly necessary in today's technology-dependent society. Administrative apathy and inadequate resources have resulted in poorly run investigations marred by an overreliance on automated forensic programs or evidence contamination, corruption, or destruction. Although resources do not appear to be forthcoming, administrators must establish forensic computer science capabilities, evaluating the feasibility of partnering law enforcement personnel with civilian experts and relying on the cooperation of corporate entities. Such collaboration is essential for the successful prosecution of computer-related crime. Proper training must begin with a basic understanding of computer structure and data management. Indeed, administrators must recognize that the practice of sending officers to one-week software certification courses may soon be self-defeating as forensic computer science garners credibility as a discipline. In addition, all departments should develop laboratories for the preservation, analysis, and reporting of computer-related crime.

In order to establish forensic capabilities, officers tasked with the investigation of computer-related crime must first identify the minimum requirements, including necessary housing and equipment. The information contained within this chapter should provide some guidance. Environmentally controlled work and storage space, recovery and analysis of hardware and software, and computer training represent the minimal elements necessary for the establishment of a computer crime unit.

DISCUSSION QUESTIONS

1. What factors should be considered by administrators in developing SOP for computer investigations?
2. What are some of the problems traditionally associated with finding digital evidence?
3. Generally speaking, what are the five categories of software which may be useful in an investigation?
4. What are some of the traditional problems associated with computer investigations?
5. In the most basic sense, what is the structure of information storage?
6. How can the integrity of data be verified by investigators?
7. What does FAT represent, and why is it important in computer investigations?
8. What are the minimum requirements for building a bare bones forensic laboratory?

RECOMMENDED READING

- Anson, Steven (2007). *Mastering Windows Network Forensics and Investigation.* Sybex: New Jersey.
- Bunting, Steve (2007). *EnCase Computer Forensics— The Official EnCe: Encase Certified Examiner Study Guide.* Sybex: New Jersey.

- Carrier, Brian (2005). *File System Forensic Analysis.* Addison-Wesley Professional: New Jersey.
- Jones, Keith J., Bejtlich, Richard; Rose, Curtis W.; Farmer, Dan; Venema, Wietse; and Carrier, Brian (2007). *Computer Forensics Library Boxed Set.* Addison-Wesley Professional: New Jersey.
- Leigland, Ryan and Krings, Axel (2004). A Formalization of Digital Forensics. *International Journal of Digital Evidence,* 3(2): 1–32. Available at *www.ijde.org.*
- Long, Johnny (2008). *No Tech Hacking.* Syngress: Massachusetts.

WEB RESOURCES

- http://www.nist.gov – link to the homepage of the National Institute of Standards and Training, a non-regulatory federal agency housed within the U.S. Department of Commerce. Employing close to 3,000 scientists, engineers, technicians, and support staff, the Institute was created to promote U.S. innovation and industrial competitiveness by advancing measurement science, standards, and technology. The site provides access to a plethora of publications involving computer forensics. In addition, NIST houses the Computer Forensics Tool Testing (CFTT) Project Web site.
- http://www.cftt.nist.gov/project_overview.htm – link to the homepage of the Computer Forensics Tool Testing Project. The project is designed to define requirements for specific types or classes of computer forensics tools (i.e., disk imaging, password cracking, write blockers, etc.). The creation of such standards will ensure the validity and universality of forensic platforms and will establish scientific acceptance as required for the introduction of evidence under *Daubert/Frye.*
- www.crazytrain.com – link to a site devoted to Linux forensic tools. The site also includes links to various papers and presentations regarding Linux forensics.
- www.maresware.com – homepage of Maresware forensic software. The site provides access to various articles and news regarding developments in computer forensics. In addition, it provides links to various other forensic resources, like hash sets, and a variety of other free software.
- www.guidancesoftware.com – homepage of Guidance Software, vendor of assorted forensic software. The site provides access to various law articles and legal news regarding forensic software. The site also provides access to various whitepapers and articles on forensic practices and tool testing.

- www.forensicfocus.com – a site dedicated to the discussion of emerging issues in computer forensics, it provides access to various bulletin boards and white papers. Discussion board topics have included the evaluation of emerging tools and general topics involved in computer investigations.
- www.thetrainingco.com – the homepage of The Training Company, an organization which provides law enforcement training and sponsors a yearly conference on TechnoSecurity. The site provides information on conferences and provides links to the group's publications. Known as a friend of law enforcement, the group offers scholarships for law enforcement attendees.
- www.us-cert.gov – the homepage of the United States Computer Emergency Readiness Team is a partnership between the Department of Homeland Security and the public and private sectors. The site provides access to countless white papers discussing computer forensics and maintains links to other resources.

ENDNOTES

[1] Rosenblatt, Kenneth S. (1995). *High-Technology Crime: Investigating Cases Involving Computers*. KSK Publications: San Jose, CA.

[2] Ibid, p. 24.

[3] According to many experts, including Dan Mares, software works in the bell curve. This functionality is adequate for average users. However, investigators often confront extreme situations! Thus, it is essential for software to be tested and retested and retested, including as many extreme conditions as possible. Investigators should test their own software library for flaws, creating a range of files from zero bytes to a very large maximum file size. This allows investigators to testify that they are fully aware of the potential failures of their software and where these flaws are likely to occur.

[4] This is not intended to be a comprehensive introduction to computer science. Rather, the following should provide the reader with a brief look at the components of a computer system which are most relevant to computer investigations. It is intended to simply familiarize the reader with common terms used in computer investigations.

[5] Kovacich, Gerald L. and Boni, William C. (2000). *High-Technology Crime Investigator's Handbook: Working in the Global Information Environment*. Butterworth-Heinemann: Boston, MA.

[6] Sammes, Tony and Jenkinson, Brian (2000). *Forensic Computing: A Practitioner's Guide*. Springer-Verlag: London.

[7] Though it is the most common, it must be noted that ASCII is not the only set of associations in use. Windows systems, for example, use the Windows ANSI code, while electronic organizers and personal information managers use a particularized modified version of ASCII. In addition, a two-byte code known as Unicode is increasing in popularity.

[8] For a comprehensive explanation of interpretative schemes, including Little Endian and Big Endian, floating decimal points, and the like, see Sammes, Tony and Jenkinson, Brian (2000). *Forensic Computing: A Practitioner's Guide*, Springer-Verlag: London.

[9] *File swap*, also important in forensic investigations, is that data which is stored on hard disk drive due to limited virtual memory (i.e., when working, if there is not enough space for all applications, data may be "swapped" in order to make room).

[10] Available at *http://www.pcguide.com/ref/hdd/file/structMBR-c.html*.

[11] Some technical documents refer to the first sector on the disk as the master boot sector or master boot record, which contains the master boot code, which is the code that enables the computer to start to boot, and the partition table, which is a four-entry table.

[12] For an introduction to Unix or Linux tools, readers may go to *http://www.opensourceforensics.org/tools/unix.html* or *www.crazytrain.com*, respectively.

[13] Available at *http://www.guidancesoftware.com/downloads/getpdf.aspx?fl=.pdf*.

[14] The author does not make any endorsements, express or otherwise, of individual software packages. Individual agencies should test all software to prepare themselves for courtroom examination. In addition, the lists provided here are far from comprehensive. Rather, they represent those software packages which are most popular.

[15] While some imaging tools provide mechanisms for checking their own output, investigators should be aware that many of them change the boot record. For example, Safeback's verification process changes the boot record when used with defaults. In fact, Safeback has been known to change bootable slave drives into non-bootable ones. Unfortunately, many investigators are not aware of this, as the program is designed to bypass boot records so that these changes are not readily apparent. Relatively speaking, these changes are inconsequential. However, investigators *must* know the entire process or face impeachment in court. Thus, investigators should test the software themselves, thoroughly preparing themselves for court testimony. Defense attorneys questioning investigators on these changes may inadvertently enhance the reputation of the investigator they are trying to destroy in cases where the investigator has done his/her homework.

[16] NIJ (2004). *Forensic Examination of Digital Evidence: A Guide for Law Enforcement*. NIJ Special Report. U.S. Department of Justice, Office of Justice Programs.

[17] Ibid.

[18] Ibid.

CHAPTER 11

Searching and Seizing Computer-Related Evidence

Chapter Outline

LEARNING OBJECTIVES

After reading this chapter, you will be able to do the following:

✓ Discuss the seven general categories of personnel that may be at a computer-related crime scene.

✓ Familiarize yourself with the tools of the trade of computer related crime scene investigation.

✓ Gain knowledge on the concerns of preservation of digital evidence.

✓ Develop comprehension on why documentation is so important.

✓ Understand SMEAC and how it applies to computer investigation.

✓ Become aware of the activities of investigators when approaching computer-related crime scenes and on scene.

KEY TERMS AND CONCEPTS

- bagging and tagging
- computer components
- hex editors
- imaging
- mainframes
- magnetic tape storage units
- minicomputers
- no-knock warrants
- probable cause
- secondary warrants
- seizure
- SMEAC
- toolkit
- trace evidence

● TRADITIONAL PROBLEMS ASSOCIATED WITH FINDING DIGITAL EVIDENCE

Unlike traditional investigations in which forensic experts are tasked with analysis of criminal evidence, computer-related investigations often require role multiplicity on the part of investigators. In fact, computer crime investigators are often forced to act as case supervisors, investigators, crime scene technicians, and forensic scientists. Such duality is further exacerbated by characteristics unique to digital evidence. First and foremost, digital evidence is especially volatile and voluminous, susceptible to climatic or environmental factors as well as human error. It may be vulnerable to power surges, electromagnetic fields, or extreme temperatures. Unlike traditional evidence in which analysis of small samples is utilized to preserve the totality of the evidence, assessment of digital evidence requires evaluation of the whole, making investigative mistakes quite costly. In fact, this characteristic may increase the potential of liability for criminal investigators if mistakes result in loss of critical data. Such is not the case with traditional evidentiary matters. (Mishandling of powdered substances or serological material rarely results in catastrophic damage to business operations, as does the destruction of business records or accounting spreadsheets.) The sheer volume of digital evidence further complicates its recovery, making it virtually impossible to conduct on-scene analysis. As such, investigators often overlook the significance of certain material or seize information which is not included in the warrant application. (Imagine searching for a stolen diamond ring at Chicago's O'Hare International Airport—securing the airport, ceasing all mobility, questioning all individuals present, searching every area, and releasing the scene in a timely manner.)

Digital evidence is also unique in its level of camouflage possibilities, lending itself to concealment by individuals desiring to hide information. In essence, computer ne'er-do-wells may hide incriminating evidence in plain sight without damaging its utility. This is in direct contrast to many types of traditional evidence (imagine hiding cocaine by mixing it with sugar.). In fact, the software community and other interest groups are actively campaigning and creating tools counterproductive to computer investigations. Traditionally, individuals well-trained in computers could recover files relatively easily, using tools such as Norton Utilities' Unerase. It was a rare occurrence when systems and data were configured with multiple levels of security. The advent of encryption and steganography programs has made the process of recovering data increasingly complex. Currently, adequate tools exist to break through most of these layers. However, one look at hacker and civil libertarian pages reveals a new trend in software—ensuring privacy from all, but especially their self-identified nemesis, the government.

Self-destructive programs are also readily available for private consumption, allowing users to sabotage their own systems upon unauthorized access. This may be likened to a cache of explosives with a triggering mechanism. Unfortunately for law enforcement, these characteristics create an inauspicious environment for the standardization of procedures. Indeed, the method of analysis of computer evidence is always contingent upon case characteristics. In some cases, for example, it may be necessary to shut a computer off to prevent remote destruction, while in others the action of disconnecting the power supply may result in irreparable damage to computer programs and the corresponding data.

Finally, technology is outpacing law-enforcement training. In an ideal situation, investigative units would have individuals devoted exclusively to technological development and training, while others are equally dedicated to on-site analysis. The first group, of course, would be responsible for passing their knowledge on to their compatriots. Unfortunately, this is almost impossible. As we stated before, departmental resources often preclude adequate training. Even those departments that have substantial resources cannot devote a multitude of investigators to this task. In addition, until a plateau is reached in computer technology (which does not seem likely in the foreseeable future), any training passed on would become obsolete moments after dissemination. Thus, significant problems exist regarding the discovery and analysis of digital evidence.

Investigative agencies should develop strict search-and-seizure policies for computer-related scenes to reduce the potential for evidence contamination or destruction by untrained personnel. Computer crime investigators and/or computer experts should be present at all scenes in which digital evidence may be collected. Their presence and direction will be essential during both the investigation and the courtroom process. Coupled with the establishment of a forensic lab, such practices should minimize potentially negative outcomes.

Why Is Digital Evidence Important?

- BTK serial murderer Dennis Rader terrorized Wichita, Kansas, for 30 years until evidence on a computer disk led police to the former church council president and Cub Scout leader.
- Scott Peterson's computer contained a map of the island where his wife's body was found and revealed that he had shopped online for a boat, studied water currents, and bought a gift for his mistress.
- David Leslie Fuller's computers showed that he had stalked three other teenage girls before he abducted, raped, and murdered 13-year-old Kacie Woody, whom he met in an online chat room.[1]

PRE-SEARCH ACTIVITIES

Regardless of case characteristics, the construction and maintenance of a technologically sound forensic laboratory is the foundation for successful case disposition. Once in place, a forensic laboratory is critical for the analysis of computer-related evidence and courtroom presentation. However, even the best forensic laboratory and analyst may be rendered moot if the investigation is conducted in a haphazard manner or exhibits disregard for legal specifications. Thus, pre-analysis activity is equally important and worthy of comparable attention to detail. This includes all pre-search activities (i.e., warrant preparation, intelligence gathering, assembling an execution team, planning the search, and assigning responsibilities) and on-scene processing (i.e., executing the warrant, securing the scene, evidence collection and preservation, and the transportation of evidence).

As stated, all phases of evidence identification, collection, preservation, and analysis are necessarily interdependent and will directly impact the success of a criminal prosecution regardless of case characteristics. Computer crime investigators, like their nontechnological counterparts, should remember that advance planning ensures the success of evidence collection. Proper intelligence gathering, for example, enables the investigative unit to collect the right experts, evidence containers, forensic software, and the like, while providing a blueprint for the corresponding warrant application. Thus, all investigators should carefully evaluate the scene in question and familiarize themselves with case parameters. Tools specifically designed to facilitate the collection of this type of evidence include: the *USA Patriot Act*, the *Foreign Intelligence Surveillance Act*, and the *Communications Assistance for Law Enforcement Act*, which *requires* telephone companies, Internet service providers (ISPs), and other

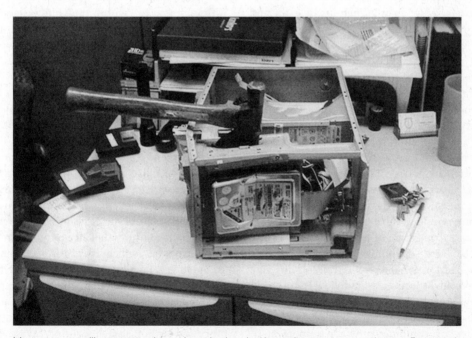

Many suspects will attempt to thwart investigations by destroying computer equipment. Fortunately for investigators, they will often forget to destroy corresponding media. In this case, the suspect had copied photographs of his underage stepdaughter onto media found at the scene. (*Photo Courtesy of James Doyle/NYPD*, ret.)

communication carriers to provide technical assistance to carry out a legitimate law-enforcement mission. Technological aspects notwithstanding, investigators may also rely on proven techniques for intelligence gathering, such as surveillance, undercover reconnaissance, informants, criminal histories, known photographs, and the like. Utility checks or architectural archives, for example, may be helpful in securing blueprints, floor plans, or maps of the area in question—essential not only for scene security but also for their illustration of electrical and telephone outlets.

As much as possible, an investigator should attempt to determine the location, size, type, and number of computers at a suspect scene. This is especially critical in voluminous searches for warrant preparation. Dumpster diving (i.e., the processing of trash) may provide a wealth of information in developing a schematic of suspect machines as individuals, even those criminally minded, will often discard this type of information or even incriminating evidence. In addition, their refuse may be helpful in gathering passwords or personal information on suspects. Investigators should be cautioned that even the most innocuous of material (e.g., packaging material, discarded media, system reports, software manuals, post-it notes, and social facts for password cracking) may provide assistance in a computer crime case. Such materials may also be useful in demonstrating knowledge and proving intent in a criminal court.

Social engineering and informants may also be used to secure this type of information, providing investigators with pertinent information such as type and number of computers and storage devices, operating systems employed, as well as schedules of applicable personnel and their personal histories. Surreptitious role-playing may be especially effective, as individuals routinely give out sensitive information to representatives of the Telephone company, service or security provider, or computer/network support staff. Once this information is obtained, investigators should prepare their tool kit accordingly—adding additional media, cords or connections, and

appropriate drivers to their boot diskettes. However, this does not suggest that other items be removed. Rather, investigators should take the opportunity to double up certain types of media known to be at the scene. Remember, the best time to get the equipment needed is *before* you arrive.

Warrant Preparation and Application

Intelligence gathering is critical to the development of a comprehensive warrant. When available, operating systems, storage devices, and hardware specifications should be included in warrant applications. Such articulation insures that searches are tailored to the particulars of the case at hand, and that evidence collected within the parameters of the warrant will withstand future judicial scrutiny. As with other issues in the investigation of computer-related crime, there are no givens in computer search warrants. Each case will vary based on scene characteristics and corresponding judicial jurisdiction. Although they are within the same system, federal circuit courts have issued widely differing opinions. Thus, investigators must be aware of the corresponding legislative and jurisprudential climate in their area and structure their application accordingly.

As warrants provide a cornucopia of legal issues at the trial level, the importance of warrant preparation cannot be overstated. Thus, any warrant application should be reviewed by as many specialists (i.e., computer investigators, legal counsel, etc.) as possible prior to magistrate approval. This ensures that it will include all of the relevant protections and language. In addition, it ensures that all equipment, media, and incidentals which may prove evidentiary are included. Finally, it breeds a familiarity on the part of the investigator, which ensures judicial approval. (Unlike other criminal search warrant applications, which are routinely processed without much scrutiny, investigators should painstakingly point out the essentials to any judicial officer. This includes explaining terminology and defining case characteristics.

This makes the warrant itself more defensible in court. However, it does not negate the possibility of issues related to the actual execution of the said warrant.) Remember, the first step in the preparation of any warrant application is the operationalization of the crime itself and, more specifically, defining the role of the computer in it. Such characterizations necessarily outline the scope of the corresponding search and seizure and are essential for the establishment of probable cause.

Probable Cause

As in noncomputer cases, three elements of probable cause must be clearly articulated to an appropriate magistrate in order to secure a warrant: *probable cause* that a crime has been committed, *probable cause* that evidence of a crime exists, and *probable cause* that extant evidence resides in a particular location. Thus, successful applications clearly demonstrate the rationale for the criminal investigation and the justifications of the requested search and/or seizure. Such considerations will dictate the scope of the warrant. For example, demonstrations that the computer in question represents the instrumentality of the crime will provide investigators with broader search powers than will one in which the computer was simply a repository of evidence. It is recommended, then, that investigators clearly establish not only the role played by a suspect computer or its components, but any reasonable role *they might have played.* This will grant them greater discretion in the search and seizure of the equipment. In cases of child pornographers, for example, investigators could reasonably argue that the seizure of the defendant's monitor and printer is necessary to view the images as the defendant would. (It is strongly recommended that investigators attempt to include graphic files in all search warrant applications as a cornucopia of child pornography is often found inadvertently.) In nonpornography cases when the original warrant is predicated on criminal behavior in which evidence is not normally found in graphic images, examiners may be able to articulate their rationale for looking at these types of files, by explaining methods of hiding data through file extension manipulation, steganography, and the like.

Seizing Equipment

Probable cause notwithstanding, investigators must also justify the **seizure** of equipment which does not necessarily represent an instrument of the crime. As warrants are issued under the provisions found within the Fourth Amendment, it is essential that investigators clearly substantiate any requests for seizures of equipment. This will minimize claims of unconstitutional deprivations. It is highly recommended that investigators request explicit permission to seize all hardware and storage devices that are constitutionally justifiable, as on-site analysis might negate the utilization of some forensic approaches. (Investigators should be aware that such requests are often denied in cases where equipment is essential for business operations.) As always, fruits of the crime, criminal contraband, and those items criminally possessed may be seized without judicial authority.

On-Site vs. Off-Site Searches

Based on case characteristics, investigators must determine if on-site or off-site searches need to be conducted. Each type has its advantages and disadvantages. On-site searches allow interviewing of witnesses based on developing evidence, yet may be impossible if there are multiple computers or large drive computers or excessive media. On the other hand, off-site searches allow investigators to proceed at their leisure, ensuring that evidence is not overlooked. However, legal issues may arise. Thus, investigators must clearly articulate (prior to arrival at the scene) what items are to be seized and which require on-site evaluation.

No-Knock Warrants

If exigent circumstances dictate it, a request for a "no-knock" warrant should be included in the application. As always, exigent circumstances would include the nature of the offense (violent vs. nonviolent), the potential for evidence destruction, the sophistication and maturity of the target, and the absence of resident. With the vulnerability of computer data, investigators should be able to present a case to the magistrate for rapid entry if the suspect has prior knowledge of the search or if he/she has the technical expertise to destroy evidence. Although these types of warrants are much harder to justify and are closely scrutinized by the courts, investigators should attempt to obtain one in any situation in which case characteristics dictate it.

Secondary/Multiple Warrants

In many cases involving computer-related evidence, multiple warrants may be required. In cases of stolen components, for example, the *contents* of the suspect computer would fall squarely outside the boundaries of the most applicable warrants. Additional warrants may also be necessitated in cases where investigators inadvertently uncover evidence of a secondary crime not included in the original warrant. For example, investigators searching a computer for drug-related spreadsheets but inadvertently uncover images of child pornography will need to obtain a **secondary warrant** to search for additional images. (Although many investigators have attempted to apply the "plain view" doctrine to such material, the courts have not agreed. *United States* v. *Carey*.[2]) In fact, secondary or multiple warrants are quite common in computer-related investigations, and investigators should be encouraged to seek additional judicial permission whenever the applicability of the original warrant is questionable.

Multiple warrants are also encouraged in cases involving networked computers. However, this may be problematic as investigators may be unaware of the physical location of the storage

The examination of a single computer file provided critical information for officials in Wichita, Kansas, investigating the BTK killer. To taunt police, BTK sent a letter to a local television station boasting of his exploits. Examination of the document's metadata revealed the name of the document's author (Dennis) and the organization's name (Christ Lutheran Church) associated with the software. The original file was located on a floppy seized during the subsequent search of the church.[3] In 2005, Dennis Rader, former Cub Scout leader, pleaded guilty and confessed to ten counts of murder. The city of Wichita found peace after decades of fear. (*Travis Heying/AP Wide World Photos*)

facility. If unknown, investigators should inform the magistrate that there may be an additional location. In some cases, magistrates will agree to expand the scope of the warrant to include non-specific areas contingent upon discoveries at the scene. In those cases where such permission is denied, investigators should request additional warrants once the physicality is determined. As a general rule, investigators should raise the possibility of off-site storage in the original warrant to strengthen any subsequent applications. Finally, additional warrants may be necessitated in cases involving locked or encrypted files, as heightened expectations of privacy apply. This is true even in warrantless consent searches if a suspect refuses to reveal the password for protected areas.

Summarily, investigators should be cautioned against broad or generalized on-site searches. Warrant applications should be characterized by a degree of specificity such that a reasonable officer can clearly differentiate between searchable and nonsearchable areas. Although some investigators proclaim the merits of vagueness and obfuscation, suggesting that this increases their investigative authority, such generalities may lead to the judicial nullification of the original warrant. Remember: it is far easier to obtain a secondary warrant based on emerging facts, than to build a case in which all of the evidence has been discarded due to a faulty warrant. (Luckily, many criminals will commingle criminal evidence or contraband and legitimate documents, an area typically outside the purview of Fourth Amendment protection.)

Plan Preparation and Personnel Gathering

The case supervisor should develop a preliminary plan of attack prior to assembling the relevant investigators. Once a team is in place, a brainstorming session(s) which exhaustively analyzes all of the issues involved in the particular case should be held to clarify roles and responsibilities and generate a comprehensive strategy. As always, written plans are highly recommended as they enable investigators to study them in depth, providing them with a global perspective of the mission at hand, while clearly delineating individual tasks. (It is also recommended that these plans be accompanied by bulleted checklists and marking instruments, as mechanisms for individual accountability have proven most effective in other areas.) At a minimum, such plans should follow the five-paragraph military order **SMEAC** (see box) and will vary depending on case characteristics determined during preliminary intelligence gathering.

On-Scene Personnel

As with traditional investigations, the deployment of personnel and the allocation of responsibilities are critical to the success of any investigation. In computer-related investigations, there are seven general categories of players. It is important to note that these categories are not mutually exhaustive or exclusive, and certain individuals may experience duality of expectations. In addition, the list provided is intended to serve as an optimal guideline. However, investigators should recognize the necessary limitations imposed by departmental resources and plan accordingly.

S.ituation—clearly define the 'who' and 'what' of the investigation. This includes number of individuals and computers, types of equipment, geographical location, and perhaps most importantly, the background of the suspects, and any dangerous situations which may arise.

M.ission—what is the optimal case scenario? What do investigators want to happen? For example, is it desirable to conduct the search while others are present? If so, surveillance prior to arrival is necessary to ascertain prime hours.

E.xecution—How will the mission be accomplished?

A.venues of approach and escape—How will investigators enter the scene? How will investigators exit? In the event of an emergency, what is the safest escape route? Where should the media be directed to? Remember that all cases are different. Some may require the use of SWAT. In those cases, civilian personnel should be kept away from the scene until it is secure. Case supervisors should provide detailed maps to investigators prior to arriving at the scene. Preferably, these maps should include the location of doors, elevators, obstacles, parking facilities, and the like. Suspects or suspect equipment should be clearly identified on each map.

C.ommunications—How will investigators communicate at the scene? How will investigators communicate to the department? Who is the primary point of contact? All of these things are extremely important in any criminal investigation. But in computer cases, where cellular phones and traditional radios may create electromagnetic fields and static electricity, it is essential that they are considered.

- **Case Supervisor(s)**—Without exception, on-scene supervisors should be the most experienced ones, with minimum qualifications including: acting as an investigator in a variety of previous cases and situations, the ability to assume control and command respect, and the ability to effectively communicate to varying populations in a professional and articulate manner. In departments which do not have experienced computer investigators, assignment of a civilian expert and experienced criminal investigator as co-case supervisors is recommended. (Although this kind of situation has proven incendiary in other types of cases, most officers are willing to defer to the technological expertise of computer experts.) Individual responsibilities for this position(s) include, but are not limited to, information dissemination, interaction with media, personnel scheduling and team compilation, equipment preparation, and of course, overall supervision. Both law enforcement and civilian experts employed in this capacity should remain onsite until scene closure. (Some texts argue that civilian experts are not required beyond initial entry and scene securement.)

- **Arrest Team**—Although individuals involved in computer crime are often dismissed as nonviolent or physically weak, all execution teams should be prepared for the worst-case scenario. Certainly case characteristics may indicate a lower vigilance threshold, but all executions should include an armed contingent experienced in arrest situations. This team's responsibilities should include arresting suspects and subsequent custodial transportation.

- **Scene Security Team**—Usually comprised of patrol officers, this team's primary responsibility lies with scene security. As in noncomputer criminal investigations, the ability to prevent evidence contamination should be considered a top priority. As

such, it is important that these individuals create a visible (preferably uniformed) barrier against scene contamination, evidence destruction, and media impropriety. Although this is more often than not a thankless task, the members of this team should be carefully selected by the team leader.

- **Interview and Interrogation Team**—Although the number of individuals assigned to this team will vary based on case characteristics, this team should be comprised of members experienced in information gathering. As the name implies, this team is responsible for interviewing witnesses and interrogating suspects. As such, it is essential that these individuals possess exceptional communication skills, especially because the traditional interviewee in these cases may have advance warning. The importance of an adequately staffed interview and interrogation team in computer-related investigations cannot be overstated. In fact, many child pornographers have confessed at the scene when confronted with evidence of their activity, while others have willingly provided passwords and the like to avoid possible damage to their equipment. (Interestingly, many computer criminals do not realize the legal ramifications of their actions, naively believing that their computers will be returned to them unchanged and that their lives will return to normal.)

- **Sketch and Photo Team**—Like the interview and interrogation team, individuals assigned to this team should be carefully screened for investigative experience. These individuals should be as meticulous as possible, as these sketches may be subpoenaed. In addition, their documentation may be used for recreation or reconstruction purposes. Their responsibilities include diagramming and photographing the entire scene, including criminal evidence, and when possible, videotaping the activities of the on-scene investigators.

- **Physical Search Team**—Case characteristics including the size of the crime scene and the multiplicity of machines will dictate the number of individuals assigned to this unit. In large searches, one officer per room should suffice, as case supervisors should limit the number of personnel on a scene to the absolute minimum to curtail possible scene contamination. The primary responsibility of this team is to identify and mark any and all potential evidence. They are *not* responsible for the collection of such evidence. These individuals should be well versed in types of computer evidence, possible locations, and such. (Although some authors (e.g., Clark & Diliberto, 1996) suggest that these officers do not need to be "computer experts," this author suggests that all team members be selected for their familiarity with computers.)

- **Seizure Team**—Unlike other areas of the investigative unit, assignment to this particular responsibility should be reserved for experienced computer investigators. These individuals are responsible for **bagging and tagging**. Due to the fragility of evidence, it is absolutely essential that individuals handling this step be experienced computer investigators. This team is responsible for imaging the drive, dismantling the computer, and labeling and recording of all relevant evidence. This team should be present at all times during scene processing. (Remember:seizure is the *last* step!) Ideally, this team is comprised of at least two investigators who have extensive computer forensic training. Since this is not possible in most departments, the team should be comprised of at least one seasoned investigator and one computer expert. This is important because computer experts are not usually aware of the legal aspects of investigations,

particularly those dealing with chain of custody and the preservation of criminal evidence. (Many civilians are experts at finding hidden data but are unable to articulate the process implemented.) Thus, officers must be present to ensure proper documentation.

Regardless of team assignment, it is imperative that notification of responsibilities and scheduled activities occur as soon as possible. Such forewarning, including written instructions and expectations, enables team members to prepare themselves and collect the necessary equipment, as well as providing an opportunity for

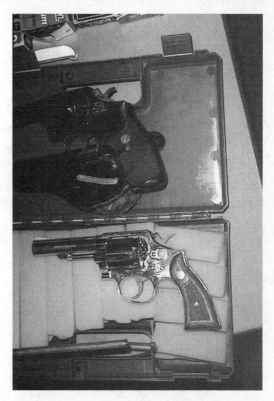

Although they are often perceived as non-dangerous, many computer criminals pose the same risk as traditional suspects. These guns, found in a computer-related search, prove that investigators should be wary of all suspects, not just those on the street. (*Photo Courtesy of James Doyle/NYPD, ret.*)

asking questions. Final pre-raid briefings should address any concerns and should include cautionary admonitions. All team members should be reminded that technological climate aside, traditional procedures for crime scene investigation remain sacrosanct. Thus, officer safety and evidence preservation remain top priorities, and conventional distrust of suspects should guide their on-scene behavior.

Preparing a Toolkit

As with noncomputer-related investigations, the preparation and maintenance of a forensic toolkit is essential for task accomplishment. Such toolkits should be compiled with materials and equipment found within the in-house forensic laboratory, but they are hardly universal. Case characteristics and scene demographics uncovered during intelligence gathering will dictate the specific elements to be included, as well as the necessary quantity. **Toolkit** preparation should

always be initiated with the collection of basic materials found in traditional criminal investigations and culminate with the assemblage of those unique to computer investigations. Investigators should remember that the value of equipment is only appreciated when it is not available. (Remember: it is impossible to be *too* prepared, so it is not only acceptable but also preferred to compile more equipment than necessary.)

Traditional Equipment

1. **Evidence tape**—used to mark the perimeter of the crime scene; it not only prevents entry by individuals external to the investigation, but also induces caution among on-scene personnel.
2. **Packing tape**—used to secure evidence containers.
3. **Evidence storage containers and labels**—although standard evidence labels are appropriate for computer-related evidence, special care should be

As stated throughout the text, the investigation of computer-related crime is similar to the investigation of non-computer-related crime. Thus, much of the material necessary for traditional scene processing, including evidence labels, is also necessary in computer cases. (*Photo Courtesy of James Doyle/NYPD, ret.*)

devoted to the packaging materials used in these investigations, as evidence may be especially vulnerable. (Although the optimum packaging material (i.e., original) is often unavailable, investigators may solicit similar materials from computer stores, large corporations, and universities.) Additional packaging materials include, diskette sleeves for protecting floppies, a multitude of folding boxes and paper bags, and antistatic peanuts.

4. **Miscellaneous writing and labeling materials**—used to label evidence, maintain the chain of custody, and document scene characteristics.

   a. Materials to sketch the crime scene (i.e., graph paper, ruler, pencils, etc.).

   b. Blank forms, including inventory, evidence booking, search warrant templates, etc.

   c. Writing utensils (e.g., pens, markers, and highlighters). Indelible markers, such as laundry pens, are especially useful for marking floppies.

   d. Labels.

   e. Note cards (usually 3–5).

   f. Stick-on circles for marking evidence.

   g. Adhesive numbers or large labels for marking cards and cables.

5. **Sanitary materials**—used to prevent evidence contamination and to protect investigators from unsanitary environments. Such materials include, rubber gloves, bleach, and disposable wipes.

6. **Flashlight**—used in the event of a power outage or to illuminate dark areas (particularly useful under desks, behind equipment, and the like).

7. **Extra batteries**—used to ensure continuity of investigative equipment, including, but not limited to, cameras, flashlights, cellular telephones, tape recorders, etc.

8. **List of contacts**—including contact information about software support, computer experts, hardware manufacturers, magistrate's office, and support organizations (e.g., HTCIA and FCIC).

9. **Mobile carts or evidence transport units**—used to transport multiple containers and heavy equipment and investigative equipment.

10. **Wireless communications**—used as mode of communication and point of contact while on-scene. (Investigators should not use suspect phone.)

11. **Photographic equipment (camera, batteries, extra film)**—used to produce visual documentation of crime scene. Such equipment should be provided to investigators as well as scene photographers, while the latter should be equipped with magnification capabilities. As always, scenes should also be videotaped if departmental resources permit.

12. **Nonmagnetic screwdrivers and hex wrenches**—used to open computer boxes. Often overlooked, such tools are necessary for getting to the guts of the computer. However, investigators should be aware that in rare cases electric screwdrivers emit enough magnetic fields to erase data, and so manual tools are preferred.

13. **Small diagonal cutters**—used for cutting nylon wire ties which are commonly utilized to secure multiple wires for organizational purposes.

14. **Hammer or nail puller**—used for removing nails which secure multiple wires.

Computer-Specific Equipment and Materials

1. **Multiple boot disks**—used to avoid self-destructive programs employed by the suspect and to minimize changes to a suspect drive (i.e., during the routine boot process, disk space is reassigned and file slack may be overwritten). It is highly recommended that investigators maintain custom boot disks which will boot to controlled specifications. At an absolute minimum, investigators should

have a Windows 98 boot disk with imaging capabilities. Investigators should include a Terminate and Stay Resident (TSR) virus shield on their investigative systems and on any boot disks taken to the scene. Some examples include McAfee's *VSHIELD* and *FPROT*. Investigators should remember to update this file on a regular basis. Unlike other programs traditionally found on boot disks which do not necessitate updating, the antivirus software should be the most current. Boot disks should also include storage enhancement programs and popular drivers for computer peripherals. A custom boot disk should boot to controlled specifications.

2. **Backup hardware and miscellaneous computer peripherals**
   a. They are the external devices and corresponding media to capture image of suspect drive. They may vary based on case characteristics (e.g., size and number of suspect drives, amount of data) and departmental resources. Such devices may include, but is not limited to, secondary hard drives.
   b. Color scanner—used to record potential evidence which may not be seized.
   c. Color printer and an assortment of computer paper—used to capture potential evidence residing in print buffers in those cases where on-scene printers are not included within the specifications of the applicable warrant. Printers may also be used to print additional forms, labels, and the like.

3. **Anti-virus software**—used for the documentation and validation of suspect machines and the prevention of infection of forensic machines.

4. **Imaging software**—used for the preservation of the original evidence. As mentioned previously, all forensic analysis should be conducted on the forensic image, ensuring the integrity of the suspect data.

5. **Application software**.

6. **Forensic software**—used for on-site evidence analysis (discussed in greater detail in the previous chapter).
   a. **Viewers**—enable investigators to quickly scan the contents of large numbers of computer files, providing, among other things, a rapid mechanism for identification of criminal contraband.
   b. **Text editors**—enable investigators to quickly search for keywords applicable to the current investigation.
   c. **Hex editors**—enable investigators to view files in hexadecimal formats and quickly search for files which may have been intentionally manipulated or which have been erased or deleted.
   d. **Password crackers**—enable investigators to circumvent many security measures employed by the suspect.
   e. **Verification software**—used to demonstrate the validity of the imaged drive.
   f. **Time/date programs**—verify the system time on the suspect machine.
   g. **Wiping programs**—enables investigators to completely delete (i.e., wipe) files representing criminal contraband if seizure is not possible.
   h. **Locking programs**—ensures data integrity, preventing intentional or accidental manipulation of data.
   i. **Fuzzy logic tools**.
   j. **File cataloging and indexing**—compartmentalizing evidence for ease in further analysis and organization.
   k. **Recovery**—enables investigators to retrieve data from corrupted media, including hidden and deleted files.

7. **Extra media**—used for a variety of purposes including: copying potential digital evidence and creating additional boot disks.

8. **Extra cables, serial port connectors, and gender changers**—used for connecting forensic units to suspect machine.

9. **Extension cords and/or power strips**—used to connect machines to power supplies.

10. **Surge protectors and/or UPS (uninterruptible power supply)**—used to ensure electrical and telephonic continuity to prevent possible destruction of computer data.

11. **Open purchase order**—although difficult to secure, optimal situations provide open purchase orders as the unexpected may occur. While investigators are strongly encouraged to provide for any possible situation and prepare investigative toolkits accordingly, they are often confounded by those situations which they had deemed *impossible*.

ON-SCENE ACTIVITIES

The investigation of computer-related crime requires the same level of preparation and evaluation as do traditional ones. They are neither more intensive nor more demanding on average than nontechnological investigations. They simply require different skills on the part of investigators. As such, the investigative process should mirror conventional methods. Careful handling of evidence, attention to detail, and professionalism should remain paramount considerations, and the unexpected should be expected in all cases. (As discussed in the preceding chapter, pre-search activities often establish the solvability of a particular case. Haphazard investigations are rarely successful, regardless of case content.) Every investigation, for example, should begin with the development of a plan to accomplish the mission at hand, as well as to secure personnel and evidence. Minimal requirements of such plans should include approaching and securing the crime scene, documentation of scene activities,

discovery and identification of potential evidence, the collection and retrieval of such material, and finally, the processing or analysis of potential evidence.

Knock, Notice, and Document

The first step taken at the majority of crime scenes involves the execution of the search warrant (i.e., *knock*, *notice*, and *document*). As in other cases, investigators must announce their presence, their interest, and their intentions, unless extraneous considerations exist which suggests heightened vulnerability of evidence or enhanced risk to the security of team personnel or civilians. (Careful pre-search planning should reveal potential threats, and requests for no-knock warrants should be included in warrant preparation.) To prevent any questions as to their practices, it is highly recommended that this (and the remainder of the investigation) be videotaped whenever possible. Such documentation provides authenticity to their claims, and more importantly, refreshes the memory of investigators when final case disposition is extended. This process can be called *Knock*, *Notice*, and *Document*.

Securing the Crime Scene

The next step in any investigation is the securing of the crime scene. As in noncomputer cases, scene security is perhaps one of the most important, yet often overlooked, factors in the successful prosecution of a suspect. Questions arising from chain of custody, scene contamination, and officer error can all but negate the most compelling of scientific evidence. Thus, it is essential that due regard be given to this step of the investigation. Unlike traditional crime scenes which are often identified and secured by patrol officers, the majority of computer-related crime scenes are such that advanced planning is possible. As such, scene security measures are often tailored to unique case characteristics and are determined prior to arrival at the scene.

Knowledge of case characteristics also enables investigators to determine their method of evidence canvassing (i.e., circular, grid, sector, or triangulation).

Upon scene, several actions must take place simultaneously at an absolute minimum (Remember: there are no absolutes in computer forensics, or police work in general, for that matter. Case characteristics will dictate proper procedures and determine potential problems. Thus, the following is not intended to serve as an all-inclusive list. Rather, it represents the absolute minimum activities which should occur upon arrival at the scene).

1. Dangerous individuals or safety hazards must be immediately recognized and contained.
2. All computers must be located and secured.
3. All personnel must be removed from the immediate area of the evidence.
4. Network connections must be ascertained and appropriate action taken. (Depending on the particular case, the network administrator may prove to be quite helpful in this respect. She/he may immediately disable network access, preventing possible remote destruction.)
5. All suspects should be immediately separated and escorted to a predetermined location.
6. All computers should be protected by a police officer. This is necessary to ensure that the computer is not manipulated in any way—remotely or not. While many of the concerns involve remote destruction, it is not always possible to sever network connections immediately. Thus, some computers may remain vulnerable to outside actions.

As securing computer crime scenes includes consideration of not only traditional hazards but also electronic threats, it is imperative that investigators identify threats that might exist from nontraditional sources and/or remote locations. Potential hazards may include booby-trapped drives and remote access. Hacker systems, in particular, should be approached with due caution. Luckily, these systems, on average, are relatively easy to identify. Workspaces littered with food and beverage debris, evidence of an individual spending large amounts of time with their computer, may signal the presence of a hacker system. Homemade systems, an assortment of atypical computer devices, or open computer boxes (i.e., computer casings, not cardboard containers) are additional beacons. Other hints in or around computer areas may include the presence of hacking literature (e.g., *Phrack, Legion of Doom Technical Journal, Activist Times Incorporated, P/HUN*) or war dialers, and software cracking programs, Trojan horses, and philes from Cult of the Dead Cow located on a suspect device are a sure sign.[4]

Determining the Need for Additional Assistance

Once the scene is secured, team supervisors must evaluate the capabilities of the personnel present during warrant execution. Assuming that proper pre-search routines included adequate intelligence gathering, this step may not be necessary, although team leaders should be prepared for the unexpected at all times as criminal investigations tend to adhere to Murphy's Law. Even the most prolific computer crime investigators, for example, confront certain systems outside of their expertise. Thus, outside assistance should be requested if any of the following systems are to be analyzed and if departmental personnel lack certification.

1. **Mainframes** are usually found in large organizations or governmental institutions. They are usually contained in one area with sophisticated air conditioning and power systems. When serving warrants on **mainframes**, investigators should seek the assistance of the system programmer. If the one onsite is not reliable or is actually a target of the investigation, investigators should contact the

manufacturer. They usually have technical support available 24-hours a day.

2. **Minicomputers** are similar to mainframes which require a specially trained staff to maintain. Again, if investigators are not comfortable with the current administrator, they contact the manufacturer or vendor.

3. **Specialty and Hacker Computers**—usually identified by its appearance, a hacker or specialty computer may be characterized by drives without covers, unusual connections, various external media, or cluttered work space. Often times, hacker systems, in particular, will be surrounded by food wrappers, soda cans, ash trays, and the like, betraying the user's lifestyle. These systems should be approached with great caution as hackers take pains to protect their own systems from intrusions. Investigators who have no experience with these systems should call an expert for assistance. At the minimum, investigators should secure the computer from any and all suspects. In addition, investigators should ascertain the presence of modulating capability, prohibiting contacts with telephones.

Scene Processing

Once the scene has been thoroughly secured and all necessary personnel have been employed, the next step in any criminal investigation involves scene processing. Although case characteristics may alter the significance or length of each individual step, the single most important aspect of scene processing in all cases is proper documentation, as investigative tactics and collection procedures may be dissected in open court. This is especially true in computer cases. Defense attorneys, relying on the traditional stereotype of technologically retarded officers, may attempt to discredit investigators by grilling them not only on procedures, but also on the justification of these procedures. Unwary investigators may find

themselves unprepared to answer technologically direct questions. As such, investigators should carefully document *every* step taken during the investigation. At a minimum, such noncomputer-specific documentation should include:

- the date, time, and location of the search, and a chronological timeline of all investigative steps taken during the process
- the identity of all individuals present at the scene upon arrival
- the identity of all investigative personnel assisting in scene processing (including names, ranks, and badge numbers of all officers)
- names, positions, and contact information for nondepartmental personnel
- descriptions and locations of all computers, devices, or media located throughout the search (including CPUs, monitors, keyboards, external storage devices, etc.)
- physical condition of all computer equipment located at the scene, including visible damage (this may be especially important to protect the corresponding department from allegations of abuse)
- presence of and status of network connections and the presence of a dial tone in cases where modems are used for connection purposes
- identification of all material or equipment which is seized
- detailed description of the scene
- status of all computers at the scene, including a description of what the computer is doing (i.e., off/on, connected to the Internet, open documents and programs, etc.)
- chronological timeline of all investigative clues and developing leads; date, time, and description of any investigative software used, and a brief justification
- whether the potential for external destruction (including mechanical, weather, magnetic) exists
- a detailed chain of custody report

In addition, investigators at the scene should document any computer-specific information available which does not require intrusion, such as open documents, desktop, tree structure, system ID, and time/date of computer clock.

Capturing the entire process on videotape is *highly* recommended, although it is not necessary to enable the audio recording capability. (In fact, audio recordings are highly discouraged as conversations between or reactions of investigators may contain profanity or comments viewed as inappropriate or unprofessional by a civilian jury.) This practice allows officers to revisit the scene as often as necessary. In addition, it makes a permanent record of all of the actions that were taken and all of the evidence that was uncovered. This may prove especially important if the computer evidence is somehow altered or destroyed during or after the investigative process. A computer screen depicting child pornography which is caught on tape, for example, may prove invaluable if the data is erased through remote detonation or careless handling. Finally, it provides a pictorial representation of the appearance and position of objects at the scene and supports the testimony of investigating officers.

Such documentation may provide them with inalienable credibility with judicial officials and, perhaps more importantly, jurors. In addition, such practices provide the chain of custody necessary for evidence validity. This may be especially important in cases where violations of the Electronic Communication Privacy Act are alleged. Thus, every step of the investigation should be clearly articulated. (In addition, proper pre-search activities should inculcate the specifics of the case and, most importantly, the limitations of the applicable search warrant. Investigators should be very clear on the types of evidence which are searchable, and those which may be seized *prior* to scene processing.) This is especially important in computer investigations as case characteristics and evolving evidence all but negate traditional notions of routinization. (Remember: any of the following variables may alter the methodology of scene processing: computer operating systems, status of computers, status of network connections, types of network connections, active software applications, advance knowledge of or on-scene discovery of self-destructive programs, assessment of other types of computer vulnerability (e.g., electrical surges and weather considerations), and warrant permissibility (i.e., breadth and scope)).

Photograph/Video

As stated previously, the golden rule for any successful criminal investigation should be: *document, document, document.* Photographs and videos are an integral part of the documentation process, and they should occur at every stage of scene processing. As in traditional crime scene investigations, it is absolutely imperative that the complete computer crime scene be photographed

---

Minimum Things to Document

1. Date, time, and description of computer, including physical damage.
2. Identifying information on all investigative personnel.
3. Identifying information on all individuals present (e.g., potential witnesses and suspects).
4. All investigative clues uncovered and developing leads.
5. Investigative software used.
6. Chronology of all actions taken.
7. Type and status of network connection.
8. Verification of network connection.
9. Status of computer.
10. Computer activity (including open documents and active software).
11. Computer desktop.
12. System date/time.
13. Tree structure (if possible).
14. Image verification.
15. Chain of custody.

As with traditional crime scenes, proper documentation of the scene is extremely important. Computer evidence requires additional photographs, and particular attention should be given to the state of the computer prior to seizure. Such documentation includes, but is not limited to: computer connections, screen activity, etc. (*Photo Courtesy of James Doyle/NYPD, ret.*)

prior to evidence collection. (To reiterate, complementary videographic documentation is highly encouraged.) This allows investigators to fully document their actions and the state of the evidence during scene processing. This may nullify

defense arguments that officers contaminated or corrupted criminal evidence. Regardless of approach, investigators should pay extra attention to the configuration of computer equipment, including connections, and most importantly, the back of the computer. This practice serves several purposes. First, it enables investigators to fully document to the court the manner in which the scene was processed. Second, it serves as a refresher for investigators called to testify months or years after the fact. And, finally, it enables investigators to duplicate the original state of the computer in court. These photographs should include close-ups and distant shots, and evidence should be illustrated in a contextual manner, using common objects as references. (Remember: photographs and videotapes may either serve as an alibi or signal an investigator's death knell. Investigators should be instructed to act as if they were performing live for the public or the jury—because they are).

Sketching the Scene

Sketching a crime scene is essential in any criminal investigation. It provides an overview of the state of the scene and acts as corroboration for investigative field notes and scene photographs. Because extraneous objects may be omitted from crime-scene sketches and not from photographs, sketches represent a more focused illustration of the applicable evidence. All sketches should include: name and rank of investigator; time, date, case number, and crime classification; name, rank, and/or identification of any and all persons providing assistance for the artist (i.e., those assisting with measurement, etc.); and orientation of

---

Computer-Specific Things to Photograph

1. Entire system configuration.
2. Front, back, and sides of computer.
3. Electrical wires, outlet configuration, and cable connections.
4. Corresponding media.
5. Printer status.
6. Attached hardware and peripherals.
7. Computer screen—this is essential as the data stored in RAM will be lost once the computer is unplugged.
8. Connection to the phone.
9. Any unusual characteristics (i.e., hiding places, written passwords, etc.).

NonComputer-Specific Things to Photograph

1. Entire scene.
2. Bookshelves—may give clues as to the level of sophistication of the suspect, possible passwords, and the like.
3. Desks and area surrounding computer.
4. Notes, stickies, and paper products surrounding computer.

all evidence, including compass direction, landmarks, position in building, etc. In the interest of efficiency, original sketches should be made in pencil, and investigators should not attempt to draw everything to scale. The documentation of measurements and the like will allow for sketch clean-up at a later time. (However, investigators should remember that even rough sketches may be subpoenaed and are treated as permanent recordings.) Measurements should extend along fixed and identifiable points, and objects must remain stationary during the measurement process.

Identifying Potential Evidence

Perhaps the most challenging of all aspects of computer crime scene processing is the identification of potential evidence external to the computer itself. Often times, investigators, in their haste to identify evidence residing on a suspect drive, will overlook trace evidence and other forms of information which may be critical to a successful investigation. As such, traditional scene practices like reviewing paper documents at the scene, dusting for fingerprints, or looking for hair and fiber may be sensible actions. In addition, this type of evidence is essential for physically placing the suspect at the scene. Assuming that the scene has been physically and electronically secured and that there is no immediate threat to human life, investigators should gather **trace evidence** prior to seizure of electronic evidence. As always, investigators should take due regard to ensure that such evidence is not altered or destroyed by careless handling of keyboards, power supplies, and the like.

In addition to trace evidence, investigators should also be alert for the presence of other types of material which may circumstantially link a suspect to a particular crime or reveal clues which further or advance an investigation (e.g., passwords). Computer printouts, software packaging, and post-it notes might contain criminal evidence, as even computer criminals use paper for record-keeping purposes. Software manuals, for example, may provide a wealth of assistance in criminal investigations, as they are often a popular place for hiding passwords. These manuals and the contact numbers for technical support found within them might also prove critical for investigators faced with software which is outdated or outside their expertise. Finally, these manuals or packaging might indicate the types of software residing upon a suspect system, signaling the sophistication of the user and the appropriate level of caution to be exercised by investigators; and alerting investigators to hidden programs. Thus, investigators should exhaustively search for documentary evidence, both direct and circumstantial, and other noncomputer-specific materials at the scene in addition to targeted systems.

Computer Components, the most recognizable of all computer evidence, include hard drives, keyboards, monitors, modems, printers, graphic cards, assorted storage devices, etc. In most investigations, a plethora of direct and circumstantial evidence may be located on a suspect hard drive. The presence of a library of pornographic representations of children, for example, may directly link a suspect to peddling in child pornography, while a review of cache files may circumstantially link him to a multitude of sites facilitating the transfer of such material. Both types of evidence might also be contained in computer peripherals like printers, where evidentiary documents are directly linked to a specific computer with individual characteristics (i.e., dot matrix with indelible "I", etc.) or circumstantially used to discuss class characteristics of printed material (i.e., laser, ink jet, dot matrix, daisy wheel, thermal printers, etc.). (As such, investigators should use caution not to disable or disconnect a printer which is currently running until the evidentiary value is ascertained. In addition, printers which are currently disabled should be powered on as print buffers might contain criminal evidence.)

Direct and/or circumstantial evidence might also reside on storage media in the same manner as it does on the hard drive. **Magnetic tape storage units**, mostly used as backup devices for large amounts of data, for example, may contain large portions of hard drives. They may also be useful in the collaboration of evidence collected at the scene, negating challenges by the defense that the hard drive was manipulated or altered by law enforcement. Other types of mass storage devices (e.g., compact discs, digital versatile disks, or USB flash drives) may also serve the same function, and all should be treated as potential evidence regardless of written labels. However, investigators should be aware of the limitations of the corresponding warrant and the particular jurisdictional climate in which it was issued. A good rule of thumb in all computer investigations (especially during the warrant preparation) is to include *assorted media* in the list of items to be searched and/or seized. Whenever authorized, investigators should seize *all* external storage devices. In searches predicated on a warrant authorizing the seizure of *related media* only, investigators should randomly sample several devices to ascertain the accuracy of their labeling scheme. Such sampling should also include those items appearing to be audio recordings (i.e., music CDs), as a case can be made that they might contain criminal evidence (i.e., hiding in plain sight is often best). (Remember: Actions which are reasonable in nature and scope are more likely to withstand judicial scrutiny.)

Assorted computer components might also prove valuable as circumstantial evidence. The presence of active modems or network connections, for example, clearly illustrates the computer's ability to communicate with others, while the presence of CD/DVD burners demonstrates the device's capacity for mass production of copyrighted material. Investigators should also be alert to those items which are not directly attached to a suspect system. Assorted computer paraphernalia, like extra hard drives, computer cords, connection devices, or power strips might reveal the recent presence of a computer at a scene in which the computer was removed by the suspect prior to the search. Although circumstantial at best, this type of testimony coupled with corroborative evidence like eyewitness testimony may result in the successful prosecution of a suspect.

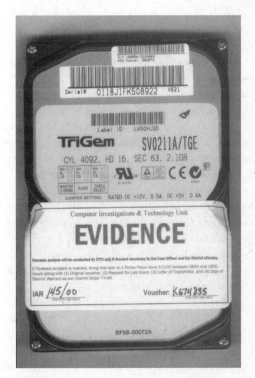

In order to preserve the integrity of the evidence, investigators should clearly label each item. Evidence labels, like the one shown here, are ideal in computer cases in which evidence may be quite fragile. (*Photo Courtesy of James Doyle/NYPD, ret.*)

Locating Evidence

As stated, not all the evidence involved in computer-related investigations is computer-specific. In fact, items which appear to bear little relevance to case characteristics may be those which are most critical to the investigation. Paper documents, crumpled sticky notes, well-worn books, materials found within or around computer work areas may prove to be critical for successful prosecution. Thus, even those investigators who are largely unfamiliar with computer-related criminal activity or the evidence that surrounds it can employ traditional crime scene investigation tactics, with some variations, by focusing on some of the following areas:

Desktops—Desktops may be a virtual cornucopia of evidence including messages, memos, monthly bills or statements, notes, ledgers, computer media, and equipment, manuals, containers, radios, tapes, televisions, and numerous office supplies. (Remember: Much of this information has traditionally been overlooked in computer seizures. While this may seem a mundane task initially, the potential of finding incriminating evidence may make it a gratifying one.)

Monitors—Computer monitors have proven a popular place for passwords. This is especially true for multiple system users. Because some systems require different passwords for security purposes and others require users to change their passwords frequently, many users simply tape them to their monitors. Other items which may be taped to a computer monitor include Web addresses, phone numbers, appointments, and the like. (Monitors should also be carefully evaluated to ascertain if the monitor itself has images burned onto its surface. Although this applies more to monochrome monitors and is, in fact, most unusual in this era of screen savers and advanced technology, investigators should study the screens of all suspect machines.)

Keyboards—Notes and passwords may also be taped to the computer keyboard. Investigators should always inspect the underside of the keyboard and other computer components, as suspects have been known to tape passwords, diskettes, and the like in these locations.

Telephone—Like monitors and keyboards, telephones have proven a popular place for passwords, appointments, phone numbers, and the like. Some individuals have even taped codes for voice messaging to the receiver.

Wallets or Purses—While some evidence found in purses, such as electronic organizers or Palm Pilots, may seem obvious, investigators should be careful in searching the entire contents, making notes along the way. Information such as student IDs, credit card numbers, birthdates, or pocket organizers may be useful in cracking passwords. (Remember: Many individuals tend to pick one combination of letters or numbers for all their password needs. Thus, slips of paper, social security cards, and driver's license may carry information vital for cracking protected systems.)

Clothing—Just as traditional crime-scene investigation involves a search of the suspect's clothing, so should technological investigations. In the computer-oriented world in which we live, computer media have often replaced briefcases. Thus, critical evidence may be found within a suspect's coat or shirt pocket in the form of a computer diskette.

Trash Cans, Recycle Bins, and Other Garbage Containers—Alert investigators have been known to discover valuable evidence in refuse containers. Hard copy printouts of computer produced documents may include incriminating evidence. In addition, handwritten notes may reveal passwords, location of files, or criminal networks. Even documents which have been shredded may prove invaluable to investigators, as some devices fail to separate the shredded documents—neatly folding the shredded item on top of itself. Thus, a little scotch tape and some patience may go a long way. Other items found may include the perforated edges of computer paper and computer packaging products. These items may be important indicators of what type of computer equipment should be at the scene, sometimes alerting investigators to their absence. Investigators should carefully evaluate all paper products for possible evidence. Although this may seem a daunting and often thankless endeavor, computer diskettes, spread sheets, and password listings are but a few of the items which have been found carefully taped to the pages of novels, medical books, software manuals, and computerized printouts.

Printers—Much like hard drives or other storage media, hard disk print buffers and print spooler devices retain data until it is written over. Thus, the last image printed by a laser printer may be retrievable, while traditional ribboned printers (found primarily on older machines) maintain evidence on the ribbon itself.

Inside the computer—As expected, the majority of evidence in a computer-related crime resides within or upon a computer component. While the recovery of such evidence will be discussed in the next chapter, investigators should be aware that all storage devices and input/output devices are potential gold mines of information. Thus, nontechnical investigators or nonspecialists should treat all computer components and paraphernalia with utmost caution.

Seizure and Documentation of Evidence

Once evidence has been identified, it is necessary to determine if the evidence is actually seizable. While some things may be seized on their face (i.e., contraband, fruits of the crime, items criminally possessed, etc.), others may not. Investigators, especially those inexperienced in computer investigations, should read the applicable warrant carefully, familiarizing themselves thoroughly with its specifications and limitations, *prior to* its execution. Whenever possible, each individual investigator or team of investigators should physically maintain in their possession a copy of the warrant throughout the duration of the investigation, as techno-warrants may be quite lengthy. As with traditional investigations, personnel should collect and preserve all evidence with extreme caution—assuring court admissibility. If, for example, an item which is found appears to

contain criminal evidence but is not included in the warrant, its seizure should only occur if the original warrant is formally amended or (more likely) a secondary warrant is issued. (Remember: waiting an hour for a judge's signature may seem inconvenient and more than a little annoying, but it pales in comparison to the days, weeks, months, or even years of work that can be dismissed in a jurisprudential second.)

Once the determination is made that evidence may be seized, the collection process should be initiated with the **imaging** (i.e., duplicated byte for byte, bit for bit) of drives onto clean media (preferably new). It is absolutely essential that this process be conducted on all hard drives prior to analysis or removal with tested forensic software packages or with clean boot disks previously prepared. If boot disks are employed, they should minimally contain any and all system drivers, applicable software, virus protection, and write-blocking programs. (Remember: write-blocking is necessary to negate challenges of corruption or contamination.) Verification of such images should also be conducted prior to evidence removal as forensic analysis should only be conducted on such images, preserving the original evidence in its entirety.[5] Many software packages, some commercially available, provide both imaging and verification utilities.

Secured computers (i.e., safe from destruction—remote or actual) which are on should not be turned off until the scene is photographed and properly documented, unless the imminent hazards to data outweigh the need for documentation. The current state of the computer and the monitor should be carefully noted prior to powering down. Some investigators also suggest copying all open documents to an external storage device prior to powering down. They should not simply turn the power off on the computer. In some cases, investigators have unwittingly turned the computer off, thus destroying potential evidence. This is especially problematic if the suspect is using an uninterruptible power supply and is working solely in memory.

FORENSIC EXAMINATION OF DIGITAL EVIDENCE: A GUIDE FOR LAW ENFORCEMENT · NIJ

Image Archive Information

Archive Method: Direct to Tape ☐   NTBackup ☐   Tar ☐   Other :* _____   Compressed? ☐
Attach appropriate worksheet for backup method used.
Tape Type: DAT 24 ☐   Dat 40 ☐   DLT ☐*   Other *:   _____   Number Used:

*Requires Lab Director Approval

Analysis Platform Information

Operating Systems Used: DOS ☐   Windows ☐   Mac ☐   *nix ☐   Other: _____
　　　　Version: _____

Analysis Software Base: I-Look ☐   EnCase ☐   DOS Utilities ☐   *nix Utilities ☐   Other:*
　　　　Version: _____

Restored Work Copy/Image Validated: Yes ☐   No ☐

List of utilities used other than base

Utility	Version	Purpose

Analysis Milestones

Milestone	Remarks	Initials
Run Anti-Virus Scan		
Full File List with Meta Data		
Identify Users/Logons/ISP Accounts, etc.		
Browse File System		
Keyword/String Search		
Web/E-mail Header Recovery		
Recover & Examine Free/Slack Space		
Examine Swap		
Unerase/Recover Deleted Files		
Execute Programs as Needed		
Examine/Recover Mail/Chat		
Crack Passwords		

Hard Drive Evidence Worksheet　　　　　　　　　　　　　　　　Page 2 of 2

The documentation of imaging should include all relevant information and include information regarding image verification procedures. The above form, compiled by the National Institute of Justice, is both straightforward and comprehensive and should accompany computer evidence.

However, circumstances may be such that remote manipulation or destruction of data is a distinct possibility. In these situations, investigators will have to evaluate the advantages and disadvantages of imaging drives prior to disconnecting them. If, for example, investigators are unable to disconnect a target computer from a network interface, they may wish to sacrifice the memory in RAM and pull the plug in the back of the computer. (Remember: if it is determined that a computer should be disconnected, always pull the plug from the back of the computer itself. This saves investigators the extended time it may take to locate the power outlet and, more importantly, eliminates the possibility that they may miss an uninterruptible power supply.) Regardless of approach, investigators should be aware that powering down may lead to more complicated analysis at the lab. (On Windows 2000, for example, a simple check mark in the *Advanced* section of the *File Properties* window enables encryption of files and entire folders while running invisibly in the background. Thus, if the user chooses to encrypt documents and temporary files, then pulling the plug would lead to automatic encryption of working files. Although password crackers could be utilized, investigators must consider the possibility that those files would be permanently inaccessible.)

As always, documentation is essential. All case notes, materials, etc. should be written in ink—requiring initialized verification for subsequent alteration or modification. In addition, notes should be of a comprehensive nature—enabling any investigator to clearly articulate the process, procedures, and investigative steps undertaken throughout initial scene processing. Although often overlooked, the importance of comprehensiveness can not be overstated. As the criminal justice process is often slow and convoluted, individuals may be asked to testify in cases with which they are completely unfamiliar. In addition, proper documentation will eradicate many of the judicial headaches that may be encountered under cross-examination.

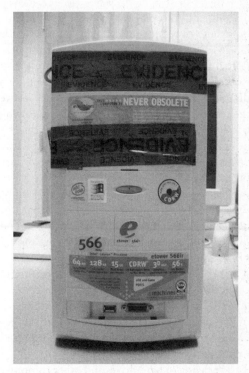

To avoid accidental contamination of evidence, drive openings should be inaccessible. Evidence tape, included in investigator toolkits, may accomplish this goal. (*Photo Courtesy of James Doyle/NYPD, ret.*)

Bagging and Tagging

Like any scientific evidence, great care must be exercised when collecting and preserving crime scene evidence. The chain of custody and continuity of possession must be maintained at all times for court admissibility. Investigators should adhere to standard operating procedures for custodial evidence collection—keeping in mind that routinization enhances witness credibility and evidence validity. Although policies and procedures vary by department, certain things remain constant.

Once images have been taken and verified, investigators should carefully label all components of the computer system and corresponding computer media and connections. Investigators should place coordinating labels on both ends of every cable and the corresponding outlets. Empty outlets should always be labeled as such to simplify physical reconfiguration at the lab or in the courtroom. Empty disk slots should be filled with a floppy containing a disabling program and taped closed to secure the read/write heads in the floppy drives during transport and to prevent accidental access by noninvestigative personnel. (Investigators may write-block drives in the autoexec.bat or use programs like Maresware's *DISABLE* which will disable a computer's keyboard, lock the computer upon start up, and alert the user that this device is forensic evidence.) This process, and the remainder of the evidence collection, should be videotaped whenever possible. If investigators are using traditional methods, they should carefully photograph all of the evidence after labeling, paying particular attention to the back of the computer. This enables investigators to recreate the entire system in the lab and, more importantly, in the courtroom.

Packaging of hard drives and other computer components should be undertaken with great care and be consistent with traditional collection methods. Latex gloves, for example, should be employed as to not contaminate fingerprints or other potential trace evidence, and a detailed shipping manifest which includes the date and time of shipping, the contents of each box, and the name or identification of the individual loading each box should be created. (This process is essential for maintaining the chain of custody and should ease the loading and unloading of often voluminous evidence.) Each individual piece of evidence should be carefully marked by the officer or investigator who collects it, and all components from a single computer system should be packaged together. This marking should never damage or impair the value of evidence or limit the number or type of examinations which may be conducted by experts. Although some investigators have adopted the practice of scratching initials, date, and the like on objects recovered, this is not recommended in computer cases.

As mentioned previously, computer components and media are more fragile than some traditional forms of evidence. Thus, marking materials should be nondestructive or intrusive. Computer wires and connection ports should be carefully labeled with colored tape prior to removal or disconnection. Computer diskettes and covered components may also be marked with colored tape and stored in appropriate sleeves. Minimum information should include the investigator's initials, date found, and location of evidence. When available, original packaging is the best form of container. (Investigators may also wish to include extra packaging materials in their evidence kits.) Other appropriate forms of containment include static-free paper products. In a pinch, standard paper envelopes may be used, but all packaging materials should be carefully labeled to maintain the chain of custody.

As stated, the maintenance of the chain of custody is essential for any successful prosecution. However, it is not the only consideration in computer-related investigations. Contamination and corruption, a consideration in all criminal cases, may be more so in computer cases, because of the fragile nature of the data. Thus, traditional methods are not always appropriate. Like blood and other liquid evidence which is vulnerable to environmental factors, computer media may be inadvertently destroyed if exposed to extreme temperatures or careless handling. Although newer computer equipment and removable storage devices are less sensitive than the dinosaurs of old, they may still be damaged when exposed to certain conditions. As a general rule, the following factors must be considered in computer-related investigations:

Temperature—Heat poses one of the greatest threats to computer evidence. Investigators should take care not to place computer components or media near excessive heat or direct sunlight. Although hardware is not as susceptible, media are especially vulnerable to intemperate environments. Several well-documented cases have been hopelessly lost because investigators

General Checklist for Evidence Preservation

Resources permitting, agencies should strive to create computer-specific evidence rooms. This prevents the potential for evidence corruption, contamination, and destruction. These environments should be climate-controlled, dust-free, and large enough to store equipment for extended periods. The following list is provided for agencies without these capabilities.

1. Temperatures should reach no higher than 90° F and no lower than 60° F.
2. Environments should (as much as possible) be dust-free. Additional security may be provided by paper packaging or coverings.
3. Environments should be free from magnetic fields. If possible, computer evidence should not be stored in proximity to electromagnetic fields. (A compass may be used to test for magnetic fields.)
4. Environments should be free from corrosive elements, such as those commonly found in arson investigations (i.e., accelerants, etc.).
5. Evidence should be stored on nonplastic shelving, preferably made of wood.
6. Environments should be static-free. Simple precautions may include avoidance of carpet, plastic shelving or containers, excessively dry environments, etc.
7. Upon arrival at storage facility, tags and identifying materials should be verified and properly marked for easy identification.
8. Evidence should be stored together so that investigators may find all components quickly and easily.

left computer evidence in their cars. Obvious damage included warped diskettes, melted tapes, and the like, but further damage may occur when damaged media are not immediately recognized and introduced into other computer equipment. Lost data and damaged equipment are but two of the possible results from exposure. The fallout of such disregard may include lost cases, thousands of investigative dollars wasted, and perpetrators set free.

Magnetic Fields—Any type of magnetic field poses a potentially calamitous risk to computer media and hardware. Although unlikely, even low-level magnetic pulses, such as those emitted from car radios and transmitters may create an environment hazardous to computer-related evidence. Such situations may cause information erasure. Other hazards may include electric motors, speakers, magnetic clips, or even refrigerator magnets. (Due to the sheer volume of potential evidence, some investigators have attempted to photocopy computer media as a form of scene documentation. This may prove fatal to an investigation. *Do not* photocopy any computer evidence. Photographic or videotaped evidence is not only preferred, it is a necessity!)

Static Electricity—An additional hazard to computer components or data involves static electricity. Traditional plastic evidence bags, for example, may generate levels of static electricity dangerous to computer media. Because of the magnetic components previously discussed, static electricity which may appear to be little more than a nuisance in other situations (e.g., clinging garments and low-level shocks) can irreparably damage critical evidence. Thus, evidence should be collected in paper evidence bags. Some manufacturers of collection materials have even developed special containers for this very purpose. Static electricity may also pose a danger to circuit boards and exposed wires. Investigators may not recognize this danger until computer equipment does not function properly. Unfortunately, by then, it is too late. Static electricity and the destruction of data in cases with exposed wires are not the only dangers. High voltage and exposed wires also pose a significant risk to human life.

Oil, Dirt, and Dust—Investigators have long known that introducing foreign elements to a crime scene may irrevocably contaminate or corrupt potential evidence. Accordingly, evidence technicians have traditionally taken precautionary measures by collecting things such as gloves, hair and shoe coverings, and the like. However, these things, while protecting traditional forms of evidence, create unacceptable levels of static electricity to computer evidence. Investigators should be acutely aware of the dangers posed by common oils found on palms and fingertips. Special care should be exercised when dealing with damaged media or exposed tape, heads, or drives. (Remember: Contamination is contagious—exposing other elements to damaged or corrupted components may spread the problem.)

Additional Environmental Characteristics—Although the fragility of computer equipment may appear obvious, past cases reveal that this is not the case. Investigators have been known to stack heavy objects on top of computer equipment, thus damaging the hard drive and destroying criminal evidence. Others have been known to place computer equipment in dusty or dirty environments. (Remember: If you would not be comfortable in an environment, neither is the computer.) Attempt to place related materials singularly on appropriate shelving in a climate-controlled, dust-free environment.

Interviewing Witnesses

While at the scene, investigators should interview witnesses for information which furthers the investigation itself or which relate to ownership, possession, or the chain of custody. As criminal defendants often deny possession of or access to criminal evidence located on a computer, it is essential to collect evidence which establishes a connection between them and the criminal evidence. At the same time, investigators must trace the custody or usage of the equipment by individuals other than the suspect. In other words, investigators must establish a comprehensive history of the suspect equipment to defeat challenges based on chain of custody. This is especially true in cases in which a third party discovered, and perhaps even investigated, criminal evidence prior to notifying law enforcement authorities. Although case characteristics will determine

specific context and parameters of the questioning of such witness, investigators should seek answers to the following questions:

- What types of digital evidence have been collected prior to the involvement of law enforcement? For example, in a cyberstalking case, does a hardcopy version of the e-mail exist? Is an electronic copy available? Does it contain full header information?
- How was the evidence discovered?
- Who handled the evidence? (Note: could be multiple individuals)
- Who controlled the digital evidence after it was examined and before it was given to authorities?
- When and how was the digital evidence collected and stored?
- Where was the evidence when it was collected?
- What type of equipment held the digital evidence?
- Who had access to the equipment?
- Who owned the equipment?
- Was the equipment shared?
- Was information retrieved from a network?
- Was information password protected?
- Who had access to password-protected information?
- Is the data located at an offsite location?
- Who may be responsible for the incident? Why do you think so?
- What actions have been taken to identify, collect, preserve, or analyze the data and the devices involved?[6]

Investigators should be as meticulous as possible in documenting the chain of custody. At a minimum, this should include the name, address, contact information, company position, or personal relationship of all individuals.

Scene Departure and Transportation of Evidence to Lab

Once the evidence has been properly collected and loaded into appropriate vehicles for transportation, investigators should follow traditional procedures for exiting a crime scene (e.g., physically securing the scene and removal of recovery equipment). Prior to leaving, investigators should re-photograph the crime scene to avoid allegations of police misconduct. Upon arrival at the lab, shipping manifests should be checked over carefully, and all items should be properly accounted for. (In addition, investigators should note the condition of the boxes upon unloading, erring on the side of caution.) These manifests should remain with the evidence at all times, and should, in fact, be treated as evidence in and of themselves. Once accounted for, all incoming evidence should be entered into the appropriate evidence control systems and assigned to a location or examiner to await analysis.

◉ CONCLUSIONS

Although many departments lack sufficient resources to adequately staff full-time computer crime units, traditional procedures for criminal investigations may be utilized by supervisory personnel in high-tech cases to ensure proper evidence collection and analysis. Investigations involving computer-related evidence should be approached in much the same manner as traditional investigations. Irrespective of case characteristics, the success of criminal investigations and subsequent prosecutions largely hinges upon both pre-search activities (i.e., warrant preparation, intelligence gathering, assembling an execution team, planning the search, and assigning responsibilities) and on-scene processing (i.e., execution of the warrant, securing the scene, evidence collection and preservation, and the transportation of evidence). Proper planning in advance ensures the successful collection of relevant evidence.

Traditionally, investigations involving computer-related evidence were often difficult due to a lack of qualified personnel and an absence of forensic laboratories. Untrained officers would routinely overlook, contaminate, or destroy potentially critical evidence. As the discipline of computer forensics evolves, such situations have diminished, but they have not been completely eliminated. The establishment of forensic laboratories, the assignment of specific personnel, and the partnering with civilian experts should continue to reduce such occurrences. In fact, careful planning and meticulous oversight should provide all departments with a platform for successful prosecution.

DISCUSSION QUESTIONS

1. What does the acronym SMEAC stand for, and how does it apply to computer investigations?
2. What are the seven general categories of personnel which may be necessary at a computer-related crime scene?
3. What items should be placed in on-scene toolkits? Which are mandatory and which will vary due to case characteristics?
4. Why is proper scene documentation so critical in criminal investigations? What are some basic guidelines?
5. What are some unusual situations that may require additional or specialized assistance?
6. Generally speaking, what are the basic steps of crime-scene processing?
7. Where should investigators look for evidence in computer-related cases?
8. What are some unique concerns in preservation of digital evidence?

RECOMMENDED READING

- DOJ (2007). *Digital Evidence in the Courtroom: A Guide for Law Enforcement and Prosecutors*. NIJ Special Report. U.S. Department of Justice: Office of Justice Programs. Washington, DC.
- Farmer, Dan and Venema, Wietse (2004). *Digital Discovery*. Addison-Wesley Professional: Ohio.
- Lyle, James (2003). "NIST CFTT: Testing Disk Imaging Tools." *International Journal of Digital Evidence*, 1(4). Available at *www.ijde.org*.
- Turnbull, Benjamin; Blundell, Barry; and Slay, Jill (2006). "Google Desktop as a Source of Digital Evidence." *International Journal of Digital Evidence*, 5(1): 1–12. Available at *www.ijde.org*.

- Wang, S. and Kao, D. (2007, May). "Internet Forensics on the Basis of Evidence Gathering with Peep Attacks." *Computer Standards & Interfaces*, *29*(4), 423–429.

WEB RESOURCES

- www.ijde.org – homepage to the *International Journal of Digital Evidence*. The site maintains the entire collection of articles published since its inception.
- www.ncjrs.gov – homepage to the National Criminal Justice Research Service, a federally funded resource offering justice information to support research, policy, and program development worldwide. It is sponsored by the U.S. Department of Justice and is housed within the Office of Justice Programs. The site provides abstracts or full-text articles on a variety of criminal justice topics. In addition, it provides announcements for funding opportunities.
- www.iacptechnology.org – a division of the International Association of Chiefs of Police, this site provides access to various articles on technology and criminal justice.
- http://www.gocsi.com/ – Computer Security Institute (CSI) serves the needs of Information Security Professionals through membership, educational events, security surveys, and awareness tools. Joining CSI provides you with high quality CSI publications, discounts on CSI conferences, access to online archives, career development, networking opportunities and more.

ENDNOTES

[1] Ritter, Nancy (2006). "Digital Evidence: How Law Enforcement Can Level the Playing Field with Criminals." *NIJ Journal*, *254*. Available at *http://www.ojp.usdoj.gov/nij/journals/254/digital_evidence.html*. Retrieved from the Internet on October 10, 2007.

[2] *United States* v. *Carey*, 172 F.3d 1268; 1999 U.S. App. LEXIS 7197; 1999 Colo. J.C.A.R. 2287.

[3] Kessler, Gary (2005). *The Role of Computer Forensics in Law Enforcement*. Available at: *http://www.garykessler.net/library/role_of_computer_forensics.html*. Retrieved from the Internet on October 10, 2007.

[4] A knowledgeable computer criminal might create a number of batch files which can perform unusual and nefarious tasks. Once the actual analysis of a system begins, investigators may also wish to look at the size of the autoexec.bat file, directories labeled "bats," "batches," "belfry" (i.e., home for the real flying rodents) or the like, and caches of hacker sites—often identified by the unique language or orthography found within them (e.g., use of the numeral "0" in place of the letter "O," "Z" in place of "s," "ph" in place of "f," etc.).

[5] Although common sense should tell investigators to properly check to see if the resulting image is readable, many rely on the copying program's statements. Thus, a good rule of thumb for investigators is to thoroughly check and recheck all copied files and imaged drives prior to scene release. In addition, CD-R's should be tested independently, as some programs show copied files in their directory, but give no indication of the functionality of such copy.

[6] DOJ (2007). *Digital Evidence in the Courtroom: A Guide for Law Enforcement and Prosecutors*. NIJ Special Report. U.S. Department of Justice: Office of Justice Programs: Washington, DC.

CHAPTER 12

Processing of Evidence and Report Preparation

Chapter Outline

LEARNING OBJECTIVES

After reading this chapter you will be able to do the following:

✓ Explore completely the aspects of data analysis.

✓ Understand CMOS passwords and their uses.

✓ Gain knowledge on the ways in which investigators can gather information from hard drives by circumventing CMOS passwords.

✓ Understand the preparation process that investigators go through to formally present the findings of their analysis of digital evidence.

✓ Develop further understanding of the importance of documentation of computer forensic investigators.

KEY TERMS AND CONCEPTS

- artifacts
- ASCII
- CMOS password
- default passwords
- compressed files

- erased files
- hidden files
- jumpers
- key disks
- partition tables

- pulling the battery
- steganographic container
- steganographic message
- storage enhancement
- user/system data

While many investigations will focus primarily on evidence stored on a suspect CPU, others will concentrate exclusively on a variety of storage media, and still others will include a combination of both. In all cases, automated or manual recovery efforts are appropriate (we will not rehash the argument as to which is better, although many investigators may be tempted to use automated programs due to their quick and painless operation). Whatever the case may be, investigation of floppies should be separate from CPU processing. Due to the voluminous nature of some cases, it is imperative that investigative procedures remain the same (as much as possible) across investigations. This will ensure a continuity across investigations and enhance testimonial validity. In addition, it will reduce confusion and increase the efficiency and subsequent effectiveness of the search. (However, agencies must be cautioned that formal policies may actually be detrimental to successful prosecution in some cases. Thus, departments should scrupulously develop generalized policies which encompass provisions for unique circumstances.)

Regardless of the software employed, investigators must thoroughly capture a complete schematic of the suspect system, keeping detailed notices to assist them with often delayed courtroom presentation. Such documentation must include any and all changes made to the data collected including justifications for modifications. In addition, this documentation should include a schematic of evidence volatility, providing justification for deviations from SOP. (As in all criminal investigations, evidence should be categorized by its inflammability, corrosiveness, or volatile characteristics.) Keep in mind that all analysis activities should be conducted with a forensic machine, due to the possibility of intentional sabotage or accidental contamination or destruction.

● ASPECTS OF DATA ANALYSIS

As stated previously, every computer investigation is different, but one rule remains the same: *document, document, document!* Other than that, procedures may vary depending upon departmental resources, expertise of personnel, and exigent circumstances. Again, each agency should develop its own investigative policy (formal or informal) and follow it as closely as possible. This is not to suggest, however, that one policy can completely account for all circumstances that may arise. Rather, it may be analogized to a coach's playbook, which changes weekly once the competition has been rated and evaluated.

The importance of documentation can not be overstated. Judicial oversight and defense challenges require that scrupulous attention be directed toward the documentation of any and all activities conducted on a particular piece of evidence. As such, analysts should continue the documentation process which was initiated by the evidence technicians or on-scene investigators by retrieving and updating the evidence logs. At a minimum, lab analysis should include the name, rank, and identifying information for any individual tasked with the analysis of such evidence; the condition of the evidence upon delivery to the analyst; the date and time of evidence arrival and return; and the name, rank, and identifying information of the person delivering such evidence. (As with traditional criminal investigations, any investigator or individual wishing access to the evidence *must* sign the evidence out. Once this process is completed, investigators or analysts may retrieve the digital information that may reside therein.)

As stated previously, contemporary criminal behavior often requires the analysis of computer materials. Using a variety of software packages, it is now possible to thoroughly analyze all of the information on each piece of storage media. Depending on the amount of media under analysis, this process can be quite cumbersome. In addition, case characteristics may preclude the most comprehensive manual search. Indeed, many investigators prefer to use automated programs like Expert Witness due to its ability to quickly analyze large disks. In addition, case

characteristics may be such that it is unnecessary to search every single file (although it is always recommended). For example, in a child pornography case where hard-copy photographs were accompanied by desktop child pornography and a directory entitled "child porn," which contained 400 depictions of child pornography, a thorough search of slack space and file swap may not be compelling. However, it may contain addresses, phone numbers, or other evidence which may incriminate others. Evidence notwithstanding, investigators should properly document all forensic software utilized, analysis techniques employed, damaged or compromised media (i.e., bad sectors, physically damaged diskettes, etc.), and evidence recovered. This documentation process should continue throughout the investigation process and should not be completed until final case disposition has been achieved.

Establish Forensically Sterile Conditions

All media used in the analysis of computer evidence must be forensically sterile for courtroom purposes. Investigators must be able to testify as to the condition of all media prior to the imaging process. As such, it is highly recommended that all media used for imaging purposes be brand new and forensically wiped prior to analysis, as some manufacturers have sold refurbished equipment as new. However, due to limited resources, this process may not be possible for poorly funded agencies. In this case, used media should be forensically wiped clean of data using software that meets DOD standards. This will prevent data corruption from previous use and data contamination from destructive programs. In addition, the condition of all physical drives should be verified prior to analysis. Media which contain damaged areas (i.e., sector, clusters, etc.) should not be utilized. However, it must be reiterated that new media which has been forensically wiped is *highly* recommended.

Investigating Windows System

Criminal evidence may reside on a variety of systems and in a variety of locations. On Windows systems, there are two types of data files which might be of interest to investigators. The first of these, **user/system data**, includes files which are intentionally added to the system through installation or user creation. The second type, **artifacts**, are system-generated files which are created for operational purposes (e.g., log files and temporary files).

USER/SYSTEM DATA	ARTIFACTS
User profiles–Data that pertains to or was created by an individual user.	**Metadata**–In its strictest sense, metadata is data about data. Such informational data includes data on file modification, access, creation, revision, and deletion dates. It has two types: *system metadata*–operating system dependant and which contains information about the file. *Application metadata*–information embedded within the file itself. This final type is transient, moving with the file.
Program files–Software applications that were installed in the computer.	**Windows system registry**–database employed with Windows operating system which store configuration information.
Temporary files (**temp file**)–Temporary data files that were created by applications.	**Event logs or log files**–files which record and document any significant occurrence in a system or program.
Special application-level files–includes Internet history and e-mail.	**Swap files**–computer memory files written to the hard drive.
	Printer spool–information stored in buffers awaiting printing.
	Recycle Bin–temporary location of deleted files

Ensure Legitimacy and Capabilities of Analysis Tools

Licenses for all forensic software that is expected to be employed in the analysis of suspect media should be verified prior to actual analysis. This process, often overlooked, is critical for witness credibility. (Imagine the embarrassment that would result if it was revealed that the software employed was not properly licensed and was being illegally used by law enforcement authorities.) Unfortunately, many investigators fail to appreciate the importance of the nuances found in many licensing agreements, using unlicensed shareware programs indiscriminately or making duplicate copies of single-user forensic suites.

Investigators should also validate any forensic software to be used—testing the software at the extremes and familiarizing themselves with its capabilities. (Too often, investigators simply trust the documentation provided by the manufacturer.) Again, this practice is critical for courtroom testimony. Although many defense attorneys are not currently knowledgeable about forensic software and practices, this situation is sure to change. Thus, investigators must be able to articulate the limitations of the analysis tools and the steps that were taken to identify them. Simplistic practices could include, for example, the intentional manipulation of data in a multitude of places on a variety of levels, such as hiding data in unused clusters and file slack or using

Investigators should always verify that proper imaging has occurred prior to analysis. (*Courtesy of James Doyle/NYPD, ret.*)

an editing program to intentionally mark clusters as bad or deleted files.

Physical Examination

Just as on-scene investigators note the condition of the suspect equipment, so should the forensic examiner. This physical examination should note any damage or markings and record class characteristics, such as its make, model, etc. In addition, attached peripherals, wires, or storage media (e.g., floppy disk) should also be noted. This enhances the credibility of the chain of custody.

Creation and Verification of Image

Assuming that an image was not secured at the crime scene, analysts should create one prior to any forensic analysis. (Remember: all examinations and analysis should be conducted on this image, leaving the original forensically pure.) In ideal situations, images should only be created on forensic machines. This preserves the integrity of the original evidence, prevents data contamination, and establishes the veracity of the subsequent analysis.

Assuming that BIOS passwords do not interfere with the investigation, the imaging of drives should always be initiated by booting the suspect drive from a previously verified forensic floppy as some users will configure their system to make modifications or erase data if third-party access is determined.[1] (As discussed in Chapter 10, there are a variety of imaging programs available to law enforcement investigators, and all forensic labs should be equipped with at least two such programs. Analysts should choose the one with which they are the most comfortable.) This forensic floppy should contain the applicable operating system, as well as a means for locking the hard drive prior to imaging. (This mechanism, often referred to as write-blocking, prevents the destruction, contamination, or corruption of original media and can be accomplished with many of the popular imaging programs, disk management software, or simple DOS commands.) Forensic boot disks should also include applicable storage enhancement programs (e.g., Stacker™, DoubleSpace™, and PKZip™), drivers for external media and printers, and an assortment of drivers and software programs determined from good pre-seizure surveillance or by evaluation of the suspect's CONFIG.SYS and AUTOEXEC.BAT files.

Investigators may also wish to consider including batch files which generally evaluate all computers for court purposes. This is especially important for those officers conducting manual analysis of forensic evidence. Such batch files would make life easier for an investigator who is processing several drives at once and those who do this type of analysis on a daily basis. In addition, they may provide a platform of consistency that validates their procedures to the court. Generally speaking, this batch file would enable investigators to establish a step-by-step preliminary investigative process which runs programs in a specified order. This saves time and, perhaps more importantly, establishes a general process for all investigations. This may prove critical under cross-examination. (For example, a defense attorney may question the applicability of the plain view doctrine if a search for transactional information reveals child pornography. If an investigator can demonstrate that she/he always sorts documents by file extension or that a thumbnail program is always executed against a suspect computer, she/he may successfully defeat the challenge.) In fact, batch files may be created to incorporate all of the forensic software employed, including write-blocking, imaging and verification, disk management, time/date authentication, virus scan, etc. In addition to any batch files or independent forensic tools, boot

disks should always include virus protection in order to protect departmental computers. However, investigators should *never* "cure" the virus on the suspect media. The importance of preserving original evidence can not be overstated. This step simply allows investigators to protect their own systems. Thus, investigators should include a Terminate and Stay Resident (TSR) virus shield on their investigative systems and on any boot disks employed. Some examples include McAfee's VSHIELD and FPROT. Investigators should remember to update this file on a regular basis. Unlike other programs traditionally found on boot disks which do not necessitate updating, the virus protection employed should be the most current one.

In the rare case where investigators cannot remove a suspect drive (i.e., permission to seize is not granted, suspect drive is intrinsically necessary for system maintenance, etc.), they may be confounded by the presence of a **CMOS password**. Currently, CMOS RAM, traditionally stored in a Motorola module used for permanently storing setup information, is found in the peripheral controller buffer via an external battery (often a coin-size Sony "lithium disk"). In many Intel chip sets, except the Pentium II boards, the PIIX4 component acts as the host, offering an additional 128 bytes via ports 72 hours/73 hours and allowing for the read/write protection of sectors 38h to 3Fh with a "write once bit." (This protection can be set via software but needs

Detection of Malware

In computer investigations, it is not unusual to discover malicious programs on suspect machines. Such programs can be intentionally installed by users to thwart computer investigation or may have been installed without the owner's knowledge. In either event, computer investigators must detect such programs to successfully defend the authenticity of collected evidence. For example, suspects might deny responsibility, claiming that incriminating evidence was placed on their computer via a Trojan. Demonstrating the absence of such applications will go a long way in defeating this claim. While a variety of anti-virus may be purchased commercially, *Gargoyle*, a Wetstone technology program, was specifically designed for forensic investigations. It is capable of conducting quick searches for known contraband and hostile programs on both stand-alone system and network resources. It may even scan within archive files (i.e., .zip; .rar; .jar; .war; .enc; etc.) and provide Windows Vista Support.

to be reset through a hardware reset.) Thus, to bypass BIOS passwords, investigators must erase or circumvent the CMOS RAM. While many inexperienced investigators have panicked in this situation, others believe that they can attack, and eventually crack, them. This has proven extremely shortsighted in some situations. While some of these passwords have been cracked using "social engineering" or default passwords, many have not. In these situations, investigators who are even slightly apprehensive should stop and contact an expert. CMOS passwords are not invincible and may be circumvented using a variety of methods including, but not limited to, jumping, pulling the battery, default passwords, social engineering, and suspect interrogation.[2]

Jumping the CMOS Password

While other types of passwords may be defeated using traditional password cracking software, CMOS passwords often require hardware manipulation on the part of the investigator. CMOS (or "boot") passwords are designed to be the first line of defense for users, thus preventing individuals from booting the computer's operating system. Therefore, it is impossible to circumvent with traditional means. However, one effective means of circumventing the CMOS is to simply "jump" it. (To locate the correct jumper, investigators may wish to read the motherboard's manual.) **Jumpers**, located either by the BIOS or elsewhere on the motherboard, may be utilized to bypass protections found in the CMOS. *Jumping* the CMOS involves the manipulation of hardware in which the password is cleared after the jumper has been reset. In these cases, investigators should look for the jumper often labeled "Clear RTC" or "Clear CMOS" or "PWRD." Once located, this jumper can be manipulated by turning the computer off for a couple of minutes, and then restarting after returning the "jumper" to its original position. (Some motherboards will automatically turn themselves on again after flashing the BIOS.) However, if no manual is available, and

the jumper is not obvious, investigators must identify the jumper through basic trial and error. Things to look for: jumpers which are isolated; those that are located near the BIOS; and those which may be switched. Investigators should only change one jumper at a time. In the event that the jumper is not adequately defined or the investigator is not familiar with system configuration, other approaches should be considered. For example, if a Dallas clock ending in A (ex. DS1287A) is present and a clear jumper cannot be located, investigators may ground the 21st pin to clear RAM.

Short Circuiting the Chip

Like the pulling of the battery, the short-circuiting of the BIOS chip will enable investigators to defeat the boot process. Generally, this process involved short-circuiting two pins of the BIOS chip for a few seconds. Although not recommended, this process can be accomplished with a paper clip or electric wire. Common examples include: CHIPS P82C206—(square) pins 12 and 32 (the first and last pins of the bottom edge of the chip) or pins 74 and 75 (the two pins on the upper left corner); OPTIF82C206 (rectangle)—pins 3 and 26 (third pin from left side and fifth pin from right side on the bottom right; Dallas DS12885S, Benchmarq bq3258S, Hitachi HD146818AP, Samsung KS82C6818A, pins 12 and 24; and Motorola MC146818AP, pins 12 and 24 or 12 and 20). In all cases, investigators should remember to turn the computer off during the process.

Pulling the Battery

Investigators may also pull the CMOS battery, as the memory will be lost after a period of time. In these cases, the battery should be disconnected for at least 24 hours. (If time permits, investigators should wait a longer period of time just to be sure.) This entails opening the case on the central processing unit (CPU) and removing the CMOS battery. (However, this approach may not be possible in cases where the battery is soldered onto the CPU.) Unfortunately, such action could result in damage to other portions of the CMOS which are essential for evidence recovery. Thus, investigators should be extremely careful when using this approach. (Investigators should also remember that notebooks often have two batteries: one buffering battery exchange and one supplyings the clock and CMOS RAM.) If investigators find that any of the above practice has resulted in modification of memory and hard drives, it will be necessary to manually reconfigure the system. Although this practice is different on some computers, many allow users to enter the setup program by depressing [F2]. Other systems may require the combination [Ctrl] [Alt] [Esc]. (If neither of these is successful, a simple call to the manufacturer may provide the solution.) Fortunately, most systems will prompt the user once they recognize that they are misconfigured. Investigators should pay careful attention to the information provided during the boot process and any information which may be located upon the hard drive's cover. Important—this new configuration may also require the Windows installation CD (i.e., it may find new hardware).

Default Passwords

Like other areas of data security, CMOS passwords may also be circumvented in many cases through the use of default passwords installed as backdoors by the manufacturer (see above). Fortunately for law enforcement, many original equipment manufacturers (OEMs) employ these standardized default passwords (often extremely simplistic) which are commonly available on the Net.

Social Engineering/Brute Force

By far, the most time-consuming (and exasperating) method of circumventing CMOS passwords involves the use of social engineering and brute force. This methodology requires meticulous investigation by law enforcement authorities. As mentioned previously, it involves traditional investigative practices, requiring the manual input of every possible personal computation. Such analysis begins and ends with the information compiled through the investigation of the suspect.

Key Disks

Some computers allow a BIOS bypass by inserting a **key disk** in the floppy disk drive while booting. Toshiba laptops, for example, enable users to bypass the BIOS by creating a key disk. To create a key disk, take a standard floppy and change the first five bytes of the second sector (the one after the boot sector) using a hex editor to 4B 45 59 00 00. (The first three bytes are the ASCII for "KEY.") This will enable the investigator to set his or her own password.

Image Verification

All images should be verified prior to analysis. Fortunately, most imaging programs provide verification capabilities. This verification is necessary to avoid evidentiary challenges of contamination or corruption. As discussed in Chapter 9, a variety of levels of verification are available, and while CRC comparisons have traditionally remained unchallenged, the MD5 hash and the SHA (Secure Hash Algorithm) are much more robust.

Some Standardized Bios Passwords

AWARD BIOS—AWARD SW; AWARD SW, Award SW, AWARD PW, award, awkward, J64 j256, j262, j332, j322, 01322222, 589589, 589721, 595595, 598598, HLT, SER, SKY_FOX, aLLy, aLLY, Condo, CONCAT, TTPTHA, aPAf, KDD, ZBAAACA, ZAAADA, ZJAAADC, djonet

AMI BIOS—AMI, A.M.I., AMI SW, AMI_SW, BIOS, PASSWORD, HEWITT RAND, Oder

Others—LKWPETER, lkwpeter, BIOSTAR, biostar, BIOSSTAR, biosstar, ALFAROME, Syxz, Wodj

Note—in some European keyboards, the American underscore (i.e., "_") is actually represented by a "?"—so AWARD_SW would become AWARD?SW

Logical Examination

Once a verified image has been created, investigators should logically examine the contents for criminal evidence. (In many cases, analysis of physical drives may not be necessary.) This includes the verification of **partition tables** and disk information (i.e., storage, hidden files, etc.). (Remember: There may be only one bootable partition per drive, located at cylinder = 0, head = 0, sector = 1.) This process may be conducted with fully automated programs or manually with programs like *DiskEdit*™. This procedure is essential as computer hard disks and storage devices are structured in such a way that evidence can reside at various levels within the structure of the disk. Because the intentional modification of disk structure and obfuscation of data is commonly discovered in the investigation of computer-related crime, investigators should be equipped with programs to view partition information, clusters, sectors, drives, directories, and hidden and **erased files**. Such views may reveal the presence of hidden files or even entire partitions. A logical analysis, for example, enables investigators to look for spatial discrepancies between logical and physical drives, possibly revealing hidden partitions.

Restoration of Files

As previously discussed, criminals may hide any and all incriminating data residing on their computer. Luckily, the majority of criminals are either technologically incompetent or technologically naive, often "hiding" data in obvious places (i.e., changing file extensions, creating innocuous file names, marking clusters as "bad" or deleted, etc.) while assuming the totality of deletion. Thus, all forensic laboratories should be equipped with software capable of recovering deleted, erased, and **compressed files**. While fully automated forensic suites include these capabilities, investigators should be comfortable with manual recovery programs like *Norton Utilities*™ *Unerase* and understand the process that the operating system employs to erase files. This could prove critical during a rigorous cross-examination, questioning

an investigator's competence. DOS platforms, for example, will change the first character of a file name to the Greek Sigma (denoted by hexadecimal E5) to "inform" the computer that the space originally designated for this file is no longer needed (This also enables investigators to identify all deleted files.) DOS then zeros out what a specified cluster pointed to and proceeds to zero out the remaining links to the original chain in the FAT. Norton's *UnErase*™ attempts to recover these files by replacing the Sigma with a valid ASCII character, identifying the number of clusters necessary, locating the corresponding unallocated clusters, and updating the FAT. This process, however, is not always as successful as investigators would like it to be. In fact, the ability to recover deleted files depends on a variety of factors including time lapsed since deletion, usage of system, etc. Thus, investigators may also use a disk editor to reconstruct files by manually employing the same methods.

Although a relatively elementary and unsophisticated approach to hiding data, some suspects may also attempt to hide data by simply using the operating system's "hidden" attribute or by altering the applicable file extensions.[3] For example, child pornographers may "hide" pornographic images by designating them as text files (i.e., JPG to TXT) by simply changing their name. They may also hinder recognition of a file by using a hexadecimal editor to change the file signature, which is a sequence of bytes at the beginning of a file that specifically indicates the type of file. Although the file will be unreadable until the signature sequence is restored, investigators may employ programs like *Mareswares HexDump* and *DISKCAT*™, identifying and reconciling contrary file signatures. Fortunately, many computer criminals are unsophisticated in their attempts at hiding incriminating material, and most forensic packages easily identify this very simplistic technique. However, other situations are a bit more complicated.

In some cases, investigators may confront untenable situations in which the data has been intentionally and "permanently" destroyed by

A Sampling of Disk/Text/Hex Editors

- **Hexd***—available at *www.dmres.com*, this series of programs is designed to either display and/or edit files or disk sectors. The programs will take a file/sector and display the hexadecimal equivalent of the characters in the file. The programs, Hexedit and Hex_sect, enable users to edit in ASCII or hex mode.
- **VEDIT** and **VEDIT Pro64**—available at *www.vedit. com*, this product provides editing capabilities for any Windows, DOS, UNIX, or Mac text files, as well as ASCII, EBCDIC, and hex files. In addition, the program allows for the processing of voluminous files. VEDIT

may edit, translate, and sort 2 Gigs of information, while VEDIT Pro64 has no limitations, according to the vendor.
- **WINHEX**—available at *http://www.winhex.com/winhex/index-m.html*, this product is a hexadecimal editor for Windows which provides native support for FAT, NATFS, Ext2/3, ReiserFS, Reiser4, UFS, CDFS, and UDF.
- **010 Editor**—available at *www.sweetscape.com/010editor/*, this product allows for the viewing and editing of large files. Written in a GUI environment, many users find this editor to be easy to use.

employing "wiping programs." These programs, commercially available, remove multiple layers of data and may require special chemical processing. Such handling is almost always outside the budgetary constraints of any investigative agency and is only employed in cases which involve national security. However, many popular wiping programs do allow recovery of some portion of information for the savvy investigators. For example, *BCWIPE*™ destroys slack space and file swap but fails to remove the volume label from the disk. It also fails to wipe the last two sectors of the drive, allowing viewing by a collection of viewers like *Norton Utilities*™. In addition, renamed files are designated by a wipe extension.

Finally, data may be concealed through the use of sophisticated software which is designed exclusively to hide data in plain sight using the least significant bit (LSB). One such category of software, steganography, allows users to effectively hide the content of selected files in others. Popular software programs like *S-Tools*™ and *StegoSuite*™ enable users to hide images and text within wave and graphic files. Thus, file viewers which typically allow investigators to physically view the contents of a document would only display the *container* (i.e., the picture or sound file) and not necessarily the suspect data (**Steganographic** messages have two parts: the **container**, which is the file which conceals data; and the **message**, which is the actual data.) Due to the randomness

of algorithmic manipulation employed in steganography programs, there is no commercially available software which will detect the presence of files imbedded in other files. Unfortunately, this requires investigators to manually evaluate all graphics and wave files (i.e., they must use the suspect program to evaluate all appropriate files, looking for a positive response). Thus, investigators must look for the presence of steganography software to discover the very presence of hidden images. Investigators may discover these types of files by looking for files created with "S" code or by looking for unusually sized applications. (Investigators should consider that the best containers are busy programs, like complex photographs, while the worst are simple ones, like a two color image. In addition, sound files (e.g., WAVE) sometimes prove to be a bonanza for law enforcement as suspects may place a continuous stream of data in a sound file, forgetting that there are periods of silence.) Unfortunately, recovery of these programs may be further complicated by secure passwords.

Listing of Files

As part of the documentary process, investigators should list all files on the suspect drive after the recovery of erased, deleted, hidden, and compressed files. Disk editors are particularly useful here as they provide tree structures which display all files and their origination path.

Steganography Detection

It is more than ironic that most investigators decry the notion that steganography is increasing in popularity among criminals. Remember, steganography is extremely difficult to detect and is *invisible* to the naked eye. Traditionally, there were no commercial tools available to identify even the presence of steganography. However, WetStone Technologies has created a variety of products that may be employed to investigate, detect, analyze, and recover digital steganography. *Stego Suite*, a combination of four products, is capable of identifying the presence of steganography without prior knowledge of the steganography algorithm that might have been used in the target file. Such blind steganography detection is exclusive to *Stego Suite*.

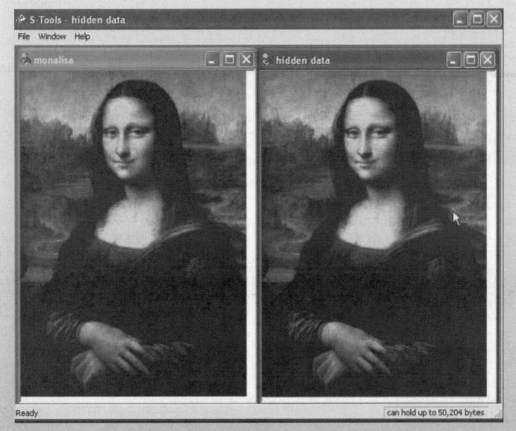

In the above illustration, a user employing *S-Tools* has hidden information within an image of the *Monalisa*. The image on the left is the original image, while the image on the right contains a hidden document. Can you tell the difference?

Examine Unallocated Space for Data Remnants

Often times, investigators may find additional evidence residing in unallocated clusters which were not intentionally manipulated by suspects.

As discussed in Chapter 8, DOS and Windows™ operating systems use fixed clusters depending on the size of the disk (i.e., an entire cluster is used for any given file regardless of the file's size).[4] Thus, files of a size not sufficient to fill the

---

Encryption and Steganography: What's the difference?

Encryption

Long used by government officials to protect national security, encryption technology has evolved dramatically with the introduction of computers. In fact, private consumers now use it routinely to protect their own sensitive information. In its most basic form, "encryption" refers to the process of converting a message from its original form ("plaintext") into an indecipherable or scrambled form ("ciphertext"). Most encryption programs use an algorithm to mathematically transform data, decipherable only to those individuals or entities holding an access key. This access key acts as a password. The security of encryption programs varies with the strength of the algorithm and the key.

Steganography

The practice of hiding information from discovery is not unique to the computer age. The word actually is a derivative from the Greek *steganos* for hidden words, where it was a common practice to place wax over words to hide them from detection. Steganography was also practiced by the Chinese who would tattoo messages on the bald head of soldiers and allow the natural re-growth of hair to conceal the messages. Contemporary practices are far more sophisticated. However, they still rely on the ignorance of investigative authorities for their success.

Like encryption, steganography involves the securing of information through the manipulation of data. Unlike encryption, which prevents access to specified data through the use of ciphertext, steganography is designed to hide the data from view.

---

designated space of a cluster are still allocated the entire space on a cluster, leaving unused or *slack* space. Consequently, remnants of files which may have contained criminal evidence may be recoverable. Although remnants of graphic and image files may not be particularly helpful, vestiges of text files may contain evidence including passwords. Fully automated programs like *EnCase*™ are designed to evaluate slack, and several manual programs like *GetSlack*™ may be used to perform the same function as well as providing a mechanism for contextual analysis. Again, case characteristics will dictate the forensic methodology employed.

Unlocking Files

Unlike the CMOS password, software and document passwords do not affect the startup of the computer and may be encountered by investigators on a variety of different levels. These passwords, designed to prevent access to special documents, programs, or compressed files, actually serve to encrypt information. In order to circumvent these types of passwords, cracking dictionaries or software is the tool of choice. These password programs are actually compilations of dictionaries and characters. They attempt to "guess" the password by inputting combinations of standard words, common characters, and lower and upper case levels. These password-cracking programs operate by comparing hash values of files. Thus, passphrases are almost impossible to crack. However, some powerful software cracking software like Access Data's *Password Recovery Toolkit*™ and *Distributed Network Attack* allow investigators to create dictionaries from the suspect drive, simply by entering the imaged drive. Although time consuming, this may allow the recovery of such passphrases.

Unfortunately, not all passwords can be cracked. Strong encryption programs like PGP and Triple DES have proven resilient to all available crackers. In fact, PGP is so confident in their ability to remain unbreakable that they have made their source code available to the public. It is programs like these that have prompted Congress to propose third-party key requirements (i.e., forcing users to provide a third person with their password). Having said this, however, it may still be possible to identify passwords through intensive analysis. Some forensic utilities, for example, enable investigators to *sniff* the hard drive the same way that hackers have sniffed identifications and passwords (e.g., Access Data and Entomb). Remember, passwords may actually be secreted away on the computer, thereby providing investigators an opportunity to find them. These passwords may reside in slack space or swap files or may be attached to other files as attachments or riders (i.e., Multiple Data Streams). Thus, investigators may wish to create a dictionary out of the file swap or slack space. (Most forensic crackers allow for the importation of investigator-created dictionaries.)

If time is of the essence, investigators may also wish to manually evaluate these areas and identify anomalies. In other cases, it may be possible to identify other passwords on a suspect computer in traditional ways. For example, investigators may identify Word files that are password protected and crack them using traditional methods. Once investigators have secured one password, they may try it on those files that are heavily encrypted, such as the PGP files. (It is often surprising how individuals will use the same password for a variety of files.)

Brute Force/Social Engineering

If the above techniques have not produced any measure of success, investigators may also try developing a profile of the suspect or the suspect computer and manually attempt password cracking. Many individuals use common or everyday words to secure their documents. Other favorites include pet's name, pet's breed, mother's name, father's name, siblings, birthdays, social security numbers, favorite sports team or figure, school name or mascot, place of birth, favorite color, boy/girlfriend's name, spouse's name, suspect's middle name, literary figures, favorite television program or movie, etc. Think of your own passwords. Chances are that someone who knew you well would be able to guess them in their entirety or at least guess the root of the password. Thus,

social engineering is a good method for all criminal investigations, especially computer-related investigations.

Program Defaults and Program-Specific Crackers

Investigators may also find it useful to compile a list of standardized defaults for password location. For example, in *Simple Accounting for Windows*™ 6.0 and 7.0, the password resides in the .asc file. In *Simple* 6.0, entity name is at offset 290–434 and the password is contained in 38 bytes from offset 252–289. For *Simple* 7.0, the password is still in the 38 bytes right before the entity name in the .asc file but the offset is different. Investigators may find it useful to contact vendor support to identify program particularities, eventually developing their own list. Investigators may also find that the Web provides a plethora of this sort of information for the diligent. Finally, investigators may wish to compile a library of program-specific password crackers. These programs reveal or circumvent the password by simply locating it with the same program defaults. These include *WordCrack*™ and *ZipCrack*™. However, investigative agencies which have the financial wherewithal to purchase the comprehensive forensic suites may not find this necessary.

Examination of User Data Files

Once all data have been preserved and/or recovered, investigators should then examine the contents of those files that are within the parameters of the warrant and consistent with case characteristics (i.e., warrants issued in drug cases, for example, may not allow for the examination of graphic files). File viewers and text searching utilities are especially useful for this purpose. File viewers, for example, allow investigators to view the front page of all documents. In addition, many allow users to quickly identify graphics files regardless of assigned file extension. This is particularly helpful to investigators searching for child pornography. Text searching utilities, on the other hand, enable investigators to search through innumerable documents for words or phrases consistent with their evidentiary expectations. Moreover, many utilities provide *fuzzy logic* capabilities in which input derivatives are also identified. These tools usually provide investigators with data location (cluster, sector, and offset) and allow investigators to pipe the information to an evidentiary file. However, they can prove relatively useless if the keyword list employed is poorly prepared.

According to many investigators, the construction of an adequate keyword list is one of the most difficult, and potentially time consuming, tasks necessary in computer investigations. Such lists must be consistent with warrant specifications and particular to case characteristics. Effective lists may be described as a balance of vagueness—vague enough to identify all files that may contain criminal evidence, but not so vague that false hits are numerous. Investigators should avoid common terminology and look to case particularities to identify appropriate terms, including characteristics of the suspect or victim (i.e., name, nicknames, etc.) and aspects of the crime (i.e., location, methodology, etc.). In cases involving child pornography, for example, investigators may wish to avoid terms like "kid" or "sex", because of the potential for false hits.

Investigators should also examine the contents of the autoexec.bat file. Reliance upon automated recovery programs overlooks the obvious—the suspect's computer may be booby-trapped in some way. In addition, important information of a nondestructive nature may reside there. For example, commands in the autoexec.bat may indicate that routine back-ups were made, leading investigators to search for additional media.

Piping of Evidence

Although the majority of evidence recovered in a computer case is admissible only in that form, investigators should make hard copies of any file which may be introduced. This includes word-processing documents, spreadsheets, graphics, movie clips, rogue programs, etc. Investigators should also be careful to make hard copies of directory and subdirectory trees. Finally, all results should be sequentially numbered. It is highly recommended that investigators employ the Bates numbering system, as judicial officials are familiar with its schematics.

Examination of Executable Programs

Examination of executable programs is essential for evidentiary validity. Identification of Trojans, for example, may prove critical in child pornography cases where the suspect argues that she/he was unaware of the images residing on the computer. Because programs like *Back Orifice*, *Deep Throat*, and *NetBus* allow total remote access to compromised machines,[5] investigators must account for their presence, or lack thereof. While some software is commercially available to identify such programs, they are most often program-specific. For example, *NetBuster* identifies and locates *NetBus*

File Viewers

- **CompuPic**—available at *www.photodex.com*, this commercial viewer provides an assortment of viewing and browsing options. In addition, it allows users to acquire pictures from digital cameras or scanners. *Price*: $79.95.
- **Conversions Plus**—available at *www.dataviz.com*, this commercial viewer is capable of reading MAC formats.
- **Thumbs Plus**—available at *www.cerious.com*, this commercial viewer includes searching, organizing, and cataloging of graphics, multimedia, and font files. It provides for thumbnails and batch editing and may be run on Windows systems.

- **Quick View Plus**—available at *www.inso.com*, this commercial viewer allows users to access, view, and print any document (e.g., text, spreadsheet, graphic, database, presentation, compressed files, and HTML) irrespective of creative platform. QVP keeps all page-level attributes intact, including columns, headers/footers, page numbers, footnotes, embedded graphics, and OLE objects. Finally, QVP supports hyperlinked documents, provided it has access to related files.

Examining External Storage Devices

Like the investigation of computer hard drives, there are no absolutes in the processing of removable storage media. However, informal, generalized guidelines similar to those discussed above may be employed. (Agencies should be hesitant to formally introduce investigative procedures due to the volatile and intangible nature of computer forensics, and the absolutism often demanded in judicial settings.)

only. Unfortunately, most of these Trojans were developed by computer hackers and can prove quite tricky to find. *Back Orifice*, for example, was created by the Cult of the Dead Cow at a hacker's conference (DEFCON7), and later versions allow users to hide the program virtually anywhere. Thus, it is essential that investigators familiarize themselves with the process of Trojan identification.

Document, document, document—As mentioned previously, the one constant in computer forensics is the need for documentation. At a minimum, documentation should include, the name and rank of all investigative personnel involved in the analysis; time, date, and place of analysis; methodology employed; physical description of media; and all files found on each. This may be done in a variety of ways. The best known (i.e., DOS) is probably the most cumbersome. While this method is relatively easy (a variation of directory, subdirectory, and hidden commands), the printouts tend to be overwhelming. Other programs such as *PowerDesk*™, *Norton Utilities*™, and Mareswares *DiskCat*™ simplify data and beautify possible exhibits, while enabling investigators to search for files by name, date, size, or type. As stated previously, hard drives are not the only source of computer evidence. Storage media, in particular, may be a virtual treasure chest for the experienced investigator. However, the same protections that were necessary to protect the robustness of evidence found on the hard drive apply in the case of floppy diskettes.

In order to identify potential evidence on computer floppies, investigators must first protect the data on the disk from corruption or destruction. The easiest way to do this, of course, is to write-block the entire disk by sliding the plastic lock tab located on the bottom left of a standard 1.44-mb diskette down. To further protect the evidence, it is strongly recommended that investigators also slide a plastic tie through the slot and secure it. This will prevent any accidental manipulation of data. In fact, investigators should be trained to treat all diskettes as if they were unlocked, further ensuring the sanctity of the data. Once the evidence is protected, investigators should image the disk. This can be done with a variety of file management software programs such as *Norton Utilities*™ and *AnaDisk*™. As with the analysis of the hard drive, all forensic analysis should be conducted on verified forensic images. Once such images are obtained, the procedures for evidence recovery are very similar to those employed with the hard drive.

Returning Equipment

Once analysis has been completed, all material or equipment which has proven to be irrelevant or superfluous should be returned upon request, as the courts have recognized that the deprivation of computer equipment and data stored therein may provide unacceptable hardship to individuals and corporations, especially in situations where no opportunity is afforded for duplication (Winick, 1994). Indeed, with the increasing reliance upon computer technology, individuals or corporations may face significant economic hazards including bankruptcy. As such, they have argued that continuing deprivation constitutes unreasonable police action once evidence recovery is achieved. In fact, only those computers or equipment which fall under legal forfeit may be held without risk of violating the PPA or incurring civil liability (*Mora* v.*United States*, 955 F.2d 156 (2nd Cir., 1992)). However, it is permissible, and necessary, to "wipe" all contraband from returned equipment.

Evidence from Internet Activity[6]

Once computers have been properly imaged and verified, investigative steps will vary based on individual case characteristics. However, almost any case may involve the Internet in some way. As noted by the National Institute of Justice, criminals may use the Internet for a variety of reasons, including, but not limited to:

- trading or sharing of information (i.e., documents, photographs, movies, graphics, software, etc.)
- concealing their identity
- assuming another identity
- identifying and gathering information on victims
- communication with co-conspirators
- distributing information or misinformation
- coordinating meetings, meeting sites, or parcel drops[7]

As such, criminal evidence may reside in a variety of places, and even those things which appear to be innocuous at first might later prove important. As mentioned previously, investigators must be able to document a relationship between the suspect and the evidence. Such links might be located in the following areas: IP addresses or domain names; e-mails and IMs; and Internet history. While most forensic packages previously discussed contain the ability to search for these things, stand-alone programs, Web sites, or court processes such as those listed below may also be used.

- **Tracing IP addresses or domain names**— Although there are a variety of programs commercially available, three free programs have proven popular among law enforcement due to their reliability. All of these programs can be located at the following sites: *www.network-tools. com*; *www.samspade.org*; *www.geektools.com*; and *www.dnsstuff.com*.

1. **whois**—a tool which can query a database that includes domain names, IP addresses, and points of contact, including names, postal addresses, and telephone numbers.
2. **traceroute**—a tool designed to trace the path a packet takes upon traveling from one device to another. It is often used to narrow down the geographic location of a particular device.
3. **nslookup**—a tool which is capable of querying a domain name server for a particular name. This tool is not altogether reliable and should only be employed as an investigative tool and not as a demonstration of proof.

- **User Accounts, E-mails,** and **IM**—registered owners of e-mail accounts may be located through subpoena and court processes. However, identification of user accounts may be accomplished through data analysis of the questioned evidence. *FTK's* data carving and e-mail recovery tools may be employed toward this end. Linking a suspect machine to a particular individual may be accomplished through an analysis of the file headers.
- **Websites** and **Internet History**—most automated forensic packages allow investigators to view the Web history of a suspect drive. In many cases, entire Web pages can be viewed. In others, only partial pages may remain. In still others, only the Web site address is recoverable. If investigators can identify the date that a particular address was accessed, they may use the WayBackMachine to view the page as the suspect did.

Note: The **WayBackMachine** is located at *http://www.archive.org/web/web.php* (or may be accessed by simply typing "waybackmachine" into the address bar). The site is an Internet archive which provides access to two billion archived pages.

NON-WINDOWS OPERATING SYSTEMS

Although most forensic investigations on personal computers are conducted on Windows platforms, there are occasions when other operating systems are present. Unfortunately, many local agencies may not have the resources to process and analyze such data and may have to rely upon outside experts. The two most common non-Windows operating systems relevant to computer forensics are: *Macintosh* and *Unix/Linux*.

Macintosh Operating System

The Macintosh operating system was designed by Apple computers and is currently used by Macintosh computers bearing the Apple logo. Although more contemporary users are familiar with Windows products, Macintosh computers are largely responsible for the popularization of graphical user interfaces (GUI). Traditionally, Macintosh systems were incompatible with other systems and were susceptible to data loss. Today, Macs are increasingly popular due to increased interoperability, savvy advertising, and graphics capability. In addition, they are attractive to users who prefer seamless integration and enhanced stability.

Due to market demand, most computer forensics specialists concentrate their efforts on Windows machines. As such, there are more commercially available forensic packages for Windows than Mac. However, there are some products that have been employed on Macintosh machines.

- **Imaging.** As in investigations involving Windows platforms, preservation of the original drive is essential. The creation of a forensic copy should be accomplished without booting the suspect computer or mounting the physical disk onto an investigative machine. In order to accomplish this, the forensic Mac should have disk arbitration disabled.[8] This can be accomplished by copying the *diskarbitrationd.plist*

file in the */etc/mach/_init.d* directory to an alternate location and deleting the original. Once this is accomplished, investors can connect to the target hard drive by either using Target Disk Mode or by removing the hard drive and connecting it via an external enclosure. Investigators may then use the *dd* command from the terminal or *dcfldd* to create the image.[9] (Investigators may prefer to use *dcfldd*, an open source Unix tool, which provides for simultaneous imaging and image verification.) A further option would be *MacQuisition*, a tool developed by Black Bag Technologies.

- **Finding Evidence.** Like Windows machines, Macintoshes can contain a plethora of criminal evidence. While much of this evidence can often be located in obvious places, some may reside in unallocated space. Case characteristics will dictate other areas of interest. For example, in cases involving security breaches, investigators may wish to examine the startup items, cron tabs, and assorted configuration files and logs. In addition, evidence may reside within images, history and temp, cache files, and executable code.[10]

- **Forensic Toolkits**
  1. **Black Bag Technologies Mac Forensic Software** is a comprehensive toolkit designed for Mac OS X. The suite is a one-stop shop for most investigations and includes imaging, recovery, and analysis tools. The 19 utilities contained within the package include provisions for text searching, directory browsing, viewing images, examination of file headers and metadata, and data segmentation.
  2. **MacForensicsLab** is similar to Black Bag's suite of tools. Operating within a self-contained environment, it has additional utilities which provide for automatic notetaking and reporting. Thus, users may prepare comprehensive, professional reports for courtroom presentation. Finally, the program provides

powerful search tools. Investigators can employ string searches to identify credit card and social security numbers; or skin tone searches to identify pornographic material.

Linux/Unix Operating Systems

As discussed in Chapter 2, Linux-based operating systems are gaining in popularity due to its inexpensive nature and subsequent increases in software applications. Linux approaches system files, data files, and user accounts differently than Windows based systems. For example, while there may be multiple users with administrator access in Windows, there is only one administrator account in Linux. Although individual user accounts may be created in this platform, the root account maintains complete control of the system. In addition, Linux systems are different in that they are characterized by a unified file system on three partitions: *root, boot,* and *swap.*[11]

There are a variety of operating systems running on Linux/Unix-based kernels. Some of the commercial products are Red Hat, SUSE Linux, Solaris, HP UNIX, and IBM's AIX. In addition, there are other variants in the field which are based on open-source operating systems. Both commercial and open-source (i.e., *in the wild*) systems largely approach the file system in the same way. By enabling *VFS*(**virtual file system**) within the kernel itself, a common set of data structures may be used. As such, a Linux system will contain much of the searching and indexing tools necessary in forensic examinations. For example, *Grep*, a character-based search tool, may be employed in text and string searches. Like cases involving Windows systems, case characteristics will dictate the search specifications and parameters. Below is a *sampling* of files which may contain criminal evidence:

- **/etc/passwd**—this file contains information on every account created on the suspect machine. This information includes:
  1. Account ID
  2. Encrypted password

  3. Numeric UserID (UID)
  4. Numeric GroupID (GID)
  5. Account information (typically the user's name)
  6. Home directory
  7. Login shell
- **/etc/shadow**—If the installation is configured to use shadow passwords, this file would contain the encrypted password and associated user account information. This file is accessible via root privileges only. An asterisk symbol (*) serves as a placeholder for the encrypted password. Information regarding password management is also contained herein.
- **/etc/hosts**—This file contains local domain name system (DNS) entries. This DNS list may be used to evaluate Web activity.
- **/etc/sysconfig**—This file contains assorted configuration files like, configuration of peripherals, scripts running at boot, etc.
- **/etc/syslog/conf**—This file contains information which identifies the location of log files.
- **/home/useraccountID/Trash**—When a particular user account ID is entered, investigators can access that user's trash. This folder contains deleted files which have not been permanently released to unallocated space (i.e., emptying the trash).

As stated, Linux operating systems contain many tools which may be employed in a forensic examination of a suspect machine. In addition, there are some Linux forensic tools available to investigators. These include:

- *Maresware: Linux Forensics.* Available at *www.dmares.com*
- *The Farmer's Boot CD.* Available at *www.forensicbootcd.com/*
- *SMART.* Available at *www.asrdata.com.*
- *The Sleuth Kit* (TSK), *The Coroner's Toolkit* (TCT) and *Autopsy.* Available at *www.sleuthkit.org.*

PDA FORENSICS

As mobile devices become more and more like minicomputers, there is a dawning realization that they may contain criminal evidence. Indeed, as Americans become less attached to hardwired devices, a demand for PDA forensics has emerged. While this section is not intended to provide an exhaustive accounting of all issues and technologies associated with PDAs, it is intended to familiarize the reader with device structure, emerging issues, and generic practices.

Generally speaking, most PDAs have similar features and capabilities. They contain system-level microprocessors; read-only memory (ROM); random access memory (RAM); multiple hardware keys and interfaces; touch sensitive, liquid crystal display; and support memory cards and peripherals. Most also contain the capability for wireless communications like infrared, Bluetooth, or WiFi.[12] However, devices will vary by their technical and physical characteristics as well as their expansion capabilities (i.e., I/O and memory card slots, device expansion sleeves, and external hardware interfaces). By design, all PDAs support basic Personal Information Management applications which provide users with organizational tools like Address Books, Appointments, Mailboxes, and Memo Management. They are generally categorized by their operating system: Palm OS; Pocket PC; or Linux-based.

The issues involved with forensically processing PDAs are the same that are found in traditional investigations of computer systems. The maintenance of the chain of custody, image verification, and evidence integrity are essential elements in criminal courts and must be carefully documented. While there are some tools out there which are capable of copying and searching data, it is highly recommended that only forensically designed products are used. Investigators should have imaging, verification, and analysis programs in their toolkits. (As both physical and logical extractions have advantages

and disadvantages, investigators should obtain both.) The leader in such software is generally considered to be Paraben Software.

- **Device Seizure**—Created by Paraben Software, *Device Seizure* is a combination of two earlier products. This new tool includes Palm DD Command Line Acquisition and supports PDAs using the following operating systems: Palm OS; Windows CE/Pocket PC/Mobile 4.x and earlier, BlackBerry 4.x and earlier, and Symbian 6.0. It also supports Garmin GPS devices. It also comes with full flashers, new model support, improved manufacturer support, and new cables added to the accompanying toolbox. The platform also provides for both logical and physical acquisitions and ensures data integrity through write blocking. More information is available at *www.paraben-forensics.com*.

REPORT PREPARATION AND FINAL DOCUMENTATION

The development of a forensic laboratory and the collection and analysis of digital evidence is critical in criminal investigations. However, successful prosecution of computer-related offenses often hinges upon formal reporting and the competency and credibility of courtroom witnesses. Incomplete reports or inconsistent testimony can negate even the best run investigations. Witnesses who are uncertain as to all aspects of their analysis or hesitant in their findings may be discredited or impeached during cross-examination. In addition, evidence may be ruled inadmissible if a proper chain of custody can not be established. Thus, it is essential that investigators are properly trained in all methods employed and maintain comprehensive logs of their activities. Such logs include both traditional and computer-generated reports. Traditional documents typically include, documents relating

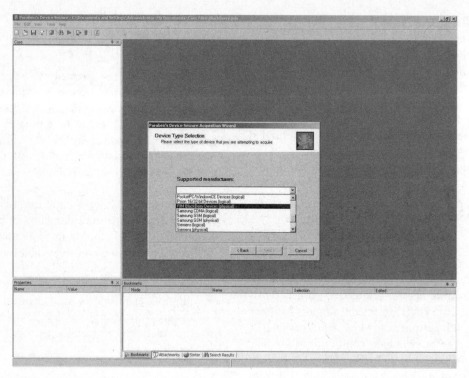

Like forensic packages designed for computer drives, Paraben's *Device Seizure* is presented in a GUI format, making it extremely popular among investigators.

to the chain of custody of physical evidence, logs of crime scene activity and evidence collection procedures, and the like. Computer-generated reports, on the other hand, typically involve those activities associated with data analysis.

Traditionally, written logs of forensic practices were necessary as investigators moved between various tools to conduct their analysis. Currently, most forensic packages are capable of creating logs and subsequent reports automatically. While many contemporary investigators eschew the traditional approach, it is recommended that both strategies are employed to enhance the credibility and veracity of the investigation. At a minimum, all reports involving data analysis should include the date, time, and identification of investigative personnel for the following events:

- Evidence seizure—should also include description of the physical condition of the

seized evidence including, but not limited to, extraneous defects, hardware configuration, and Internet connections)
- Digital imaging and verification—should also include the software employed
- Application of forensic software—including, but not limited to, text searching, restoration of files, indexing, file viewers, data carving, e-mail viewers, etc.
- Special techniques or unique problems encountered
- Consultation with outside sources

The two most popular forensic suites for Windows platforms, Access Data's Forensic Tool Kit (FTK) and Guidance Software's EnCase, are capable of logging all activities and creating comprehensive reports automatically. Below is an example of the summary sheet for an investigation using FTK.

NIJ | SPECIAL REPORT / APR. 04

Hard Drive Evidence Worksheet

Case Number: _____   Exhibit Number: _____

Laboratory Number: _____   Control Number: _____

Hard Drive #1 Label Information [Not Available ☐]   Hard Drive #2 Label Information [Not Available ☐]

Manufacturer: _____	Manufacturer: _____
Model: _____	Model: _____
Serial Number: _____	Serial Number: _____
Capacity: _____ Cylinders: _____	Capacity: _____ Cylinders: _____
Heads: _____ Sectors: _____	Heads: _____ Sectors: _____
Controller Rev. _____	Controller Rev. _____
IDE ☐ 50 Pin SCSI ☐	IDE ☐ 50 Pin SCSI ☐
68 Pin SCSI ☐ 80 Pin SCSI ☐ Other ☐	68 Pin SCSI ☐ 80 Pin SCSI ☐ Other ☐
Jumper: Master ☐ Slave ☐ Cable Select ☐ Undetermined ☐	Jumper: Master ☐ Slave ☐ Cable Select ☐ Undetermined ☐

Hard Drive #1 Parameter Information

DOS FDisk ☐   PTable ☐   PartInfo ☐   Linux FDisk ☐   SafeBack ☐   EnCase ☐   Other: _____

Capacity: _____   Cylinders: _____   Heads: _____   Sectors: _____

LBA Addressable Sectors: _____   Formatted Drive Capacity: _____

Volume Label: _____

Partitions

Name:	Bootable?	Start:	End:	Type:
_____	☐	_____	_____	_____
_____	☐	_____	_____	_____
_____	☐	_____	_____	_____
_____	☐	_____	_____	_____

Hard Drive #2 Parameter Information

DOS FDisk ☐   PTable ☐   PartInfo ☐   Linux FDisk ☐   SafeBack ☐   EnCase ☐   Other: _____

Capacity: _____   Cylinders: _____   Heads: _____   Sectors: _____

LBA Addressable Sectors: _____   Formatted Drive Capacity: _____

Volume Label: _____

Partitions

Name:	Bootable?	Start:	End:	Type:
_____	☐	_____	_____	_____
_____	☐	_____	_____	_____
_____	☐	_____	_____	_____
_____	☐	_____	_____	_____

Hard Drive Evidence Worksheet   Page 1 of 2

● CONCLUSIONS

As previously discussed, investigators should maintain a variety of forensic tools, including both automated and manual programs. Both are necessary, although many investigators appear to be overly reliant upon one-stop programs. In fact, automated analysis tools are designed to be useful to virtually anyone, including unskilled investigators. In the words of a seasoned examiner, "anyone can pick the low-hanging fruit". Case characteristics and situational variables will

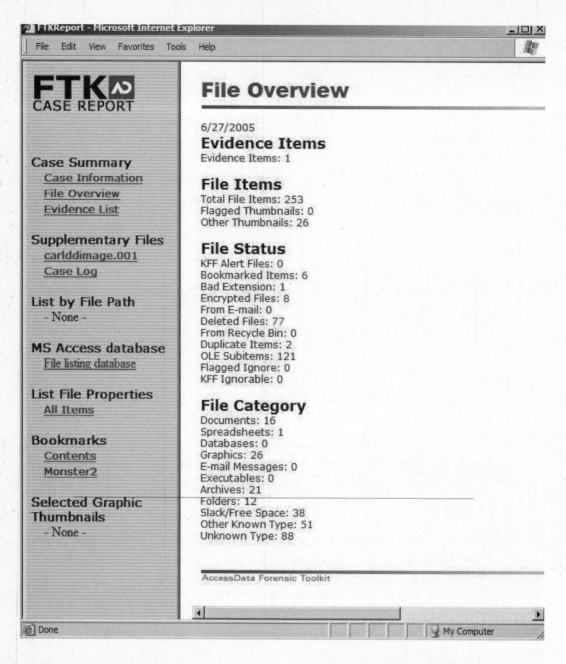

dictate the level and sophistication of the search necessary. Certainly, cases involving threats to national security are such that an exhaustive examination of all available materials is all but mandated. Simple cases involving 40 counts of child pornography in which the criminal evidence clearly resides on a suspect's desktop may not require such detail. Irrespective of the tools selected, a familiarity with computer operating systems and the mechanics of data storage is essential to withstand court challenges as to an investigator's competence.

DISCUSSION QUESTIONS

1. What are the basic steps in data analysis?
2. What are some basic strategies for defeating CMOS passwords?
3. Discuss the forensic toolkits used on non-Windows operating systems.
4. What are some of the advantages and disadvantages of automated forensic packages?
5. Describe the final preparations that investigators go through before they present the evidence found analysis of digital evidence.
6. Discuss why in the field of computer forensics it is important to document the findings.

RECOMMENDED READING

- Davis, Chris; Philipp, Aaron; and Cowen, David (2004). *Hacking Exposed: Secrets & Solutions: Computer Forensics.* McGraw-Hill: Ohio.
- DOJ (2007). *Investigations Involving the Internet and Computer Networks.* National Institute of Justice: Office of Justice Programs.
- Hoe, Nah Soo (2005). *Linux End User Training Materials.* Asian Pacific Development Information Programme. May be retrieved from the Internet at *http://linux.about.com/gi/dynamic/offsite.htm?zi = 1/XJ&sdn = linux&zu = http%3A%2F%2Fwww.apdip.net.*
- Hosmer, Chet (2006). Discovering Hidden Data. *Journal of Digital Forensic Practice,* 1:47–56.
- Jansen, Wayne and Ayers, Rick (2004). *Guidelines on PDA Forensics: Recommendations of the National Institute of Standards and Technology.* NIST: Special Publication 800–72. National Institute of Standards and Technology, U.S. Department of Commerce: Gaithersburg, MD.
- NIJ (2007). *Investigations Involving the Internet and Computer Networks.* NIJ: Special Report. U.S. Department of Justice: Office of Justice Programs, Washington, DC.

WEB RESOURCES

- http://www.maresware.com/maresware/linksto_forensic_tools.htm#graphic – page provides a listing of and linking to an assortment of forensic software and hardware.
- www.ojp.usdoj.gov/nij – the homepage of the Office of Justice Programs of the U.S. Department of Justice,

the site provides links to assorted publications in computer forensics. In addition, the site contains links to other government resources on crime and justice.

- www.apdip.net – the homepage of the Asia-Pacific Development Information Programme of the United Nations Development Programme and host of the International Open Source Network. The site contains links to various government resources. It also provides access to numerous white papers and articles, videos, and multimedia products on operating systems and computer forensics.
- www.crazytrain.com – the homepage of Thomas Rude, the site contains links to various articles on computer forensics for Linux.

ENDNOTES

[1] During the boot process of a computer, the operating system is loaded first, followed by other programs. These programs allow users to interact with the computer in a specific manner. As such, these programs should also be included on a boot disk to prevent destruction of data (possibly evidence) located in file slack and ROM.

[2] While there are other hardware solutions to defeating a CMOS password, they are extremely invasive and go beyond the introductory parameters established in this text. Once again, it must be emphasized that this text is not intended to serve as a primer for computer forensics. Rather, it is intended to provide a brief overview of the issues involved in the investigation of computer-related crime.

[3] File extensions are identifiers designated by DOS located after the period which indicate the type of file included therein. For example, the extension DOC in the file ILOVEYOU.DOC would indicate that the file was textual in nature (i.e., a word processing document).

[4] It should be noted that NT uses a much smaller default cluster of either 4 or 8K.

[5] Generally speaking, these types of Trojans come in two parts: the *client* and the *server*. The *client* portion of the program is the one which allows users to remotely access other machines, while the *server* is the portion which *serves* (i.e., provides) information to the client. Most often, the *server* is surreptitiously delivered and executed by unsuspecting victims.

[6] This section is not intended to serve as a comprehensive guide for conducting Internet investigations, as parameters of the book preclude this. For a complete discussion of Internet investigations, see NIJ (2007). *Investigations Involving the Internet and Computer Networks.* NIJ: Special Report. U.S. Department of Justice: Office of Justice Programs, Washington, DC.

[7] NIJ (2007). *Investigations Involving the Internet and Computer Networks.*

[8] "Disk arbitration" is used by Mac OS X Panther (10.3 +) to mount disks automatically at startup and when they are detected.

[9] Faas, Ryan (2007). *Mac OS X Security Part 1: Investigating Security Breaches and Illegal Use.* Available at: *http://*

www.peachpit.com/articles/article.aspx?p = 706210&seqNum = 3. Retrieved from the Internet on October 12, 2007.

[10]Ibid.

[11]Volonino, Linda; Anzaldua, Reynaldo; and Godwin, Jana (2007). *Computer Forensics: Principles and Practices*. Prentice Hall: New Jersey.

[12]Jansen, Wayne and Ayers, Rick (2004). *Guidelines on PDA Forensics: Recommendations of the National Institute of Standards and Technology*. NIST: Special Publication 800–72. National Institute of Standards and Technology, U.S. Department of Commerce: Gaithersburg, MD.

CHAPTER 13

Conclusions and Future Issues

Chapter Outline

LEARNING OBJECTIVES

After reading this chapter, you will be able to do the following:

✓ Explore traditional problems associated with the investigation and prosecution of computer-related crime.
✓ Discuss strategies to minimize the impact of computer-related crimes.
✓ Discuss approaches to combating Internet crime.
✓ Recognize emerging trends in wireless communications.
✓ Develop an understanding of societal expectations of decency on the Internet.
✓ Explore issues associated with data mining.

KEY TERMS AND CONCEPTS

- data mining
- interoperability
- *Daubert/Frye* challenges
- data stripping

As stated in previous chapters, the advent of technology has vastly changed the modus operandi of certain criminal elements. Indeed, advances have changed the very physical environment in which crime occurs. Whereas physical environments traditionally presented necessary spatial and demographic limitations, the intangibility of electronic communications and commerce exponentially increases illicit possibilities while negating the efficacy of conventional preventive measures. Thieves no longer must concern themselves with the necessary risks associated with the physical removal of massive amounts of stolen merchandise, including their physical presence or the collection of co-conspirators, transportation device, and storage locations. Vandals may generate mass destruction totaling billions without ever leaving the comfort of their home or office. The *Code Red Worm*, for example, cost companies over $2.6 billion worldwide, while estimates place the damages associated with the *Love Bug* as high as $8.7 billion. In fact, the emergence of wireless technology has created an almost ethereal criminal network, in which ghostlike entities emerge ephemerally to wreak their deviant havoc and escape to their digital netherworld. (Such translucence coupled with corresponding perceptions of invincibility has even proven seductive to seemingly average individuals, creating a new breed of first-time criminals.) As such, every aspect of the criminal justice processing of the same must display levels of ingenuity, comparable to the virtuosity exhibited by these emerging entrepreneurs. Unfortunately, such has not been the case.

TRADITIONAL PROBLEMS AND RECOMMENDATIONS

For the most part, the investigation and prosecution of computer-related crime has been hindered by a lack of nomenclature, due primarily to the reluctance of the Supreme Court to interpret emerging legislative actions. As such, investigators, prosecutors, and even trial courts have no basis for determining the legality of either questioned behavior or law enforcement actions. Thus, universal definitions of computer-related crime and computer privacy must be established.

Establishing Technology-Neutral Legislation

The development of computer-specific legislation must be undertaken in a manner that ensures uniformity in application and interpretation irrespective of jurisdictional climate. At the same time, emerging legislation must be generic enough to encompass advances in technology, assuring that application to tomorrow's technology is possible. Just as the applicability of the *Wire Act* has been questioned regarding its implementation for Internet crimes committed via cable modems (as opposed to telephone communications), the advent of wireless communications poses new questions altogether. Thus, legislators should develop technology-neutral legislation, which narrowly defines (and emphasizes) elemental issues like intent, while providing a broad platform for methodology employed. In addition, such legislation should identify traditional challenges in the analysis of digital evidence and provide justifications for the potential of protracted examination of computer materials (e.g., voluminous nature of computer containers, password-protected information, damaged media, and lack of resources.).

Establishing Accountability for Internet Users

Legislation must also be enacted that ensures confidentiality for those who seek it for legitimate purposes, but that denies blanket anonymity. This would allow legitimate surfers the luxury to browse the Web anonymously for all practical purposes, safely concealing their identities from criminals and government officials alike, while providing a mechanism for law enforcement to pursue those predators, criminals, or terrorists who attempt to mask their illegitimate activities. This is especially important in the wake of the events of 9/11. It is imperative that our interest in the globalization of information and communication not supersede the interests of national security. Unfortunately, such a balance is difficult to achieve.

Democratic principles mandate elevated expectations of privacy in private activities which are often counterproductive to law enforcement interests. Moreover, the foundations of open markets and capitalist ideologies require a communication tool which provides a medium for worldwide dissemination, heretofore unavailable prior to the introduction of the World Wide Web. Thus, the development of enforcement-friendly legislation which encourages economic growth consistent with an emerging global market and which does not stifle individual expression is a difficult task at best. Legislatures must also struggle with issues of state sovereignty, taking care that the role of the federal government is that of mediator, not dictator.

Increasing Public Awareness and Research Capabilities

Traditionally, computer-related crime has not garnered significant attention from most sectors of society which fail to recognize the insidious nature of the phenomenon. Thus, a comprehensive effort must be undertaken to educate all levels of the community, including politicians, teachers, law-enforcement officials, individual consumers, and children. Such awareness must include the potential of computer crime, creating an appreciation of the dangers inherent in such activities (i.e., everyone must see both the threat and the exponential growth associated with computer crime). Once established, this collective understanding should result in additional funding for computer-related initiatives and increase public reporting and cooperation. In addition, baseline measurements of prevalence and typologies of offenders should be established. One possible solution would be to amend one of the two empirical measures of crime: the FBI's Uniform Crime Report (UCR) and the National Crime Survey (NCS). This would enable officials to classify incidents and offenders, increasing the efficiency and effectiveness of subsequent investigations. (Without such baseline data on incidents, offenders, forensic problems, and case outcomes, identification of regional or national trends is all but impossible, and the development of evidence analysis capabilities is unlikely.) Moreover, available information should include a comprehensive national directory of technical experts, forensic examiners, academic resources, and external granting institutions, as well as local information including a who's who of electronic crime investigators, unit managers, prosecutors, laboratory technicians, manufacturers, and expert witnesses. Such a compilation of data, when presented as an online clearinghouse, should encourage information-sharing among investigators and agencies alike.

Increasing Inter-Agency and Intra-Departmental Cooperation

Although the law enforcement culture has long been characterized by a lack of communication and cooperation among agencies, the lack of resources available to combat computer-related crime mandates increasing the number of multi-jurisdictional task forces and central reporting stations. While law enforcement agencies have recently formed such collaborative efforts, much is left to be done. Local agencies, in particular, should develop formal alliances with better funded and better trained state and federal agencies. The federal government, on the other hand, must make resources available to these same municipal administrators seeking technological assistance. This includes concentrated dissemination of grant solicitations, as well as technical guidance to the municipal administrators. Task forces already in place should independently seek external funding and should include at least one individual versed in the art of grant writing. Utilization of central reporting stations (both regional and national) should be increased, as duplication of effort dramatically decreases the efficacy of even the most dedicated of efforts. Such clearinghouses should mirror (and work in concert with) the federal system in which regional U.S. Attorneys' offices are required to report all ongoing investigations to one central location (i.e., the Computer Crime Section of the Department of Justice). To further conserve resources, these stations should serve multiple tasks, such as serving as a 24-hour support line, equipped to handle general legal inquiries and provide onsite management assistance for electronic crime units and task forces. (Inter-agency collaboration notwithstanding, investigators must also secure cooperation *within* their own department, increasing awareness of the potentiality of digital evidence and its corresponding vulnerability. Furthermore, investigators must obtain executive support so that resources may be allocated without reservation. Until such a time, computer-related criminal investigations will remain substandard.)

Developing Relationships Between Investigative Agencies and the Private Sector

All levels of the law enforcement community must also seek out and establish partnerships with the high-tech industry for a variety of reasons. First and foremost, law enforcement agencies will remain overworked, understaffed, poorly funded, and technologically deficient due to the continuing struggle for external funding. High-tech corporations, with their unlimited resources and highly trained personnel, may alleviate some of this problem by donating equipment and expertise to their local agencies. In addition, these entities may be called upon to develop software requisite to the law enforcement mission like IP tracking systems, editing and searching tools, and general investigative utilities. Partnerships which emphasize ethical accountability may also result in the development of materials which preclude the proliferation of inappropriate material through filtering and professional accountability. For example, the Electronic Commerce and Consumer Protection Group (which includes AOL, American Express, AT&T, Dell, Visa, Microsoft, IBM, etc.) is currently developing jurisdictional regulations to address consumer protection in a global marketplace. Their goals include the development of a code of conduct among e-tailers to facilitate e-commerce within a secure environment, and the retention of data to identify online predators. Finally, such teamwork will necessarily result in increased reporting of criminal victimization among corporate targets, thus making it easier to develop baseline data for empirical measurement.

Developing International Cooperation

Traditionally, several problems and troublesome questions have erupted concerning international procedures for the preservation of digital evidence. One of the most ambiguous areas involves the search and seizure of computer networks, as it is questionable whether, and to what extent, the right to search and seize a specific computer installation includes the right to search databases that are accessible by this installation but that are situated in other premises. The importance of such questions has reached astronomical proportions, as more and more individuals and corporations are implementing offsite storage databases to protect proprietary information. Thus, pivotal questions include the international sovereignty over the stored data and the accessibility of the information by investigating agencies. Thus, it is questionable whether and to what extent the right to search and seize a specific computer installation includes the right to search databases that are accessible by this installation but that are situated in other premises.

Effective international consortia must be established and global treaties implemented so that jurisdictional disputes do not compromise the interest of justice. Unfortunately, such collaboration must overcome traditional problems including, cultural stereotypes and multi-cultural tensions; a lack of global consensus on criminal behavior and human rights; a lack of expertise in criminal justice and legal communities; competing interests; a lack of extradition and mutual assistance treaties; a lack of synchronized law enforcement efforts; and finally, jurisdictional disputes regarding original sovereignty in cases of dual criminality. While some of these traditional barriers may be overcome through perseverance and a universal understanding of the insidious nature of computer-related criminal activity, others may not. However, officials should attempt to establish an increased number of Multi-Lingual Assistance Treaties (MLATs) which address jurisdictional inconsistencies. Without these, international legal assistance is governed by domestic mutual legal assistance laws and practices, which includes the *letters rogatory* process (A *letter rogatory* is a letter request for assistance from one country's judicial authority to that of another country). Such practices are not only unworkable in most cases, but they require individualized intervention of federal authorities, a situation sure to result in increased backlogs and case overload. In the absence of MLATs, federal authorities should develop formal alliances with enforcement components of other nations. The Organization for Economic Cooperation and Development (OECD), for example, recognized that cultural differences must be overcome when circumstances dictate, publishing a report that evaluated existing laws among international communities and suggesting revisions of same

which would establish a minimum list of abuses that all member countries would prohibit and prosecute.

Unfortunately, member countries have been slow to react to such international mandates, citing jurisdictional sovereignty and American imperialism. Other efforts, highly supported by the United States, have been widely criticized. On January 21, 1997, Janet Reno urged the P8 Senior Experts' Group on Transnational Crime to develop international laws and a *global legal support regime*. She encouraged countries to develop a global understanding with international cooperation firmly entrenched. These efforts would include the preservation of evidence which resided on foreign soil. However, this effort has been unduly criticized by smaller countries who are concerned about American imperialism. Government officials must continue their pursuit of international cooperation and collaborations. At a minimum, a generalized understanding with other international communities which allows for investigation and subsequent prosecution of computer crime must be achieved.

Standardization of Accreditation or Expertise

Due to the inexperience of legislative authorities and the inconsistency of judicial estimation, law enforcement authorities must establish a standard of accreditation and/or expertise of forensic methodologies and examiners. As in any emerging discipline, such standardization would decrease **Daubert/Frye challenges** to the recovery of digital evidence. (Such challenges issued to emerging or untested scientific methods require a variety of thresholds, many of which have not yet been achieved in the emerging field of computer forensics.) Thus, the discipline should attempt to identify and address each of the following questions:

1. Can the techniques involved in data recovery be empirically tested?
2. Have they been subjected to peer review and publication?

3. Does the theory or technique have the potential for a high rate of error?
4. Does the technique enjoy a general acceptance within the scientific community?

Such challenges can only be met through the development of professional associations and academic publishing which provide a means of discourse among analysts. (The standard does not require a universal acceptance or rigorous testing by *all* experts in the field, but it does require a mechanism for empirical testing and debate.) Although the resources associated with the development of independent research outlets could prove insurmountable at the present time, practitioners should evaluate the feasibility of amalgamation with established forensic science associations. As an alternative, funds could be solicited from federal monies or technology companies. Such funds could then be invested in an interest-bearing endowment, much like specialized chairs in university settings. Regardless, law enforcement administrators and legislators should develop innovative strategies to increase revenues available to law enforcement to establish high-tech investigative capabilities.

It must be noted that the standardization of computer forensics cannot be accomplished overnight. Like all recognized disciplines, it must be founded on a solid framework of scientific inquiry. Computer forensic "doc-in-a-box" organizations that tout certificates of accreditation are most often self-serving entities more concerned with capitalism and free enterprise than law enforcement interests. Self-proclaimed "experts" may actually hinder prosecutorial efforts by utilization of unrecognized methodologies. In fact, true experts are much harder to find than the multitude of individuals who have anointed themselves as the computer-forensic messiahs. Many of the latter category do not display any evidence of expertise (or humility), while the former are those individuals who recognized their own limitations and concede that technology is far outpacing investigative capabilities. Thus, any development of an accreditation process should utilize those individuals who are respected among their peers and include a combination of investigators and forensic programmers.[1] Such an entity would bring professionalism to computer investigations, extend awareness among the community, and decrease the likelihood of successful evidentiary challenges.

Miscellaneous

As more and more individuals are using the Internet in their daily lives, it is critical for law enforcement to establish a visible presence on the Web. All departments, for example, should create and maintain a departmental Web page, illustrating their commitment to contemporary problems and providing a mechanism for community input. In this way, technology can be used to foster positive relations with the community and establish a system conducive to anonymous reporting (i.e., the same perception of anonymity that encourages criminals creates a comfort zone for those wishing to come forward with information but are reluctant to be identified). In addition, it allows departments to publicize their mission statements, promote departmental initiatives, enhance their ability to update community residents (including the photographic display of missing persons and wanted individuals), and provide a mechanism for communication in emergency situations (i.e., severe weather, etc.).

ADDITIONAL APPROACHES TO INTERNET CRIME

Computer crime is increasing at an exponential rate as criminals move more of their operations to the cyberworld. Of significant concern to authorities is the increase in money laundering, organized crime, and denial of service (DOS) attacks as they threaten consumer confidence, and through extension, the global economy. Unfortunately, the borderless nature of the Internet has made it extraordinarily difficult to

Technology: The New Center of Gravity for Law Enforcement in the Information Age

Al Lewis

The purpose of this paper is to demonstrate how technology can be leveraged to create a more effective law enforcement organizational model—an organization capable of effectively combating today's cyber-based threat to national security.

The twenty-first century, like those before, has brought great change to the world. The proliferation of technology, combined with the Internet as the new communications medium, is the greatest catalyst of these changes. Technology has created an era of mobility, making location transparent to the individual. The Internet has re-defined the speed in which the world communicates, making near-real-time communications the norm. The significance of this is that information has become the new currency. This is the fundamental characteristic of the Information Age.

Information was important before the Internet, but oftentimes the information was not actionable. Consider the British commanders during the American Revolution. If a commander had to convey battlefield issues of strategic importance to the King, he had to send a message, by ship, back to England. In this case, even though the information might have been important, it was hardly actionable. The result was the information did not have an immediate impact on the battlefield.

The Threat

Technology has made information actionable, thus exponentially increasing its value. Information has become more important than actual currency. Information has become synonymous with National Security. Therefore, technology, information, and national security are inextricably linked. The relationship between technology, information, and national security has led to the creation of the cyber-based criminal. The cyber-based criminal can encompass the lone criminal, skilled hackers, organized crime, and nation-state sponsored spies as well as terrorists.

> The gravest danger to freedom lies at the crossroads of radicalism and technology. When the spread of chemical and biological and nuclear weapons, along with ballistic missile technology—when that occurs, even weak states and small groups could attain a catastrophic power to strike great nations. Our enemies have declared this very intention, and have been caught seeking these terrible weapons. They want the capability to blackmail us, or to harm us, or to harm our friends—and we will oppose them with all our power. (President Bush, 2002)

Indeed the most significant threat facing national security is the trifecta formed by the convergence of the skilled hacker, organized criminal elements, and the terror-based extremist. Hence, the modern cyber-based criminal element is amorphous in nature, ranging from the virtually inept to the most dedicated, and highest skilled members of modern society.

Law enforcement organizations are overburdened bureaucracies that have traditionally been reactive to crime. The mission of law enforcement has and remains to protect and serve the people from the criminal element. In the past, this linear process focused almost entirely on solving a crime once it had been committed. Prevention was an afterthought and manifested itself in a police presence, providing an outward deterrent to would-be criminals. Unfortunately, the volatile nature of cyberspace does not tolerate time well. Law enforcement organizations must shift from reactive to proactive enforcement methodologies to combat the ever-changing cybersphere. The shift in methodology for law enforcement organizations is not an esoteric one. Law enforcement must trim the bureaucracies and leverage technology in order to remain viable.

In the Web site Wikipedia, The Free Encyclopedia (2006), the center of gravity for the military is defined as ". . . those characteristics, capabilities, or locations from which a military force derives its freedom of action, physical strength, or will to fight." Law enforcement must define technology as its center of gravity. Technology is the great equalizer.

Many of today's law enforcement agencies are steeped in tradition, hierarchical in organization, controlled by bureaucracy, and limited in jurisdiction and resources. Conversely, the cyber-based criminal element is an enemy with seemingly unlimited resources, a nonhierarchical communications network, and limited infrastructure overhead. The modern cyber-based criminal is also unlimited by geography and virtually free from attribution for crimes committed.

By adopting technology as its center of gravity, law enforcement agencies can break free from the cycle of "too little too late." Technology facilitates a streamlined, efficient use of resources, while enabling a faster, more effective horizontal communications model.

(*Continued*)

The New Model

Consider a law enforcement agency that uses online collaboration, knowledge management, and data mining as their business communications model. The agency would be able to effectively function across all three operational modes indicative of a law enforcement organization: reactive (incident response), crisis management, and prevention (proactive).

For example, a federal law enforcement agency with the mission of protecting a high-ranking official during a public speech could use technology to enhance the overall event security, throughout the aforementioned three operational phases.

Prevention. In this scenario, prior to the event, the agency, leveraging current geospatial information, maps out the venue for the event. A line of sight analysis is conducted based on satellite imagery surrounding the podium, in order to identify potential areas of vulnerability to handgun, shotgun, and rifle ranges. Then, a blast simulation is conducted for the average payload of a foot mobile suicide bomber and for a vehicle-mounted bomb; these concentric patterns are used to formulate a barrier plan around the podium. Additionally, the geospatial maps are used to devise the most effective (protective) route in and from the event. Additionally, a variety of secure networked modes of communication are established for the duration of the event, and extensive coordination has been made covering all jurisdictional issues, and a large de-confliction effort has been established.

Incident response. During the event, a suspicious individual is identified by a surveillance team. The team is able to communicate in real-time to an enforcement team, which is in constant contact with the operations center. As the enforcement team moves to intercept the suspicious person, the protective team is updated and given the location of the incident as one of the line of sight checkpoints. The protective team moves to obscure the line of sight to the protectee as the enforcement team arrives at location of the suspicious individual. The enforcement team is able to identify the person and have a complete criminal history of him or her while conducting a field interview.

Crisis management. During the event, a nearby explosion occurs and a large plume of gas accumulates in the air. The protective team reports the incident to the operations center as they begin evacuation of the protectee. The operations center runs a plume analysis, based on the wind and weather, and determines the safest route for the evacuation of the protectee is different from the primary evacuation route. The operations center notifies and re-routes the protective team during the evacuation. Simultaneously, the operations center has coordinated with the 9/11 center and local authorities to assist in coordinating the evacuation of the civilians and subsequent bomb investigation.

By leveraging technology, the agency was able to reduce risk through preventative measures, enhance planning and preparation, communicate effectively during a crisis, and increase the safety of the populace during the event. Additionally, technology will facilitate the subsequent bomb investigation through a variety of means.

Summarily, today's cyber-base criminal adopts rapidly to take advantage of emerging technologies in furtherance of their devious activities. Law enforcement organizations must compensate for limited resources through proper application of technology in order to effectively combat the cyber-based criminal and enhance national security.

References

Center of gravity (military). (2006, March 24). In *Wikipedia, The Free Encyclopedia.* Available at *http://en.wikipedia. org/w/index.php?title = Center_of_gravity_%28military% 29&oldid = 45336382.* Retrieved from the Internet on June 6, 2006 at 12:31.

President Bush, George W. (September 17, 2002). *The National Security Strategy of the United States of America, 5*(1): 17. Available at *http://www.whitehouse.gov/nsc/nss5.html.* Retrieved from the Internet on June 6, 2006.

police. Thus, law enforcement authorities must partner with cyber citizens to properly address the phenomenon. In a perfect world, such collaboration would be heartily embraced by both citizens and corporate entities. However, private and capitalist interests often discourage such participation, and legislation is needed to overcome such reluctance. Such legislation should address the following areas:

- **Utilization of existing forfeiture statutes**—Federal legislation provides for the seizure of all assets of a legitimate business which facilitates the laundering of money obtained in an illegal enterprise. Even legitimate revenue can be seized if it is intermingled with laundered funds as it serves to conceal or otherwise disguise illegal money.

- **Accountability of ISP's Hosts and E-businesses**—Legislation must include new accountability statutes which enable authorities to civilly punish ISPs, hosts or other e-businesses which facilitate illegal activity. As the standard of proof in such cases is relatively low (i.e., preponderance of the evidence), online businesses should comply. In particular, legislation which mandates accountability of SMTP servers should be developed to reduce the number of DOS attacks. To wit, the imposition of monetary fines should be levied against operators running SMTP servers with open relays or unrestricted, anonymous-access FTP servers.

- **Know your customer**—Legislation must encourage a grassroots approach in the business community. Those engaged in e-commerce need to be educated and recognize that the dangers associated with organized crime's infiltration of e-commerce. "Know your customer" statutes should require businesses to (1) know their customers; (2) assure their identity; and (3) require transparency.

FUTURE TRENDS AND EMERGING CONCERNS

As illustrated throughout the text, the identification, investigation, and prosecution of computer-related crime are accompanied by a myriad of unique problems. Unfortunately, it is anticipated that these problems will be further exacerbated by emerging technologies. Legal questions regarding decency and privacy are but two of the issues sure to plague future administrators. Advances in wireless communications and encryption technology will further complicate the legal landscape, and the increasing convergence of audio, video, and digital data will present new challenges for criminal investigators.

Wireless Communications

Although cellular telephones have been around for quite some time, the reduction of costs and the increase in communication quality have vastly expanded their audience and created a society increasingly reliant on technology. Fortunately for law enforcement, tapping into wireless communications has proven far easier than traditional telephonic exchanges for two primary reasons: (1) it is easier to identify a suspect's cellular provider than to predict which pay phone a suspect will use; and, (2) the Supreme Court has refused to recognize an expectation of privacy in wireless communications. Moreover, it provides data on the cell site of the

---

Educating the Public

In addition to the passage of legislation targeting corporate facilitators of online crime, the government must continue to educate the public. To reiterate, the war against computer-related crime must be fought on all fronts.

Tips for Individuals

- Use a blended data security platform which incorporates anti-virus, firewall, intrusion detection, and vulnerability management. This will significantly enhance your level

of security and identify if the computer has been compromised.
- Update security patches and virus definitions as they emerge to keep the protection current.
- Create passwords which include letters and numbers, avoiding words which appear in the dictionary.
- Change passwords often.
- Never view, open, or execute any e-mail attachment unless you are sure of its contents and are expecting it.
- Don't fall prey to phishing scams and hoaxes.

sender or recipient, and provides a mechanism for locating a particular phone, a capability which has been significantly enhanced by recently passed FCC regulations which require all providers to have the capability of locating phones within a 40-foot radius for longitude, latitude, and altitude. However, the increase in wireless communications has also complicated investigations and developed new avenues for criminal behavior. Earth-based gateways of the satellite systems which service the United States, for example, may actually reside outside its jurisdictional boundaries making them almost impossible to police. In addition, the decreasing costs associated with cellular service have encouraged the use of "disposable phones" in the furtherance of a virtual cornucopia of criminal activity, while the sheer marketability of wireless communications has attracted representatives from criminal syndicates.

It is anticipated that the increased proliferation of wireless devices will be accompanied by an increase in viruses and contaminants for PDA's and cell phones. Spam, often used as a delivery vehicle for malware, will also increase. While the first cell phone virus was created to prove that this could be done, others are far more insidious. Like computer viruses, cell phone viruses are represented as unwanted executable files that are contagious after infection. They are spread via smart phones with connection and data capabilities in one of three ways: Internet downloads, Bluetooth wireless connection, and multimedia messaging service. Fortunately, wide-scale infection has not been realized due to the large number of proprietary operating systems. However, it is anticipated that large-scale infections will rise as universal operating systems emerge.

Data Hiding: Remote Storage, Encryption, and the Like

As if the advent of wireless technologies was not enough to hinder law enforcement efforts, data hiding practices, precipitated by warnings from privacy advocates, present unique challenges. The increase of remote storage facilities (i.e., virtual islands of information unattached and, thus, unregulated by a sovereign state), for example, may be especially troublesome to law enforcement authorities for a variety of reasons. First, it does not seem likely that the Supreme Court will uphold the constitutionality of search warrants for non-particularized locations of remote areas of data storage (i.e., a search warrant for any location of remote data). Thus, investigators may be unable to access incriminating information. Second, the lack of physicality obscures jurisdictional boundaries,

A Sampling of Cell Phone Viruses

- Cabir.A
  - Date of Release—June 2004
  - Affected systems—Symbian Series 60 phones
  - Method of dispersal—Bluetooth
  - Payload—none
- Skulls.A
  - Date of Release—November 2004
  - Affected systems—various Symbian systems
  - Method of dispersal—Internet download
  - Payload—disables all phone functions with the exception of sending and receiving messages.
- Commwarrior.A
  - Date of Release—January 2005
  - Affected systems—Symbian Series 60 phones

  - Method of dispersal—Bluetooth and MMS
  - Payload—sends MMS messages to everyone in phonebook
- Fontal.A
  - Date of Release—April 2005
  - Affected systems—Symbian Series 60 phones
  - Method of dispersal—Internet download
  - Payload—disables phone by locking phone in startup mode

Online Stock Manipulation

The Internet has invigorated the entire industry of stock scams. Now there isn't much scam activity that happens off-line.

—Kevin Lichtman, President of FinanicalWeb.com.

Con artists looking to make a fast buck have been around forever, as have the suckers who fall for their scams. But the Internet has altered the way the game is played; the bad guys have mastered new techniques for touting frauds on the Web, spamming scams through e-mail, and talking up hot investment tips on bulletin boards.

The one-time success of Net stocks and the perception that anyone can get rich on the Internet are making the job of scam artists even easier. Plenty of money-losing Internet companies with minimal track records and hazy business plans have been underwritten by reputable brokerage firms, and their stock prices have shot up hundreds of percent a day. Meanwhile, con artists are peddling copycat companies of their own, and investors can find it difficult to differentiate between companies with legitimate potential and scams designed to part them from their money.

making it unclear as to who is the prevailing legal authority. And, finally, hyper-privacy individuals or businesses may utilize *data stripping* methods, where data is fragmented and placed on various servers.

The emergence of over-the-counter encryption technology may also prove problematic for law enforcement officials. As these packages become more available and consumers become more concerned with privacy and/or security, it appears inevitable that encrypted files, folders, and/or drives will become more commonplace in criminal investigations. Unfortunately, advances in encryption technology coupled with the easing of export regulations may make it all but impossible to access questionable data. However, the events of 9/11 may make the passage of anti-encryption legislation more likely, as it has been discovered that communications between the conspirators were encrypted with PGP.

Finally, the increasing availability of anonymizer-type technology and disposable e-mail accounts may further complicate criminal investigations. Like the other technologies discussed, these tools are becoming more popular as more and more consumers become concerned with the security of proprietary and personal information. While the majority of those individuals employing these mechanisms are concerned with protecting themselves from online predators and fraudsters, many deviants utilize them to hide their activities from law enforcement authorities.

New Investigative Technologies and the Constitution

As with other areas of technology, the introduction of surveillance software and methodologies has resulted in various legal questions unanswered by traditional legislation or judicial action. One such question involves the use of software which captures every action undertaken by an individual user of a suspect machine (i.e., key loggers).

Case in point: Does the implantation of key logging software by government officials violate the wiretap statute? What is the legal standard for obtaining judicial permission (i.e., court order, warrant, etc.)? In a recent crackdown on organized crime families in the Philadelphia area, government agents armed with a warrant copied the contents of a personal computer located at Merchant Services, a company allegedly owned by Nicky Scarfo, Jr. However, they were unable to access the information in a file ("Factors") which was encrypted with PGP. So they obtained a court order to return to the location. Subsequently, they installed a key logger on the same machine and secured the password necessary to decrypt the said file. This resulted in a three-count indictment. Government is refusing to identify the methodology used, stating that it is not important. Scarfo's attorneys, on the other hand, claim that this knowledge is necessary to determine whether a wiretap order should have been secured.

Governing Decency and Virtual Pornography

Courts have been increasingly cautious and consistently ambiguous regarding the level of protection afforded online communications and in defining indecency and vulgarity on the Web. However, it appears unlikely that a universal definition will soon emerge as content-restrictive legislation has failed judicial scrutiny. Thus, numerous bills have been proposed which involve the use of "E-chip" blocking software. Such devices would be distributed by ISPs and would serve as information filters. Unfortunately, similar measures have been widely criticized as they are incapable of distinguishing between legitimate, educational information and profane or indecent material. Other proposals which include rating systems for sites are equally unworkable as there is no agency for enforcement. Finally, none of the proposals provide for the regulation of simulated behavior or virtual images.

Until recently, the thought that the computer (or any other device) could enable users to act out fantasies in a real-life context appeared preposterous. However, some authors suggest that individual users may utilize advances in technology to engage in virtual behavior which in the real world may be felonious. Indeed, society has already witnessed inroads into computer-generated images. Movies as early as *Jurassic Park* and *Total Recall* have successfully utilized computer-generated animation, while digital remastering has produced the re-release of George Lucas' *Star Wars* trilogy. In fact, some individuals argue that the use of synthetic actors may be the wave of the future as the technology becomes more available and less expensive. This would allow producers to reduce the rising costs of salaries, while at the same time, providing a "safe" way to conduct dangerous stunts. This same technology could also be used in illegitimate markets—allowing pornography peddlers to go beyond the scope of traditional decency standards. At some point, for example, it will be possible to generate realistic images of children engaging in sexual activity or create snuff films, where the computer-generated "victim" is killed

during sexual acts. Some even suggest that the near future will bring technology capable of simulating actual sexual intercourse. Appropriately placed sensors in gloves and body coverings coupled with sophisticated programs and virtual helmets would literally enable the user to experience sexual arousal with an inanimate object.

> Some promoters of virtual reality see a new, safe, clean way to have sexual encounters. Eventually users will be able to don a suit, gloves, and goggles, and have sex with their computer. Inside the goggles are tiny video monitors that would project computer-generated images, and the suit and gloves would have sensors to react to every move of the user. Users will be able to buy, rent, or make their own life-like sex partners and do with them whatever they please . . . . we don't have the sticky stuff that comes with real life, no more AIDS, no more intersubjective rivalries, no more otherness . . . there's no more (real) sex, and therefore there will be no more failure.[2]

Such capabilities will necessarily increase the number of individuals acting out fantastical situations that would violate criminal statutes in the absence of abstract dimensions. It may be argued that such increases may result in amplifications in real-world situations, creating an environment conducive to the exploitation and victimization of children in particular. Thus, legislation must be created to establish acceptable parameters of computer activity. Unfortunately, civil libertarians will continue to argue that virtual victimization is a legal impossibility and will continue to promote the eradication of any censorship legislation regardless of design.

Data Mining and Increased Interoperability

The evolution of computer crime investigations has revealed that the prevention and detection of computer-related criminal activity is extremely difficult. Criminals, not bound by considerations of law and cultural norms, have employed various methods to perpetrate their nefarious schemes. In response, law enforcement agencies have had to employ similar tactics to identify and thwart their endeavors. Such approaches, however, have not always been embraced by privacy advocates. In recent years, packet sniffing and data-mining programs have proven to be favorite targets of organizations like EPIC and the ACLU.

Data mining may be defined as a comprehensive analysis of large data sets designed to uncover patterns and relationships. Analysis tools include, but are not limited to: statistical models, mathematical algorithms, and artificial intelligence. According to the Government Accountability Office, 52 government agencies have launched nearly 200 data-mining programs, with 91 percent of these employed by law enforcement or counterterrorism.[3] While most of these projects are designed to enhance services and improve customer relations, others are employed to analyze intelligence and identify terrorists.

Although the potential for intelligence gathering by law enforcement is tremendous, there are some significant limitations. First, data mining often lacks contexts. Although it is capable of revealing patterns, it fails to identify causal relationships or depth and strength of connections. For example, programs to identify known terrorists may include analysis of factors like: propensity to purchase last-minute flights or one-way tickets. While terrorists may display this characteristic, so might an individual with a sick child. While terrorists might visit sites displaying violent rhetoric, so might academics interested in the same phenomenon.

Data mining is often limited by its lack of quality control, as there is no differentiation between good and bad data sources. The factors affecting data quality include: presence of duplicate records;

lack of data standards; timeliness of updates; and, of course, human error. The effectiveness of data mining may be enhanced by cleaning up data which has been compromised. Investigators should employ the following practices to reduce false positives:

- removal of duplicate records
- normalization or standardization of data appearance
- accounting for missing data points
- removal of unnecessary data fields
- identification of anomalous data points.

Data mining practices have also been criticized for *mission creep*, as there appears to be a tendency to use mined data for things other than that which it was intended. It increases the potential for mistakes and false conclusions, as the data may be utilized by a third party or an entity with a mission which is inconsistent with the original purpose of the collection. These problems are exacerbated in cases where data mining is used by authorities for predictive purposes. In fact, predictive data mining requires a significant number of known instances, which might not be available in law enforcement operations. For example, patterns of consumer purchasing emerge after analysis of millions of records. Thus, employing predictive data mining to identify crime trends or suspected terrorists may be inappropriate. This problem is further compounded by the interoperability of data mining software and services across agencies. This lack of universality often causes a loss of appropriate data or misinterpretation of the results. In order to remedy such inconsistencies, a universal structure should be developed and utilized.

A Sampling of Data Mining Projects

Department of Education—compares its databases with those of the FBI to verify identities in *Project Strikeback*.

Department of Defense—mines the intelligence community and the Internet to identify foreign terrorists or their supporters in their *Verity K2 Enterprise* program.

National Security Agency—employs software by Cogito, Inc., which is capable of analyzing phone records and other voluminous data.

Reducing Cyber Vulnerability and Increasing National Security—Recommendations from the National Infrastructure Advisory Council[4]

1. Direct lead agencies to work with each of the critical sectors to more closely examine the risks and vulnerabilities of providing critical services over network-based systems.
2. Direct DHS and the Sector Specific Agencies to identify potential failure points across federal government systems. Encourage the private sector to perform similar cross-sector analysis in collaboration with DHS, as long as DHS can assure protection of sensitive, proprietary results.
3. Encourage sector and cross-sector coordinating groups to establish and/or support existing cyber security best practices or standards for their respective sectors.
4. Direct DHS to sponsor cross-sector activities to promote a better understanding of the cross-sector vulnerability impacts of a cyber attack.
5. Direct federal agencies to include cyber attack scenarios and protective measures in their disaster recovery planning. Encourage sector coordinating groups to include cyber attack scenarios and protective measures in their disaster recovery planning.
6. Encourage law enforcement organizations to prosecute cyber criminals and identity thieves, as well as publicize efforts to do so.
7. Promote awareness of cyber security best practices as the corporate, government, small business, university, and individual levels.

Data mining by government agencies has been attacked by privacy advocates who argue that the practice violates various constitutional rights due to the problems discussed above. As a result, various bills have been proposed which would eliminate the mining of data by government agencies. Although the majority of such proposed legislation have been defeated, the proliferation of the same indicates a growing concern among the public and its representatives. Thus, it is essential that authorities address such concerns and develop a universal structure of language of data.

CONCLUSIONS

Unquestionably, advances in technology increase the potentiality and renovate the methodology of traditional criminal behavior. Just as the automobile vastly expanded the landscape of the criminal underworld, the advent of cyberspace and the ability to communicate globally has exponentially broadened the potentiality of criminal activity. Although some authors predicted that *"cybercrimes w(ould)l peak and then decrease"* (e.g., Parker, 1998), there is no empirical evidence to support this supposition. In fact, the streamlining of proprietary data coupled with society's increasing reliance on computer technology is sure to create an environment ripe for criminal entrepreneurs.

It seems entirely plausible that a certain level of street crime will be supplanted by technological alternatives as the profitability and anonymity of cybercrime become well known. In fact, a marked increase in narcotics trafficking and fencing of stolen property has been noted on the Web in recent years. Unfortunately, the criminal justice system is unequipped to deal with such transference. The lack of appropriate legislation and the lack of resources allocated to this area of criminal activity can only be exacerbated by social and judicial indifference to the dangers of computer-related crime. Thus, it is essential that the potentiality of computer-related crime and the insidious nature of the phenomenon be recognized and addressed by all sectors of the community.

DISCUSSION QUESTIONS

1. What can legislators do to assist law enforcement in the area of computer-related crime?
2. What can law enforcement agencies do to enhance their investigative capabilities?

3. What are some potential benefits and pitfalls of formal accreditation of forensic examiners?
4. What are some emerging issues in the area of high-tech crime? Why are these problematic, and what proactive measures can be implemented to lessen their negative impact?

WEB RESOURCES

- www.us-cert.gov – the homepage of the United States Computer Emergency Readiness Team, a partnership between the Department of Homeland Security and the public and private sectors. The site provides numerous links to other government resources and provides access to various articles and research studies involving computer-related incidents. The site also provides access to US-CERT's quarterly publications which evaluate current issues and project future trends.
- www.privacyrights.org – homepage of the Privacy Rights Clearinghouse, a nonprofit consumer information and advocacy organization, the site contains a comprehensive chronology of data breaches affecting U.S. residents. It also contains links to government records and numerous publications concerning computer security and informational privacy.

ENDNOTES

[1]The following individuals were but a few examples of experts which the author had the privilege of conversing with during the preparation of this manuscript. All of them recognized the importance of networking, and all would probably object to the characterization as "expert." Danny Mares, *Marsware*; Joe Mykytyn; Chip Johnson, *State Law Enforcement Division (SLED)*; Jimmy Doyle, *NYPD*; Sunny Parmar, *RCMP*, Bruce Simmons, *Mitre*).

[2]Johnson, David (1994). Why the Possession of Computer-Generated Child Pornography 4 (311). Available at *www. lexisnexis.com*. Retrieved from the Internet on October 11, 2007.

[3]Mohammed, Arshad and Goo Sara Kehaulani (2006). Government Increasingly Turning to Data Mining: Peek into Private Lives May Help in Hunt for Terrorists. The Washington Post (June 15, 2006). Available at *www.washingtonpost.com*.

[4]National Infrastructure Advisory Council (2006). *National Infrastructure Protection Plan*. Department of Homeland Security: Washington, DC.

CASES CITED

44 Liquormart, Inc. v. *Rhode Island*, 517 U.S. 484 (1996).

Andersen Consulting LLP v. *UOP and Bickel and Brewer*, 991 F. Supp.1041 (1998).

Ashcroft v. *Free Speech Coalition*, 535 U.S. 234 (2002).

Bernstein v. *United States Department of Justice* (1999, 9th Circuit 9716686).

Casino City, Inc. v. *United States Department of Justice*, No. 04-557-B-M3 (M.D. La. August 7, 2004). Available at *http://ww2.casinocitypress. com/complaintfiledon8-9-04.pdf.*

Central Hudson Gas and Electric v. *Public Service Commission of New York*, 447 U.S. 557 (1980).

Coolidge v. *New Hampshire*, 403 U.S. 443, 465, 29 L.Ed. 2d 564, 91 S.Ct. 2022 (1971).

Doe v. *MySpace, Inc.*, No. A-06-CA-983-SS (W.D. Tex. 2007).

Ex parte Jackson, 96 U.S. 727 (1877).

FCC v. *Pacifica Foundation*, 438 U.S. 726 (1978).

Fraser v. *Nationwide Mutual Insurance* (decided March, 2001) United States District Court for the Eastern District of Pennsylvania. # 98-CV-6726.

The Free Speech Colation v. *Reno* (9th Cir., 1999)–(198 F.3d 1083, 9th Cir., 1999) #97-16536.

Gues v. *Leis*, 255 F.3d 325 (6th Cir., 2001).

Ginsberg v. *New York*, 390 U.S. 629 (1968).

Hester v. *United States*, 265 U.S. 57.

Hoffa v. *U.S.*, 385 *United States* 293 (1966).

In re Subpoena Duces Tecum, 846 F. Supp. 11 (S.D.N.Y., 1994).

Florida v. *Jimeno*, 500 U.S. 248, 251 (1991).

Jacobellis v. *Ohio*, 378 U.S. 184 (1964).

Junger v. *Daley*, 1998 WL 388972 (N.D. Ohio, 1998).

Karn v. *U.S. Department of State*, 107 F.3d 923 (D.C.Cir. 1997).

Katz v. *United States* 389 U.S. 347 (1967).

Lewis v. *United States*, 385 U.S. 206 (1980).

Maryland v. *Garrison*, 480 U.S. 79 (1987).

Miller v. *California*, 413 U.S. 15 (1973).

New York v. *Ferber*, 458 U.S. 747 (1982).

Olmstead v. *United States*, 277 U.S. 438 (1928).

Osborne v. *Ohio*, 495 U.S. 103 (1990).

Posadas de Puerto Rico Associates v. *Tourism Co. Of Puerto Rico*, 478 U.S. 328 (1986).

Rawlings v. *Kentucky*, 448 U.S. 98; 100 S.Ct. 2556; 1980 U.S. Lexis 142; 65 L. Ed. 2d 633.

Regina v. *Hicklin*, 1868 L. R. 3 Q. B. 360 (1857).

Reno v. *ACLU*, 521 U.S. 844 (1997).

Rios v. *United States*, 364 U.S. 253 (1960).

Roth v. *United States*, 354 U.S. 476 (1957).

Sable Communications, Inc. v. *FCC*, 492 U.S. 115 (1989).

Stanley v. *Georgia*, 394 U.S. 557(1969).

Steve Jackson Games, Inc. v. *U.S. Secret Service et al.*, 36 F.3d 457, 463 (5th Cir., 1994).

Sweezy v. *New Hampshire*, 354 U.S. 234 (1957).

Timothy R. McVeigh v. *William S. Cohen et al.* 983 F. Supp. 215 (1998). District of Columbia.

United States v. *Abbell*, 914 F. Supp. 519 (S.D.Fla. 1995).

United States v. *Acheson*, 195 F.3d 645 (11th Cir., 1999).

United States v. *Barth*, 26 F. Supp. 2d 929 (U.S. Dist. Lexis 18316) (U.S. District Court for the Western District of Texas, Midland–Odessa Division).

United States v. *Block*, 590 F.2d 5335 (4th Cir., 1978).

United States v. *Carey*, 172 F.3d 1268; 1999 U.S. App. LEXIS 7197; 1999 Colo.J.C.A.R. 2287 (10th Cir., 1999).

United States v. *Charbonneau*, 979 F. Supp. 1177 (S.D. Ohio, 1997).

United States v. *Dichiarinte*, 445 F.2d 126 (7th Cir., 1971).

United States v. *Elliott*, 107 F.3d 810, 815 (10th Cir., 1997).

United States v. *Gawrysiak*, 972 F. Supp. 853 (D.N.J. 1997).

United States v. *Gutierrez-Hermosillo*, 142 F.3d 1225, 1231 (10th Cir), cert. Denied, 119 S.Ct. 230 (1998).

United States v. *Hambrick*, 55 F. Supp. 2d 504 (W.D. Va. 1999).

United States v. *Hersch*, CR-A-93-10339-2, 1994 WL 568728.

United States v. *Hilton*, 167 F.3d 61 (1st Cir., 1999).

United States v. *Hunter*, 13 F. Supp. 2d 574 (D.Vt. 1998)—privileges.

United States v. *Kennerley*, 209 F. 119, 120 (S.D.N.Y. 1913).

United States v. *Kim* 27 F.3d 947, 956 (Third Cir., 1994).

United States v. *Lee*, 274 U.S. 559 (1982).

United States v. *Lyons*, 992 F.2d 1029 (10th Cir., 1993).

United States v. *Maxwell*, 42 M.J. 568 (1995) United States Air Force Court of Criminal Appeals.

United States v. *Mento*, #99-4813 (4th Cir., 2000).

United States v. *Meriwether*, 917 F.2d 955, 960 (6th Cir., 1990).

United States v. *Miller*, 425 U.S. 435, 443 (1976).

United States v. *Monroe*, 50 M.J. 550 (A.F.C.C.A., 1999).

United States v. *Pervaz*, 118 F.3d 1 (1st Cir., 1997).

United States v. *Reyes*, 922 F. Supp. 818, 836 (S.D.N.Y., 1996); 798 F. F.2D 380, 383 (10th Cir., 1986).

United States v. *Ross*, 456 U.S. 798, 820–822 (1982).

United States v. *Sassani*, 1998 WL 89875 (4th Cir., March 4) (Per curiam) (unpublished decision), cert. denied, 119 S.Ct. 276 (1998).

United States v. *Schaefer*, 87 F.3d 562, 569 (1st Cir., 1996).

United States v. *Stribling*, 94 F.3d 321, 324 (Seventh Cir., 1996).

United States v. *Thomas*, 74 F.3d. 701 (Sixth Cir., 1996).

United States v. *Torch*, 609 F.2d 1088, 1090 (Fourth Cir., 1979)—seizing hardware.

United States v. *Turner* (1st Cir.) *http://laws.find-law.com/1st/981258.html.*

Warden v. *Hayden*, 387 U.S. 294 (1967).

Weeks v. *United States*, 232 U.S. 383 (1914).

Wesley College v. *Leslie Pitts, Bettina Ferguson, and Keith Hudson*, 974 F. Supp. 375 (1997)—United States District Court for the District of Delaware.

WORKS CITED

Adams, Jo-Ann M. (1996). "Controlling Cyberspace: Applying the Computer Fraud and Abuse Act to the Internet." *Santa Clara Computer and High Technology Law Journal*, *12*(403). Available at *www.lexis-nexis.com* (last accessed on November 1, 2001).

Allison, Stuart F.H.; Schuck, Amie M.; and Lersch, Kim Michelle (2004). "Exploring the Crime of Identity Theft: Prevalence, Clearance Rates, and Victim/Offender Characteristics." *Journal of Criminal Justice, 33*(19–29).

Andreano, Frank P. (1999). "The Evolution of Federal Computer Crime Policy: The Ad Hoc Approach to an Ever-Changing Problem." *American Journal of Criminal Law*, *27*(81). Lexis-Nexis.

Baker, Glenn D. (1993). "Trespassers will be prosecuted: Computer Crime in the 1990's." *Computer/Law Journal*, *12*(61). Available at *www.westdoc.com.*

Baladi, Joe (1999). "Buidling Castles Made of Glass: Security on the Internet." *University of Arkansas at Little Rock Law Review, 21*(251).

Baldas, Tresa (2005). " 'Fear Factor' Promotes Identity Theft Suits." *New York Law Journal*, May 12, 2005. Available at *http://web2.infotrac.galegroup.com.*

Bank, David (2005). "Security Breaches of Customers' Data Trigger Lawsuits." *The Wall Street Journal*, July 21, 2005: B1.

Bates, Jim (1997). "Fundamentals of Computer Forensics." *International Journal of Forensic Computing.* Available at *www.forensic-computing.com/archives/fundamentals.html* (last accessed on May 20, 2000).

Benoliel, Daniel (2005). "Law, Geography and Cyberspace: The Case of On-Line Territorial Privacy." *Cardozo Arts and Entertainment Law*

Journal, *23*(125). Available at *www.Lexis-Nexis.com*.

Bergelt, Kelley (2003). "Stimulation by Simulation: Is there Really any Difference Between Actual and Virtual Child Pornography? The Supreme Court Gives Pornographers a New Vehicle for Satisfaction." *Capitol University Law Review*, *31*(565).

Berinator, Scott (2002). "The Truth About Cyberterrorism." *CIO Magazine*. Available at *www.cio.com/archive/031502/truth.html*.

Bernstein, Richard (2005). "Must the Children be Sacrificed: The Tension Between Emerging Imaging Technology, Free Speech and Protecting Children." *Rutgers Computer and Technology Law Journal*, *31*(406). Available at *www.lexisnexis.com*.

Bosworth, Martin H. (2006). *Teens Arrested in VA Laptop Theft: Feds Drop Offer of Free Credit Monitoring for Veterans*. ConsumerAffairs.com.

Britz, Marjie T. (2004). *Cybercrime and Computer Forensic Science*. Prentice-Hall: New Jersey.

Britz, Marjie T. (2006). *The Emerging Face of Organized Crime*. A paper presented at the 2006 Cybercrime Summit, Kennesaw State University.

Britz, Marjie T. (2008). *Criminal Evidence*. Allyn & Bacon: Upper Saddle River, NJ.

Broadhurst, Roderic (2006). "Developments in the Global Law Enforcement of Cyber-Crime." *Policing: An International Journal of Police Strategies and Management*, *29*(3): 408–433.

Cassell, Bryan-Low (2005). "Ukraine Captures Key Suspect Tied to Identity Theft." *The Wall Street Journal*, July 19, 2005: B9.

Center for Democracy & Technology (2000). "Encryption Litigation." Available at *wysiwyg://99/http://www.cdt.org/cypto/litigation/* (last accessed on May 15, 2000).

Center for Strategic and International Studies, Global Organized Crime Project (1998). "Cybercrime . . . Cyberterrorism . . . Cyber-warefare: Averting an Electronic Waterloo." Washington, DC.

Chittenden, Maurice (2000). "Security Alert as Thief Grabs Military Laptop." *The Sunday Times News*. May 21, 2000. Available at *www.the-times.co.uk/ . . . pages/sti/2000/05021/stinwenws01039.html* (last accessed on November 2, 2000).

Clark, Franklin and Diliberto, Ken (1996). *Investigating Computer Crime*. CRC Press: Boca Raton, FL.

Clarke, Catherine Therese (1996). "Innovation and the Information Environment: From CrimINet to Cyber-Perp: Toward an Inclusive Approach to Policing the Evolving Criminal Mens Rea on the Internet." *Oregon Law Review*, *75*(191): 1–46. Available at *www.lexis-nexis.com* (last accessed on November 20, 1999).

Coacher, LeEllen (1999). "Permitting Systems Protection Monitoring: When the Government Can Look and What It Can See." *Air Force Law Review*, *46*(155).

Cohen, Fred (2001). "Information Protection." Opening Keynote Presentation of the annual meetings of the Techno-Security conference, Myrtle Beach, SC, April 23, 2001.

Coll, Steve; Glasser, Susan B.; and Tate, Julie (2005). Terrorists Turn to the Web as Base of Operations. *Washington Post*, September 9, 2005. Available at *www.crime-research.org/articles/terrorists_turn/*.

Combs, Cindy C. (2007). *Terrorism in the Twenty-First Century* (4th Ed). Prentice-Hall: Upper Saddle River, NJ.

Coombes, Andrea (2005). "MarketWatch: Identity Thieves Target College Aid." *The Wall Street Journal*. October 23: 4.

Debat, Alexis (2006). "Al Qaeda's Web of Terror." *ABC News*. March 10, 2006.

DeMarco, Robert T. (2004). "FBI Opens New Computer Crime Lab." *Computer Crime Research Center*, July 1, 2004. Available at *www.crime-research.org*.

Dempsey, James X. (1997). "Communications Privacy in the Digital Age: Revitalizing the Federal Wiretap Laws to Enhance Privacy." *Albany Law Journal of Science and Technology*, *8*(1). Available at *www.cdt.org/publications/lawreview/1997albany.shtml* (last accessed on August 10, 2007).

Department of Defense (May 20, 2003). *Report to Congress Regarding the Terrorism Informational Awareness Program, Detailed Information*. Available at *http://wyden.senate.gov/leg_issues/reports/darpa_tia_summary.pdf* (last accessed on May 15, 2007).

Department of Defense. December 12, 2003. *Information Technology Management: Terrorism Information Awareness Project* (D2004-033).

Digital Telephony and Law Enforcement Access to Advanced Telecommunications Technologies and Services: Joint Hearings on H.R. 4922 and S. 2375 Before the Subcommittee on Technology and the Law of the Senate Committee on the Judiciary and the Subcommittee on Civil and Constitutional Rights of the House Committee on the Judiciary, 103rd Congress 6 (1994).

Dittrich, David (1999). "The *stacheldraht* Distributed Denial of Service Attack Tool." Written December 31, 1999. Available at *http://packetstorm.securify.com/distributed/stacheldraht.analysis* (last accessed on February 12, 2001 at 2:37 p.m.).

Doherty, Kelly M. (1999). "*www.obscenity.com:* An Analysis of Obscenity and Indecency Regulation on the Internet." *Akron Law Review*, *32*(259). Available at *http://web.lexis-nexis.com* (last accessed on January 22, 2001 at 4:04 p.m.).

DOJ (1997). "Report on the Availability of Bomb-making Information, The Extent to which Its Dissemination may be Subject to Regulations Consistent with the First Amendment to the United States Constitution." Office of Legislative Affairs, April 29, 1997.

DOJ (November 25, 2000). Texas Woman Pleads Guilty to Operating Ring that Trafficked in Counterfeit Microsoft Software. Available at *www.cybercrime.gov/mos.htm* (last accessed on October 19, 2000).

DOJ (November 28, 2000). Emulex Hoaxer Indicted for Using Bogus Press Release and Internet Service to Drive Down Price of Stock. Available at *www.cybercrime.gov/emulex.htm* (last accessed on October 19, 2000).

DOJ (2000). Computer Crime and Intellectual Property Section (CCIPS): Prosecuting Crimes Facilitated by Computers and by the Interent. Available at *www.cybercrime.gov/crimes.html* (last accessed on October 2, 2000).

DOJ (2004). *Nineteen Individuals Indicted in Internet "Carding" Conspiracy: Shadowcrew Organization Called "One-Stop Online Marketplace for Identity Theft"*. Press Release. October 28, 2004. Available at *http://www.usdoj.gov/opa/pr/2004/October/04_crm_726.htm*. Retrieved from the Internet on October 15, 2007.

DOJ (2006). *Fact Sheet: The Work of the President's Identity Theft Task Force.* September 19, 2006. Available at *www.usdoj.gov*.

DOJ (2007). *Digital Evidence in the Courtroom: A Guide for Law Enforcement and Prosecutors.* NIJ Special Report. U.S. Department of Justice. Office of Justice Programs: Washington, DC.

DOJ (2007). *What are Identity Theft and Identity Fraud.* Available at *http://www.usdoj.gov/criminal/fraud/idtheft.html#What%20Are%20Identity%20Theft%20and%20Identity* (last accessed on January 10, 2007).

Douglas, Karen M.; McGarty, Craig; Bliuc, Ana-Maria; and Girish, Lala (2005). "Understanding Cyberhate: Social Competition and Social Creativity in Online White Supremacist Groups." *Social Science Computer Review*, *23*(1): 68–76.

Doyle, Charles (2002). *The USA Patriot Act: A Legal Analysis.* CRS Report for Congress. Available at *http://www.fas.org/irp/crs/RL31377.pdf*.

Ehrenfeld, Rachel (2002). *Funding Terrorism: Sources and Methods.* A paper presented at the Los Alamos National Laboratory, March 25–29.

EnCase Legal Journal (April, 2000). *Encase Legal Journal*, *1*(3): 1–16. Guidance Software, Inc.

Faas, Ryan (2007). *Mac OS X Security Part 1: Investigating Security Breaches and Illegal Use.* Available at *http://www.peachpit.com/articles/article.aspx?p=706210&seqNum=3*. Retrieved from the Internet on October 12, 2007.

Financial Action Task Force (2006). Report on New Payment Methods. *Financial Action Task Force Report.* October 13, 2006. Available at *www.fatf-gafi.org*.

FitzGerald, Nick (1995). "Frequently Asked Questions on Virus-L/comp.virus". Available at *www.bocklabs.wisc.edu/~janda/virl_faq.html#B01* (last accessed on May 15, 2000).

Fu, Kevin (1996). "Crime and Law in Cyberspace." DOJ/Training Session, The Sixth Conference on Computer, Freedom and Privacy, MIT, Cambridge, MA.

GAO (2002). *Identity Fraud: Prevalence and Links to Alien Illegal Activities.* Before the Subcommittee on Crime, Terrorism and Homeland Security and the Subcommittee on Immigration, Border Security, and Claims, Committee on the Judiciary, House of Representatives. United States General Accounting Office. Available at *http://www.consumer.gov/idtheft/pdf/gao-d02830t.pdf* (last accessed on May 5, 2007).

Geating, Gary (1998). "First Amendment: b) Obscenity and Other Unprotected Speech: Free Speech Coalition v. Reno." *Berkeley Technology Law Journal, 13*(389). Available at *www.lexis-nexis.com* (last accessed on January 22, 2001).

Gindin, Susan E. (1999). *Guide to E-Mail and the Internet in the Workplace.* Bureau of National Affairs: Washington, DC.

Glasner, Joanna (2000). "Typo-loving Squatter Squashed." Available at *www.wired.com/news/business/0,1367,39888,00.html* (last accessed on November 1, 2000).

Golubov, Dmitro Ivanovich (2005). "Ukraine Captures Key Suspect Tied to Identity Theft." *The Wall Street Journal,* July 19, 2005: B9.

Gordon, Gary R. and Willox, Norman A. (2003). *Identity Fraud: A Critical National and Global Threat: A Joint Project of the Economic Crime Institute of Utica College and LexisNexis, a Division of Reed Elsevier Inc.* Electronic Crime Institute: Utica, NY.

Grennan, Sean; Britz, Marjie T.; Rush, Jeff; and Barker, Tom (2000). *Gangs: An International Approach.* Prentice-Hall: Upper Saddle River, NJ.

Grennan, Sean and Britz, Marjie T. (2007). *Organized Crime: A Worldwide Perspective.* Prentice-Hall: Upper Saddle River, NJ.

Guidance Software (1999). *EnCase: Secure and Analyze Computer Evidence—User's Guide,* Guidance Software, Inc: Pasadena, CA.

Hall, Mark (2000). "Reno Calls for Network Targeting Net Crime." *Computerworld, 34*(3): 17.

Harbert, Tam (1999). "Guard Dog Supreme." *Electronic Business, 25*(5): 56–60.

Hinde, Steven (2005). "Identity Theft and Fraud". *Computer Fraud and Security.* (June): 18–20.

Hinde, Steven (2005). "Identity Theft: The Fight." *Computer Fraud and Security.* (May): 6–7.

Hinde, Stephen (2006). "Identity Theft: Theft, Loss and Giveaways." *Computer Fraud & Security.* (May): 18–20.

Hinduja, Sameer (2004). "Perceptions of Local and State Law Enforcement Concerning the Role of Computer Crime *Hinduja* Investigative Teams." *Policing: An International Journal of Police Strategies and Management, 27*(3): 341–357.

Holt, Theresa J. (2004). "The Fair and Accurate Credit Transactions Act: New Tool to Fight Identity Theft." *Business Horizons, 47*(5): 3–6.

Homer-Dixon, Thomas (2002). "The Rise of Complex Terrorism." *Foreign Policy, 128*: 52–62.

Hosmer, Chet (2006). "Discovering Hidden Data." *Journal of Digital Forensic Practice, 1*: 47–56.

Howard, Ty E. (2004). "Don't Cache Out Your Case: Prosecuting Child Pornography Possession Laws Based on Images Located in temporary Internet Files." *Berkeley Technology Law Journal, 19*(1227). Available at *www.lexisnexis.com.*

ICE (2006). *Document and Benefit Fraud Investigations: Document and Benefit Fraud Task Forces.* U.S. Immigration and Customs Enforcement. December 6, 2006. Available at *www.ice.gov/pi/news/factsheets/dbf061211.htm* (last accessed on May 12, 2007).

Icove, David; Seger, Karl; and VonStorch William (1995). *Computer Crime: A Crimefighter's Handbook.* O'Reilly & Associates, Inc.: Sebastopol, California.

Jacques, Stephen C. (1997). "Comment: Reno v. ACLU: Insulating the Internet, the First Amendment, and the Marketplace of Ideas." *The American University Law Review, 46*: 1945–1998.

Jansen, Wayne and Ayers, Rick (2004). *Guidelines on PDA Forensics: Recommendations of the National Institute of Standards and Technology.* NIST: Special Publication 800-72. National Institute of Standards and Technology, U.S. Department of Commerce: Gaithersburg, MD.

Jenkins, B. (1975). *International Terrorism.* Los Angeles, CA: Crescent Publication.

Johnson, David (1994). "Why the Possession of Computer-Generated Child Pornography 4(311)." Available at *http://web.lexisnexis.com/universal/docu ... zS&_md5+aba61b17e6c9c7f8 aoe836f07b620293* (last accessed on February 7, 2001).

Kaplan, Eben (2006). *Terrorists and the Internet*. Council on Foreign Relations. Available at *www.cfr.org/publiction/10005* (last accessed on December 31, 2006).

Katel, Peter (2005). "Identify Theft: Can Congress Give Americans Better Protection?" *CQ Researcher*, 15(22). Available at *http://library2.cqpress.com/cqrearcher/* (last accessed on August 5, 2006).

Keefe, Bob (2005). *Forget "Kid" Stuff—Organized Crime's Moving Online*. Seattle Post-Intelligencer. February 22, 2005. Available at *http://seattlepi.nwsource.com/national/213069_onlinecrime22.html* (last accessed on February 28, 2007).

Keizer, Gregg (2005). *Keyloggers Foiled in Attempted $423 Million Bank Heist*. TechWeb. Available at *http://www.techweb.com/wire/security/159901593*. Retrieved from the Internet on September 15, 2007.

Kerr, Donald M. (July 4, 2000). Statement for the Record on *Internet and Data Interception Capabilities Developed by FBI* before the United States House of Representatives: The Committee on the Judiciary Subcommittee on the Constitution, Washington, DC. Available at *www.fbi.gov/pressrm/congress/congressoo/kerr072400.htm* (last accessed on February 12, 2001).

Kerr, Donald M. (September 6, 2000b). Statement for the Record on *Carnivore Diagnostic Tool* before the United States Sentate: The Committee on the Judiciary, Washington, DC. Available at *www.fbi.gov/pressrm/congress/congressoo/kerr090600.htm*.

Kerr, Orin S. (2001). *Computer Crime and Intellectual Property Section (CCIPS) and Seizing Computers and Obtaining Electronic Evidence in Criminal Investigations. www.cybercrime.gov/searchmanual.htm* (last accessed on January 16, 2001).

Kluger, Jeffrey (June 24, 2000). "Extortion on the Internet." *Time* 155(3): 56.

Kornegay, James Nicholas (2006). "Protecting Our Children and the Constitution: An Analysis of the 'Virtual' Child Pornography Provisions of the PROTECT Act of 2003." *William and Mary Law Review*, 47(2129). Available at *www.lexisnexis.com*.

Kovacich, Gerald L. and Boni, William C. (2000). *High-Technology Crime Investigator's Handbook: Working in the Global Information Environment*. Butterworth-Heinemann: Boston, MA.

Krause, William J. (2004). *Terrorist Identification, Screening, and Tracking under Homeland Security Presidential Directive 6*. CRS Report for Congress: RL32366.

Kutz, Gregory D. (2006). *Border Security: Continued Weaknesses in Screening Entrants into the United States*. Testimony before the Committee of Finance, U.S. Senate, August 2, 2006. Available at *http://finance.senate.gov/hearings/testimony/2005test/080206gk.pdf* (last accessed on May 15, 2007).

LaFave, Wayne R. (1996). "Computers, Urinals, and the Fourth Amendment: Confessions of a Patron Saint." *Michigan Law Review*, 94(8): 2553–2589.

Levin, Robert B. (1995). "The Virtual Fourth Amendment: Searches and Seizures in Cyberspace." *Maryland Bar Journal*, XXVII(3): 2–5.

Lewis, James A. (2002). *Assessing the Risks of Cyber Terrorism, Cyber War and Other Cyber Threats*. Center for Strategic and International Studies.

Lewis, James A. (2006). *McAfee Virtual Criminology Report: North American Study into Organized Crime and the Internet*. McAfee. Available at *http://www.mcafee.com/us/threat_center/white_paper.html*. Retrieved from the Internet on June 30, 2007.

Lindner, Anne (2006). "First Amendment as Last Resort: The Internet Gambling Industry's Bid to Advertise in the United States." *Saint Louis University Law Journal*, 50(1289). Available at *www.lexisnexis.com*.

Linnhoff, Stefan and Langenderfer (2004). "Identity Theft Legislation: The Fair and Accurate Credit Transactions Act of 2003 and the Road Not Taken." *The Journal of Consumer Affairs*, 38(2): 204–216.

Litton/TASC (2000). *Computer Forensics Investigations*. Litton/TASC: Chantilly, VA.

Lynch, Jennifer (2005). "Identity Theft in Cyberspace: Crime Control Methods and Their Effectiveness in Combating Phishing Attacks." *Berkeley Technology Law Journal, 20*(1): 259–300.

Mahnaimi, Uzi (2000). "Israeli Spies Tapped Clinton E-mail." *The Sunday Times: Foreign News*, May 21, 2000. Available at *www.the-times.co.uk/ . . . pages/sti/2000/05/21/stifgnusa02003.htm* (last accessed on November 15, 2000).

Manion, Mark and Goodrum, Abby (2000). "Terrorism and Civil Disobedience: Toward a Hactivist Ethic." *Computers and Society* (June): 14–19.

Manjoo, Farhad (2000). "Hacker Finds Hole in Netscape Communicator." *Wired News*. Available at *www.wired.com/news/technology* (last accessed on November 15, 2000 at 2:30 p.m.).

McAfee (2005). *McAfee Virtual Criminology Report: North American Study into Organized Crime and the Internet*. Available at *www.mcafee.com*.

McClintick, James (2005). "Web-Surfing in Chilly Waters: How the Patiot Act's Amendments to the Pen Register Statute Burden Freedom of Inquiry." *American University Journal of Gender, Social Policy and the Law, 13*(353). Available at *www.lexisnexis.com*.

Meeks, Brock N. (2000). *FBI's Carnivore has Partners: Declassified Documents Reveal E-mail Snoop Program Details*. Available at *www.msnbc.com/new/47749.asp?0nm=T19&vpl=1*.

Merlis, Steven E. (2005). "Preserving Internet Expression While Protecting Our Children: Solutions Following *Ashcroft* v. *ACLU*." *Northwestern Journal of Technology and Intellectual Property, 4*(117). Available at *www.lexisnexis.com*.

Metchik, Eric (1997). "A Typology of Crime on the Internet." *Security Journal, 9*: 27–31.

Mitchell, Daniel J. (2002). "U.S. Government Agencies Confirm that Low-Tax Jurisdictions Are Not Money Laundering Havens." *Prosperitas, II*(I): 1–7.

Mitchell, Stevan D. and Banker, Elizabeth A. (1998). "Private Intrusion Response." *Harvard Journal of Law and Technology*, 11(699).

Mohammed, Arshad and Goo Sara Kehaulani (2006). *Government Increasingly Turning to Data Mining: Peek into Private Lives May Help in Hunt for Terrorists*. The Washington Post. June 15, 2006 Available at *www.washingtonpost.com*.

Musgrove, Mike (1999). "Suit Targets DVD-Copying Software: Industry Group Seeks to Block Breaking of Security System." Available at *www.washingtonpost.com/wp-srv/Wplate/1999-12/29/0261-12299-idx.html* (last accessed on January 13, 2000).

Mykyten, Joe (2000). Personal communications. Duluth, Georgia. July, 18–23.

Newman, Graeme R. (2004). "Identity Theft." *Problem-Oriented Guides for Police: Problem Specific Guides Series, 25*. Available at *www.cops.usdoj.gov*.

Nicholson, Laura J.; Shebar, Tom F.; and Weinberg, Meredith R. (2000). "Computer Crimes: Annual White Collar Crime Survey." *American Criminal Law Review*. Available at *http://www.accessmylibrary.com/coms2/summary_0286-28748235_ITM*. Retrieved from the Internet on August 10, 2007.

Noblett, Michael G.; Pollitt, Mark M.; and Presley, Lawrence A. (2000). "Recovering and Examining Computer Forensic Evidence." *Forensic Science Communications, 2*(4). Available at *www.fbi.gov/programs/labs/fsc/current/computer.htm* (last accessed on November 6, 2000).

Orenstein, David (1999). "Standard in Works for Sharing E-Customer Data: Ability to Easily Share Information Alarms Privacy Experts, Despite Planned Guidelines." *Computerworld*. November 22, 1999, p. 2.

Packard, Ashley (2000). "Does Proposed Federal Cyberstalking Legislation Meet Constitutional Requirements?" *Communications Law and Policy, 5*(505). Available at *www.lexis-nexis.com* (last accessed on February 20, 2001).

Paget, Francois (2007). "Identity Theft." *White Paper*, January. McAfee. Available at *www.mcafee.com/us/local_content/white_papers/wp_id_theft_en.pdf*. Retrieved from the Internet on August 8, 2007.

Parker, Donn B. (1998). *Fighting Computer Crime: A New Framework for Protecting Information*. John Wiley & Sons, Inc.: New York, NY.

Pastrikos, Catherine (2004). "Identity Theft Statutes: Which Will Protect Americans the Most?" *Albany Law Review*, 67(4): 1137–1157.

Perl, Michael W. (2003). "It's Not Always about the Money: Why the State Identity Theft Laws Fail to Adequately Address Criminal Record Identity Theft." *Journal of Criminal Law and Criminology*, 94(1): 169–208.

Ping, He (2004). "New Trends in Money Laundering—From the Real World to Cyberspace." *Journal of Money Laundering Control*, 8(1): 48–55.

Phillippsohn, Steven (2001). "The Dangers of New Technology—Laundering on the Internet." *Journal of Money Laundering Control*, 5(1): 87–95.

Power, Richard (2000). *Tangled Web: Tales of Digital Crime for the Shadows of Cyberspace*. Que Publishing: New York.

Radcliff, Deborah (December 14, 1998). "Crime in the 21st Century." *Infoworld*, 20(50): 65–66.

Radcliff, Deborah (August 9, 1999). "Typing a Byte Out of Crime." *Computerworld*, 33(22): 32–33.

Randall, Neil (1999). "How Viruses Work: Understanding How Viruses Work Is the First Step in Defending Against Them." *PC Magazine*, p. 1. February 9, 1999.

Rappaport, Kim L. (1998). "In the Wake of Reno v. ACLU: The Continued Struggle in Western Constitutional Democracies with Internet Censorship and Freedom of Speech Online." *American University International Law Review*, 13(765). Available at *www.lexis-nexis.com*.

Reno, Janet (January 21, 1997). Keynote Address by U.S. Attorney General Janet Reno on High-Tech and Computer Crime. Delivered at the Meeting of the P8 Senior Experts' Group on Transnational Organized Crime. Chantilly, VA. Available at *http://www.usdoj.gov/criminal/cybercrime/agfranc. htm* (last accessed on October 3, 2000).

Reese, Lloyd F. (2004). "Black Ice: The Invisible Threat of Cyber-Terrorism." *Security Management*, 48(9): 212–213.

Rider, Barry (2001). "Cyber-Organized Crime: The Impact of Information Technology on Organized Crime." *Journal of Financial Crime*, 8(4): 332–347.

Rodriguez, Alexander (1998). "All Bark, No Byte: Employee E-Mail Privacy Rights in the Private Sector Workplace." *Emory Law Journal*, 47: 1439–1473.

Rosenblatt, Kenneth S. (1995). *High-Technology Crime: Investigating Cases Involving Computers*. KSK Publications: San Jose, CA.

Rutgers University (2004). *The Thief Is in the Mail*. Identity Theft Resolution Center. Available at *http://www.identitytheft911-sunj.com/articles/article.ext?sp=49*.

Sammes, Tony and Jenkinson, Brian (2000). *Forensic Computing: A Practitioner's Guide*. Springer-Verlag: London.

Schmidt-Sandwick, Robin (2003). Supreme Court Strikes Down Two Provisions of the Child Pornography Prevention Act (CPPA), Leaving Virtual Child Pornography Virtually Unregulated. *Ashcroft* v. *Free Speech Coalition*, 122 S. Ct. 1389 (2002). *North Dakota Law Review*, 79(175). Available at *www.lexisnexis.com*.

SEARCH (2000). *The Investigation of Computer Crime*. The National Consortium for Justice Information and Statistics: Sacramento, CA.

Seifert, Jeffrey W. (2007). *Data Mining and Homeland Security: An Overview*. CRS Report for Congress. Order Code RL 31798 (January 18, 2007).

Shelby, Senator Richard C. (2005). *The Financial Services Industry's Responsibilities and Role in Preventing Identity Theft and Protecting Sensitive Financial Information*. Hearing of the Senate Banking, Housing, and Urban Affairs Committee Subject. September 22, 2005. Available at *www.lexis-nexis.com*.

Shelley, Louise (1997). *Threat from International Organized Crime and Terrorism*. Congressional Testimony before the House Committee on International Relations. (October 1, 1997).

Shelley, Louise (2000). "The Nexus of Organized Criminals and Terrorists". *International Annals of Criminology*, 40(1–2): 85–91.

Shnier, Mitchell (1998). *Computer Dictionary*. Que Corporation, Indianapolis, IN.

Soma, John T.; Banker, Elizabeth A.; and Smith, Alexander R. (1996). "Computer Crime: Substantive Statutes & Technical & Search Considerations." *The Air Force Law Review*, 39(225). Lexis-Nexis—Available at *http://web.lexisnexis.com/universe/docu . . . zS&_md5=754b013cfb0e7bead5108ab532fd080d* (last accessed on August 13, 2007).

Southern Poverty Law Center (2006). "L.A. Blackouts." *Intelligence Reports*, Winter (124): 1–73.

Spernow, Bill (2001). "A Cutting Edge Look at Enhancing Security for the Enterprise." A paper presented at the annual meetings of the Techno-Security conference, Myrtle Beach, SC, April 23, 2001.

Stafford, Marla Royne (2004). "Identity Theft: Laws, Crimes, and Victims." *The Journal of Consumer Affairs*, 38(2): 201–203.

Stambaugh, Hollis; Beupre, David S.; Baker, Richard; Cassady, Wayne; and Williams, Wayne P. (2001). "Electronic Crime Needs Assessment for State and Local Law Enforcement." DOJ # 98-DT-R-076. Washington, DC: NIJ.

State of New Jersey Commission of Investigation (2004). "The Changing Face of Organized Crime in New Jersey." *Trends in Organized Crime*, 8(2).

Sterling, Bruce (1994). *The Hacker Crackdown: Law and Disorder on the Electronic Frontier.* Available at *http://www.mit.edu/hacker/hacker.html* (last accessed on August 13, 2007).

Stevens, Gina and Doyle, Charles (2003). *Privacy: An Overview of Federal Statutes Governing Wiretapping and Electronic Eavesdropping.* Report for Congress: #98-326. Available at *http://www.epic.org/privacy/wiretap/98-326.pdf.* Retrieved from the Internet on October 7, 2007.

Sullivan, Bob (June 21, 2000). "Protesters to Nike: Just Hack It!" MSNBC. Available at *www.zdnet.com . . . tories/news/0,4586,2592093,00.html* (last accessed on February 12, 2001).

Sullivan, Scott (June 1999). "Policing the Internet." *FBI Law Enforcement Bulletin*, pp. 18–21.

SWGDE (Scientific Working Group on Digital Evidence) (1999). Digital Evidence: Standards and Principles. A paper presented at the International Hi-Tech Crime and Forensics Conference in London, England, October 4–7, 1999. Available at *www.Fbi.gov/programs/lab/fsc/backissu/april2000/swgde.htm* (last accessed on November 10, 2000).

Symantec (1997). *Norton Utilities for DOS: Definitions.*

Taylor, Chris (June 14, 1999). "Geeks vs. G-men." *Time*, 64.

Taylor, Chris (November 1, 1999). "Hacker's Delight." *Time*, 154(18): 18.

Tharp, Paul (2005). "UPS Says "Oops!'—Citi Loses Financial Records of 3.9M Customers." *The New York Post*, (June 7): 41.

Tien, Lee (2005). "Doors, Envelopes, and Encryption: The Uncertain Role of Precautions in Fourth Amendment Law." *DePaul Law Review*, 54(873). Available at *www.lexisnexis.com.*

TRAC (2003). "Criminal Terrorism Enforcement Since the 9/11/01 Attacks." *A TRAC Special Report* (December 8, 2003). Available at *http://trac.syr.edu/tracreports/terrorism/report031208.html#figure2* (last accessed on December 2, 2006).

Transportation Security Administration (March 11, 2003). *TSA's CAPPS II Gives Equal Weight to Privacy, Security.* Press Release. Available at *www.tsa.gov* (last accessed on May 15, 2007).

Tsfati, Yariv and Weimann, Gabriel (2002). "*www.terrorism.com:* Terror on the Internet." *Studies in Conflict and Terrorism*, 25: 317–332.

Tuerkheimer, Frank M. (1993). "The Underpinnings of Privacy Protection." *Communications of the ACM*, 36(8): 69–74.

Tyson, Ann Scott and Lee, Christopher (2006). "Data Theft Affected Most in Military: National Security Concerns Raised." *Washingtonpost.com* (p. A01). Available at *http://www.washingtonpost.com/wp-dyn/content/article/2006/06/06/AR2006060601332.html* (last accessed on November 30, 2006).

United States Coast Guard (2005). Transcript from *The Subcommittee on Coast Guard and Maritime Transportation Hearing on Coast Guard Law Enforcement.* June 15, 2005. Available at *http://www.house.gov/transportation/cgmt/06-15-05/06-15-05memo.html#PURPOSE.*

United States Customs and Border Protection (2007). "Overview of the Visa Waiver Program." *ID and Entry for Foreign Nationals.* Available at *http://www.cbp.gov/xp/cgov/travel/ id_visa/vwp/vwp.xml* (last accessed on January 1, 2007).

United States Department of Justice (March, 2000). "The Electronic Frontier: The Challenge of Unlawful Conduct Involving the Use of the Internet-A report of the President's Working Group on Unlawful Conduct on the Internet."

United States of America Federal Trade Commission Complaint. *In the Matter of CardSystems Solutions, Inc., a corporation.* Docket No. C-052-3148. Available at *http://www.ftc.gov/os/caselist/0523148/0523148complaint.pdf.*

United States General Accounting Office (1998). "Critical Infrastructure Protection: Comprehensive Strategy Can Draw on Year 2000 Experience." DOC # GAOAIMD—00-1, Washington, DC: 8.

United Nations (2000). "United Nations Manual on the prevention and Control of Computer-related Criteria." *International Review of Criminal Policy*, *43 & 44.* Available at *www.ifs.univie.ac.at/~pr2gq1/rev4344.html* (last accessed on May 31, 2006).

Weinberg, J. (2006). "Everyone's a Winner: Regulating, Not Prohibiting, Internet Gambling." *Southwestern University Law Review, 35*(2): 293–326.

Williams, Phil (2004). Department of Homeland Security, Office of Inspector General, Office of Information Technology. DHS Challenges in Consolidating Terrorist Watch List Information.

Winick, Raphael (1994). "Searches and Seizures of Computers and Computer Data." *Harvard Journal of Law and Technology, 8*(1): 75–128.

Wischnowsky, Dave (2006). "Identity Theft of MLB Players Alleged." *The Chicago Tribune* (December 20, 2006). Available at *www.chicagotribune.com* (last accessed on February 22, 2007).

Wolak, Janis; Finkelhor, David; and Mitchell, Kimberly J. (2005). *Child-Pornography Possessors Arrested in Internet-Related Crimes: Findings from the National Juvenile Online Victimization study.* National Center for Missing and Exploited Children. Availble at: *www.missingkids.com.* Retrieved from the Internet on August 17, 2007.

Wright, Benjamin (2004). "Internet Break-Ins: New Legal Liability". *Computer Law and Security Report, 20*(3): 171–174.

Zanini, Michele (1999). "Middle Eastern Terrorism and Netwar." *Studies in Conflict and Terrorism, 22*: 247–256.